A TREASURY OF
AMERICAN
POETRY

A TREASURY OF AMERICAN POETRY

....

EDITED BY
ALLEN MANDELBAUM &
ROBERT D. RICHARDSON, JR.

GRAMERCY BOOKS
NEW YORK

This 2003 edition published by Gramercy Books, an imprint of
Random House Value Publishing, a division of Random House, Inc.,
New York, by arrangement with Bantam Books.

Gramercy is a registered trademark and the colophon
is a trademark of Random House, Inc.

Random House
New York • Toronto • London • Sydney • Auckland
www.randomhouse.com

Interior design by Glen M. Edelstein

Printed and bound in the United States of America

[Previously published as *Three Centuries of American Poetry*.]

Library of Congress Cataloging-in-Publication Data
Three centuries of American poetry, 1620-1923.
A treasury of American poetry / edited by Allen Mandelbaum
and Robert D. Richardson, Jr.
p. cm.
Originally published under title: Three centuries of American poetry,
1620-1923. New York : Bantam Books, 1999.
Includes index.
ISBN 0-517-22153-5
1. American poetry. 2. United States—Poetry. I. Mandelbaum, Allen,
1926- II. Richardson, Robert D., 1934- III. Title.

PS584 .T48 2003
811.008—dc21
2002033876

10 9 8 7 6 5 4 3 2 1

TO THE ROARING WIND

What syllable are you seeking,
Vocalissimus,
In the distances of sleep?
Speak it.

—Wallace Stevens

ACKNOWLEDGMENTS

Special thanks are due to Nathan Eddy, who proofed much of the manuscript, to Megan Carnes, who ran down many citations, to Rosie Clevidence for early encouragement that we were going in the right direction, to Karl Kirchwey for suggestions about Stickney, to Joe Reed for a host of useful suggestions, and to Patty Cowell and her invaluable work with American women poets. Thanks also to the splendid team at Bantam, to Glen Edelstein for making the book look right, to Janet Biehl for superior copy-editing, to Katie Hall for vital encouragement and keeping it all together and coherent, and to Toni Burbank for her long-standing faith and enthusiasm for the project. Lily Saade at Wake Forest University has done a heroic job of making a text out of the mass of suggestions and the reams of paper generated by the compilers. It was she who first licked the wild cub into shape and made it look like a book.

Allen Mandelbaum
Robert D. Richardson, Jr.
June, 1998

CONTENTS

III · YOUNG AMERICA: THE ROMANTIC ERA: 1826–1859

xviii

V - THE ERA OF RECONSTRUCTION AND EXPANSION: 1870–1900

VI · THE ADVENT OF THE MODERN: 1901–1922

INTRODUCTIONS

ON THE CANON OF AMERICAN POETRY

There ain't no canon. There ain't going to be any canon. There never has been a canon. That's the canon.

This formulation (which I make bold to take from Gertrude Stein's famous comment on her philosophy, "There ain't any answer, etc.") is literally true. It is now more than two hundred years since the appearance of the first anthology of American verse: Elihu H. Smith's *American Poems* of 1793. Of the fifteen poets and sixty-five poems in that volume, only two poets (Joel Barlow and Philip Freneau) and only one poem (Freneau's "Hurricane") have survived to stand in the present anthology. Of the fifty-five poets represented in the 1840 *Gems of American Poetry,* only one is represented here, and that one is Clement Moore, the author of "A Visit from St. Nicholas."

By 1900 there was so much American poetry to choose from that extreme anthological principles were invoked. E. C. Stedman's *American Anthology* of 1900 included works by 537 poets, while C. H. Page's *The Chief American Poets* (1905) whittled that number down to nine. If Stedman seems unfocused, Page seems rash. Page included Bryant, Poe, Emerson, Longfellow, Whittier, Holmes, Lowell, Whitman, and Lanier. No Bradstreet, no Taylor, no Dickinson, no Melville, no Robinson. In the cases of Taylor and Dickinson, we are simply lucky that the twentieth century discovered and printed poetry that was unknown in its own day. In the cases of Bradstreet, Melville, and Robinson, one can only say that taste changes. It is difficult to find a single American poet, currently considered important, who has not, at some time, for some reason, been left out. The anthology called *Parnassus* (1874), edited by Ralph Waldo Emerson and his daughter Edith, inexplicably contains no poetry by Whitman. Oscar Williams's and Edwin Honig's *Major American Poets* (1962) contains no T. S. Eliot because Eliot's publisher's policy at the time was "not to allow Mr. Eliot's poetry to appear in paperback books selling for less than $1.75."

More discoveries will be made and taste will change. An anthology of American poetry a hundred years from now will be as different from this one as this one is from either Stedman's or Page's. This volume is not intended to set a seal upon the past. It is meant, rather, as an invitation to the reader of today and to those poets whose names we do not yet know. "In our ordinary states of mind," Emerson once observed, "we deem not only letters in general but the most famous books part of a pre-established harmony, fatal, unalterable. . . . But Man is critic of all these also and should treat the entire extant product of the human intellect as only one age, revisable, corrigible, reversible by him."

The canon is dead. Long live the canon.

Robert D. Richardson, Jr.

Middletown, Connecticut

August 1998

OF THOSE "WHO LIVE
AND SPEAK FOR AYE"

Wallace Stevens urges: "Speak it." But speech has many variants: murmur, chant, song, bluster, malediction, hymn, psalm—modes that conjure not a chorus but a fraternity-sorority of soloists. The patient work of many blessèd editors has in our present century amplified the speech of earlier centuries, giving Bradstreet, Taylor, Dickinson, Melville, and many others fuller voice, restoring neglected words.

Faced with those words, the reader-hearer is often more ecumenical than the poet. T. S. Eliot needs to bracket/browbeat the Romantics and hosanna the Metaphysical soloists; but the reader can listen attentively, sympathetically to both Shelley and Donne. Thus this American anthology is, if anything, ecumenical: two tastes, two long—and often different—experiences with texts combined in shaping it.

Taste is perhaps more kin to opinion than it is to thought. But we have tried to think through the vicissitudes of taste and to ingather poetic speech that conjures the speaker in a way that reaches us today. We have sought those words that ask to be read aloud.

We have moved as often as possible past the anthological tendency/ itch to gather snippets; and where—of necessity—we have cut, we hope that our selections invite to fuller reconnaissance. The Puritan register, its anxious colloquy with an all-powerful Lord, is amply represented— allowing us to see, above all in Edward Taylor, the energy that declares man's puniness and then subverts that declaration with percussive creativity. We have mined the resources of Longfellow's taletelling, his fluent narrative, and given space, too, to his elegiac awareness of the futilities woven into the mind of the narrator. The declarative "I" of Whitman—as well as his shadowed, self-questioning self—are here; so, too, is the adroit, investigative "I" of Dickinson—her barbed lyre. In the post-Puritan age of the pensioned god, we have drawn fully on that replete rabbi, Wallace Stevens, one who shuns the "I" but is obsessed with the third person, not least the penetrating "she" who "says" and "hears" in "Sunday Morning."

We have grouped our many soloists in historical chapters-cantos- contexts, stages in America's way(s); and we have ordered the endnotes, too, in accord with the birth dates of the poets. In sectioning off those time contexts, we have remembered that "speech" also includes the quiet domestic solos that invited attention in the parlor and those cadenzas that stirred applause in the music hall. And outdoors, beneath the heavens, we have not neglected the impassioned plaint that rose from the fields of slavery, and from the people whom our hunger for land and our labors dispossessed.

In sum, the poet is not a historian, but his voice begins where the historian's begins. He breathes in time. Aloud.

Loud enough to enter our significant present as we conjure the vicissitudes of an America still coming to terms with its varied selves—reaching beyond hygienic homiletics, slick Sunday supplements, and small beer.

The gamut of registers and content which that reaching involves is indeed wide: this book, then, is a sampling, but one that is, we hope, both broad and detailed.

Allen Mandelbaum

Wake Forest University
&
University of Turin

August 1998

I
THE COLONIAL
ERA:
TO 1775

JOHN SMITH
(c.1580–1631)

The Sea Marke

Aloofe, aloofe, and come no neare
    the dangers doe appeare;
Which if my ruine had not beene
    you had not seene:
I onely lie upon this shelfe
    to be a mark to all
    which on the same might fall,
That none may perish but my selfe.

If in or outward you be bound,
    doe not forget to sound;
Neglect of that was cause of this
    to steare amisse.
The Seas were calme, the wind was faire,
    that made me so secure,
    that now I must indure
All weathers be they foule or faire.

The Winters cold, the Summers heat,
    alternatively beat
Upon my bruised sides, that rue
    because too true
That no releefe can ever come.
    But why should I despair
    being promised so faire
That there shall be a day of Dome.

ROGER WILLIAMS
(1603–1683)

Of Eating and Entertainment

    Coarse bread and water's most their fare,
    O England's diet fine;
Thy cup runs o'er with plenteous store
    Of wholesome beer and wine.

Sometimes God gives them fish or flesh,
    Yet they're content without;
And what comes in, they part to friends
    And strangers round about.

God's providence is rich to His,
    Let none distrustful be;
In wilderness, in great distress,
    These ravens have fed me.

ANNE BRADSTREET
(c.1612–1672)

The Author to Her Book

Thou ill-form'd offspring of my feeble brain,
Who after birth did'st by my side remain,
Till snatcht from thence by friends, less wise then true
Who thee abroad, expos'd to publick view,
Made thee in raggs, halting to th' press to trudge,
Where errors were not lessened (all may judg).
At thy return my blushing was not small,
My rambling brat (in print) should mother call,
I cast thee by as one unfit for light,
Thy Visage was so irksome in my sight;
Yet being mine own, at length affection would
Thy blemishes amend, if so I could:
I wash'd thy face, but more defects I saw,
And rubbing off a spot, still made a flaw.
I stretcht thy joynts to make thee even feet,
Yet still thou run'st more hobling then is meet;
In better dress to trim thee was my mind,
But nought save home-spun Cloth, i'th' house I find.
In this array, 'mongst Vulgars mayst thou roam,
In Criticks hands, beware thou dost not come;
And take thy way where yet thou art not known,
If for thy Father askt, say, thou hadst none:
And for thy Mother, she alas is poor,
Which caus'd her thus to send thee out of door.

To My Dear and Loving Husband

If ever two were one, then surely we.
If ever man were lov'd by wife, then thee;
If ever wife was happy in a man,
Compare with me ye women if you can.
I prize thy love more than whole Mines of gold,
Or all the riches that the East doth hold.
My love is such that Rivers cannot quench,
Nor ought but love from thee, give recompence.
Thy love is such I can no way repay,
The heavens reward thee manifold I pray.
Then while we live, in love lets so persever,
That when we live no more, we may live ever.

Some Verses upon the Burning of Our House, July 10th, 1666

In silent night when rest I took,
For sorrow neer I did not look,
I waken'd was with thundring nois
And Piteous shreiks of dreadfull voice.
That fearfull sound of fire and fire,
Let no man know is my Desire.

I, starting up, the light did spye,
And to my God my heart did cry
To strengthen me in my Distresse
And not to leave me succourlesse.
Then coming out beheld a space,
The flame consume my dwelling place.

And, when I could no longer look,
I blest his Name that gave and took,
That layd my goods now in the dust:
Yea so it was, and so 'twas just.
It was his own: it was not mine;
Far be it that I should repine.

He might of All justly bereft,
But yet sufficient for us left.
When by the Ruines oft I past,
My sorrowing eyes aside did cast,
And here and there the places spye
Where oft I sate, and long did lye.

Here stood that Trunk, and there that chest;
There lay that store I counted best:
My pleasant things in ashes lye,
And them behold no more shall I.
Under thy roof no guest shall sitt,
Nor at thy Table eat a bitt.

No pleasant tale shall 'ere be told,
Nor things recounted done of old.
No Candle 'ere shall shine in Thee,
Nor bridegroom's voice ere heard shall bee.
In silence ever shalt thou lye;
Adeiu, Adeiu; All's vanity.

Then streight I 'gin my heart to chide,
And did thy wealth on earth abide?
Didst fix thy hope on mouldring dust,
The arm of flesh didst make thy trust?
Raise up thy thoughts above the skye
That dunghill mists away may flie.

Thou hast an house on high erect,
Fram'd by that mighty Architect,
With glory richly furnished,
Stands permanent though this bee fled.
It's purchased, and paid for too
By him who hath enough to doe.

A Prise so vast as is unknown,
Yet, by his Gift, is made thine own.
Ther's wealth enough, I need no more;
Farewell my Pelf, farewell my Store.
The world no longer let me Love,
My hope and Treasure lyes Above.

Epitaphs for Queen Elizabeth

Her Epitaph.
Here sleeps THE Queen; this is the royall bed.
O'th' Damask Rose, sprung from the white and red,
Whose sweet perfume fills the all-filling aire,
This Rose is withered, once so lovely faire,
On neither tree did grow such Rose before,
The greater was our gain, our losse the more.

Another

Here lies the pride of Queens, pattern of Kings,
So blaze it fame, here's feathers for thy wings,
Here lies the envy'd, yet unparralell'd Prince,
Whose living vertues speak (though dead long since)
If many worlds, as that fantastick framed,
In every one, be her great glory famed.

Contemplations

1

Some time now past in the Autumnal Tide,
When *Phoebus* wanted but one hour to bed,
The trees all richly clad, yet void of pride,
Were gilded o're by his rich golden head.
Their leaves & fruits seem'd painted, but was true
Of green, of red, of yellow, mixed hew,
Rapt were my sences at this delectable view.

2

I wist not what to wish, yet sure thought I,
If so much excellence abide below;
How excellent is he that dwells on high?
Whose power and beauty by his works we know.
Sure he is goodness, wisdome, glory, light,
That hath this under world so richly dight:
More Heaven then Earth was here, no winter & no night.

3

Then on a stately Oak I cast mine Eye,
Whose ruffling top the Clouds seem'd to aspire;
How long since thou wast in thine Infancy?
Thy strength, and stature, more thy years admire,
Hath hundred winters past since thou wast born?
Or thousand since thou brakest thy shell of horn,
If so, all these as nought, Eternity doth scorn.

4

Then higher on the glistening Sun I gaz'd,
Whose beams was shaded by the leavie Tree,
The more I look'd, the more I grew amaz'd,
And softly said, what glory's like to thee?
Soul of this world, this Universes Eye,
No wonder, some made thee a Deity:
Had I not better known, (alas) the same had I.

5

Thou as a Bridegroom from thy Chamber rushes,
And as a strong man, joyes to run a race,
The morn doth usher thee, with smiles & blushes,
The Earth reflects her glances in thy face.
Birds, insects, Animals with Vegative,
Thy heat from death and dulness doth revive:
And in the darksome womb of fruitful nature dive.

6

Thy swift Annual, and diurnal Course,
Thy daily streight, and yearly oblique path,
Thy pleasing fervor, and thy scorching force,
All mortals here the feeling knowledg hath.
Thy presence makes it day, thy absence night,
Quaternal Seasons caused by thy might:
Hail Creature, full of sweetness, beauty & delight.

7

Art thou so full of glory, that no Eye
Hath strength, thy shining Rayes once to behold?
And is thy splendid Throne erect so high?
As to approach it, can no earthly mould.
How full of glory then must thy Creator be?
Who gave this bright light luster unto thee:
Admir'd, ador'd for ever, be that Majesty.

8

Silent alone, where none or saw, or heard,
In pathless paths I lead my wandring feet,
My humble Eyes to lofty Skyes I rear'd
To sing some Song, my mazed Muse thought meet.
My great Creator I would magnifie,
That nature had, thus decked liberally:
But Ah, and Ah, again, my imbecility!

9

I heard the merry grashopper then sing,
The black clad Cricket, bear a second part,
They kept one tune, and plaid on the same string,
Seeming to glory in their little Art.
Shall Creatures abject, thus their voices raise?
And in their kind resound their makers praise:
Whilst I as mute, can warble forth no higher layes.

10

When present times look back to Ages past,
And men in being fancy those are dead,
It makes things gone perpetually to last,
And calls back moneths and years that long since fled
It makes a man more aged in conceit,
Then was *Methuselah,* or's grand-sire great:
While of their persons & their acts his mind doth treat.

11

Sometimes in *Eden* fair, he seems to be,
Sees glorious *Adam* there made Lord of all,
Fancyes the Apple, dangle on the Tree,
That turn'd his Sovereign to a naked thral.
Who like a miscreant's driven from that place,
To get his bread with pain, and sweat of face:
A penalty impos'd on his backsliding Race.

12

Here sits our Grandame in retired place,
And in her lap, her bloody *Cain* new born,
The weeping Imp oft looks her in the face,
Bewails his unknown hap, and fate forlorn;
His Mother sighs, to think of Paradise,
And how she lost her bliss, to be more wise,
Believing him that was, and is, Father of lyes.

13

Here *Cain* and *Abel* come to sacrifice,
Fruits of the Earth, and Fatlings each do bring,
On *Abels* gift the fire descends from Skies,
But no such sign on false *Cain's* offering;
With sullen hateful looks he goes his wayes.
Hath thousand thoughts to end his brothers dayes,
Upon whose blood his future good he hopes to raise.

14

There *Abel* keeps his sheep, no ill he thinks,
His brother comes, then acts his fratricide,
The Virgin Earth, of blood her first draught drinks
But since that time she often hath been cloy'd;
The wretch with gastly face and dreadful mind,
Thinks each he sees will serve him in his kind,
Though none on Earth but kindred near then could he find.

15

Who fancyes not his looks now at the Barr,
His face like death, his heart with horror fraught,
Nor Male-factor ever felt like warr,
When deep dispair, with wish of life hath fought,
Branded with guilt, and crusht with treble woes,
A Vagabond to Land of *Nod* he goes,
A City builds, that wals might him secure from foes.

16

Who thinks not oft upon the Fathers ages.
Their long descent, how nephews sons they saw,
The starry observations of those Sages,
And how their precepts to their sons were law,
How Adam sigh'd to see his Progeny,
Cloath'd all in his black sinfull Livery,
Who neither guilt, nor yet the punishment could fly.

17

Our life compare we with their length of dayes
Who to the tenth of theirs doth now arrive?
And though thus short, we shorten many wayes,
Living so little while we are alive;
In eating, drinking, sleeping, vain delight
So unawares comes on perpetual night,
And puts all pleasures vain unto eternal flight.

18

When I behold the heavens as in their prime,
And then the earth (though old) stil clad in green,
The stones and trees, insensible of time,
Nor age nor wrinkle on their front are seen;
If winter come, and greeness then do fade,
A Spring returns, and they more youthfull made;
But Man grows old, lies down, remains where once he's laid.

19

By birth more noble then those creatures all,
Yet seems by nature and by custome curs'd,
No sooner born, but grief and care makes fall
That state obliterate he had at first:
Nor youth, nor strength, nor wisdom spring again
Nor habitations long their names retain,
But in oblivion to the final day remain.

20

Shall I then praise the heavens, the trees, the earth
Because their beauty and their strength last longer
Shall I wish there, or never to had birth,
Because they're bigger, & their bodyes stronger?
Nay, they shall darken, perish, fade and dye,
And when unmade, so ever shall they lye,
But man was made for endless immortality.

21

Under the cooling shadow of a stately Elm
Close sate I by a goodly Rivers side,
Where gliding streams the Rocks did overwhelm;
A lonely place, with pleasures dignifi'd.
I once that lov'd the shady woods so well,
Now thought the rivers did the trees excel,
And if the sun would ever shine, there would I dwell.

22

While on the stealing stream I fixt mine eye,
Which to the long'd for Ocean held its course,
I markt, nor crooks, nor rubs that there did lye
Could hinder ought, but still augment its force:
O happy Flood, quoth I, that holds thy race
Till thou arrive at thy beloved place,
Nor is it rocks or shoals that can obstruct thy pace.

23

Nor is't enough, that thou alone may'st slide,
But hundred brooks in thy cleer waves do meet,
So hand in hand along with thee they glide
To *Thetis* house, where all imbrace and greet:
Thou Emblem true, of what I count the best,
O could I lead my Rivolets to rest,
So may we press to that vast mansion, ever blest.

24

Ye Fish which in this liquid Region 'bide,
That for each season, have your habitation,
Now salt, now fresh where you think best to glide
To unknown coasts to give a visitation,
In Lakes and ponds, you leave your numerous fry,
So nature taught, and yet you know not why,
You watry folk that know not your felicity.

25

Look how the wantons frisk to task the air,
Then to the colder bottome streight they dive,
Eftsoon to *Neptun's* glassie Hall repair
To see what trade they great ones there do drive,
Who forrage o're the spacious sea-green field,
And take the trembling prey before it yield,
Whose armour is their scales, their spreading fins their shield.

26

While musing thus with contemplation fed,
And thousand fancies buzzing in my brain,
The sweet-tongu'd Philomel percht ore my head,
And chanted forth a most melodious strain
Which rapt me so with wonder and delight,
I judg'd my hearing better then my sight,
And wisht me wings with her a while to take my flight.

27

O merry Bird (said I) that fears no snares,
That neither toyles nor hoards up in thy barn,
Feels no sad thoughts nor cruciating cares
To gain more good, or shun what might thee harm
Thy cloaths ne're wear, thy meat is every where,
Thy bed a bough, thy drink the water cleer,
Reminds not what is past, nor whats to come dost fear.

28

The dawning morn with songs thou dost prevent,
Sets hundred notes unto thy feathered crew,
So each one tunes his pretty instrument,
And warbling out the old, begin anew,
And thus they pass their youth in summer season,
Then follow thee into a better Region,
Where winter's never felt by that sweet airy legion.

29

Man at the best a creature frail and vain,
In knowledg ignorant, in strength but weak,
Subject to sorrows, losses, sickness, pain,
Each storm his state, his mind, his body break,
From some of these he never finds cessation,
But day or night, within, without, vexation,
Troubles from foes, from friends, from dearest, near'st Relation.

30
And yet this sinfull creature, frail and vain,
This lump of wretchedness, of sin and sorrow,
This weather-beaten vessel wrackt with pain,
Joyes not in hope of an eternal morrow;
Nor all his losses, crosses and vexation,
In weight, in frequency and long duration
Can make him deeply groan for that divine Translation.

31
The Mariner that on smooth waves doth glide,
Sings merrily, and steers his Barque with ease,
As if he had command of wind and tide,
And now becomes great Master of the seas;
But suddenly a storm spoiles all the sport,
And makes him long for a more quiet port,
Which 'gainst all adverse winds may serve for fort.

32
So he that faileth in this world of pleasure,
Feeding on sweets, that never bit of th' sowre,
That's full of friends, of honour and of treasure,
Fond fool, he takes this earth ev'n for heav'ns bower.
But sad affliction comes & makes him see
Here's neither honour, wealth, or safety;
Only above is found all with security.

33
O Time the fatal wrack of mortal things,
That draws oblivions curtains over kings,
Their sumptuous monuments, men know them not,
Their names without a Record are forgot,
Their parts, their ports, their pomp's all laid in th' dust
Nor wit nor gold, nor buildings scape times rust;
But he whose name is grav'd in the white stone
Shall last and shine when all of these are gone.

from The Four Ages of Man

OLD AGE

My memory is short, and braine is dry.
My Almond-tree (gray haires) doth flourish now,
And back, once straight, begins apace to bow.
My grinders now are few, my sight doth faile
My skin is wrinkled, and my cheeks are pale.
No more rejoyce, at musickes pleasant noyse.

The Prologue

I
To sing of Wars, of Captaines, and of Kings,
Of Cities founded, Common-wealths begun,
For my mean Pen, are too superiour things,
And how they all, or each, their dates have run:
Let Poets, and Historians set these forth,
My obscure Verse, shal not so dim their worth.

2
But when my wondring eyes, and envious heart,
Great *Bartas* sugar'd lines doe but read o're;
Foole, I doe grudge, the Muses did not part
'Twixt him and me, that over-fluent store;
A *Bartas* can, doe what a *Bartas* wil,
But simple I, according to my skill.

3
From School-boyes tongue, no Rhethorick we expect,
Nor yet a sweet Consort, from broken strings,
Nor perfect beauty, where's a maine defect,
My foolish, broken, blemish'd Muse so sings;
And this to mend, alas, no Art is able,
'Cause Nature made it so irreparable.

4
Nor can I, like that fluent sweet tongu'd *Greek*
Who lisp'd at first, speake afterwards more plaine
By Art, he gladly found what he did seeke,
A full requitall of his striving paine:
Art can doe much, but this maxime's most sure,
A weake or wounded braine admits no cure.

5
I am obnoxious to each carping tongue,
Who sayes, my hand a needle better fits,
A Poets Pen, all scorne, I should thus wrong;
For such despight they cast on female wits:
If what I doe prove well, it wo'nt advance,
They'l say its stolne, or else, it was by chance.

6
But sure the antick *Greeks* were far more milde,
Else of our Sex, why feigned they those nine,
And poesy made, *Calliope's* owne childe,
So 'mongst the rest, they plac'd the Arts divine:
But this weake knot they will full soone untye,
The *Greeks* did nought, but play the foole and lye.

7
Let *Greeks* be *Greeks,* and Women what they are,
Men have precedency, and still excell,
It is but vaine, unjustly to wage war,
Men can doe best, and Women know it well;
Preheminence in each, and all is yours,
Yet grant some small acknowledgement of ours.

8
And oh, ye high flown quils, that soare the skies,
And ever with your prey, still catch your praise,
If e're you daigne these lowly lines, your eyes
Give wholsome Parsley wreath, I aske no Bayes:
This meane and unrefined stuffe of mine,
Will make your glistering gold but more to shine.

Anagrams

An Anagram.
Anna Bradestreate.
Deer Neat *An Bartas.*
So *Bartas* like thy fine spun Poems been,
That *Bartas* name will prove an Epicene.
* * *
Another.
Anne Bradstreate.
Artes bred neat *An.*

MICHAEL WIGGLESWORTH
(1631–1705)

from The Day of Doom

1
Still was the night, Serene and Bright,
    when all Men sleeping lay;
Calm was the season, and carnal reason
    thought so 'twould last for ay.
Soul, take thine ease, let sorrow cease,
    much good thou hast in store;
This was their Song, their Cups among,
    the Evening before.

5
For at midnight brake forth a Light,
    which turn'd the night to day,
And speedily an hideous cry
    did all the world dismay.
Sinners awake, their hearts do ake,
    trembling their loynes surprizeth;
Amaz'd with fear, by what they hear,
    each one of them ariseth.

6
They rush from Beds with giddy heads,
    and to their windows run,
Viewing this light, which shines more bright
    then doth the Noon-day Sun.
Straightway appears (they see't with tears)

the Son of God most dread;
Who with his Train comes on amain
    To Judge both Quick and Dead.

21
Thus every one before the Throne
    of Christ the Judge is brought,
Both righteous and impious
    that good or ill had wrought.
A separation, and diff'ring station
    by Christ appointed is
(To sinners sad) 'twixt good and bad,
    'twixt Heirs of woe and bliss.

25
Christ's Flock of Lambs there also stands,
    whose Faith was weak, yet true;
All sound Believers (Gospel receivers)
    whose Grace was small, but grew:
And them among an Infant throng
    of Babes, for whom Christ dy'd;
Whom for his own, by wayes unknown
    to men, he sanctify'd.

52
The glorious Judge will priviledge
    nor Emperour, nor King:
But every one that hath mis-done
    doth into Judgment bring.
And every one that hath mis-done,
    the Judge impartially
Condemneth to eternal wo,
    and endless misery.

JOHN COTTON
OF 'QUEEN'S CREEK'
(1640–1669)

Bacons Epitaph

Death why soe crewill! what, no other way
To manifest thy splleene, but thus to slay
Our hopes of safety; liberty, our all
Which, through thy tyrany, with him must fall
To its late Caoss? Had thy riged force
Bin delt by retale, and not thus in gross
Griefe had bin silent: Now wee must complaine
Since thou, in him, hast more then thousand slane
Whose lives and safetys did so much depend
On him there lif, with him there lives must end.
    If't be a sin to thinke Death brib'd can bee
Wee must be guilty; say twas bribery
Guided the fatall shaft. Verginias foes,
To whom for secrit crimes just vengeance owes
Disarved plagues, dreding their just disart
Corrupted Death by Parasscellcian art
Him to destroy; whose well tride curage such,
There heartless harts, nor arms, nor strength could touch.
    Who now must heale those wounds, or stop that blood
The Heathen made, and drew into a flood?
Who i'st must please our Cause? nor Trump nor Drum
Nor Deputations; these alass are dumb,
And Cannot speake. Our Arms (though nere so strong)
Will want the aide of his Commanding tongue,
Which Conquer'd more than Ceaser: He orethrew
Onely the outward frame; this Could subdue
The ruged workes of nature. Soules repleate
With dull Child could, he'd annemate with heate
Drawne forth of reasons Lymbick. In a word
Marss and Minerva both in him Concurd
For arts, for arms, whose pen and sword alike,
As Catos did, my admireation strike
In to his foes; while they confess withall
It was there guilt stil'd him a Criminall.
Onely this difference doth from truth proceed:
They in the guilt, he in the name must bleed,
While none shall dare his Obseques to sing
In disarv'd measures, untill time shall bring
Truth Crown'd with freedom, and from danger free,

To sound his praises to posterity.
Here let him rest; while wee this truth report,
Hee's gon from hence unto a higher Court
To pleade his Cause: where he by this doth know
Whether to Ceaser hee was friend, or foe.

EDWARD TAYLOR
(1642–1729)

Prologue

Lord, Can a Crumb of Dust the Earth outweigh,
    Outmatch all mountains, nay the Chrystall Sky?
Imbosom in't designs that shall Display
    And trace into the Boundless Deity?
    Yea hand a Pen whose moysture doth guild ore
    Eternall Glory with a glorious glore.

If it its Pen had of an Angels Quill,
    And Sharpend on a Pretious Stone ground tite,
And dipt in Liquid Gold, and mov'de by Skill
    In Christall leaves should golden Letters write
    It would but blot and blur yea jag, and jar
    Unless thou mak'st the Pen, and Scribener.

I am this Crumb of Dust which is design'd
    To make my Pen unto thy Praise alone,
And my dull Phancy I would gladly grinde
    Unto an Edge on Zions Pretious Stone.
    And Write in Liquid Gold upon thy Name
    My Letters till thy glory forth doth flame.

Let not th'attempts breake down my Dust I pray
    Nor laugh thou them to scorn but pardon give.
Inspire this Crumb of Dust till it display
    Thy Glory through't: and then thy dust shall live.
    Its failings then thou'lt overlook I trust,
    They being Slips slipt from thy Crumb of Dust.

Thy Crumb of Dust breaths two words from its breast,
    That thou wilt guide its pen to write aright
To prove thou art, and that thou art the best
    And shew thy Properties to shine most bright.
    And then thy Works will shine as flowers on Stems
    Or as in Jewellary Shops, do jems.

from GODS DETERMINATIONS

The Preface

    Infinity, when all things it beheld
In Nothing, and of Nothing all did build,
Upon what Base was fixt the Lath, wherein
He turn'd this Globe, and riggalld it so trim?
Who blew the Bellows of his Furnace Vast?
Or held the Mould wherein the world was Cast?
Who laid its Corner Stone? Or whose Command?
Where stand the Pillars upon which it stands?
Who Lac'de and Fillitted the earth so fine,
With Rivers like green Ribbons Smaragdine?
Who made the Sea's its Selvedge, and it locks
Like a Quilt Ball within a Silver Box?
Who Spread its Canopy? Or Curtains Spun?
Who in this Bowling Alley bowld the Sun?
Who made it always when it rises set
To go at once both down, and up to get?
Who th'Curtain rods made for this Tapistry?
Who hung the twinckling Lanthorns in the Sky?
Who? who did this? or who is he? Why, know
Its Onely Might Almighty this did doe.
His hand hath made this noble worke which Stands
His Glorious Handywork not made by hands.
Who spake all things from nothing; and with ease
Can speake all things to nothing, if he please.
Whose Little finger at his pleasure Can
Out mete ten thousand worlds with halfe a Span:
Whose Might Almighty can by half a looks
Root up the rocks and rock the hills by th'roots.
Can take this mighty World up in his hande,
And shake it like a Squitchen or a Wand.
Whose single Frown will make the Heavens shake
Like as an aspen leafe the Winde makes quake.
Oh! what a might is this Whose single frown

Doth shake the world as it would shake it down?
Which All from Nothing fet, from Nothing, All:
Hath All on Nothing set, lets Nothing fall
Gave All to nothing Man indeed, whereby
Through nothing man all might him Glorify.
In Nothing then imbosst the brightest Gem
More pretious than all pretiousness in them.
But Nothing man did throw down all by Sin:
And darkened that lightsom Gem in him.
    That now his Brightest Diamond is grown
    Darker by far than any Coalpit Stone.

from PREPARATORY MEDITATIONS: FIRST SERIES

The Reflexion

Lord, art thou at the Table Head above
    Meat, Med'cine, sweetness, sparkling Beautys to
Enamour Souls with Flaming Flakes of Love,
    And not my Trencher, nor my Cup o'reflow?
    Be n't I a bidden Guest? Oh! sweat mine Eye.
    Oreflow with Teares: Oh! draw thy fountains dry.

Shall I not smell thy sweet, oh! Sharons Rose?
    Shall not mine Eye salute thy Beauty? Why?
Shall thy sweet leaves their Beautious sweets upclose?
    As halfe ashamde my sight should on them ly?
    Woe's me! for this my sighs shall be in grain
    Offer'd on Sorrows Altar for the same.

Had not my Soule's thy Conduit, Pipes stopt bin
    With mud, what Ravishment would'st thou Convay?
Let Graces Golden Spade dig till the Spring
    Of tears arise, and cleare this filth away.
    Lord, let thy spirit raise my sighings till
    These Pipes my soule do with thy sweetness fill.

Earth once was Paradise of Heaven below
    Till inkefac'd sin had it with poyson stockt
And Chast this Paradise away into
    Heav'ns upmost Loft, and it in Glory Lockt.
    But thou, sweet Lord, hast with thy golden Key
    Unlockt the Doore, and made, a golden day.

Once at thy Feast, I saw thee Pearle-like stand
　　'Tween Heaven, and Earth where Heavens Bright glory all
In streams fell on thee, as a floodgate and,
　　Like Sun Beams through thee on the World to Fall.
　　Oh! sugar sweet then! my Deare sweet Lord, I see
　　Saints' Heavens-lost Happiness restor'd by thee.

Shall Heaven, and Earth's bright Glory all up lie
　　Like Sun Beams bundled in the sun, in thee?
Dost thou sit Rose at Table Head, where I
　　Do sit, and Carv'st no morsell sweet for mee?
　　So much before, so little now! Sprindge, Lord,
　　Thy Rosie Leaves, and me their Glee afford.

Shall not thy Rose my Garden fresh perfume?
　　Shall not thy Beauty my dull Heart assaile?
Shall not thy golden gleams run through this gloom?
　　Shall my black Velvet Mask thy fair Face Vaile?
　　Pass o're my Faults: shine forth, bright sun: arise
　　Enthrone thy Rosy-selfe within mine Eyes.

[6] Another Meditation at the same Time

Am I thy Gold? Or Purse, Lord, for thy Wealth;
　　Whether in mine, or mint refinde for thee?
Ime counted so, but count me o're thyselfe,
　　Lest gold washt face, and brass in Heart I bee.
　　I Feare my Touchstone touches when I try
　　Mee, and my Counted Gold too overly.

Am I new minted by thy Stamp indeed?
　　Mine Eyes are dim; I cannot clearly see.
Be thou my Spectacles that I may read
　　Thine Image, and Inscription stampt on mee.
　　If thy bright Image do upon me stand
　　I am a Golden Angell in thy hand.

Lord, make my Soule thy Plate: thine Image bright
　　Within the Circle of the same enfoile.
And on its brims in golden Letters write
　　Thy Superscription in an Holy style.
　　Then I shall be thy Money, thou my Hord:
　　Let me thy Angell bee, bee thou my Lord.

[8] Meditation. Joh. 6.51. I am the Living Bread

I kening through Astronomy Divine
    The Worlds bright Battlement, wherein I spy
A Golden Path my Pensill cannot line,
    From that bright Throne unto my Threshold ly.
    And while my puzzled thoughts about it pore
    I finde the Bread of Life in't at my doore.

When that this Bird of Paradise put in
    This Wicker Cage (my Corps) to tweedle praise
Had peckt the Fruite forbad: and so did fling
    Away its Food; and lost its golden dayes;
    It fell into Celestiall Famine sore:
    And never could attain a morsell more.

Alas! alas! Poore Bird, what wilt thou doe?
    The Creatures field no food for Souls e're gave.
And if thou knock at Angells dores they show
    An Empty Barrell : they no soul bread have.
    Alas! Poore Bird, the Worlds White Loafe is done.
    And cannot yield thee here the smallest Crumb.

In this sad state, God's Tender Bowells run
    Out streams of Grace: And he to end all strife
The Purest Wheate in Heaven, his deare-dear Son
    Grinds, and kneads up into this Bread of Life.
    Which Bread of Life from Heaven down came and stands
    Disht on thy Table up by Angells Hands.

Did God mould up this Bread in Heaven, and bake,
    Which from his table came, and to thine goeth?
Doth he bespeake thee thus, This Soule Bread take.
    Come Eate thy fill of this thy Gods White Loafe?
    Its Food too fine for Angells, yet come, take
    And Eate thy fill. Its Heavens Sugar Cake.

What Grace is this knead in this Loafe? This thing
    Souls are but petty things it to admire.
Yee Angells, help: This fill would to the brim
    Heav'ns whelm'd-down Chrystall meele Bowle, yea and
        higher.
This Bread of Life dropt in thy mouth, doth Cry.
Eate, Eate me, Soul, and thou shalt never dy.

from [22] Meditation. Phil. 2.9. God hath Highly Exalted him

When thy Bright Beams, my Lord, do strike mine Eye,
    Methinkes I then could truely Chide out right
My Hide bound Soule that stands so niggardly
    That scarce a thought gets glorified by't.
    My Quaintest Metaphors are ragged Stuff,
Making the Sun seem like a Mullipuff.

Its my desire, thou shouldst be glorifi'de:
    But when thy Glory shines before mine eye,
I pardon Crave, lest my desire be Pride.
    Or bed thy Glory in a Cloudy Sky.
    The Sun grows wan; and Angells palefac'd shrinke,
Before thy Shine, which I besmeere with Inke.

But shall the Bird sing forth thy Praise, and shall
    The little Bee present her thankfull Hum?
But I who see thy shining Glory fall
    Before mine Eyes, stand Blockish, Dull, and Dumb?
    Whether I speake, or speechless stand, I spy,
    I faile thy Glory: therefore pardon Cry.

But this I finde; My Rhymes do better suite
    Mine own Dispraise than tune forth praise to thee.
Yet being Chid, whether Consonant, or Mute,
    I force my Tongue to tattle, as you see.
    That I thy glorious Praise may Trumpet right,
    Be thou my Song, and make Lord, mee thy Pipe.

. . . .

from [7] Meditation. Ps. 105.17. He sent a man before them, even Joseph, who was sold etc.

All Dull, my Lord, my Spirits flat, and dead
   All water sockt and sapless to the skin.
Oh! Screw mee up and make my Spirits bed
    Thy quickening vertue For my inke is dim,
    My pensill blunt. Doth Joseph type out thee?
    Haraulds of Angells sing out, Bow the Knee.

. . . .

from [35] Meditation. Joh. 15.5. Without me yee can do nothing

My Blessed Lord, that Golden Linck that joyns
   My Soule, and thee, out blossoms on't this Spruice
Peart Pronown MY more spiritous than wines,
    Rooted in Rich Relation, Graces Sluce.
    This little Voice feasts mee with fatter Sweets
    Than all the Stars that pave the Heavens Streets.

It hands me All, my heart, and hand to thee
   And up doth lodge them in thy persons Lodge
And as a Golden bridg ore it to mee
    Thee, and thine All to me, and never dodge.
    In this small Ship a mutuall Intrest sayles
    From Heaven and Earth, by th'holy Spirits gales.

Thy Ware to me's so rich, should my Returns
   Be packt in sparkling Metaphors, out stilld
From Zion's garden flowers, by fire that burns
    Aright, of Saphire Battlements up filld
    And sent in Jasper Vialls it would bee
    A pack of guilded Non-Sense unto thee.

. . . .

from [36] Meditation. Col. 1.18. He is the Head
of the Body

. . . .

My Metaphors are but dull Tacklings tag'd
　　With ragged Non-Sense. Can such draw to thee
My stund affections all with Cinders clag'd,
　　If thy bright beaming headship touch not mee?
　　If that thy headship shines not in mine eyes,
　　My heart will fuddled ly with worldly toyes.

. . . .

from [43] Meditation. Rom. 9.5. God blessed
forever

When, Lord, I seeke to shew thy praises, then
　　Thy shining Majesty doth stund my minde,
Encramps my tongue and tongue ties fast my Pen,
　　That all my doings, do not what's designd.
　　My Speeche's Organs are so trancifide
　　My words stand startld, can't thy praises stride.

Nay Speeches Bloomery can't from the Ore
　　Of Reasons mine, melt words for to define
Thy Deity, nor t'deck the reechs that sore
　　From Loves rich Vales, sweeter than hony rhimes.
　　Words though the finest twine of reason, are
　　Too Course a web for Deity to ware.

Words Mentall are syllabicated thoughts:
　　Words Orall but thoughts Whiffld in the Winde.
Words Writ, are incky, Goose quill-slabbred draughts,
　　Although the fairest blossoms of the minde.
　　Then can such glasses cleare enough descry
　　My Love to thee, or thy rich Deity?

Words are befould, Thoughts filthy fumes that smoake,
 From Smutty Huts, like Will-a-Wisps that rise
From Quaugmires, run ore bogs where frogs do Croake,
 Lead all astray led by them by the eyes.
 My muddy Words so dark thy Deity,
 And cloude thy Sun-Shine, and its Shining Sky.

. . . .

from [77] Meditation. Zech. 9.11. The Pit wherein is no water

. . . .

A Pit indeed of Sin: No water's here:
 Whose bottom's furthest off from Heaven bright,
And is next doore to Hell Gate, to it neer:
 And here I dwell in sad and solemn night,
 My Gold-Fincht Angell Feathers dapled in
 Hells Scarlet Dy fat, blood red grown with Sin.

I in this Pit all Destitute of Light
 Cram'd full of Horrid Darkness, here do Crawle
Up over head, and Eares, in Nauseous plight:
 And Swinelike Wallow in this mire, and Gall:
 No Heavenly Dews nor Holy Waters drill:
 Nor Sweet Aire Brieze, nor Comfort here distill.

Here for Companions, are Fears, Heart-Achs, Grief
 Frogs, Toads, Newts, Bats, Horrid Hob-Goblins, Ghosts:
Ill Spirits haunt this Pit: and no reliefe:
 Nor Coard can fetch me hence in Creatures Coasts.
 I who once lodgd at Heavens Palace Gate
 With full Fledgd Angells, now possess this fate.

But yet, my Lord, thy golden Chain of Grace
 Thou canst let down, and draw mee up into
Thy Holy Aire, and Glory's Happy Place.
 Out from these Hellish damps and pit so low.
 And if thy Grace shall do't, My Harp I'le raise,
 Whose Strings toucht by this Grace, Will twang thy praise.

[THE LIKENINGS OF EDWARD TAYLOR:
A GATHERING OF TROPES]

from PREPARATORY MEDITATIONS: FIRST SERIES

from [3] Meditation. Can. 1.3. Thy Good Ointment

But Woe is mee! who have so quick a Sent
    To Catch perfumes pufft out from Pincks, and Roses
And other Muscadalls, as they get Vent,
    Out of their Mothers Wombs to bob our noses.
    And yet thy sweet perfume doth seldom latch
    My Lord, within my Mammulary Catch.

Am I denos'de? or doth the Worlds ill sents
    Engarison my nosthrills narrow bore?
Or is my smell lost in these Damps it Vents?
    And shall I never finde it any more?
    Or is it like the Hawks, or Hownds whose breed
    Take stincking Carrion for Perfume indeed?

This is my Case. All things smell sweet to mee:
    Except thy sweetness, Lord. Expell these damps.
Breake up this Garison: and let me see
    Thy Aromaticks pitching in these Camps.
    Oh! let the Clouds of thy sweet Vapours rise,
    And both my Mammularies Circumcise.

Shall Spirits thus my Mammularies suck?
    (As Witches Elves their teats,) and draw from thee
My Dear, Dear Spirit after fumes of muck?
    Be Dunghill Damps more sweet than Graces bee?
    Lord, clear these Caves. These Passes take, and keep.
    And in these Quarters lodge thy Odours sweet.

. . . .

from [39] Meditation. from 1 Joh. 2.1. If any man sin, we have an Advocate.

My Sin! my Sin, My God, these Cursed Dregs,
    Green, Yellow, Blew streakt Poyson hellish, ranck,
Bubs hatcht in natures nest on Serpents Eggs,
    Yelp, Cherp and Cry; they set my Soule a Cramp.
    I frown, Chide, strik and fight them, mourn and Cry
To Conquour them, but cannot them destroy.

I cannot kill nor Coop them up: my Curb
    'S less than a Snaffle in their mouth: my Rains
They as a twine thrid, snap: by hell they're spurd:
    And load my Soule with swagging loads of pains.
    Black Imps, young Divells, snap, bite, drag to bring
And pick mee headlong hells dread Whirle Poole in.

. . . .

from PREPARATORY MEDITATIONS: SECOND SERIES

from [5] Meditation on Gal. 3.16. And to thy Seed Which is Christ.

. . . .

Lord with thine Altars Fire, mine Inward man
    Refine from dross: burn out my sinfull guise
And make my Soul thine Altars Drippen pan
    To Catch the Drippen of thy Sacrifice.
    This is the Unction thine receive; the which
    Doth teach them all things of an happy pitch.

Thy Altars Fire burns not to ashes down
    This Offering. But it doth roast it here.
This is thy Roastmeate cooked up sweet, brown,
    Upon thy table set for Souls good cheer.
    The Drippen, and the meate are royall fair
    That fatten Souls, that with it welcomd are.

My Trencher, Lord, with thy Roast Mutton dress:
  And my dry Bisket in thy Dripping Sap.
And feed my Soul with thy Choice Angell Mess:
  My heart thy Praise, Will, tweedling Larklike tap.
  My florid notes, like Tenderills of Vines
  Twine round thy Praise, plants sprung in true Love's Mines.

from [18] Meditation. Heb. 13.10. Wee have an Altar

A Bran, a Chaff, a very Barly yawn,
  An Husk, a Shell, a Nothing, nay yet Worse,
A Thistle, Bryer prickle, pricking Thorn
  A Lump of Lewdeness, Pouch of Sin, a purse
  Of Naughtiness, I am, yea what not Lord?
  And wilt thou be mine Altar? and my bord?

Mine Heart's a Park or Chase of sins: Mine Head
  'S a Bowling Alley. Sins play Ninehole here.
Phansy's a Green: sin Barly breaks in't led.
  Judgment's a pingle. Blindeman's Buff's plaid there.
  Sin playes at Coursey Parke within my Minde.
  My Wills a Walke in which it aires what's blinde.

Sure then I lack Atonement. Lord me help.
  Thy Shittim Wood ore laid With Wealthy brass
Was an Atoning altar, and sweet smelt:
  But if ore laid with pure pure gold it was
  It was an Incense Altar, all perfum'd
  With Odours, wherein Lord thou thus was bloom'd.

. . . .

from [25] Meditation. Numb. 28.4.9. One Lamb shalt thou offer in the Morning, and the other at Even. And on the Sabbath day two Lambs etc.

Guilty, my Lord, What can I more declare?
  Thou knowst the Case, and Cases of my Soule.
Box of tinder: Sparks that falling o're
  Set all on fire, and worke me all in Shoals.
  A Pouch of Passion is my Pericarde.
  Sparks fly when ere my Flint and Steele strike hard.

I am a Dish of Dumps: yea ponderous dross,
  Black blood all clotted, burdening my heart,
That Anger's anvill, and my bark bears moss.
  My Spirits soakt are drunke with blackish Art.
  If any Vertue stir, it is but feeble.
  Th'Earth Magnet is, my heart's the trembling needle.

My Mannah breedeth Worms: Thoughts fly blow'd are.
  My heart's the Temple of the God of Flies.

. . . .

from [67B] Meditation. Mal. 4.2. With Healing in His Wings

. . . .

The Fiery Darts of Satan stob my heart.
  His Punyards Thrusts are deep, and venom'd too.
His Arrows wound my thoughts, Words, Works, each part
  They all a bleeding ly by th' Stobs, and rue.
  His Aire I breath in, poison doth my Lungs.
  Hence come Consumptions, Fevers, Head pains: Turns.

Yea, Lythargy, the Apoplectick Stroke:
  The Catochee, Soul Blindness, Surdity,
Ill tongue, Mouth Ulcers, Frog, the Quinsie Throate
  The Palate Fallen, Wheezings, Pleurisy.
  Heart Ach, the Syncopee, bad stomach tricks
  Gaul Tumors, Liver grown; spleen evills Cricks.

The Kidny toucht, The Iliak, Colick Griefe
  The Ricats, Dropsy, Gout, the Scurvy, Sore
The Miserere Mei. O Reliefe
  I want and would, and beg it at thy doore.
  O! Sun of Righteousness Thy Beams bright, Hot
  Rafter a Doctors, and a Surgeons Shop.

. . . .

from [75] Meditation. Phil. 3 Ult. Our Vile Bodie

. . . .

Here is a Mudwall tent, whose Matters are
    Dead Elements, which mixt make dirty trade:
Which with Life Animall are wrought up faire
    A Living mudwall by Gods holy Spade.
    Yet though a Wall alive all spruice, and crouce
    Its Base, and Vile. And baseness keeps its House.

Nature's Alembick 't is, Its true: that stills
    The Noblest Spirits terrene fruits possess,
Yet, oh! the Relicks in the Caldron will
    Proove all things else, Guts, Garbage, Rotteness.
    And all its pipes but Sincks of nasty ware
    That foule Earths face, and do defile the aire.

A varnisht pot of putrid excrements,
    And quickly turns to excrements itselfe,
By natures Law: but, oh! there therein tents
    A sparke immortall and no mortall elfe.
    An Angell bright here in a Swine Sty dwell!
    What Lodge of Wonders's this? What tongue can tell?

But, oh! how doth this Wonder still encrease?
    The Soule Creeps in't. And by it's too defil'd.
Are both made base, and vile, can have no peace
    Without, nor in: and's of its Shine beguil'd.
    And though this Spirit in it dwells yet here
    Its glory will not dwell with such sad geere.

Both grac'd together, and disgrac'd. Sad Case.
    What now becomes of Gods Electing Love?
This now doth raise the Miracle apace,
    Christ doth step in, and Graces Art improove.
    He kills the Leprosy that taints the Walls:
    And sanctifies the house before it falls.

. . . .

Oh! make my Body, Lord, Although its vile,
    Thy warehouse where Grace doth her treasures lay.
And Cleanse the house and ery Room from Soile.
    Deck all my Rooms with thy rich Grace I pray.
    If thy free Grace doth my low tent, perfume,
    I'll sing thy Glorious praise in ery room.

Upon a Spider Catching a Fly

Thou sorrow, venom Elfe.
   Is this thy play,
To spin a web out of thyselfe
    To catch a Fly?
      For Why?

I saw a pettish wasp
   Fall foule therein.
Whom yet thy Whorle pins did not clasp
   Lest he should fling
     His sting.

But as affraid, remote
   Didst stand hereat
And with thy little fingers stroke
   And gently tap
     His back.

Thus gently him didst treate
   Lest he should pet,
And in a froppish, waspish heate
   Should greatly fret
     Thy net.

Whereas the silly Fly,
   Caught by its leg
Thou by the throate tookst hastily
   And 'hinde the head
     Bite Dead.

This goes to pot, that not
   Nature doth call.
Strive not above what strength hath got
   Lest in the brawle
     Thou fall.

This Frey seems thus to us.
   Hells Spider gets
His intrails spun to whip Cords thus
   And wove to nets
     And sets.

To tangle Adams race
    In's stratigems
To their Destructions, spoil'd, made base
    By venom things
        Damn'd Sins.

But mighty, Gracious Lord
    Communicate
Thy Grace to breake the Cord, afford
    Us Glorys Gate
        And State.

We'l Nightingaile sing like
    When pearcht on high
In Glories Cage, thy glory, bright,
    And thankfully,
        For joy.

Huswifery

Make me, O Lord, thy Spining Wheele compleate.
    Thy Holy Worde my Distaff make for mee.
Make mine Affections thy Swift Flyers neate
    And make my Soule thy holy Spoole to bee.
    My Conversation make to be thy Reele
    And reele the yarn thereon spun of thy Wheele.

Make me thy Loome then, knit therein this Twine:
    And make thy Holy Spirit, Lord, winde quills:
Then weave the Web thyselfe. The yarn is fine.
    Thine Ordinances make my Fulling Mills.
    Then dy the same in Heavenly Colours Choice,
    All pinkt with Varnisht Flowers of Paradise.

Then cloath therewith mine Understanding, Will,
    Affections, Judgment, Conscience, Memory
My Words, and Actions, that their shine may fill
    My wayes with glory and thee glorify.
    Then mine apparell shall display before yee
    That I am Cloathd in Holy robes for glory.

Upon Wedlock, And Death of Children

A Curious Knot God made in Paradise,
  And drew it out inamled neatly Fresh.
It was the True-Love Knot, more sweet than spice
  And set with all the flowres of Graces dress.
  Its Weddens Knot, that ne're can be unti'de.
  No Alexanders Sword can it divide.

The slips here planted, gay and glorious grow:
  Unless an Hellish breath do sindge their Plumes.
Here Primrose, Cowslips, Roses, Lilies blow
  With violets and Pinkes that voide perfumes.
  Whose beautious leaves ore laid with Hony Dew.
  And chanting birds Cherp out sweet Musick true.

When in this Knot I planted was, my Stock
  Soon knotted, and a manly flower out brake.
And after it my branch again did knot
  Brought out another Flowre its sweet breathd mate.
  One knot gave one tother the tothers place.
  Whence Checkling smiles fought in each others face.

But oh! a glorious hand from glory came
  Guarded with Angells, soon did Crop this flowre
Which almost tore the root up of the same
  At that unlookt for, Dolesome, darksome houre.
  In Pray're to Christ perfum'de it did ascend,
  And Angells bright did it to heaven tend.

But pausing on't, this sweet perfum'd my thought,
  Christ would in Glory have a Flowre, Choice, Prime,
And having Choice, chose this my branch forth brought.
  Lord take't. I thanke thee, thou takst ought of mine,
  It is my pledg in glory, part of mee
  Is now in it, Lord, glorifi'de with thee.

But praying ore my branch, my branch did sprout
  And bore another manly flower, and gay
And after that another, sweet brake out,
  The which the former hand soon got away.
  But oh! the tortures, Vomit, screechings, groans,
  And six weeks Fever would pierce hearts like stones.

Griefe o're doth flow: and nature fault would finde
    Were not thy Will, my Spell Charm, Joy, and Gem:
That as I said, I say, take, Lord, they're thine.
    I piecemeal pass to Glory bright in them.
    I joy, may I sweet Flowers for Glory breed,
    Whether thou getst them green, or lets them seed.

RICHARD STEERE
(1643–1721)

from A Monumental Memorial of Marine Mercy

    Since Every *Quill* is silent to Relate
What being known must needs be wonder'd at
I take the boldness to present your *Eye*
With Safty's *Prospect* in Extremity,
Which tho not Cloath'd with *Academick* Skill,
Or lofty Raptures of *Poet's* Quill;
But wrapt in *raggs,* through which your eyes may see
The *Naked* Truth in plain simplicitee.
    I without further prologue *Lanch with* ink
With Captain *Balston* in th' *Adventure Pinck;*

. . . .

    The Two and twentieth day much *wind* did blow,
When in the *Downs* we let our *Anchor* goe,
But it *came home:* we our *Shift Anchor Cast,*
Which *(insignificant) came home* as fast,
And we were driven up *alongst* the *Side*
Of a *Ship* there, which did at *Anchor* ride,
Our *Anchor* took her *Cable,* and did pass
Up with a speedy motion to her *Hass,*
Which at their *Bows* they *Cutting* from the *Cable,*
And t'other *Anchor* being too unable
To bring us up, broke in the *shank,* and we
Again (by Violence) *Drove out to Sea;*
We thought to *Anchor* then in *Poulstone Bay,*
And let our *small Bower go* without delay,
Which like a rotten stick was quickly broke
(When once it came to strain) both *flewks & stock,*
Neither *Shift-Anchor, Best* nor yet *Small Bower*
To *Bring us up* had strength enough or power;

And in the Afternoon the *winds* Restrain
Their furious *Blasts,* now only did remain
Our small *Cedge Anchor,* (unto which we must
Our *Lives,* our *Ship,* and all her *Cargo* trust,)
Which *Letting go,* Heav'ns care did so provide,
That we that *Ebb* secure in safety *Ride;*
From which our apprehensions may Inspect,
How the *Great* God by *Small* meanes doth protect,
Whose strength can make our strongest *cables* weak,
Our *Cobwebs* strong, no earthly strein can break.

. . . .

And so Return into the *Downs* again,
And weighing thence, favour'd with *winds* and *floods,*
Our *selves* in Safety with our *ship* and *goods*
The *Twenty fifth* (assisted by the Lord)
Arriv'd at *London* and at *Ratcliff Moor'd.*

THOMAS MAULE
(c.1645–1724)

To Cotton Mather, from a Quaker

Hebrew, Greek or Latin, I have not,
Learning have, which by the Truth I got
As in true verse, here is this time to thee,
The Truth of which thou in my verse may see.
While thou keep on thy lying Trade to gain:
I thee withstand, the Truth for to maintain;
A Servant fit thou art for evil work,
To deal well sharp with thee will not thee hurt?
Thou Lives at ease, while others Plow and Sow,
Their labour give, for what well do not know,
The love of Money leads thee for to preach:
Keep that from thee, thou wil't no longer teach;
And as to all thy Marchandizing ware,
Such men that buy, their Souls have but ill fare.
Which Trade of thine cannot continue long,
As men see thy deceit will from thee throng:
And those that live to God will search thee out;
Yea, those of thy own Trade will help to rout;
For those of thy own Trade much disagree.

Which shews their fall is near, Gods People see,
It is a Money Trade that with some wit,
With which dishonest men themselves do fit:
Thou hath thy masters way to deal with *Maule,*
As in thy Book without thy name at all,
That is, to *Boston* Wood, the Gallows there:
It shews thou art both void of Grace and fear;
A better way he finds to deal with thee;
To do some good, as all men hear may see,
To leave deceit, and in some boat to row,
Until a good be, then unto preaching go:
If boating work, with thee will not agree;
Take other honest Trade, and honest be.
As for thy Trade of preaching we all see,
It starves mens Souls, and also purses free.
But if resolve not with the Truth to dwell:
Thou must take part with them that go to Hell;
Many things I have against thee more,
And value not the study of thy store.
Thou at the first hath wrong with me begun,
Truth will me right so far may see it done.
Which to conclude with Letters of my name;
That thou may certain be from whom it came.

EBENEZER COOKE
(1667–c.1732)

from The Sot-weed Factor

CONDEMN'D by Fate to way-ward Curse,
Of Friends unkind, and empty Purse;
Plagues worse then fill'd *Pandora's* Box,
I took my leave of *Albion's* Rocks:
With heavy Heart, concern'd that I
Was forc'd my Native Soil to fly,
And the *Old World* must bid good-buy.
But Heav'n ordain'd it should be so,
And to repine is vain, we know.
Freighted with Fools, from, *Plymouth* sound,
To *Mary-Land* our Ship was bound;
Where we arriv'd in dreadful Pain,
Shock'd by the Terrors of the Main;

. . . .

These *Sot-weed* Planters crowd the Shoar,
In Hew as tawny as a Moor;
Figures, so strange, no God design'd
To be a Part of Humane Kind:
But wanton Nature, void of Rest,
Moulded the brittle Clay in Jest.
At last, a Fancy very odd
Took me, this was the Land of *Nod,*
Planted at first when Vagrant *Cain,*
His Broter had unjustly slain;
Then, conscious of the Crime he'd done,
From Vengeance dire, he hither run;
And in a Hut supinely dwelt,
The first in *Furs* and *Sotweed* dealt.
And ever since that Time, this Place,
Has harbour'd a detested Race;
Who, when they could not thrive at Home,
For Refuge to these Worlds did roam.

BENJAMIN FRANKLIN
(1706–1790)

Epitaph in Bookish Style.

The Body
of
Benjamin Franklin
Printer
(Like the cover of an old book
Its contents torn out
And stript of its lettering and gilding)
Lies here, food for worms.
But the work shall not be lost
For it will (as he believed) appear once more
In a new and more elegant edition
Revised and corrected
by
The Author.

Jane Colman Turell

(1708–1735)

You Beauteous Dames

    You beauteous dames, if that my love you see,
With eager steps conduct him here to me,
Tell him no joy to me you can impart,
And that no pain is like a bleeding heart.
Say I am sick of love, and moaning lie,
Whilst the sad echo to my groans reply,
    Who is thy love? the scornful maids reply,
And for what form waste you your bloom in sighs?
Let's know the man, if he be worth your care,
Or does deserve the tender love you bear.
    Whilst your request with pleasure I obey,
Your strict attention give to what I say.
My love excels all that's on earth call'd fair,
As the bright sun excels the meanest star.
His head is wisdom's spacious theatre,
Riches of grace and beauty there appear.
A down his shoulders with becoming pride
Falls fine hair in beauteous ringlets tied.
His sparkling eyes in splendent luster vie
With the twin stars that grace the azure sky.
His cheeks excel the fragrant blushing rose
Which in the fruitful vale of Sharon grows.
His lips like lilies in their flow'ry bloom
Yield a sweet odor and a rich perfume.
His ivory arms more charming to behold
Than orient pearls, encas'd in shining gold.
His well turn'd legs like stately pillars stand
Of marble, polish'd by a curious hand.
His mien is noble and august his air,
His countenance as Lebanon does appear.

from An Invitation Into the Country, In Imitation of Horace

. . . .

     Though my small incomes never can afford,
Like wealthy Celsus to regale a Lord;
No ivory tables groan beneath the weight
Of sumptuous dishes, serv'd in massy plate;
The forest ne'er was search'd for food for me,
Not from my hounds the timorous hare does flee:
No leaden thunder strikes the fowl in air,
Nor from my shaft the winged death do fear:
With silken nets I ne'er the lake despoil,
Nor with my bait the larger fish beguile.
No luscious sweet-meats, by my servants plac'd
In curious order, e'er my table grac'd:
To please the taste, no rich Burgundian wine,
In crystal glasses on my side-board shine;
The luscious sweets of fair Canaries' Isle
Ne'er fill'd my casks, nor in my flagons smile:
No wine, but what does from my apples flow,
My frugal house on any can bestow:
Except when Cesar's birth-day does return,
And joyful fires throughout the village burn;
The moderate each takes his cheerful glass,
And our good wishes to Augustus pass.

. . . .

ANONYMOUS

The Cameleon Lover
(1732)

If what the *Curious* have observ'd be true,
That the *Cameleon* will assume the *Hue*
Of all the Objects that approach its *Touch;*
No Wonder then, that the *Amours* of *such*
Whose *Taste* betrays them to a close Embrace
With the *dark* Beauties of the *Sable* Race,
(Stain'd with the Tincture of the *Sooty* Sin,)
Imbibe the *Blackness* of their *Charmer's* Skin.

The Cameleon's Defence
(1732)

All Men have Follies, which they blindly trace
Thro' the dark Turnings of a dubious Maze:
But happy those, who, by a prudent Care,
Retreat betimes, from the fallacious Snare.
The eldest Sons of Wisdom were not free,
From the same Failure you condemn in Me.
If as the Wisest of the Wise have err'd,
I go astray and am condemn'd unheard,
My Faults you too severely reprehend,
More like a rigid Censor than a Friend.
Love is the Monarch Passion of the Mind,
Knows no Superior, by no Laws confin'd;
But triumphs still, impatient of Controul,
O'er all the proud Endowments of the Soul.

FRANCIS HOPKINSON
(1737–1791)

O'er the Hills

O'er the hills far away, at the birth of the morn,
I hear the full tone of the sweet sounding horn;
The sportsmen with shoutings all hail the new day,
And swift run the hounds o'er the hills far away.
Across the deep valley their course they pursue,
And rush through the thickets yet silver'd with dew;
Nor hedges nor ditches their speed can delay—
Still sounds the sweet horn o'er the hills far away.

DANIEL BLISS
(1740–1806)

Epitaph of John Jack

God wills us free; man wills us slaves.
I will as God wills; God's will be done.
Here lies the body of
    JOHN JACK
A native of Africa who died
March 1773, aged about 60 years.
Tho' born in a land of slavery,
He was born free.
Tho' he lived in a land of liberty,
He lived a slave.
Till by his honest, tho' stolen, labors,
He acquired the source of slavery,
Which gave him his freedom;
Tho' not long before
Death, the grand tyrant,
Gave him his final emancipation,
And set him on a footing with kings.
Tho' a slave to vice,
He practised those virtues
Without which kings are but slaves.

ANONYMOUS

The Country School

    Put to the door—the school's begun—
Stand in your places every one,—
Attend,———
Read in the bible,—tell the place,—
"Job twentieth and the seventeenth varse,—
Caleb, begin. *And—he—shall—suck—*
Sir,—Moses got a pin and stuck——
Silence,—stop Caleb—Moses! here!
What's this complaint? *I didn't, Sir,—*
Hold up your hand,—What is't a pin?
O dear, I won't do so agin.
Read on. *The increase of his h—h—horse—*

Hold: H, O, U, S, E, spells house.
Sir, what's this word? for I can't tell it.
Can't you indeed! Why, spell it. *Spell it.*
Begin yourself, I say. *Who, I?*
Yes, try. Sure you can spell it. *Try.*
Go, take your seats and primers, go,
You sha'n't abuse the bible so.

Will pray Sir Master mend my pen?
Say, Master, that's enough.—Here, Ben,
Is this your copy? Can't you tell?
Set all your letters parallel.
I've done my sum—'tis just a groat—
Let's see it.—*Master, m' I g' out?*
Yes,—bring some wood in—What's that noise?
It isn't I, Sir, it's them boys.——

Come Billy, read—What's that? *That's A—*
Sir, Jim has snatch'd my rule away——
Return it, James.—Here, rule with this—
Billy, read on,—*That's crooked S.*
Read in the spelling-book—Begin—
The boys are out—Then call them in—
My nose bleeds, mayn't I get some ice,
And hold it in my breeches?—Yes.
John, keep your seat. *My sum is more—*
Then do't again—Divide by four,
By twelve, and twenty—Mind the rule.
Now speak, Manassah, and spell tool.
I can't—Well try—*T, W, L.*
Not wash'd your hands yet, boody, ha?
You had your orders yesterday.
Give me the ferrule, hold your hand.
Oh! Oh! There,—mind my next command.

The grammar read. Tell where the place is.
C sounds like K in cat and cases.
My book is torn. The next.—*Here not—*
E final makes it long—say note.
What are the stops and marks, Susannah?
*Small points, Sir.——*And how many, Hannah?
Four, Sir. How many, George? You look:
Here's more than fifty in my book.
How's this? Just come, Sam? *Why I've been—*
Who knocks? *I don't know, Sir.* Come in.
"Your most obedient, Sir?" And yours.
Sit down, Sir. Sam, put to the doors.

What do you bring to tell that's new!
"Nothing, that's either strange or true.
"What a prodigious school! I'm sure
"You've got a hundred here, or more.
"A word, Sir, if you please." I will—
You girls, till I come in be still.

    "Come, we can dance to night—so you
"Dismiss your brain-distracting crew,
"And come—For all the girls are there.
"We'll have a fiddle and a player."
Well, mind and have the sleigh-bells sent,
I'll soon dismiss my regiment.

    Silence! The second class must read.
As quick as possible—proceed.
Not found your book yet? Stand—be fix'd—
The next read, stop—the next—the next.
You need not read again, tis well.
Come Tom and Dick, choose sides to spell.

Will this word do? Yes, Tom spell dunce.
Sit still there, all you little ones.
I've got a word, Well, name it. *Gizzard.*
You spell it Sampson.—G, I, Z.
Spell conscience, Jack. K, O, N,
S, H, U, N, T, S.—Well done!
Put out the next.—*Mine is folks.*
Tim, spell it.—P, H, O, U, X.
O shocking! Have you all try'd? No.
Say Master, but no matter, go—
Lay by your books—and you, Josiah,
Help Jed to make the morning fire.

SONGS AND HYMNS: TO 1775

The Lord to Mee a Shepherd Is
(The Bay Psalm Book, 1640)

The Lord to mee a shepheard is,
    want therefore shall not I.
Hee in the folds of tender-grasse,
    doth cause mee downe to lie:
To waters calme me gently leads

Restore my soule doth hee:
    he doth in paths of righteousnes:
    for his names sake leade mee.
Yea though in valley of deaths shade
    I walk, none ill I'le feare:
    because thou art with mee, thy rod,
    and staffe my comfort are.
For mee a table thou hast spread,
    in presense of my foes:
    thou dost annoynt my head with oyle,
    my cup it over-flowes.
Goodness & mercy surely shall
    all my dayes follow mee:
    and in the Lords house I shall dwell
    so long as dayes shall bee.

A Whaling Song
(John Osborn, n.d.)

When spring returns with western gales,
    And gentle breezes sweep
The ruffling seas, we spread our sails
    To plough the wat'ry deep.

For killing northern whales prepared,
    Our nimble boats on board,
With craft and rum (our chief regard)
    And good provisions stored,

Cape Cod, our dearest, native land,
    We leave astern, and lose
Its sinking cliffs and lessening sands,
    While Zephyr gently blows.

. . . .

When eastward, clear of Newfoundland,
    We stem the frozen pole.
We see the icy islands stand,
    The northern billows roll.

. . . .

A mighty whale we rush upon,
    And in our irons throw:
She sinks her monstrous body down
    Among the waves below.

. . . .

She thrashes with her tail around,
    And blows her redd'ning breath;
She breaks the air, a deaf'ning sound,
    While ocean groans beneath.

From numerous wounds, with crimson flood
    She stains the frothy seas,
And grasps, and blows her latest blood,
    While quivering life decays.

With joyful hearts we see her die,
    And on the surface lay;
While all with eager haste apply,
    To save our deathful prey.

Christ the Apple-Tree
(Anonymous, 1761)

The tree of life my soul hath seen,
Laden with fruit, and always green:
The trees of nature fruitless be,
Compar'd with Christ the apple-tree.

His beauty doth all things excel:
By faith I know, but ne'er can tell,
The glory which I now can see,
In Jesus Christ the apple-tree.

For happiness I long have sought,
And pleasure dearly I have bought:
I miss'd of all; but now I see
'Tis found in Christ the apple-tree.

I'm weary'd with my former toil,
Here I will sit and rest a while:
Under the shadow I will be,
Of Jesus Christ the apple-tree.

With great delight I'll make my stay,
There's none shall fright my soul away:
Among the sons of men I see
There's none like Christ the apple-tree.

I'll sit and eat this fruit divine,
It cheers my heart like spirit'al wine;
And now this fruit is sweet to me,
That grows on Christ the apple-tree.

This fruit doth make my soul to thrive,
It keeps my dying faith alive;
Which makes my soul in haste to be
With Jesus Christ the apple-tree.

Springfield Mountain
(Irma Townsend Ireland, 1761)

On Springfield Mountains there did dwell
A likeley youth was known full well
Lieutenant Merrick onley son
A likeley youth near twenty-one.

One Friday morning he did go
in to the medow and did mow
A round or two then he did feal
A pisen serpent at his heal.

When he received his deadly wond
he dropt hi sythe apon the ground
And strate for home was his intent
Calling aloude still as he went,

tho all around his voys wase hered
but none of his friends to him apierd
they thought it was some workman calld
And there poor Timothy alone must fall.

So soon his Carfull father went
To seak his son with discontent
and there hes fond onley son he found
ded as a stone apon the ground.

And there he lay down sopose to rest
Withe both his hands Acrost his brest
his mouth and eyes Closed fast
And there poor man he slept his last.

his father vieude his track with greate concern
Where he had run across the corn
Uneven tracks where he did go
did apear to stagger two and frow.

The seventh of August sixty-one
this fatull axandint was done
Let this a warning be to all
to be prepared when God does call.

Let Tyrants Shake
(William Billings, 1770)

Let tyrants shake their iron rod,
And slavery clank her galling chains.
We fear them not; we trust in God;
New England's God forever reigns.

When God inspired us for the fight
Their ranks were broke, their lines were forced;
Their ships were shattered in our sight
Or swiftly driven from our coast.

The foe comes on with haughty stride;
Our troops advance with martial noise.
Their veterans flee before our youth,
And generals yield to beardless boys.

What grateful offerings shall we bring?
What shall we render to the Lord?
Loud halleluiahs let us sing.
And praise his name on every chord.

Wak'd by the Gospel's Joyful Sound

(Samson Occom, 1774)

Wak'd by the gospel's joyful sound,
My soul in guilt and thrall I found,
   Exposed to endless woe:
Eternal truth aloud proclaim'd,
The sinner must be born again,
   Or else to ruin go.

Surpris'd I was, but could not tell
Which way to shun the gates of hell,
   For they were drawing near:
I strove indeed, but all in vain—
The sinner must be born again,
   Still sounded in my ear.

Then to the law I flew for help;
But still the weight of guilt I felt,
   And no relief I found:
While death eternal gave me pain,
The sinner must be born again,
   Did loud as thunder sound.

God's justice now I did behold,
And guilt lay heavy on my soul—
   It was a heavy load!
I read my Bible; it was plain
The sinner must be born again,
   Or feel the wrath of God.

I heard some tell how Christ did give
His life, to let the sinner live;
   But him I could not see:
This solemn truth did still remain—
The sinner must be born again,
   Or dwell in misery.

But as my soul, with dying breath,
Was gasping in eternal death,
   Christ Jesus I did spy:
Free grace and pardon he proclaim'd;
The sinner then was born again,
   With raptures I did cry.

The Angels in the world above,
And saints can witness to the love,
 Which then my soul enjoy'd.
My soul did mount on faith, its wing,
And glory, glory, did I sing,
 To Jesus Christ my Lord.

Come, needy sinners, hear me tell
What boundless love in Jesus dwell,
 How Mercy doth abound;
Let none of mercy doubting stand,
Since I the chief of sinners am,
 Yet I have mercy found.

II

REVOLUTION
AND THE EARLY
REPUBLIC:
1775–1825

JOHN TRUMBULL
(1750–1831)

from M'FINGAL

from The Town-Meeting, A.M.

When Yankies, skill'd in martial rule,
First put the British troops to school;
Instructed them in warlike trade,
And new manoeuvres of parade,
The true war-dance of Yankee reels,
And *manual exercise* of heels;
Made them give up, like saints complete,
The arm of flesh, and trust the feet,
And work, like Christians undissembling,
Salvation out, by fear and trembling;
Taught Percy fashionable races,
And modern modes of Chevy-Chases:
From Boston, in his best array,
Great 'Squire M'FINGAL took his way,
And graced with ensigns of renown,
Steer'd homeward to his native town.
    His high descent our heralds trace
From Ossian's famed Fingalian race:
For though their name some part may lack,
Old Fingal spelt it with a MAC;
Which great M'Pherson, with submission,
We hope will add the next edition.
    His fathers flourish'd in the Highlands
Of Scotia's fog-benighted islands;
Whence gain'd our 'Squire two gifts by right,
Rebellion, and the Second-sight.
Of these, the first, in ancient days,
Had gain'd the noblest palm of praise,
'Gainst kings stood forth and many a crown'd head
With terror of its might confounded;
Till rose a king with potent charm
His foes by meekness to disarm,
Whom every Scot and Jacobite
Strait fell in love with at first sight;
Whose gracious speech with aid of pensions,
Hush'd down all murmurs of dissensions,
And with the sound of potent metal

Brought all their buzzing swarms to settle;
Who rain'd his ministerial manna,
Till loud Sedition sung hosanna;
The grave Lords-Bishops and the Kirk
United in the public work;
Rebellion, from the northern regions,
With Bute and Mansfield swore allegiance;
All hands combin'd to raze, as nuisance,
Of church and state the Constitutions,
Pull down the empire, on whose ruins
They meant to edify their new ones;
Enslave th' Amer'can wildernesses,
And rend the provinces in pieces.
With these our 'Squire, among the valiant'st,
Employ'd his time, and tools and talents,
And found this new rebellion pleasing
As his old king-destroying treason.

 Nor less avail'd his optic sleight,
And Scottish gift of second-sight.
No ancient sybil, famed in rhyme,
Saw deeper in the womb of time;
No block in old Dodona's grove
Could ever more orac'lar prove.
Nor only saw he all that could be,
But much that never was, nor would be;
Whereby all prophets far outwent he,
Though former days produced a plenty:
For any man with half an eye
What stands before him can espy;
But optics sharp it needs, I ween,
To see what is not to be seen.
As in the days of ancient fame,
Prophets and poets were the same,
And all the praise that poets gain
Is for the tales they forge and feign:
So gain'd our 'Squire his fame by seeing
Such things, as never would have being;
Whence he for oracles was grown
The very tripod of his town.
Gazettes no sooner rose a lie in,
But strait he fell to prophesying;
Made dreadful slaughter in his course,
O'erthrew provincials, foot and horse,
Brought armies o'er, by sudden pressings,
Of Hanoverians, Swiss and Hessians,
Feasted with blood his Scottish clan,

And hang'd all rebels to a man,
Divided their estates and pelf,
And took a goodly share himself.
All this with spirit energetic,
He did by second-sight prophetic.

. . . .

PHILIP FRENEAU
(1752–1832)

from George the Third's Soliloquy

. . . .

France aids them now, a desperate game I play,
And hostile Spain will do the same, they say;
My armies vanquished, and my heroes fled,
My people murmuring, and my commerce dead,
My shattered navy pelted, bruised, and clubbed,
By Dutchmen bullied, and by Frenchmen drubbed,
My name abhorred, my nation in disgrace,
How should I act in such a mournful case!
My hopes and joys are vanished with my coin,
My ruined army, and my lost Burgoyne!
What shall I do—confess my labours vain,
Or whet my tusks, and to the charge again!
But where's my force—my choicest troops are fled,
Some thousands crippled, and a myriad dead—
If I were owned the boldest of mankind,
And hell with all her flames inspired my mind,
Could I at once with Spain and France contend,
And fight the rebels on the world's green end?—

. . . .

from The House of Night—A Vision

I

Trembling I write my dream, and recollect
A fearful vision at the midnight hour;
So late, Death o'er me spread his sable wings,
Painted with fancies of malignant power!

6

By some sad means, when Reason holds no sway,
Lonely I rov'd at midnight o'er a plain
Where murmuring streams and mingling rivers flow
Far to their springs, or seek the sea again.

8

Dark was the sky, and not one friendly star
Shone from the zenith or horizon, clear,
Mist sate upon the woods, and darkness rode
In her black chariot, with a wild career.

9

And from the woods the late resounding note
Issued of the loquacious Whip-poor-will,
Hoarse, howling dogs, and nightly roving wolves
Clamour'd from far off cliffs invisible.

10

Rude, from the wide extended Chesapeke
I heard the winds the dashing waves assail,
And saw from far, by picturing fancy form'd,
The black ship travelling through the noisy gale.

11

At last, by chance and guardian fancy led,
I reach'd a noble dome, rais'd fair and high,
And saw the light from upper windows flame,
Presage of mirth and hospitality.

12

And by that light around the dome appear'd
A mournful garden of autumnal hue,
Its lately pleasing flowers all drooping stood
Amidst high weeds that in rank plenty grew.

109

O'er a dark field I held my dubious way
Where Jack-a-lanthorn walk'd his lonely round,
Beneath my feet substantial darkness lay,
And screams were heard from the distemper'd ground.

110

Nor look'd I back, till to a far off wood,
Trembling with fear, my weary feet had sped—
Dark was the night, but at the inchanted dome
I saw the infernal windows flaming red.

111

And from within the howls of Death I heard,
Cursing the dismal night that gave him birth,
Damning his ancient sire, and mother sin,
Who at the gates of hell, accursed, brought him forth.

117

Dim burnt the lamp, and now the phantom Death
Gave his last groans in horror and despair—
"All hell demands me hence,"—he said, and threw
The red lamp hissing through the midnight air.

118

Trembling, across the plain my course I held,
And found the grave-yard, loitering through the gloom,
And, in the midst, a hell-red, wandering light,
Walking in fiery circles round the tomb.

125

At distance far approaching to the tomb,
By lamps and lanthorns guided through the shade,
A coal-black chariot hurried through the gloom,
Spectres attending, in black weeds array'd.

128

Before the hearse Death's chaplain seem'd to go,
Who strove to comfort, what he could, the dead;
Talk'd much of Satan, and the land of woe,
And many a chapter from the scriptures read.

132

What is this Death, ye deep read sophists, say?—
Death is no more than one unceasing change;
New forms arise, while other forms decay,
Yet all is Life throughout creation's range.

133
The towering Alps, the haughty Appenine,
The Andes, wrapt in everlasting snow,
The Appalachian and the Ararat
Sooner or later must to ruin go.

134
Hills sink to plains, and man returns to dust,
That dust supports a reptile or a flower;
Each changeful atom by some other nurs'd
Takes some new form, to perish in an hour.

135
Too nearly join'd to sickness, toils, and pains,
(Perhaps for former crimes imprison'd here)
True to itself the immortal soul remains,
And seeks new mansions in the starry sphere.

136
When Nature bids thee from the world retire,
With joy thy lodging leave, a fated guest;
In Paradise, the land of thy desire,
Existing always, always to be blest.

from The British Prison Ship

Two hulks on Hudson's stormy bosom lie,
Two, farther south, affront the pitying eye—
There, the black *Scorpion* at her mooring rides,
There, *Strombolo* swings, yielding to the tides;
Here, bulky *Jersey* fills a larger space,
And *Hunter,* to all hospitals disgrace—
Thou, *Scorpion,* fatal to thy crowded throng,
Dire theme of horror and Plutonian song,
Requir'st my lay—thy sultry decks I know,
And all the torments that exist below!
The briny wave that Hudson's bosom fills
Drain'd through her bottom in a thousand rills,
Rotten and old, replete with sighs and groans,
Scarce on the waters she sustain'd her bones;
Here, doom'd to toil, or founder in the tide,
At the moist pumps incessantly we ply'd,
Here, doom'd to starve, like famish'd dogs we tore
The scant allowance, that our tyrants bore.

. . . .

60

One master o'er the murdering tribe was plac'd,
By him the rest were honour'd or disgrac'd;—
Once, and but once, by some strange fortune led
He came to see the dying and the dead—
He came—but anger so deform'd his eye,
And such a faulchion glitter'd on his thigh,
And such a gloom his visage darken'd o'er,
And two such pistols in his hands he bore!
That, by the gods!—with such a load of steel
He came, we thought, to murder, not to heal.

. . . .

Each day, at least three carcases we bore,
And scratch'd them graves along the sandy shore;
By feeble hands the shallow graves were made,
No stone memorial o'er the corpses laid;
In barren sands, and far from home, they lie,
No friend to shed a tear, when passing by;
O'er the mean tombs insulting Britons tread,
Spurn at the sand, and curse the rebel dead.

The Vanity of Existence—To Thyrsis

In youth, gay scenes attract our eyes,
    And not suspecting their decay
Life's flowery fields before us rise,
    Regardless of its winter day.

But vain pursuits and joys as vain,
    Convince us life is but a dream.
Death is to wake, to rise again
    To that true life you best esteem.

So nightly on some shallow tide,
    Oft have I seen a splendid show;
Reflected stars on either side,
    And glittering moons were seen below.

But when the tide had ebbed away,
    The scene fantastic with it fled,
A bank of mud around me lay,
    And sea-weed on the river's bed.

The Hurricane

Happy the man who, safe on shore,
    Now trims, at home, his evening fire;
Unmov'd, he hears the tempests roar,
    That on the tufted groves expire:
Alas! on us they doubly fall,
Our feeble barque must bear them all.

Now to their haunts the birds retreat,
    The squirrel seeks his hollow tree,
Wolves in their shaded caverns meet,
    All, all are blest but wretched we—
Foredoomed a stranger to repose,
No rest the unsettled ocean knows.

While o'er the dark abyss we roam,
    Perhaps, with last departing gleam,
We saw the sun descend in gloom,
    No more to see his morning beam;
But buried low, by far too deep,
On coral beds, unpitied, sleep!

But what a strange, uncoasted strand
    Is that, where fate permits no day—
No charts have we to mark that land,
    No compass to direct that way—
What Pilot shall explore the realm,
What new Columbus take the helm!

While death and darkness both surround,
    And tempests rage with lawless power,
Of friendship's voice I hear no sound,
    No comfort in this dreadful hour—
What friendship can in tempests be,
What comforts on this raging sea?

The barque, accustomed to obey,
    No more the trembling pilots guide:
Alone she gropes her trackless way,
    While mountains burst on either side—
Thus, skill and science both must fall;
And ruin is the lot of all.

The Wild Honey Suckle

Fair flower, that dost so comely grow,
Hid in this silent, dull retreat,
Untouched thy honied blossoms blow,
Unseen thy little branches greet:
    No roving foot shall crush thee here,
    No busy hand provoke a tear.

By Nature's self in white arrayed,
She bade thee shun the vulgar eye,
And planted here the guardian shade,
And sent soft waters murmuring by;
    Thus quietly thy summer goes,
    Thy days declining to repose.

Smit with those charms, that must decay,
I grieve to see your future doom;
They died—nor were those flowers more gay,
The flowers that did in Eden bloom;
    Unpitying frosts, and Autumn's power
    Shall leave no vestige of this flower.

From morning suns and evening dews
At first thy little being came:
If nothing once, you nothing lose,
For when you die you are the same;
    The space between, is but an hour,
    The frail duration of a flower.

The Indian Burying Ground

In spite of all the learned have said,
    I still my old opinion keep;
The *posture,* that *we* give the dead,
    Points out the soul's eternal sleep.

Not so the ancients of these lands—
    The Indian, when from life released,
Again is seated with his friends,
    And shares again the joyous feast.

His imaged birds, and painted bowl,
    And venison, for a journey dressed,
Bespeak the nature of the soul,
    ACTIVITY, that knows no rest.

His bow, for action ready bent,
    And arrows, with a head of stone,
Can only mean that life is spent,
    And not the old ideas gone.

Thou, stranger, that shalt come this way,
    No fraud upon the dead commit—
Observe the swelling turf, and say
    They do not *lie,* but here they *sit.*

Here still a lofty rock remains,
    On which the curious eye may trace
(Now wasted, half, by wearing rains)
    The fancies of a ruder race.

Here still an aged elm aspires,
    Beneath whose far-projecting shade
(And which the Shepherd still admires)
    The children of the forest played!

There oft a restless Indian queen
    (Pale *Shebah,* with her braided hair)
And many a barbarous form is seen
    To chide the man that lingers there.

By midnight moons, o'er moistening dews,
    In habit for the chase arrayed,
The hunter still the deer pursues,
    The hunter and the deer, a shade!

And long shall timorous fancy see
    The painted chief, and pointed spear,
And Reason's self shall bow the knee
    To shadows and delusions here.

On the Uniformity and Perfection of Nature

On one fix'd point all nature moves,
Nor deviates from the track she loves;
Her system, drawn from reason's source,
She scorns to change her wonted course.

Could she descend from that great plan
To work unusual things for man,
To suit the insect of an hour—
This would betray a want of power,

Unsettled in its first design
And erring, when it did combine
The parts that form the vast machine,
The figures sketch'd on nature's scene.

Perfections of the great first cause
Submit to no contracted laws,
But all-sufficient, all-supreme,
Include no trivial views in them.

Who looks through nature with an eye
That would the scheme of heaven descry,
Observes her constant, still the same,
In all her laws, through all her frame.

No imperfection can be found
In all that is, above, around,—
All, nature made, in reason's sight
Is order all, and *all is right*.

Epitaph for Jonathan Robbins

Reader,
If thou be a Christian and a Freeman,
consider
By what unexampled causes
It has become necessary to construct
This Monument
of national degradation
and
Individual Injustice
which is erected
To the Memory of a Citizen of the United States
JONATHAN ROBBINS, Mariner;
A native of Danbury, in the pious and industrious state of
Connecticut:
who,
Under the Presidency of John Adams,
And by his advice,
Timothy Pickering being Secretary of State,
Was delivered up to the British government,
By whom he was ignominiously put to death;
because,
Though an American Citizen,
He was barbarously forced into the service of his country's
worst enemy,

And compelled to fight
Against his conscience and his country's good,
On board the British frigate Hermione,
Commanded by a monster of the name of Pigot,
He
Bravely asserted his right to freedom as a man, and boldly
extricated himself from the bondage of his tyrannical
oppressors,
After devoting them to merited destruction.
If you are a Seaman,
Pause:—
Cast your eyes into your soul and ask,
If you had been as Robbins was
What would you have done?
What ought you not to do?
And look at Robbins
Hanging at a British yard-arm!
He was your comrade—
And as true a tar as ever strapped a block:
He was your fellow-citizen
And as brave a heart as bled at Lexington or Trenton.
Like you,
He was a member of a Republic
Proud of past glories,
and
Boastful of national honour, virtue, and independence.
Like him,
You may one day be trussed up, to satiate British vengeance;
Your heinous crime,
Daring to prefer danger or death
To a base bondage—
Alas poor Robbins!
Alas poor Liberty!
Alas my country!

PHILLIS WHEATLEY
(c.1753–1784)

To the University of Cambridge in New England, America

While an intrinsic ardor prompts to write,
The muses promise to assist my pen;
'Twas not long since I left my native shore
The land of errors, and *Egyptian* gloom:
Father of mercy, 'twas thy gracious hand
Brought me in safety from those dark abodes.

    Students, to you 'tis giv'n to scan the heights
Above, to traverse the ethereal space,
And mark the systems of revolving worlds.
Still more, ye sons of science ye receive
The blissful news by messengers from heav'n,
How *Jesus'* blood for your redemption flows.
See him with hands out-stretcht upon the cross;
Immense compassion in his bosom glows;
He hears revilers, nor resents their scorn:
What matchless mercy in the Son of God!
When the whole human race by sin had fall'n,
He deign'd to die that they might rise again,
And share with him in the sublimest skies,
Life without death, and glory without end.

    Improve your privileges while they stay,
Ye pupils, and each hour redeem, that bears
Or good or bad report of you to heav'n.
Let sin, that baneful evil to the soul,
By you be shunn'd, nor once remit your guard;
Suppress the deadly serpent in its egg.
Ye blooming plants of human race devine,
An *Ethiop* tells you 'tis your greatest foe;
Its transient sweetness turns to endless pain,
And in immense perdition sinks the soul.

America

New England first a wilderness was found
Till for a continent 'twas destin'd round
From feild to feild the savage monsters run
E'r yet Brittania had her work begun
Thy Power, O Liberty, makes strong the weak
And (wond'rous instinct) Ethiopians speak
Sometimes by Simile, a victory's won
A certain lady had an only son
He grew up daily virtuous as he grew
Fearing his Strength which she undoubted knew
She laid some taxes on her darling son
And would have laid another act there on
Amend your manners I'll the taxes remove
Was said with seeming Sympathy and Love
By many Scourges she his goodness try'd
Untill at length the Best of Infants cry'd
He wept, Brittania turn'd a senseless ear
At last awaken'd by maternal fear
Why weeps americus why weeps my Child
Thus spake Brittania, thus benign and mild
My dear mama said he shall I repeat—
Then Prostrate fell, at her maternal feet
What ails the rebel, great Brittania Cry'd
Indeed said he you have no cause to Chide
You see each day my fluent tears my food.
Without regard, what no more English blood?
Was length of time drove from our English viens.
The kindred he to Great Brittania deigns?
Tis thus with thee O Brittain keeping down
New English force, thou fear'st his Tyranny and thou didst frown
He weeps afresh to feel this Iron chain
Turn, O Brittania claim thy child again
Riecho Love drive by thy powerful charms
Indolence Slumbering in forgetful arms
See Agenoria diligent imploys
Her sons, and thus with rapture she replys
Arise my sons with one consent arise
Lest distant continents with vult'ring eyes
Should charge America with Negligence
They praise Industry but no pride commence
To raise their own Profusion, O Britain See
By this New England will increase like thee

JOEL BARLOW
(1754–1812)

from The Hasty Pudding

Omne tulit punctum qui miscuit utile dulci.
He makes a good breakfast who mixes pudding with molasses.

CANTO I

Ye Alps audacious, thro' the Heavens that rise,
To cramp the day and hide me from the skies;
Ye Gallic flags, that o'er their heights unfurl'd,
Bear death to kings, and freedom to the world,
I sing not you. A softer theme I chuse,
A virgin theme, unconscious of the Muse,
But fruitful, rich, well suited to inspire
The purest frenzy of poetic fire.
    Despise it not, ye Bards to terror steel'd,
Who hurl'd your thunders round the epic field;
Nor ye who strain your midnight throats to sing
Joys that the vineyard and the still-house bring;
Or on some distant fair your notes employ,
And speak of raptures that you ne'er enjoy.
I sing the sweets I know, the charms I feel,
My morning incense, and my evening meal,
The sweets of Hasty-Pudding. Come, dear bowl,
Glide o'er my palate, and inspire my soul.
The milk beside thee, smoking from the kine,
Its substance mingled, married in with thine,
Shall cool and temper thy superior heat,
And save the pains of blowing while I eat.
    Oh! could the smooth, the emblematic song
Flow like thy genial juices o'er my tongue,
Could those mild morsels in my numbers chime,
And, as they roll in substance, roll in rhyme,
No more thy aukward unpoetic name
Should shun the Muse, or prejudice thy fame;
But rising grateful to the accustom'd ear,
All Bards should catch it, and all realms revere!
    Assist me first with pious toil to trace
Thro' wrecks of time thy lineage and thy race;
Declare what lovely squaw, in days of yore,

(Ere great Columbus sought thy native shore)
First gave thee to the world; her works of fame
Have liv'd indeed, but liv'd without a name.
Some tawny Ceres, goddess of her days,
First learn'd with stones to crack the well-dry'd maize,
Thro' the rough sieve to shake the golden show'r,
In boiling water stir the yellow flour.
The yellow flour, bestrew'd and stir'd with haste,
Swell in the flood and thickens to a paste,
Then puffs and wallops, rises to the brim,
Drinks the dry knobs that on the surface swim:
The knobs at last the busy ladle breaks,
And the whole mass its true consistence takes.

     Could but her sacred name, unknown so long,
Rise like her labors, to the sons of song,
To her, to them, I'd consecrate my lays,
And blow her pudding with the breath of praise.
If 'twas Oella, whom I sang before,
I here ascribe her one great virtue more.
Not thro' the rich Peruvian realms alone
The fame of Sol's sweet daughter should be know,
But o'er the world's wide climes should live secure,
Far as his rays extend, as long as they endure.

     Dear Hasty-Pudding, what unpromis'd joy
Expands my heart, to meet thee in Savoy:
Doom'd o'er the world thro' devious paths to roam,
Each clime my country, and each house my home,
My soul is sooth'd, my cares have found an end,
I greet my long-lost, unforgotten friend.

     For thee thro' Paris, that corrupted town,
How long in vain I wandered up and down,
Where shameless Bacchus, with his drenching hoard
Cold from his cave usurps the morning board.
London is lost in smoke and steep'd in tea;
No Yankey there can lisp the name of thee:
The uncouth word, a libel on the town,
Would call a proclamation from the crown.
For climes oblique, that fear the sun's full rays,
Chill'd in their fogs, exclude the generous maize;
A grain whose rich luxuriant growth requires
Short gentle showers, and bright etherial fires.

     But here tho' distant from our native shore,
With mutual glee we meet and laugh once more,
The same! I know thee by that yellow face,
That strong complexion of true Indian race,
Which time can never change, nor soil impair,
Nor Alpine snows, nor Turkey's morbid air;

For endless years, thro' every mild domain,
Where grows the maize, there thou art sure to reign.
      But man, more fickle, the bold licence claims,
In different realms to give thee different names.
Thee the soft nations round the warm Levant
Palanta call, the French of course *Polante;*
E'en in thy native regions, how I blush
To hear the Pennsylvanians call thee *Mush!*
On Hudson's banks, while men of Belgic spawn
Insult and eat thee by the name *suppawn.*
All spurious appellations, void of truth:
I've better known thee from my earliest youth,
Thy name is *Hasty-Pudding!* thus our sires
Were wont to greet thee fuming from their fires;
And while they argu'd in thy just defence
With logic clear, they thus explained the sense:—
"In *haste* the boiling cauldron o'er the blaze,
"Receives and cooks the ready-powder'd maize;
"In *haste* 'tis serv'd, and then in equal *haste,*
"With cooling milk, we make the sweet repast.
"No carving to be done, no knife to grate
"The tender ear, and wound the stony plate;
"But the smooth spoon, just fitted to the lip,
"And taught with art the yielding mass to dip,
"By frequent journies to the bowl well stor'd,
"Performs the hasty honors of the board."
Such is thy name, significant and clear,
A name, a sound to every Yankey dear,
But most to me, whose heart and palate chaste
Preserve my pure hereditary taste.
      There are who strive to stamp with disrepute
The luscious food, because it feeds the brute;
In tropes of high-strain'd wit, while gaudy prigs
Compare thy nursling man to pamper'd pigs;
With sovereign scorn I treat the vulgar jest,
Nor fear to share thy bounties with the beast.
What though the generous cow gives me to quaff
The milk nutritious; am I then a calf?
Or can the genius of the noisy swine,
Tho' nurs'd on pudding, thence lay claim to mine?
Sure the sweet song, I fashion to thy praise,
Runs more melodious than the notes they raise.
      My song resounding in its grateful glee,
No merit claims; I praise myself in thee.
My father lov'd thee through his length of days:
For thee his fields were shaded o'er with maize;
From thee what health, what vigour he possest,

Ten sturdy freemen sprung from him attest;
Thy constellation rul'd my natal morn,
And all my bones were made of Indian corn.
Delicious grain! whatever form it take,
To roast or boil, to smother or to bake,
In every dish 'tis welcome still to me,
But most, my Hasty-Pudding, most in thee.
    Let the green Succatash with thee contend,
Let beans and corn their sweetest juices blend,
Let butter drench them in its yellow tide,
And a long slice of bacon grace their side;
Not all the plate, how fam'd soe'er it be,
Can please my palate like a bowl of thee.
    Some talk of Hoe-cake, fair Virginia's pride,
Rich Johnny-cake this mouth has often tri'd;
Both please me well, their virtues much the same;
Alike their fabric, as allied their fame,
Except in dear New-England, where the last
Receives a dash of pumpkin in the paste,
To give it sweetness and improve the taste.
But place them all before me, smoaking hot,
The big round dumplin rolling from the pot;
The pudding of the bag, whose quivering breast,
With suet lin'd leads on the Yankey feast;
The Charlotte brown, within whose crusty sides
A belly soft the pulpy apple hides;
The yellow bread, whose face like amber glows,
And all of Indian that the bake-pan knows—
You tempt me not—my fav'rite greets my eyes,
To that lov'd bowl my spoon by instinct flies.

. . . .

from THE VISION OF COLUMBUS

. . . .

    There reigns a prince, whose hand the sceptre claims,
Thro' a long lineage of imperial names;
Where the brave roll of following Incas trace
The distant father of their realm and race,
Immortal Capac. He in youthful pride,
With fair Oella, his illustrious bride,
In virtuous guile, proclaim'd their birth begun,
From the pure splendors of their God, the sun;

With power and dignity a throne to found,
Fix the mild sway and spread their arts around;
Crush the dire Gods that human victims claim,
And point all worship to a nobler name;
With cheerful rites, the due devotions pay
To the bright beam, that gives the changing day.
　　On this fair plan, the children of the skies
Bade, in the wild, a growing empire rise;
Beneath their hand, and sacred to their fame,
Rose yon fair walls, that meet the solar flame.
Succeeding sovereigns spread their bounds afar,
By arts of peace and temper'd force of war;
Till these surrounding realms the sceptre own,
And grateful millions hail the genial sun.

. . . .

　　In those blank periods, where no man can trace
The gleams of thought that first illumed his race,
His errors, twined with science, took their birth
And forged their fetters for this child of earth.
And when, as oft, he dared expand his view
And work with nature on the line she drew,
Some monster, gender'd in his fears, unmann'd
His opening soul and marr'd the works he plann'd.
Fear, the first passion of his helpless state,
Redoubles all the woes that round him wait,
Blocks nature's path and sends him wandering wide,
Without a guardian and without a guide.
　　Beat by the storm, refresht by gentle rain,
By sunbeams cheer'd or foundered in the main,
He bows to every force he can't control,
Endows them all with intellect and soul,
With passions various, turbulent and strong,
Rewarding virtue and avenging wrong,
Gives heaven and earth to their supernal doom
And swells their sway beyond the closing tomb.
Hence rose his gods, that mystic monstrous lore
Of blood-stain'd altars of priestly power,
Hence blind credulity on all dark things,
False morals hence and hence the yoke of kings.

. . . .

Accustom'd thus to bow the suppliant head
And reverence powers that shake his heart with dread,
His pliant faith extends with easy ken
From heavenly hosts to heaven-anointed men;
The sword, the tripod join their mutual aids
To film his eyes with more impervious shades,
Create a sceptred idol and enshrine
The robber chief in attributes divine,
Arm the new phantom with the nation's rod
And hail the dreadful delegate of God.

. . . .

The mask of priesthood and the mace of kings,
Lie trampled in the dust; for here at last
Fraud, folly, error all their emblems cast.
Each envoy here unloads his wearied hand
Of some old idol from his native land;
One flings a pagod on the mingled heap,
One lays a crescent, one a cross to sleep;
Swords, sceptres, mitres, crowns and globes and stars.
Codes of false fame and stimulants to wars
Sink in the settling mass; since guile began,
These are the agents of the woes of man.

. . . .

from THE COLUMBIAD

. . . .

From slavery then your rising realms to save,
Regard the master, notice not the slave;
Consult alone for freemen, and bestow
Your best, your only cares, to keep them so.
Tyrants are never free; and, small and great,
All masters must be tyrants soon or late;
So nature works; and oft the lordling knave
Turns out at once a tyrant and a slave,
Struts, cringes, bullies, begs, as courtiers must,
Makes one a god, another threads in dust,
Fears all alike, and filches whom he can,
But knows no equal, finds no friend in man.
Ah! would you not be slaves, with lords and kings,
Then be not masters; there the danger springs.

The whole crude system that torments this earth,
Of rank, privation, privilege of birth,
False honor, fraud, corruption, civil jars,
The rage of conquest and the curse of wars,
Pandora's total shower, all ills combined
That erst o'erwhelm'd and still distress mankind,
Box'd up secure in your deliberate hand,
Wait your behest, to fix or fly this land.
　　Equality of Right is nature's plan;
And following nature is the march of man.
Whene'er he deviates in the least degree,
When, free himself, he would be more than free,
The baseless column, rear'd to bear his bust,
Falls as he mounts, and whelms him in the dust.

. . . .

　　Mark modern Europe with her feudal codes,
Serfs, villains, vassals, nobles, kings and gods,
All slaves of different grades, corrupt and curst
With high and low, for senseless rank athirst,
Wage endless wars; not fighting to be free,
But *cujum pecus,* whose base herd they'll be.
　　Too much of Europe, here transplanted o'er,
Nursed feudal feelings on your tented shore,
Brought sable serfs from Afric, call'd it gain,
And urged your sires to forge the fatal chain.
But now, the tents o'erturn'd, the war dogs fled,
Now fearless Freedom rears at last her head
Matcht with celestial Peace,—my friends, beware
To shade the splendors of so bright a pair;
Complete their triumph, fix their firm abode,
Purge all privations from your liberal code,
Restore their souls to men, give earth repose,
And save your sons from slavery, wars and woes.

. . . .

Yankee Doodle
(Anonymous, 1775)

Father and I went down to camp
Along with Captain Goodwin,
And there we saw the men and boys
As thick as hasty pudding.

> *Yankee Doodle, keep it up,*
> *Yankee Doodle dandy!*
> *Mind the music and the steps,*
> *And with the girls be handy!*

There was Captain Washington
Upon a slapping stallion,
Giving orders to his men,
I guess there was a million.

And there they had a swamping gun
As big as a log of maple,
On a deuced little cart,
A load for father's cattle.

And every time they fired it off,
It took a horn of powder;
It made a noise like father's gun,
Only a nation louder.

And there I saw a little keg,
Its heads were made of leather—
They knocked upon it with little sticks
To call the folks together.

The troopers, too, would gallop up
And fire right in our faces,
It scared me almost half to death
To see them run such races.

But I can't tell you half I saw;
They kept up such a smother,
So I took off my hat, made a bow,
And scampered home to mother.

The Yankee Man-of-War
(Anonymous, 1778)

'T is of a gallant Yankee ship that flew the stripes and stars,
And the whistling wind from the west-nor'-west blew through the
    pitch pine-spars;
With her starboard tacks aboard, my boys, she hung upon the gale;
On an autumn night we raised the light on the old Head of Kinsale.

It was a clear and cloudless night, and the wind blew steady and
    strong,
As gayly over the sparkling deep our good ship bowled along;
With the foaming seas beneath her bow the fiery waves she spread,
And bending low her bosom of snow, she buried her lee cat-head.

There was no talk of short'ning sail by him who walked the poop,
And under the press of her pond'ring jib, the boom bent like a hoop!
And the groaning water-ways told the strain that held her stout main-
    tack,
But he only laughed as he glanced aloft at a white silvery track.

The mid-tide meets in the Channel waves that flow from shore to
    shore,
And the mist hung heavy upon the land from Featherstone to
    Dunmore,
And that sterling light in Tusker Rock where the old bell tolls each
    hour,
And the beacons light that shone so bright was quench'd on
    Waterford Tower.

What looms upon our starboard bow? What hangs upon the breeze?
'T is time our good ship hauled her wind abreast the old Saltees,
For by her ponderous press of sail and by her consorts four
We saw our morning visitor was a British man-of-war.

Up spake our noble Captain then, as a shot ahead of us past—
"Haul snug your flowing courses! lay your topsail to the mast!"
Those Englishmen gave three loud hurrahs from the deck of their
    covered ark,
And we answered back by a solid broad-side from the decks of our
    patriot bark.

"Out boom! out booms!" our skipper cried, "out booms and give her
  sheet,"
And the swiftest keel that was ever launched shot ahead of the British
  fleet,
And amidst a thundering shower of shot, with stun'-sails hoisting
  away,
Down the North Channel Paul Jones did steer just at the break of
  day.

See! How the Nations Rage Together
(Richard Allen, 1801)

See! how the nations rage together,
Seeking of each other's blood;
See how the scriptures are fulfilling!
Sinners awake and turn to God.

We see the fig-tree budding;
You that in open ruin lie,
Behold the leaves almost appearing,
Awake! behold your end is nigh.

We read of wars, and great commotions,
To come *before* that *dreadful day;*
Sinners quit *your sinful courses,*
And trifle not your time away.

Consider now the desolation,
And the shortness of your time;
Since there's none but a dark ocean,
For all that don't repent in time,

Ye ministers that wait on *preaching,*
Teachers and exhorters too,
Don't you see *your harvest wasting,*
Arise, there is no rest for you,

O think upon that strict commandment,
God has on his teachers laid:
The sinner's blood that dies unwarned,
Shall fall upon the teacher's head.

Arise *dear brethren, let's be doing,*
See *the nations in distress;*
The Lord of hosts forbid their ruin,
Before their *day of grace is past.*

To see the land lie in confusion,
Looks dreadful in our mortal eye;
But O dear sinners, that is nothing,
To when the day of doom draws nigh.

To see the Lord in clouds descending,
Saints and angels guard him round;
The saints from earth will rise to meet
But sinners speechless at his frown.

To see the mountains a burning,
Mountains and hills must forward fly;
The moon in blood, the stars a falling,
And comets blazing thro' the sky.

O sinners! that's not all that's dreadful,
Before your Judge you must appear;
To answer for your past transactions,
How you ran your courses here.

The book of Conscience will be open'd
And you character read therein;
The sentence is, depart ye cursed,
And every saint will cry, Amen.

O Lord, forbid that this our nation,
That this should be their dreadful case;
O sinners turn and find salvation,
While now he offers you free grace.

'Tis now you have a gospel morning,
And yet the lamp holds out to burn;
'Tis now you have sufficient warning,
O sinners! sinners! will you turn?

I Love Thy Kingdom, Lord

(Timothy Dwight, 1801)

"I love thy Kingdom, Lord,
    The house of thine abode,
The Church our blest Redeemer saved
    With his own precious blood.

"I love thy Church, O God:
    Her walls before thee stand,
Dear as the apple of thine eye
    And graven on thy hand.

"If e'er to bless thy sons
    My voice or hands deny,
These hands let useful skill forsake,
    This voice in silence die.

"If e'er my heart forget
    Her welfare or her woe,
Let every joy this heart forsake,
    And every grief o'erflow.

"For her my tears shall fall,
    For her my prayers ascend;
To her my cares and toils be given
    Till toils and cares shall end.

"Beyond my highest joy
    I prize her heavenly ways,
Her sweet communion, solemn vows,
    Her hymns of love and praise.

"Jesus, thou Friend Divine,
    Our Saviour and our King,
Thy hand from every snare and foe
    Shall great deliverance bring.

"Sure as thy truth shall last,
    To Zion shall be given
The brightest glories earth can yield,
    And brighter bliss of heaven."

Poor Wayfaring Stranger
(Anonymous, n.d.)

I'm just a poor wayfaring stranger,
A-trav'ling through this world of woe,
But there's no sickness, toil or danger
In that bright land to which I go.
    I'm going there to see my father,
    I'm going there no more to roam,
    I'm just a-going over Jordan,
    I'm just a-going over home.

I'm just a poor wayfaring stranger,
A-trav'ling through this world of woe,
But there's no sickness, toil or danger
In that bright land to which I go.
    I'm going there to see my mother,
    She said she'd meet me when I come;
    I'm just a-going over Jordan,
    I'm just a-going over home.

Walk Softly
(Shaker Hymn, n.d.)

When we assemble here to worship God,
To sing his praises and to hear his word
    We will walk softly.

With purity of heart; and with clean hands,
Our souls are free, we're free from Satan's bands
    We will walk softly.

While we are passing thro' the sacred door,
Into the fold where Christ has gone before,
    We will walk softly.

We'll worship and bow down we will rejoice
And when we hear the shepherd's gentle voice
    We will walk softly.

I Will Bow and Be Simple
(Shaker Hymn, n.d.)

I will bow and be simple
I will bow and be free
I will bow and be humble
Yea bow like the willow-tree
I will bow this is the token
I will wear the easy yoke
I will bow and be broken
Yea I'll fall upon the rock.

Home, Sweet Home
(John Howard Payne, 1823)

'Mid pleasures and palaces though we may roam,
Be it ever so humble there's no place like home!
A charm from the skies seems to hallow us there,
Which, seek through the world, is ne'er met with elsewhere.

> Home! Home! Sweet, sweet home!
> There's no place like home!
> There's no place like home!

An exile from home splendor dazzles in vain;
Oh, give me my lowly thatch'd cottage again!
The birds singing gaily that came at my call;
Give me them with the peace of mind dearer than all.
(Chorus)

O Thou, to Whom in Ancient Time
(John Pierpont, 1824)

"O Thou, to whom, in ancient time,
    The lyre of Hebrew bards was strung,
Whom kings adored in song sublime,
    And prophets praised with glowing tongue;

"Not now on Zion's height alone
    Thy favored worshiper may dwell,
Nor where, at sultry noon, thy Son
    Sat weary by the patriarch's well.

"From every place below the skies,
　　The grateful song, the fervent prayer,
The incense of the heart, may rise
　　To heaven, and find acceptance there.

"O Thou, to whom, in ancient time,
　　The lyre of prophet bards was strung,
To Thee at last, in every clime,
　　Shall temples rise, and praise be sung."

III

YOUNG AMERICA: THE ROMANTIC ERA: 1826–1859

WILLIAM CULLEN BRYANT
(1794–1878)

Thanatopsis

To him who in the love of Nature holds
Communion with her visible forms, she speaks
A various language; for his gayer hours
She has a voice of gladness, and a smile
And eloquence of beauty, and she glides
Into his darker musings, with a mild
And healing sympathy, that steals away
Their sharpness, ere he is aware. When thoughts
Of the last bitter hour come like a blight
Over thy spirit, and sad images
Of the stern agony, and shroud, and pall,
And breathless darkness, and the narrow house,
Make thee to shudder, and grow sick at heart;—
Go forth, under the open sky, and list
To Nature's teachings, while from all around—
Earth and her waters, and the depths of air—
Comes a still voice—Yet a few days, and thee
The all-beholding sun shall see no more
In all his course; nor yet in the cold ground,
Where thy pale form was laid, with many tears,
Nor in the embrace of ocean, shall exist
Thy image. Earth, that nourished thee, shall claim
Thy growth, to be resolved to earth again,
And, lost each human trace, surrendering up
Thine individual being, shalt thou go
To mix forever with the elements,
To be a brother to the insensible rock
And to the sluggish clod, which the rude swain
Turns with his share, and treads upon. The oak
Shall send his roots abroad, and pierce thy mould.

Yet not to thine eternal resting-place
Shalt thou retire alone, nor couldst thou wish
Couch more magnificent. Thou shalt lie down
With patriarchs of the infant world—with kings,
The powerful of the earth—the wise, the good,
Fair forms, and hoary seers of ages past,
All in one mighty sepulchre. The hills
Rock-ribbed and ancient as the sun,—the vales
Stretching in pensive quietness between;

The venerable woods—rivers that move
In majesty, and the complaining brooks
That make the meadows green; and, poured round all,
Old Ocean's gray and melancholy waste,—
Are but the solemn decorations all
Of the great tomb of man. The golden sun,
The planets, all the infinite host of heaven,
Are shining on the sad abodes of death,
Through the still lapse of ages. All that tread
The globe are but a handful to the tribes
That slumber in its bosom.—Take the wings
Of morning, pierce the Barcan wilderness,
Or lose thyself in the continuous woods
Where rolls the Oregon, and hears no sound,
Save his own dashings—yet the dead are there:
And millions in those solitudes, since first
The flight of years began, have laid them down
In their last sleep—the dead reign there alone.
So shalt thou rest, and what if thou withdraw
In silence from the living, and no friend
Take note of thy departure? All that breathe
Will share thy destiny. The gay will laugh
When thou art gone, the solemn brood of care
Plod on, and each one as before will chase
His favorite phantom; yet all these shall leave
Their mirth and their employments, and shall come
And make their bed with thee. As the long train
Of ages glide away, the sons of men,
The youth in life's green spring, and he who goes
In the full strength of years, matron and maid,
The speechless babe, and the gray-headed man—
Shall one by one be gathered to thy side,
By those, who in their turn shall follow them.

So live, that when thy summons comes to join
The innumerable caravan, which moves
To that mysterious realm, where each shall take
His chamber in the silent halls of death,
Thou go not, like the quarry-slave at night,
Scourged to his dungeon, but, sustained and soothed
By an unfaltering trust, approach thy grave,
Like one who wraps the drapery of his couch
About him, and lies down to pleasant dreams.

from The Prairies

These are the gardens of the Desert, these
The unshorn fields, boundless and beautiful,
For which the speech of England has no name—
The Prairies. I behold them for the first,
And my heart swells, while the dilated sight
Takes in the encircling vastness. Lo! they stretch,
In airy undulations, far away,
As if the ocean, in his gentlest swell,
Stood still, with all his rounded billows fixed,
And motionless forever.—Motionless?—
No—they are all unchained again. The clouds
Sweep over with their shadows, and, beneath,
The surface rolls and fluctuates to the eye;
Dark hollows seem to glide along and chase
The sunny ridges.

. . . .

Still this great solitude is quick with life.
Myriads of insects, gaudy as the flowers
They flutter over, gentle quadrupeds,
And birds, that scarce have learned the fear of man,
Are here, and sliding reptiles of the ground,
Startlingly beautiful. The graceful deer
Bounds to the wood at my approach. The bee,
A more adventurous colonist than man,
With whom he came across the eastern deep,
Fills the savannas with his murmurings,
And hides his sweets, as in the golden age,
Within the hollow oak. I listen long
To his domestic hum, and think I hear
The sound of that advancing multitude
Which soon shall fill these deserts. From the ground
Comes up the laugh of children, the soft voice
Of maidens, and the sweet and solemn hymn
Of Sabbath worshippers. The low of herds
Blends with the rustling of the heavy grain
Over the dark brown furrow. All at once
A fresher wind sweeps by, and breaks my dream,
And I am in the wilderness alone.

Green River

When breezes are soft and skies are fair,
I steal an hour from study and care,
And hie me away to the woodland scene,
Where wanders the stream, with waters of green,
As if the bright fringe of herbs on its brink
Had given their stain to the waves they drink;
And they, whose meadows it murmurs through,
Have named the stream from its own fair hue.

Yet pure its waters—its shallows are bright
With colored pebbles and sparkles of light,
And clear the depths where its eddies play,
And dimples deepen and whirl away,
And the plane-tree's speckled arms o'er-shoot
The swifter current that mines its root,
Through whose shifting leaves, as you walk the hill,
The quivering glimmer of sun and rill
With a sudden flash on the eye is thrown,
Like the ray that streams from the diamond-stone.
Oh, loveliest there the spring days come,
With blossoms, and birds, and wild-bees' hum;
The flowers of summer are fairest there,
And freshest the breath of the summer air;
And sweetest the golden autumn day
In silence and sunshine glides away.

Yet, fair as thou art, thou shunnest to glide,
Beautiful stream! by the village side;
But windest away from haunts of men,
To quiet valley and shaded glen;
And forest, and meadow, and slope of hill,
Around thee, are lonely, lovely, and still;
Lonely—save when, by thy rippling tides,
From thicket to thicket the angler glides,
Or the simpler comes, with basket and book,
For herbs of power on thy banks to look;
Or haply, some idle dreamer, like me,
To wander, and muse, and gaze on thee,
Still—save the chirp of birds that feed
On the river cherry and seedy reed,
And thy own wild music gushing out
With mellow murmur of fairy shout,
From dawn to the blush of another day,
Like traveller singing along his way.

That fairy music I never hear,
Nor gaze on those waters so green and clear,
And mark them winding away from sight,
Darkened with shade or flashing with light,
While o'er them the vine to its thicket clings,
And the zephyr stoops to freshen his wings,
But I wish that fate had left me free
To wander these quiet haunts with thee,
Till the eating cares of earth should depart,
And the peace of the scene pass into my heart;
And I envy thy stream, as it glides along
Through its beautiful banks in a trance of song.

Though forced to drudge for the dregs of men,
And scrawl strange words with the barbarous pen,
And mingle among the jostling crowd,
Where the sons of strife are subtle and loud—
I often come to this quiet place,
To breathe the airs that ruffle thy face,
And gaze upon thee in silent dream,
For in thy lonely and lovely stream
An image of that calm life appears
That won my heart in my greener years.

To Cole, the Painter, Departing for Europe

Thine eyes shall see the light of distant skies;
  Yet, COLE! thy heart shall bear to Europe's strand
  A living image of our own bright land,
Such as upon thy glorious canvas lies;
Lone lakes—savannas where the bison roves—
  Rocks rich with summer garlands—solemn streams—
  Skies, where the desert eagle wheels and screams—
Spring bloom and autumn blaze of boundless groves.
Fair scenes shall greet thee where thou goest—fair,
  But different—everywhere the trace of men,
  Paths, homes, graves, ruins, from the lowest glen
To where life shrinks from the fierce Alpine air.
  Gaze on them, till the tears shall dim thy sight,
  But keep that earlier, wilder image bright.

Lydia H. Sigourney
(1791–1865)

The Indian's Welcome to the Pilgrim Fathers

Above them spread a stranger sky;
    Around, the sterile plain;
The rock-bound coast rose frowning nigh;
    Beyond,—the wrathful main:
Chill remnants of the wintry snow
    Still choked the encumbered soil,
Yet forth those Pilgrim Fathers go
    To mark their future toil.

'Mid yonder vale their corn must rise
    In summer's ripening pride,
And there the church-spire woo the skies
    Its sister-school beside.
Perchance mid England's velvet green
    Some tender thought reposed,
Though nought upon their stoic mien
    Such soft regret disclosed.

When sudden from the forest wide
    A red-bowed chieftain came,
With towering form, and haughty stride,
    And eye like kindling flame:
No wrath he breathed, no conflict sought,
    To no dark ambush drew,
But simply to the Old World brought
    The welcome of the New.

That welcome was a blast and ban
    Upon thy race unborn;
Was there no seer,—thou fated Man!—
    Thy lavish zeal to warn?
Thou in thy fearless faith didst hail
    A weak, invading band,
But who shall heed thy children's wail
    Swept from their native land?

Thou gav'st the riches of thy streams,
    The lordship o'er thy waves,
The region of thine infant dreams
    And of thy father's graves,—
But who to yon proud mansions, piled
    With wealth of earth and sea,
Poor outcast from thy forest wild,
    Say, who shall welcome thee?

from The Stars

Make friendship with the stars.
                                Go forth at night,
And talk with Aldebaran, where he flames
In the cold forehead of the wintry sky.
Turn to the sister Pleiades, and ask
If there be death in Heaven? A blight to fall
Upon the brightness of unfrosted hair?
A severing of fond hearts? A place of graves?
Our sympathies are with you, stricken stars,
Clustering so closely round the lost one's place.
Too well we know the hopeless toil to hide
The chasm in love's fond circle. The lone seat
Where the meek grandsire, with his silver locks,
Reclined so happily; the fireside chair
Whence the fond mother fled; the cradle turn'd
Against the wall, and empty; well we know
The untold anguish, when some dear one falls.
How oft the life-blood trickling from our hearts,
Reveals a kindred spirit torn away!
Tears are our birth-right, gentle sister rain,
And more we love you, if like us ye mourn.
—Ho! bold Orion, with thy lion-shield;
What tidings from the chase? what monster slain?
Runn'st thou a tilt with Taurus? or dost rear
Thy weapon for more stately tournament?
'Twere better, sure, to be a son of peace
Among those quiet stars, than raise the rout
Of rebel tumult, and of wild affray,
Or feel ambition with its scorpion sting
Transfix thy heel, and like Napoleon fall.
Fair queen, Cassiopeia! is thy court
Well peopled with chivalric hearts, that pay
Due homage to thy beauty? Thy levee,
Is it still throng'd as in thy palmy youth?
Is there no change of dynasty? No dread

Of revolution 'mid the titled peers
That age on age have served thee? Teach us how
To make our sway perennial, in the hearts
Of those who love us, so that when our bloom
And spring-tide wither, they in phalanx firm
May gird us round, and make life's evening bright.

. . . .

Death of an Infant

Death found strange beauty on that polished brow,
And dashed it out. There was a tint of rose
On cheek and lip. He touched the veins with ice,
And the rose faded. Forth from those blue eyes
There spake a wishful tenderness, a doubt
Whether to grieve or sleep, which innocence
Alone may wear. With ruthless haste he bound
The silken fringes of those curtaining lids
For ever. There had been a murmuring sound
With which the babe would claim its mother's ear,
Charming her even to tears. The spoiler set
The seal of silence. But there beamed a smile,
So fixed, so holy, from that cherub brow,
Death gazed, and left it there. He dared not steal
The signet ring of Heaven.

GEORGE MOSES HORTON
(c.1797–c.1883)

Early Affection

I lov'd thee from the earliest dawn,
    When first I saw thy beauty's ray,
And will, until life's eve comes on,
    And beauty's blossom fades away;
And when all things go well with thee,
With smiles and tears remember me.

I'll love thee when thy morn is past,
    And wheedling gallantry is o'er,
When youth is lost in ages blast,
    And beauty can ascend no more,
And when life's journey ends with thee,
O, then look back and think of me.

I'll love thee with a smile or frown,
    'Mid sorrow's gloom or pleasure's light,
And when the chain of life runs down,
    Pursue thy last eternal flight,
When thou hast spread thy wing to flee,
Still, still, a moment wait for me.

I'll love thee for those sparkling eyes,
    To which my fondness was betray'd,
Bearing the tincture of the skies,
    To glow when other beauties fade,
And when they sink too low to see,
Reflect an azure beam on me.

EDWARD COOTE PINKNEY
(1802–1828)

On Parting

Alas! our pleasant moments fly
    On rapid wings away,
While those recorded with a sigh,
    Mock us by long delay.

Time,—envious time,—loves not to be
    In company with mirth,
But makes malignant pause to see
    The work of pain on earth.

RALPH WALDO EMERSON
(1803–1882)

The Sphinx

The Sphinx is drowsy,
    Her wings are furled:
Her ear is heavy,
    She broods on the world.
"Who'll tell me my secret,
    The ages have kept?—
I awaited the seer
    While they slumbered and slept:—

"The fate of the man-child,
    The meaning of man;
Known fruit of the unknown;
    Dædalian plan;
Out of sleeping a waking,
    Out of waking a sleep;
Life death overtaking;
    Deep underneath deep?

"Erect as a sunbeam,
    Upspringeth the palm;
The elephant browses,
    Undaunted and calm;
In beautiful motion
    The thrush plies his wings;
Kind leaves of his covert,
    Your silence he sings.

"The waves, unashamèd,
    In difference sweet,
Play glad with the breezes,
    Old playfellows meet;
The journeying atoms,
    Primordial wholes,
Firmly draw, firmly drive,
    By their animate poles.

"Sea, earth, air, sound, silence,
    Plant, quadruped, bird,
By one music enchanted,
    One deity stirred,—
Each the other adorning,
    Accompany still;
Night veileth the morning,
    The vapor the hill.

"The babe by its mother
    Lies bathèd in joy;
Glide its hours uncounted,—
    The sun is its toy;
Shines the peace of all being,
    Without cloud, in its eyes;
And the sum of the world
    In soft miniature lies.

"But man crouches and blushes,
    Absconds and conceals;
He creepeth and peepeth,
    He palters and steals;
Infirm, melancholy,
    Jealous glancing around,
An oaf, an accomplice,
    He poisons the ground.

"Out spoke the great mother,
    Beholding his fear;—
At the sound of her accents
    Cold shuddered the sphere:—
'Who, has drugged my boy's cup?
    Who, has mixed my boy's bread?
Who, with sadness and madness,
    Has turned my child's head?' "

I heard a poet answer
    Aloud and cheerfully,
"Say on, sweet Sphinx! thy dirges
    Are pleasant songs to me.
Deep love lieth under
    These pictures of time;
They fade in the light of
    Their meaning sublime.

"The fiend that man harries
    Is love of the Best;
Yawns the pit of the Dragon,
    Lit by rays from the Blest.
The Lethe of Nature
    Can't trance him again,
Whose soul sees the perfect,
    Which his eyes seek in vain.

"To vision profounder,
    Man's spirit must dive;
His aye-rolling orb
    At no goal will arrive;
The heavens that now draw him
    With sweetness untold,
Once found,—for new heavens
    He spurneth the old.

"Pride ruined the angels,
    Their shame them restores;
Lurks the joy that is sweetest
    In stings of remorse.
Have I a lover
    Who is noble and free?—
I would he were nobler
    Than to love me.

"Eterne alternation
    Now follows, now flies;
And under pain, pleasure,—
    Under pleasure, pain lies.
Love works at the centre,
    Heart-heaving alway;
Forth speed the strong pulses
    To the borders of day.

"Dull Sphinx, Jove keep thy five wits;
    Thy sight is growing blear;
Rue, myrrh and cummin for the Sphinx,
    Her muddy eyes to clear!"
The old Sphinx bit her thick lip,—
    Said, "Who taught thee me to name?
I am thy spirit, yoke-fellow;
    Of thine eye I am eyebeam.

"Thou art the unanswered question;
    Couldst see thy proper eye,
Alway it asketh, asketh;
    And each answer is a lie.
So take thy quest through nature,
    It through thousand natures ply;
Ask on, thou clothed eternity;
    Time is the false reply."

Uprose the merry Sphinx,
    And crouched no more in stone;
She melted into purple cloud,
    She silvered in the moon;
She spired into a yellow flame;
    She flowered in blossoms red;
She flowed into a foaming wave:
    She stood Monadnoc's head.

Thorough a thousand voices
    Spoke the universal dame;
"Who telleth one of my meanings
    Is master of all I am."

Each and All

Little thinks, in the field, yon red-cloaked clown
Of thee from the hill-top looking down;
The heifer that lows in the upland farm,
Far-heard, lows not thine ear to charm;
The sexton, tolling his bell at noon,
Deems not that great Napoleon
Stops his horse, and lists with delight,
Whilst his files sweep round yon Alpine height;
Nor knowest thou what argument
Thy life to thy neighbor's creed has lent.
All are needed by each one;
Nothing is fair or good alone.
I thought the sparrow's note from heaven,
Singing at dawn on the alder bough;
I brought him home, in his nest, at even;
He sings the song, but it cheers not now,
For I did not bring home the river and sky;—
He sang to my ear,—they sang to my eye.
The delicate shells lay on the shore;
The bubbles of the latest wave
Fresh pearls to their enamel gave,

And the bellowing of the savage sea
Greeted their safe escape to me.
I wiped away the weeds and foam,
I fetched my sea-born treasures home;
But the poor, unsightly, noisome things
Had left their beauty on the shore
With the sun and the sand and the wild uproar.
The lover watched his graceful maid,
As 'mid the virgin train she strayed,
Nor knew her beauty's best attire
Was woven still by the snow-white choir.
At last she came to his hermitage,
Like the bird from the woodlands to the cage;—
The gay enchantment was undone,
A gentle wife, but fairy none.
Then I said, 'I covet truth;
Beauty is unripe childhood's cheat;
I leave it behind with the games of youth:'—
As I spoke, beneath my feet
The ground-pine curled its pretty wreath,
Running over the club-moss burrs;
I inhaled the violet's breath;
Around me stood the oaks and firs;
Pine-cones and acorns lay on the ground;
Over me soared the eternal sky,
Full of light and of deity;
Again I saw, again I heard,
The rolling river, the morning bird;—
Beauty through my senses stole;
I yielded myself to the perfect whole.

Hamatreya

Bulkeley, Hunt, Willard, Hosmer, Meriam, Flint,
Possessed the land which rendered to their toil
Hay, corn, roots, hemp, flax, apples, wool and wood.
Each of these landlords walked amidst his farm,
Saying, ' 'T is mine, my children's and my name's.
How sweet the west wind sounds in my own trees!
How graceful climb those shadows on my hill!
I fancy these pure waters and the flags
Know me, as does my dog: we sympathize;
And, I affirm, my actions smack of the soil.'

Where are these men? Asleep beneath their grounds:
And strangers, fond as they, their furrows plough.
Earth laughs in flowers, to see her boastful boys
Earth-proud, proud of the earth which is not theirs;
Who steer the plough, but cannot steer their feet
Clear of the grave.
They added ridge to valley, brook to pond,
And sighed for all that bounded their domain;
'This suits me for a pasture; that's my park;
We must have clay, lime, gravel, granite-ledge,
And misty lowland, where to go for peat.
The land is well,—lies fairly to the south.
'T is good, when you have crossed the sea and back,
To find the sitfast acres where you left them.'
Ah! the hot owner sees not Death, who adds
Him to his land, a lump of mould the more.
Hear what the Earth says:—

EARTH-SONG

'Mine and yours;
Mine, not yours.
Earth endures;
Stars abide—
Shine down in the old sea;
Old are the shores;
But where are old men?
I who have seen much,
Such have I never seen.

'The lawyer's deed
Ran sure,
In tail,
To them, and to their heirs
Who shall succeed,
Without fail,
Forevermore.

'Here is the land,
Shaggy with wood,
With its old valley,
Mound and flood.
But the heritors?—

Fled like the flood's foam.
The lawyer, and the laws,
And the kingdom,
Clean swept herefrom.

'They called me theirs,
Who so controlled me;
Yet every one
Wished to stay, and is gone,
How am I theirs,
If they cannot hold me,
But I hold them?'

When I heard the Earth-song
I was no longer brave;
My avarice cooled
Like lust in the chill of the grave.

The Rhodora

In May, when sea-winds pierced our solitudes,
I found the fresh Rhodora in the woods,
Spreading its leafless blooms in a damp nook,
To please the desert and the sluggish brook.
The purple petals, fallen in the pool,
Made the black water with their beauty gay;
Here might the red-bird come his plumes to cool,
And court the flower that cheapens his array.
Rhodora! if the sages ask thee why
This charm is wasted on the earth and sky,
Tell them, dear, that if eyes were made for seeing,
Then Beauty is its own excuse for being:
Why thou wert there, O rival of the rose!
I never thought to ask, I never knew:
But, in my simple ignorance, suppose
The self-same Power that brought me there brought you.

The Snowstorm

Announced by all the trumpets of the sky,
Arrives the snow, and, driving o'er the fields,
Seems nowhere to alight: the whited air
Hides hills and woods, the river, and the heaven,
And veils the farm-house at the garden's end.

The sled and traveller stopped, the courier's feet
Delayed, all friends shut out, the housemates sit
Around the radiant fireplace, enclosed
In a tumultuous privacy of storm.

Come see the north wind's masonry.
Out of an unseen quarry evermore
Furnished with tile, the fierce artificer
Curves his white bastions with projected roof
Round every windward stake, or tree, or door.
Speeding, the myriad-handed, his wild work
So fanciful, so savage, nought cares he
For number or proportion. Mockingly,
On coop or kennel he hangs Parian wreaths;
A swan-like form invests the hidden thorn;
Fills up the farmer's lane from wall to wall,
Maugre the farmer's sighs; and at the gate
A tapering turret overtops the work.
And when his hours are numbered, and the world
Is all his own, retiring, as he were not,
Leaves, when the sun appears, astonished Art
To mimic in slow structures, stone by stone,
Built in an age, the mad wind's night-work,
The frolic architecture of the snow.

Ode Inscribed to W. H. Channing

Though loath to grieve
The evil time's sole patriot,
I cannot leave
My honied thought
For the priest's cant,
Or statesman's rant.

If I refuse
My study for their politique,
Which at the best is trick,
The angry Muse
Puts confusion in my brain.

But who is he that prates
Of the culture of mankind,
Of better arts and life?
Go, blindworm, go,
Behold the famous States

Harrying Mexico
With rifle and with knife!

Or who, with accent bolder,
Dare praise the freedom-loving mountaineer?
I found by thee, O rushing Contoocook!
And in thy valleys, Agiochook!
The jackals of the negro-holder.

The God who made New Hampshire
Taunted the lofty land
With little men;—
Small bat and wren
House in the oak:—
If earth-fire cleave
The upheaved land, and bury the folk,
The southern crocodile would grieve.
Virtue palters; Right is hence;
Freedom praised, but hid;
Funeral eloquence
Rattles the coffin-lid.

What boots thy zeal,
O glowing friend,
That would indignant rend
The northland from the south?
Wherefore? to what good end?
Boston Bay and Bunker Hill
Would serve things still;—
Things are of the snake.

The horseman serves the horse,
The neatherd serves the neat,
The merchant serves the purse,
The eater serves his meat;
'T is the day of the chattel,
Web to weave, and corn to grind;
Things are in the saddle,
And ride mankind.

There are two laws discrete,
Not reconciled,—
Law for man, and law for thing;
The last builds town and fleet,
But it runs wild,
And doth the man unking.

'T is fit the forest fall,
The steep be graded,
The mountain tunnelled,
The sand shaded,
The orchard planted,
The glebe tilled,
The prairie granted,
The steamer built.

Let man serve law for man;
Live for friendship, live for love,
For truth's and harmony's behoof;
The state may follow how it can,
As Olympus follows Jove.

    Yet do not I implore
The wrinkled shopman to my sounding woods,
Nor bid the unwilling senator
Ask votes of thrushes in the solitudes.
Every one to his chosen work;—
Foolish hands may mix and mar;
Wise and sure the issues are.
Round they roll till dark is light,
Sex to sex, and even to odd;—
The over-god
Who marries Right to Might,
Who peoples, unpeoples,—
He who exterminates
Races by stronger races,
Black by white faces,—
Knows to bring honey
Out of the lion;
Grafts gentlest scion
On pirate and Turk.

The Cossack eats Poland,
Like stolen fruit;
Her last noble is ruined,
Her last poet mute:
Straight, into double band
The victors divide;
Half for freedom strike and stand;—
The astonished Muse finds thousands at her side.

Give All to Love

Give all to love;
Obey thy heart;
Friends, kindred, days,
Estate, good-fame,
Plans, credit and the Muse,—
Nothing refuse.

'T is a brave master;
Let it have scope:
Follow it utterly,
Hope beyond hope:
High and more high
It dives into noon,
With wing unspent,
Untold intent;
But it is a god,
Knows its own path
And the outlets of the sky.

It was never for the mean;
It requireth courage stout.
Souls above doubt,
Valor unbending,
It will reward,—
They shall return
More than they were,
And ever ascending.

Leave all for love;
Yet, hear me, yet,
One word more thy heart behoved,
One pulse more of firm endeavor,—
Keep thee to-day,
To-morrow, forever,
Free as an Arab
Of thy beloved.

Cling with life to the maid;
But when the surprise,
First vague shadow of surmise
Flits across her bosom young,
Of a joy apart from thee,
Free be she, fancy-free;
Nor thou detain her vesture's hem,

Nor the palest rose she flung
From her summer diadem.

Though thou loved her as thyself,
As a self of purer clay,
Though her parting dims the day,
Stealing grace from all alive;
Heartily know,
When half-gods go,
The gods arrive.

Bacchus

Bring me wine, but wine which never grew
In the belly of the grape,
Or grew on vine whose tap-roots, reaching through
Under the Andes to the Cape,
Suffer no savor of the earth to scape.

Let its grapes the morn salute
From a nocturnal root,
Which feels the acrid juice
Of Styx and Erebus;
And turns the woe of Night,
By its own craft, to a more rich delight.

We buy ashes for bread;
We buy diluted wine;
Give me of the true,—
Whose ample leaves and tendrils curled
Among the silver hills of heaven
Draw everlasting dew;
Wine of wine,
Blood of the world,
Form of forms, and mould of statures,
That I intoxicated,
And by the draught assimilated,
May float at pleasure through all natures;
The bird-language rightly spell,
And that which roses say so well.

Wine that is shed
Like the torrents of the sun
Up the horizon walls,
Or like the Atlantic streams, which run
When the South Sea calls.

Water and bread,
Food which needs no transmuting,
Rainbow-flowering, wisdom-fruiting,
Wine which is already man,
Food which teach and reason can.

Wine which Music is,—
Music and wine are one,—
That I, drinking this,
Shall hear far Chaos talk with me;
Kings unborn shall walk with me;
And the poor grass shall plot and plan
What it will do when it is man.
Quickened so, will I unlock
Every crypt of every rock.

I thank the joyful juice
For all I know;—
Winds of remembering
Of the ancient being blow,
And seeming-solid walls of use
Open and flow.

Pour, Bacchus! the remembering wine;
Retrieve the loss of me and mine!
Vine for vine be antidote,
And the grape requite the lote!
Haste to cure the old despair,—
Reason in Nature's lotus drenched,
The memory of ages quenched;
Give them again to shine;
Let wine repair what this undid;
And where the infection slid,
A dazzling memory revive;
Refresh the faded tints,
Recut the aged prints,
And write my old adventures with the pen
Which on the first day drew,
Upon the tablets blue,
The dancing Pleiads and eternal men.

Blight

Give me truths;
For I am weary of the surfaces,
And die of inanition. If I knew
Only the herbs and simples of the wood,
Rue, cinquefoil, gill, vervain and agrimony,
Blue-vetch and trillium, hawkweed, sassafras,
Milkweeds and murky brakes, quaint pipes and sun-dew,
And rare and virtuous roots, which in these woods
Draw untold juices from the common earth,
Untold, unknown, and I could surely spell
Their fragrance, and their chemistry apply
By sweet affinities to human flesh,
Driving the foe and stablishing the friend,—
O, that were much, and I could be a part
Of the round day, related to the sun
And planted world, and full executor
Of their imperfect functions.
But these young scholars, who invade our hills,
Bold as the engineer who fells the wood,
And travelling often in the cut he makes,
Love not the flower they pluck, and know it not,
And all their botany is Latin names.
The old men studied magic in the flowers,
And human fortunes in astronomy,
And an omnipotence in chemistry,
Preferring things to names, for these were men,
Were unitarians of the united world,
And, wheresoever their clear eye-beams fell,
They caught the footsteps of the SAME. Our eyes
Are armed, but we are strangers to the stars,
And strangers to the mystic beast and bird,
And strangers to the plant and to the mine.
The injured elements say, 'Not in us;'
And night and day, ocean and continent,
Fire, plant and mineral say, 'Not in us;'
And haughtily return us stare for stare.
For we invade them impiously for gain;
We devastate them unreligiously,
And coldly ask their pottage, not their love.
Therefore they shove us from them, yield to us
Only what to our griping toil is due;
But the sweet affluence of love and song,
The rich results of the divine consents
Of man and earth, of world beloved and lover,

The nectar and ambrosia, are withheld;
And in the midst of spoils and slaves, we thieves
And pirates of the universe, shut out
Daily to a more thin and outward rind,
Turn pale and starve. Therefore, to our sick eyes,
The stunted trees look sick, the summer short,
Clouds shade the sun, which will not tan our hay,
And nothing thrives to reach its natural term;
And life, shorn of its venerable length,
Even at its greatest space is a defeat,
And dies in anger that it was a dupe;
And, in its highest noon and wantonness,
Is early frugal, like a beggar's child;
Even in the hot pursuit of the best aims
And prizes of ambition, checks its hand,
Like Alpine cataracts frozen as they leaped,
Chilled with a miserly comparison
Of the toy's purchase with the length of life.

Dirge

I reached the middle of the mount
    Up which the incarnate soul must climb,
And paused for them, and looked around,
    With me who walked through space and time.

Five rosy boys with morning light
    Had leaped from one fair mother's arms,
Fronted the sun with hope as bright,
    And greeted God with childhood's psalms.

Knows he who tills this lonely field
    To reap its scanty corn,
What mystic fruit his acres yield
    At midnight and at morn?

In the long sunny afternoon
    The plain was full of ghosts;
I wandered up, I wandered down,
    Beset by pensive hosts.

The winding Concord gleamed below,
    Pouring as wide a flood
As when my brothers, long ago,
    Came with me to the wood.

But they are gone,—the holy ones
    Who trod with me this lovely vale;
The strong, star-bright companions
    Are silent, low and pale.

My good, my noble, in their prime,
    Who made this world the feast it was,
Who learned with me the lore of time,
    Who loved this dwelling-place!

They took this valley for their toy,
    They played with it in every mood;
A cell for prayer, a hall for joy,—
    They treated Nature as they would.

They colored the horizon round;
    Stars flamed and faded as they bade,
All echoes hearkened for their sound,—
    They made the woodlands glad or mad.

I touch this flower of silken leaf,
    Which once our childhood knew;
Its soft leaves wound me with a grief
    Whose balsam never grew.

Hearken to yon pine-warbler
    Singing aloft in the tree!
Hearest thou, O traveller,
    What he singeth to me?

Not unless God made sharp thine ear
    With sorrow such as mine,
Out of that delicate lay could'st thou
    Its heavy tale divine.

'Go, lonely man,' it saith;
    'They loved thee from their birth;
Their hands were pure, and pure their faith,—
    There are no such hearts on earth.

'Ye drew one mother's milk,
    One chamber held ye all;
A very tender history
    Did in your childhood fall.

'You cannot unlock your heart,
    The key is gone with them;
The silent organ loudest chants
    The master's requiem.'

Threnody

The South-wind brings
Life, sunshine and desire,
And on every mount and meadow
Breathes aromatic fire;
But over the dead he has no power,
The lost, the lost, he cannot restore;
And, looking over the hills, I mourn
The darling who shall not return.

I see my empty house,
I see my trees repair their boughs;
And he, the wondrous child,
Whose silver warble wild
Outvalued every pulsing sound
Within the air's cerulean round,—
The hyacinthine boy, for whom
Morn well might break and April bloom,
The gracious boy, who did adorn
The world whereinto he was born,
And by his countenance repay
The favor of the loving Day,—
Has disappeared from the Day's eye;
Far and wide she cannot find him;
My hopes pursue, they cannot bind him.
Returned this day, the South-wind searches,
And finds young pines and budding birches;
But finds not the budding man;
Nature, who lost, cannot remake him;
Fate let him fall, Fate can't retake him;
Nature, Fate, men, him seek in vain.

And whither now, my truant wise and sweet,
O, whither tend thy feet?
I had the right, few days ago,
Thy steps to watch, thy place to know:
How have I forfeited the right?
Hast thou forgot me in a new delight?
I hearken for thy household cheer,
O eloquent child!

Whose voice, an equal messenger,
Conveyed thy meaning mild.
What though the pains and joys
Whereof it spoke were toys
Fitting his age and ken,
Yet fairest dames and bearded men,
Who heard the sweet request,
So gentle, wise and grave,
Bended with joy to his behest
And let the world's affairs go by,
A while to share his cordial game,
Or mend his wicker wagon-frame,
Still plotting how their hungry ear
That winsome voice again might hear;
For his lips could well pronounce
Words that were persuasions.

Gentlest guardians marked serene
His early hope, his liberal mien;
Took counsel from his guiding eyes
To make this wisdom earthly wise.
Ah, vainly do these eyes recall
The school-march, each day's festival,
When every morn my bosom glowed
To watch the convoy on the road;
The babe in willow wagon closed,
With rolling eyes and face composed;
With children forward and behind,
Like Cupids studiously inclined;
And he the chieftain paced beside,
The centre of the troop allied,
With sunny face of sweet repose,
To guard the babe from fancied foes.
The little captain innocent
Took the eye with him as he went;
Each village senior paused to scan
And speak the lovely caravan.
From the window I look out
To mark thy beautiful parade,
Stately marching in cap and coat
To some tune by fairies played;—
A music heard by thee alone
To works as noble led thee on.

Now Love and Pride, alas! in vain,
Up and down their glances strain.
The painted sled stands where it stood;
The kennel by the corded wood;
His gathered sticks to stanch the wall
Of the snow-tower, when snow should fall;
The ominous hole he dug in the sand,
And childhood's castles built or planned;
His daily haunts I well discern,—
The poultry-yard, the shed, the barn,—
And every inch of garden ground
Paced by the blessed feet around,
From the roadside to the brook
Whereinto he loved to look.
Step the meek fowls where erst they ranged;
The wintry garden lies unchanged;
The brook into the stream runs on;
But the deep-eyed boy is gone.

On that shaded day,
Dark with more clouds than tempests are,
When thou didst yield thy innocent breath
In birdlike heavings unto death,
Night came, and Nature had not thee;
I said, 'We are mates in misery.'
The morrow dawned with needless glow; ·
Each snowbird chirped, each fowl must crow;
Each tramper started; but the feet
Of the most beautiful and sweet
Of human youth had left the hill
And garden,—they were bound and still.
There's not a sparrow or a wren,
There's not a blade of autumn grain,
Which the four seasons do not tend
And tides of life and increase lend;
And every chick of every bird,
And weed and rock-moss is preferred.
O ostrich-like forgetfulness!
O loss of larger in the less!
Was there no star that could be sent,
No watcher in the firmament,
No angel from the countless host
That loiters round the crystal coast,
Could stoop to heal that only child,
Nature's sweet marvel undefiled,
And keep the blossom of the earth,
Which all her harvests were not worth?

Not mine,—I never called thee mine,
But Nature's heir,—if I repine,
And seeing rashly torn and moved
Not what I made, but what I loved,
Grow early old with grief that thou
Must to the wastes of Nature go,—
'T is because a general hope
Was quenched, and all must doubt and grope.
For flattering planets seemed to say
This child should ills of ages stay,
By wondrous tongue, and guided pen,
Bring the flown Muses back to men.
Perchance not he but Nature ailed,
The world and not the infant failed.
It was not ripe yet to sustain
A genius of so fine a strain,
Who gazed upon the sun and moon
As if he came unto his own,
And, pregnant with his grander thought,
Brought the old order into doubt.
His beauty once their beauty tried;
They could not feed him, and he died,
And wandered backward as in scorn,
To wait an æon to be born.
Ill day which made this beauty waste,
Plight broken, this high face defaced!
Some went and came about the dead;
And some in books of solace read;
Some to their friends the tidings say;
Some went to write, some went to pray;
One tarried here, there hurried one;
But their heart abode with none.
Covetous death bereaved us all,
To aggrandize one funeral.
The eager fate which carried thee
Took the largest part of me:
For this losing is true dying;
This is lordly man's down-lying,
This his slow but sure reclining,
Star by star his world resigning.

O child of paradise,
Boy who made dear his father's home,
In whose deep eyes
Men read the welfare of the times to come,
I am too much bereft.
The world dishonored thou hast left.

O truth's and nature's costly lie!
O trusted broken prophecy!
O richest fortune sourly crossed!
Born for the future, to the future lost!

The deep Heart answered, 'Weepest thou?
Worthier cause for passion wild
If I had not taken the child.
And deemest thou as those who pore,
With aged eyes, short way before,—
Think'st Beauty vanished from the coast
Of matter, and thy darling lost?
Taught he not thee—the man of eld,
Whose eyes within his eyes beheld
Heaven's numerous hierarchy span
The mystic gulf from God to man?
To be alone wilt thou begin
When worlds of lovers hem thee in?
To-morrow, when the masks shall fall
That dizen Nature's carnival,
The pure shall see by their own will,
Which overflowing Love shall fill,
'T is not within the force of fate
The fate-conjoined to separate.
But thou, my votary, weepest thou?
I gave thee sight—where is it now?
I taught thy heart beyond the reach
Of ritual, bible, or of speech;
Wrote in thy mind's transparent table,
As far as the incommunicable;
Taught thee each private sign to raise
Lit by the supersolar blaze.
Past utterance, and past belief,
And past the blasphemy of grief,
The mysteries of Nature's heart;
And though no Muse can these impart,
Throb thine with Nature's throbbing breast,
And all is clear from east to west.

'I came to thee as to a friend;
Dearest, to thee I did not send
Tutors, but a joyful eye,
Innocence that matched the sky,
Lovely locks, a form of wonder,
Laughter rich as woodland thunder,
That thou might'st entertain apart
The richest flowering of all art:

And, as the great all-loving Day
Through smallest chambers takes its way,
That thou might'st break thy daily bread
With prophet, savior and head;
That thou might'st cherish for thine own
The riches of sweet Mary's Son,
Boy-Rabbi, Israel's paragon.
And thoughtest thou such guest
Would in thy hall take up his rest?
Would rushing life forget her laws,
Fate's glowing revolution pause?
High omens ask diviner guess;
Not to be conned to tediousness
And know my higher gifts unbind
The zone that girds the incarnate mind.
When the scanty shores are full
With Thought's perilous, whirling pool;
When frail Nature can no more,
Then the Spirit strikes the hour:
My servant Death, with solving rite,
Pours finite into infinite.
Wilt thou freeze love's tidal flow,
Whose streams through Nature circling go?
Nail the wild star to its track
On the half-climbed zodiac?
Light is light which radiates,
Blood is blood which circulates,
Life is life which generates,
And many-seeming life is one,—
Wilt thou transfix and make it none?
Its onward force too starkly pent
In figure, bone and lineament?
Wilt thou, uncalled, interrogate,
Talker! the unreplying Fate?
Nor see the genius of the whole
Ascendant in the private soul,
Beckon it when to go and come,
Self-announced its hour of doom?
Fair the soul's recess and shrine,
Magic-built to last a season;
Masterpiece of love benign,
Fairer that expansive reason
Whose omen 't is, and sign.
Wilt thou not ope thy heart to know
What rainbows teach, and sunsets show?
Verdict which accumulates
From lengthening scroll of human fates,

Voice of earth to earth returned,
Prayers of saints that inly burned,—
Saying, *What is excellent,*
As God lives, is permanent;
Hearts are dust, hearts' loves remain;
Heart's love will meet thee again.
Revere the Maker; fetch thine eye
Up to his style, and manners of the sky.
Not of adamant and gold
Built he heaven stark and cold;
No, but a nest of bending reeds,
Flowering grass and scented weeds;
Or like a traveller's fleeing tent,
Or bow above the tempest bent;
Built of tears and sacred flames,
And virtue reaching to its aims;
Built of furtherance and pursuing,
Not of spent deeds, but of doing.
Silent rushes the swift Lord
Through ruined systems still restored,
Broadsowing, bleak and void to bless,
Plants with worlds the wilderness;
Waters with tears of ancient sorrow
Apples of Eden ripe to-morrow.
House and tenant go to ground,
Lost in God, in Godhead found.'

Concord Hymn

By the rude bridge that arched the flood,
  Their flag to April's breeze unfurled,
Here once the embattled farmers stood
  And fired the shot heard round the world.

The foe long since in silence slept;
  Alike the conqueror silent sleeps;
And Time the ruined bridge has swept
  Down the dark stream which seaward creeps.

On this green bank, by this soft stream,
  We set to-day a votive stone;
That memory may their deed redeem,
  When, like our sires, our sons are gone.

Spirit, that made those heroes dare
  To die, and leave their children free,
Bid Time and Nature gently spare
  The shaft we raise to them and thee.

Brahma

If the red slayer think he slays,
  Or if the slain think he is slain,
They know not well the subtle ways
  I keep, and pass, and turn again.

Far or forgot to me is near;
  Shadow and sunlight are the same;
The vanished gods to me appear;
  And one to me are shame and fame.

They reckon ill who leave me out;
  When me they fly, I am the wings;
I am the doubter and the doubt,
  And I the hymn the Brahmin sings.

The strong gods pine for my abode,
  And pine in vain the sacred Seven;
But thou, meek lover of the good!
  Find me, and turn thy back on heaven.

Boston Hymn

The word of the Lord by night
To the watching Pilgrims came,
As they sat by the seaside,
And filled their hearts with flame.

God said, I am tired of kings,
I suffer them no more;
Up to my ear the morning brings
The outrage of the poor.

Think ye I made this ball
A field of havoc and war,
Where tyrants great and tyrants small
Might harry the weak and poor?

My angel,—his name is Freedom,—
Choose him to be your king;
He shall cut pathways east and west
And fend you with his wing.

Lo! I uncover the land
Which I hid of old time in the West,
As the sculptor uncovers the statue
When he has wrought his best;

I show Columbia, of the rocks
Which dip their foot in the seas
And soar to the air-borne flocks
Of clouds and the boreal fleece.

I will divide my goods;
Call in the wretch and slave:
None shall rule but the humble,
And none but Toil shall have.

I will have never a noble,
No lineage counted great;
Fishers and choppers and ploughmen
Shall constitute a state.

Go, cut down trees in the forest
And trim the straightest boughs;
Cut down trees in the forest
And build me a wooden house.

Call the people together,
The young men and the sires,
The digger in the harvest-field,
Hireling and him that hires;

And here in a pine state-house
They shall choose men to rule
In every needful faculty,
In church and state and school.

Lo, now! if these poor men
Can govern the land and sea
And make just laws below the sun,
As planets faithful be.

And ye shall succor men;
'T is nobleness to serve;
Help them who cannot help again:
Beware from right to swerve.

I break your bonds and masterships,
And I unchain the slave:
Free be his heart and hand henceforth
As wind and wandering wave.

I cause from every creature
His proper good to flow:
As much as he is and doeth,
So much he shall bestow.

But, laying hands on another
To coin his labor and sweat,
He goes in pawn to his victim
For eternal years in debt.

To-day unbind the captive,
So only are ye unbound;
Lift up a people from the dust,
Trump of their rescue, sound!

Pay ransom to the owner
And fill the bag to the brim.
Who is the owner? The slave is owner,
And ever was. Pay him.

O North! give him beauty for rags,
And honor, O South! for his shame;
Nevada! coin thy golden crags
With Freedom's image and name.

Up! and the dusky race
That sat in darkness long,—
Be swift their feet as antelopes,
And as behemoth strong.

Come, East and West and North,
By races, as snow-flakes,
And carry my purpose forth,
Which neither halts nor shakes.

My will fulfilled shall be,
For, in daylight or in dark,
My thunderbolt has eyes to see
His way home to the mark.

Days

Daughters of Time, the hypocritic Days,
Muffled and dumb like barefoot dervishes,
And marching single in an endless file,
Bring diadems and fagots in their hands.
To each they offer gifts after his will,
Bread, kingdoms, stars, and sky that holds them all.
I, in my pleachéd garden, watched the pomp,
Forgot my morning wishes, hastily
Took a few herbs and apples, and the Day
Turned and departed silent. I, too, late,
Under her solemn fillet saw the scorn.

Terminus

It is time to be old,
To take in sail:—
The god of bounds,
Who sets to seas a shore,
Came to me in his fatal rounds,
And said: 'No more!
No farther shoot
Thy broad ambitious branches, and thy root.
Fancy departs: no more invent;
Contract thy firmament
To compass of a tent.
There's not enough for this and that,
Make thy option which of two;
Economize the failing river,
Not the less revere the Giver,
Leave the many and hold the few.
Timely wise accept the terms,
Soften the fall with wary foot;
A little while
Still plan and smile,
And,—fault of novel germs,—
Mature the unfallen fruit.
Curse, if thou wilt, thy sires,
Bad husbands of their fires,

Who, when they gave thee breath,
Failed to bequeath
The needful sinew stark as once,
The Baresark marrow to thy bones,
But left a legacy of ebbing veins,
Inconstant heat and nerveless reins,—
Amid the Muses, left thee deaf and dumb,
Amid the gladiators, halt and numb.'

    As the bird trims her to the gale,
I trim myself to the storm of time,
I man the rudder, reef the sail,
Obey the voice at eve obeyed at prime:
'Lowly faithful, banish fear,
Right onward drive unharmed;
The port, well worth the cruise, is near,
And every wave is charmed.'

Experience

THE lords of life, the lords of life,—
I saw them pass
In their own guise,
Like and unlike,
Portly and grim,—
Use and Surprise,
Surface and Dream,
Succession swift and spectral Wrong,
Temperament without a tongue,
And the inventor of the game
Omnipresent without name;—
Some to see, some to be guessed,
They marched from east to west:
Little man, least of all,
Among the legs of his guardians tall,
Walked about with puzzled look.
Him by the hand dear Nature took,
Dearest Nature, strong and kind,
Whispered, 'Darling, never mind!
To-morrow they will wear another face,
The founder thou; these are thy race!'

from Quatrains

POET [I]

Ever the Poet *from* the land
Steers his bark and trims his sail;
Right out to sea his courses stand,
New worlds to find in pinnace frail.

POET [II]

To clothe the fiery thought
In simple words succeeds,
For still the craft of genius is
To mask a king in weeds.

SHAKSPEARE

I see all human wits
Are measured but a few;
Unmeasured still my Shakspeare sits,
Lone as the blessed Jew.

MEMORY

Night-dreams trace on Memory's wall
Shadows of the thoughts of day,
And thy fortunes, as they fall,
The bias of the will betray.

CLIMACTERIC

I am not wiser for my age,
Nor skilful by my grief;
Life loiters at the book's first page,—
Ah! could we turn the leaf.

Unity

Space is ample, east and west,
But two cannot go abreast,
Cannot travel in it two:
Yonder masterful cuckoo
Crowds every egg out of the nest,
Quick or dead, except its own;
A spell is laid on sod and stone,
Night and Day were tampered with,
Every quality and pith
Surcharged and sultry with a power
That works its will on age and hour.

Circles

Nature centres into balls,
And her proud ephemerals,
Fast to surface and outside,
Scan the profile of the sphere;
Knew they what that signified,
A new genesis were here.

But Nature whistled with all her winds,
Did as she pleased and went her way.

from Life

Him strong Genius urged to roam,
Stronger Custom brought him home.

from The Exile

. . . .

I have an arrow that will find its mark,
A mastiff that will bite without a bark.

SARAH HELEN WHITMAN

(1803–1878)

from The Past

"So fern, und doch so nah."
—Goethe

Thick darkness broodeth o'er the world:
The raven pinions of the Night,
Close on her silent bosom furled,
Reflect no gleam of Orient light.
E'en the wild Norland fires that mocked
The faint bloom of the eastern sky,
Now leave me, in close darkness locked,
To-night's weird realm of fantasy.

Borne from pale shadow-lands remote,
A morphean music, wildly sweet,
Seems, on the starless gloom, to float,
Like the white-pinioned Paraclete.
Softly into my dream it flows,
Then faints into the silence drear;
While from the hollow dark outgrows
The phantom Past, pale gliding near.

. . . .

To——

Vainly my heart had with thy sorceries striven:
It had no refuge from my love,—no Heaven
But in thy fatal presence;—from afar
It owned thy power and trembled like a star
O'erfraught with light and splendor. Could I deem
How dark a shadow should obscure its beam?—
Could I believe that pain could ever dwell
Where thy bright presence cast its blissful spell?
Thou wert my proud palladium;—could I fear
The avenging Destinies when thou wert near?—
Thou wert my Destiny;—thy song, thy fame,
The wild enchantments clustering round thy name,
Were my soul's heritage, its royal dower;
Its glory and its kingdom and its power!

ELIZABETH OAKES-SMITH
(1806–1893)

Annihilation

Doubt, cypress crowned, upon a ruined arch
    Amid the shapely temple overthrown,
Exultant, stays at length her onward march:
    Her victim, all with earthliness o'ergrown,
Hath sunk himself to earth to perish there;
    His thoughts are outward, all his love a blight,
Dying, deluding, are his hopes, though fair—
    And death, the spirit's everlasting night.
Thus, midnight travellers, on some mountain steep
    Hear far above the avalanche boom down,
Starting the glacier echoes from their sleep,
    And lost in glens to human foot unknown—
The death-plunge of the lost come to their ear,
And silence claims again her region cold and drear.

JOHN GREENLEAF WHITTIER
(1807–1892)

Telling the Bees

Here is the place; right over the hill
    Runs the path I took;
You can see the gap in the old wall still,
    And the stepping-stones in the shallow brook.

There is the house, with the gate red-barred,
    And the poplars tall;
And the barn's brown length, and the cattle-yard,
    And the white horns tossing above the wall.

There are the beehives ranged in the sun;
    And down by the brink
Of the brook are her poor flowers, weed-o'errun,
    Pansy and daffodil, rose and pink.

A year has gone, as the tortoise goes,
    Heavy and slow;
And the same rose blows, and the same sun glows,
    And the same brook sings of a year ago.

There's the same sweet clover-smell in the breeze;
    And the June sun warm
Tangles his wings of fire in the trees,
    Setting, as then, over Fernside farm.

I mind me how with a lover's care
    From my Sunday coat
I brushed off the burrs, and smoothed my hair,
    And cooled at the brookside my brow and throat.

Since we parted, a month had passed,—
    To love, a year;
Down through the beeches I looked at last
    On the little red gate and the well-sweep near.

I can see it all now,—the slantwise rain
    Of light through the leaves,
The sundown's blaze on her window-pane,
    The bloom of her roses under the eaves.

Just the same as a month before,—
    The house and the trees,
The barn's brown gable, the vine by the door,—
    Nothing changed but the hives of bees.

Before them, under the garden wall,
    Forward and back,
Went drearily singing the chore-girl small,
    Draping each hive with a shred of black.

Trembling, I listened: the summer sun
    Had the chill of snow;
For I knew she was telling the bees of one
    Gone on the journey we all must go!

Then I said to myself, "My Mary weeps
    For the dead to-day:
Haply her blind old grandsire sleeps
    The fret and the pain of his age away."

But her dog whined low; on the doorway sill,
　　With his cane to his chin,
The old man sat; and the chore-girl still
　　Sung to the bees stealing out and in.

And the song she was singing ever since
　　In my ear sounds on:—
"Stay at home, pretty bees, fly not hence!
　　Mistress Mary is dead and gone!"

from SNOW-BOUND—A WINTER IDYL

The sun that brief December day
Rose cheerless over hills of gray,
And, darkly circled, gave at noon
A sadder light than waning moon.
Slow tracing down the thickening sky
Its mute and ominous prophecy,
A portent seeming less than threat,
It sank from sight before it set.
A chill no coat, however stout,
Of homespun stuff could quite shut out,
A hard, dull bitterness of cold,
That checked, mid-vein, the circling race
Of life-blood in the sharpened face,
The coming of the snow-storm told.
The wind blew east; we heard the roar
Of Ocean on his wintry shore,
And felt the strong pulse throbbing there
Beat with low rhythm our inland air.

Meanwhile we did our nightly chores,—
Brought in the wood from out of doors,
Littered the stalls, and from the mows
Raked down the herd's-grass for the cows:
Heard the horse whinnying for his corn;
And, sharply clashing horn on horn,
Impatient down the stanchion rows
The cattle shake their walnut bows;
While, peering from his early perch
Upon the scaffold's pole of birch,
The cock his crested helmet bent
And down his querulous challenge sent.

Unwarmed by any sunset light
The gray day darkened into night,
A night made hoary with the swarm
And whirl-dance of the blinding storm,
As zigzag, wavering to and fro,
Crossed and recrossed the wingèd snow:
And ere the early bedtime came
The white drift piled the window-frame,
And through the glass the clothes-line posts
Looked in like tall and sheeted ghosts.

So all night long the storm roared on:
The morning broke without a sun;
In tiny spherule traced with lines
Of Nature's geometrics signs,
In starry flake, and pellicle,
All day the hoary meteor fell;
And, when the second morning shone,
We looked upon a world unknown,
On nothing we could call our own.
Around the glistening wonder bent
The blue walls of the firmament,
No cloud above, no earth below,—
A universe of sky and snow!
The old familiar sights of ours
Took marvellous shapes; strange domes and towers
Rose up where sty or corn-crib stood,
Or garden-wall, or belt of wood;
A smooth white mound the brush-pile showed,
A fenceless drift what once was road;
The bridle-post an old man sat
With loose-flung coat and high cocked hat;
The well-curb had a Chinese roof;
And even the long sweep, high aloof,
In its slant splendor, seemed to tell
Of Pisa's leaning miracle.

A prompt, decisive man, no breath
Our father wasted: "Boys a path!"
Well pleased, (for when did farmer boy
Count such a summons less than joy?)
Our buskins on our feet we drew;
With mittened hands, and caps drawn low,
To guard our necks and ears from snow,
We cut the solid whiteness through.
And, where the drift was deepest, made

A tunnel walled and overlaid
With dazzling crystal: we had read
Of rare Aladdin's wondrous cave,
And to our own his name we gave,
With many a wish the luck were ours
To test his lamp's supernal powers.
We reached the barn with merry din,
And roused the prisoned brutes within.
The old horse thrust his long head out,
And grave with wonder gazed about;
The cock his lusty greeting said,
And forth his speckled harem led;
The oxen lashed their tails, and hooked,
And mild reproach of hunger looked;
The hornëd patriarch of the sheep,
Like Egypt's Amun roused from sleep,
Shook his sage head with gesture mute,
And emphasized with stamp of foot.

All day the gusty north-wind bore
The loosening drift its breath before;
Low circling round its southern zone,
The sun through dazzling snow-mist shone.
No church-bell lent its Christian tone
To the savage air, no social smoke
Curled over woods of snow-hung oak.
A solitude made more intense
By dreary-voicëd elements,
The shrieking of the mindless wind,
The moaning tree-boughs swaying blind,
And on the glass the unmeaning beat
Of ghostly finger-tips of sleet.
Beyond the circle of our hearth
No welcome sound of toil or mirth
Unbound the spell, and testified
Of human life and thought outside.
We minded that the sharpest ear
The buried brooklet could not hear,
The music of whose liquid lip
Had been to us companionship,
And, in our lonely life, had grown
To have an almost human tone.

. . . .

So days went on: a week had passed
Since the great world was heard from last.
The Almanac we studied o'er,
Read and reread our little store
Of books and pamphlets, scarce a score;
One harmless novel, mostly hid
From younger eyes, a book forbid,
And poetry, (or good or bad,
A single book was all we had,)
Where Ellwood's meek, drab-skirted Muse,
    A stranger to the heathen Nine,
    Sang, with a somewhat nasal whine,
The wars of David and the Jews.
At last the floundering carrier bore
The village paper to our door.
Lo! broadening outward as we read,
To warmer zones the horizon spread
In panoramic length unrolled
We saw the marvels that it told.
Before us passed the painted Creeks,
    And daft McGregor on his raids
    In Costa Rica's everglades.
And up Taygetos winding slow
Rode Ypsilanti's Mainote Greeks,
A Turk's head at each saddle-bow!
Welcome to us its week-old news,
Its corner for the rustic Muse,
    Its monthly gauge of snow and rain,
Its record, mingling in a breath
The wedding bell and dirge of death:
Jest, anecdote, and love-lorn tale,
The latest culprit sent to jail;
Its hue and cry of stolen and lost,
Its vendue sales and goods at cost,
    And traffic calling loud for gain.
We felt the stir of hall and street,
The pulse of life that round us beat;
The chill embargo of the snow
Was melted in the genial glow;
Wide swung again our ice-locked door,
And all the world was ours once more!

Clasp, Angel of the backward look
    And folded wings of ashen gray
    And voice of echoes far away,
The brazen covers of thy book;
The weird palimpsest old and vast,

Wherein thou hid'st the spectral past;
Where, closely mingling, pale and glow
The characters of joy and woe;
The monographs of outlived years,
Or smile-illumed or dim with tears,
    Green hills of life that slope to death,
And haunts of home, whose vistaed trees
Shade off to mournful cypresses
    With the white amaranths underneath.
Even while I look, I can but heed
    The restless sands' incessant fall,
Importunate hours that hours succeed,
Each clamorous with its own sharp need,
    And duty keeping pace with all.
Shut down and clasp the heavy lids;
I hear again the voice that bids
The dreamer leave his dream midway
For larger hopes and graver fears:
Life greatens in these later years,
The century's aloe flowers to-day!

Yet, haply, in some lull of life,
Some Truce of God which breaks its strife,
The worldling's eyes shall gather dew,
    Dreaming in throngful city ways
Of winter joys his boyhood knew;
And dear and early friends—the few
Who yet remain—shall pause to view
    These Flemish pictures of old days;
Sit with me by the homestead hearth,
And stretch the hands of memory forth
    To warm them at the wood-fire's blaze!
And thanks untraced to lips unknown
Shall greet me like the odors blown
From unseen meadows newly mown,
Or lilies floating in some pond,
Wood-fringed, the wayside gaze beyond;
The traveller owns the grateful sense
Of sweetness near, he knows not whence,
And, pausing, takes with forehead bare
The benediction of the air.

Ichabod

So fallen! so lost! the light withdrawn
      Which once he wore!
The glory from his gray hairs gone
      Forevermore!

Revile him not, the Tempter hath
      A snare for all;
And pitying tears, not scorn and wrath,
      Befit his fall!

Oh, dumb be passion's stormy rage,
      When he who might
Have lighted up and led his age,
      Falls back in night.

Scorn! would the angels laugh, to mark
      A bright soul driven,
Fiend-goaded, down the endless dark,
      From hope and heaven!

Let not the land once proud of him
      Insult him now,
Nor brand with deeper shame his dim,
      Dishonored brow.

But let its humbled sons, instead,
      From sea to lake,
A long lament, as for the dead,
      In sadness make.

Of all we loved and honored, naught
      Save power remains;
A fallen angel's pride of thought,
      Still strong in chains.

All else is gone; from those great eyes
      The soul has fled:
When faith is lost, when honor dies,
      The man is dead!

Then, pay the reverence of old days
      To his dead fame;
Walk backward, with averted gaze,
      And hide the shame!

The Fruit Gift

Last night, just as the tints of autumn's sky
   Of sunset faded from our hills and streams,
   I sat, vague listening, lapped in twilight dreams,
To the leaf's rustle, and the cricket's cry.
Then, like that basket, flush with summer fruit,
Dropped by the angels at the Prophet's foot,
Came, unannounced, a gift of clustered sweetness,
   Full-orbed, and glowing with the prisoned beams
Of summery suns, and rounded to completeness
By kisses of the south-wind and the dew.
Thrilled with a glad surprise, methought I knew
The pleasure of the homeward-turning Jew,
When Eshcol's clusters on his shoulders lay,
Dropping their sweetness on his desert way.

I said, "This fruit beseems no world of sin.
   Its parent vine, rooted in Paradise,
   O'ercrept the wall, and never paid the price
   Of the great mischief,—an ambrosial tree,
Eden's exotic, somehow smuggled in,
   To keep the thorns and thistles company."
Perchance our frail, sad mother plucked in haste
   A single vine-slip as she passed the gate,
Where the dread sword alternate paled and burned,
   And the stern angel, pitying her fate,
Forgave the lovely trespasser, and turned
Aside his face of fire; and thus the waste
And fallen world hath yet its annual taste
Of primal good, to prove of sin the cost,
And show by one gleaned ear the mighty harvest lost.

Abraham Davenport

In the old days (a custom laid aside
With breeches and cocked hats) the people sent
Their wisest men to make the public laws.
And so, from a brown homestead, where the Sound
Drinks the small tribute of the Mianas,
Waved over by the woods of Rippowams,
And hallowed by pure lives and tranquil deaths,
Stamford sent up to the councils of the State
Wisdom and grace in Abraham Davenport.

'Twas on a May-day of the far old year
Seventeen hundred eighty, that there fell
Over the bloom and sweet life of the Spring,
Over the fresh earth and the heaven of noon,
A horror of great darkness, like the night
In day of which the Norland sagas tell,—
The Twilight of the Gods. The low-hung sky
Was black with ominous clouds, save where its rim
Was fringed with a dull glow, like that which climbs
The crater's sides from the red hell below.
Birds ceased to sing, and all the barnyard fowls
Roosted; the cattle at the pasture bars
Lowed, and looked homeward; bats on leathern wings
Flitted abroad; the sounds of labor died;
Men prayed, and women wept; all ears grew sharp
To hear the doom-blast of the trumpet shatter
The black sky, that the dreadful face of Christ
Might look from the rent clouds, not as He looked
A loving guest at Bethany, but stern
As Justice and inexorable Law.

Meanwhile in the old State House, dim as ghosts,
Sat the lawgivers of Connecticut,
Trembling beneath their legislative robes.
"It is the Lord's Great Day! Let us adjourn,"
Some said; and then, as if with one accord,
All eyes were turned to Abraham Davenport.
He rose, slow cleaving with his steady voice
The intolerable hush. "This well may be
The Day of Judgment which the world awaits;
But be it so or not, I only know
My present duty, and my Lord's command
To occupy till He come. So at the post
Where He hath set me in His providence,
I choose, for one, to meet Him face to face,—
No faithless servant frightened from my task,
But ready when the Lord of the harvest calls;
And therefore, with all reverence, I would say,
Let God do His work, we will see to ours.
Bring in the candles." And they brought them in.

Then by the flaring lights the Speaker read,
Albeit with husky voice and shaking hands,
An act to amend an act to regulate
The shad and alewive fisheries. Whereupon
Wisely and well spake Abraham Davenport,
Straight to the question, with no figures of speech

Save the ten Arab signs, yet not without
The shrewd dry humor natural to the man:
His awe-struck colleagues listening all the while,
Between the pauses of his argument,
To hear the thunder of the wrath of God
Break from the hollow trumpet of the cloud.

And there he stands in memory to this day,
Erect, self-poised, a rugged face, half seen
Against the background of unnatural dark,
A witness to the ages as they pass,
That simple duty hath no place for fear.

_____

He ceased: just then the ocean seemed
    To lift a half-faced moon in sight;
And, shore-ward, o'er the waters gleamed,
    From crest to crest, a line of light,
Such as of old, with solemn awe,
    The fishers by Gennesaret saw,
When dry-shod o'er it walked the Son of God,
Tracking the waves with light where'er his sandals trod.

Silently for a space each eye
    Upon that sudden glory turned:
Cool from the land the breeze blew by,
    The tent-ropes flapped, the long beach churned
Its waves to foam; on either hand
    Stretched, far as sight, the hills of sand;
With bays of marsh, and capes of bush and tree,
The wood's black shore-line loomed beyond the meadowy sea.

. . . .

The Slave-Ships

"That fatal, that perfidious Bark
Built in th' eclipse, and rigg'd with curses dark."
                    MILTON'S *Lycidas*

"All ready?" cried the captain;
    "Ay, ay!" the seamen said;
"Heave up the worthless lubbers,—
    The dying and the dead."
Up from the slave-ship's prison
    Fierce, bearded heads were thrust:

"Now let the sharks look to it,—
    Toss up the dead ones first!"

Corpse after corpse came up,—
    Death had been busy there;
Where every blow is mercy,
    Why should the spoiler spare?
Corpse after corpse they cast
    Sullenly from the ship,
Yet bloody with the traces
    Of fetter-link and whip.

Gloomily stood the captain,
    With his arms upon his breast,
With his cold brow sternly knotted
    And his iron lip compressed.
"Are all the dead dogs over?"
    Growled through that matted lip;
"The blind ones are no better,
    Let's lighten the good ship."

Hark! from the ship's dark bosom,
    The very sounds of hell!
The ringing clank of iron,
    The maniac's short, sharp yell!
The hoarse, low curse, throat-stifled;
    The starving infant's moan,
The horror of a breaking heart
    Poured through a mother's groan.

Up from that loathsome prison
    The stricken blind ones came;
Below, had all been darkness,
    Above, was still the same.
Yet the holy breath of heaven
    Was sweetly breathing there,
And the heated brow of fever
    Cooled in the soft sea air.

"Overboard with them, shipmates!"
    Cutlass and dirk were plied;
Fettered and blind, one after one,
    Plunged down the vessel's side.
The sabre smote above,
    Beneath, the lean shark lay,
Waiting with wide and bloody jaw
    His quick and human prey.

God of the earth! what cries
    Rang upward unto thee?
Voices of agony and blood,
    From ship-deck and from sea.
The last dull plunge was heard,
    The last wave caught its stain,
And the unsated shark looked up
    For human hearts in vain.
       *   *   *
Red glowed the western waters,
    The setting sun was there,
Scattering alike on wave and cloud
    His fiery mesh of hair.
Amidst a group in blindness,
    A solitary eye
Gazed, from the burdened slaver's deck,
    Into that burning sky.

"A storm," spoke out the gazer,
    "Is gathering and at hand;
Curse on 't, I 'd give my other eye
    For one firm rood of land."
And then he laughed, but only
    His echoed laugh replied,
For the blinded and the suffering
    Alone were at his side.

Night settled on the waters,
    And on a stormy heaven,
While fiercely on that lone ship's track
    The thunder-gust was driven.
"A sail!—thank God, a sail!"
    And as the helmsman spoke,
Up through the stormy murmur
    A shout of gladness broke.

Down came the stranger vessel,
    Unheeding on her way,
So near that on the slaver's deck
    Fell off her driven spray.
"Ho! for the love of mercy,
    We're perishing and blind!"
A wail of utter agony
    Came back upon the wind:

"Help us! for we are stricken
    With blindness every one;
Ten days we 've floated fearfully,
    Unnoting star or sun.
Our ship 's the slaver Leon,—
    We 've but a score on board;
Our slaves are all gone over,—
    Help, for the love of God!"

On livid brows of agony
    The broad red lightning shone;
But the roar of wind and thunder
    Stifled the answering groan;
Wailed from the broken waters
    A last despairing cry,
As, kindling in the stormy light,
    The stranger ship went by.

                *   *   *

In the sunny Guadaloupe
    A dark-hulled vessel lay,
With a crew who noted never
    The nightfall or the day.
The blossom of the orange
    Was white by every stream,
And tropic leaf, and flower, and bird
    Were in the warm sunbeam.

And the sky was bright as ever,
    And the moonlight slept as well,
On the palm-trees by the hillside,
    And the streamlet of the dell:
And the glances of the Creole
    Were still as archly deep,
And her smiles as full as ever
    Of passion and of sleep.

But vain were bird and blossom,
    The green earth and the sky,
And the smile of human faces,
    To the slaver's darkened eye;
At the breaking of the morning,
    At the star-lit evening time,
O'er a world of light and beauty
    Fell the blackness of his crime.

The Christian Slave

A Christian! going, gone!
Who bids for God's own image? for his grace,
With that poor victim of the market-place,
    Hath in her suffering won?

My God! can such things be?
Hast Thou not said that whatsoe'er is done
Unto Thy weakest and Thy humblest one
    Is even done to Thee?

In that sad victim, then,
Child of Thy pitying love, I see Thee stand;
Once more the jest-word of a mocking band,
    Bound, sold, and scourged again!

A Christian up for sale!
Wet with her blood your whips, o'ertask her frame,
Make her life loathsome with your wrong and shame,
    Her patience shall not fail!

A heathen hand might deal
Back on your heads the gathered wrong of years:
But her low, broken prayer and nightly tears,
    Ye neither heed nor feel.

Con well thy lesson o'er,
Thou prudent teacher, tell the toiling slave
No dangerous tale of Him who came to save
    The outcast and the poor.

But wisely shut the ray
Of God's free Gospel from her simple heart,
And to her darkened mind alone impart
    One stern command, Obey!

So shalt thou deftly raise
The market price of human flesh; and while
On thee, their pampered guest, the planters smile,
    Thy church shall praise.

Grave, reverend men shall tell
From Northern pulpits how thy work was blest,
While in that vile South Sodom first and best,
    Thy poor disciples sell.

Oh, shame! the Moslem thrall,
Who, with his master, to the Prophet kneels,
While turning to the sacred Kebla feels
    His fetters break and fall.

    Cheers from the turbaned Bey
Of robber-peopled Tunis! he hath torn
The dark slave-dungeons open, and hath borne
    Their inmates into day:

    But our poor slave in vain
Turns to the Christian shrine his aching eyes;
Its rites will only swell his market price,
    And rivet on his chain.

    God of all right! how long
Shall priestly robbers at Thine altar stand,
Lifting in prayer to Thee the bloody hand
    And haughty brow of wrong?

    Oh, from the fields of cane,
From the low rice-swamp, from the trader's cell;
From the black slave-ship's foul and loathsome hell,
    And coffle's weary chain;

    Hoarse, horrible, and strong,
Rises to Heaven that agonizing cry,
Filling the arches of the hollow sky,
    How long, O God, how long?

from Yorktown

    . . . .

Lo! fourscore years have passed; and where
The Gallic bugles stirred the air,
And, through breached batteries, side by side,
To victory stormed the hosts allied,
And brave foes grounded, pale with pain,
The arms they might not lift again,
As abject as in that old day
The slave still toils his life away.

Oh, fields still green and fresh in story,
Old days of pride, old names of glory,
Old marvels of the tongue and pen,
Old thoughts which stirred the hearts of men,
Ye spared the wrong; and over all
Behold the avenging shadow fall!
Your world-wide honor stained with shame,—
Your freedom's self a hollow name!

Where's now the flag of that old war?
Where flows its stripe? Where burns its star?
Bear witness, Palo Alto's day,
Dark Vale of Palms, red Monterey,
Where Mexic Freedom, young and weak,
Fleshes the Northern eagle's beak;
Symbol of terror and despair,
Of chains and slaves, go seek it there!

Laugh, Prussia, midst thy iron ranks!
Laugh, Russia, from thy Neva's banks!
Brave sport to see the fledgling born
Of Freedom by its parent torn!
Safe now is Speilberg's dungeon cell,
Safe drear Siberia's frozen hell:
With Slavery's flag o'er both unrolled,
What of the New World fears the Old?

HENRY WADSWORTH LONGFELLOW
(1807–1882)

Hymn to the Night

I heard the trailing garments of the Night
    Sweep through her marble halls!
I saw her sable skirts all fringed with light
    From the celestial walls!

I felt her presence, by its spell of might,
    Stoop o'er me from above;
The calm, majestic presence of the Night,
    As of the one I love.

I heard the sounds of sorrow and delight,
    The manifold, soft chimes,
That fill the haunted chambers of the Night,
    Like some old poet's rhymes.

From the cool cisterns of the midnight air,
    My spirit drank repose;
The fountain of perpetual peace flows there,—
    From those deep cisterns flows.

O holy Night! from thee I learn to bear
    What man has borne before!
Thou layest thy finger on the lips of Care,
    And they complain no more.

Peace! Peace! Orestes-like I breathe this prayer!
    Descend with broad-winged flight,
The welcome, the thrice-prayed for, the most fair,
    The best-beloved Night!

A Psalm of Life
What the heart of the young man said to the psalmist

Tell me not, in mournful numbers,
    Life is but an empty dream!—
For the soul is dead that slumbers,
    And things are not what they seem.

Life is real! Life is earnest!
    And the grave is not its goal;
Dust thou art, to dust returnest,
    Was not spoken of the soul.

Not enjoyment, and not sorrow,
    Is our destined end or way;
But to act, that each to-morrow
    Find us farther than to-day.

Art is long, and Time is fleeting,
    And our hearts, though stout and brave,
Still, like muffled drums, are beating
    Funeral marches to the grave.

In the world's broad field of battle,
    In the bivouac of Life,
Be not like dumb, driven cattle!
    Be a hero in the strife!

Trust no Future, howe'er pleasant!
    Let the dead Past bury its dead!

The Wreck of the Hesperus

It was the schooner Hesperus,
    That sailed the wintry sea;
And the skipper had taken his little daughter,
    To bear him company.

Blue were her eyes as the fairy-flax,
    Her cheeks like the dawn of day,
And her bosom white as the hawthorn buds,
    That ope in the month of May.

The skipper he stood beside the helm,
    His pipe was in his mouth,
And he watched how the veering flaw did blow
    The smoke now West, now South.

Then up and spake an old Sailòr,
    Had sailed to the Spanish Main,
"I pray thee, put into yonder port,
    For I fear a hurricane.

"Last night, the moon had a golden ring,
    And to-night no moon we see!"
The skipper, he blew a whiff from his pipe,
    And a scornful laugh laughed he.

Colder and louder blew the wind,
    A gale from the Northeast,
The snow fell hissing in the brine,
    And the billows frothed like yeast.

Down came the storm, and smote amain
    The vessel in its strength;
She shuddered and paused, like a frighted steed,
    Then leaped her cable's length.

"Come hither! come hither! my little daughtèr,
    And do not tremble so;
For I can weather the roughest gale
    That ever wind did blow."

He wrapped her warm in his seaman's coat
    Against the stinging blast;
He cut a rope from a broken spar,
    And bound her to the mast.

"O father! I hear the church-bells ring,
    Oh say, what may it be?"
" 'T is a fog-bell on a rock-bound coast!"—
    And he steered for the open sea.

"O father! I hear the sound of guns,
    Oh say, what may it be?"
"Some ship in distress, that cannot live
    In such an angry sea!"

"O father! I see a gleaming light,
    Oh say, what may it be?"
But the father answered never a word,
    A frozen corpse was he.

Lashed to the helm, all stiff and stark,
    With his face turned to the skies,
The lantern gleamed through the gleaming snow
    On his fixed and glassy eyes.

Then the maiden clasped her hands and prayed
    That savèd she might be;
And she thought of Christ, who stilled the wave,
    On the Lake of Galilee.

And fast through the midnight dark and drear,
    Through the whistling sleet and snow,
Like a sheeted ghost, the vessel swept
    Tow'rds the reef of Norman's Woe.

And ever the fitful gusts between
    A sound came from the land;
It was the sound of the trampling surf
    On the rocks and the hard sea-sand.

The breakers were right beneath her bows,
    She drifted a dreary wreck,
And a whooping billow swept the crew
    Like icicles from her deck.

She struck where the white and fleecy waves
    Looked soft as carded wool,
But the cruel rocks, they gored her side
    Like the horns of an angry bull.

Her rattling shrouds, all sheathed in ice,
    With the masts went by the board;
Like a vessel of glass, she stove and sank,
    Ho! ho! the breakers roared!

At daybreak, on the bleak sea-beach,
    A fisherman stood aghast,
To see the form of a maiden fair,
    Lashed close to a drifting mast.

The salt sea was frozen on her breast,
    The salt tears in her eyes;
And he saw her hair, like the brown seaweed,
    On the billows fall and rise.

Such was the wreck of the Hesperus,
    In the midnight and the snow!
Christ save us all from a death like this,
    On the reef of Norman's Woe!

Excelsior

The shades of night were falling fast,
As through an Alpine village passed
A youth, who bore, 'mid snow and ice,
A banner with strange device,
      Excelsior!

His brow was sad; his eye beneath
Flashed like a falchion from its sheath,
And like a silver clarion rung
The accents of that unknown tongue,
      Excelsior!

In happy homes he saw the light
Of household fires gleam warm and bright;
Above, the spectral glaciers shone,
And from his lips escaped a groan,
      Excelsior!

"Try not the Pass!" the old man said;
"Dark lowers the tempest overhead,
The roaring torrent is deep and wide!"
And loud that clarion voice replied,
      Excelsior!

"Oh stay," the maiden said, "and rest
Thy weary head upon this breast!"
A tear stood in his bright blue eye,
But still he answered, with a sigh,
      Excelsior!

"Beware the pine-tree's withered branch!
Beware the awful avalanche!"
This was the peasant's last Good-night,
A voice replied, far up the height,
      Excelsior!

At break of day, as heavenward
The pious monks of St. Bernard
Uttered the oft-repeated prayer,
A voice cried through the startled air,
      Excelsior!

A traveller, by the faithful hound,
Half-buried in the snow was found,
Still grasping in his hand of ice
That banner with the strange device,
     Excelsior!

There in the twilight cold and gray,
Lifeless, but beautiful, he lay,
And from the sky, serene and far,
A voice fell, like a falling star,
     Excelsior!

The Slave in the Dismal Swamp

In dark fens of the Dismal Swamp
    The hunted Negro lay;
He saw the fire of the midnight camp,
And heard at times a horse's tramp
    And a bloodhound's distant bay.

Where will-o'-the-wisps and glow-worms shine,
    In bulrush and in brake;
Where waving mosses shroud the pine,
And the cedar grows, and the poisonous vine
    Is spotted like the snake;

Where hardly a human foot could pass,
    Or a human heart would dare,
On the quaking turf of the green morass
He crouched in the rank and tangled grass,
    Like a wild beast in his lair.

A poor old slave, infirm and lame;
    Great scars deformed his face;
On his forehead he bore the brand of shame,
And the rags, that hid his mangled frame,
    Were the livery of disgrace.

All things above were bright and fair,
    All things were glad and free;
Lithe squirrels darted here and there,
And wild birds filled the echoing air
    With songs of Liberty!

On him alone was the doom of pain,
    From the morning of his birth;
On him alone the curse of Cain
Fell, like a flail on the garnered grain,
    And struck him to the earth!

The Warning

Beware! The Israelite of old, who tore
    The lion in his path,—when, poor and blind,
He saw the blessed light of heaven no more,
    Shorn of his noble strength and forced to grind
In prison, and at last led forth to be
A pander to Philistine revelry,—

Upon the pillars of the temple laid
    His desperate hands, and in its overthrow
Destroyed himself, and with him those who made
    A cruel mockery of his sightless woe;
The poor, blind Slave, the scoff and jest of all,
Expired, and thousands perished in the fall!

There is a poor, blind Samson in this land,
    Shorn of his strength and bound in bonds of steel,
Who may, in some grim revel, raise his hand,
    And shake the pillars of this Commonweal,
Till the vast Temple of our liberties
A shapeless mass of wreck and rubbish lies.

The Arrow and the Song

I shot an arrow into the air,
It fell to earth, I knew not where;
For, so swiftly it flew, the sight
Could not follow it in its flight.

I breathed a song into the air,
It fell to earth, I knew not where;
For who has sight so keen and strong,
That it can follow the flight of song?

Long, long afterward, in an oak
I found the arrow, still unbroke;
And the song, from beginning to end,
I found again in the heart of a friend.

Mezzo Cammin

Half of my life is gone, and I have let
    The years slip from me and have not fulfilled
    The aspiration of my youth, to build
    Some tower of song with lofty parapet.
Not indolence, nor pleasure, nor the fret
    Of restless passions that would not be stilled,
    But sorrow, and a care that almost killed,
    Kept me from what I may accomplish yet;
Though, halfway up the hill, I see the Past
    Lying beneath me with its sounds and sights,—
    A city in the twilight dim and vast,
With smoking roofs, soft bells, and gleaming lights,—
    And hear above me on the autumnal blast
    The cataract of Death far thundering from the heights.

from FRAGMENTS

December 18, 1847

Soft through the silent air descend the feathery snow-flakes;
White are the distant hills, white are the neighboring fields;
Only the marshes are brown, and the river rolling among them
Weareth the leaden hue seen in the eyes of the blind.

August 4, 1856

A lovely morning, without the glare of the sun,
the sea in great commotion, chafing and foaming.

So from the bosom of darkness our days come roaring and gleaming,
    Chafe and break into foam, sink into darkness again.
But on the shores of Time each leaves some trace of its passage,
    Though the succeeding wave washes it out from the sand.

Elegiac Verse XII

Wisely the Hebrews admit no Present tense in their language;
    While we are speaking the word, it is already the Past.

Jugurtha

How cold are thy baths, Apollo!
    Cried the African monarch, the splendid,
As down to his death in the hollow
    Dark dungeons of Rome he descended,
    Uncrowned, unthroned, unattended;
How cold are thy baths, Apollo!

How cold are thy baths, Apollo!
    Cried the Poet, unknown, unbefriended,
As the vision, that lured him to follow,
    With the mist and the darkness blended,
    And the dream of his life was ended;
How cold are thy baths, Apollo!

The Cross of Snow

In the long, sleepless watches of the night,
    A gentle face—the face of one long dead—
    Looks at me from the wall, where round its head
    The night-lamp casts a halo of pale light.
Here in this room she died; and soul more white
    Never through martyrdom of fire was led
    To its repose; nor can in books be read
    The legend of a life more benedight.
There is a mountain in the distant West
    That, sun-defying, in its deep ravines
    Displays a cross of snow upon its side.
Such is the cross I wear upon my breast
    These eighteen years, through all the changing scenes
And seasons, changeless since the day she died.

The Sound of the Sea

The sea awoke at midnight from its sleep,
    And round the pebbly beaches far and wide
    I heard the first wave of the rising tide
    Rush onward with uninterrupted sweep;
A voice out of the silence of the deep,
    A sound mysteriously multiplied
    As of a cataract from the mountain's side,
    Or roar of winds upon a wooded steep.
So comes to us at times, from the unknown
    And inaccessible solitudes of being,

The rushing of the sea-tides of the soul;
And inspirations, that we deem our own,
Are some divine foreshadowing and foreseeing
    Of things beyond our reason or control.

Chaucer

An old man in a lodge within a park;
    The chamber walls depicted all around
    With portraitures of huntsman, hawk, and hound,
    And the hurt deer. He listeneth to the lark,
Whose song comes with the sunshine through the dark
    Of painted glass in leaden lattice bound;
    He listeneth and he laugheth at the sound,
    Then writeth in a book like any clerk.
He is the poet of the dawn, who wrote
    The Canterbury Tales, and his old age
    Made beautiful with song; and as I read
I hear the crowing cock, I hear the note
    Of lark and linnet, and from every page
    Rise odors of ploughed field or flowery mead.

Divina Commedia

I
Oft have I seen at some cathedral door
    A laborer, pausing in the dust and heat,
    Lay down his burden, and with reverent feet
    Enter, and cross himself, and on the floor
Kneel to repeat his paternoster o'er;
    Far off the noises of the world retreat;
    The loud vociferations of the street
    Become an undistinguishable roar.
So, as I enter here from day to day,
    And leave my burden at this minster gate,
    Kneeling in prayer, and not ashamed to pray,
The tumult of the time disconsolate
    To inarticulate murmurs dies away,
    While the eternal ages watch and wait.

2

How strange the sculptures that adorn these towers!
    This crowd of statues, in whose folded sleeves
    Birds build their nests; while canopied with leaves
    Parvis and portal bloom like trellised bowers,
And the vast minster seems a cross of flowers!
    But fiends and dragons on the gargoyled eaves
    Watch the dead Christ between the living thieves,
    And, underneath, the traitor Judas lowers!
Ah! from what agonies of heart and brain,
    What exultations trampling on despair,
    What tenderness, what tears, what hate of wrong,
What passionate outcry of a soul in pain,
    Uprose this poem of the earth and air,
    This mediæval miracle of song!

3

I enter, and I see thee in the gloom
    Of the long aisles, O poet saturnine!
    And strive to make my steps keep pace with thine.
    The air is filled with some unknown perfume;
The congregation of the dead make room
    For thee to pass; the votive tapers shine;
    Like rooks that haunt Ravenna's groves of pine
    The hovering echoes fly from tomb to tomb;
From the confessionals I hear arise
    Rehearsals of forgotten tragedies,
    And lamentations from the crypts below;
And then a voice celestial that begins
    With the pathetic words, "Although your sins
    As scarlet be," and ends with "as the snow."

4

With snow-white veil and garments as of flame,
    She stands before thee, who so long ago
    Filled thy young heart with passion and the woe
    From which thy song and all its splendors came;
And while with stern rebuke she speaks thy name,
    The ice about thy heart melts as the snow
    On mountain heights, and in swift overflow
    Comes gushing from thy lips in sobs of shame.
Thou makest full confession; and a gleam,
    As of the dawn on some dark forest cast,
    Seems on thy lifted forehead to increase;
Lethe and Eunoe—the remembered dream
    And the forgotten sorrow—bring at last
    That perfect pardon which is perfect peace.

5

I lift mine eyes, and all the windows blaze
    With forms of Saints and holy men who died,
    Here martyred and hereafter glorified;
    And the great Rose upon its leaves displays
Christ's Triumph, and the angelic roundelays,
    With splendor upon splendor multiplied;
    And Beatrice again at Dante's side
    No more rebukes, but smiles her words of praise.
And then the organ sounds, and unseen choirs
    Sing the old Latin hymns of peace and love
    And benedictions of the Holy Ghost;
And the melodious bells among the spires
    O'er all the house-tops and through heaven above
    Proclaim the elevation of the Host!

6

O star of morning and of liberty!
    O bringer of the light, whose splendor shines
    Above the darkness of the Apennines,
    Forerunner of the day that is to be!
The voices of the city and the sea,
    The voices of the mountains and the pines,
    Repeat thy song, till the familiar lines
    Are footpaths for the thought of Italy!
Thy flame is blown abroad from all the heights,
    Through all the nations, and a sound is heard,
    As of a mighty wind, and men devout,
Strangers of Rome, and the new proselytes,
    In their own language hear thy wondrous word,
    And many are amazed and many doubt.

Snow-flakes

Out of the bosom of the Air,
    Out of the cloud-folds of her garments shaken,
Over the woodlands brown and bare,
    Over the harvest-fields forsaken,
        Silent, and soft, and slow
        Descends the snow.

Even as our cloudy fancies take
    Suddenly shape in some divine expression,
Even as the troubled heart doth make
    In the white countenance confession,
        The troubled sky reveals
        The grief it feels.

This is the poem of the air,
    Slowly in silent syllables recorded;
This is the secret of despair,
    Long in its cloudy bosom hoarded,
        Now whispered and revealed
        To wood and field.

The Children's Hour

Between the dark and the daylight,
    When the night is beginning to lower,
Comes a pause in the day's occupations,
    That is known as the Children's Hour.

I hear in the chamber above me
    The patter of little feet,
The sound of a door that is opened,
    And voices soft and sweet.

From my study I see in the lamplight,
    Descending the broad hall stair,
Grave Alice, and laughing Allegra,
    And Edith with golden hair.

A whisper, and then a silence:
    Yet I know by their merry eyes
They are plotting and planning together
    To take me by surprise.

A sudden rush from the stairway,
    A sudden raid from the hall!
By three doors left unguarded
    They enter my castle wall!

They climb up into my turret
    O'er the arms and back of my chair;
If I try to escape, they surround me;
    They seem to be everywhere.

They almost devour me with kisses,
    Their arms about me entwine,
Till I think of the Bishop of Bingen
    In his Mouse-Tower of the Rhine!

Do you think, O blue-eyed banditti,
    Because you have scaled the wall,
Such an old mustache as I am
    Is not a match for you all!

I have you fast in my fortress,
    And will not let you depart,
But put you down into the dungeon
    In the round-tower of my heart.

And there will I keep you forever,
    Yes, forever and a day,
Till the walls shall crumble to ruin,
    And moulder in dust away!

Sandalphon

Have you read in the Talmud of old,
In the Legends the Rabbins have told
    Of the limitless realms of the air,
Have you read it,—the marvellous story
Of Sandalphon, the Angel of Glory,
    Sandalphon, the Angel of Prayer?

How, erect, at the outermost gates
Of the City Celestial he waits,
    With his feet on the ladder of light,
That, crowded with angels unnumbered,
By Jacob was seen, as he slumbered
    Alone in the desert at night?

The Angels of Wind and of Fire
Chant only one hymn, and expire
    With the song's irresistible stress;
Expire in their rapture and wonder,
As harp-strings are broken asunder
    By music they throb to express.

But serene in the rapturous throng,
Unmoved by the rush of the song,
　　With eyes unimpassioned and slow,
Among the dead angels, the deathless
Sandalphon stands listening breathless
　　To sounds that ascend from below;—

From the spirits on earth that adore,
From the souls that entreat and implore
　　In the fervor and passion of prayer;
From the hearts that are broken with losses,
And weary with dragging the crosses
　　Too heavy for mortals to bear.

And he gathers the prayers as he stands,
And they change into flowers in his hands,
　　Into garlands of purple and red;
And beneath the great arch of the portal,
Through the streets of the City Immortal
　　Is wafted the fragrance they shed.

　　It is but a legend, I know,—
A fable, a phantom, a show,
　　Of the ancient Rabbinical lore;
Yet the old mediæval tradition,
The beautiful, strange superstition,
　　But haunts me and holds me the more.

When I look from my window at night,
And the welkin above is all white,
　　All throbbing and panting with stars,
Among them majestic is standing
Sandalphon the angel, expanding
　　His pinions in nebulous bars.

And the legend, I feel, is a part
Of the hunger and thirst of the heart,
　　The frenzy and fire of the brain,
That grasps at the fruitage forbidden,
The golden pomegranates of Eden,
　　To quiet its fever and pain.

My Lost Youth

Often I think of the beautiful town
    That is seated by the sea;
Often in thought go up and down
The pleasant streets of that dear old town,
    And my youth comes back to me.
        And a verse of a Lapland song
        Is haunting my memory still:
        "A boy's will is the wind's will,
And the thoughts of youth are long, long thoughts."

I can see the shadowy lines of its trees,
    And catch, in sudden gleams,
The sheen of the far-surrounding seas,
And islands that were the Hesperides
    Of all my boyish dreams.
        And the burden of that old song,
        It murmurs and whispers still:
        "A boy's will is the wind's will,
And the thoughts of youth are long, long thoughts."

I remember the black wharves and the slips,
    And the sea-tides tossing free;
And Spanish sailors with bearded lips,
And the beauty and mystery of the ships,
    And the magic of the sea.
        And the voice of that wayward song
        Is singing and saying still:
        "A boy's will is the wind's will,
And the thoughts of youth are long, long thoughts."

I remember the bulwarks by the shore,
    And the fort upon the hill;
The sunrise gun, with its hollow roar,
The drum-beat repeated o'er and o'er,
    And the bugle wild and shrill.
        And the music of that old song
        Throbs in my memory still:
        "A boy's will is the wind's will,
And the thoughts of youth are long, long thoughts."

I remember the sea-fight far away,
    How it thundered o'er the tide!
And the dead captains, as they lay
In their graves, o'erlooking the tranquil bay
    Where they in battle died.

And the sound of that mournful song
　　Goes through me with a thrill:
"A boy's will is the wind's will,
And the thoughts of youth are long, long thoughts."

I can see the breezy dome of groves,
　　The shadows of Deering's Woods;
And the friendships old and the early loves
Come back with a Sabbath sound, as of doves
　　In quiet neighborhoods.
　　　　And the verse of that sweet old song,
　　　　It flutters and murmurs still:
　　"A boy's will is the wind's will,
And the thoughts of youth are long, long thoughts."

I remember the gleams and glooms that dart
　　Across the school-boy's brain;
The song and the silence in the heart,
That in part are prophecies, and in part
　　Are longings wild and vain
　　　　And the voice of that fitful song
　　　　Sings on, and is never still:
　　"A boy's will is the wind's will,
And the thoughts of youth are long, long thoughts."

There are things of which I may not speak;
　　There are dreams that cannot die;
There are thoughts that make the strong heart weak,
And bring a pallor into the cheek,
　　And a mist before the eye.
　　　　And the words of that fatal song
　　　　Come over me like a chill:
　　"A boy's will is the wind's will,
And the thoughts of youth are long, long thoughts."

Strange to me now are the forms I meet
　　When I visit the dear old town;
But the native air is pure and sweet,
And the trees that o'ershadow each well-known street,
　　As they balance up and down,
　　　　Are singing the beautiful song,
　　　　Are sighing and whispering still:
　　"A boy's will is the wind's will,
And the thoughts of youth are long, long thoughts."

And Deering's Woods are fresh and fair,
    And with joy that is almost pain
My heart goes back to wander there,
And among the dreams of the days that were,
    I find my lost youth again.
        And the strange and beautiful song,
        The groves are repeating it still:
        "A boy's will is the wind's will,
And the thoughts of youth are long, long thoughts."

Haunted Houses

All houses wherein men have lived and died
    Are haunted houses. Through the open doors
The harmless phantoms on their errands glide,
    With feet that make no sound upon the floors.

We meet them at the doorway, on the stair,
    Along the passages they come and go,
Impalpable impressions on the air,
    A sense of something moving to and fro.

There are more guests at table than the hosts
    Invited; the illuminated hall
Is thronged with quiet, inoffensive ghosts,
    As silent as the pictures on the wall.

The stranger at my fireside cannot see
    The forms I see, nor hear the sounds I hear;
He but perceives what is; while unto me
    All that has been is visible and clear.

We have no title-deeds to house or lands;
    Owners and occupants of earlier dates
From graves forgotten stretch their dusty hands,
    And hold in mortmain still their old estates.

The spirit-world around this world of sense
    Floats like an atmosphere, and everywhere
Wafts through these earthly mists and vapors dense
    A vital breath of more ethereal air.

Our little lives are kept in equipoise
    By opposite attractions and desires;
The struggle of the instinct that enjoys,
    And the more noble instinct that aspires.

These perturbations, this perpetual jar
    Of earthly wants and aspirations high,
Come from the influence of an unseen star,
    An undiscovered planet in our sky.

And as the moon from some dark gate of cloud
    Throws o'er the sea a floating bridge of light,
Across whose trembling planks our fancies crowd
    Into the realm of mystery and night,—

So from the world of spirits there descends
    A bridge of light, connecting it with this,
O'er whose unsteady floor, that sways and bends,
    Wander our thoughts above the dark abyss.

from EVANGELINE

This is the forest primeval. The murmuring pines and the hemlocks,
Bearded with moss, and in garments green, indistinct in the twilight,
Stand like Druids of eld, with voices sad and prophetic,
Stand like harpers hoar, with beards that rest on their bosoms.
Loud from its rocky caverns, the deep-voiced neighboring ocean
Speaks, and in accents disconsolate answers the wail of the forest.

This is the forest primeval; but where are the hearts that beneath it
Leaped like the roe, when he hears in the woodland the voice of the
    huntsman?
Where is the thatch-roofed village, the home of Acadian farmers,—
Men whose lives glided on like rivers that water the woodlands,
Darkened by shadows of earth, but reflecting an image of heaven?
Waste are those pleasant farms, and the farmers forever departed!
Scattered like dust and leaves, when the mighty blasts of October
Seize them, and whirl them aloft, and sprinkle them o'er the ocean.
Naught but tradition remains of the beautiful village of Grand-Pré.

Ye who believe in affection that hopes, and endures, and is patient,
Ye who believe in the beauty and strength of woman's devotion,
List to the moral tradition, still sung by the pines of the forest;
List to a Tale of Love in Acadie, home of the happy.

. . . .

from THE SONG OF HIAWATHA

Hiawatha's Fasting

. . . .

On the fourth day of his fasting
In his lodge he lay exhausted;
From his couch of leaves and branches
Gazing with half-open eyelids,
Full of shadowy dreams and visions,
On the dizzy, swimming landscape,
On the gleaming of the water,
On the splendor of the sunset.
    And he saw a youth approaching,
Dressed in garments green and yellow,
Coming through the purple twilight,
Through the splendor of the sunset;
Plumes of green bent o'er his forehead,
And his hair was soft and golden.
    Standing at the open doorway,
Long he looked at Hiawatha,
Looked with pity and compassion
On his wasted form and features,
And, in accents like the sighing
Of the South-Wind in the tree-tops,
Said he, "O my Hiawatha!
All your prayers are heard in heaven,
For you pray not like the others;
Not for greater skill in hunting,
Not for greater craft in fishing,
Not for triumph in the battle,
Nor renown among the warriors,
But for profit of the people,
For advantage of the nations.
    "From the Master of Life descending,
I, the friend of man, Mondamin,
Come to warn you and instruct you,
How by struggle and by labor
You shall gain what you have prayed for.
Rise up from your bed of branches,
Rise, O youth, and wrestle with me!"
    Faint with famine, Hiawatha
Started from his bed of branches,
From the twilight of his wigwam
Forth into the flush of sunset

Came, and wrestled with Mondamin;
At his touch he felt new courage
Throbbing in his brain and bosom,
Felt new life and hope and vigor
Run through every nerve and fibre.

. . . .

Thrice they wrestled there together
In the glory of the sunset,
Till the darkness fell around them,
Till the heron, the Shuh-shuh-gah,
From her nest among the pine-trees,
Uttered her loud cry of famine,
And Mondamin paused to listen.
Tall and beautiful he stood there,
In his garments green and yellow;
To and fro his plumes above him
Waved and nodded with his breathing,
And the sweat of the encounter
Stood like drops of dew upon him.
And he cried, "O Hiawatha!
Bravely have you wrestled with me,
Thrice have wrestled stoutly with me,
And the Master of Life, who sees us,
He will give to you the triumph!"
Then he smiled, and said: "To-morrow
Is the last day of your conflict,
Is the last day of your fasting.
You will conquer and o'ercome me;
Make a bed for me to lie in,
Where the rain may fall upon me,
Where the sun may come and warm me;
Strip these garments, green and yellow,
Strip this nodding plumage from me,
Lay me in the earth, and make it
Soft and loose and light above me.
"Let no hand disturb my slumber,
Let no weed nor worm molest me,
Let not Kahgahgee, the raven,
Come to haunt me and molest me,
Only come yourself to watch me,
Till I wake, and start, and quicken,
Till I leap into the sunshine."

. . . .

On the morrow came Nokomis,
On the seventh day of his fasting,
Came with food for Hiawatha,
Came imploring and bewailing,
Lest his hunger should o'ercome him,
Lest his fasting should be fatal.

But he tasted not, and touched not,
Only said to her, "Nokomis,
Wait until the sun is setting,
Till the darkness falls around us,
Till the heron, the Shuh-shuh-gah,
Crying from the desolate marshes,
Tells us that the day is ended."

Homeward weeping went Nokomis,
Sorrowing for her Hiawatha,
Fearing lest his strength should fail him,
Lest his fasting should be fatal.
He meanwhile sat weary waiting
For the coming of Mondamin,
Till the shadows, pointing eastward,
Lengthened over field and forest,
Till the sun dropped from the heaven,
Floating on the waters westward,
As a red leaf in the Autumn
Falls and floats upon the water,
Falls and sinks into its bosom.

And behold! the young Mondamin,
With his soft and shining tresses,
With his garments green and yellow,
With his long and glossy plumage,
Stood and beckoned at the doorway;
And as one in slumber walking,
Pale and haggard, but undaunted,
From the wigwam Hiawatha
Came and wrestled with Mondamin.

Round about him spun the landscape,
Sky and forest reeled together,
And his strong heart leaped within him,
As the sturgeon leaps and struggles
In a net to break its meshes.
Like a ring of fire around him
Blazed and flared the red horizon,
And a hundred suns seemed looking
At the combat of the wrestlers.

Suddenly upon the greensward
All alone stood Hiawatha,
Panting with his wild exertion,

Palpitating with the struggle;
And before him breathless, lifeless,
Lay the youth, with hair dishevelled,
Plumage torn, and garments tattered,
Dead he lay there in the sunset.

And victorious Hiawatha
Made the grave as he commanded,
Stripped the garments from Mondamin,
Stripped his tattered plumage from him,
Laid him in the earth, and made it
Soft and loose and light above him;
And the heron, the Shuh-shuh-gah,
From the melancholy moorlands,
Gave a cry of lamentation,
Gave a cry of pain and anguish!

Homeward then went Hiawatha
To the lodge of old Nokomis,
And the seven days of his fasting
Were accomplished and completed.
But the place was not forgotten
Where he wrestled with Mondamin;
Nor forgotten nor neglected
Was the grave where lay Mondamin,
Sleeping in the rain and sunshine,
Where his scattered plumes and garments
Faded in the rain and sunshine.

Day by day did Hiawatha
Go to wait and watch beside it;
Kept the dark mould soft above it,
Kept it clean from weeds and insects,
Drove away, with scoffs and shoutings,
Kahgahgee, the king of ravens.

Till at length a small green feather
From the earth shot slowly upward,
Then another and another,
And before the Summer ended
Stood the maize in all its beauty,
With its shining robes about it,
And its long, soft, yellow tresses;
And in rapture Hiawatha
Cried aloud, "It is Mondamin!
Yes, the friend of man, Mondamin!"

Then he called to old Nokomis
And Iagoo, the great boaster,
Showed them where the maize was growing,
Told them of his wondrous vision,
Of his wrestling and his triumph,

Of this new gift to the nations,
Which should be their food forever.
    And still later, when the Autumn
Changed the long, green leaves to yellow,
And the soft and juicy kernels
Grew like wampum hard and yellow,
Then the ripened ears he gathered,
Stripped the withered husks from off them,
As he once had stripped the wrestler,
Gave the first Feast of Mondamin,
And made known unto the people
This new gift of the Great Spirit.

The Jewish Cemetery at Newport

How strange it seems! These Hebrews in their graves,
    Close by the street of this fair seaport town,
Silent beside the never-silent waves,
    At rest in all this moving up and down!

The trees are white with dust, that o'er their sleep
    Wave their broad curtains in the south wind's breath,
While underneath these leafy tents they keep
    The long, mysterious Exodus of Death.

And these sepulchral stones, so old and brown,
    That pave with level flags their burial-place,
Seem like the tablets of the Law, thrown down
And broken by Moses at the mountain's base.

The very names recorded here are strange,
    Of foreign accent, and of different climes;
Alvares and Rivera interchange
    With Abraham and Jacob of old times.

"Blessed be God! for he created Death!"
    The mourners said, "and Death is rest and peace;"
Then added, in the certainty of faith,
    "And giveth Life that nevermore shall cease."

Closed are the portals of their Synagogue,
    No Psalms of David now the silence break,
No Rabbi reads the ancient Decalogue
    In the grand dialect the Prophets spake.

Gone are the living, but the dead remain,
    And not neglected; for a hand unseen,
Scattering its bounty, like a summer rain,
    Still keeps their graves and their remembrance green.

How came they here? What burst of Christian hate,
What persecution, merciless and blind,
    Drove o'er the sea—that desert desolate—
These Ishmaels and Hagars of mankind?

They lived in narrow streets and lanes obscure,
    Ghetto and Judenstrass, in mirk and mire;
Taught in the school of patience to endure
    The life of anguish and the death of fire.

All their lives long, with the unleavened bread
    And bitter herbs of exile and its fears,
The wasting famine of the heart they fed,
    And slaked its thirst with marah of their tears.

Anathema maranatha! was the cry
    That rang from town to town, from street to street;
At every gate the accursed Mordecai
    Was mocked and jeered, and spurned by Christian feet.

Pride and humiliation hand in hand
    Walked with them through the world where'er they went;
Trampled and beaten were they as the sand,
    And yet unshaken as the continent.

For in the background figures vague and vast
    Of patriarchs and of prophets rose sublime,
And all the great traditions of the Past
    They saw reflected in the coming time.

And thus forever with reverted look
    The mystic volume of the world they read,
Spelling it backward, like a Hebrew book,
    Till life became a Legend of the Dead.

But ah! what once has been shall be no more!
    The groaning earth in travail and in pain
Brings forth its races, but does not restore,
    And the dead nations never rise again.

from Monologue: The Last Judgment
from Part Third, IV

. . . .

In happy hours, when the imagination
Wakes like a wind at midnight, and the soul
Trembles in all its leaves, it is a joy
To be uplifted on its wings, and listen
To the prophetic voices in the air
That call us onward. Then the work we do
Is a delight, and the obedient hand
Never grows weary. But how different is it
In the disconsolate, discouraged hours,
When all the wisdom of the world appears
As trivial as the gossip of a nurse
In a sick-room, and all our work seems useless.

. . . .

from In the Coliseum

All things must have an end; the world itself
Must have an end, as in a dream I saw it.
There came a great hand out of heaven, and touched
The earth, and stopped it in its course. The seas
Leaped, a vast cataract, into the abyss;
The forests and fields slid off, and floated
Like wooded islands in the air. The dead
Were hurled forth from their sepulchres; the living
Were mingled with them, and themselves were dead,—
All being dead; and the fair, shining cities
Dropped out like jewels from a broken crown.
Naught but the core of the great globe remained,
A skeleton of stone. And over it
The wrack of matter drifted like a cloud,
And then recoiled upon itself, and fell
Back on the empty world, that with the weight
Reeled, staggered, righted, and then headlong plunged
Into the darkness, as a ship, when struck
By a great sea, throws off the waves at first

On either side, then settles and goes down
Into the dark abyss, with her dead crew.

———————

The Grave

For thee was a house built
Ere thou wast born,
For thee was a mould meant
Ere thou of mother camest.
But it is not made ready,
Nor its depth measured,
Nor is it seen
How long it shall be.
Now I bring thee
Where thou shalt be;
Now I shall measure thee,
And the mould afterwards.

    Thy house is not
Highly timbered,
It is unhigh and low;
When thou art therein,
The heel-ways are low,
The side-ways unhigh.
The roof is built
Thy breast full nigh,
So thou shalt in mould
Dwell full cold,
Dimly and dark.

    Doorless is that house,
And dark it is within;
There thou art fast detained
And Death hath the key.
Loathsome is that earth-house,
And grim within to dwell.
There thou shalt dwell,
And worms shall divide thee.

Thus thou art laid,
And leavest thy friends;
Thou hast no friend,
Who will come to thee,
Who will ever see
How that house pleaseth thee;
Who will ever open
The door for thee,
And descend after thee;
For soon thou art loathsome
And hateful to see.

————

from TALES OF A WAYSIDE INN

The Landlord's Tale: Paul Revere's Ride

Listen, my children, and you shall hear
Of the midnight ride of Paul Revere,
On the eighteenth of April, in Seventy-five;
Hardly a man is now alive
Who remembers that famous day and year.

He said to his friend, "If the British march
By land or sea from the town to-night,
Hang a lantern aloft in the belfry arch
Of the North Church tower as a signal light,—
One, if by land, and two, if by sea;
And I on the opposite shore will be,
Ready to ride and spread the alarm
Through every Middlesex village and farm,
For the country folk to be up and to arm."

Then he said, "Good-night!" and with muffled oar
Silently rowed to the Charlestown shore,
Just as the moon rose over the bay,
Where swinging wide at her moorings lay
The Somerset, British man-of-war;
A phantom ship, with each mast and spar
Across the moon like a prison bar,
And a huge black hulk, that was magnified
By its own reflection in the tide.

Meanwhile, his friend, through alley and street,
Wanders and watches with eager ears,
Till in the silence around him he hears
The muster of men at the barrack door,
The sound of arms, and the tramp of feet,
And the measured tread of the grenadiers,
Marching down to their boats on the shore.

Then he climbed the tower of the Old North Church,
By the wooden stairs, with stealthy tread,
To the belfry-chamber overhead,
And startled the pigeons from their perch
On the sombre rafters, that round him made
Masses and moving shapes of shade,—
By the trembling ladder, steep and tall,
To the highest window in the wall,
Where he paused to listen and look down
A moment on the roofs of the town,
And the moonlight flowing over all.

Beneath, in the churchyard, lay the dead,
In their night-encampment on the hill,
Wrapped in silence so deep and still
That he could hear, like a sentinel's tread,
The watchful night-wind, as it went
Creeping along from tent to tent,
And seeming to whisper, "All is well!"
A moment only he feels the spell
Of the place and the hour, and the secret dread
Of the lonely belfry and the dead;
For suddenly all his thoughts are bent
On a shadowy something far away,
Where the river widens to meet the bay,—
A line of black that bends and floats
On the rising tide, like a bridge of boats.

Meanwhile, impatient to mount and ride,
Booted and spurred, with a heavy stride
On the opposite shore walked Paul Revere.
Now he patted his horse's side,
Now gazed at the landscape far and near,
Then, impetuous, stamped the earth,
And turned and tightened his saddle-girth;
But mostly he watched with eager search
The belfry-tower of the Old North Church,
As it rose above the graves on the hill,
Lonely and spectral and sombre and still.

And lo! as he looks, on the belfry's height
A glimmer, and then a gleam of light!
He springs to the saddle, the bridle he turns,
But lingers and gazes, till full on his sight
A second lamp in the belfry burns!

A hurry of hoofs in a village street,
A shape in the moonlight, a bulk in the dark,
And beneath, from the pebbles, in passing, a spark
Struck out by a steed flying fearless and fleet:
That was all! And yet, through the gloom and the light,
The fate of a nation was riding that night;
And the spark struck out by that steed, in his flight,
Kindled the land into flame with its heat.

He has left the village and mounted the steep,
And beneath him, tranquil and broad and deep,
Is the Mystic, meeting the ocean tides;
And under the alders that skirt its edge,
Now soft on the sand, now loud on the ledge,
Is heard the tramp of his steed as he rides.

It was twelve by the village clock,
When he crossed the bridge into Medford town.
He heard the crowing of the cock,
And the barking of the farmer's dog,
And felt the damp of the river fog,
That rises after the sun goes down.

It was one by the village clock,
When he galloped into Lexington.
He saw the gilded weathercock
Swim in the moonlight as he passed,
And the meeting-house windows, blank and bare,
Gaze at him with a spectral glare,
As if they already stood aghast
At the bloody work they would look upon.

It was two by the village clock,
When he came to the bridge in Concord town.
He heard the bleating of the flock,
And the twitter of birds among the trees,
And felt the breath of the morning breeze
Blowing over the meadows brown.
And one was safe and asleep in his bed
Who at the bridge would be first to fall,

Who that day would be lying dead,
Pierced by a British musket-ball.

You know the rest. In the books you have read,
How the British Regulars fired and fled,—
How the farmers gave them ball for ball,
From behind each fence and farm-yard wall,
Chasing the red-coats down the lane,
Then crossing the fields to emerge again
Under the trees at the turn of the road,
And only pausing to fire and load.

So through the night rode Paul Revere;
And so through the night went his cry of alarm
To every Middlesex village and farm,—
A cry of defiance and not of fear,
A voice in the darkness, a knock at the door,
And a word that shall echo forevermore!
For, borne on the night-wind of the Past,
Through all our history, to the last,
In the hour of darkness and peril and need,
The people will waken and listen to hear
The hurrying hoof-beats of that steed,
And the midnight message of Paul Revere.

The Spanish Jew's Tale:
The Legend of Rabbi Ben Levi

Rabbi Ben Levi, on the Sabbath, read
A volume of the Law, in which it said,
"No man shall look upon my face and live."
And as he read, he prayed that God would give
His faithful servant grace with mortal eye
To look upon His face and yet not die.

Then fell a sudden shadow on the page,
And, lifting up his eyes, grown dim with age,
He saw the Angel of Death before him stand,
Holding a naked sword in his right hand.
Rabbi Ben Levi was a righteous man,
Yet through his veins a chill of terror ran.
With trembling voice he said, "What wilt thou here?"
The Angel answered, "Lo! the time draws near
When thou must die; yet first, by God's decree,
Whate'er thou askest shall be granted thee."

Replied the Rabbi, "Let these living eyes
First look upon my place in Paradise."

Then said the Angel, "Come with me and look."
Rabbi Ben Levi closed the sacred book,
And rising, and uplifting his gray head,
"Give me thy sword," he to the Angel said,
"Lest thou shouldst fall upon me by the way."
The Angel smiled and hastened to obey,
Then led him forth to the Celestial Town,
And set him on the wall, whence, gazing down,
Rabbi Ben Levi, with his living eyes,
Might look upon his place in Paradise.

Then straight into the city of the Lord
The Rabbi leaped with the Death-Angel's sword,
And through the streets there swept a sudden breath
Of something there unknown, which men call death.
Meanwhile the Angel stayed without, and cried,
"Come back!" To which the Rabbi's voice replied,
"No! in the name of God, whom I adore,
I swear that hence I will depart no more!"

Then all the Angels cried, "O Holy One,
See what the son of Levi here hath done!
The kingdom of Heaven he takes by violence,
And in Thy name refuses to go hence!"
The Lord replied, "My Angels, be not wroth;
Did e'er the son of Levi break his oath?
Let him remain; for he with mortal eye
Shall look upon my face and yet not die."

Beyond the outer wall the Angel of Death
Heard the great voice, and said, with panting breath,
"Give back the sword, and let me go my way."
Whereat the Rabbi paused, and answered, "Nay!
Anguish enough already hath it caused
Among the sons of men." And while he paused
He heard the awful mandate of the Lord
Resounding through the air, "Give back the sword!"

The Rabbi bowed his head in silent prayer,
Then said he to the dreadful Angel, "Swear
No human eye shall look on it again;
But when thou takest away the souls of men,
Thyself unseen, and with an unseen sword,
Thou wilt perform the bidding of the Lord."

The Angel took the sword again, and swore,
And walks on earth unseen forevermore.

The Spanish Jew's Tale: Azrael

King Solomon, before his palace gate
At evening, on the pavement tessellate
Was walking with a stranger from the East,
Arrayed in rich attire as for a feast,
The mighty Runjeet-Sing, a learned man,
And Rajah of the realms of Hindostan.
And as they walked the guest became aware
Of a white figure in the twilight air,
Gazing intent, as one who with surprise
His form and features seemed to recognize;
And in a whisper to the king he said:
"What is yon shape, that, pallid as the dead,
Is watching me, as if he sought to trace
In the dim light the features of my face?"

The king looked, and replied: "I know him well;
It is the Angel men call Azrael,
'T is the Death Angel; what hast thou to fear?"
And the guest answered: "Lest he should come near,
And speak to me, and take away my breath!
Save me from Azrael, save me from death!
O king, that hast dominion o'er the wind,
Bid it arise and bear me hence to Ind."

The king gazed upward at the cloudless sky,
Whispered a word, and raised his hand on high,
And lo! the signet-ring of chrysoprase
On his uplifted finger seemed to blaze
With hidden fire, and rushing from the west
There came a mighty wind, and seized the guest
And lifted him from earth, and on they passed,
His shining garments streaming in the blast,
A silken banner o'er the walls upreared,
A purple cloud, that gleamed and disappeared.
Then said the Angel, smiling: "If this man
Be Rajah Runjeet-Sing of Hindostan,
Thou hast done well in listening to his prayer;
I was upon my way to seek him there."

Delia

Sweet as the tender fragrance that survives,
When martyred flowers breathe out their little lives,
Sweet as a song that once consoled our pain,
But never will be sung to us again,
Is thy remembrance. Now the hour of rest
Hath come to thee. Sleep, darling; it is best.

Dedication

Nothing that is shall perish utterly,
     But perish only to revive again
     In other forms, as clouds restore in rain
     The exhalations of the land and sea.
Men build their houses from the masonry
     Of ruined tombs; the passion and the pain
     Of hearts, that long have ceased to beat, remain
     To throb in hearts that are, or are to be.
So from old chronicles, where sleep in dust
     Names that once filled the world with trumpet tones,
     I build this verse; and flowers of song have thrust
Their roots among the loose disjointed stones,
     Which to this end I fashion as I must.
     Quickened are they that touch the Prophet's bones.

LUCRETIA DAVIDSON
(1808–1825)

The Fear of Madness

There is something which I dread,
     It is a dark, a fearful thing;
It steals along with withering tread,
     Or sweeps on wild destruction's wing.

That thought comes o'er me in the hour
     Of grief, of sickness, or of sadness;
'Tis not the dread of death—'tis more,
     It is the dread of madness.

O! may these throbbing pulses pause,
    Forgetful of their feverish course;
May this hot brain, which, burning, glows
    With all its fiery whirlpool's force,

Be cold, and motionless, and still,
    A tenant of its lowly bed,
But let not dark delirium steal—
[*Unfinished*]

EDGAR ALLAN POE
(1809–1849)

Sonnet—to Science

Science! true daughter of Old Time thou art!
    Who alterest all things with thy peering eyes.
Why preyest thou thus upon the poet's heart,
    Vulture, whose wings are dull realities?
How should he love thee? or how deem thee wise,
    Who wouldst not leave him in his wandering
To seek for treasure in the jewelled skies,
    Albeit he soared with an undaunted wing?
Hast thou not dragged Diana from her car?
    And driven the Hamadryad from the wood
To seek a shelter in some happier star?
    Hast thou not torn the Naiad from her flood,
The Elfin from the green grass, and from me
The summer dream beneath the tamarind tree?

To Helen

Helen, thy beauty is to me
    Like those Nicéan barks of yore,
That gently, o'er a perfumed sea,
    The weary, way-worn wanderer bore
    To his own native shore.

On desperate seas long wont to roam,
    Thy hyacinth hair, thy classic face,
Thy Naiad airs have brought me home
    To the glory that was Greece,
And the grandeur that was Rome.

Lo! in yon brilliant window-niche
      How statue-like I see thee stand,
      The agate lamp within thy hand!
Ah, Psyche, from the regions which
      Are Holy-Land!

Israfel

In Heaven a spirit doth dwell
      "Whose heart-strings are a lute;"
None sing so wildly well
As the angel Israfel,
And the giddy stars (so legends tell)
Ceasing their hymns, attend the spell
      Of his voice, all mute.

Tottering above
      In her highest noon,
      The enamoured moon
Blushes with love,
      While, to listen, the red levin
      (With the rapid Pleiads, even,
      Which were seven,)
      Pauses in Heaven.

And they say (the starry choir
      And the other listening things)
That Israfeli's fire
Is owing to that lyre
      By which he sits and sings—
The trembling living wire
Of those unusual strings.

But the skies that angel trod,
      Where deep thoughts are a duty—
Where Love's a grown-up God—
      Where the Houri glances are
Imbued with all the beauty
      Which we worship in a star.

Therefore, thou art not wrong,
      Israfeli, who despisest
An unimpassioned song;
To thee the laurels belong,
      Best bard, because the wisest!
Merrily live, and long!

The ecstasies above
    With thy burning measures suit—
Thy grief, thy joy, thy hate, thy love,
    With the fervour of thy lute—
    Well may the stars be mute!

Yes, Heaven is thine; but this
    Is a world of sweets and sours;
    Our flowers are merely—flowers,
And the shadow of thy perfect bliss
    Is the sunshine of ours.

If I could dwell
Where Israfel
    Hath dwelt, and he where I,
He might not sing so wildly well
    A mortal melody,
While a bolder note than this might swell
    From my lyre within the sky.

The City in the Sea

Lo! Death has reared himself a throne
In a strange city lying alone
Far down within the dim West,
Where the good and the bad and the worst and the best
Have gone to their eternal rest.
There shrines and palaces and towers
(Time-eaten towers that tremble not!)
Resemble nothing that is ours.
Around, by lifting winds forgot,
Resignedly beneath the sky
The melancholy waters lie.

No rays from the holy heaven come down
On the long night-time of that town;
But light from out the lurid sea
Streams up the turrets silently—
Gleams up the pinnacles far and free
Up domes—up spires—up kingly halls—
Up fanes—up Babylon-like walls—
Up shadowy long-forgotten bowers
Of sculptured ivy and stone flowers—
Up many and many a marvellous shrine
Whose wreathéd friezes intertwine
The viol, the violet, and the vine.

Resignedly beneath the sky
The melancholy waters lie.
So blend the turrets and shadows there
That all seem pendulous in air,
While from a proud tower in the town
Death looks gigantically down.

There open fanes and gaping graves
Yawn level with the luminous waves;
But not the riches there that lie
In each idol's diamond eye—
Not the gaily-jewelled dead
Tempt the waters from their bed;
For no ripples curl, alas!
Along that wilderness of glass—
No swellings tell that winds may be
Upon some far-off happier sea—
No heavings hint that winds have been
On seas less hideously serene.

But lo, a stir is in the air!
The wave—there is a movement there!
As if the towers had thrust aside,
In slightly sinking, the dull tide—
As if their tops had feebly given
A void within the filmy Heaven.
The waves have now a redder glow—
The hours are breathing faint and low—
And when, amid no earthly moans,
Down, down that town shall settle hence,
Hell, rising from a thousand thrones,
Shall do it reverence.

The Haunted Palace

In the greenest of our valleys
    By good angels tenanted,
Once a fair and stately palace—
    Radiant palace—reared its head.
In the monarch Thought's dominion—
    It stood there!
Never seraph spread a pinion
    Over fabric half so fair!

Banners yellow, glorious, golden,
    On its roof did float and flow—
(This—all this—was in the olden
    Time long ago)
And every gentle air that dallied,
    In that sweet day,
Along the ramparts plumed and pallid,
    A wingéd odor went away.

Wanderers in that happy valley,
    Through two luminous windows, saw
Spirits moving musically,
    To a lute's well-tunéd law,
Round about a throne where, sitting,
    Porphyrogene,
In state his glory well befitting
    The ruler of the realm was seen.

And all with pearl and ruby glowing
    Was the fair palace door,
Through which came flowing, flowing, flowing,
    And sparkling evermore,
A troop of Echoes whose sweet duty
    Was but to sing,
In voices of surpassing beauty,
    The wit and wisdom of their king.

But evil things, in robes of sorrow,
    Assailed the monarch's high estate.
(Ah, let us mourn!—for never morrow
    Shall dawn upon him, desolate!)
And round about his home the glory
    That blushed and bloomed,
Is but a dim-remembered story
    Of the old-time entombed.

And travellers, now, within that valley,
    Through the encrimsoned windows see
Vast forms that move fantastically
    To a discordant melody,
While, like a ghastly rapid river,
    Through the pale door
A hideous throng rush out forever
    And laugh—but smile no more.

Sonnet, Silence

There are some qualities—some incorporate things,
    That have a double life, which thus is made
A type of that twin entity which springs
    From matter and light, evinced in solid and shade.
There is a two-fold *Silence*—sea and shore—
    Body and Soul. One dwells in lonely places,
    Newly with grass o'ergrown; some solemn graces,
Some human memories and tearful lore,
Render him terrorless: his name's "No more."
He is the corporate Silence: dread him not!
    No power hath he of evil in himself;
But should some urgent fate (untimely lot!)
    Bring thee to meet his shadow (nameless elf,
That haunteth the lone regions where hath trod
No foot of man,) commend thyself to God!

The Conqueror Worm

Lo! 'tis a gala night
    Within the lonesome latter years!
An angel throng, bewinged, bedight
    In veils, and drowned in tears,
Sit in a theatre, to see
    A play of hopes and fears,
While the orchestra breathes fitfully
    The music of the spheres.

Mimes, in the form of God on high,
    Mutter and mumble low,
And hither and thither fly—
    Mere puppets they, who come and go
At bidding of vast formless things
    That shift the scenery to and fro,
Flapping from out their Condor wings
    Invisible Wo!

That motley drama—oh, be sure
    It shall not be forgot!
With its Phantom chased for evermore,
    By a crowd that seize it not,
Through a circle that ever returneth in
    To the self-same spot,
And much of Madness, and more of Sin,
    And Horror the soul of the plot.

But see, amid the mimic rout
    A crawling shape intrude!
A blood-red thing that writhes from out
    The scenic solitude!
It writhes!—it writhes!—with mortal pangs
    The mimes become its food,
And seraphs sob at vermin fangs
    In human gore imbued.

Out—out are the lights—out all!
    And, over each quivering form,
The curtain, a funeral pall,
    Comes down with the rush of a storm,
While the angels, all pallid and wan,
    Uprising, unveiling, affirm
That the play is the tragedy, "Man,"
    And its hero the Conqueror Worm.

Lenore

Ah, broken is the golden bowl!
    The spirit flown forever!
Let the bell toll!—A saintly soul
    Glides down the Stygian river!
And let the burial rite be read—
    The funeral song be sung—
A dirge for the most lovely dead
    That ever died so young!
        And, Guy de Vere,
        Hast *thou* no tear?
           Weep now or nevermore!
      See, on yon drear
      And rigid bier,
        Low lies thy love Lenore!

"Yon heir, whose cheeks of pallid hue
    With tears are streaming wet,
Sees only, through
Their crocodile dew,
    A vacant coronet—
        False friends! ye loved her for her wealth
        And hated her for her pride,
        And, when she fell in feeble health,
        Ye blessed her—that she died.
          How *shall* the ritual, then, be read?
          The requiem *how* be sung

For her most wrong'd of all the dead
That ever died so young?"

Peccavimus!
But rave not thus!
   And let the solemn song
Go up to God so mournfully that *she* may feel no wrong!
      The sweet Lenore
      Hath "gone before"
         With young hope at her side,
            And thou art wild
            For the dear child
      That should have been thy bride—
         For her, the fair
         And debonair,
      That now so lowly lies—
      The life still there
      Upon her hair,
         The death upon her eyes.

"Avaunt!—to-night
My heart is light—
   No dirge will I upraise,
But waft the angel on her flight
   With a Pæan of old days!
      Let *no* bell toll!
      Lest her sweet soul,
         Amid its hallow'd mirth,
         Should catch the note
         As it doth float
      Up from the damned earth—
         To friends above, from fiends below,
            th' indignant ghost is riven—
         From grief and moan
         To a gold throne
      Beside the King of Heaven!"

The Raven

Once upon a midnight dreary, while I pondered, weak and weary,
Over many a quaint and curious volume of forgotten lore—
While I nodded, nearly napping, suddenly there came a tapping,
As of some one gently rapping, rapping at my chamber door—
" 'Tis some visitor," I muttered, "tapping at my chamber door—
      Only this and nothing more."

Ah, distinctly I remember it was in the bleak December;
And each separate dying ember wrought its ghost upon the floor.
Eagerly I wished the morrow;—vainly I had sought to borrow
From my books surcease of sorrow—sorrow for the lost Lenore—
For the rare and radiant maiden whom the angels name Lenore—
    Nameless *here* for evermore.

And the silken, sad, uncertain rustling of each purple curtain
Thrilled me—filled me with fantastic terrors never felt before;
So that now, to still the beating of my heart, I stood repeating
" 'Tis some visitor entreating entrance at my chamber door—
Some late visitor entreating entrance at my chamber door;—
    This it is and nothing more."

Presently my soul grew stronger; hesitating then no longer,
"Sir," said I, "or Madam, truly your forgiveness I implore;
But the fact is I was napping, and so gently you came rapping,
And so faintly you came tapping, tapping at my chamber door,
That I scarce was sure I heard you"—here I opened wide the door;—
    Darkness there and nothing more.

Deep into that darkness peering, long I stood there wondering,
                                        fearing,
Doubting, dreaming dreams no mortal ever dared to dream before;
But the silence was unbroken, and the stillness gave no token,
And the only word there spoken was the whispered word, "Lenore?"
This I whispered, and an echo murmured back the word, "Lenore!"
    Merely this and nothing more.

Back into the chamber turning, all my soul within me burning,
Soon again I heard a tapping somewhat louder than before.
"Surely," said I, "surely that is something at my window lattice;
Let me see, then, what thereat is, and this mystery explore—
Let my heart be still a moment and this mystery explore;—
    'Tis the wind and nothing more!"

Open here I flung the shutter, when, with many a flirt and flutter,
In there stepped a stately Raven of the saintly days of yore;
Not the least obeisance made he; not a minute stopped or stayed he;
But, with mien of lord or lady, perched above my chamber door—
Perched upon a bust of Pallas just above my chamber door—
    Perched, and sat, and nothing more.

Then this ebony bird beguiling my sad fancy into smiling,
By the grave and stern decorum of the countenance it wore,
"Though thy crest be shorn and shaven, thou," I said, "art sure no
craven,
Ghastly grim and ancient Raven wandering from the Nightly shore—
Tell me what thy lordly name is on the Night's Plutonian shore!"
Quoth the Raven "Nevermore."

Much I marvelled this ungainly fowl to hear discourse so plainly,
Though its answer little meaning—little relevancy bore;
For we cannot help agreeing that no living human being
Ever yet was blessed with seeing bird above his chamber door—
Bird or beast upon the sculptured bust above his chamber door,
With such name as "Nevermore."

But the Raven, sitting lonely on the placid bust, spoke only
That one word, as if his soul in that one word he did outpour.
Nothing farther then he uttered—not a feather then he fluttered—
Till I scarcely more than muttered "Other friends have flown before—
On the morrow *he* will leave me, as my Hopes have flown before."
Then the bird said "Nevermore."

Startled at the stillness broken by reply so aptly spoken,
"Doubtless," said I, "what it utters is its only stock and store
Caught from some unhappy master whom unmerciful Disaster
Followed fast and followed faster till his songs one burden bore—
Till the dirges of his Hope that melancholy burden bore
Of 'Never—nevermore.' "

But the Raven still beguiling my sad fancy into smiling,
Straight I wheeled a cushioned seat in front of bird, and bust and
door;
Then, upon the velvet sinking, I betook myself to linking
Fancy unto fancy, thinking what this ominous bird of yore—
What this grim, ungainly, ghastly, gaunt, and ominous bird of yore
Meant in croaking "Nevermore."

This I sat engaged in guessing, but no syllable expressing
To the fowl whose fiery eyes now burned into my bosom's core;
This and more I sat divining, with my head at ease reclining
On the cushion's velvet lining that the lamp-light gloated o'er,
But whose velvet-violet lining with the lamp-light gloating o'er,
She shall press, ah, nevermore!

Then, methought, the air grew denser, perfumed from an unseen
censer
Swung by seraphim whose foot-falls tinkled on the tufted floor.
"Wretch," I cried, "thy God hath lent thee—by these angels he hath
sent thee
Respite—respite and nepenthe from thy memories of Lenore;
Quaff, oh quaff this kind nepenthe and forget this lost Lenore!"
Quoth the Raven "Nevermore."

"Prophet!" said I, "thing of evil!—prophet still, if bird or devil!—
Whether Tempter sent, or whether tempest tossed thee here ashore,
Desolate yet all undaunted, on this desert land enchanted—
On this home by Horror haunted—tell me truly, I implore—
Is there—is there balm in Gilead?—tell me—tell me, I implore!"
Quoth the Raven "Nevermore."

"Prophet!" said I, "thing of evil!—prophet still, if bird or devil!
By that Heaven that bends above us—by that God we both adore—
Tell this soul with sorrow laden if, within the distant Aidenn,
It shall clasp a sainted maiden whom the angels name Lenore—
Clasp a rare and radiant maiden whom the angels name Lenore."
Quoth the Raven "Nevermore."

"Be that word our sign of parting, bird or fiend!" I shrieked,
upstarting—
"Get thee back into the tempest and the Night's Plutonian shore!
Leave no black plume as a token of that lie thy soul hath spoken!
Leave my loneliness unbroken!—quit the bust above my door!
Take thy beak from out my heart, and take thy form from
off my door!"
Quoth the Raven "Nevermore."

And the Raven, never flitting, still is sitting, *still* is sitting
On the pallid bust of Pallas just above my chamber door;
And his eyes have all the seeming of a demon's that is dreaming,
And the lamp-light o'er him streaming throws his shadow
on the floor;
And my soul from out that shadow that lies floating on the floor
Shall be lifted—nevermore!

Ulalume—A Ballad

The skies they were ashen and sober;
    The leaves they were crispéd and sere—
    The leaves they were withering and sere:
It was night, in the lonesome October
    Of my most immemorial year:
It was hard by the dim lake of Auber,
    In the misty mid region of Weir:—
It was down by the dank tarn of Auber,
    In the ghoul-haunted woodland of Weir.

Here once, through an alley Titanic,
    Of cypress, I roamed with my Soul—
    Of cypress, with Psyche, my Soul.
These were days when my heart was volcanic
    As the scoriac rivers that roll—
    As the lavas that restlessly roll
Their sulphurous currents down Yaanek,
    In the ultimate climes of the Pole—
That groan as they roll down Mount Yaanek,
    In the realms of the Boreal Pole.

Our talk had been serious and sober,
    But our thoughts they were palsied and sere—
    Our memories were treacherous and sere;
For we knew not the month was October,
    And we marked not the night of the year—
    (Ah, night of all nights in the year!)
We noted not the dim lake of Auber,
    (Though once we had journeyed down here)
We remembered not the dank tarn of Auber,
    Nor the ghoul-haunted woodland of Weir.

And now, as the night was senescent,
    And star-dials pointed to morn—
    As the star-dials hinted of morn—
At the end of our path a liquescent
    And nebulous lustre was born,
Out of which a miraculous crescent
    Arose with a duplicate horn—
Astarte's bediamonded crescent,
    Distinct with its duplicate horn.

And I said—"She is warmer than Dian;
    She rolls through an ether of sighs—
    She revels in a region of sighs.
She has seen that the tears are not dry on
    These cheeks where the worm never dies,
And has come past the stars of the Lion,
    To point us the path to the skies—
    To the Lethean peace of the skies—
Come up, in despite of the Lion,
    To shine on us with her bright eyes—
Come up, through the lair of the Lion,
    With love in her luminous eyes."

But Psyche, uplifting her finger,
    Said—"Sadly this star I mistrust—
    Her pallor I strangely mistrust—
Ah, hasten!—ah, let us not linger!
    Ah, fly!—let us fly!—for we must."
In terror she spoke; letting sink her
    Wings till they trailed in the dust—
In agony sobbed; letting sink her
    Plumes till they trailed in the dust—
    Till they sorrowfully trailed in the dust.

I replied—"This is nothing but dreaming.
    Let us on, by this tremulous light!
    Let us bathe in this crystalline light!
Its Sibyllic splendor is beaming
    With Hope and in Beauty to-night—
    See!—it flickers up the sky through the night!
Ah, we safely may trust to its gleaming
    And be sure it will lead us aright—
We surely may trust to a gleaming
    That cannot but guide us aright
Since it flickers up to Heaven through the night."

Thus I pacified Psyche and kissed her,
    And tempted her out of her gloom—
    And conquered her scruples and gloom;
And we passed to the end of the vista—
    But were stopped by the door of a tomb—
    By the door of a legended tomb:—
And I said—"What is written, sweet sister,
    On the door of this legended tomb?"
    She replied—"Ulalume—Ulalume!—
    'T is the vault of thy lost Ulalume!"

Then my heart it grew ashen and sober
    As the leaves that were crispéd and sere—
    As the leaves that were withering and sere—
And I cried—"It was surely October,
    On *this* very night of last year,
    That I journeyed—I journeyed down here!—
    That I brought a dread burden down here—
    On this night, of all nights in the year,
    Ah, what demon hath tempted me here?
Well I know, now, this dim lake of Auber—
    This misty mid region of Weir:—
Well I know, now, this dank tarn of Auber—
    This ghoul-haunted woodland of Weir."

Said we, then—the two, then—"Ah, can it
    Have been that the woodlandish ghouls—
    The pitiful, the merciful ghouls,
To bar up our way and to ban it
    From the secret that lies in these wolds—
    From the thing that lies hidden in these wolds—
Have drawn up the spectre of a planet
    From the limbo of lunary souls—
This sinfully scintillant planet
    From the Hell of the planetary souls?"

The Bells

I

        Hear the sledges with the bells—
            Silver bells!
What a world of merriment their melody foretells!
        How they tinkle, tinkle, tinkle,
            In the icy air of night!
        While the stars that oversprinkle
        All the Heavens, seem to twinkle
    ₁   With a crystalline delight;
        Keeping time, time, time,
        In a sort of Runic rhyme,
To the tintinabulation that so musically wells
    From the bells, bells, bells, bells,
            Bells, bells, bells—
        From the jingling and the tinkling of the bells.

2
Hear the mellow wedding bells—
　　Golden bells!
What a world of happiness their harmony foretells!
　　Through the balmy air of night
　　How they ring out their delight!—
　　　From the molten-golden notes
　　　　And all in tune,
　　　What a liquid ditty floats
　　To the turtle-dove that listens while she gloats
　　　On the moon!
　　Oh, from out the sounding cells
What a gush of euphony voluminously wells!
　　　How it swells!
　　　How it dwells
　　On the Future!—how it tells
　　Of the rapture that impels
　To the swinging and the ringing
　　Of the bells, bells, bells!—
Of the bells, bells, bells, bells,
　　Bells, bells, bells—
To the rhyming and the chiming of the bells!

3
　　Hear the loud alarum bells—
　　　Brazen bells!
What tale of terror, now, their turbulency tells!
　　In the startled ear of Night
　　How they scream out their affright!
　　　Too much horrified to speak,
　　　They can only shriek, shriek,
　　　　Out of tune,
In a clamorous appealing to the mercy of the fire—
In a mad expostulation with the deaf and frantic fire,
　　　Leaping higher, higher, higher,
　　　With a desperate desire
　　And a resolute endeavor
　　Now—now to sit, or never,
　By the side of the pale-faced moon.
　　　Oh, the bells, bells, bells!
　　　What a tale their terror tells
　　　　Of despair!
　　How they clang and clash and roar!
　　What a horror they outpour
　　　In the bosom of the palpitating air!
　　　Yet the ear, it fully knows,
　　　　By the twanging

And the clanging,
How the danger ebbs and flows:—
Yes, the ear distinctly tells,
In the jangling
And the wrangling,
How the danger sinks and swells,
By the sinking or the swelling in the anger of the bells—
Of the bells—
Of the bells, bells, bells, bells,
Bells, bells, bells—
In the clamor and the clangor of the bells.

4
Hear the tolling of the bells—
Iron bells!
What a world of solemn thought their monody compels!
In the silence of the night
How we shiver with affright
At the melancholy meaning of the tone!
For every sound that floats
From the rust within their throats
Is a groan.
And the people—ah, the people
They that dwell up in the steeple
All alone,
And who, tolling, tolling, tolling,
In that muffled monotone,
Feel a glory in so rolling
On the human heart a stone—
They are neither man nor woman—
They are neither brute nor human,
They are Ghouls:—
And their king it is who tolls:—
And he rolls, rolls, rolls, rolls
A Pæan from the bells!
And his merry bosom swells
With the Pæan of the bells!
And he dances and he yells;
Keeping time, time, time,
In a sort of Runic rhyme,
To the Pæan of the bells—
Of the bells:—
Keeping time, time, time,
In a sort of Runic rhyme,
To the throbbing of the bells—
Of the bells, bells, bells—
To the sobbing of the bells:—

Keeping time, time, time,
    As he knells, knells, knells,
In a happy Runic rhyme,
    To the rolling of the bells—
Of the bells, bells, bells:—
    To the tolling of the bells—
Of the bells, bells, bells, bells,
    Bells, bells, bells—
To the moaning and the groaning of the bells.

A Dream Within a Dream

Take this kiss upon the brow!
And, in parting from you now,
Thus much let me avow—
You are not wrong, who deem
That my days have been a dream;
Yet if hope has flown away
In a night, or in a day,
In a vision, or in none,
Is it therefore the less *gone*?
All that we see or seem
Is but a dream within a dream.

I stand amid the roar
Of a surf-tormented shore,
And I hold within my hand
Grains of the golden sand—
How few! yet how they creep
Through my fingers to the deep,
While I weep—while I weep!
O God! can I not grasp
Them with a tighter clasp?
O God! can I not save
One from the pitiless wave?
Is *all* that we see or seem
But a dream within a dream?

For Annie

Thank Heaven! the crisis—
    The danger is past,
And the lingering illness
    Is over at last—
And the fever called "Living"
    Is conquered at last.

Sadly, I know
    I am shorn of my strength,
And no muscle I move
    As I lie at full length—
But no matter!—I feel
    I am better at length.

And I rest so composedly,
    Now, in my bed,
That any beholder
    Might fancy me dead—
Might start at beholding me,
    Thinking me dead.

The moaning and groaning,
    The sighing and sobbing,
Are quieted now,
    With that horrible throbbing
At heart:—ah, that horrible,
    Horrible throbbing!

The sickness—the nausea—
    The pitiless pain—
Have ceased, with the fever
    That maddened my brain—
With the fever called "Living"
    That burned in my brain.

And oh! of all tortures
    That torture the worst
Has abated—the terrible
    Torture of thirst
For the napthaline river
    Of Passion accurst:—
I have drank of a water
    That quenches all thirst:—

Of a water that flows,
　　With a lullaby sound,
From a spring but a very few
　　Feet under ground—
From a cavern not very far
　　Down under ground.

And ah! let it never
　　Be foolishly said
That my room it is gloomy
　　And narrow my bed;
For man never slept
　　In a different bed—
And, to *sleep*, you must slumber
　　In just such a bed.

My tantalized spirit
　　Here blandly reposes,
Forgetting, or never
　　Regretting its roses—
Its old agitations
　　Of myrtles and roses:

For now, while so quietly
　　Lying, it fancies
A holier odor
　　About it, of pansies—
A rosemary odor,
　　Commingled with pansies—
With rue and the beautiful
　　Puritan pansies.

And so it lies happily,
　　Bathing in many
A dream of the truth
　　And the beauty of Annie—
Drowned in a bath
　　Of the tresses of Annie.

She tenderly kissed me,
　　She fondly caressed,
And then I fell gently
　　To sleep on her breast—
Deeply to sleep
　　From the heaven of her breast.

When the light was extinguished,
　　She covered me warm,
And she prayed to the angels
　　To keep me from harm—
To the queen of the angels
　　To shield me from harm.

And I lie so composedly,
　　Now, in my bed,
(Knowing her love)
　　That you fancy me dead—
And I rest so contentedly,
　　Now in my bed,
(With her love at my breast)
　　That you fancy me dead—
That you shudder to look at me,
　　Thinking me dead:—

But my heart it is brighter
　　Than all of the many
Stars in the sky,
　　For it sparkles with Annie—
It glows with the light
　　Of the love of my Annie—
With the thought of the light
　　Of the eyes of my Annie.

Eldorado

　　Gaily bedight,
　　A gallant knight,
In sunshine and in shadow,
　　Had journeyed long,
　　Singing a song,
In search of Eldorado.

　　But he grew old—
　　This knight so bold—
And o'er his heart a shadow
　　Fell, as he found
　　No spot of ground
That looked like Eldorado.

And, as his strength
Failed him at length
He met a pilgrim shadow—
"Shadow," said he,
"Where can it be—
This land of Eldorado?"

"Over the Mountains
Of the Moon,
Down the Valley of the Shadow,
Ride, boldly ride,"
The shade replied,—
"If you seek for Eldorado!"

Annabel Lee

It was many and many a year ago,
In a kingdom by the sea,
That a maiden there lived whom you may know
By the name of Annabel Lee;—
And this maiden she lived with no other thought
Than to love and be loved by me.

I was a child and *she* was a child,
In this kingdom by the sea;
But we loved with a love that was more than love—
I and my Annabel Lee—
With a love that the wingéd seraphs in Heaven
Coveted her and me.

And this was the reason that, long ago,
In this kingdom by the sea,
A wind blew out of a cloud, chilling
My beautiful Annabel Lee;
So that her high-born kinsmen came
And bore her away from me,
To shut her up in a sepulchre,
In this kingdom by the sea.

The angels, not half so happy in Heaven,
Went envying her and me—
Yes!—that was the reason (as all men know,
In this kingdom by the sea)
That the wind came out of the cloud by night,
Chilling and killing my Annabel Lee.

But our love it was stronger by far than the love
    Of those who were older than we—
    Of many far wiser than we—
And neither the angels in Heaven above,
    Nor the demons down under the sea,
Can ever dissever my soul from the soul
    Of the beautiful Annabel Lee:—

For the moon never beams, without bringing me dreams
    Of the beautiful Annabel Lee;
And the stars never rise, but I feel the bright eyes
    Of the beautiful Annabel Lee:—
And so, all the night-tide, I lie down by the side
Of my darling—my darling—my life and my bride,
    In her sepulchre there by the sea—
    In her tomb by the sounding sea.

[May 1849]

Monody on Doctor Olmsted

If this prime ass is with his brother worms—
Forgive the license of the *clASSic* terms!—
I hope they'll make a "black-board" of his face
And make it minus all but its grimace,
That devilish simper which he frequent wore
When, with the glibness of a saint, he swore,
That, "His last work was plainer far than dirt"—
As tainting too, thou muddy-headed squirt!
Plain—dead level—flat—they are the same—
At him, ye worms! till appetite is lame.

OLIVER WENDELL HOLMES
(1809–1894)

from An After-Dinner Poem
(Terpsichore)

Skins of flayed authors, husks of dead reviews,
The turn-coat's clothes, the office-seeker's shoes,
Scraps from cold feasts, where conversation runs
Through mouldy toasts to oxidated puns,
And grating songs a listening crowd endures,

Rasped from the throats of bellowing amateurs;
Sermons, whose writers played such dangerous tricks
Their own heresiarchs called them heretics,
(Strange that one term such distant poles should link,
The Priestleyan's copper and the Puseyan's zinc);
Poems that shuffle with superfluous legs
A blindfold minuet over addled eggs,
Where all the syllables that end in èd,
Like old dragoons, have cuts across the head;
Essays so dark Champollion might despair
To guess what mummy of a thought was there,
Where our poor English, striped with foreign phrase,
Looks like a zebra in a parson's chaise;
Lectures that cut our dinners down to roots,
Or prove (by monkeys) men should stick to fruits,—
Delusive error, as at trifling charge
Professor Gripes will certify at large;
Mesmeric pamphlets, which to facts appeal,
Each fact as slippery as a fresh-caught eel;
And figured heads, whose hieroglyphs invite
To wandering knaves that discount fools at sight:
Such things as these, with heaps of unpaid bills,
And candy puffs and homoeopathic pills,
And ancient bell-crowns with contracted rim,
And bonnets hideous with expanded brim,
And coats whose memory turns the sartor pale,
Their sequels tapering like a lizard's tale,—
How might we spread them to the smiling day,
And toss them, fluttering like the new-mown hay,
To laughter's light or sorrow's pitying shower,
Were these brief minutes lengthened to an hour.

The narrow moments fit like Sunday shoes,—
How vast the heap, how quickly must we choose!
A few small scraps from out his mountain mass
We snatch in haste, and let the vagrant pass.
This shrunken CRUST that Cerberus could not bite,
Stamped (in one corner) "Pickwick copyright,"
Kneaded by youngsters, raised by flattery's yeast,
Was once a loaf, and helped to make a feast.
He for whose sake the glittering show appears
Has sown the world with laughter and with tears,
And they whose welcome wets the bumper's brim
Have wit and wisdom,—for they all quote him.
So, many a tongue the evening hour prolongs
With spangled speeches,—let alone the songs;
Statesmen grow merry, lean attorneys laugh,

And weak teetotals warm to half and half,
And beardless Tullys, new to festive scenes,
Cut their first crop of youth's precocious greens,
And wits stand ready for impromptu claps,
With loaded barrels and percussion caps,
And Pathos, cantering through the minor keys,
Waves all her onions to the trembling breeze;
While the great Feasted views with silent glee
His scattered limbs in Yankee fricassee.

Aestivation

In candent ire the solar splendor flames;
The foles, languescent, pend from arid rames;
His humid front the cive, anheling, wipes,
And dreams of erring on ventiferous ripes.

How dulce to vive occult to mortal eyes,
Dorm on the herb with none to supervise,
Carp the suave berries from the crescent vine,
And bibe the flow from longicaudate kine!

To me, alas! no verdurous visions come,
Save yon exiguous pool's conferva-scum,—
No concave vast repeats the tender hue
That laves my milk-jug with celestial blue!

Me wretched! Let me curr to quercine shades!
Effund your albid hausts, lactiferous maids!
Oh, might I vole to some umbrageous clump,—
Depart,—be off,—excede,—evade,—erump!

Ballad of the Oysterman

It was a tall young oysterman lived by the river-side,
His shop was just upon the bank, his boat was on the tide;
The daughter of a fisherman, that was so straight and slim,
Lived over on the other bank, right opposite to him.

It was the pensive oysterman that saw a lovely maid,
Upon a moonlight evening, a-sitting in the shade;
He saw her wave her handkerchief, as much as if to say,
"I'm wide awake, young oysterman, and all the folks away."

Then up arose the oysterman, and to himself said he,
"I guess I'll leave the skiff at home, for fear that folks should see;
I read it in the story-book, that, for to kiss his dear,
Leander swam the Hellespont,—and I will swim this here."

And he has leaped into the waves, and crossed the shining stream,
And he has clambered up the bank, all in the moonlight gleam;
Oh there were kisses sweet as dew, and words as soft as rain,—
But they have heard her father's step, and in he leaps again!

Out spoke the ancient fisherman,—"Oh, what was that, my
daughter?"
" 'T was nothing but a pebble, sir, I threw into the water."
"And what is that, pray tell me, love, that paddles off so fast?"
"It's nothing but a porpoise, sir, that's been a-swimming past."

Out spoke the ancient fisherman,—"Now bring me my harpoon!
I'll get into my fishing-boat, and fix the fellow soon."
Down fell the pretty innocent, as falls a snow-white lamb,
Her hair drooped round her pallid cheeks, like seaweed on a clam.

Alas for those two loving ones! she waked not from her swound,
And he was taken with the cramp, and in the waves was drowned;
But Fate has metamorphosed them, in pity of their woe,
And now they keep an oyster-shop for mermaids down below.

The Chambered Nautilus

This is the ship of pearl, which, poets feign,
    Sails the unshadowed main,—
    The venturous bark that flings
On the sweet summer wind its purpled wings
In gulfs enchanted, where the Siren sings,
    And coral reefs lie bare,
Where the cold sea-maids rise to sun their streaming hair.

Its webs of living gauze no more unfurl;
    Wrecked is the ship of pearl!
    And every chambered cell,
Where its dim dreaming life was wont to dwell,
As the frail tenant shaped his growing shell,
    Before thee lies revealed,—
Its irised ceiling rent, its sunless crypt unsealed!

Year after year beheld the silent toil
    That spread his lustrous coil;
    Still, as the spiral grew,
He left the past year's dwelling for the new,
Stole with soft step its shining archway through,
    Built up its idle door,
Stretched in his last-found home, and knew the old no more.

Thanks for the heavenly message brought by thee,
    Child of the wandering sea,
    Cast from her lap, forlorn!
From thy dead lips a clearer note is born
Than ever Triton blew from wreathèd horn!
    While on mine ear it rings,
Through the deep caves of thought I hear a voice that sings:—

Build thee more stately mansions, O my soul,
    As the swift seasons roll!
    Leave thy low-vaulted past!
Let each new temple, nobler than the last,
Shut thee from heaven with a dome more vast,
    Till thou at length art free,
Leaving thine outgrown shell by life's unresting sea!

The Deacon's Masterpiece

OR, THE WONDERFUL "ONE-HOSS SHAY"—
A LOGICAL STORY

Have you heard of the wonderful one-hoss shay,
That was built in such a logical way
It ran a hundred years to a day,
And then, of a sudden, it—ah, but stay,
I'll tell you what happened without delay,
Scaring the parson into fits,
Frightening people out of their wits,—
Have you ever heard of that, I say?

Seventeen hundred and fifty-five.
Georgius Secundus was then alive,—
Snuffy old drone from the German hive.
That was the year when Lisbon-town
Saw the earth open and gulp her down,
And Braddock's army was done so brown,
Left without a scalp to its crown.

It was on the terrible Earthquake-day
That the Deacon finished the one-hoss shay.

Now in building of chaises, I tell you what,
There is always *somewhere* a weakest spot,—
In hub, tire, felloe, in spring or thill,
In panel, or crossbar, or floor, or sill,
In screw, bolt, thoroughbrace,—lurking still,
Find it somewhere you must and will,—
Above or below, or within or without,—
And that's the reason, beyond a doubt,
That a chaise *breaks down,* but does n't *wear out.*

But the Deacon swore (as Deacons do,
With an "I dew vum," or an "I tell *yeou*")
He would build one shay to beat the taown
'N' the keounty 'n' all the kentry raoun';
It should be so built that it *could n'* break daown:
"Fur," said the Deacon, " 't's mighty plain
Thut the weakes' place mus' stan' the strain;
'N' the way t' fix it, uz I maintain,
         Is only jest
T' make that place uz strong uz the rest."

So the Deacon inquired of the village folk
Where he could find the strongest oak,
That could n't be split nor bent nor broke,—
That was for spokes and floor and sills;
He sent for lancewood to make the thills;
The crossbars were ash, from the straightest trees,
The panels of white-wood, that cuts like cheese,
But lasts like iron for things like these;
The hubs of logs from the "Settler's ellum,"—
Last of its timber,—they could n't sell 'em,
Never an axe had seen their chips,
And the wedges flew from between their lips,
Their blunt ends frizzled like celery-tips;
Step and prop-iron, bolt and screw,
Spring, tire, axle, and linchpin too,
Steel of the finest, bright and blue;
Thoroughbrace bison-skin, thick and wide;
Boot, top, dasher, from tough old hide
Found in the pit when the tanner died.
That was the way he "put her through."
"There!" said the Deacon, "naow she'll dew!"

Do! I tell you, I rather guess
She was a wonder, and nothing less!
Colts grew horses, beards turned gray,
Deacon and deaconess dropped away,
Children and grandchildren—where were they?
But there stood the stout old one-hoss shay
As fresh as on Lisbon-earthquake-day!

Eighteen hundred;—it came and found
The Deacon's masterpiece strong and sound.
Eighteen hundred increased by ten;—
"Hahnsum kerridge" they called it then.
Eighteen hundred and twenty came;—
Running as usual; much the same.
Thirty and forty at last arrive,
And then come fifty, and FIFTY-FIVE.

Little of all we value here
Wakes on the morn of its hundredth year
Without both feeling and looking queer.
In fact, there's nothing that keeps its youth,
So far as I know, but a tree and truth.
(This is a moral that runs at large;
Take it.—You're welcome.—No extra charge.)

FIRST OF NOVEMBER,—the Earthquake-day,—
There are traces of age in the one-hoss shay,
A general flavor of mild decay,
But nothing local, as one may say.
There could n't be,—for the Deacon's art
Had made it so like in every part
That there was n't a chance for one to start.
For the wheels were just as strong as the thills,
And the floor was just as strong as the sills,
And the panels just as strong as the floor,
And the whipple-tree neither less nor more,
And the back crossbar as strong as the fore,
And spring and axle and hub *encore.*
And yet, *as a whole,* it is past a doubt
In another hour it will be *worn out!*

First of November; 'Fifty-five!
This morning the parson takes a drive.
Now, small boys, get out of the way!
Here comes the wonderful one-hoss shay,
Drawn by a rat-tailed ewe-necked bay.
"Huddup!" said the parson.—Off went they.

The parson was working his Sunday's text,—
Had got to *fifthly,* and stopped perplexed
At what the—Moses—was coming next.
All at once the horse stood still,
Close by the meet'n'-house on the hill.
First a shiver, and then a thrill,
Then something decidedly like a spill,—
And the parson was sitting upon a rock,
At half past nine by the meet'n'-house clock,—
Just the hour of the Earthquake shock!
What do you think the parson found,
When he got up and stared around?
The poor old chaise in a heap or mound,
As if it had been to the mill and ground!
You see, of course, if you're not a dunce,
How it went to pieces all at once,—
All at once, and nothing first,—
Just as bubbles do when they burst.

End of the wonderful one-hoss shay.
Logic is logic. That's all I say.

The Last Leaf

I saw him once before,
As he passed by the door,
          And again
The pavement stones resound,
As he totters o'er the ground
          With his cane.

They say that in his prime,
Ere the pruning-knife of Time
          Cut him down,
Not a better man was found
By the Crier on his round
          Through the town.

But now he walks the streets,
And he looks at all he meets
          Sad and wan,
And he shakes his feeble head,
That it seems as if he said,
          "They are gone."

The mossy marbles rest
On the lips that he has prest
    In their bloom,
And the names he loved to hear
Have been carved for many a year
    On the tomb.

My grandmamma has said—
Poor old lady, she is dead
    Long ago—
That he had a Roman nose,
And his cheek was like a rose
    In the snow.

But now his nose is thin,
And it rests upon his chin
    Like a staff,
And a crook is in his back,
And a melancholy crack
    In his laugh.

I know it is a sin
For me to sit and grin
    At him here;
But the old three-cornered hat,
And the breeches, and all that,
    Are so queer!

And if I should live to be
The last leaf upon the tree
    In the spring,
Let them smile, as I do now,
At the old forsaken bough
    Where I cling.

Old Ironsides

Ay, tear her tattered ensign down!
    Long has it waved on high,
And many an eye has danced to see
    That banner in the sky;
Beneath it rung the battle shout,
    And burst the cannon's roar;—
The meteor of the ocean air
    Shall sweep the clouds no more.

Her deck, once red with heroes' blood,
    Where knelt the vanquished foe,
When winds were hurrying o'er the flood,
    And waves were white below,
No more shall feel the victor's tread,
    Or know the conquered knee;—
The harpies of the shore shall pluck
    The eagle of the sea!

Oh better that her shattered hulk
    Should sink beneath the wave;
Her thunders shook the mighty deep,
    And there should be her grave;
Nail to the mast her holy flag,
    Set every threadbare sail,
And give her to the god of storms,
    The lightning and the gale!

Peau de Chagrin of State Street

How beauteous is the bond
In the manifold array
Of its promises to pay,
While the eight per cent it gives
And the rate at which one lives
    Correspond!

But at last the bough is bare
Where the coupons one by one
Through their ripening days have run,
And the bond, a beggar now,
Seeks investment anyhow,
    Anywhere!

The Poet Grows Old

How I cut the fresh branches of succulent rhyme
In the spring of my years, my asparagus time!
To clip them, to bind them, how light was the toil,
As each morning they sprouted afresh from the soil!

Spring passed, still my pages of silver-shod lines
Filled up like the pods on my marrow fat vines;
Uncared for they grew and unasked for they came,—
The peas and the poems,—with both 'twas the same.

And when the last crop on the meadow was mown,
When the apples were ripe, when the song-birds had flown,
My harvest of verse was awaiting me still
For the corn-field stood ready my basket to fill.

But winter has come with his icicle-spear
And built his white throne on the grave of the year
The blossoms are snowflakes he flings to the gale
And the seed that he casts in the furrow is hail.

The fields are all bare and the harvest is o'er
I come with my sickle and basket no more;
But a rusty old spade, and I prospect around
For the bread-fruit of Erin that grows underground.

THOMAS HOLLEY CHIVERS
(1809–1858)

The Shell

1
What is it makes thy sound unto my ear
    So mournful, Angel of the mighty Sea?
Is it the soul of her who once was here,
    Speaking affection, through thy lips, to me?

2
Oh! from my childhood this has been to me
    A mystery which no one could solve!—It sounds
And sorrows for the Sea incessantly—
    Telling the grief with which my soul abounds!

3
Here, in its labyrinthine curve, it leaves
    The foot-prints of its song in many dyes;
And here, incessantly, it ever weaves
    The rainbow-tissue of its melodies.

4
When any harsher sound disturbs me here,
    In my lamentings in this world for thee,
I will apply it to my listening ear,
    And think it is thy soul come down to me.

MARGARET FULLER
(1810–1850)

Let me Gather from the Earth

Let me gather from the Earth, one full grown fragrant flower,
Let it bloom within my bosom through its one blooming hour.
Let it die within my bosom and to its parting breath
Mine shall answer, *having lived,* I shrink not now from death.
It is this niggard halfness that turns my heart to stone,
'Tis the cup seen, not tasted, that makes the infant moan.
Let me for once press firm my lips upon the moment's brow,
Let me for once distinctly feel *I am all happy now,*
And bliss shall seal a blessing upon that moment's brow.

Winged Sphinx

Through brute nature upward rising,
    Seed up-striving to the light,
Revelations still surprising,
    My inwardness is grown insight.
    Still I slight not those first stages,
Dark but God-directed Ages;
    In my nature leonine
Labored & learned a Soul divine;
    Put forth an aspect Chaste, Serene,
Of nature virgin mother queen;
    Assumes at last the destined wings,
Earth & heaven together brings;
    While its own form the riddle tells
That baffled all the wizard spells
    Drawn from intellectual wells,
Cold waters where truth never dwells:
    —It was fable told you so;—
    Seek her in common daylight's glow.

FRANCES S. OSGOOD
(1811–1859)

He Bade me be Happy

He bade me "Be happy," he whisper'd "Forget me;"
    He vow'd my affection was cherish'd in vain.
"Be happy!" "Forget me!" I would, if he'd let me—
    Why will he keep coming to say so again?

He came—it was not the first time, by a dozen—
    To take, as he said, "an eternal adieu;"
He went, and, for comfort, I turn'd to—my cousin,
    When back stalk'd the torment his vows to renew.

"You must love me no longer!" he said but this morning.
    "I love you no longer!" I meekly replied.
"Is this my reward?" he cried; "falsehood and scorning
    From her who was ever my idol, my pride!"

ELLEN STURGIS HOOPER
(1812–1848)

I Slept and Dreamed

I slept, and dreamed that life was Beauty;
I woke, and found that life was Duty.
Was thy dream then a shadowy lie?
Toil on, sad heart, courageously,
And thou shalt find thy dream to be
A noonday light and truth to thee.

JONES VERY
(1813–1880)

The Dead

I see them crowd on crowd they walk the earth
Dry, leafless trees no Autumn wind laid bare;
And in their nakedness find cause for mirth,
And all unclad would winter's rudeness dare;
No sap doth through their clattering branches flow,
Whence springing leaves and blossoms bright appear;
Their hearts the living God have ceased to know,
Who gives the springtime to th'expectant year;
They mimic life, as if from him to steal
His glow of health to paint the livid cheek;
They borrow words for thoughts they cannot feel,
That with a seeming heart their tongue may speak;
And in their show of life more dead they live
Than those that to the earth with many tears they give.

Thy Better Self

I am thy other self, what thou wilt be,
When thou art I, the one seest now;
In finding thy true self thou wilt find me,
The springing blade, where now thou dost but plough.
I am thy neighbor, a new house I've built,
Which thou as yet hast never entered in;
I come to call thee; come in when thou wilt,
The feast is always ready to begin.
Thou should'st love me, as thou dost love thyself,
For I am but another self beside;
To show thee him thou lov'st in better health,
What thou would'st be, when thou to him hast died;
Then visit me, I make thee many a call;
Nor live I near to thee alone, but all.

Enoch

I looked to find a man who walked with God,
Like the translated patriarch of old;—
Though gladdened millions on His footstool trod,
Yet none with him did such sweet converse hold;
I heard the wind in low complaint go by

That none his melodies like him could hear;
Day unto day spoke wisdom from on high,
Yet none like David turned a willing ear;
God walked alone unhonored through the earth;
For Him no heart-built temple open stood,
The soul forgetful of her nobler birth
Had hewn him lofty shrines of stone and wood,
And left unfinished and in ruins still
The only temple he delights to fill.

The Latter Rain

The latter rain, it falls in anxious haste
Upon the sun-dried fields and branches bare,
Loosening with searching drops the rigid waste
As if it would each root's lost strength repair;
But not a blade grows green as in the spring,
No swelling twig puts forth its thickening leaves;
The robins only mid the harvests sing
Pecking the grain that scatters from the sheaves;
The rain falls still—the fruit all ripened drops,
It pierces chestnut burr and walnut shell,
The furrowed fields disclose the yellow crops,
Each bursting pod of talents used can tell,
And all that once received the early rain
Declare to man it was not sent in vain.

The Eagles

The eagles gather on the place of death
So thick the ground is spotted with their wings,
The air is tainted with the noisome breath
The wind from off the field of slaughter brings;
Alas! no mourners weep them for the slain,
But all unburied lies the naked soul;
The whitening bones of thousands strew the plain,
Yet none can now the pestilence controul;
The eagles gathering on the carcase feed,
In every heart behold their half-formed prey;
The battened wills beneath their talons bleed,
Their iron beaks without remorse must slay;
Till by the sun no more the place is seen,
Where they who worshipped idol gods have been.

The New Man

The hands must touch and handle many things,
The eyes long waste their glances all in vain;
The feet course still in idle, mazy rings,
E'er man himself, the lost, shall back regain;
The hand that ever moves, the eyes that see,
While day holds out his shining lamp on high,
And strait as flies the honey-seeking bee,
Direct the feet to unseen flowers they spy,
These, when they come, the man revealed from heaven,
Shall labor all the day in quiet rest,
And find at eve the covert duly given,
Where with the bird they find sweet sleep and rest;
That shall their wasted strength to health restore,
And bid them seek the morn the hills and fields once more.

CHRISTOPHER CRANCH
(1813–1892)

Enosis

Thought is deeper than all speech,
    Feeling deeper than all thought;
Souls to souls can never teach
    What unto themselves was taught.

We are spirits clad in veils;
    Man by man was never seen;
All our deep communing fails
    To remove the shadowy screen.

Heart to heart was never known;
    Mind with mind did never meet;
We are columns left alone,
    Of a temple once complete.

Like the stars that gem the sky,
    Far apart, though seeming near,
In our light we scattered lie;
    All is thus but starlight here.

What is social company
    But a babbling summer stream?
What our wise philosophy
    But the glancing of a dream?

Only when the sun of love
    Melts the scattered stars of thought;
Only when we live above
    What the dim-eyed world hath taught;

Only when our souls are fed
    By the Fount which gave them birth,
And by inspiration led,
    Which they never drew from earth,

We like parted drops of rain
    Swelling till they meet and run,
Shall be all absorbed again,
    Melting, flowing into one.

December

No more the scarlet maples flash and burn
    Their beacon-fires from hilltop and from plain;
The meadow-grasses and the woodland fern
    In the bleak woods lie withered once again.

The trees stand bare, and bare each stony scar
    Upon the cliffs; half frozen glide the rills;
The steel-blue river like a scimitar
    Lies cold and curved between the dusky hills.

Over the upland farm I take my walk,
    And miss the flaunting flocks of golden-rod;
Each autumn flower a dry and leafless stalk,
    Each mossy field a track of frozen sod.

I hear no more the robin's summer song
    Through the gray network of the wintry woods;
Only the cawing crows that all day long
    Clamor about the windy solitudes.

Like agate stones upon earth's frozen breast,
    The little pools of ice lie round and still;
While sullen clouds shut downward east and west
    In marble ridges stretched from hill to hill.

Come once again, O southern wind,—once more
    Come with thy wet wings flapping at my pane;
Ere snow-drifts pile their mounds about my door,
    One parting dream of summer bring again.

Ah, no! I hear the windows rattle fast;
    I see the first flakes of the gathering snow,
That dance and whirl before the northern blast.
    No countermand the march of days can know.

December drops no weak, relenting tear,
    By our fond summer sympathies ensnared;
Nor from the perfect circle of the year
    Can even winter's crystal gems be spared.

The Autumn Rain

1
Roof and spire and darkened vane
Steep and soak in the night-long rain
That drips through the barns on the golden grain;
And a drowning mist sweeps over the plain,
And spatters with mud the rutted lane
And the dead flower stalks that bud not again.

2
Wind-driven drops of the autumn rain,
Beat, beat on the window-pane!
Beat, beat, sorrowful rain!
Drive through the night o'er the desolate plain!
Beat and sob to the old refrain,
And weep for the years that come not again.

3
Years, with your mingling of joy and of pain,—
Joys long forgotten, and cares that remain;
Hopes lying stranded and choked in the drain
Of the down-rushing river of fate,—I would fain
Sigh with the night-wind and weep with the rain,
For ye come not again!—ye come not again!

HENRY DAVID THOREAU
(1817–1862)

Love Equals Swift and Slow

Love equals swift and slow
    And high and low—
Racer and lame—
    The hunter and his game.

Light-Winged Smoke

Light-winged Smoke, Icarian bird,
Melting thy pinions in thy upward flight,
Lark without song, and messenger of dawn,
Circling above the hamlets as thy nest;
Or else, departing dream, and shadowy form
Of midnight vision, gathering up thy skirts;
By night star-veiling, and by day
Darkening the light and blotting out the sun;
Go thou my incense upward from this hearth,
And ask the gods to pardon this clear flame.

Though All the Fates

Though all the fates should prove unkind,
Leave not your native land behind.
The ship, becalmed, at length stands still;
The steed must rest beneath the hill;
But swiftly still our fortunes pace
To find us out in every place.

The vessel, though her masts be firm,
Beneath her copper bears a worm;
Around the cape, across the line,
Till fields of ice her course confine;
It matters not how smooth the breeze,
How shallow or how deep the seas,
Whether she bears Manilla twine,
Or in her hold Madeira wine,
Or China teas, or Spanish hides,
In port or quarantine she rides;
Far from New England's blustering shore,

New England's worm her hulk shall bore,
And sink her in the Indian seas,
Twine, wine, and hides, and China teas.

Salmon Brook

Salmon Brook,
Penichook,
Ye sweet waters of my brain,
When shall I look,
Or cast the hook,
In your waves again?

Silver eels,
Wooden creels,
These the baits that still allure,
And dragon-fly
That floated by,
May they still endure?

I Am a Parcel of Vain Strivings

I am a parcel of vain strivings tied
By a chance bond together,
Dangling this way and that, their links
Were made so loose and wide,
Methinks,
For milder weather.

A bunch of violets without their roots,
And sorrel intermixed,
Encircled by a wisp of straw
Once coiled about their shoots,
The law
By which I'm fixed.

A nosegay which Time clutched from out
Those fair Elysian fields,
With weeds and broken stems, in haste,
Doth make the rabble rout
That waste
The day he yields.

And here I bloom for a short hour unseen,
  Drinking my juices up,
 With no root in the land
   To keep my branches green,
     But stand
   In a bare cup.

Some tender buds were left upon my stem
   In mimicry of life,
 But ah! the children will not know,
   Till time has withered them,
     The woe
   With which they're rife.

But now I see I was not plucked for naught,
   And after in life's vase
 Of glass set while I might survive,
   But by a kind hand brought
     Alive
   To a strange place.

That stock thus thinned will soon redeem its hours,
   And by another year,
 Such as God knows, with freer air,
   More fruits and fairer flowers
     Will bear,
   While I droop here.

All Things Are Current Found

All things are current found
On earthly ground,
Spirits and elements
Have their descents.

Night and day, year on year,
High and low, far and near,
These are our own aspects,
These are our own regrets.

Ye gods of the shore,
Who abide evermore,
I see you far headland,
Stretching on either hand;

I hear the sweet evening sounds
From your undecaying grounds;
Cheat me no more with time,
Take me to your clime.

My Life Has Been the Poem

My life has been the poem I would have writ,
But I could not both live and utter it.

Any Fool Can Make a Rule

Any fool can make a rule
And every fool will mind it.

I Am Bound, I Am Bound

I am bound, I am bound, for a distant shore,
By a lonely isle, by a far Azore,
There it is, there it is, the treasure I seek,
On the barren sands of a desolate creek.

The Poet's Delay

In vain I see the morning rise,
    In vain observe the western blaze,
Who idly look to other skies,
    Expecting life by other ways.

Amidst such boundless wealth without,
    I only still am poor within,
The birds have sung their summer out,
    But still my spring does not begin.

Shall I then wait the autumn wind,
    Compelled to seek a milder day,
And leave no curious nest behind,
    No woods still echoing to my lay?

William Ellery Channing
(1818–1901)

from The Earth Spirit

Then spoke the Spirit of the Earth,
    Her gentle voice like a soft water's song;—
None from my loins have ever birth,
    But what to joy and love belong;
I faithful am, and give to thee
Blessings great, and give them free.
    I have woven shrouds of air
        In a loom of hurrying light,
    For the trees which blossoms bear,
        And gilded them with sheets of bright;
I fall upon the grass like love's first kiss,
I make the golden flies and their fine bliss.
        I paint the hedge-rows in the lane,
And clover white and red the pathways bear,
        I laugh aloud in sudden gusts of rain,
To see the ocean lash himself in air . . .

. . . .

American Indian Poems: 1826–1859

Chant to the Fire-fly

(Chippewa original)
Wau wau tay see!
Wau wau tay see!
E mow e shin
Tahe bwau ne baun-e wee!
Be eghaun—be eghaun—ewee!
Wau wau tay see!
Wau wau tay see!
Was sa koon ain je gun.
Was sa koon ain je gun.

(Literal translation)
Flitting-white-fire-insect! waving-white-fire-bug!
give me light before I go to bed! give me light
before I go to sleep. Come, little dancing white-
fire-bug! Come, little flitting white-fire-beast!
Light me with your bright white-flame-instrument
—your little candle.

(Literary translation)
Fire-fly, fire-fly! bright little thing,
Light me to bed, and my song I will sing.
Give me your light, as you fly o'er my head,
That I may merrily go to my bed.
Give me your light o'er the grass as you creep,
That I may joyfully go to my sleep.
Come, little fire-fly, come, little beast—
Come! and I'll make you tomorrow a feast.
Come, little candle that flies as I sing,
Bright little fairy-bug—night's little king;
Come, and I'll dance as you guide me along,
Come, and I'll pay you, my bug, with a song.

From the South: I

(Chippewa original)
From the south they come,
The birds, the warlike birds,
        With sounding wings.

I wish to change myself
To the body of that swift bird.

I throw away my body in the strife.

From the South: II

(Chippewa original)
From the south they came, Birds of War—
Hark! to their passing scream.
I wish the body of the fiercest,
As swift, as cruel, as strong.
I cast my body to the chance of fighting.
Happy shall I be to lie in that place,
In that place where the fight was,
Beyond the enemy's line.

The Lament of the Captive
(Richard Henry Wilde, 1819)

My life is like the summer rose
    That opens to the morning sky,
And, ere the shades of evening close,
    Is scattered on the ground to die:
Yet on that rose's humble bed
The softest dews of night are shed;
As if she wept such waste to see—
But none shall drop a tear for me!

My life is like the autumn leaf
    That trembles in the moon's pale ray,
Its hold is frail—its date is brief—
    Restless, and soon to pass away:
Yet when that leaf shall fall and fade,
The parent tree will mourn its shade,
The wind bewail the leafless tree,
But none shall breathe a sigh for me!

My life is like the print, which feet
    Have left on TAMPA'S desert strand,
Soon as the rising tide shall beat,
    Their track will vanish from the sand:
Yet, as if grieving to efface
All vestige of the human race,
On that lone shore loud moans the sea,
But none shall thus lament for me!

A Visit from St. Nicholas
(Clement Moore, 1823)

'Twas the night before Christmas, when all through the house
Not a creature was stirring, not even a mouse;
The stockings were hung by the chimney with care,
In hopes that ST. NICHOLAS soon would be there;
The children were nestled all snug in their beds,
While visions of sugar-plums danced in their heads;
And mamma in her 'kerchief, and I in my cap,
Had just settled our brains for a long winter's nap,
When out on the lawn there arose such a clatter,
I sprang from the bed to see what was the matter.
Away to the window I flew like a flash,

Tore open the shutters and threw up the sash.
The moon on the breast of the new-fallen snow
Gave the lustre of mid-day to objects below,
When, what to my wondering eyes should appear,
But a miniature sleigh, and eight tiny reindeer,
With a little old driver, so lively and quick,
I knew in a moment it must be St. Nick.
More rapid than eagles his coursers they came,
And he whistled, and shouted, and called them by name;
"Now, *Dasher!* now, *Dancer!* now, *Prancer* and *Vixen!*
On, *Comet!* on, *Cupid!* on, *Donder* and *Blitzen!*
To the top of the porch! to the top of the wall!
Now dash away! dash away! dash away all!"
As dry leaves that before the wild hurricane fly,
When they meet with an obstacle, mount to the sky;
So up to the house-top the coursers they flew,
With the sleigh full of Toys, and St. Nicholas too.
And then, in a twinkling, I heard on the roof
The prancing and pawing of each little hoof.
As I drew in my head, and was turning around,
Down the chimney St. Nicholas came with a bound.
He was dressed all in fur, from his head to his foot,
And his clothes were all tarnished with ashes and soot;
The bundle of Toys he had flung on his back,
And he looked like a pedler just opening his pack.
His eyes—how they twinkled! his dimples how merry!
His cheeks were like roses, his nose like a cherry!
His droll little mouth was drawn up like a bow,
And the beard of his chin was as white as the snow;
The stump of a pipe he held tight in his teeth,
And the smoke it encircled his head like a wreath;
He had a broad face and a little round belly,
That shook when he laughed, like a bowlful of jelly.
He was chubby and plump, a right jolly old elf,
And I laughed when I saw him, in spite of myself;
A wink of his eye and a twist of his head,
Soon gave me to know I had nothing to dread;
He spoke not a word, but went straight to his work,
And filled all the stockings; then turned with a jerk,
And laying his finger aside of his nose,
And giving a nod, up the chimney he rose;
He sprang to his sleigh, to his team gave a whistle,
And away they all flew like the down of a thistle.
But I heard him exclaim, ere he drove out of sight,
"Happy Christmas to all, and to all a goodnight."

The Old Oaken Bucket
(Samuel Woodworth, 1826)

How dear to this heart are the scenes of my childhood,
  When fond recollection presents them to view!—
The orchard, the meadow, the deep-tangled wildwood,
  And every loved spot which my infancy knew!
The wide-spreading pond, and the mill that stood by it;
  The bridge, and the rock where the cataract fell;
The cot of my father, the dairy-house nigh it;
  And e'en the rude bucket that hung in the well.
The old oaken bucket, the iron-bound bucket,
The moss-covered bucket, which hung in the well.

That moss-covered vessel I hailed as a treasure;
  For often at noon, when returned from the field,
I found it the source of an exquisite pleasure—
  The purest and sweetest that Nature can yield.
How ardent I seized it, with hands that were glowing,
  And quick to the white-pebbled bottom it fell!
Then soon, with the emblem of truth overflowing,
  And dripping with coolness, it rose from the well—
The old oaken bucket, the iron-bound bucket.
The moss-covered bucket arose from the well.

How sweet from the green, mossy brim to receive it,
  As, poised on the curb, it inclined to my lips!
Not a full, blushing goblet could tempt me to leave it,
  The brightest that beauty or revelry sips.
And now, far removed from the loved habitation,
  The tear of regret will intrusively swell,
As Fancy reverts to my father's plantation,
  And sighs for the bucket that hangs in the well—
The old oaken bucket, the iron-bound bucket,
The moss-covered bucket that hangs in the well!

Mary Had a Little Lamb
(Sarah Josepha Hale, 1830)

Mary had a little lamb,
  Its fleece was white as snow;
And everywhere that Mary went,
  The lamb was sure to go.

He followed her to school one day,
　　Which was against the rule;
It made the children laugh and play
　　To see a lamb at school.

And so the teacher turned him out,
　　But still he lingered near,
And waited patiently about
　　Till Mary did appear.

And then he ran to her, and laid
　　His head upon her arm,
As if he said, "I'm not afraid—
　　You'll keep me from all harm."

"What makes the lamb love Mary so?"
　　The eager children cry.
"Oh, Mary loves the lamb, you know,"
　　The teacher did reply.

"And you each gentle animal
　　In confidence may bind,
And make them follow at your call,
　　If you are only kind."

America
(Samuel Francis Smith, 1831)

My country, 'tis of thee,
Sweet land of liberty,
Of thee I sing;
Land where my fathers died,
Land of the Pilgrim's pride,
From ev'ry mountainside
Let freedom ring!

My native country, thee,
Land of the noble free,
Thy name I love;
I love thy rocks and rills,
Thy woods and templed hills;
My heart with rapture thrills,
Like that above.

Let music swell the breeze,
And ring from all the trees
Sweet freedom's song.
Let mortal tongues awake;
Let all that breathe partake;
Let rocks their silence break,
The sound prolong.

Our father's God, to Thee,
Author of liberty,
To Thee we sing.
Long may our land be bright
With freedom's holy light;
Protect us by Thy might,
Great God, our King!

Woodman, Spare That Tree
(George Pope Morris, 1837)

Woodman, spare that tree!
Touch not a single bough!
In youth it sheltered me,
And I'll protect it now.

'Twas my forefather's hand
That placed it near his cot;
There, woodman, let it stand,
Thy ax shall harm it not!

That old familiar tree,
Whose glory and renown
Are spread o'er land and sea,
And wouldst thou hew it down?

Woodman, forbear thy stroke!
Cut not its earth-bound ties!
Oh! spare that aged oak,
Now towering to the skies.

When but an idle boy
I sought its grateful shade;
In all their gushing joy
Here too my sisters played.

My mother kissed me here
My father pressed my hand—
Forgive this foolish tear,
But let that old oak stand!

My heart-strings round thee cling,
Close as thy bark, old friend!
Here shall the wild-bird sing,
And still thy branches bend.

Old tree, the storm still brave!
And, woodman, leave the spot!
While I've a hand to save,
Thy ax shall harm it not.

Nearer My God to Thee
(Sarah F. Adams, 1841)

Nearer, my God, to thee,
    Nearer to Thee!
E'en tho' it be a cross
    That raiseth me,
Still all my song shall be,
Nearer, my God, to thee,
Nearer, my God, to thee,
    Nearer to thee!

Tho' like a wanderer,
    The sun gone down,
Darkness be over me,
    My rest a stone,
Yet in my dreams I'd be
Nearer, my God, to thee,
Nearer, my God, to thee,
    Nearer to thee.

There let the way appear
    Steps unto heaven;
All that thou sendest me
    In mercy given;
Angels to beckon me
Nearer, my God, to thee,
Nearer, my God, to thee,
    Nearer to thee.

Then, with my waking thoughts
 Bright with thy praise,
Out of my stony griefs
 Bethel I'll raise;
So by my woes to be
Nearer, my God, to thee,
Nearer, my God, to thee,
 Nearer to thee.

Or if on joyful wing
 Cleaving the sky,
Sun, moon, and stars forgot,
 Upwards I fly,
Still all my song shall be,
Nearer, my God, to thee,
Nearer, my God, to thee,
 Nearer to thee!

Old Dan Tucker
(Daniel Decatur Emmett, 1841)

I come to town de udder night,
I hear de noise an' saw de fight;
De watchman was a-running round,
Cryin': "Old Dan Tucker's come to town."

Chorus
So get out de way,
Ole Dan Tucker!
Get out de way,
Ole Dan Tucker!
Get out de way,
Ole Dan Tucker,
You're too late to come to supper.

Dan Tucker is a nice old man,
He used to ride our darby ram;
He sent him whizzin' down de hill,
If he hadn't got up, he'd lay dar still.

Old Dan Tucker an' I got drunk,
He fell in de fire an' kick up a chunk,
De charcoal got inside he shoe,
Lor' bless you, honey, how de ashes flew!

I went to town to buy some goods,
I lost myself in a piece of woods;
De night was dark. I had to suffer,
It froze de heel of Daniel Tucker.

Tucker was a hardened sinner,
He nebber said his grace at dinner;
De old sow squeal, de pigs did squall,
He whole hog wid de tail and all.

And now Ole Dan is a gone sucker,
And nebber can go home to supper;
Old Dan, he has had his last ride,
And de banjo's buried by his side.

The Blue Tail Fly
or Jimmy Cracked Corn
(Daniel Decatur Emmett?, 1846)

O when you come in summer time,
To South Carlinar's sultry clime,
If in de shade you chance to lie,
You'll soon find out de blue tail fly,
An scratch 'im wid a brier too.

Dere's many kind ob dese here tings,
From different sort ob insects springs;
Some hatch in June, and some July,
But August fotches de blue tail fly
    An scratch 'im wid a brier too.

When I was young I used to wait
On Massa's table an hand de plate;
I'de pass de bottle when he dry,
And brush away de blue tail fly,
    And scratch 'im wid a brier too.

Den arter dinner massa sleep,
He bid me vigilance to keep;
An when he gwine to shut he eye,
He tell me watch de blue tail fly,
    And scratch 'im wid a brier too.

When he ride in de arternoon,
I foller wid a hickory broom;
De poney being berry shy,
When bitten by de blue tail fly,
    And scratch 'im wid a brier too.

One day he rode aroun de farm,
De flies so numerous did swarm;
One chance to bite 'im on de thigh,
De debble take dat blue tail fly,
    And scratch 'im wid a brier too.

De poney run, he jump, an pitch,
An tumble massa in de ditch;
He died, an de Jury wonder why,
De verdict was de "blue tail fly,"
    And scratch 'im wid a brier too.

Dey laid 'im under a simmon tree,
His epitaph am dar to see;
Beneath dis stone I'm forced to lie,
All by de means ob de blue tail fly,
    And scratch 'im wid a brier too.

Ole Massa's gone, now let him rest,
Dey say all tings am for de best;
I neber shall forget till de day I die,
Ole Massa an de blue tail fly,
    And scratch 'im wid a brier too.

De hornet gets in your eyes an nose,
De 'skeeter bites y'e through your close,
De galinipper sweeten high,
But wusser yet de blue tail fly,
    And scratch 'im wid a brier too.

Oh, Susanna!
(Stephen Foster, 1848)

I came from Alabama wid my banjo on my knee;
I'm g'wan to Lou'sianna, my true love for to see.
It rain'd all night the day I left, the weather, it was dry;
The sun so hot I froze to death; Susanna don't you cry.

I had a dream de odder night, when eb'ryt'ing was still;
I thought I saw Susanna a-coming down de hill.
De buckwheat cake war in her mouth, de tear was in her eye;
Says I: "I'm coming from de South, Susanna, don't you cry."

I soon will be in New Orleans, and den I'll look all round,
And when I find Susanna, I'll fall upon the ground.
But if I do not find her, dis darky'll surely die;
And when I'm dead and buried, Susanna, don't you cry.

Chorus
Oh, Susanna!
Oh, don't you cry for me;
I've come from Alabama
Wid my banjo on my knee.

Camptown Races
(Stephen Foster, 1850)

De Camptown ladies sing dis song, doodah! doodah!
De Camptown race track five miles long, oh, doodahday!
I come down dah wid my hat caved in, doodah! doodah!
I go back home wid a pocket full of tin, oh, doodahday!

Chorus
Gwine to run all night!
Gwine to run all day!
I'll bet my money on de bobtail nag,
Somebody bet on de bay.

De long-tail filly and de big black hoss, doodah! doodah!
Dey fly de track and dey both cut across, oh, doodah-day!
De blind hoss stickin' in a big mudhole, doodah! doodah!
Can't touch bottom wid a ten-foot pole, oh, doodah-day!

Old muley cow come onto de track, doodah! doodah!
De bobtail fling her ober his back, oh, doodah-day!
Den fly along like a railroad car, doodah! doodah!
Runnin' a race wid a shootin' star, oh, doodah-day!

See dem flyin' on a ten-mile heat, doodah! doodah!
Round de race track, den repeat, oh, dooday-day!
I win my money on de bobtail nag, doodah! doodah!
I keep my money in an old tow bag, oh, doodah-day!

It Came Upon the Midnight Clear

(Edmund Hamilton Sears, 1850)

It came upon the midnight clear,
    That glorious song of old,
From angels bending near the earth,
    To touch their harps of gold:
'Peace on the earth, good-will to men,
    From heav'n's all gracious King.'
The world in solemn stillness lay
    To hear the angels sing.

Still thro' the cloven skies they come,
    With peaceful wings unfurled;
And still their heavenly music floats
    O'er all the weary world:
Above its sad and lowly plains
    They bend on hovering wing,
And ever o'er its Babel sounds
    The blessèd angels sing.

But with the woes of sin and strife
    The world has suffered long;
Beneath the angel-strain have rolled
    Two thousand years of wrong;
And man, at war with man, hears not
    The love song which they bring:
O hush the noise, ye men of strife,
    And hear the angels sing!

And ye, beneath life's crushing load
    Whose forms are bending low,
Who toil along the climbing way,
    With painful steps and slow,—
Look now; for glad and golden hours
    Come swiftly on the wing:
O rest beside the weary road,
    And hear the angels sing!

For, lo! the days are hastening on
    By prophet bards foretold,
When with the ever-circling years
    Comes round the age of gold:
When peace shall over all the earth
    Its ancient splendors fling,
And the whole world give back the song
    Which now the angels sing.

The E-ri-e
(Anonymous, c.1850)

We were forty miles
Forget it I never sha
What a terrible storr
On the E-ri-e Canal.

Refrain
Oh the E-ri-e was a
The gin was getting
    And I scarcely tl
    We'll get a drinl
Till we get to Buffal
Till we get to Buffal

We were loaded do
We were chuck up :
And the captain he ʌᴏᴏᴋᴇᴅ ᴅᴏ
With his goddam wicked eye.

Oh the girls are in the Police Gazette,
The crew are all in jail;
I'm the only living sea cook's son
That's left to tell the tale.

Turkey in the Straw
(Anonymous, 1851)

As I was a-gwine down the road,
Tired team and a heavy load,
Crack my whip and the leader sprung;
I says day-day to the wagon tongue.
    Turkey in the straw, turkey in the hay,
    Roll 'em up and twist 'em up a high tuckahaw,
    And hit 'em up a tune called Turkey in the Straw.

Went out to milk and I didn't know how,
I milked the goat instead of the cow.
A monkey sittin' on a pile of straw
A-winkin' at his mother-in-law.
    Turkey in the straw, turkey in the hay,
    Roll 'em up and twist 'em up a high tuckahaw,
    And hit 'em up a tune called Turkey in the Straw.

Met Mr. Catfish comin' down stream,
Says Mr. Catfish, "What does you mean?"
Caught Mr. Catfish by the snout
And turned Mr. Catfish wrong side out.
    Turkey in the straw, turkey in the hay,
    Roll 'em up and twist 'em up a high tuckahaw,
    And hit 'em up a tune called Turkey in the Straw.

Came to the river and I couldn't get across
Paid five dollars for an old blind hoss
Wouldn't go ahead, nor he wouldn't stand still
So he went up and down like an old saw mill.
    Turkey in the straw, turkey in the hay,
    Roll 'em up and twist 'em up a high tuckahaw,
    And hit 'em up a tune called Turkey in the Straw.

As I came down the new cut road
Met Mr. Bullfrog, met Miss Toad
And every time Miss Toad would sing
Ole Bullfrog cut a pigeon wing.
    Turkey in the straw, turkey in the hay,
    Roll 'em up and twist 'em up a high tuckahaw,
    And hit 'em up a tune called Turkey in the Straw.

O I jumped in the seat, and I gave a little yell,
The horses run away, broke the wagon all to hell;
Sugar in the gourd and honey in the horn,
I never was so happy since the hour I was born.
    Turkey in the straw, turkey in the hay,
    Roll 'em up and twist 'em up a high tuckahaw,
    And hit 'em up a tune called Turkey in the Straw.

Listen to the Mocking Bird
(Septimus Winner, 1855)

When the charms of spring awaken, awaken, awaken,
When the charms of spring awaken,
And the mocking bird is singing on the bough,
I feel like one forsaken, forsaken, forsaken,
I feel like one forsaken,
Since my Hally is no longer with me now.

Listen to the mocking bird, listen to the mocking bird,
The mocking bird still singing o'er her grave
Listen to the mocking bird, listen to the mocking bird,
Still singing where the weeping willows wave.

I'm dreaming now of Hally, sweet Hally, sweet Hally;
I'm dreaming now of Hally,
For the thought of her is one that never dies
She's sleeping in the valley, the valley, the valley;
She's sleeping in the valley,
And the mocking bird is singing where she lies.

Ah well I yet remember, remember, remember;
Ah well I yet remember,
When we gathered in the cotton side by side;
'Twas in the mild September, September, September,
'Twas in the mild September,
And the mocking bird was singing far and wide.

Jingle Bells
(John Pierpont, 1857)

Dashing thro' the snow
In a one-horse open sleigh,
O'er the fields we go,
Laughing all the way;
Bells on bob-tail ring,
Making spirits bright;
What fun it is to ride and sing
A sleighing song tonight!

(Refrain)
Jingle Bells! Jingle Bells!
Jingle all the way!
Oh, what fun it is to ride
In an one-horse open sleigh!

Day or two ago
I thought I'd take a ride,
And soon Miss Fannie Bright
Was seated by my side;
The horse was lean and lank,
Misfortune seem'd his lot,
He got into a drifted bank,
And we, we got upsot.

Now the ground is white,
Go it while you're young;
Take the girls tonight,
And sing this sleighing song;
Just get a bob-tailed nag,
Two-forty for his speed,
Then hitch him to an open sleigh,
And crack! you'll take the lead.

The Yellow Rose of Texas
(Anonymous, 1858)

There's a yellow rose in Texas that I am going to see,
No other darkey knows her, no darkey only me;
She cried so when I left her, it like to broke my heart,
And if I ever find her we never more will part.

Chorus
    She's the sweetest rose of color this darkey ever knew,
    Her eyes are bright as diamonds, they sparkle like the dew,
    You may talk about your Dearest May, and sing of Rosa Lee,
    But the yellow rose of Texas beats the belles of Tennessee.

Where the Rio Grande is flowing, and the starry skies are bright,
She walks along the river in the quiet summer night;
She thinks if I remember when we parted long ago,
I promised to come back again, and not to leave her so.

(Chorus)
Oh, now I'm going to find her, for my heart is full of woe,
And we'll sing the song together, that we sung so long ago;
We'll play the banjo gaily, and we'll sing the songs of yore,
And the yellow rose of Texas shall be mine forevermore.

Sweet Betsey from Pike
(John A. Stone, 1858)

Oh, don't you remember sweet Betsey from Pike,
Who crossed the big mountains with her lover Ike,
With two yoke of cattle, a large yellow dog,
A tall shanghai rooster and one spotted hog.

Singing, goodbye, Pike County, farewell for awhile,
We'll come back again when we've panned out our pile,
Singing tooral lal, looral lal, looral lal lay,
Singing tooral lal, looral lal, looral lal lay.

One evening quite early they camped on the Platte,
'Twas near by the road on a green shady flat,
Where Betsey, sore-footed, lay down to repose,
While with wonder Ike gazed on his Pike County rose.

Their wagon broke down with a terrible crash,
And out on the prairie rolled all kinds of trash;
A few little baby clothes done up with great care—
'Twas rather suspicious, though all on the square.

The shanghai ran off and the cattle all died;
That morning the last piece of bacon was fried;
Poor Ike was discouraged, and Betsey got mad,
The dog drooped his tail and looked wondrously sad.

They stopped at Salt Lake to inquire the way,
When Brigham declared that sweet Betsey should stay;
But Betsey got frightened and ran like a deer,
While Brigham stood pawing the ground like a steer.

They soon reached the desert, where Betsey gave out,
And down in the sand she lay rolling about;
While Ike, half distracted, looked on with surprise,
Saying, "Betsey, get up, you'll get sand in your eyes."

Sweet Betsey got up in a great deal of pain,
Declared she'd go back to Pike County again;
But Ike gave a sigh, and they fondly embraced,
And they traveled along with his arm round her waist.

They suddenly stopped on a very high hill,
With wonder looked upon old Placerville;
Ike sighed when he said, and he cast his eyes down,
"Sweet Betsey, my darling, we've got to Hangtown."

Long Ike and Sweet Betsey attended a dance,
Ike wore a pair of his Pike County pants;
Sweet Betsey was covered with ribbons and rings;
Says Ike, "You're an angel, but where are your wings?"

A miner said, "Betsey, will you dance with me?"
"I will that, old hoss, if you don't make too free;
But don't dance me hard, do you want to know why?
Dog on you! I'm chock full of strong alkali!"

This Pike County couple got married, of course,
And Ike became jealous—obtained a divorce;
Sweet Betsey, well satisfied, said with a shout,
"Goodbye, you big lummox, I'm glad you've backed out!"

Stand Up, Stand Up for Jesus
(George Duffield, Jr., 1858)

"Stand up, stand up for Jesus!
    Ye soldiers of the cross;
Lift high his royal banner,
    It must not suffer loss.
From victory unto victory
    His army he shall lead,
Till every foe is vanquished
    And Christ is Lord indeed.

"Stand up, stand up for Jesus!
    The solemn watchword hear;
If while ye sleep he suffers,
    Away with shame and fear;
Where'er ye meet with evil,
    Within you or without,
Charge for the God of Battles,
    And put the foe to rout!

"Stand up, stand up for Jesus!
    The trumpet call obey;
Forth to the mighty conflict,
    In this his glorious day:
Ye that are men, now serve him,
    Against unnumbered foes;
Let courage rise with danger,
    And strength to strength oppose.

"Stand up, stand up for Jesus!
    Stand in his strength alone;
The arm of flesh will fail you,
    Ye dare not trust your own:
Put on the gospel armor,
    Each piece put on with prayer;

Where duty calls, or danger,
    Be never wanting there.

"Stand up, stand up for Jesus!
    Each soldier to his post;
Close up the broken column,
    And shout through all the host:
Make good the loss so heavy,
    In those that still remain,
And prove to all around you,
    That death itself is gain.

"Stand up, stand up for Jesus!
    The strife will not be long;
This day the noise of battle,
    The next the victor's song:
To him that overcometh,
    A crown of life shall be;
He with the King of glory
    Shall reign eternally."

IV

THE CIVIL WAR
ERA: 1860–1870

WALT WHITMAN
(1819–1892)

One's-Self I sing

One's-Self I sing, a simple separate person,
Yet utter the word Democratic, the word En-Masse.

Of physiology from top to toe I sing,
Not physiognomy alone nor brain alone is worthy for the Muse, I
    say the Form complete is worthier far,
The Female equally with the Male I sing.

Of Life immense in passion, pulse, and power,
Cheerful, for freest action form'd under the laws divine,
The Modern Man I sing.

To the States

To the States or any one of them, or any city of the States, *Resist
    much, obey little,*
Once unquestioning obedience, once fully enslaved,
Once fully enslaved, no nation, state, city of this earth, ever after-
    ward resumes its liberty.

The Ship Starting

Lo, the unbounded sea,
On its breast a ship starting, spreading all sails, carrying even her
    moonsails,
The pennant is flying aloft as she speeds she speeds so stately—
    below emulous waves press forward,
They surround the ship with shining curving motions and foam.

Song of Myself (1891–1892 ed.)

1
I celebrate myself, and sing myself,
And what I assume you shall assume,
For every atom belonging to me as good belongs to you.

I loafe and invite my soul,
I lean and loafe at my ease observing a spear of summer grass.
My tongue, every atom of my blood, form'd from this soil, this air,
Born here of parents born here from parents the same, and their
    parents the same,
I, now thirty-seven years old in perfect health begin,
Hoping to cease not till death.

Creeds and schools in abeyance,
Retiring back a while sufficed at what they are, but never forgotten,
I harbor for good or bad, I permit to speak at every hazard,
Nature without check with original energy.

2

Houses and rooms are full of perfumes, the shelves are crowded with
    perfumes,
I breathe the fragrance myself and know it and like it,
The distillation would intoxicate me also, but I shall not let it.

The atmosphere is not a perfume, it has no taste of the distillation, it
    is odorless,
It is for my mouth forever, I am in love with it,
I will go to the bank by the wood and become undisguised and
    naked,
I am mad for it to be in contact with me.
The smoke of my own breath,
Echoes, ripples, buzz'd whispers, love-root, silk-thread, crotch and
    vine,
My respiration and inspiration, the beating of my heart, the passing of
    blood and air through my lungs,
The sniff of green leaves and dry leaves, and of the shore and dark-
    color'd sea-rocks, and of hay in the barn,
The sound of the belch'd words of my voice loos'd to the eddies of
    the wind,
A few light kisses, a few embraces, a reaching around of arms,
The play of shine and shade on the trees as the supple boughs wag,
The delight alone or in the rush of the streets, or along the fields and
    hill-sides,
The feeling of health, the full-noon trill, the song of me rising from
    bed and meeting the sun.

Have you reckon'd a thousand acres much? have you reckon'd the
    earth much?
Have you practis'd so long to learn to read?
Have you felt so proud to get at the meaning of poems?

Stop this day and night with me and you shall possess the origin of all
poems,
You shall possess the good of the earth and sun, (there are millions of
suns left,)
You shall no longer take things at second or third hand, nor look
through the eyes of the dead, nor feed on the spectres in books,
You shall not look through my eyes either, nor take things from me,
You shall listen to all sides and filter them from your self.

3
I have heard what the talkers were talking, the talk of the beginning
and the end,
But I do not talk of the beginning or the end.

There was never any more inception than there is now,
Nor any more youth or age than there is now,
And will never be any more perfection than there is now,
Nor any more heaven or hell than there is now.

Urge and urge and urge,
Always the procreant urge of the world.

Out of the dimness opposite equals advance, always substance and
increase, always sex,
Always a knit of identity, always distinction, always a breed of life.

To elaborate is no avail, learn'd and unlearn'd feel that it is so.

Sure as the most certain sure, plumb in the uprights, well entretied,
braced in the beams,
Stout as a horse, affectionate, haughty, electrical,
I and this mystery here we stand.

Clear and sweet is my soul, and clear and sweet is all that is not my
soul.

Lack one lacks both, and the unseen is proved by the seen,
Till that becomes unseen and receives proof in its turn.

Showing the best and dividing it from the worst age vexes age,
Knowing the perfect fitness and equanimity of things, while they
discuss I am silent, and go bathe and admire myself.

Welcome is every organ and attribute of me, and of any man hearty
and clean,
Not an inch nor a particle of an inch is vile, and none shall be less
familiar than the rest.

I am satisfied—I see, dance, laugh, sing;

As the hugging and loving bed-fellow sleeps at my side through the
    night, and withdraws at the peep of the day with stealthy tread,

Leaving me baskets cover'd with white towels swelling the house with
    their plenty,

Shall I postpone my acceptation and realization and scream at my
    eyes,

That they turn from gazing after and down the road,

And forthwith cipher and show me to a cent,

Exactly the value of one and exactly the value of two, and which is
    ahead?

4

Trippers and askers surround me,

People I meet, the effect upon me of my early life or the ward and
    city I live in, or the nation,

The latest dates, discoveries, inventions, societies, authors old and
    new,

My dinner, dress, associates, looks, compliments, dues,

The real or fancied indifference of some man or woman I love,

The sickness of one of my folks or of myself, or ill-doing or loss or
    lack of money, or depressions or exaltations,

Battles, the horrors of fratricidal war, the fever of doubtful news, the
    fitful events;

These come to me days and nights and go from me again,

But they are not the Me myself.

Apart from the pulling and hauling stands what I am,

Stands amused, complacent, compassionating, idle, unitary,

Looks down, is erect, or bends an arm on an impalpable certain rest,

Looking with side-curved head curious what will come next,

Both in and out of the game and watching and wondering at it.

Backward I see in my own days where I sweated through fog with
    linguists and contenders,

I have no mockings or arguments, I witness and wait.

5

I believe in you my soul, the other I am must not abase itself to you,

And you must not be abased to the other.

Loafe with me on the grass, loose the stop from your throat,

Not words, not music or rhyme I want, not custom or lecture, not
    even the best,

Only the lull I like, the hum of your valvèd voice.

I mind how once we lay such a transparent summer morning,
How you settled your head athwart my hips and gently turn'd over
upon me,
And parted the shirt from my bosom-bone, and plunged your tongue
to my bare-stript heart,
And reach'd till you felt my beard, and reach'd till you held my feet.

Swiftly arose and spread around me the peace and knowledge that
pass all the argument of the earth,
And I know that the hand of God is the promise of my own,
And I know that the spirit of God is the brother of my own,
And that all the men ever born are also my brothers, and the women
my sisters and lovers,
And that a kelson of the creation is love,
And limitless are leaves stiff or drooping in the fields,
And brown ants in the little wells beneath them,
And mossy scabs of the worm fence, heap'd stones, elder, mullein and
poke-weed.

6
A child said *What is the grass?* fetching it to me with full hands;
How could I answer the child? I do not know what it is any more
than he.

I guess it must be the flag of my disposition, out of hopeful green
stuff woven.

Or I guess it is the handkerchief of the Lord,
A scented gift and remembrancer designedly dropt,
Bearing the owner's name someway in the corners, that we may see
and remark, and say *Whose?*
Or I guess the grass is itself a child, the produced babe of the
vegetation.

Or I guess it is a uniform hieroglyphic,
And it means, Sprouting alike in broad zones and narrow zones,
Growing among black folks as among white,
Kanuck, Tuckahoe, Congressman, Cuff, I give them the same, I
receive them the same.

And now it seems to me the beautiful uncut hair of graves.

Tenderly will I use you curling grass,
It may be you transpire from the breasts of young men,
It may be if I had known them I would have loved them,
It may be you are from old people, or from offspring taken soon out
    of their mothers' laps,
And here you are the mothers' laps.

This grass is very dark to be from the white heads of old mothers,
Darker than the colorless beards of old men,
Dark to come from under the faint red roofs of mouths.

O I perceive after all so many uttering tongues,
And I perceive they do not come from the roofs of mouths for
    nothing.

I wish I could translate the hints about the dead young men and
    women,
And the hints about old men and mothers, and the offspring taken
    soon out of their laps.

What do you think has become of the young and old men?
And what do you think has become of the women and children?

They are alive and well somewhere,
The smallest sprout shows there is really no death,
And if ever there was it led forward life, and does not wait at the end
    to arrest it,
And ceas'd the moment life appear'd.

All goes onward and outward, nothing collapses,
And to die is different from what any one supposed, and luckier.

7
Has any one supposed it lucky to be born?
I hasten to inform him or her it is just as lucky to die, and I know it.

I pass death with the dying and birth with the new-wash'd babe, and
    am not contain'd between my hat and boots,
And peruse manifold objects, no two alike and every one good,
The earth good and the stars good, and their adjuncts all good.

I am not an earth nor an adjunct of an earth,
I am the mate and companion of people, all just as immortal and
    fathomless as myself,
(They do not know how immortal, but I know.)

Every kind for itself and its own, for me mine male and female,
For me those that have been boys and that love women,
For me the man that is proud and feels how it stings to be slighted,
For me the sweet-heart and the old maid, for me mothers and the mothers of mothers,
For me lips that have smiled, eyes that have shed tears,
For me children and the begetters of children.

Undrape! you are not guilty to me, nor stale nor discarded,
I see through the broadcloth and gingham whether or no,
And am around, tenacious, acquisitive, tireless, and cannot be shaken away.

8
The little one sleeps in its cradle,
I lift the gauze and look a long time, and silently brush away flies with my hand.

The youngster and the red-faced girl turn aside up the busy hill,
I peeringly view them from the top.

The suicide sprawls on the bloody floor of the bedroom,
I witness the corpse with its dabbled hair, I note where the pistol has fallen.

The blab of the pave, tires of carts, sluff of boot-soles, talk of the promenaders,
The heavy omnibus, the driver with his interrogating thumb, the clank of the shod horses on the granite floor,
The snow-sleighs, clinking, shouted jokes, pelts of snow-balls,
The hurrahs for popular favorites, the fury of rous'd mobs,
The flap of the curtain'd litter, a sick man inside borne to the hospital,
The meeting of enemies, the sudden oath, the blows and fall,
The excited crowd, the policeman with his star quickly working his passage to the centre of the crowd,
The impassive stones that receive and return so many echoes,
What groans of over-fed or half-starv'd who fall sunstruck or in fits,
What exclamations of women taken suddenly who hurry home and give birth to babes,
What living and buried speech is always vibrating here, what howls restrain'd by decorum,
Arrests of criminals, slights, adulterous offers made, acceptances, rejections with convex lips,
I mind them or the show or resonance of them—I come and I depart.

9
The big doors of the country barn stand open and ready,
The dried grass of the harvest-time loads the slow-drawn wagon,
The clear light plays on the brown gray and green intertinged,
The armfuls are pack'd to the sagging mow.

I am there, I help, I came stretch'd atop of the load,
I felt its soft jolts, one leg reclined on the other,
I jump from the cross-beams and seize the clover and timothy,
And roll head over heels and tangle my hair full of wisps.

10
Alone far in the wilds and mountains I hunt,
Wandering amazed at my own lightness and glee,
In the late afternoon choosing a safe spot to pass the night,
Kindling a fire and broiling the fresh-kill'd game,
Falling asleep on the gather'd leaves with my dog and gun by my side.

The Yankee clipper is under her sky-sails, she cuts the sparkle and
    scud,
My eyes settle the land, I bend at her prow or shout joyously from the
    deck.

The boatmen and clam-diggers arose early and stopt for me,
I tuck'd my trowser-ends in my boots and went and had a good time;
You should have been with us that day round the chowder-kettle.

I saw the marriage of the trapper in the open air in the far west, the
    bride was a red girl,
Her father and his friends sat near cross-legged and dumbly smoking,
    they had moccasins to their feet and large thick blankets hanging
    from their shoulders,
On a bank lounged the trapper, he was drest mostly in skins, his
    luxuriant beard and curls protected his neck, he held his bride by
    the hand,
She had long eyelashes, her head was bare, her coarse straight locks
    descended upon her voluptuous limbs and reach'd to her feet.

The runaway slave came to my house and stopt outside,
I heard his motions crackling the twigs of the woodpile,
Through the swung half-door of the kitchen I saw him limpsy and
    weak,
And went where he sat on a log and led him in and assured him,
And brought water and fill'd a tub for his sweated body and bruis'd
    feet,
And gave him a room that enter'd from my own, and gave him some
    coarse clean clothes,

And remember perfectly well his revolving eyes and his awkwardness,
And remember putting plasters on the galls of his neck and ankles;
He staid with me a week before he was recuperated and pass'd north,
I had him sit next me at table, my fire-lock lean'd in the corner.

11

Twenty-eight young men bathe by the shore,
Twenty-eight young men and all so friendly;
Twenty-eight years of womanly life and all so lonesome.

She owns the fine house by the rise of the bank,
She hides handsome and richly drest aft the blinds of the window.

Which of the young men does she like the best?
Ah the homeliest of them is beautiful to her.

Where are you off to, lady? for I see you,
You splash in the water there, yet stay stock still in your room.

Dancing and laughing along the beach came the twenty-ninth bather,
The rest did not see her, but she saw them and loved them.

The beards of the young men glisten'd with wet, it ran from their
     long hair,
Little streams pass'd all over their bodies.

An unseen hand also pass'd over their bodies,
It descended tremblingly from their temples and ribs.

The young men float on their backs, their white bellies bulge to the
     sun, they do not ask who seizes fast to them,
They do not know who puffs and declines with pendant and bending
     arch,
They do not think whom they souse with spray.

12

The butcher-boy puts off his killing-clothes, or sharpens his knife at
     the stall in the market,
I loiter enjoying his repartee and his shuffle and break-down.

Blacksmiths with grimed and hairy chests environ the anvil,
Each has his main-sledge, they are all out, there is a great heat in the
     fire.

From the cinder-strew'd threshold I follow their movements,
The lithe sheer of their waists plays even with their massive arms,
Overhand the hammers swing, overhand so slow, overhand so sure,
They do not hasten, each man hits in his place.

13
The negro holds firmly the reins of his four horses, the block swags
    underneath on its tied-over chain,
The negro that drives the long dray of the stone-yard, steady and tall
    he stands pois'd on one leg on the string-piece,
His blue shirt exposes his ample neck and breast and loosens over his
    hip-band,
His glance is calm and commanding, he tosses the slouch of his hat
    away from his forehead,
The sun falls on his crispy hair and mustache, falls on the black of his
    polish'd and perfect limbs.

I behold the picturesque giant and love him, and I do not stop there,
I go with the team also.

In me the caresser of life wherever moving, backward as well as
    forward sluing,
To niches aside and junior bending, not a person or object missing,
Absorbing all to myself and for this song.

Oxen that rattle the yoke and chain or halt in the leafy shade, what is
    that you express in your eyes?
It seems to me more than all the print I have read in my life.

My tread scares the wood-drake and wood-duck on my distant and
    day-long ramble,
They rise together, they slowly circle around.

I believe in those wing'd purposes,
And acknowledge red, yellow, white, playing within me,
And consider green and violet and the tufted crown intentional,
And do not call the tortoise unworthy because she is not something
    else,
And the jay in the woods never studied the gamut, yet trills pretty
    well to me,
And the look of the bay mare shames silliness out of me.

14
The wild gander leads his flock through the cool night,
Ya-honk he says, and sounds it down to me like an invitation,
The pert may suppose it meaningless, but I listening close,
Find its purpose and place up there toward the wintry sky.

The sharp-hoof'd moose of the north, the cat on the house-sill, the
     chickadee, the prairie-dog,
The litter of the grunting sow as they tug at her teats,
The brood of the turkey-hen and she with her half-spread wings,
I see in them and myself the same old law.

The press of my foot to the earth springs a hundred affections,
They scorn the best I can do to relate them.

I am enamour'd of growing out-doors,
Of men that live among cattle or taste of the ocean or woods,
Of the builders and steerers of ships and the wielders of axes and
     mauls, and the drivers of horses,
I can eat and sleep with them week in and week out.

What is commonest, cheapest, nearest, easiest, is Me,
Me going in for my chances, spending for vast returns,
Adorning myself to bestow myself on the first that will take me,
Not asking the sky to come down to my good will,
Scattering it freely forever.

15
The pure contralto sings in the organ loft,
The carpenter dresses his plank, the tongue of his foreplane whistles
     its wild ascending lisp,
The married and unmarried children ride home to their Thanksgiving
     dinner,
The pilot seizes the king-pin, he heaves down with a strong arm,
The mate stands braced in the whale-boat, lance and harpoon are
     ready,
The duck-shooter walks by silent and cautious stretches,
The deacons are ordain'd with cross'd hands at the altar,
The spinning-girl retreats and advances to the hum of the big wheel,
The farmer stops by the bars as he walks on a First-day loafe and
     looks at the oats and rye,
The lunatic is carried at last to the asylum a confirm'd case,
(He will never sleep any more as he did in the cot in his mother's
     bed-room;)
The jour printer with gray head and gaunt jaws works at his case,
He turns his quid of tobacco while his eyes blurr with the manuscript;
The malform'd limbs are tied to the surgeon's table,
What is removed drops horribly in a pail;
The quadroon girl is sold at the auction-stand, the drunkard nods by
     the bar-room stove,
The machinist rolls up his sleeves, the policeman travels his beat, the
     gate-keeper marks who pass,

The young fellow drives the express-wagon, (I love him, though I do not know him;)

The half-breed straps on his light boots to compete in the race,

The western turkey-shooting draws old and young, some lean on their rifles, some sit on logs,

Out from the crowd steps the marksman, takes his position, levels his piece;

The groups of newly-come immigrants cover the wharf or levee,

As the woolly-pates hoe in the sugar-field, the overseer views them from his saddle,

The bugle calls in the ball-room, the gentlemen run for their partners, the dancers bow to each other,

The youth lies awake in the cedar-roof'd garret and harks to the musical rain,

The Wolverine sets traps on the creek that helps fill the Huron,

The squaw wrapt in her yellow-hemm'd cloth is offering moccasins and bead-bags for sale,

The connoisseur peers along the exhibition-gallery with half-shut eyes bent sideways,

As the deck-hands make fast the steamboat the plank is thrown for the shore-going passengers,

The young sister holds out the skein while the elder sister winds it off in a ball, and stops now and then for the knots,

The one-year wife is recovering and happy having a week ago borne her first child,

The clean-hair'd Yankee girl works with her sewing-machine or in the factory or mill,

The paving-man leans on his two-handed rammer, the reporter's lead flies swiftly over the note-book, the sign-painter is lettering with blue and gold,

The canal boy trots on the tow-path, the book-keeper counts at his desk, the shoemaker waxes his thread,

The conductor beats time for the band and all the performers follow him,

The child is baptized, the convert is making his first professions,

The regatta is spread on the bay, the race is begun, (how the white sails sparkle!)

The drover watching his drove sings out to them that would stray,

The pedler sweats with his pack on his back, (the purchaser higgling about the odd cent;)

The bride unrumples her white dress, the minute-hand of the clock moves slowly,

The opium-eater reclines with rigid head and just-open'd lips,

The prostitute draggles her shawl, her bonnet bobs on her tipsy and pimpled neck,

The crowd laugh at her blackguard oaths, the men jeer and wink to each other,

(Miserable! I do not laugh at your oaths nor jeer you;)
The President holding a cabinet council is surrounded by the great
    Secretaries,
On the piazza walk three matrons stately and friendly with twined
    arms,
The crew of the fish-smack pack repeated layers of halibut in the
    hold,
The Missourian crosses the plains toting his wares and his cattle,
As the fare-collector goes through the train he gives notice by the
    jingling of loose change,
The floor-men are laying the floor, the tinners are tinning the roof, the
    masons are calling for mortar,
In single file each shouldering his hod pass onward the laborers;
Seasons pursuing each other the indescribable crowd is gather'd, it is
    the fourth of Seventh-month, (what salutes of cannon and small
    arms!)
Seasons pursuing each other the plougher ploughs, the mower mows,
    and the winter-grain falls in the ground;
Off on the lakes the pike-fisher watches and waits by the hole in the
    frozen surface,
The stumps stand thick round the clearing, the squatter strikes deep
    with his axe,
Flatboatmen make fast towards dusk near the cotton-wood or pecan-
    trees,
Coon-seekers go through the regions of the Red river or through
    those drain'd by the Tennessee, or through those of the Arkansas,
Torches shine in the dark that hangs on the Chattahooche or
    Altamahaw,
Patriarchs sit at supper with sons and grandsons and great-grandsons
    around them,
In walls of adobie, in canvas tents, rest hunters and trappers after
    their day's sport,
The city sleeps and the country sleeps,
The living sleep for their time, the dead sleep for their time,
The old husband sleeps by his wife and the young husband sleeps by
    his wife;
And these tend inward to me, and I tend outward to them,
And such as it is to be of these more or less I am,
And of these one and all I weave the song of myself.

16
I am of old and young, of the foolish as much as the wise,
Regardless of others, ever regardful of others,
Maternal as well as paternal, a child as well as a man,
Stuff'd with the stuff that is coarse and stuff'd with the stuff that is
    fine,

One of the Nation of many nations, the smallest the same and the
    largest the same,
A Southerner soon as a Northerner, a planter nonchalant and
    hospitable down by the Oconee I live,
A Yankee bound my own way ready for trade, my joints the limberest
    joints on earth and the sternest joints on earth,
A Kentuckian walking the vale of the Elkhorn in my deer-skin
    leggings, a Louisianian or Georgian,
A boatman over lakes or bays or along coasts, a Hoosier, Badger,
    Buckeye;
At home on Kanadian snow-shoes or up in the bush, or with
    fishermen off Newfoundland,
At home in the fleet of ice-boats, sailing with the rest and tacking,
At home on the hills of Vermont or in the woods of Maine, or the
    Texan ranch,
Comrade of Californians, comrade of free North-Westerners, (loving
    their big proportions,)
Comrade of raftsmen and coalmen, comrade of all who shake hands
    and welcome to drink and meat,
A learner with the simplest, a teacher of the thoughtfullest,
A novice beginning yet experient of myriads of seasons,
Of every hue and caste am I, of every rank and religion,
A farmer, mechanic, artist, gentleman, sailor, quaker,
Prisoner, fancy-man, rowdy, lawyer, physician, priest.

I resist any thing better than my own diversity,
Breathe the air but leave plenty after me,
And am not stuck up, and am in my place.

(The moth and the fish-eggs are in their place,
The bright suns I see and the dark suns I cannot see are in their
    place,
The palpable is in its place and the impalpable is in its place.)

17
These are really the thoughts of all men in all ages and lands, they are
    not original with me,
If they are not yours as much as mine they are nothing, or next to
    nothing,
If they are not the riddle and the untying of the riddle they are
    nothing,
If they are not just as close as they are distant they are nothing.

This is the grass that grows wherever the land is and the water is,
This the common air that bathes the globe.

18
With music strong I come, with my cornets and my drums,
I play not marches for accepted victors only, I play marches for
    conquer'd and slain persons.

Have you heard that it was good to gain the day?
I also say it is good to fall, battles are lost in the same spirit in which
    they are won.

I beat and pound for the dead,
I blow through my embouchures my loudest and gayest for them.

Vivas to those who have fail'd!
And to those whose war-vessels sank in the sea!
And to those themselves who sank in the sea!
And to all generals that lost engagements, and all overcome heroes!
And the numberless unknown heroes equal to the greatest heroes
    known!

19
This is the meal equally set, this the meat for natural hunger,
It is for the wicked just the same as the righteous, I make
    appointments with all,
I will not have a single person slighted or left away,
The kept-woman, sponger, thief, are hereby invited,
The heavy-lipp'd slave is invited, the venerealee is invited;
There shall be no difference between them and the rest.

This is the press of a bashful hand, this the float and odor of hair,
This the touch of my lips to yours, this the murmur of yearning,
This the far-off depth and height reflecting my own face,
This the thoughtful merge of myself, and the outlet again.

Do you guess I have some intricate purpose?
Well I have, for the Fourth-month showers have, and the mica on the
    side of a rock has.

Do you take it I would astonish?
Does the daylight astonish? does the early redstart twittering through
    the woods?
Do I astonish more than they?

This hour I tell things in confidence,
I might not tell everybody, but I will tell you.

20

Who goes there? hankering, gross, mystical, nude;
How is it I extract strength from the beef I eat?

What is a man anyhow? what am I? what are you?

All I mark as my own you shall offset it with your own,
Else it were time lost listening to me.

I do not snivel that snivel the world over,
That months are vacuums and the ground but wallow and filth.

Whimpering and truckling fold with powders for invalids, conformity,
    goes to the fourth-remov'd,
I wear my hat as I please indoors or out.

Why should I pray? why should I venerate and be ceremonious?

Having pried through the strata, analyzed to a hair, counsel'd with
    doctors and calculated close,
I find no sweeter fat than sticks to my own bones.

In all people I see myself, none more and not one a barley-corn less,
And the good or bad I say of myself I say of them.

I know I am solid and sound,
To me the converging objects of the universe perpetually flow,
All are written to me, and I must get what the writing means.

I know I am deathless,
I know this orbit of mine cannot be swept by a carpenter's compass,
I know I shall not pass like a child's carlacue cut with a burnt stick at
    night.

I know I am august,
I do not trouble my spirit to vindicate itself or be understood,
I see that the elementary laws never apologize,
(I reckon I behave no prouder than the level I plant my house by,
    after all.)

I exist as I am, that is enough,
If no other in the world be aware I sit content,
And if each and all be aware I sit content.

One world is aware and by far the largest to me, and that is myself,
And whether I come to my own to-day or in ten thousand or ten
    million years,
I can cheerfully take it now, or with equal cheerfulness I can wait.

My foothold is tenon'd and mortis'd in granite,
I laugh at what you call dissolution,
And I know the amplitude of time.

21
I am the poet of the Body and I am the poet of the Soul,
The pleasures of heaven are with me and the pains of hell are with
    me,
The first I graft and increase upon myself, the latter I translate into a
    new tongue.

I am the poet of the woman the same as the man,
And I say it is as great to be a woman as to be a man,
And I say there is nothing greater than the mother of men.

I chant the chant of dilation or pride,
We have had ducking and deprecating about enough,
I show that size is only development.

Have you outstript the rest? are you the President?
It is a trifle, they will more than arrive there every one, and still pass
    on.

I am he that walks with the tender and growing night,
I call to the earth and sea half-held by the night.

Press close bare-bosom'd night—press close magnetic nourishing
    night!
Night of south winds—night of the large few stars!
Still nodding night—mad naked summer night.

Smile O voluptuous cool-breath'd earth!
Earth of the slumbering and liquid trees!
Earth of departed sunset—earth of the mountains misty-topt!
Earth of the vitreous pour of the full moon just tinged with blue!
Earth of shine and dark mottling the tide of the river!
Earth of the limpid gray of clouds brighter and clearer for my sake!
Far-swooping elbow'd earth—rich apple-blossom'd earth!
Smile, for your lover comes.

Prodigal, you have given me love—therefore I to you give love!
O unspeakable passionate love.

22

You sea! I resign myself to you also—I guess what you mean,
I behold from the beach your crooked inviting fingers,
I believe you refuse to go back without feeling of me,
We must have a turn together, I undress, hurry me out of sight of the
    land,
Cushion me soft, rock me in billowy drowse,
Dash me with amorous wet, I can repay you.

Sea of stretch'd ground-swells,
Sea breathing broad and convulsive breaths,
Sea of the brine of life and of unshovell'd yet always-ready graves,
Howler and scooper of storms, capricious and dainty sea,
I am integral with you, I too am of one phase and of all phases.

Partaker of influx and efflux I, extoller of hate and conciliation,
Extoller of amies and those that sleep in each others' arms.

I am he attesting sympathy,
(Shall I make my list of things in the house and skip the house that
    supports them?)

I am not the poet of goodness only, I do not decline to be the poet of
    wickedness also.

What blurt is this about virtue and about vice?
Evil propels me and reform of evil propels me, I stand indifferent,
My gait is no fault-finder's or rejecter's gait,
I moisten the roots of all that has grown.

Did you fear some scrofula out of the unflagging pregnancy?
Did you guess the celestial laws are yet to be work'd over and
    rectified?

I find one side a balance and the antipodal side a balance,
Soft doctrine as steady help as stable doctrine,
Thoughts and deeds of the present our rouse and early start.

This minute that comes to me over the past decillions,
There is no better than it and now.

What behaved well in the past or behaves well to-day is not such a
    wonder,
The wonder is always and always how there can be a mean man or an
    infidel.

23
Endless unfolding of words of ages!
And mine a word of the modern, the word En-Masse.

A word of the faith that never balks,
Here or henceforward it is all the same to me, I accept Time
  absolutely.

It alone is without flaw, it alone rounds and completes all,
That mystic baffling wonder alone completes all.

I accept Reality and dare not question it,
Materialism first and last imbuing.

Hurrah for positive science! long live exact demonstration!
Fetch stonecrop mixt with cedar and branches of lilac,
This is the lexicographer, this the chemist, this made a grammar of
  the old cartouches,
These mariners put the ship through dangerous unknown seas,
This is the geologist, this works with the scalpel, and this is a
  mathematician.

Gentlemen, to you the first honors always!
Your facts are useful, and yet they are not my dwelling,
I but enter by them to an area of my dwelling.

Less the reminders of properties told my words,
And more the reminders they of life untold, and of freedom and
  extrication,
And make short account of neuters and geldings, and favor men and
  women fully equipt,
And beat the gong of revolt, and stop with fugitives and them that
  plot and conspire.

24
Walt Whitman, a kosmos, of Manhattan the son,
Turbulent, fleshy, sensual, eating, drinking and breeding,
No sentimentalist, no stander above men and women or apart from
  them,
No more modest than immodest.

Unscrew the locks from the doors!
Unscrew the doors themselves from their jambs!

Whoever degrades another degrades me,
And whatever is done or said returns at last to me.

Through me the afflatus surging and surging, through me the current
  and index.

I speak the pass-word primeval, I give the sign of democracy,
By God! I will accept nothing which all cannot have their counterpart
  of on the same terms.

Through me many long dumb voices,
Voices of the interminable generations of prisoners and slaves,
Voices of the diseas'd and despairing and of thieves and dwarfs,
Voices of cycles of preparation and accretion,
And of the threads that connect the stars, and of wombs and of the
  father-stuff,
And of the rights of them the others are down upon,
Of the deform'd, trivial, flat, foolish, despised,
Fog in the air, beetles rolling balls of dung.

Through me forbidden voices,
Voices of sexes and lusts, voices veil'd and I remove the veil,
Voices indecent by me clarified and transfigur'd.

I do not press my fingers across my mouth,
I keep as delicate around the bowels as around the head and heart,
Copulation is no more rank to me than death is.

I believe in the flesh and the appetites,
Seeing, hearing, feeling, are miracles, and each part and tag of me is a
  miracle.

Divine am I inside and out, and I make holy whatever I touch or am
  touch'd from,
The scent of these arm-pits aroma finer than prayer,
This head more than churches, bibles, and all the creeds.

If I worship one thing more than another it shall be the spread of my
  own body, or any part of it,
Translucent mould of me it shall be you!
Shaded ledges and rests it shall be you!
Firm masculine colter it shall be you!
Whatever goes to the tilth of me it shall be you!
You my rich blood! your milky stream pale strippings of my life!
Breast that presses against other breasts it shall be you!
My brain it shall be your occult convolutions!
Root of wash'd sweet-flag! timorous pond-snipe! nest of guarded
  duplicate eggs! it shall be you!
Mix'd tussled hay of head, beard, brawn, it shall be you!
Trickling sap of maple, fibre of manly wheat, it shall be you!

Sun so generous it shall be you!
Vapors lighting and shading my face it shall be you!
You sweaty brooks and dews it shall be you!
Winds whose soft-tickling genitals rub against me it shall be you!
Broad muscular fields, branches of live oak, loving lounger in my
    winding paths, it shall be you!
Hands I have taken, face I have kiss'd, mortal I have ever touch'd, it
    shall be you.

I dote on myself, there is that lot of me and all so luscious,
Each moment and whatever happens thrills me with joy,
I cannot tell how my ankles bend, nor whence the cause of my
    faintest wish,
Nor the cause of the friendship I emit, nor the cause of the friendship
    I take again.

That I walk up my stoop, I pause to consider if it really be,
A morning-glory at my window satisfies me more than the metaphysics
    of books.

To behold the day-break!
The little light fades the immense and diaphanous shadows,
The air tastes good to my palate.

Hefts of the moving world at innocent gambols silently rising freshly
    exuding,
Scooting obliquely high and low.

Something I cannot see puts upward libidinous prongs,
Seas of bright juice suffuse heaven.

The earth by the sky staid with, the daily close of their junction,
The heav'd challenge from the east that moment over my head,
The mocking taunt, See then whether you shall be master!

25
Dazzling and tremendous how quick the sun-rise would kill me,
If I could not now and always send sun-rise out of me.

We also ascend dazzling and tremendous as the sun,
We found our own O my soul in the calm and cool of the daybreak.

My voice goes after what my eyes cannot reach,
With the twirl of my tongue I encompass worlds and volumes of
    worlds.

Speech is the twin of my vision, it is unequal to measure itself,
It provokes me forever, it says sarcastically,
Walt you contain enough, why don't you let it out then?

Come now I will not be tantalized, you conceive too much of
    articulation,
Do you not know O speech how the buds beneath you are folded?
Waiting in gloom, protected by frost,
The dirt receding before my prophetical screams,
I underlying causes to balance them at last,
My knowledge my live parts, it keeping tally with the meaning of all
    things,
Happiness, (which whoever hears me let him or her set out in search
    of this day.)

My final merit I refuse you, I refuse putting from me what I really am,
Encompass worlds, but never try to encompass me,
I crowd your sleekest and best by simply looking toward you.

Writing and talk do not prove me,
I carry the plenum of proof and every thing else in my face,
With the hush of my lips I wholly confound the skeptic.

26
Now I will do nothing but listen,
To accrue what I hear into this song, to let sounds contribute
    toward it.

I hear bravuras of birds, bustle of growing wheat, gossip of flames,
    clack of sticks cooking my meals,
I hear the sound I love, the sound of the human voice,
I hear all sounds running together, combined, fused or following,
Sounds of the city and sounds out of the city, sounds of the day and
    night,
Talkative young ones to those that like them, the loud laugh of work-
    people at their meals,
The angry base of disjointed friendship, the faint tones of the sick,
The judge with hands tight to the desk, his pallid lips pronouncing a
    death-sentence,
The heave'e'yo of stevedores unlading ships by the wharves, the
    refrain of the anchor-lifters,
The ring of alarm-bells, the cry of fire, the whirr of swift-streaking
    engines and hose-carts with premonitory tinkles and color'd lights,
The steam-whistle, the solid roll of the train of approaching cars,
The slow march play'd at the head of the association marching two
    and two,

(They go to guard some corpse, the flag-tops are draped with black
muslin.)

I hear the violoncello, ('tis the young man's heart's complaint,)
I hear the key'd cornet, it glides quickly in through my ears,
It shakes mad-sweet pangs through my belly and breast.

I hear the chorus, it is a grand opera,
Ah this indeed is music—this suits me.

A tenor large and fresh as the creation fills me,
The orbic flex of his mouth is pouring and filling me full.

I hear the train'd soprano (what work with hers is this?)
The orchestra whirls me wider than Uranus flies,
It wrenches such ardors from me I did not know I possess'd them,
It sails me, I dab with bare feet, they are lick'd by the indolent waves,
I am cut by bitter and angry hail, I lose my breath,
Steep'd amid honey'd morphine, my windpipe throttled in fakes of
death,
At length let up again to feel the puzzle of puzzles,
And that we call Being.

27
To be in any form, what is that?
(Round and round we go, all of us, and ever come back thither,)
If nothing lay more develop'd the quahaug in its callous shell were
enough.

Mine is no callous shell,
I have instant conductors all over me whether I pass or stop,
They seize every object and lead it harmlessly through me.

I merely stir, press, feel with my fingers, and am happy,
To touch my person to some one else's is about as much as I can
stand.

28
Is this then a touch? quivering me to a new identity,
Flames and ether making a rush for my veins,
Treacherous tip of me reaching and crowding to help them,
My flesh and blood playing out lightning to strike what is hardly
different from myself,
On all sides prurient provokers stiffening my limbs,
Straining the udder of my heart for its withheld drip,
Behaving licentious toward me, taking no denial,
Depriving me of my best as for a purpose,

Unbuttoning my clothes, holding me by the bare waist,
Deluding my confusion with the calm of the sunlight and pasture-
    fields,
Immodestly sliding the fellow-senses away,
They bribed to swap off with touch and go and graze at the edges of
    me,
No consideration, no regard for my draining strength or my anger,
Fetching the rest of the herd around to enjoy them a while,
Then all uniting to stand on a headland and worry me.

The sentries desert every other part of me,
They have left me helpless to a red marauder,
They all come to the headland to witness and assist against me.

I am given up by traitors,
I talk wildly, I have lost my wits, I and nobody else am the greatest
    traitor,
I went myself first to the headland, my own hands carried me there.

You villain touch! what are you doing? my breath is tight in its throat,
Unclench your floodgates, you are too much for me.

29
Blind loving wrestling touch, sheath'd hooded sharp-tooth'd touch!
Did it make you ache so, leaving me?

Parting track'd by arriving, perpetual payment of perpetual loan,
Rich showering rain, and recompense richer afterward.

Sprouts take and accumulate, stand by the curb prolific and vital,
Landscapes projected masculine, full-sized and golden.

30
All truths wait in all things,
They neither hasten their own delivery nor resist it,
They do not need the obstetric forceps of the surgeon,
The insignificant is as big to me as any,
(What is less or more than a touch?)

Logic and sermons never convince,
The damp of the night drives deeper into my soul.

(Only what proves itself to every man and woman is so,
Only what nobody denies is so.)

A minute and a drop of me settle my brain,
I believe the soggy clods shall become lovers and lamps,
And a compend of compends is the meat of a man or woman,
And a summit and flower there is the feeling they have for each other,
And they are to branch boundlessly out of that lesson until it becomes
    omnific,
And until one and all shall delight us, and we them.

31
I believe a leaf of grass is no less than the journey-work of the stars,
And the pismire is equally perfect, and a grain of sand, and the egg of
    the wren,
And the tree-toad is a chef-d'oeuvre for the highest,
And the running blackberry would adorn the parlors of heaven,
And the narrowest hinge in my hand puts to scorn all machinery,
And the cow crunching with depress'd head surpasses any statue,
And a mouse is miracle enough to stagger sextillions of infidels.

I find I incorporate gneiss, coal, long-threaded moss, fruits, grains,
    esculent roots,
And am stucco'd with quadrupeds and birds all over,
And have distanced what is behind me for good reasons,
But call any thing back again when I desire it.

In vain the speeding or shyness,
In vain the plutonic rocks send their old heat against my approach,
In vain the mastodon retreats beneath its own powder'd bones,
In vain objects stand leagues off and assume manifold shapes,
In vain the ocean settling in hollows and the great monsters lying low,
In vain the buzzard houses herself with the sky,
In vain the snake slides through the creepers and logs,
In vain the elk takes to the inner passes of the woods,
In vain the razor-bill'd auk sails far north to Labrador,
I follow quickly, I ascend to the nest in the fissure of the cliff.

32
I think I could turn and live with animals, they are so placid and self-
    contain'd,
I stand and look at them long and long.

They do not sweat and whine about their condition,
They do not lie awake in the dark and weep for their sins,
They do not make me sick discussing their duty to God,
Not one is dissatisfied, not one is demented with the mania of owning
    things,

Not one kneels to another, nor to his kind that lived thousands of
    years ago,
Not one is respectable or unhappy over the whole earth.

So they show their relations to me and I accept them,
They bring me tokens of myself, they evince them plainly in their
    possession.

I wonder where they get those tokens,
Did I pass that way huge times ago and negligently drop them?

Myself moving forward then and now and forever,
Gathering and showing more always and with velocity,
Infinite and omnigenous, and the like of these among them,
Not too exclusive toward the reachers of my remembrancers,
Picking out here one that I love, and now go with him on brotherly
    terms.

A gigantic beauty of a stallion, fresh and responsive to my caresses,
Head high in the forehead, wide between the ears,
Limbs glossy and supple, tail dusting the ground,
Eyes full of sparkling wickedness, ears finely cut, flexibly moving.

His nostrils dilate as my heels embrace him,
His well-built limbs tremble with pleasure as we race around and
    return.
I but use you a minute, then I resign you, stallion,
Why do I need your paces when I myself out-gallop them?
Even as I stand or sit passing faster than you.

33
Space and Time! now I see it is true, what I guess'd at,
What I guess'd when I loaf'd on the grass,
What I guess'd while I lay alone in my bed,
And again as I walk'd the beach under the paling stars of the
    morning.

My ties and ballasts leave me, my elbows rest in sea-gaps,
I skirt sierras, my palms cover continents,
I am afoot with my vision.

By the city's quadrangular houses—in log huts, camping with
    lumbermen,
Along the ruts of the turnpike, along the dry gulch and rivulet bed,
Weeding my onion-patch or hoeing rows of carrots and parsnips,
    crossing savannas, trailing in forests,
Prospecting, gold-digging, girdling the trees of a new purchase,

Scorch'd ankle-deep by the hot sand, hauling by boat down the
  shallow river,
Where the panther walks to and fro on a limb overhead, where the
  buck turns furiously at the hunter,
Where the rattlesnake suns his flabby length on a rock, where the
  otter is feeding on fish,
Where the alligator in his tough pimples sleeps by the bayou,
Where the black bear is searching for roots or honey, where the
  beaver pats the mud with his paddle-shaped tail;
Over the growing sugar, over the yellow-flower'd cotton plant, over
  the rice in its low moist field,
Over the sharp-peak'd farm house, with its scallop'd scum and slender
  shoots from the gutters,
Over the western persimmon, over the long-leav'd corn, over the
  delicate blue-flower flax,
Over the white and brown buckwheat, a hummer and buzzer there
  with the rest,
Over the dusky green of the rye as it ripples and shades in the breeze;
Scaling mountains, pulling myself cautiously up, holding on by low
  scragged limbs,
Walking the path worn in the grass and beat through the leaves of the
  brush,
Where the quail is whistling betwixt the woods and the wheat-lot,
Where the bat flies in the Seventh-month eve, where the great gold-
  bug drops through the dark,
Where the brook puts out of the roots of the old tree and flows to
  the meadow,
Where cattle stand and shake away flies with the tremulous
  shuddering of their hides,
Where the cheese-cloth hangs in the kitchen, where andirons straddle
  the hearth-slab, where cobwebs fall in festoons from the rafters;
Where trip-hammers crash, where the press is whirling its cylinders,
Wherever the human heart beats with terrible throes under its ribs,
Where the pear-shaped balloon is floating aloft, (floating in it myself
  and looking composedly down,)
Where the life-car is drawn on the slip-noose, where the heat hatches
  pale-green eggs in the dented sand,
Where the she-whale swims with her calf and never forsakes it,
Where the steam-ship trails hind-ways its long pennant of smoke,
Where the fin of the shark cuts like a black chip out of the water,
Where the half-burn'd brig is riding on unknown currents,
Where shells grow to her slimy deck, where the dead are corrupting
  below;
Where the dense-starr'd flag is borne at the head of the regiments,
Approaching Manhattan up by the long-stretching island,
Under Niagara, the cataract falling like a veil over my countenance,
Upon a door-step, upon the horse-block of hard wood outside,

Upon the race-course, or enjoying picnics or jigs or a good game of
   baseball,
At he-festivals, with blackguard gibes, ironical license, bull-dances,
   drinking, laughter,
At the cider-mill tasting the sweets of the brown mash, sucking the
   juice through a straw,
At apple-peelings wanting kisses for all the red fruit I find,
At musters, beach-parties, friendly bees, huskings, house-raisings;
Where the mocking-bird sounds his delicious gurgles, cackles,
   screams, weeps,
Where the hay-rick stands in the barn-yard, where the dry-stalks are
   scatter'd, where the brood-cow waits in the hovel,
Where the bull advances to do his masculine work, where the stud to
   the mare, where the cock is treading the hen,
Where the heifers browse, where geese nip their food with short jerks,
Where sun-down shadows lengthen over the limitless and lonesome
   prairie,
Where herds of buffalo make a crawling spread of the square miles
   far and near,
Where the humming-bird shimmers, where the neck of the long-lived
   swan is curving and winding,
Where the laughing-gull scoots by the shore, where she laughs her
   near-human laugh,
Where bee-hives range on a gray bench in the garden half hid by the
   high weeds,
Where band-neck'd partridges roost in a ring on the ground with
   their heads out,
Where burial coaches enter the arch'd gates of a cemetery,
Where winter wolves bark amid wastes of snow and icicled trees,
Where the yellow-crown'd heron comes to the edge of the marsh at
   night and feeds upon small crabs,
Where the splash of swimmers and divers cools the warm noon,
Where the katy-did works her chromatic reed on the walnut-tree over
   the well,
Through patches of citrons and cucumbers with silver-wired leaves,
Through the salt-lick or orange glade, or under conical firs,
Through the gymnasium, through the curtain'd saloon, through the
   office or public hall;
Pleas'd with the native and pleas'd with the foreign, pleas'd with the
   new and old,
Pleas'd with the homely woman as well as the handsome,
Pleas'd with the quakeress as she puts off her bonnet and talks
   melodiously,
Pleas'd with the tune of the choir of the whitewash'd church,
Pleas'd with the earnest words of the sweating Methodist preacher,
   impress'd seriously at the camp-meeting;

Looking in at the shop windows of Broadway the whole forenoon,
  flatting the flesh of my nose on the thick plate glass,
Wandering the same afternoon with my face turn'd up to the clouds,
  or down a lane or along the beach,
My right and left arms round the sides of two friends, and I in the
  middle;
Coming home with the silent and dark-cheek'd bush-boy, (behind me
  he rides at the drape of the day,)
Far from the settlements studying the print of animals' feet, or the
  moccasin print,
By the cot in the hospital reaching lemonade to a feverish patient,
Nigh the coffin'd corpse when all is still, examining with a candle;
Voyaging to every port to dicker and adventure,
Hurrying with the modern crowd as eager and fickle as any,
Hot toward one I hate, ready in my madness to knife him,
Solitary at midnight in my back yard, my thoughts gone from me a
  long while,
Walking the old hills of Judæa with the beautiful gentle God by my
  side,
Speeding through space, speeding through heaven and the stars,
Speeding amid the seven satellites and the broad ring, and the
  diameter of eighty thousand miles,
Speeding with tail'd meteors, throwing fire-balls like the rest,
Carrying the crescent child that carries its own full mother in its belly,
Storming, enjoying, planning, loving, cautioning,
Backing and filling, appearing and disappearing,
I tread day and night such roads.

I visit the orchards of spheres and look at the product,
And look at quintillions ripen'd and look at quintillions green.

I fly those flights of a fluid and swallowing soul,
My course runs below the soundings of plummets.

I help myself to material and immaterial,
No guard can shut me off, no law prevent me.

I anchor my ship for a little while only,
My messengers continually cruise away or bring their returns to me.

I go hunting polar furs and the seal, leaping chasms with a pike-
  pointed staff, clinging to topples of brittle and blue.

I ascend to the foretruck,
I take my place late at night in the crow's-nest,
We sail the arctic sea, it is plenty light enough,
Through the clear atmosphere I stretch around on the wonderful
  beauty,
The enormous masses of ice pass me and I pass them, the scenery is
  plain in all directions,
The white-topt mountains show in the distance, I fling out my fancies
  toward them,
We are approaching some great battle-field in which we are soon to
  be engaged,
We pass the colossal outposts of the encampment, we pass with still
  feet and caution,
Or we are entering by the suburbs some vast and ruin'd city,
The blocks and fallen architecture more than all the living cities of the
  globe.

I am a free companion, I bivouac by invading watchfires,
I turn the bridegroom out of bed and stay with the bride myself,
I tighten her all night to my thighs and lips.

My voice is the wife's voice, the screech by the rail of the stairs,
They fetch my man's body up dripping and drown'd.

I understand the large hearts of heroes,
The courage of present times and all times,
How the skipper saw the crowded and rudderless wreck of the steam-
  ship, and Death chasing it up and down the storm,
How he knuckled tight and gave not back an inch, and was faithful of
  days and faithful of nights,
And chalk'd in large letters on a board, *Be of good cheer, we will not
  desert you;*
How he follow'd with them and tack'd with them three days and
  would not give it up,
How he saved the drifting company at last,
How the lank loose-gown'd women look'd when boated from the side
  of their prepared graves,
How the silent old-faced infants and the lifted sick, and the sharp-
  lipp'd unshaved men;
All this I swallow, it tastes good, I like it well, it becomes mine,
I am the man, I suffer'd, I was there.

The disdain and calmness of martyrs,
The mother of old, condemn'd for a witch, burnt with dry wood, her
  children gazing on,
The hounded slave that flags in the race, leans by the fence, blowing,
  cover'd with sweat,

The twinges that sting like needles his legs and neck, the murderous
    buckshot and the bullets,
All these I feel or am.

I am the hounded slave, I wince at the bite of the dogs,
Hell and despair are upon me, crack and again crack the marksmen,
I clutch the rails of the fence, my gore dribs, thinn'd with the ooze of
    my skin,
I fall on the weeds and stones,
The riders spur their unwilling horses, haul close,
Taunt my dizzy ears and beat me violently over the head with whip-
    stocks.

Agonies are one of my changes of garments,
I do not ask the wounded person how he feels, I myself become the
    wounded person,
My hurts turn livid upon me as I lean on a cane and observe.

I am the mash'd fireman with breast-bone broken,
Tumbling walls buried me in their debris,
Heat and smoke I inspired, I heard the yelling shouts of my
    comrades,
I heard the distant click of their picks and shovels,
They have clear'd the beams away, they tenderly lift me forth.

I lie in the night air in my red shirt, the pervading hush is for my
    sake,
Painless after all I lie exhausted but not so unhappy,
White and beautiful are the faces around me, the heads are bared of
    their fire-caps,
The kneeling crowd fades with the light of the torches.

Distant and dead resuscitate,
They show as the dial or move as the hands of me, I am the clock
    myself.

I am an old artillerist, I tell of my fort's bombardment,
I am there again.

Again the long roll of the drummers,
Again the attacking cannon, mortars,
Again to my listening ears the cannon responsive.

I take part, I see and hear the whole,
The cries, curses, roar, the plaudits for well-aim'd shots,
The ambulanza slowly passing trailing its red drip,
Workmen searching after damages, making indispensable repairs,
The fall of grenades through the rent roof, the fan-shaped explosion,
The whizz of limbs, heads, stone, wood, iron, high in the air.

Again gurgles the mouth of my dying general, he furiously waves with
    his hand,
He gasps through the clot *Mind not me—mind—the entrenchments.*

34
Now I tell what I knew in Texas in my early youth,
(I tell not the fall of Alamo,
Not one escaped to tell the fall of Alamo,
The hundred and fifty are dumb yet at Alamo,)
'Tis the tale of the murder in cold blood of four hundred and twelve
    young men.

Retreating they had form'd in a hollow square with their baggage for
    breastworks,
Nine hundred lives out of the surrounding enemy's, nine times their
    number, was the price they took in advance,
Their colonel was wounded and their ammunition gone,
They treated for an honorable capitulation, receiv'd writing and seal,
    gave up their arms and march'd back prisoners of war.

They were the glory of the race of rangers,
Matchless with horse, rifle, song, supper, courtship,
Large, turbulent, generous, handsome, proud, and affectionate,
Bearded, sunburnt, drest in the free costume of hunters,
Not a single one over thirty years of age.

The second First-day morning they were brought out in squads and
    massacred, it was beautiful early summer,
The work commenced about five o'clock and was over by eight.

None obey'd the command to kneel,
Some made a mad and helpless rush, some stood stark and straight,
A few fell at once, shot in the temple or heart, the living and dead lay
    together,
The maim'd and mangled dug in the dirt, the new-comers saw them
    there,
Some half-kill'd attempted to crawl away,
These were despatch'd with bayonets or batter'd with the blunts of
    muskets,

A youth not seventeen years old seiz'd his assassin till two more came
    to release him,
The three were all torn and cover'd with the boy's blood.

At eleven o'clock began the burning of the bodies;
That is the tale of the murder of the four hundred and twelve young
    men.

35
Would you hear of an old-time sea-fight?
Would you learn who won by the light of the moon and stars?
List to the yarn, as my grandmother's father the sailor told it to me.

Our foe was no skulk in his ship I tell you, (said he,)
His was the surly English pluck, and there is no tougher or truer, and
    never was, and never will be;
Along the lower'd eve he came horribly raking us.

We closed with him, the yards entangled, the cannon touch'd,
My captain lash'd fast with his own hands.

We had receiv'd some eighteen pound shots under the water,
On our lower-gun-deck two large pieces had burst at the first fire,
    killing all around and blowing up overhead.

Fighting at sun-down, fighting at dark,
Ten o'clock at night, the full moon well up, our leaks on the gain, and
    five feet of water reported,
The master-at-arms loosing the prisoners confined in the after-hold to
    give them a chance for themselves.

The transit to and from the magazine is now stopt by the sentinels,
They see so many strange faces they do not know whom to trust.

Our frigate takes fire,
The other asks if we demand quarter?
If our colors are struck and the fighting done?

Now I laugh content, for I hear the voice of my little captain,
We have not struck, he composedly cries, *we have just begun our part
of the fighting.*

Only three guns are in use,
One is directed by the captain himself against the enemy's main-mast,
Two well serv'd with grape and canister silence his musketry and clear
    his decks.

The tops alone second the fire of this little battery, especially the
    main-top,
They hold out bravely during the whole of the action.

Not a moment's cease,
The leaks gain fast on the pumps, the fire eats toward the powder-
    magazine.

One of the pumps has been shot away, it is generally thought we are
    sinking.

Serene stands the little captain,
He is not hurried, his voice is neither high nor low,
His eyes give more light to us than our battle-lanterns.

Toward twelve there in the beams of the moon they surrender to us.

36
Stretch'd and still lies the midnight,
Two great hulls motionless on the breast of the darkness,
Our vessel riddled and slowly sinking, preparations to pass to the one
    we have conquer'd,
The captain on the quarter-deck coldly giving his orders through a
    countenance white as a sheet,
Near by the corpse of the child that serv'd in the cabin,
The dead face of an old salt with long white hair and carefully curl'd
    whiskers,
The flames spite of all that can be done flickering aloft and below,
The husky voices of the two or three officers yet fit for duty,
Formless stacks of bodies and bodies by themselves, dabs of flesh
    upon the masts and spars,
Cut of cordage, dangle of rigging, slight shock of the soothe of waves,
Black and impassive guns, litter of powder-parcels, strong scent,
A few large stars overhead, silent and mournful shining,
Delicate sniffs of sea-breeze, smells of sedgy grass and fields by the
    shore, death-messages given in charge to survivors,
The hiss of the surgeon's knife, the gnawing teeth of his saw,
Wheeze, cluck, swash of falling blood, short wild scream, and long,
    dull, tapering groan,
These so, these irretrievable.

37
You laggards there on guard! look to your arms!
In at the conquer'd doors they crowd! I am possess'd!
Embody all presences outlaw'd or suffering,
See myself in prison shaped like another man,
And feel the dull unintermitted pain.

For me the keepers of convicts shoulder their carbines and keep
  watch,
It is I let out in the morning and barr'd at night.

Not a mutineer walks handcuff'd to jail but I am handcuff'd to him
  and walk by his side,
(I am less the jolly one there, and more the silent one with sweat on
  my twitching lips.)

Not a youngster is taken for larceny but I go up too, and am tried
  and sentenced.
Not a cholera patient lies at the last gasp but I also lie at the last
  gasp,
My face is ash-color'd, my sinews gnarl, away from me people retreat.

Askers embody themselves in me and I am embodied in them,
I project my hat, sit shame-faced, and beg.

38
Enough! enough! enough!
Somehow I have been stunn'd. Stand back!
Give me a little time beyond my cuff'd head, slumbers, dreams,
  gaping,
I discover myself on the verge of a usual mistake.

That I could forget the mockers and insults!
That I could forget the trickling tears and the blows of the bludgeons
  and hammers!
That I could look with a separate look on my own crucifixion and
  bloody crowning.

I remember now,
I resume the overstaid fraction,
The grave of rock multiplies what has been confided to it, or to any
  graves,
Corpses rise, gashes heal, fastenings roll from me.

I troop forth replenish'd with supreme power, one of an average
  unending procession,
Inland and sea-coast we go, and pass all boundary lines,
Our swift ordinances on their way over the whole earth,
The blossoms we wear in our hats the growth of thousands of years.

Eleves, I salute you! come forward!
Continue your annotations, continue your questionings.

39
The friendly and flowing savage, who is he?
Is he waiting for civilization, or past it and mastering it?

Is he some Southwesterner rais'd out-doors? is he Kanadian?
Is he from the Mississippi country? Iowa, Oregon, California?
The mountains? prairie-life, bush-life? or sailor from the sea?

Wherever he goes men and women accept and desire him,
They desire he should like them, touch them, speak to them, stay with
    them.

Behavior lawless as snow-flakes, words simple as grass, uncomb'd
    head, laughter, and naiveté,
Slow-stepping feet, common features, common modes and emanations,
They descend in new forms from the tips of his fingers,
They are wafted with the odor of his body or breath, they fly out of
    the glance of his eyes.

40
Flaunt of the sunshine I need not your bask—lie over!
You light surfaces only, I force surfaces and depths also.

Earth! you seem to look for something at my hands,
Say, old top-knot, what do you want?

Man or woman, I might tell how I like you, but cannot,
And might tell what it is in me and what it is in you, but cannot,
And might tell that pining I have, that pulse of my nights and days.

Behold, I do not give lectures or a little charity,
When I give I give myself.

You there, impotent, loose in the knees,
Open your scarf'd chops till I blow grit within you,
Spread your palms and lift the flaps of your pockets,
I am not to be denied, I compel, I have stores plenty and to spare,
And any thing I have I bestow.

I do not ask who you are, that is not important to me,
You can do nothing and be nothing but what I will infold you.

To cotton-field drudge or cleaner of privies I lean,
On his right cheek I put the family kiss,
And in my soul I swear I never will deny him.

On women fit for conception I start bigger and nimbler babes,
(This day I am jetting the stuff of far more arrogant republics.)

To any one dying, thither I speed and twist the knob of the door,
Turn the bed-clothes toward the foot of the bed,
Let the physician and the priest go home.

I seize the descending man and raise him with resistless will,
O despairer, here is my neck,
By God, you shall not go down! hang your whole weight upon me.

I dilate you with tremendous breath, I buoy you up,
Every room of the house do I fill with an arm'd force,
Lovers of me, bafflers of graves.

Sleep—I and they keep guard all night,
Not doubt, not decease shall dare to lay finger upon you,
I have embraced you, and henceforth possess you to myself,
And when you rise in the morning you will find what I tell you is so.

41
I am he bringing help for the sick as they pant on their backs,
And for strong upright men I bring yet more needed help.

I heard what was said of the universe,
Heard it and heard it of several thousand years;
It is middling well as far as it goes—but is that all?

Magnifying and applying come I,
Outbidding at the start the old cautious hucksters,
Taking myself the exact dimensions of Jehovah,
Lithographing Kronos, Zeus his son, and Hercules his grandson,
Buying drafts of Osiris, Isis, Belus, Brahma, Buddha,
In my portfolio placing Manito loose, Allah on a leaf, the crucifix
    engraved,
With Odin and the hideous-faced Mexitli and every idol and image,
Taking them all for what they are worth and not a cent more,
Admitting they were alive and did the work of their days,
(They bore mites as for unfledg'd birds who have now to rise and fly
    and sing for themselves,)
Accepting the rough deific sketches to fill out better in myself,
    bestowing them freely on each man and woman I see,
Discovering as much or more in a framer framing a house,
Putting higher claims for him there with his roll'd-up sleeves driving
    the mallet and chisel,
Not objecting to special revelations, considering a curl of smoke or a
    hair on the back of my hand just as curious as any revelation,

Lads ahold of fire-engines and hook-and-ladder ropes no less to me
  than the gods of the antique wars,
Minding their voices peal through the crash of destruction,
Their brawny limbs passing safe over charr'd laths, their white
  foreheads whole and unhurt out of the flames;
By the mechanic's wife with her babe at her nipple interceding for
  every person born,
Three scythes at harvest whizzing in a row from three lusty angels
  with shirts bagg'd out at their waists,
The snag-tooth'd hostler with red hair redeeming sins past and to
  come,
Selling all he possesses, traveling on foot to fee lawyers for his brother
  and sit by him while he is tried for forgery;
What was strewn in the amplest strewing the square rod about me,
  and not filling the square rod then,
The bull and the bug never worshipp'd half enough,
Dung and dirt more admirable than was dream'd,
The supernatural of no account, myself waiting my time to be one of
  the supremes,
The day getting ready for me when I shall do as much good as the
  best, and be as prodigious;
By my life-lumps! becoming already a creator,
Putting myself here and now to the ambush'd womb of the shadows.

42
A call in the midst of the crowd,
My own voice, orotund sweeping and final.

Come my children,
Come my boys and girls, my women, household and intimates,
Now the performer launches his nerve, he has pass'd his prelude on
  the reeds within.

Easily written loose-finger'd chords—I feel the thrum of your climax
  and close.

My head slues round on my neck,
Music rolls, but not from the organ,
Folks are around me, but they are no household of mine.

Ever the hard unsunk ground,
Ever the eaters and drinkers, ever the upward and downward sun,
  ever the air and the ceaseless tides,
Ever myself and my neighbors, refreshing, wicked, real,
Ever the old inexplicable query, ever that thorn'd thumb, that breath
  of itches and thirsts,

Ever the vexer's *hoot! hoot!* till we find where the sly one hides and
    bring him forth,
Ever love, ever the sobbing liquid of life,
Ever the bandage under the chin, ever the trestles of death.

Here and there with dimes on the eyes walking,
To feed the greed of the belly the brains liberally spooning,
Tickets buying, taking, selling, but in to the feast never once going,
Many sweating, ploughing, thrashing, and then the chaff for payment
    receiving,
A few idly owning, and they the wheat continually claiming.

This is the city and I am one of the citizens,
Whatever interests the rest interests me, politics, wars, markets,
    newspapers, schools,
The mayor and councils, banks, tariffs, steamships, factories, stocks,
    stores, real estate and personal estate.

The little plentiful manikins skipping around in collars and tail'd
    coats,
I am aware who they are, (they are positively not worms or fleas,)
I acknowledge the duplicates of myself, the weakest and shallowest is
    deathless with me,
What I do and say the same waits for them,
Every thought that flounders in me the same flounders in them.

I know perfectly well my own egotism,
Know my omnivorous lines and must not write any less,
And would fetch you whoever you are flush with myself.

Not words of routine this song of mine,
But abruptly to question, to leap beyond yet nearer bring;
This printed and bound book—but the printer and the printing-office
    boy?
The well-taken photographs—but your wife or friend close and solid
    in your arms?
The black ship mail'd with iron, her mighty guns in her turrets—but
    the pluck of the captain and engineers?
In the houses the dishes and fare and furniture—but the host and
    hostess, and the look out of their eyes?
The sky up there—yet here or next door, or across the way?
The saints and sages in history—but you yourself?
Sermons, creeds, theology—but the fathomless human brain,
And what is reason? and what is love? and what is life?

43
I do not despise you priests, all time, the world over,
My faith is the greatest of faiths and the least of faiths,
Enclosing worship ancient and modern and all between ancient and
   modern,
Believing I shall come again upon the earth after five thousand years,
Waiting responses from oracles, honoring the gods, saluting the sun,
Making a fetich of the first rock or stump, powowing with sticks in
   the circle of obis,
Helping the llama or brahmin as he trims the lamps of the idols,
Dancing yet through the streets in a phallic procession, rapt and
   austere in the woods a gymnosophist,
Drinking mead from the skull-cup, to Shastas and Vedas admirant,
   minding the Koran,
Walking the teokallis, spotted with gore from the stone and knife,
   beating the serpent-skin drum,
Accepting the Gospels, accepting him that was crucified, knowing
   assuredly that he is divine,
To the mass kneeling or the puritan's prayer rising, or sitting patiently
   in a pew,
Ranting and frothing in my insane crisis, or waiting dead-like till my
   spirit arouses me,
Looking forth on pavement and land, or outside of pavement and
   land,
Belonging to the winders of the circuit of circuits.

One of that centripetal and centrifugal gang I turn and talk like a man
   leaving charges before a journey.

Down-hearted doubters dull and excluded,
Frivolous, sullen, moping, angry, affected, dishearten'd, atheistical,
I know every one of you, I know the sea of torment, doubt, despair
   and unbelief.

How the flukes splash!
How they contort rapid as lightning, with spasms and spouts of
   blood!

Be at peace bloody flukes of doubters and sullen mopers,
I take my place among you as much as among any,
The past is the push of you, me, all, precisely the same,
And what is yet untried and afterward is for you, me, all, precisely the
   same.

I do not know what is untried and afterward,
But I know it will in its turn prove sufficient, and cannot fail.

Each who passes is consider'd, each who stops is consider'd, not a
single one can it fail.

It cannot fail the young man who died and was buried,
Nor the young woman who died and was put by his side,
Nor the little child that peep'd in at the door, and then drew back
and was never seen again,
Nor the old man who has lived without purpose, and feels it with
bitterness worse than gall,
Nor him in the poor house tubercled by rum and the bad disorder,
Nor the numberless slaughter'd and wreck'd, nor the brutish koboo
call'd the ordure of humanity,
Nor the sacs merely floating with open mouths for food to slip in,
Nor any thing in the earth, or down in the oldest graves of the earth,
Nor any thing in the myriads of spheres, nor the myriads of myriads
that inhabit them,
Nor the present, nor the least wisp that is known.

44
It is time to explain myself—let us stand up.

What is known I strip away,
I launch all men and women forward with me into the Unknown.

The clock indicates the moment—but what does eternity indicate?

We have thus far exhausted trillions of winters and summers,
There are trillions ahead, and trillions ahead of them.

Births have brought us richness and variety,
And other births will bring us richness and variety.

I do not call one greater and one smaller,
That which fills its period and place is equal to any.

Were mankind murderous or jealous upon you, my brother, my sister?
I am sorry for you, they are not murderous or jealous upon me,
All has been gentle with me, I keep no account with lamentation,
(What have I to do with lamentation?)

I am an acme of things accomplish'd, and I am encloser of things to
be.

My feet strike an apex of the apices of the stairs,
On every step bunches of ages, and larger bunches between the steps,
All below duly travel'd, and still I mount and mount.

Rise after rise bow the phantoms behind me,
Afar down I see the huge first Nothing, I know I was even there,
I waited unseen and always, and slept through the lethargic mist,
And took my time, and took no hurt from the fetid carbon.

Long I was hugg'd close—long and long.

Immense have been the preparations for me,
Faithful and friendly the arms that have help'd me.

Cycles ferried my cradle, rowing and rowing like cheerful boatmen,
For room to me stars kept aside in their own rings,
They sent influences to look after what was to hold me.

Before I was born out of my mother generations guided me,
My embryo has never been torpid, nothing could overlay it.

For it the nebula cohered to an orb,
The long slow strata piled to rest it on,
Vast vegetables gave it sustenance,
Monstrous sauroids transported it in their mouths and deposited it
    with care.

All forces have been steadily employ'd to complete and delight me,
Now on this spot I stand with my robust soul.

45
O span of youth! ever-push'd elasticity!
O manhood, balanced, florid and full.

My lovers suffocate me,
Crowding my lips, thick in the pores of my skin,
Jostling me through streets and public halls, coming naked to me at
    night,
Crying by day *Ahoy!* from the rocks of the river, swinging and
    chirping over my head,
Calling my name from flower-beds, vines, tangled underbrush,
Lighting on every moment of my life,
Bussing my body with soft balsamic busses,
Noiselessly passing handfuls out of their hearts and giving them to be
    mine.

Old age superbly rising! O welcome, ineffable grace of dying days!

Every condition promulges not only itself, it promulges what grows
    after and out of itself,
And the dark hush promulges as much as any.

I open my scuttle at night and see the far-sprinkled systems,
And all I see multiplied as high as I can cipher edge but the rim of
    the farther systems.

Wider and wider they spread, expanding, always expanding,
Outward and outward and forever outward.

My sun has his sun and round him obediently wheels,
He joins with his partners a group of superior circuit,
And greater sets follow, making specks of the greatest inside them.

There is no stoppage and never can be stoppage,
If I, you, and the worlds, and all beneath or upon their surfaces, were
    this moment reduced back to a pallid float, it would not avail in
    the long run,
We should surely bring up again where we now stand,
And surely go as much farther, and then farther and farther.

A few quadrillions of eras, a few octillions of cubic leagues, do not
    hazard the span or make it impatient,
They are but parts, any thing is but a part.

See ever so far, there is limitless space outside of that,
Count ever so much, there is limitless time around that.

My rendezvous is appointed, it is certain,
The Lord will be there and wait till I come on perfect terms,
The great Camerado, the lover true for whom I pine will be there.

46
I know I have the best of time and space, and was never measured
    and never will be measured.

I tramp a perpetual journey, (come listen all!)
My signs are a rain-proof coat, good shoes, and a staff cut from the
    woods,
No friend of mine takes his ease in my chair,
I have no chair, no church, no philosophy,
I lead no man to a dinner-table, library, exchange,
But each man and each woman of you I lead upon a knoll,
My left hand hooking you round the waist,
My right hand pointing to landscapes of continents and the public
    road.

Not I, not any one else can travel that road for you,
You must travel it for yourself.

It is not far, it is within reach,
Perhaps you have been on it since you were born and did not know,
Perhaps it is everywhere on water and on land.

Shoulder your duds dear son, and I will mine, and let us hasten forth,
Wonderful cities and free nations we shall fetch as we go.

If you tire, give me both burdens, and rest the chuff of your hand on
    my hip,
And in due time you shall repay the same service to me,
For after we start we never lie by again.

This day before dawn I ascended a hill and look'd at the crowded
    heaven,
And I said to my spirit *When we become the enfolders of those orbs,
    and the pleasure and knowledge of every thing in them, shall we be
    fill'd and satisfied then?*
And my spirit said *No, we but level that lift to pass and continue
    beyond.*

You are also asking me questions and I hear you,
I answer that I cannot answer, you must find out for yourself.

Sit a while dear son,
Here are biscuits to eat and here is milk to drink,
But as soon as you sleep and renew yourself in sweet clothes, I kiss
    you with a good-by kiss and open the gate for your egress hence.

Long enough have you dream'd contemptible dreams,
Now I wash the gum from your eyes,
You must habit yourself to the dazzle of the light and of every
    moment of your life.

Long have you timidly waded holding a plank by the shore,
Now I will you to be a bold swimmer,
To jump off in the midst of the sea, rise again, nod to me, shout, and
    laughingly dash with your hair.

47
I am the teacher of athletes,
He that by me spreads a wider breast than my own proves the width
    of my own,
He most honors my style who learns under it to destroy the teacher.

286

The boy I love, the same becomes a man not through derived power,
    but in his own right,
Wicked rather than virtuous out of conformity or fear,
Fond of his sweetheart, relishing well his steak,
Unrequited love or a slight cutting him worse than sharp steel cuts,
First-rate to ride, to fight, to hit the bull's eye, to sail a skiff, to sing a
    song or play on the banjo,
Preferring scars and the beard and faces pitted with small-pox over all
    latherers,
And those well-tann'd to those that keep out of the sun.

I teach straying from me, yet who can stray from me?
I follow you whoever you are from the present hour,
My words itch at your ears till you understand them.

I do not say these things for a dollar or to fill up the time while I wait
    for a boat,
(It is you talking just as much as myself, I act as the tongue of you,
Tied in your mouth, in mine it begins to be loosen'd.)

I swear I will never again mention love or death inside a house,
And I swear I will never translate myself at all, only to him or her
    who privately stays with me in the open air.

If you would understand me go to the heights or water-shore,
The nearest gnat is an explanation, and a drop or motion of waves a
    key,
The maul, the oar, the hand-saw, second my words.

No shutter'd room or school can commune with me,
But roughs and little children better than they.

The young mechanic is closest to me, he knows me well,
The woodman that takes his axe and jug with him shall take me with
    him all day,
The farm-boy ploughing in the field feels good at the sound of my
    voice,
In vessels that sail my words sail, I go with fishermen and seamen and
    love them.

The soldier camp'd or upon the march is mine,
On the night ere the pending battle many seek me, and I do not fail
    them,
On that solemn night (it may be their last) those that know me seek
    me.

My face rubs to the hunter's face when he lies down alone in his
    blanket,
The driver thinking of me does not mind the jolt of his wagon,
The young mother and old mother comprehend me,
The girl and the wife rest the needle a moment and forget where they
    are,
They and all would resume what I have told them.

48

I have said that the soul is not more than the body,
And I have said that the body is not more than the soul,
And nothing, not God, is greater to one than one's self is,
And whoever walks a furlong without sympathy walks to his own
    funeral drest in his shroud,
And I or you pocketless of a dime may purchase the pick of the earth,
And to glance with an eye or show a bean in its pod confounds the
    learning of all times,
And there is no trade or employment but the young man following it
    may become a hero,
And there is no object so soft but it makes a hub for the wheel'd
    universe,
And I say to any man or woman, Let your soul stand cool and
    composed before a million universes.

And I say to mankind, Be not curious about God,
For I who am curious about each am not curious about God,
(No array of terms can say how much I am at peace about God and
    about death.)

I hear and behold God in every object, yet understand God not in the
    least,
Nor do I understand who there can be more wonderful than myself.

Why should I wish to see God better than this day?
I see something of God each hour of the twenty-four, and each
    moment then,
In the faces of men and women I see God, and in my own face in the
    glass,
I find letters from God dropt in the street, and every one is sign'd by
    God's name,
And I leave them where they are, for I know that wheresoe'er I go,
Others will punctually come for ever and ever.

49

And as to you Death, and you bitter hug of mortality, it is idle to try
    to alarm me.

To his work without flinching the accoucheur comes,
I see the elder-hand pressing receiving supporting,
I recline by the sills of the exquisite flexible doors,
And mark the outlet, and mark the relief and escape.

And as to you Corpse I think you are good manure, but that does not
    offend me,
I smell the white roses sweet-scented and growing,
I reach to the leafy lips, I reach to the polish'd breasts of melons.

And as to you Life I reckon you are the leavings of many deaths,
(No doubt I have died myself ten thousand times before.)

I hear you whispering there O stars of heaven,
O suns—O grass of graves—O perpetual transfers and promotions,
If you do not say any thing how can I say any thing?

Of the turbid pool that lies in the autumn forest,
Of the moon that descends the steeps of the soughing twilight,
Toss, sparkles of day and dusk—toss on the black stems that decay in
    the muck,
Toss to the moaning gibberish of the dry limbs.

I ascend from the moon, I ascend from the night,
I perceive that the ghastly glimmer is noonday sunbeams reflected,
And debouch to the steady and central from the offspring great or
    small.

50
There is that in me—I do not know what it is—but I know it is in
    me.

Wrench'd and sweaty—calm and cool then my body becomes,
I sleep—I sleep long.

I do not know it—it is without name—it is a word unsaid,
It is not in any dictionary, utterance, symbol.

Something it swings on more than the earth I swing on,
To it the creation is the friend whose embracing awakes me.

Perhaps I might tell more. Outlines! I plead for my brothers and
    sisters.

Do you see O my brothers and sisters?
It is not chaos or death—it is form, union, plan—it is eternal life—it
    is Happiness.

51

The past and present wilt—I have fill'd them, emptied them,
And proceed to fill my next fold of the future.

Listener up there! what have you to confide to me?
Look in my face while I snuff the sidle of evening,
(Talk honestly, no one else hears you, and I stay only a minute
    longer.)

Do I contradict myself?
Very well then I contradict myself,
(I am large, I contain multitudes.)

I concentrate toward them that are nigh, I wait on the door-slab.

Who has done his day's work? who will soonest be through with his
    supper?
Who wishes to walk with me?

Will you speak before I am gone? will you prove already too late?

52

The spotted hawk swoops by and accuses me, he complains of my gab
    and my loitering.

I too am not a bit tamed, I too am untranslatable,
I sound my barbaric yawp over the roofs of the world.

The last scud of day holds back for me,
It flings my likeness after the rest and true as any on the shadow'd
    wilds,
It coaxes me to the vapor and the dusk.

I depart as air, I shake my white locks at the runaway sun,
I effuse my flesh in eddies, and drift it in lacy jags.

I bequeath myself to the dirt to grow from the grass I love,
If you want me again look for me under your boot-soles.

You will hardly know who I am or what I mean,
But I shall be good health to you nevertheless,
And filter and fibre your blood.

Failing to fetch me at first keep encouraged,
Missing me one place search another,
I stop somewhere waiting for you.

In Paths Untrodden

In paths untrodden,
In the growth by margins of pond-waters,
Escaped from the life that exhibits itself,
From all the standards hitherto publish'd, from the pleasures,
    profits, conformities,
Which too long I was offering to feed my soul,
Clear to me now standards not yet publish'd, clear to me that my
    soul,
That the soul of the man I speak for rejoices in comrades,
Here by myself away from the clank of the world,
Tallying and talk'd to here by tongues aromatic,
No longer abash'd, (for in this secluded spot I can respond as I
    would not dare elsewhere,)
Strong upon me the life that does not exhibit itself, yet contains
    all the rest,
Resolv'd to sing no songs to-day but those of manly attachment,
Projecting them along that substantial life,
Bequeathing hence types of athletic love,
Afternoon this delicious Ninth-month in my forty-first year,
I proceed for all who are or have been young men,
To tell the secret of my nights and days,
To celebrate the need of comrades.

I Saw in Louisiana a Live-Oak Growing

I saw in Louisiana a live-oak growing,
All alone stood it and the moss hung down from the branches,
Without any companion it grew there uttering joyous leaves of
    dark green,
And its look, rude, unbending, lusty, made me think of myself,
But I wonder'd how it could utter joyous leaves standing alone
    there without its friend near, for I knew I could not,
And I broke off a twig with a certain number of leaves upon it,
    and twined around it a little moss,
And brought it away, and I have placed it in sight in my room,
It is not needed to remind me as of my own dear friends,
(For I believe lately I think of little else than of them,)
Yet it remains to me a curious token, it makes me think of manly
    love;
For all that, and though the live-oak glistens there in Louisiana
    solitary in a wide flat space,
Uttering joyous leaves all its life without a friend a lover near,
I know very well I could not.

On the Beach at Night

On the beach at night,
Stands a child with her father,
Watching the east, the autumn sky.

Up through the darkness,
While ravening clouds, the burial clouds, in black masses spreading,
Lower sullen and fast athwart and down the sky,
Amid a transparent clear belt of ether yet left in the east,
Ascends large and calm the lord-star Jupiter,
And nigh at hand, only a very little above,
Swim the delicate sisters the Pleiades.

From the beach the child holding the hand of her father,
Those burial-clouds that lower victorious soon to devour all,
Watching, silently weeps.

Weep not, child,
Weep not, my darling,
With these kisses let me remove your tears,
The ravening clouds shall not long be victorious,
They shall not long possess the sky, they devour the stars only in
    apparition,
Jupiter shall emerge, be patient, watch again another night, the
    Pleiades shall emerge,
They are immortal, all those stars both silvery and golden shall
    shine out again,
The great stars and the little ones shall shine out again, they
    endure,
The vast immortal suns and the long-enduring pensive moons
    shall again shine.

Then dearest child mournest thou only for Jupiter?
Considerest thou alone the burial of the stars?
Something there is,
(With my lips soothing thee, adding I whisper,
I give thee the first suggestion, the problem and indirection,)
Something there is more immortal even than the stars,
(Many the burials, many the days and nights, passing away,)
Something that shall endure longer even than lustrous Jupiter,
Longer than sun or any revolving satellite,
Or the radiant sisters the Pleiades.

Europe
The 72nd and 73rd Years of These States.

Suddenly out of its stale and drowsy lair, the lair of slaves,
Like lightning it le'pt forth half startled at itself,
Its feet upon the ashes and the rags, its hands tight to the throats
of kings.

O hope and faith!
O aching close of exiled patriots' lives!
O many a sicken'd heart!
Turn back unto this day and make yourselves afresh.

And you, paid to defile the People—you liars, mark!
Not for numberless agonies, murders, lusts,
For court thieving in its manifold mean forms, worming from his
simplicity the poor man's wages,
For many a promise sworn by royal lips and broken and laugh'd
at in the breaking,

Then in their power not for all these did the blows strike revenge,
or the heads of the nobles fall;
The People scorn'd the ferocity of kings.

But the sweetness of mercy brew'd bitter destruction, and the
frighten'd monarchs come back,
Each comes in state with his train, hangman, priest, tax-gatherer,
Soldier, lawyer, lord, jailer, and sycophant.

Yet behind all lowering stealing, lo, a shape,
Vague as the night, draped interminably, head, front and form, in
scarlet folds,
Whose face and eyes none may see,
Out of its robes only this, the red robes, lifted by the arm,
One finger crook'd pointed high over the top, like the head of a
snake appears.

Meanwhile corpses lie in new-made graves, bloody corpses of
young men,
The rope of the gibbet hangs heavily, the bullets of princes are
flying, the creatures of power laugh aloud,
And all these things bear fruits, and they are good.

Those corpses of young men,
Those martyrs that hang from the gibbets, those hearts pierc'd by
    the gray lead,
Cold and motionless as they seem live elsewhere with unslaughter'd
    vitality.

They live in other young men O kings!
They live in brothers again ready to defy you,
They were purified by death, they were taught and exalted.

Not a grave of the murder'd for freedom but grows seed for freedom,
    in its turn to bear seed,
Which the winds carry afar and re-sow, and the rains and the
    snows nourish.

Not a disembodied spirit can the weapons of tyrants let loose,
But it stalks invisibly over the earth, whispering, counseling,
    cautioning.

Liberty, let others despair of you—I never despair of you.

Is the house shut? is the master away?
Nevertheless, be ready, be not weary of watching,
He will soon return, his messengers come anon.

As I Ebb'd with the Ocean of Life

1
As I ebb'd with the ocean of life,
As I wended the shores I know,
As I walk'd where the ripples continually wash you Paumanok,
Where they rustle up hoarse and sibilant,
Where the fierce old mother endlessly cries for her castaways,
I musing late in the autumn day, gazing off southward,
Held by this electric self out of the pride of which I utter poems,
Was seiz'd by the spirit that trails in the lines underfoot,
The rim, the sediment that stands for all the water and all the
    land of the globe.

Fascinated, my eyes reverting from the south, dropt, to follow
    those slender windrows,
Chaff, straw, splinters of wood, weeds, and the sea-gluten,
Scum, scales from shining rocks, leaves of salt-lettuce, left by the
    tide,
Miles walking, the sound of breaking waves the other side of me,
Paumanok there and then as I thought the old thought of likenesses,

These you presented to me you fish-shaped island,
As I wended the shores I know,
As I walk'd with that electric self seeking types.

2
As I wend to the shores I know not,
As I list to the dirge, the voices of men and women wreck'd,
As I inhale the impalpable breezes that set in upon me,
As the ocean so mysterious rolls toward me closer and closer,
I too but signify at the utmost a little wash'd-up drift,
A few sands and dead leaves to gather,
Gather, and merge myself as part of the sands and drift.

O baffled, balk'd, bent to the very earth,
Oppress'd with myself that I have dared to open my mouth,
Aware now that amid all that blab whose echoes recoil upon me I
    have not once had the least idea who or what I am,
But that before all my arrogant poems the real Me stands yet
    untouch'd, untold, altogether unreach'd,
Withdrawn far, mocking me with mock-congratulatory signs and
    bows,
With peals of distant ironical laughter at every word I have written,
Pointing in silence to these songs, and then to the sand beneath.

I perceive I have not really understood any thing, not a single
    object, and that no man ever can,
Nature here in sight of the sea taking advantage of me to dart
    upon me and sting me,
Because I have dared to open my mouth to sing at all.

3
You oceans both, I close with you,
We murmur alike reproachfully rolling sands and drift, knowing
    not why,
These little shreds indeed standing for you and me and all.

You friable shore with trails of debris,
You fish-shaped island, I take what is underfoot,
What is yours is mine my father.

I too Paumanok,
I too have bubbled up, floated the measureless float, and been
    wash'd on your shores,
I too am but a trail of drift and debris,
I too leave little wrecks upon you, you fish-shaped island.

I throw myself upon your breast my father,
I cling to you so that you cannot unloose me,
I hold you so firm till you answer me something.

Kiss me my father,
Touch me with your lips as I touch those I love,
Breathe to me while I hold you close the secret of the murmuring
    I envy.

4
Ebb, ocean of life, (the flow will return,)
Cease not your moaning you fierce old mother,
Endlessly cry for your castaways, but fear not, deny not me,
Rustle not up so hoarse and angry against my feet as I touch you
    or gather from you.

I mean tenderly by you and all,
I gather for myself and for this phantom looking down where we
    lead, and following me and mine.

Me and mine, loose windrows, little corpses,
Froth, snowy white, and bubbles,
(See, from my dead lips the ooze exuding at last,
See, the prismatic colors glistening and rolling,)
Tufts of straw, sands, fragments,
Buoy'd hither from many moods, one contradicting another,
From the storm, the long calm, the darkness, the swell,
Musing, pondering, a breath, a briny tear, a dab of liquid or soil,
Up just as much out of fathomless workings fermented and thrown,
A limp blossom or two, torn, just as much over waves floating,
    drifted at random,
Just as much for us that sobbing dirge of Nature,
Just as much whence we come that blare of the cloud-trumpets,
We, capricious, brought hither we know not whence, spread out
    before you,
You up there walking or sitting,
Whoever you are, we too lie in drifts at your feet.

The Dalliance of the Eagles

Skirting the river road, (my forenoon walk, my rest,)
Skyward in air a sudden muffled sound, the dalliance of the eagles,
The rushing amorous contact high in space together,
The clinching interlocking claws, a living, fierce, gyrating wheel,
Four beating wings, two beaks, a swirling mass tight grappling,
In tumbling turning clustering loops, straight downward falling,

Till o'er the river pois'd, the twain yet one, a moment's lull,
A motionless still balance in the air, then parting, talons loosing,
Upward again on slow-firm pinions slanting, their separate diverse
   flight,
She hers, he his, pursuing.

Cavalry Crossing a Ford

A line in long array where they wind betwixt green islands,
They take a serpentine course, their arms flash in the sun—hark
   to the musical clank,
Behold the silvery river, in it the splashing horses loitering stop to
   drink,
Behold the brown-faced men, each group, each person a picture,
   the negligent rest on the saddles,
Some emerge on the opposite bank, others are just entering the
   ford—while,
Scarlet and blue and snowy white,
The guidon flags flutter gayly in the wind.

Vigil Strange I Kept on the Field One Night

Vigil strange I kept on the field one night;
When you my son and my comrade dropt at my side that day,
One look I but gave which your dear eyes return'd with a look I
   shall never forget,
One touch of your hand to mine O boy, reach'd up as you lay on
   the ground,
Then onward I sped in the battle, the even-contested battle,
Till late in the night reliev'd to the place at last again I made my
   way,
Found you in death so cold dear comrade, found your body son
   of responding kisses, (never again on earth responding,)
Bared your face in the starlight, curious the scene, cool blew the
   moderate night-wind,
Long there and then in vigil I stood, dimly around me the battle-
   field spreading,
Vigil wondrous and vigil sweet there in the fragrant silent night,
But not a tear fell, not even a long-drawn sigh, long, long I gazed,
Then on the earth partially reclining sat by your side leaning my
   chin in my hands,
Passing sweet hours, immortal and mystic hours with you dearest
   comrade—not a tear, not a word,
Vigil of silence, love and death, vigil for you my son and my
   soldier,

As onward silently stars aloft, eastward new ones upward stole,
Vigil final for you brave boy, (I could not save you, swift was your
    death,
I faithfully loved you and cared for you living, I think we shall
    surely meet again,)
Till at latest lingering of the night, indeed just as the dawn
    appear'd,
My comrade I wrapt in his blanket, envelop'd well his form,
Folded the blanket well, tucking it carefully over head and care-
    fully under feet,
And there and then and bathed by the rising sun, my son in his
    grave, in his rude-dug grave I deposited,
Ending my vigil strange with that, vigil of night and battle-field
    dim,
Vigil for boy of responding kisses, (never again on earth
    responding,)
Vigil for comrade swiftly slain, vigil I never forget, how as day
    brighten'd,
I rose from the chill ground and folded my soldier well in his
    blanket,
And buried him where he fell.

The Wound-Dresser

I

An old man bending I come among new faces,
Years looking backward resuming in answer to children,
Come tell us old man, as from young men and maidens that love
    me,
(Arous'd and angry, I'd thought to beat the alarum, and urge
    relentless war,
But soon my fingers fail'd me, my face droop'd and I resign'd
    myself,
To sit by the wounded and soothe them, or silently watch the
    dead;)
Years hence of these scenes, of these furious passions, these
    chances,
Of unsurpass'd heroes, (was one side so brave? the other was
    equally brave;)
Now be witness again, paint the mightiest armies of earth,
Of those armies so rapid so wondrous what saw you to tell us?
What stays with you latest and deepest? of curious panics,
Of hard-fought engagements or sieges tremendous what deepest
    remains?

3
On, on I go, (open doors of time! open hospital doors!)
The crush'd head I dress, (poor crazed hand tear not the bandage
away,)
The neck of the cavalry-man with the bullet through and through
I examine,
Hard the breathing rattles, quite glazed already the eye, yet life
struggles hard,
(Come sweet death! be persuaded O beautiful death!
In mercy come quickly.)
From the stump of the arm, the amputated hand,
I undo the clotted lint, remove the slough, wash off the matter
and blood,
Back on his pillow the soldier bends with curv'd neck and side-
falling head,
His eyes are closed, his face is pale, he dares not look on the
bloody stump,
And has not yet look'd on it.

I dress a wound in the side, deep, deep,
But a day or two more, for see the frame all wasted and sinking,
And the yellow-blue countenance see.

I dress the perforated shoulder, the foot with the bullet-wound,
Cleanse the one with a gnawing and putrid gangrene, so sicken-
ing, so offensive,
While the attendant stands behind aside me holding the tray and
pail.

I am faithful, I do not give out,
The fractur'd thigh, the knee, the wound in the abdomen,
These and more I dress with impassive hand, (yet deep in my
breast a fire, a burning flame.)

4
Thus in silence in dreams' projections,
Returning, resuming, I thread my way through the hospitals,
The hurt and wounded I pacify with soothing hand,
I sit by the restless all the dark night, some are so young,
Some suffer so much, I recall the experience sweet and sad,
(Many a soldier's loving arms about this neck have cross'd and
rested,
Many a soldier's kiss dwells on these bearded lips.)

When Lilacs Last in the Dooryard Bloom'd

I

When lilacs last in the dooryard bloom'd,
And the great star early droop'd in the western sky in the night,
I mourn'd, and yet shall mourn with ever-returning spring.

Ever-returning spring, trinity sure to me you bring,
Lilac blooming perennial and drooping star in the west,
And thought of him I love.

2

O powerful western fallen star!
O shades of night—O moody, tearful night!
O great star disappear'd—O the black murk that hides the star!
O cruel hands that hold me powerless—O helpless soul of me!
O harsh surrounding cloud that will not free my soul.

3

In the dooryard fronting an old farm-house near the white-wash'd
    palings,
Stands the lilac-bush tall-growing with heart-shaped leaves of rich
    green,
With many a pointed blossom rising delicate, with the perfume
    strong I love,
With every leaf a miracle—and from this bush in the dooryard,
With delicate-color'd blossoms and heart-shaped leaves of rich
    green,
A sprig with its flower I break.

4

In the swamp in secluded recesses,
A shy and hidden bird is warbling a song.

Solitary the thrush,
The hermit withdrawn to himself, avoiding the settlements,
Sings by himself a song.

Song of the bleeding throat,
Death's outlet song of life, (for well dear brother I know,
If thou wast not granted to sing thou would'st surely die.)

5
Over the breast of the spring, the land, amid cities,
Amid lanes and through old woods, where lately the violets peep'd
    from the ground, spotting the gray debris,
Amid the grass in the fields each side of the lanes, passing the
    endless grass,
Passing the yellow-spear'd wheat, every grain from its shroud in
    the dark-brown fields uprisen,
Passing the apple-tree blows of white and pink in the orchards,
Carrying a corpse to where it shall rest in the grave,
Night and day journeys a coffin.

6
Coffin that passes through lanes and streets,
Through day and night with the great cloud darkening the land,
With the pomp of the inloop'd flags with the cities draped in black,
With the show of the States themselves as of crape-veil'd women
    standing,
With processions long and winding and the flambeaus of the night,
With the countless torches lit, with the silent sea of faces and the
    unbared heads,
With the waiting depot, the arriving coffin, and the sombre faces,
With dirges through the night, with the thousand voices rising
    strong and solemn,
With all the mournful voices of the dirges pour'd around the coffin,
The dim-lit churches and the shuddering organs—where amid
    these you journey,
With the tolling tolling bells' perpetual clang,
Here, coffin that slowly passes,
I give you my sprig of lilac.

7
(Nor for you, for one alone,
Blossoms and branches green to coffins all I bring,
For fresh as the morning, thus would I chant a song for you O
    sane and sacred death.

All over bouquets of roses,
O death, I cover you over with roses and early lilies,
But mostly and now the lilac that blooms the first,
Copious I break, I break the sprigs from the bushes,
With loaded arms I come, pouring for you,
For you and the coffins all of you O death.)

8

O western orb sailing the heaven,
Now I know what you must have meant as a month since I
  walk'd,
As I walk'd in silence the transparent shadowy night,
As I saw you had something to tell as you bent to me night after
  night,
As you droop'd from the sky low down as if to my side, (while
  the other stars all look'd on,)
As we wander'd together the solemn night, (for something I know
  not what kept me from sleep,)
As the night advanced, and I saw on the rim of the west how full
  you were of woe,
As I stood on the rising ground in the breeze in the cool trans-
  parent night,
As I watch'd where you pass'd and was lost in the netherward
  black of the night,
As my soul in its trouble dissatisfied sank, as where you sad orb,
Concluded, dropt in the night, and was gone.

9

Sing on there in the swamp,
O singer bashful and tender, I hear your notes, I hear your call,
I hear, I come presently, I understand you,
But a moment I linger, for the lustrous star has detain'd me,
The star my departing comrade holds and detains me.

10

O how shall I warble myself for the dead one there I loved?
And how shall I deck my song for the large sweet soul that has
  gone?
And what shall my perfume be for the grave of him I love?

Sea-winds blown from east and west,
Blown from the Eastern sea and blown from the Western sea, till
  there on the prairies meeting,
These and with these and the breath of my chant,
I'll perfume the grave of him I love.

11

O what shall I hang on the chamber walls?
And what shall the pictures be that I hang on the walls,
To adorn the burial-house of him I love?

Pictures of growing spring and farms and homes,
With the Fourth-month eve at sundown, and the gray smoke lucid
    and bright,
With floods of the yellow gold of the gorgeous, indolent, sinking
    sun, burning, expanding the air,
With the fresh sweet herbage under foot, and the pale green leaves
    of the trees prolific,
In the distance the flowing glaze, the breast of the river, with a
    wind-dapple here and there,
With ranging hills on the banks, with many a line against the sky,
    and shadows,
And the city at hand with dwellings so dense, and stacks of chim-
    neys,
And all the scenes of life and the workshops, and the workmen
    homeward returning.

12
Lo, body and soul—this land,
My own Manhattan with spires, and the sparkling and hurrying
    tides, and the ships,
The varied and ample land, the South and the North in the light,
    Ohio's shores and flashing Missouri,
And ever the far-spreading prairies cover'd with grass and corn.

Lo, the most excellent sun so calm and haughty,
The violet and purple morn with just-felt breezes,
The gentle soft-born measureless light,
The miracle spreading bathing all, the fulfill'd noon,
The coming eve delicious, the welcome night and the stars,
Over my cities shining all, enveloping man and land.

13
Sing on, sing on you gray-brown bird,
Sing from the swamps, the recesses, pour your chant from the
    bushes,
Limitless out of the dusk, out of the cedars and pines.

Sing on dearest brother, warble your reedy song,
Loud human song, with voice of uttermost woe.

O liquid and free and tender!
O wild and loose to my soul—O wondrous singer!
You only I hear—yet the star holds me, (but will soon depart,)
Yet the lilac with mastering odor holds me.

14

Now while I sat in the day and look'd forth,
In the close of the day with its light and the fields of spring, and
    the farmers preparing their crops,
In the large unconscious scenery of my land with its lakes and
    forests,
In the heavenly aerial beauty, (after the perturb'd winds and the
    storms,)
Under the arching heavens of the afternoon swift passing, and the
    voices of children and women,
The many-moving sea-tides, and I saw the ships how they
    sail'd,
And the summer approaching with richness, and the fields all busy
    with labor,
And the infinite separate houses, how they all went on, each with
    its meals and minutia of daily usages,
And the streets how their throbbings throbb'd, and the cities pent
    —lo, then and there,
Falling upon them all and among them all, enveloping me with the
    rest,
Appear'd the cloud, appear'd the long black trail,
And I knew death, its thought, and the sacred knowledge of
    death.

Then with the knowledge of death as walking one side of me,
And the thought of death close-walking the other side of me,
And I in the middle as with companions, and as holding the
    hands of companions,
I fled forth to the hiding receiving night that talks not,
Down to the shores of the water, the path by the swamp in the
    dimness,
To the solemn shadowy cedars and ghostly pines so still.

And the singer so shy to the rest receiv'd me,
The gray-brown bird I know receiv'd us comrades three,
And he sang the carol of death, and a verse for him I love.

From deep secluded recesses,
From the fragrant cedars and the ghostly pines so still,
Came the carol of the bird.

And the charm of the carol rapt me,
As I held as if by their hands my comrades in the night,
And the voice of my spirit tallied the song of the bird.

Come lovely and soothing death,
Undulate round the world, serenely arriving, arriving,
In the day, in the night, to all, to each,
Sooner or later delicate death.

Prais'd be the fathomless universe,
For life and joy, and for objects and knowledge curious,
And for love, sweet love—but praise! praise! praise!
For the sure-enwinding arms of cool-enfolding death.

Dark mother always gliding near with soft feet,
Have none chanted for thee a chant of fullest welcome?
Then I chant it for thee, I glorify thee above all,
I bring thee a song that when thou must indeed come, come
    unfalteringly.

Approach strong deliveress,
When it is so, when thou hast taken them I joyously sing the dead
Lost in the loving floating ocean of thee,
Laved in the flood of thy bliss O death.

From me to thee glad serenades,
Dances for thee I propose saluting thee, adornments and feastings for
    thee,
And the sights of the open landscape and the high-spread sky are
    fitting,
And life and the fields, and the huge and thoughtful night.

The night in silence under many a star,
The ocean shore and the husky whispering wave whose voice I
    know,
And the soul turning to thee O vast and well-veil'd death,
And the body gratefully nestling close to thee.

Over the tree-tops I float thee a song,
Over the rising and sinking waves, over the myriad fields and the
    prairies wide,
Over the dense-pack'd cities all and the teeming wharves and ways
I float this carol with joy, with joy to thee O death.

15
To the tally of my soul,
Loud and strong kept up the gray-brown bird,
With pure deliberate notes spreading filling the night.

Loud in the pines and cedars dim,
Clear in the freshness moist and the swamp-perfume,
And I with my comrades there in the night.

While my sight that was bound in my eyes unclosed,
As to long panoramas of visions.

And I saw askant the armies,
I saw as in noiseless dreams hundreds of battle-flags,
Borne through the smoke of the battles and pierc'd with missiles
    I saw them,
And carried hither and yon through the smoke, and torn and
    bloody,
And at last but a few shreds left on the staffs, (and all in silence,)
And the staffs all splinter'd and broken.

I saw battle-corpses, myriads of them,
And the white skeletons of young men, I saw them,
I saw the debris and debris of all the slain soldiers of the war,
But I saw they were not as was thought,
They themselves were fully at rest, they suffer'd not,
The living remain'd and suffer'd, the mother suffer'd,
And the wife and the child and the musing comrade suffer'd,
And the armies that remain'd suffer'd.

16
Passing the visions, passing the night,
Passing, unloosing the hold of my comrades' hands,
Passing the song of the hermit bird and the tallying song of my
    soul,
Victorious song, death's outlet song, yet varying ever-altering song,
As low and wailing, yet clear the notes, rising and falling, flooding
    the night,
Sadly sinking and fainting, as warning and warning, and yet again
    bursting with joy,
Covering the earth and filling the spread of the heaven,
As that powerful psalm in the night I heard from recesses,
Passing, I leave thee lilac with heart-shaped leaves,
I leave thee there in the door-yard, blooming, returning with
    spring.

I cease from my song for thee,
From my gaze on thee in the west, fronting the west, communing
    with thee,
O comrade lustrous with silver face in the night.

Yet each to keep and all, retrievements out of the night,
The song, the wondrous chant of the gray-brown bird,
And the tallying chant, the echo arous'd in my soul,
With the lustrous and drooping star with the countenance full
    of woe,
With the holders holding my hand nearing the call of the bird,
Comrades mine and I in the midst, and their memory ever to
    keep, for the dead I loved so well,
For the sweetest, wisest soul of all my days and lands—and this
    for his dear sake,
Lilac and star and bird twined with the chant of my soul,
There in the fragrant pines and the cedars dusk and dim.

O Captain! My Captain!

O Captain! my Captain! our fearful trip is done,
The ship has weather'd every rack, the prize we sought is won,
The port is near, the bells I hear, the people all exulting,
While follow eyes the steady keel, the vessel grim and daring;
        But O heart! heart! heart!
            O the bleeding drops of red,
                Where on the deck my Captain lies,
                    Fallen cold and dead.

O Captain! my Captain! rise up and hear the bells;
Rise up—for you the flag is flung—for you the bugle trills,
For you bouquets and ribbon'd wreaths—for you the shores
    a-crowding,
For you they call, the swaying mass, their eager faces turning;
        Here Captain! dear father!
            This arm beneath your head!
                It is some dream that on the deck,
                    You've fallen cold and dead.

My Captain does not answer, his lips are pale and still,
My father does not feel my arm, he has no pulse nor will,
The ship is anchor'd safe and sound, its voyage closed and done,
From fearful trip the victor ship comes in with object won;
        Exult O shores, and ring O bells!
            But I with mournful tread,
                Walk the deck my Captain lies,
                    Fallen cold and dead.

A Noiseless Patient Spider

A noiseless patient spider,
I mark'd where on a little promontory it stood isolated,
Mark'd how to explore the vacant vast surrounding,
It launch'd forth filament, filament, filament, out of itself,
Ever unreeling them, ever tirelessly speeding them.

And you O my soul where you stand,
Surrounded, detached, in measureless oceans of space,
Ceaselessly musing, venturing, throwing, seeking the spheres to
    connect them,
Till the bridge you will need be form'd, till the ductile anchor
    hold,
Till the gossamer thread you fling catch somewhere, O my soul.

A Prairie Sunset

Shot gold, maroon and violet, dazzling silver, emerald, fawn,
The earth's whole amplitude and Nature's multiform power
    consign'd for once to colors;
The light, the general air posses'd by them—colors till now
    unknown,
No limit, confine—not the Western sky alone—the high
    meridian—North, South, all,
Pure luminous color fighting the silent shadows to the last.

The Dismantled Ship

In some unused lagoon, some nameless bay,
On sluggish, lonesome waters, anchor'd near the shore,
And old, dismasted, gray and batter'd ship, disabled, done,
After free voyages to all the seas of earth, haul'd up at last and
    hawser'd tight,
Lies rusting, mouldering.

Good-Bye My Fancy

Good-bye my fancy—(I had a word to say,
But 'tis not quite the time—The best of any man's word or say,
Is when its proper place arrives—and for its meaning,
I keep mine till the last.)

JAMES RUSSELL LOWELL
(1819–1891)

from A FABLE FOR CRITICS

[Phoebus]

Phoebus, sitting one day in a laurel tree's shade,
Was reminded of Daphne, of whom it was made,
For the god being one day too warm in his wooing,
She took to the tree to escape his pursuing;
Be the cause what it might, from his offers she shrunk,
And, Ginevra-like, shut herself up in a trunk

. . . .

"Oh, weep with me, Daphne," he sighed, "for you know it's
A terrible thing to be pestered with poets!
But, alas, she is dumb, and the proverb holds good,
She never will cry till she's out of the wood!
What would n't I give if I never had known of her?
'T were a kind of relief had I something to groan over:
If I had but some letters of hers, now, to toss over,
I might turn for the nonce a Byronic philosopher,
And bewitch all the flats by bemoaning the loss of her.
One needs something tangible, though, to begin on,—
A loom, as it were, for the fancy to spin on;
What boots all your grist? it can never be ground
Till a breeze makes the arms of the windmill go round;
(Or, if 't is a water-mill, alter the metaphors,
And say it won't stir, save the wheel be well wet afore,
Or lug in some stuff about water 'so dreamily,'—

. . . .

I called this a "Fable for Critics;" you think it's
More like a display of my rhythmical trinkets;
My plot, like an icicle, 's slender and slippery,
Every moment more slender, and likely to slip awry,
And the reader unwilling *in loco desipere*
Is free to jump over as much of my frippery
As he fancies, and, if he's a provident skipper, he

May have like Odysseus control of the gales,
And get safe to port, ere his patience quite fails . . .

. . . .

[Emerson]

"There comes Emerson first, whose rich words, every one,
Are like gold nails in temples to hang trophies on,
Whose prose is grand verse, while his verse, the Lord knows,
Is some of it pr—No, 't is not even prose;

. . . .

"But, to come back to Emerson (whom, by the way,
I believe we left waiting),—his is, we may say,
A Greek head on right Yankee shoulders, whose range
Has Olympus for one pole, for t' other the Exchange;
He seems, to my thinking (although I'm afraid
The comparison must, long ere this, have been made),
A Plotinus-Montaigne, where the Egyptian's gold mist
And the Gascon's shrewd wit cheek-by-jowl coexist;
All admire, and yet scarcely six converts he's got
To I don't (nor they either) exactly know what;
For though he builds glorious temples, 't is odd
He leaves never a doorway to get in a god.
'T is refreshing to old-fashioned people like me
To meet such a primitive Pagan as he,
In whose mind all creation is duly respected
As parts of himself—just a little projected;
And who 's willing to worship the stars and the sun,
A convert to—nothing but Emerson.

. . . .

[Channing and Thoreau]

"There comes _____, for instance; to see him 's rare sport,
Tread in Emerson's tracks with legs painfully short;
How he jumps, how he strains, and gets red in the face,
To keep step with the mystagogue's natural pace!
He follows as close as a stick to a rocket,
His fingers exploring the prophet's each pocket.
Fie, for shame, brother bard; with good fruit of your own,
Can't you let Neighbor Emerson's orchards alone?

Besides, 't is no use, you'll not find e'en a core,—
_____ has picked up all the windfalls before.
They might strip every tree, and E. never would catch 'em,
His Hesperides have no rude dragon to watch 'em;
When they send him a dishful, and ask him to try 'em;
He never suspects how the sly rogues came by 'em;
He wonders why 't is there are none such his trees on,
And thinks 'em the best he has tasted this season.

[Alcott]

"Yonder, calm as a cloud, Alcott stalks in a dream,
And fancies himself in thy groves, Academe,
With the Parthenon nigh, and the olive-trees o'er him,
And never a fact to perplex him or bore him,
With a snug room at Plato's when night comes, to walk to,
And people from morning till midnight to talk to,
And from midnight till morning, nor snore in their listening;—
So he muses, his face with the joy of it glistening,
For his highest conceit of a happiest state is
Where they'd live upon acorns, and hear him talk gratis;
And, indeed, I believe, no man ever talked better,—
Each sentence hangs perfectly poised to a letter;
He seems piling words, but there's royal dust hid
In the heart of each sky-piercing pyramid.
While he talks he is great, but goes out like a taper,
If you shut him up closely with pen, ink, and paper;
Yet his fingers itch for 'em from morning till night,
And he thinks he does wrong if he don't always write;
In this, as in all things, a lamb among men,
He goes to sure death when he goes to his pen.

. . . .

[Hawthorne]

"There is Hawthorne, with genius so shrinking and rare
That you hardly at first see the strength that is there;
A frame so robust, with a nature so sweet,
So earnest, so graceful, so lithe and so fleet,
Is worth a descent from Olympus to meet;

. . . .

He's a John Bunyan Fouqué, a Puritan Tieck;
When Nature was shaping him, clay was not granted
For making so full-sized a man as she wanted,
So, to fill out her model, a little she spared
From some finer-grained stuff for a woman prepared,
And she could not have hit a more excellent plan
For making him fully and perfectly man.
The success of her scheme gave her so much delight,
That she tried it again, shortly after, in Dwight;
Only, while she was kneading and shaping the clay,
She sang to her work in her sweet childish way,
And found, when she'd put the last touch to his soul,
That the music had somehow got mixed with the whole.

[Cooper]

"Here's Cooper, who's written six volumes to show
He's as good as a lord: well, let's grant that he's so;
If a person prefer that description of praise,
Why, a coronet's certainly cheaper than bays;
But he need take no pains to convince us he's not
(As his enemies say) the American Scott.
Choose any twelve men, and let C. read aloud
That one of his novels of which he's most proud,
And I'd lay any bet that, without ever quitting
Their box, they'd be all, to a man, for acquitting.
He has drawn you one character, though, that is new,
One wildflower he's plucked that is wet with the dew
Of this fresh Western world, and, the thing not to mince,
He has done naught but copy it ill ever since;
His Indians, with proper respect be it said,
Are just Natty Bumppo, daubed over with red,
And his very Long Toms are the same useful Nat,
Rigged up in duck pants and a sou'wester hat
(Though once in a Coffin, a good chance was found
To have slipped the old fellow away underground).
All his other men-figures are clothes upon sticks,
The *dernière chemise* of a man in a fix
(As a captain besieged, when his garrison's small,
Sets up caps upon poles to be seen o'er the wall);
And the women he draws from one model don't vary,
All sappy as maples and flat as a prairie.
When a character's wanted, he goes to the task
As a cooper would do in composing a cask;
He picks out the staves, of their qualities heedful,
Just hoops them together as tight as is needful,

And, if the best fortune should crown the attempt, he
Has made at the most something wooden and empty.

"Don't suppose I would underrate Cooper's abilities;
If I thought you'd do that, I should feel very ill at ease;
The men who have given to *one* character life
And objective existence are not very rife;
You may number them all, both prose-writers and singers,
Without overrunning the bounds of your fingers,
And Natty won't go to oblivion quicker
Than Adams the parson or Primrose the vicar.

"There is one thing in Cooper I like, too, and that is
That on manners he lectures his countrymen gratis;
Not precisely so either, because, for a rarity,
He is paid for his tickets in unpopularity.
Now he may overcharge his American pictures,
But you'll grant there's a good deal of truth in his strictures;
And I honor the man who is willing to sink
Half his present repute for the freedom to think,
And, when he has thought, be his cause strong or weak,
Will risk t' other half for the freedom to speak,
Caring naught for what vengeance the mob has in store,
Let that mob be the upper ten thousand or lower.

. . . .

[Poe]

"There comes Poe, with his raven, like Barnaby Rudge,
Three fifths of him genius and two fifths sheer fudge,
Who talks like a book of iambs and pentameters,
In a way to make people of common sense damn metres,
Who has written some things quite the best of their kind,
But the heart somehow seems all squeezed out by the mind,

[Longfellow]

Who—But hey-day! What's this? Messieurs Mathews and Poe,
You must n't fling mud-balls at Longfellow so,
Does it make a man worse that his character's such
As to make his friends love him (as you think) too much?
Why, there is not a bard at this moment alive
More willing than he that his fellows should thrive;
While you are abusing him thus, even now

He would help either one of you out of a slough;
You may say that he's smooth and all that till you're hoarse,
But remember that elegance also is force;
After polishing granite as much as you will,
The heart keeps its tough old persistency still;
Deduct all you can, *that* still keeps you at bay;
Why, he'll live till men weary of Collins and Gray.
I'm not over-fond of Greek metres in English,
To me rhyme's a gain, so it be not too jinglish,
And your modern hexameter verses are no more
Like Greek ones than sleek Mr. Pope is like Homer;
As the roar of the sea to the coo of a pigeon is,
So, compared to your moderns, sounds old Melesigenes;
I may be too partial, the reason, perhaps, o't is
That I've heard the old blind man recite his own rhapsodies,
And my ear with that music impregnate may be,
Like the poor exiled shell with the soul of the sea,
Or as one can't bear Strauss when his nature is cloven
To its deeps within deeps by the stroke of Beethoven;
But, set that aside, and 't is truth that I speak,
Had Theocritus written in English, not Greek,
I believe that his exquisite sense would scarce change a line
In that rare, tender, virgin-like pastoral Evangeline.
That's not ancient nor modern, its place is apart
Where time has no sway, in the realm of pure Art,
'T is a shrine of retreat from Earth's hubbub and strife
As quiet and chaste as the author's own life.

[Philothea (Lydia Child)]

"There comes Philothea, her face all aglow,
She has just been dividing some poor creature's woe,
And can't tell which pleases her most, to relieve
His want, or his story to hear and believe;
No doubt against many deep griefs she prevails,
For her ear is the refuge of destitute tales;
She knows well that silence is sorrow's best food,
And that talking draws off from the heart its black blood,
So she'll listen with patience and let you unfold
Your bundle of rags as 't were pure cloth of gold,
Which, indeed, it all turns to as soon as she's touched it,
And (to borrow a phrase from the nursery) *muched* it;
She has such a musical taste, she will go
Any distance to hear one who draws a long bow;
She will swallow a wonder by mere might and main,
And thinks it Geometry's fault if she's fain

To consider things flat, inasmuch as they're plain;
Facts with her are accomplished, as Frenchmen would say—
They will prove all she wishes them to either way,—
And, as fact lies on this side or that, we must try,
If we're seeking the truth, to find where it don't lie;
I was telling her once of a marvellous aloe
That for thousands of years had looked spindling and sallow,
And, though nursed by the fruitfullest powers of mud,
Had never vouchsafed e'en so much as a bud,
Till its owner remarked (as a sailor, you know,
Often will in a calm) that it never would blow,
For he wished to exhibit the plant, and designed
That its blowing should help him in raising the wind;
At last it was told him that if he should water
Its roots with the blood of his unmarried daughter
(Who was born, as her mother, a Calvinist, said,
With William Law's serious caul on her head),
It would blow as the obstinate breeze did when by a
Like decree of her father died Iphigenia;
At first he declared he himself would be blowed
Ere his conscience with such a foul crime he would load,
But the thought, coming oft, grew less dark than before,
And he mused, as each creditor knocked at his door,
If *this* were but done they would dun me no more;
I told Philothea his struggles and doubts,
And how he considered the ins and the outs
Of the visions he had, and the dreadful dyspepsy,
How he went to the seër that lives at Po'keepsie,
How the seër advised him to sleep on it first,
And to read his big volume in case of the worst,
And further advised he should pay him five dollars
For writing **hum, hum,** on his wristbands and collars;
Three years and ten days these dark words he had studied
When the daughter was missed, and the aloe had budded;
I told how he watched it grow large and more large,
And wondered how much for the show he should charge,—
She had listened with utter indifference to this, till
I told how it bloomed, and, discharging its pistil
With an aim the Eumenides dictated, shot
The botanical filicide dead on the spot;
It had blown, but he reaped not his horrible gains,
For it blew with such force as to blow out his brains,
And the crime was blown also, because on the wad,
Which was paper, was writ 'Visitation of God,'
As well as a thrilling account of the deed
Which the coroner kindly allowed me to read.

"Well, my friend took this story up just, to be sure,
As one might a poor foundling that's laid at one's door;
She combed it and washed it and clothed it and fed it,
And as if 't were her own child most tenderly bred it,
Laid the scene (of the legend, I mean) far away a-
mong the green vales underneath Himalaya,
And by artist-like touches, laid on here and there,
Made the whole thing so touching, I frankly declare
I have read it all thrice, and, perhaps I am weak,
But I found every time there were tears on my cheek.

"The pole, science tells us, the magnet controls,
But she is a magnet to emigrant Poles,
And folks with a mission that nobody knows
Throng thickly about her as bees round a rose;
She can fill up the *carets* in such, make their scope
Converge to some focus of rational hope,
And, with sympathies fresh as the morning, their gall
Can transmute into honey,—but this is not all;
Not only for those she has solace, oh say,
Vice's desperate nursling adrift in Broadway,
Who clingest, with all that is left of thee human,
To the last slender spar from the wreck of the woman,
Hast thou not found one shore where those tired drooping feet
Could reach firm mother-earth, one full heart on whose beat
The soothed head in silence reposing could hear
The chimes of far childhood throb back on the ear?
Ah, there's many a beam, from the fountain of day
That, to reach us unclouded, must pass, on its way,
Through the soul of a woman, and hers is wide ope
To the influence of Heaven as the blue eyes of Hope;
Yes, a great heart is hers, one that dares to go in
To the prison, the slave-hut, the alleys of sin,
And to bring into each, or to find there, some line
Of the never completely out-trampled divine;
If her heart at high floods swamps her brain now and then,
'T is but richer for that when the tide ebbs agen,
As, after old Nile has subsided, his plain
Overflows with a second broad deluge of grain:
What a wealth would it bring to the narrow and sour
Could they be as a Child but for one little hour!

. . . .

[Holmes]

"There's Holmes, who is matchless among you for wit;
A Leyden-jar always full-charged, from which flit
The electrical tingles of hit after hit;
In long poems 't is painful sometimes, and invites
A thought of the way the new Telegraph writes,
Which pricks down its little sharp sentences spitefully
As if you got more than you'd title to rightfully,
And you find yourself hoping its wild father Lightning
Would flame in for a second and give you a fright'ning.
He has perfect sway of what I call a sham metre,
But many admire it, the English pentameter,
And Campbell, I think, wrote most commonly worse,
With less nerve, swing, and fire in the same kind of verse,
Nor e'er achieved aught in 't so worthy of praise
As the tribute of Holmes to the grand *Marseillaise*.
You went crazy last year over Bulwer's New Timon;—
Why, if B., to the day of his dying, should rhyme on,
heaping verses on verses and tomes upon tomes,
He could ne'er reach the best point and vigor of Holmes.
His are just the fine hands, too, to weave you a lyric
Full of fancy, fun, feeling, or spiced with satiric
In a measure so kindly, you doubt if the toes
That are trodden upon are your own or your foes."

[Lowell]

"There is Lowell, who's striving Parnassus to climb
With a whole bale of *isms* tied together with rhyme,
He might get on alone, spite of brambles and boulders,
But he can't with that bundle he has on his shoulders,
The top of the hill he will ne'er come nigh reaching
Till he learns the distinction 'twixt singing and preaching;
His lyre has some chords that would ring pretty well,
But he'd rather by half make a drum of the shell,
And rattle away till he's old as Methusalem,
At the head of a march to the last new Jerusalem.

. . . .

from Introduction

. . . .

'Old Joe is gone, who saw hot Percy goad
His slow artillery up the Concord road,
A tale which grew in wonder, year by year,
As, every time he told it, Joe drew near
To the main fight, till, faded and grown gray,
The original scene to bolder tints gave way;
Then Joe had heard the foe's scared double-quick
Beat on stove drum with one uncaptured stick,
And, ere death came the lengthening tale to lop,
Himself had fired, and seen a red-coat drop;
Had Joe lived long enough, that scrambling fight
Had squared more nearly with his sense of right,
And vanquished Percy, to complete the tale,
Had hammered stone for life in Concord jail.'

. . . .

from The 'Cruetin Sarjunt

Thrash away, you'll *hev* to rattle
    On them kittle-drums o' yourn,—
'Taint a knowin' kind o' cattle
    Thet is ketched with mouldy corn;
Put in stiff, you fifer feller,
    Let folks see how spry you be,—
Guess you'll toot till you are yeller
    'Fore you git ahold o' me!

Thet air flag's a leetle rotten,
    Hope it aint your Sunday's best;—
Fact! it takes a sight o' cotton
    To stuff out a soger's chest;
Sence we farmers hev to pay fer 't,
    Ef you must wear humps like these,
Sposin' you should try salt hay fer 't,
    It would du ez slick ez grease.

from Under the Willows

. . . .

May is a pious fraud of the almanac,
A ghastly parody of real Spring
Shaped out of snow and breathed with eastern wind;
Or if, o'er-confident, she trust the date,
And, with her handful of anemones,
Herself as shivery, steal into the sun,
The season need but turn his hour-glass round,
And Winter suddenly, like crazy Lear,
Reels back, and brings the dead May in his arms,
Her budding breasts and wan dislustred front
With frosty streaks and drifts of his white beard
All overblown. Then, warmly walled with books,
While my wood-fire supplies the sun's defect,
Whispering old forest-sagas in its dreams,
I take my May down from the happy shelf
Where perch the world's rare song-birds in a row,
Waiting my choice to open with full breast,
And beg an alms of springtime, ne'er denied
Indoors by vernal Chaucer, whose fresh woods
Throb thick with merle and mavis all the years.

July breathes hot, sallows the crispy fields,
Curls up the wan leaves of the lilac-hedge,
And every eve cheats us with show of clouds
That braze the horizon's western rim, or hang
Motionless, with heaped canvas drooping idly,
Like a dim fleet by starving men besieged,
Conjectured half, and half descried afar,
Helpless of wind, and seeming to slip back
Adown the smooth curve of the oily sea.
But June is full of invitations sweet,
Forth from the chimney's yawn and thrice-read tomes
To leisurely delights and sauntering thoughts
That brook no ceiling narrower than the blue.
The cherry, drest for bridal, at my pane
Brushes, then listens, *Will he come?* The bee,
All dusty as a miller, takes his toll
Of powdery gold, and grumbles. What a day
To sun me and do nothing! Nay, I think
Merely to bask and ripen is sometimes
The student's wiser business; the brain
That forages all climes to line its cells,
Ranging both worlds on lightest wings of wish,

Will not distil the juices it has sucked
To the sweet substance of pellucid thought,
Expect for him who hath the secret learned
To mix his blood with sunshine, and to take
The winds into his pulses. Hush! 't is he!
My oriole, my glance of summer fire,
Is come at last, and, ever on the watch,
Twitches the packthread I had lightly wound
About the bough to help his housekeeping,—
Twitches and scouts by turns, blessing his luck,
Yet fearing me who laid it in his way,
Nor, more than wiser we in our affairs,
Divines the providence that hides and helps.
Heave, ho! Heave, ho! he whistles as the twine
Slackens its hold; *once more, now!* and a flash
Lightens across the sunlight to the elm
Where his mate dangles at her cup of felt.
Nor all his booty is the thread; he trails
My loosened thought with it along the air,
And I must follow, would I ever find
The inward rhyme to all this wealth of life.

. . . .

So mused I once within my willow-tent
One brave June morning, when the bluff northwest,
Thrusting aside a dank and snuffling day
That made us bitter at our neighbors' sins,
Brimmed the great cup of heaven with sparkling cheer
And roared a lusty stave; the sliding Charles,
Blue toward the west, and bluer and more blue,
Living and lustrous as a woman's eyes
Look once and look no more, with southward curve
Ran crinkling sunniness, like Helen's hair
Glimpsed in Elysium, insubstantial gold;
From blossom-clouded orchards, far away
The bobolink tinkled; the deep meadows flowed
With multitudinous pulse of light and shade
Against the bases of the southern hills,
While here and there a drowsy island rick
Slept and its shadow slept; the wooden bridge
Thundered, and then was silent; on the roofs
The sun-warped shingles rippled with the heat;
Summer on field and hill, in heart and brain,
All life washed clean in this high tide of June.

Aladdin

When I was a beggarly boy,
    And lived in a cellar damp,
I had not a friend nor a toy,
    But I had Aladdin's lamp;
When I could not sleep for the cold,
    I had fire enough in my brain,
And builded, with roofs of gold,
    My beautiful castles in Spain!

Since then I have toiled day and night,
    I have money and power good store,
But I'd give all my lamps of silver bright
    For the one that is mine no more;
Take, Fortune, whatever you choose,
    You gave, and may snatch again;
I have nothing 't would pain me to lose,
    For I own no more castles in Spain!

from Our Own—Progression F

HIS WANDERINGS AND PERSONAL ADVENTURES

. . . .

this hand-to-mouth, pert, rapid, nineteenth century;
This is the Age of Scramble; men move faster than they did
When they pried up the imperial Past's deep-dusted coffin-lid,
Searching for scrolls of precedent; the wire-tamed lightning now
Replaces Delphos—men don't leave the steamer for the scow;
What hero, were they new to-day, would ever stop to read
The Iliad, the Shanàmeh, or the Nibelungenlied?
Their public's gone, the artist Greek, the lettered Shah, the hairy
    Graf—
Folio and plesiosaur sleep well; *we* weary o'er a paragraph;
The mind moves planet-like no more, it fizzes, cracks, and bustles;
From end to end with journals dry the land o'ershadowed rustles,
As with dead leaves a winter-beech, and, with their breath-roused jars
Amused, we care not if they hide the eternal skies and stars;
Down to the general level of the Board of Brokers sinking,
The Age takes in the newspapers, or, to say sooth unshrinking,
The newspapers take in the Age, and Stocks do all the thinking.

HERMAN MELVILLE
(1819–1891)

The Portent

Hanging from the beam,
    Slowly swaying (such the law),
Gaunt the shadow on your green,
    Shenandoah!
The cut is on the crown
(Lo, John Brown),
And the stabs shall heal no more.

Hidden in the cap
    Is the anguish none can draw;
So your future veils its face,
    Shenandoah!
But the streaming beard is shown
(Weird John Brown),
The meteor of the war.

Misgivings

When ocean-clouds over inland hills
    Sweep storming in late autumn brown,
And horror the sodden valley fills,
    And the spire falls crashing in the town,
I muse upon my country's ills—
The tempest bursting from the waste of Time
On the world's fairest hope linked with man's foulest crime.

Nature's dark side is heeded now—
    (Ah! optimist-cheer disheartened flown)—
A child may read the moody brow
    Of yon black mountain lone.
With shouts the torrents down the gorges go,
And storms are formed behind the storm we feel:
The hemlock shakes in the rafter, the oak in the driving keel.

Shiloh: A Requiem

Skimming lightly, wheeling still,
  The swallows fly low
Over the field in clouded days,
  The forest-field of Shiloh—
Over the field where April rain
Solaced the parched one stretched in pain
Through the pause of night
That followed the Sunday fight
  Around the church of Shiloh—
The church so lone, the log-built one,
That echoed to many a parting groan
        And natural prayer
  Of dying foemen mingled there—
Foemen at morn, but friends at eve—
  Fame or country least their care:
(What like a bullet can undeceive!)
  But now they lie low,
While over them the swallows skim
  And all is hushed at Shiloh.

The House-Top, a Night Piece

No sleep. The sultriness pervades the air
And binds the brain—a dense oppression, such
As tawny tigers feel in matted shades,
Vexing their blood and making apt for ravage.
Beneath the stars the roofy desert spreads
Vacant as Libya. All is hushed near by.
Yet fitfully from far breaks a mixed surf
Of muffled sound, the Atheist roar of riot.
Yonder, where parching Sirius set in drought,
Balefully glares red Arson—there—and there.
The Town is taken by its rats—ship-rats
And rats of the wharves. All civil charms
And priestly spells which late held hearts in awe—
Fear-bound, subjected to a better sway
Than sway of self; these like a dream dissolve,
And man rebounds whole æons back in nature.
Hail to the low dull rumble, dull and dead,
And ponderous drag that shakes the wall.
Wise Draco comes, deep in the midnight roll
Of black artillery; he comes, though late;
In code corroborating Calvin's creed
And cynic tyrannies of honest kings;

He comes, nor parleys; and the Town, redeemed,
Gives thanks devout; nor, being thankful, heeds
The grimy slur on the Republic's faith implied,
Which holds that Man is naturally good,
And—more—is Nature's Roman, never to be
        scourged.

The Martyr
Indicative of the Passion of the People
on the 15th Day of April, 1865

Good Friday was the day
    Of the prodigy and crime,
When they killed him in his pity,
    When they killed him in his prime
Of clemency and calm—
        When with yearning he was filled
        To redeem the evil-willed,
And, though conqueror, be kind;
    But they killed him in his kindness,
    In their madness and their blindness,
And they killed him from behind.

        There is sobbing of the strong,
            And a pall upon the land;
        But the People in their weeping
            Bare the iron hand:
        Beware the People weeping
            When they bare the iron hand.

He lieth in his blood—
    The father in his face;
They have killed him, the Forgiver—
    The Avenger takes his place,
The Avenger wisely stern,
        Who in righteousness shall do
        What the heavens call him to,
And the parricides remand;
    For they killed him in his kindness
    In their madness and their blindness,
And his blood is on their hand.

There is sobbing of the strong,
   And a pall upon the land;
But the People in their weeping
      Bare the iron hand:
Beware the People weeping
   When they bare the iron hand.

The Apparition—A Retrospect

Convulsions came; and, where the field
   Long slept in pastoral green,
A goblin-mountain was upheaved
(Sure the scared sense was all deceived),
   Marl-glen and slag-ravine.

The unreserve of Ill was there,
   The clinkers in her last retreat;
But, ere the eye could take it in,
Or mind could comprehension win,
   It sunk!—and at our feet.

So, then, Solidity's a crust—
   The core of fire below;
All may go well for many a year,
But who can think without a fear
   Of horrors that happen so?

The Maldive Shark

About the Shark, phlegmatical one,
Pale sot of the Maldive sea,
The sleek little pilot-fish, azure and slim,
How alert in attendance be.
From his saw-pit of mouth, from his charnel of maw,
They have nothing of harm to dread,
But liquidly glide on his ghastly flank
Or before his Gorgonian head;
Or lurk in the port of serrated teeth
In white triple tiers of glittering gates,
And there find a haven when peril's abroad,
An asylum in jaws of the Fates!
They are friends; and friendly they guide him to prey,
Yet never partake of the treat—
Eyes and brains to the dotard lethargic and dull,
Pale ravener of horrible meat.

To Ned

Where is the world we roved, Ned Bunn?
    Hollows thereof lay rich in shade
By voyagers old inviolate thrown
    Ere Paul Pry cruised with Pelf and Trade.
To us old lads some thoughts come home
Who roamed a world young lads no more shall roam.

Nor less the satiate year impends
    When, wearying of routine-resorts,
The pleasure-hunter shall break loose,
    Ned, for our Pantheistic ports:—
Marquesas and glenned isles that be
Authentic Edens in a Pagan sea.

The charm of scenes untried shall lure,
    And, Ned, a legend urge the flight—
The Typee-truants under stars
    Unknown to Shakespeare's *Midsummer-Night;*
And man, if lost to Saturn's Age,
Yet feeling life no Syrian pilgrimage.

But, tell, shall he, the tourist, find
    Our isles the same in violet-glow
Enamouring us what years and years—
    Ah, Ned, what years and years ago!
Well, Adam advances, smart in pace,
But scarce by violets that advance you trace.

But we, in anchor-watches calm,
    The Indian Psyche's languor won,
And, musing, breathed primeval balm
    From Edens ere yet overrun;
Marvelling mild if mortal twice,
Here and hereafter, touch a Paradise.

The Berg

A DREAM

I saw a ship of martial build
(Her standards set, her brave apparel on)
Directed as by madness mere
Against a stolid iceberg steer,
Nor budge it, though the infatuate ship went down.

The impact made huge ice-cubes fall
Sullen, in tons that crashed the deck;
But that one avalanche was all—
No other movement save the foundering wreck.

Along the spurs of ridges pale,
Not any slenderest shaft and frail,
A prism over glass-green gorges lone,
Toppled; nor lace of traceries fine,
Nor pendant drops in grot or mine
Were jarred, when the stunned ship went down.
Nor sole the gulls in cloud that wheeled
Circling one snow-flanked peak afar,
But nearer fowl the floes that skimmed
And crystal beaches, felt no jar.
No thrill transmitted stirred the lock
Of jack-straw needle-ice at base;
Towers undermined by waves—the block
Atilt impending—kept their place.
Seals, dozing sleek on sliddery ledges
Slipt never, when by loftier edges
Through very inertia overthrown,
The impetuous ship in bafflement went down.

Hard Berg (methought), so cold, so vast,
With mortal damps self-overcast;
Exhaling still thy dankish breath—
Adrift dissolving, bound for death;
Though lumpish thou, a lumbering one—
A lumbering lubbard loitering slow,
Impingers rue thee and go down,
Sounding thy precipice below,
Nor stir the slimy slug that sprawls
Along thy dead indifference of walls.

Monody

To have known him, to have loved him
    After loneness long;
And then to be estranged in life,
    And neither in the wrong;
And now for death to set his seal—
    Ease me, a little ease, my song!

By wintry hills his hermit-mound
    The sheeted snow-drifts drape,
And houseless there the snow-bird flits
    Beneath the fir-trees' crape:
Glazed now with ice the cloistral vine
    That hid the shyest grape.

Fragments of a Lost Gnostic Poem
of the Twelfth Century

Found a family, build a state,
The pledged event is still the same:
Matter in end will never abate
His ancient brutal claim.

Indolence is heaven's ally here,
And energy the child of hell:
The Good Man pouring from his pitcher clear
But brims the poisoned well.

The Ravaged Villa

In shards the sylvan vases lie,
    Their links of dance undone;
And brambles wither by thy brim,
    Choked Fountain of the Sun!
The spider in the laurel spins,
    The weed exiles the flower,
And, flung to kiln, Apollo's bust
    Makes lime for Mammon's tower.

My Jacket Old

My jacket old, with narrow seam—
When the dull day's work is done
I dust it, and of Asia dream,
Old Asia of the sun!
There other garbs prevail;
Yea, lingering there, free robe and vest,
Edenic Leisure's age attest
Ere Work, alack, came in with Wail.

Pontoosuc

Crowning a bluff where gleams the lake below,
Some pillared pines in well-spaced order stand
And like an open temple show.
And here in best of seasons bland;
Autumnal noon-tide, I look out
From dusk arcades on sunshine all about.
Beyond the Lake, in upland cheer
Fields, pastoral fields and barns appear,
They skirt the hills where lonely roads
Revealed in links thro' tiers of woods
Wind up to indistinct abodes
And faery-peopled neighborhoods;
While further fainter mountains keep
Hazed in romance impenetrably deep.

Look, corn in stacks, on many a farm,
And orchards ripe in languorous charm,
As dreamy Nature, feeling sure
Of all her genial labor done,
And the last mellow fruitage won,
Would idle out her term mature;
Reposing like a thing reclined
In kinship with man's meditative mind.

For me, within the brown arcade—
Rich life, methought; sweet here in shade
And pleasant abroad in air!—But, nay,
A counter thought intrusive played,
A thought as old as thought itself,
And who shall lay it on the shelf!—
I felt the beauty bless the day
In opulence of autumn's dower;
But evanescence will not stay!
A year ago was such an hour,
As this, which but foreruns the blast
Shall sweep these live leaves to the dead leaves past.

All dies!—

I stood in revery long.
Then, to forget death's ancient wrong,
I turned me in the deep arcade,
And there by chance in lateral glade
I saw low tawny mounds in lines
Relics of trunks of stately pines

Ranked erst in colonnades where, lo!
Erect succeeding pillars show!

All dies! and not alone
The aspiring trees and men and grass;
The poet's forms of beauty pass,
And noblest deeds they are undone
Even truth itself decays, and lo,
From truth's sad ashes fraud and falsehood grow.

All dies!

The workman dies, and after him, the work;
Like to these pines whose graves I trace,
Statue and statuary fall upon their face:
In very amaranths the worm doth lurk,
Even stars, Chaldæans say, have left their place.
Andes and Apalachee tell
Of havoc ere our Adam fell,
And present Nature as a moss doth show
On the ruins of the Nature of the æons of long ago.

But look—and hark!

Adown the glade,
Where light and shadow sport at will,
Who cometh vocal, and arrayed
As in the first pale tints of morn—
So pure, rose-clear, and fresh and chill!
Some ground-pine springs her brow adorn,
The earthy rootlets tangled clinging.
Over tufts of moss which dead things made,
Under vital twigs which danced or swayed,
Along she floats, and lightly singing:

"Dies, all dies!
The grass it dies, but in vernal rain
Up it springs and it lives again;
Over and over, again and again
It lives, it dies and it lives again.
Who sighs that all dies?
Summer and winter, and pleasure and pain
And everything everywhere in God's reign,
They end, and anon they begin again:
Wane and wax, wax and wane:
Over and over and over amain

End, ever end, and begin again—
End, ever end, and forever and ever begin again!"

She ceased, and nearer slid, and hung
In dewy guise; then softlier sung:
"Since light and shade are equal set
And all revolves, nor more ye know;
Ah, why should tears the pale cheek fret
For aught that waneth here below.
Let go, Let go!"

With that, her warm lips thrilled me through,
She kissed me, while her chaplet cold
Its rootlets brushed against my brow,
With all their humid clinging mould.
She vanished, leaving fragrant breath
And warmth and chill of wedded life and death.

from CLAREL

from The Hostel

. . . .

                    Ah!
These under-formings in the mind,
Banked corals which ascend from far,
But little heed men that they wind
Unseen, unheard—till lo, the reef—
The reef and breaker, wreck and grief.
But here unlearning, how to me
Opes the expanse of time's vast sea!
Yes, I am young, but Asia old.
The books, the books not all have told.

from The Inscription

" 'Emblazoned bleak in austral skies—
A heaven remote, whose starry swarm
Like Science lights but cannot warm—
Translated Cross, hast thou withdrawn,
Dim paling too at every dawn,
With symbols vain once counted wise,

And gods declined to heraldries?
Estranged, estranged: can friend prove so?
Aloft, aloof, a frigid sign:
How far removed, thou Tree divine,
Whose tender fruit did reach so low—
Love apples of New-Paradise!
About the wide Australian sea
The planted nations yet to be—
When, ages hence, they lift their eyes,
Tell, what shall they retain of thee?
But class thee with Orion's sword?
In constellations unadored,
Christ and the Giant equal prize?
The atheist cycles—*must* they be?
Fomentors as forefathers we?'

"I, Science, I whose gain's thy loss,
I slanted thee, thou Slanting Cross."

from Prelusive

In Piranesi's rarer prints,
Interiors measurelessly strange,
Where the distrustful thought may range
Misgiving still—what mean the hints?
Stairs upon stairs which dim ascend
In series from plunged Bastiles drear—
Pit under pit; long tier on tier
Of shadowed galleries which impend
Over cloisters, cloisters without end;
The hight, the depth—the far, the near;
Ring-bolts to pillars in vaulted lanes,
And dragging Rhadamanthine chains;
These less of wizard influence lend
Than some allusive chambers closed.
      Those wards of hush are not disposed
In gibe of goblin fantasy—
Grimace—unclean diablery:
Thy wings, Imagination, span
Ideal truth in fable's seat:
The thing implied is one with man,
His penetralia of retreat—
The heart, with labyrinths replete:
In freaks of intimation see
Paul's "mystery of iniquity:"
Involved indeed, a blur of dream;

As, awed by scruple and restricted
In first design, or interdicted
By fate and warnings as might seem;
The inventor miraged all the maze,
Obscured it with prudential haze;
Nor less, if subject unto question,
The egg left, egg of the suggestion.

  Dwell on those etchings in the night,
Those touches bitten in the steel
By aqua-fortis, till ye feel
The Pauline text in gray of light;
Turn hither then and read aright.

from The Cypriote

  "Noble gods at the board
  Where lord unto lord
Light pushes the care-killing wine:
   Urbane in their pleasure,
   Superb in their leisure—
    Lax ease—
Lax ease after labor divine!

  "Golden ages eternal,
  Autumnal, supernal,
Deep mellow their temper serene:
   The rose by their gate
   Shall it yield unto fate?
    They are gods—
They are gods and their garlands keep green.

  "Ever blandly adore them;
  But spare to implore them:
They rest, they discharge them from time;
   Yet believe, light believe
   They would succor, reprieve—
    Nay, retrieve—
Might but revelers pause in the prime!"

from The Shepherd's Dale

"As cruel as a Turk: Whence came
That proverb old as the crusades?
From Anglo-Saxons. What are they?
Let the horse answer, and blockades
Of medicine in civil fray!
The Anglo-Saxons—lacking grace
To win the love of any race;
Hated by myriads dispossessed
Of rights—the Indians East and West.
These pirates of the sphere! grave looters—
Grave, canting, Mammonite freebooters,
Who in the name of Christ and Trade
(Oh, bucklered forehead of the brass!)
Deflower the world's last sylvan glade!"

from A New-Comer

[UNGAR'S HARANGUE]

"Ay, Democracy
Lops, lops; but where's her planted bed?
The future, what is that to her
Who vaunts she's no inheritor?
'Tis in her mouth, not in her heart.
The Past she spurns, though 'tis the past
From which she gets her saving part—
That Good which lets her Evil last.
Behold her whom the panders crown,
Harlot on horseback, riding down
The very Ephesians who acclaim
This great Diana of ill fame!
Arch strumpet of an impious age,
Upstart from ranker villanage,
'Tis well she must restriction taste
Nor lay the world's broad manor waste:
Asia shall stop her at the least,
That old inertness of the East.
She's limited; lacking the free
And genial catholicity
Which in Christ's pristine scheme unfurled
Grace to the city and the world."

from Ungar and Rolfe

They felt how far beyond the scope
Of elder Europe's saddest thought
Might be the New World's sudden brought
In youth to share old age's pains—
To feel the arrest of hope's advance,
And squandered last inheritance;
And cry—"To Terminus build fanes!
Columbus ended earth's romance:
No New World to mankind remains!"

Epilogue

If Luther's day expand to Darwin's year,
Shall that exclude the hope—foreclose the fear?

    Unmoved by all the claims our times avow,
The ancient Sphinx still keeps the porch of shade;
And comes Despair, whom not her calm may cow,
And coldly on that adamantine brow
Scrawls undeterred his bitter pasquinade.
But Faith (who from the scrawl indignant turns)
With blood warm oozing from her wounded trust,
Inscribes even on her shards of broken urns
The sign o' the cross—*the spirit above the dust!*

    Yea, ape and angel, strife and old debate—
The harps of heaven and dreary gongs of hell;
Science the feud can only aggravate—
No umpire she betwixt the chimes and knell:
The running battle of the star and clod
Shall run forever—if there be no God.

    Degrees we know, unknown in days before;
The light is greater, hence the shadow more;
And tantalized and apprehensive Man
Appealing—Wherefore ripen us to pain?
Seems there the spokesman of dumb Nature's train.
    But through such strange illusions have they passed
Who in life's pilgrimage have baffled striven—
Even death may prove unreal at the last,
And stoics be astounded into heaven.

Then keep thy heart, though yet but ill-resigned—
Clarel, thy heart, the issues there but mind;
That like the crocus budding through the snow—
That like a swimmer rising from the deep—
That like a burning secret which doth go
Even from the bosom that would hoard and keep;
Emerge thou mayst from the last whelming sea,
And prove that death but routs life into victory.

ALICE CARY
(1820–1871)

The Bridal Veil

We're married, they say, and you think you have won me,—
Well, take this white veil from my head, and look on me;
Here's matter to vex you, and matter to grieve you,
Here's doubt to distrust you, and faith to believe you,—
I am all as you see, common earth, common dew;
Be wary, and mould me to roses, not rue!

Ah! shake out the filmy thing, fold after fold,
And see if you have me to keep and to hold,—
Look close on my heart—see the worst of its sinning,—
It is not yours to-day for the yesterday's winning—
The past is not mine—I am too proud to borrow—
You must grow to new heights if I love you to-morrow.

I have wings flattened down and hid under my veil:
They are subtle as light—you can never undo them,
And swift in their flight—you can never pursue them,
And spite of all clasping, and spite of all bands,
I can slip like a shadow, a dream, from your hands.

Nay, call me not cruel, and fear not to take me,
I am yours for my life-time, to be what you make me,—
To wear my white veil for a sign, or a cover,
As you shall be proven my lord, or my lover;
A cover for peace that is dead, or a token
Of bliss that can never be written or spoken.

ANN PLATO

(c.1820–?)

The Natives of America

Tell me a story, father please,
And then I sat upon his knees.
Then answer'd he,—"what speech make known,
Or tell the words of native tone,
Of how my Indian fathers dwelt,
And, of sore oppression felt;
And how they mourned a land serene,
It was an ever mournful theme."

Yes, I replied,—I like to hear,
And bring my father's spirit near;
Of every pain they did forego,
Oh, please to tell me all you know.
In history often I do read,
Of pain which none but they did heed.

He thus began. "We were a happy race,
When we no tongue but ours did trace,
We were in ever peace,
We sold, we did release—
Our brethren, far remote, and far unknown,
And spake to them in silent, tender tone.
We all were then as in one band,
We join'd and took each others hand;
Our dress was suited to the clime,
Our food was such as roam'd that time,
Our houses were of sticks compos'd;
No matter,—for they us enclos'd.

But then discover'd was this land indeed
By European men; who then had need
Of this far country. Columbus came afar,
And thus before we could say Ah!
What meaneth this?—we fell in cruel hands.
Though some were kind, yet others then held bands
Of cruel oppression. Then too, foretold our chief,—
Beggars you will become—is my belief.
We sold, then some bought lands,
We altogether moved in foreign hands.

Wars ensued. They knew the handling of firearms.
Mothers spoke,—no fear this breast alarms,
They will not cruelly us oppress,
Or thus our lands possess.
Alas! it was a cruel day; we were crush'd:
Into the dark, dark woods we rush'd
To seek a refuge.

My daughter, we are now diminish'd, unknown,
Unfelt! Alas! No tender tone
To cheer us when the hunt is done;
Fathers sleep,—we're silent every one.

Oh! silent the horror, and fierce the fight,
When my brothers were shrouded in night;
Strangers did us invade—strangers destroy'd
The fields, which were by us enjoy'd.

Our country is cultur'd, and looks all sublime,
Our fathers are sleeping who lived in the time
That I tell. Oh! could I tell them my grief
In its flow, that in roaming, we find no relief.

I love my country; and shall, until death
Shall cease my breath.

Now daughter dear I've done,
Seal this upon thy memory; until the morrow's sun
Shall sink, to rise no more;
And if my years should score,
Remember this, though I tell no more."

JOSHUA McCARTER SIMPSON
(c.1820–1876)

from Away to Canada

. . . .

Grieve not, my wife—grieve not for me,
    O! do not break my heart,
For nought but cruel slavery
    Would cause me to depart.
If I should stay to quell your grief,

Your grief I would augment;
For no one knows the day that we
  Asunder might be rent.

    O! Susannah,
      Don't you cry for me—
    I'm going up to Canada,
      Where colored men are free.

I heard old master pray last night—
  I heard him pray for me;
That God would come, and in his might
  From Satan set me free;
So I from Satan would escape,
  And flee the wrath to come—
If there's a fiend in human shape,
  Old master must be one.

    O! old master,
      While you pray for me,
    I'm doing all I can to reach
      The land of Liberty.

FREDERICK GODDARD TUCKERMAN
(*1821–1873*)

from SONNETS, FIRST SERIES

VI
Not sometimes, but to him that heeds the whole
And in the Ample reads his personal page,
Laboring to reconcile, content, assuage
The vexed conditions of his heritage,
Forever waits an angel at the goal.
And ills seem but as food for spirits sage,
And greed becomes a dark apparelage,
The weed and wearing of the sacred soul.
Might I but count, but here, one watchlight spark!
But vain, O vain this turning for the light,
Vain as a groping hand to rend the dark—
I call, entangled in the night, a night
Of wind and voices, but the gusty roll
Is vague, nor comes their cheer of pilotage.

V
No! Cover not the fault. The wise revere
The judgment of the simple. Harshly flow
The words of counsel; but at the end may show
Matter and music to the unwilling ear.
But perfect grief, like love, should cast out fear
And like an o'erbrimmed river moaning go.
Yet shrinks it from the senseless chaff and chat
Of those who smile and insolently bestow
Their ignorant praise, or those who stoop and peer
To pick with sharpened fingers for a flaw,
Not ever touch the quick, nor rub the raw.
Better than this were surgery rough as that
Which, hammer and chisel in hand, at one sharp blow
Strikes out the wild tooth from a horse's jaw.

VII
His heart was in his garden; but his brain
Wandered at will among the fiery stars.
Bards, heroes, prophets, Homers, Hamilcars,
With many angels stood, his eye to gain;
The devils, too, were his familiars:
And yet the cunning florist held his eyes
Close to the ground, a tulip bulb his prize,
And talked of tan and bonedust, cutworms, grubs,
As though all Nature held no higher strain;
Or, if he spoke of art, he made the theme
Flow through boxborders, turf, and flower tubs
Or, like a garden engine's, steered the stream,
Now spouted rainbows to the silent skies,
Now kept it flat and raked the walls and shrubs.

XVIII
And change with hurried hand has swept these scenes:
The woods have fallen, across the meadow-lot
The hunter's trail and trap-path is forgot,
And fire has drunk the swamps of evergreens;
Yet for a moment let my fancy plant
These autumn hills again: the wild dove's haunt,
The wild deer's walk. In golden umbrage shut,
The Indian river runs, Quonecktacut!
Here, but a lifetime back, where falls tonight
Behind the curtained pane a sheltered light

On buds of rose or vase of violet
Aloft upon the marble mantel set,
Here in the forest-heart, hung blackening
The wolfbait on the bush beside the spring.

from SONNETS, FOURTH SERIES

VIII
Nor strange it is, to us who walk in bonds
Of flesh and time, if virtue's self awhile
Gleam dull like sunless ice; whilst graceful guile—
Blood-flecked like hamatite or diamonds
With a red inward spark—to reconcile
Beauty and evil seems and corresponds
So well with good that the mind joys to have
Full wider jet and scope: nor swings and sleeps
Forever in one cradle wearily
Like those vast weeds that off d'Acunha's isle
Wash with the surf and flap their might fronds
Mournfully to the dipping of the wave,
Yet cannot be disrupted from their deeps
By the whole heave and settle of the sea.

from The Cricket

I
The humming bee purrs softly o'er his flower;
   From lawn and thicket
The dogday locust singeth in the sun
   From hour to hour:
Each has his bard, and thou, ere day be done,
   Shalt have no wrong.
So bright that murmur mid the insect crowd,
Muffled and lost in bottom-grass, or loud
   By pale and picket:
Shall I not take to help me in my song
   A little cooing cricket?

II

The afternoon is sleepy; let us lie
Beneath these branches whilst the burdened brook,
Muttering and moaning to himself, goes by;
And mark our minstrel's carol whilst we look
Toward the faint horizon swooning blue.
    Or in a garden bower,
Trellised and trammeled with deep drapery
      Of hanging green,
      Light glimmering through—
There let the dull hop be,
Let bloom, with poppy's dark refreshing flower:
Let the dead fragrance round our temples beat,
Stunning the sense to slumber, whilst between
The falling water and fluttering wind
      Mingle and meet,
      Murmur and mix,
No few faint pipings from the glades behind,
      Or alder-thicks:
But louder as the day declines,
From tingling tassel, blade, and sheath,
Rising from nets of river vies,
      Winrows and ricks,
      Above, beneath,
      At every breath,
At hand, around, illimitably
Rising and falling like the sea,
      Acres of cricks!

. . . .

IV

So wert thou loved in that old graceful time
    When Greece was fair,
While god and hero hearkened to thy chime;
    Softly astir
Where the long grasses fringed Caÿster's lip;
Long-drawn, with glimmering sails of swan and ship,
    And ship and swan;
    Or where
    Reedy Eurotas ran.
Did that low marble teach thy tender flute
    Xenaphyle?
Its breathings mild? say! did the grasshopper
Sit golden in thy purple hair
    O Psammathe?
    Or wert thou mute,

Grieving for Pan amid the alders there?
And by the water and along the hill
That thirsty tinkle in the herbage still,
Though the lost forest wailed to horns of Arcady?

V
Like the Enchanter old—
Who sought mid the dead water's weeds and scum
For evil growths beneath the moonbeam cold,
    Or mandrake or dorcynium;
And touched the leaf that opened both his ears,
So that articulate voices now he hears
In cry of beast, or bird, or insect's hum,—
Might I but find thy knowledge in thy song!
    That twittering tongue,
Ancient as light, returning like the years.
    So might I be,
Unwise to sing, thy true interpreter
Through denser stillness and in sounder dark,
Than ere thy notes have pierced to harrow me.
    So might I stir
    The world to hark
    To thee my lord and lawgiver,
    And cease my quest:
Content to bring thy wisdom to the world;
Content to gain at last some low applause,
    Now low, now lost
Like thine from mossy stone, amid the stems and straws,
    Or garden gravemound tricked and dressed—
    Powdered and pearled
    By stealing frost—
In dusky rainbow beauty of euphorbias!
For larger would be less indeed, and like
The ceaseless simmer in the summer grass
To him who toileth in the windy field,
    Or where the sunbeams strike,
Naught in innumerable numerousness.
    So might I much possess,
    So much must yield;
But failing this, the dell and grassy dike,
The water and the waste shall still be dear,
And all the pleasant plots and places
    Where thou hast sung, and I have hung
    To ignorantly hear.
Then Cricket, sing thy song! or answer mine!
Thine whispers blame, but mine has naught but praises.
It matters not. Behold! the autumn goes,

The shadow grows,
The moments take hold of eternity;
Even while we stop to wrangle or repine
Our lives are gone—
Like thinnest mist,
Like yon escaping color in the tree;
Rejoice! rejoice! whilst yet the hours exist—
Rejoice or mourn, and let the world swing on
Unmoved by cricket song of thee or me.

The Refrigerium

Let them lie,—their day is over;
Nought but night and stillness be:
Let the slow rain come and bring
Brake and stargrass, speedwell, harebell,
All the fulness of the spring;
What reck I of friend and lover?
Foe by foe laid lovingly?

What are mounds of green earth, either?
What to me unfriendly bones
Death hath pacified and won
To a reconciled patience,
Though their very graves have run
In the blending earth together,
And the spider links the stones?

To the hills I wander, crying,
Where we stood in days of old,
Stood and saw the sunset die;
Watched through tears the passing purple,—
O my darling! misery
Has been mine; but thou wert lying
In a slumber sweet and cold.

F.E.W. HARPER
(1824–1911)

Bury Me in a Free Land

Make me a grave where'er you will,
In a lowly plain, or a lofty hill,
Make it among earth's humblest graves,
But not in a land where men are slaves.

I could not rest if around my grave
I heard the steps of a trembling slave:
His shadow above my silent tomb
Would make it a place of fearful gloom.

I could not rest if I heard the tread
Of a coffle gang to the shambles led,
And the mother's shriek of wild despair
Rise like a curse on the trembling air.

I could not sleep if I saw the lash
Drinking her blood at each fearful gash,
And I saw her babes torn from her breast,
Like trembling doves from their parent nest.

I'd shudder and start if I heard the bay
Of blood-hounds seizing their human prey,
And I heard the captive plead in vain
As they bound afresh his galling chain.

If I saw young girls from their mother's arms
Bartered and sold for their youthful charms,
My eye would flash with a mournful flame,
My death-paled cheek grow red with shame.

I would sleep, dear friends, where bloated might
Can rob no man of his dearest right;
My rest shall be calm in any grave
Where none can call his brother a slave.

I ask no monument, proud and high,
To arrest the gaze of the passers by;
All that my yearning spirit craves,
Is bury me not in a land of slaves.

The Death of Moses

. . . .

Oh never on that mountain
Was seen a lovelier sight
Than the troupe of fair young angels
That gathered 'round the dead.
With gentle hands they bore him
That bright and shining train,
From Nebo's lonely mountain
To sleep in Moab's vale.
But they sang no mournful dirges,
No solemn requiems said,
And the soft wave of their pinions
Made music as they trod.
But no one heard them passing,
None saw their chosen grave;
It was the angels secret
Where Moses should be laid.
And when the grave was finished,
They trod with golden sandals
Above the sacred spot,
And the brightest, fairest flower
Sprang up beneath their tread.
Nor broken turf, nor hillock
Did e'er reveal that grave,
And truthful lips have never said
We know where he is laid.

LUCY LARCOM
(*1824–1893*)

They Said

They said of her, "She never can have felt
    The sorrows that our deeper natures feel:"
They said, "Her placid lips have never spelt
    Hard lessons taught by Pain; her eyes reveal
    No passionate yearning, no perplexed appeal

To other eyes. Life and her heart have dealt
With her but lightly."—When the Pilgrims dwelt
    First on these shores, lest savage hands should steal
To precious graves with desecrating tread,
    The burial-field was with the ploughshare crossed,
    And there the maize her silken tresses tossed.
With thanks those Pilgrims ate their bitter bread,
    While peaceful harvests hid what they had lost.
    What if her smiles concealed from you her dead?

from November

. . . .

This is the month of sunrise skies
    Intense with molten mist and flame;
Out of the purple deeps arise
    Colors no painter yet could name:
Gold-lilies and the cardinal-flower
Were pale against this gorgeous hour.

Still lovelier when athwart the east
    The level beam of sunset falls:
The tints of wild-flowers long deceased
    Glow then upon the horizon walls;
Shades of the rose and violet
Close to their dear world lingering yet.

What idleness, to moan and fret
    For any season fair, gone by!
Life's secret is not guessed at yet;
    Veil under veil its wonders lie.
Through grief and loss made glorious
The soul of past joy lives in us.

More welcome than voluptuous gales
    This keen, crisp air, as conscience clear:
November breathes no flattering tales;
    The plain truth-teller of the year,
Who wins her heart, and he alone,
Knows she has sweetness all her own.

CHARLES GODFREY LELAND
(1824–1903)

Ballad

Der noble Ritter Hugo
    Von Schwillensaufenstein,
Rode out mit shpeer und helmet,
    Und he coom to de panks of de Rhine.

Und oop dere rose a meermaid,
    Vot hadn't got nodings on,
Und she say, "Oh, Ritter Hugo,
    Vhere you goes mit yourself alone?"

And he says, "I rides in de creenwood,
    Mit helmet und mit shpeer,
Til I cooms into em Gasthaus,
    Und dere I trinks some beer."

Und den outshpoke de maiden
    Vot hadn't got nodings on:
"I ton't dink mooch of beoplesh
    Dat goes mit demselfs alone.

"You'd petter coom down in de wasser,
    Vhere dere's heaps of dings to see,
Und hafe a shplendid tinner
    Und drafel along mit me.

"Dere you sees de fisch a schwimmin',
    Und you catches dem efery von:"—
So sang dis wasser maiden
    Vot hadn't got nodings on.

"Dere is drunks all full mit money
    In ships dat vent down of old;
Und you helpsh yourself, by dunder!
    To shimmerin' crowns of gold.

"Shoost look at dese shpoons und vatches!
    Shoost see dese diamant rings!
Coom down and fill your bockets,
    Und I'll giss you like efery dings.

"Vot you vantsh mit your schnapps und lager?
    Coom down into der Rhine!
Der ish pottles der Kaiser Charlemagne
    Vonce filled mit gold-red wine!"

Dat fetched him—he shtood all shpellpound;
    She pooled his coat-tails down,
She drawed him oonder der wasser,
    De maiden mit nodings on.

BAYARD TAYLOR
(1825–1878)

Bedouin Song

From the Desert I come to thee
    On a stallion shod with fire;
And the winds are left behind
    In thy speed of my desire.
Under the window I stand,
    And the midnight hears my cry:
I love thee, I love but thee,
    With a love that shall not die
        Till the sun grows cold,
        And the stars are old,
        And the leaves of the Judgment
            Book unfold!

Look from thy window and see
    My passion and my pain;
I lie on the sands below,
    And I faint in thy disdain.
Let the night-winds touch thy brow
    With the heat of my burning sigh,
And melt thee to hear the vow
    Of a love that shall not die
        Till the sun grows cold,
        And the stars are old,
        And the leaves of the Judgment
            Book unfold!

My steps are nightly driven,
    By the fever in my breast,
To hear from thy lattice breathed
    The word that shall give me rest.
Open the door of thy heart,
    And open thy chamber door,
And my kisses shall teach thy lips
    The love that shall fade no more
        Till the sun grows cold,
        And the stars are old,
        And the leaves of the Judgment
            Book unfold!

ROSE TERRY COOKE
(1827–1892)

Blue-beard's Closet

Fasten the chamber!
Hide the red key;
Cover the portal,
That eyes may not see.
Get thee to market,
To wedding and prayer;
Labor or revel,
The chamber is there!

In comes a stranger—
"Thy pictures how fine,
Titian or Guido,
Whose is the sign?"
Looks he behind them?
Ah! have a care!
"Here is a finer."
The chamber is there!

Fair spreads the banquet,
Rich the array;
See the bright torches
Mimicking day;
When harp and viol
Thrill the soft air,
Comes a light whisper:
The chamber is there!

Marble and painting,
Jasper and gold,
Purple from Tyrus,
Fold upon fold,
Blossoms and jewels,
Thy palace prepare:
Pale grows the monarch;
The chamber is there!

Once it was open
As shore to the sea;
White were the turrets,
Goodly to see;
All through the casements
Flowed the sweet air;
Now it is darkness;
The chamber is there!

Silence and horror
Brood on the walls;
Through every crevice
A little voice calls:
"Quicken, mad footsteps,
On pavement and stair;
Look not behind thee,
The chamber is there!"

Out of the gateway,
Through the wide world,
Into the tempest
Beaten and hurled,
Vain is thy wandering,
Sure thy despair,
Flying or staying,
The chamber is there!

HENRY TIMROD
(1828–1867)

Charleston

Calm as that second summer which precedes
    The first fall of the snow,
In the broad sunlight of heroic deeds,
    The City bides the foe.

As yet, behind their ramparts stern and proud,
    Her bolted thunders sleep—
Dark Sumter, like a battlemented cloud,
    Looms o'er the solemn deep.

No Calpe frowns from lofty cliff or scar
    To guard the holy strand;
But Moultrie holds in leash her dogs of war
    Above the level sand.

And down the dunes a thousand guns lie couched,
    Unseen, beside the flood—
Like tigers in some Orient jungle crouched
    That wait and watch for blood.

Meanwhile, through streets still echoing with trade,
    Walk grave and thoughtful men,
Whose hands may one day wield the patriot's blade
    As lightly as the pen.

And maidens, with such eyes as would grow dim
    Over a bleeding hound,
Seem each one to have caught the strength of him
    Whose sword she sadly bound.

Thus girt without and garrisoned at home,
    Day patient following day,
Old Charleston looks from roof, and spire, and dome,
    Across her tranquil bay.

Ships, through a hundred foes, from Saxon lands
    And spicy Indian ports,
Bring Saxon steel and iron to her hands,
    And Summer to her courts.

But still, along yon dim Atlantic line,
  The only hostile smoke
Creeps like a harmless mist above the brine,
  From some frail, floating oak.

Shall the Spring dawn, and she still clad in smiles,
  And with an unscathed brow,
Rest in the strong arms of her palm-crowned isles,
  As fair and free as now?

We know not; in the temple of the Fates
  God has inscribed her doom;
And, all untroubled in her faith, she waits
  The triumph or the tomb.

Ethnogenesis

I
Hath not the morning dawned with added light?
And shall not evening call another star
Out of the infinite regions of the night,
To mark this day in Heaven? At last, we are
A nation among nations; and the world
Shall soon behold in many a distant port
    Another flag unfurled!
Now, come what may, whose favor need we court?
And, under God, whose thunder need we fear?
    Thank Him who placed us here
Beneath so kind a sky—the very sun
Takes part with us; and on our errands run
All breezes of the ocean; dew and rain
Do noiseless battle for us; and the Year,
And all the gentle daughters in her train,
March in our ranks, and in our service wield
    Long spears of golden grain!
A yellow blossom as her fairy shield,
June flings her azure banner to the wind,
    While in the order of their birth
Her sisters pass, and many an ample field
Grows white beneath their steps, till now, behold,
    Its endless sheets unfold
THE SNOW OF SOUTHERN SUMMERS! Let the earth
Rejoice! beneath those fleeces soft and warm
    Our happy land shall sleep
    In a repose as deep

As if we lay intrenched behind
Whole leagues of Russian ice and Arctic storm!

2
And what if, mad with wrongs themselves have wrought,
    In their own treachery caught,
    By their own fears made bold,
    And leagued with him of old,
Who long since in the limits of the North
Set up his evil throne, and warred with God—
What if, both mad and blinded in their rage,
Our foes should fling us down their mortal gage,
And with a hostile step profane our sod!
We shall not shrink, my brothers, but go forth
To meet them, marshalled by the Lord of Hosts,
And overshadowed by the mighty ghosts
Of Moultrie and of Eutaw—who shall foil
Auxiliars such as these? Nor these alone,
    But every stock and stone
    Shall help us; but the very soil,
And all the generous wealth it gives to toil,
And all for which we love our noble land,
Shall fight beside, and through us; sea and strand,
    The heart of woman, and her hand,
Tree, fruit, and flower, and every influence,
    Gentle, or grave, or grand;
    The winds in our defence
Shall seem to blow; to us the hills shall lend
    Their firmness and their calm;
And in our stiffened sinews we shall blend
    The strength of pine and palm!

3
Nor would we shun the battle-ground,
    Though weak as we are strong;
Call up the clashing elements around,
    And test the right and wrong!
On one side, creeds that dare to teach
What Christ and Paul refrained to preach;
Codes built upon a broken pledge,
And Charity that whets a poniard's edge;
Fair schemes that leave the neighboring poor
To starve and shiver at the schemer's door,
While in the world's most liberal ranks enrolled,
He turns some vast philanthropy to gold;
Religion, taking every mortal form
But that a pure and Christian faith makes warm,

Where not to vile fanatic passion urged,
Or not in vague philosophies submerged,
Repulsive with all Pharisaic leaven,
And making laws to stay the laws of Heaven!
And on the other, scorn of sordid gain,
Unblemished honor, truth without a stain,
Faith, justice, reverence, charitable wealth,
And, for the poor and humble, laws which give,
Not the mean right to buy the right to live,
      But life, and home, and health!
To doubt the end were want of trust in God,
      Who, if he has decreed
   That we must pass a redder sea
Than that which rang to Miriam's holy glee,
      Will surely raise at need
      A Moses with his rod!

4
But let our fears—if fears we have—be still,
And turn us to the future! Could we climb
Some mighty Alp, and view the coming time,
The rapturous sight would fill
      Our eyes with happy tears!
Not only for the glories which the years
Shall bring us; not for lands from sea to sea,
And wealth, and power, and peace, though these shall be;
But for the distant peoples we shall bless,
And the hushed murmurs of a world's distress:
For, to give labor to the poor,
      The whole sad planet o'er,
And save from want and crime the humblest door,
Is one among the many ends for which
      God makes us great and rich!
The hour perchance is not yet wholly ripe
When all shall own it, but the type
Whereby we shall be known in every land
Is that vast gulf which lips our Southern strand,
And through the cold, untempered ocean pours
Its genial streams, that far off Arctic shores
May sometimes catch upon the softened breeze
Strange tropic warmth and hints of summer seas.

La Belle Juive

Is it because your sable hair
Is folded over brows that wear
At times a too imperial air;

Or is it that the thoughts which rise
In those dark orbs do seek disguise
Beneath the lids of Eastern eyes;

That choose whatever pose or place
May chance to please, in you I trace
The noblest woman of your race?

The crowd is sauntering at its ease,
And humming like a hive of bees—
You take your seat and touch the keys:

I do not hear the giddy throng;
The sea avenges Israel's wrong,
And on the wind floats Miriam's song!

You join me with a stately grace;
Music to Poesy gives place;
Some grand emotion lights your face:

At once I stand by Mizpeh's walls;
With smiles the martyred daughter falls,
And desolate are Mizpeh's halls!

Intrusive babblers come between;
With calm, pale brow and lofty mien,
You thread the circle like a queen!

Then sweeps the royal Esther by;
The deep devotion in her eye
Is looking "If I die, I die!"

You stroll the garden's flowery walks;
The plants to me are grainless stalks,
And Ruth to old Naomi talks.

Adopted child of Judah's creed,
Like Judah's daughters, true at need,
I see you mid the alien seed.

I watch afar the gleaner sweet;
I wake like Boaz in the wheat,
And find you lying at my feet!

My feet! Oh! if the spell that lures
My heart through all these dreams endures,
How soon shall I be stretched at yours!

Ode Sung at Magnolia Cemetery

1
Sleep sweetly in your humble graves,
    Sleep, martyrs of a fallen cause;
Though yet no marble column craves
    The pilgrim here to pause.

2
In seeds of laurel in the earth
    The blossom of your fame is blown,
And somewhere, waiting for its birth,
    The shaft is in the stone!

3
Meanwhile, behalf the tardy years
    Which keep in trust your storied tombs,
Behold! your sisters bring their tears,
    And these memorial blooms.

4
Small tributes! but your shades will smile
    More proudly on these wreaths to-day,
Than when some cannon-moulded pile
    Shall overlook this bay.

5
Stoop, angels, hither from the skies!
    There is no holier spot of ground
Than where defeated valor lies,
    By mourning beauty crowned!

HELEN HUNT JACKSON
(1830–1885)

Her Eyes

That they are brown, no man will dare to say
He knows. And yet I think that no man's look
Ever those depths of light and shade forsook,
Until their gentle pain warned him away.
Of all sweet things I know but one which may
Be likened to her eyes.
               When, in deep nook
Of some green field, the water of a brook
Makes lingering, whirling eddy in its way,
Round soft drowned leaves; and in a flash of sun
They turn to gold, until the ripples run
Now brown, now yellow, changing as by some
Swift spell.
             I know not with what body come
The saints. But this I know, my Paradise
Will mean the resurrection of her eyes.

EMILY DICKINSON
(1830–1886)

49

I never lost as much but twice,
And that was in the sod.
Twice have I stood a beggar
Before the door of God!

Angels—twice descending
Reimbursed my store—
Burglar! Banker—Father!
I am poor once more!

67

Success is counted sweetest
By those who ne'er succeed.
To comprehend a nectar
Requires sorest need.

Not one of all the purple Host
Who took the Flag today
Can tell the definition
So clear of Victory

As he defeated—dying—
On whose forbidden ear
The distant strains of triumph
Burst agonized and clear!

71

A throe upon the features—
A hurry in the breath—
An ecstasy of parting
Denominated "Death"—

An anguish at the mention
Which when to patience grown,
I've known permission given
To rejoin its own.

76

Exultation is the going
Of an inland soul to sea,
Past the houses—past the headlands—
Into deep Eternity—

Bred as we, among the mountains,
Can the sailor understand
The divine intoxication
Of the first league out from land?

Surgeons must be very careful
When they take the knife!
Underneath their fine incisions
Stirs the Culprit—*Life*!

130

These are the days when Birds come back—
A very few—a Bird or two—
To take a backward look.

These are the days when skies resume
The old—old sophistries of June—
A blue and gold mistake.

Oh fraud that cannot cheat the Bee—
Almost thy plausibility
Induces my belief.

Till ranks of seeds their witness bear—
And softly thro' the altered air
Hurries a timid leaf.

Oh Sacrament of summer days,
Oh Last Communion in the Haze—
Permit a child to join.

Thy sacred emblems to partake—
Thy consecrated bread to take
And thine immortal wine!

146

On such a night, or such a night,
Would anybody care
If such a little figure
Slipped quiet from its chair—

So quiet—Oh how quiet,
That nobody might know
But that the little figure
Rocked softer—to and fro—

On such a dawn, or such a dawn—
Would anybody sigh
That such a little figure
Too sound asleep did lie

For Chanticleer to wake it—
Or stirring house below—
Or giddy bird in orchard—
Or early task to do?

There was a little figure plump
For every little knoll—
Busy needles, and spools of thread—
And trudging feet from school—

Playmates, and holidays, and nuts—
And visions vast and small—
Strange that the feet so precious charged
Should reach so small a goal!

153

Dust is the only Secret—
Death, the only One
You cannot find out all about
In his "native town."

Nobody knew "his Father"—
Never was a Boy—
Hadn't any playmates,
Or "Early history"—

Industrious! Laconic!
Punctual! Sedate!
Bold as a Brigand!
Stiller than a Fleet!

Builds, like a Bird, too!
Christ robs the Nest—
Robin after Robin
Smuggled to Rest!

"Faith" is a fine invention
When Gentlemen can *see*—
But *Microscopes* are prudent
In an Emergency.

187

How many times these low feet staggered—
Only the soldered mouth can tell—
Try—can you stir the awful rivet—
Try—can you lift the hasps of steel!

Stroke the cool forehead—hot so often—
Lift—if you care—the listless hair—
Handle the adamantine fingers
Never a thimble—more—shall wear—

Buzz the dull flies—on the chamber window—
Brave—shines the sun through the freckled pane—
Fearless—the cobweb swings from the ceiling—
Indolent Housewife—in Daisies—lain!

189

It's such a little thing to weep—
So short a thing to sigh—
And yet—by Trades—the size of *these*
We men and women die!

201

Two swimmers wrestled on the spar—
Until the morning sun—
When One—turned smiling to the land—
Oh God! the Other One!

The stray ships—passing—
Spied a face—
Upon the waters borne—
With eyes in death—still begging raised—
And hands—beseeching—thrown!

210

The thought beneath so slight a film—
Is more distinctly seen—
As laces just reveal the surge—
Or Mists—the Apennine

211

Come slowly—Eden!
Lips unused to Thee—
Bashful—sip thy Jessamines—
As the fainting Bee—

Reaching late his flower,
Round her chamber hums—
Counts his nectars—
Enters—and is lost in Balms.

214

I taste a liquor never brewed—
From Tankards scooped in Pearl—
Not all the Vats upon the Rhine
Yield such an Alcohol!

Inebriate of Air—am I—
And Debauchee of Dew—
Reeling—thro endless summer days—
From inns of Molten Blue—

When "Landlords" turn the drunken Bee
Out of the Foxglove's door—
When Butterflies—renounce their "drams"—
I shall but drink the more!

Till Seraphs swing their snowy Hats—
And Saints—to windows run—
To see the little Tippler
Leaning against the—Sun—

Safe in their Alabaster Chambers—
Untouched by Morning
And untouched by Noon—
Sleep the meek members of the Resurrection—
Rafter of satin,
And Roof of stone.

Light laughs the breeze
In her Castle above them—
Babbles the Bee in a stolid Ear,
Pipe the Sweet Birds in ignorant cadence—
Ah, what sagacity perished here!
(*version of 1859*)

Safe in their Alabaster Chambers—
Untouched by Morning—
And untouched by Noon—
Lie the meek members of the Resurrection—
Rafter of Satin—and Roof of Stone!

Grand go the Years—in the Crescent—above them—
Worlds scoop their Arcs—
And Firmaments—row—
Diadems—drop—and Doges—surrender—
Soundless as dots—on a Disc of Snow—
(*version of 1861*)

234

You're right—"the way *is* narrow"—
And "difficult the Gate"—
And "few there be"—Correct again—
That "enter in—thereat"—

'Tis Costly—So are *purples*!
'Tis just the price of *Breath*—
With but the "Discount" of the *Grave*—
Termed by the *Brokers*—"*Death*"!

And after *that*—there's Heaven—
The *Good* Man's—"*Dividend*"—
And *Bad* Men—"go to Jail"—
I guess—

241

I like a look of Agony,
Because I know it's true—
Men do not sham Convulsion,
Nor simulate, a Throe—
The Eyes glaze once—and that is Death—
Impossible to feign
The Beads upon the Forehead
By homely Anguish strung.

249

Wild Nights—Wild Nights!
Were I with thee
Wild Nights should be
Our luxury!

Futile—the Winds—
To a Heart in port—
Done with the Compass—
Done with the Chart!

Rowing in Eden—
Ah, the Sea!
Might I but moor—Tonight—
In Thee!

254

"Hope" is the thing with feathers—
That perches in the soul—
And sings the tune without the words—
And never stops—at all—

And sweetest—in the Gale—is heard—
And sore must be the storm—
That could abash the little Bird
That kept so many warm—

I've heard it in the chillest land—
And on the strangest Sea—
Yet, never, in Extremity,
It asked a crumb—of Me.

There's a certain Slant of light,
Winter Afternoons—
That oppresses, like the Heft
Of Cathedral Tunes—

Heavenly Hurt, it gives us—
We can find no scar,
But internal difference,
Where the Meanings, are—

None may teach it—Any—
'Tis the Seal Despair—
An imperial affliction
Sent us of the Air—

When it comes, the Landscape listens—
Shadows—hold their breath—
When it goes, 'tis like the Distance
On the look of Death—

280

I felt a Funeral, in my Brain,
And Mourners to and fro
Kept treading—treading—till it seemed
That Sense was breaking through—

And when they all were seated,
A Service, like a Drum—
Kept beating—beating—till I thought
My Mind was going numb—

And then I heard them lift a Box
And creak across my Soul
With those same Boots of Lead, again,
Then Space—began to toll,

As all the Heavens were a Bell,
And Being, but an Ear,
And I, and Silence, some strange Race
Wrecked, solitary, here—

And then a Plank in Reason, broke,
And I dropped down, and down—
And hit a World, at every plunge,
And Finished knowing—then—

287

A Clock Stopped—
Not the Mantel's—
Geneva's farthest skill
Can't put the puppet bowing—
That just now dangled still—

An awe came on the Trinket!
The Figures hunched, with pain—
Then quivered out of Decimals—
Into Degreeless Noon—

It will not stir for Doctors—
This Pendulum of snow—
This Shopman importunes it—
While cool—concernless No—

Nods from the Gilded pointers—
Nods from the Seconds slim—
Decades of Arrogance between
The Dial life—
And Him—

288

I'm Nobody! Who are you?
Are you—Nobody—Too?
Then there's a pair of us!
Don't tell! they'd advertise—you know!

How dreary—to be—Somebody!
How public—like a Frog—
To tell one's name—the livelong June—
To an admiring Bog!

301

I reason, Earth is short—
And Anguish—absolute—
And many hurt,
But, what of that?

I reason, we could die—
The best Vitality
Cannot excel Decay,
But, what of that?

I reason, that in Heaven—
Somehow, it will be even—
Some new Equation, given—
But, what of that?

303

The Soul selects her own Society—
Then—shuts the Door—
To her divine Majority—
Present no more—

Unmoved—she notes the Chariots—pausing—
At her low Gate—
Unmoved—an Emperor be kneeling
Upon her Mat—

I've known her—from an ample nation—
Choose One—
Then—close the Valves of her attention—
Like Stone—

305

The difference between Despair
And Fear—is like the One
Between the instant of a Wreck—
And when the Wreck has been—

The Mind is smooth—no Motion—
Contented as the Eye
Upon the Forehead of a Bust—
That knows—it cannot see—

315

He fumbles at your Soul
As Players at the Keys
Before they drop full Music on—
He stuns you by degrees—
Prepares your brittle Nature
For the Ethereal Blow
By fainter Hammers—further heard—
Then nearer—Then so slow
Your Breath has time to straighten—
Your Brain—to bubble Cool—
Deals—One—imperial—Thunderbolt—
That scalps your naked Soul—
When Winds take Forests in their Paws—
The Universe—is still—

324

Some keep the Sabbath going to Church—
I keep it, staying at Home—
With a Bobolink for a Chorister—
And an Orchard, for a Dome—

Some keep the Sabbath in Surplice—
I just wear my Wings—
And instead of tolling the Bell, for Church,
Our little Sexton—sings.

God preaches, a noted Clergyman—
And the sermon is never long,
So instead of getting to Heaven, at last—
I'm going, all along.

326

I cannot dance upon my Toes—
No Man instructed me—
But oftentimes, among my mind,
A Glee possesseth me,

That had I Ballet knowledge—
Would put itself abroad
In Pirouette to blanch a Troupe—
Or lay a Prima, mad,

And though I had no Gown of Gauze—
No Ringlet, to my Hair,
Nor hopped to Audiences—like Birds,
One Claw upon the Air,

Nor tossed my shape in Eider Balls,
Nor rolled on wheels of snow
Till I was out of sight, in sound,
The House encore me so—

Nor any know I know the Art
I mention—easy—Here—
Nor any Placard boast me—
It's full as Opera—

341

After great pain, a formal feeling comes—
The Nerves sit ceremonious, like Tombs—
The stiff Heart questions was it He, that bore,
And Yesterday, or Centuries before?

The Feet, mechanical, go round—
Of Ground, or Air, or Ought—
A Wooden way
Regardless grown,
A Quartz contentment, like a stone—

This is the Hour of Lead—
Remembered, if outlived,
As Freezing persons, recollect the Snow—
First—Chill—then Stupor—then the letting go—

346

Not probable—The barest Chance—
A smile too few—a word too much
And far from Heaven as the Rest—
The Soul so close on Paradise—

What if the Bird from journey far—
Confused by Sweets—as Mortals—are—
Forget the secret of His wing
And perish—but a Bough between—
Oh, Groping feet—
Oh Phantom Queen!

352

Perhaps I asked too large—
I take—no less than skies—
For Earths, grow thick as
Berries, in my native town—

My Basket holds—just—Firmaments—
Those—dangle easy—on my arm,
But smaller bundles—Cram.

355

'Tis Opposites—entice—
Deformed Men—ponder Grace—
Bright fires—the Blanketless—
The Lost—Day's face—

The Blind—esteem it be
Enough Estate—to see—
The Captive—strangles new—
For deeming—Beggars—play—

To lack—enamor Thee—
Tho' the Divinity—
Be only
Me—

356

The Day that I was crowned
Was like the other Days—
Until the Coronation came—
And then—'twas Otherwise—

As Carbon in the Coal
And Carbon in the Gem
Are One—and yet the former
Were dull for Diadem—

I rose, and all was plain—
But when the Day declined
Myself and It, in Majesty
Were equally—adorned—

The Grace that I—was chose—
To Me—surpassed the Crown
That was the Witness for the Grace—
'Twas even that 'twas Mine—

364

The Morning after Woe—
'Tis frequently the Way—
Surpasses all that rose before—
For utter Jubilee—

As Nature did not care—
And piled her Blossoms on—
And further to parade a Joy
Her Victim stared upon—

The Birds declaim their Tunes—
Pronouncing every word
Like Hammers—Did they know they fell
Like Litanies of Lead—

On here and there—a creature—
They'd modify the Glee
To fit some Crucifixal Clef—
Some Key of Calvary—

365

Dare you see a Soul *at the White Heat?*
Then crouch within the door—
Red—is the Fire's common tint—
But when the vivid Ore
Has vanquished Flame's conditions,
It quivers from the Forge

Without a color, but the light
Of unanointed Blaze.
Least Village has its Blacksmith
Whose Anvil's even ring
Stands symbol for the finer Forge
That soundless tugs—within—
Refining these impatient Ores
With Hammer, and with Blaze
Until the Designated Light
Repudiate the Forge—

367

Over and over, like a Tune—
The Recollection plays—
Drums off the Phantom Battlements
Cornets of Paradise—

Snatches, from Baptized Generations—
Cadences too grand
But for the Justified Processions
At the Lord's Right hand.

376

Of Course—I prayed—
And did God Care?
He cared as much as on the Air
A Bird—had stamped her foot—
And cried "Give Me"—
My Reason—Life—
I had not had—but for Yourself—
'Twere better Charity
To leave me in the Atom's Tomb—
Merry, and Nought, and gay, and numb—
Than this smart Misery.

377

To lose one's faith—surpass
The loss of an Estate—
Because Estates can be
Replenished—faith cannot—

Inherited with Life—
Belief—but once—can be—
Annihilate a single clause—
And Being's—Beggary—

378

I saw no Way—The Heavens were stitched—
I felt the Columns close—
The Earth reversed her Hemispheres—
I touched the Universe—

And back it slid—and I alone—
A Speck upon a Ball—
Went out upon Circumference—
Beyond the Dip of Bell—

383

Exhilaration—is within—
There can no Outer Wine
So royally intoxicate
As that diviner Brand

The Soul achieves—Herself—
To drink—or set away
For Visitor—Or Sacrament—
'Tis not of Holiday

To stimulate a Man
Who hath the Ample Rhine
Within his Closet—Best you can
Exhale in offering.

384

No Rack can torture me—
My Soul—at Liberty—
Behind this mortal Bone
There knits a bolder One—

You cannot prick with saw—
Nor pierce with Scimitar—
Two Bodies—therefore be—
Bind One—The Other fly—

The Eagle of his Nest
No easier divest—
And gain the Sky
Than mayest Thou—

Except Thyself may be
Thine Enemy—
Captivity is Consciousness—
So's Liberty.

391

A Visitor in Marl—
Who influences Flowers—
Till they are orderly as Busts—
And Elegant—as Glass—

Who visits in the Night—
And just before the Sun—
Concludes his glistening interview—
Caresses—and is gone—

But whom his fingers touched—
And where his feet have run—
And whatsoever Mouth he kissed—
Is as it had not been—

401

What Soft—Cherubic Creatures—
These Gentlewomen are—
One would as soon assault a Plush—
Or violate a Star—

Such Dimity Convictions—
A Horror so refined
Of freckled Human Nature—
Of Deity—ashamed—

It's such a common—Glory—
A Fisherman's—Degree—
Redemption—Brittle Lady—
Be so—ashamed of Thee—

405

It might be lonelier
Without the Loneliness—
I'm so accustomed to my Fate—
Perhaps the Other—Peace—

Would interrupt the Dark—
And crowd the little Room—
Too scant—by Cubits—to contain
The Sacrament—of Him—

I am not used to Hope—
It might intrude upon—
Its sweet parade—blaspheme the place—
Ordained to Suffering—

It might be easier
To fail—with Land in Sight—
Than gain—My Blue Peninsula—
To perish—of Delight—

407

If What we could—were what we would—
Criterion—be small—
It is the Ultimate of Talk—
The Impotence to Tell—

429

The Moon is distant from the Sea—
And yet, with Amber Hands—
She leads Him—docile as a Boy—
Along appointed Sands—

He never misses a Degree—
Obedient to Her Eye
He comes just so far—toward the Town—
Just so far—goes away—

Oh, Signor, Thine, the Amber Hand—
And mine—the distant Sea—
Obedient to the least command
Thine eye impose on me—

435

Much Madness is divinest Sense—
To a discerning Eye—
Much Sense—the starkest Madness—
'Tis the Majority
In this, as All, prevail—
Assent—and you are sane—
Demur—you're straightway dangerous—
And handled with a Chain—

441

This is my letter to the World
That never wrote to Me—
The simple News that Nature told—
With tender Majesty

Her Message is committed
To Hands I cannot see—
For love of Her—Sweet—countrymen—
Judge tenderly—of Me

448

This was a Poet—It is That
Distills amazing sense
From ordinary Meanings—
And Attar so immense

From the familiar species
That perished by the Door—
We wonder it was not Ourselves
Arrested it—before—

Of Pictures, the Discloser—
The Poet—it is He—
Entitles Us—by Contrast—
To ceaseless Poverty—

Of Portion—so unconscious—
The Robbing—could not harm—
Himself—to Him—a Fortune—
Exterior—to Time—

455

Triumph—may be of several kinds—
There's Triumph in the Room
When that Old Imperator—Death—
By Faith—be overcome—

There's Triumph of the finer Mind
When Truth—affronted long—
Advance unmoved—to Her Supreme—
Her God—Her only Throng—

A Triumph—when Temptation's Bribe
Be slowly handed back—
One eye upon the Heaven renounced—
And One—upon the Rack—

Severer Triumph—by Himself
Experienced—who pass
Acquitted—from that Naked Bar—
Jehovah's Countenance—

456

So well that I can live without—
I love thee—then How well is that?
As well as Jesus?
Prove it me
That He—loved Men—
As I—love thee—

461

A Wife—at Daybreak I shall be—
Sunrise—Hast thou a Flag for me?
At Midnight, I am but a Maid,
How short it takes to make a Bride—
Then—Midnight, I have passed from thee
Unto the East, and Victory—

Midnight—Good Night! I hear them call,
The Angels bustle in the Hall—
Softly my Future climbs the Stair,
I fumble at my Childhood's prayer
So soon to be a Child no more—
Eternity, I'm coming—Sir,
Savior—I've seen the face—before!

465

I heard a Fly buzz—when I died—
The Stillness in the Room
Was like the Stillness in the Air—
Between the Heaves of Storm—

The Eyes around—had wrung them dry—
And Breaths were gathering firm
For that last Onset—when the King
Be witnessed—in the Room—

I willed my Keepsakes—Signed away
What portion of me be
Assignable—and then it was
There interposed a Fly—

With Blue—uncertain stumbling Buzz—
Between the light—and me—
And then the Windows failed—and then
I could not see to see—

485

To make One's Toilette—after Death
Has made the Toilette cool
Of only Taste we cared to please
Is difficult, and still—

That's easier—than Braid the Hair—
And make the Bodice gay—
When eyes that fondled it are wrenched
By Decalogues—away—

492

Civilization—spurns—the Leopard!
Was the Leopard—bold?
Deserts—never rebuked her Satin—
Ethiop—her Gold—
Tawny—her Customs—
She was Conscious—
Spotted—her Dun Gown—
This was the Leopard's nature—Signor—
Need—a keeper—frown?

Pity—the Pard—that left her Asia—
Memories—of Palm—
Cannot be stifled—with Narcotic—
Nor suppressed—with Balm—

501

This World is not Conclusion.
A Species stands beyond—
Invisible, as Music—
But positive, as Sound—
It beckons, and it baffles—
Philosophy—don't know—
And through a Riddle, at the last—
Sagacity, must go—
To guess it, puzzles scholars—
To gain it, Men have borne
Contempt of Generations
And Crucifixion, shown—
Faith slips—and laughs, and rallies—
Blushes, if any see—
Plucks at a twig of Evidence—
And asks a Vane, the way—
Much Gesture, from the Pulpit—
Strong Hallelujahs roll—
Narcotics cannot still the Tooth
That nibbles at the soul—

502

At least—to pray—is left—is left—
Oh Jesus—in the Air—
I know not which thy chamber is—
I'm knocking—everywhere—
Thou settest Earthquake in the South—
And Maelstrom, in the Sea—
Say, Jesus Christ of Nazareth—
Hast thou no Arm for Me?

505

I would not paint—a picture—
I'd rather be the One
Its bright impossibility
To dwell—delicious—on—
And wonder how the fingers feel
Whose rare—celestial—stir—
Evokes so sweet a Torment—
Such sumptuous—Despair—

I would not talk, like Cornets—
I'd rather be the One
Raised softly to the Ceilings—
And out, and easy on—
Through Villages of Ether—
Myself endued Balloon
By but a lip of Metal—
The pier to my Pontoon—

Nor would I be a Poet—
It's finer—own the Ear—
Enamored—impotent—content—
The License to revere,
A privilege so awful
What would the Dower be,
Had I the Art to stun myself
With Bolts of Melody!

It was not Death, for I stood up,
And all the Dead, lie down—
It was not Night, for all the Bells
Put out their Tongues, for Noon.

It was not Frost, for on my Flesh
I felt Siroccos—crawl—
Nor Fire—for just my Marble feet
Could keep a Chancel, cool—

And yet, it tasted, like them all,
The Figures I have seen
Set orderly, for Burial,
Reminded me, of mine—

As if my life were shaven,
And fitted to a frame,
And could not breathe without a key,
And 'twas like Midnight, some—

When everything that ticked—has stopped—
And Space stares all around—
Or Grisly frosts—first Autumn morns,
Repeal the Beating Ground—

But, most, like Chaos—Stopless—cool—
Without a Chance, or Spar—
Or even a Report of Land—
To justify—Despair.

511

If you were coming in the Fall,
I'd brush the Summer by
With half a smile, and half a spurn,
As housewives do, a Fly.

If I could see you in a year,
I'd wind the months in balls—
And put them each in separate Drawers,
For fear the numbers fuse—

If only Centuries, delayed,
I'd count them on my Hand,
Subtracting, till my fingers dropped
Into Van Dieman's Land.

If certain, when this life was out—
That yours and mine, should be
I'd toss it yonder, like a Rind,
And take Eternity—

But, now, uncertain of the length
Of this, that is between,
It goads me, like the Goblin Bee—
That will not state—its sting.

518

Her sweet Weight on my Heart at Night
Had scarcely deigned to lie—
When, stirring, for Belief's delight,
My Bride had slipped away—

If 'twas a Dream—made solid—just
The Heaven to confirm—
Or if Myself were dreamed of Her—
The power to presume—

With Him remain—who unto Me—
Gave—even as to All—
A Fiction superseding Faith—
By so much—as 'twas real—

536

The Heart asks Pleasure—first—
And then—Excuse from Pain—
And then—those little Anodynes
That deaden suffering—

And then—to go to sleep—
And then—if it should be
The will of its Inquisitor
The privilege to die—

569

I reckon—when I count at all—
First—Poets—Then the Sun—
Then Summer—Then the Heaven of God—
And then—the List is done—

But, looking back—the First so seems
To Comprehend the Whole—
The Others look a needless Show—
So I write—Poets—All—

Their Summer—lasts a Solid Year—
They can afford a Sun
The East—would deem extravagant—
And if the Further Heaven—

Be Beautiful as they prepare
For Those who worship Them—
It is too difficult a Grace—
To justify the Dream—

579

I had been hungry, all the Years—
My Noon had Come—to dine—
I trembling drew the Table near—
And touched the Curious Wine—

'Twas this on Tables I had seen—
When turning, hungry, Home
I looked in Windows, for the Wealth
I could not hope—for Mine—

I did not know the ample Bread—
'Twas so unlike the Crumb
The Birds and I, had often shared
In Nature's—Dining Room—

The Plenty hurt me—'twas so new—
Myself felt ill—and odd—
As Berry—of a Mountain Bush—
Transplanted—to the Road—

Nor was I hungry—so I found
That Hunger—was a way
Of Persons outside Windows—
The Entering—takes away—

640

I cannot live with You—
It would be Life—
And Life is over there—
Behind the Shelf

The Sexton keeps the Key to—
Putting up
Our Life—His Porcelain—
Like a Cup—

Discarded of the Housewife—
Quaint—or Broke—
A newer Sevres pleases—
Old Ones crack—

I could not die—with You—
For One must wait
To shut the Other's Gaze down—
You—could not—

And I—Could I stand by
And see You—freeze—
Without my Right of Frost—
Death's privilege?

Nor could I rise—with You—
Because Your Face
Would put out Jesus'—
That New Grace

Glow plain—and foreign
On my homesick Eye—
Except that You than He
Shone closer by—

They'd judge Us—How—
For You—served Heaven—You know,
Or sought to—
I could not—

Because You saturated Sight—
And I had no more Eyes
For sordid excellence
As Paradise

And were You lost, I would be—
Though My Name
Rang loudest
On the Heavenly fame—

And were You—saved—
And I—condemned to be
Where You were not—
That self—were Hell to Me—

So We must meet apart—
You there—I—here—
With just the Door ajar
That Oceans are—and Prayer—
And that White Sustenance—
Despair—

642

Me from Myself—to banish—
Had I Art—
Impregnable my Fortress
Unto All Heart—

But since Myself—assault Me—
How have I peace
Except by subjugating
Consciousness?

And since We're mutual Monarch
How this be
Except by Abdication—
Me—of Me?

650

Pain—has an Element of Blank—
It cannot recollect
When it begun—or if there were
A time when it was not—

It has no Future—but itself—
Its Infinite contain
Its Past—enlightened to perceive
New Periods—of Pain.

657

I dwell in Possibility—
A fairer House than Prose—
More numerous of Windows—
Superior—for Doors—

Of Chambers as the Cedars—
Impregnable of Eye—
And for an Everlasting Roof
The Gambrels of the Sky—

Of Visitors—the fairest—
For Occupation—This—
The spreading wide my narrow Hands
To gather Paradise—

675

Essential Oils—are wrung—
The Attar from the Rose
Be not expressed by Suns—alone—
It is the gift of Screws—

The General Rose—decay—
But this—in Lady's Drawer
Make Summer—When the Lady lie
In ceaseless Rosemary—

680

Each Life Converges to some Centre—
Expressed—or still—
Exists in every Human Nature
A Goal—

Embodied scarcely to itself—it may be—
Too fair
For Credibility's presumption
To mar—

Adored with caution—as a Brittle Heaven—
To reach
Were hopeless, as the Rainbow's Raiment
To touch—

Yet persevered toward—sure—for the Distance—
How high—
Unto the Saints' slow diligence—
The Sky—

Ungained—it may be—by a Life's low Venture—
But then—
Eternity enable the endeavoring
Again.

701

A Thought went up my mind today—
That I have had before—
But did not finish—some way back—
I could not fix the Year—

Nor where it went—nor why it came
The second time to me—
Nor definitely, what it was—
Have I the Art to say—

But somewhere—in my Soul—I know—
I've met the Thing before—
It just reminded me—'twas all—
And came my way no more—

709

Publication—is the Auction
Of the Mind of Man—
Poverty—be justifying
For so foul a thing

Possibly—but We—would rather
From Our Garret go
White—Unto the White Creator—
Than invest—Our Snow—

Thought belong to Him who gave it—
Then—to Him Who bear
Its Corporeal illustration—Sell
The Royal Air—

In the Parcel—Be the Merchant
Of the Heavenly Grace—
But reduce no Human Spirit
To Disgrace of Price—

724

It's easy to invent a Life—
God does it—every Day—
Creation—but the Gambol
Of His Authority—

It's easy to efface it—
The thrifty Deity
Could scarce afford Eternity
To Spontaneity—

The Perished Patterns murmur—
But His Perturbless Plan
Proceed—inserting Here—a Sun—
There—leaving out a Man—

729

Alter! When the Hills do—
Falter! When the Sun
Question if His Glory
Be the Perfect One—

Surfeit! When the Daffodil
Doth of the Dew—
Even as Herself—Sir—
I will—of You—

754

My Life had stood—a Loaded Gun—
In Corners—till a Day
The Owner passed—identified—
And carried Me away—

And now We roam in Sovereign Woods—
And now We hunt the Doe—
And every time I speak for Him—
The Mountains straight reply—

And do I smile, such cordial light
Upon the Valley glow—
It is as a Vesuvian face
Had let its pleasure through—

And when at Night—Our good Day done—
I guard My Master's Head—
'Tis better than the Eider-Duck's
Deep Pillow—to have shared—

To foe of His—I'm deadly foe—
None stir the second time—
On whom I lay a Yellow Eye—
Or an emphatic Thumb—

Though I than He—may longer live
He longer must—than I—
For I have but the power to kill,
Without—the power to die—

777

The Loneliness One dare not sound—
And would as soon surmise
As in its Grave go plumbing
To ascertain the size—

The Loneliness whose worst alarm
Is lest itself should see—
And perish from before itself
For just a scrutiny—

The Horror not to be surveyed—
But skirted in the Dark—
With Consciousness suspended—
And Being under Lock—

I fear me this—is Loneliness—
The Maker of the soul
Its Caverns and its Corridors
Illuminate—or seal—

785

They have a little Odor—that to me
Is metre—nay—'tis melody—
And spiciest at fading—indicate—
A Habit—of a Laureate—

847

Finite—to fail, but infinite to Venture—
For the one ship that struts the shore
Many's the gallant—overwhelmed Creature
Nodding in Navies nevermore—

861

Split the Lark—and you'll find the Music—
Bulb after Bulb, in Silver rolled—
Scantily dealt to the Summer Morning
Saved for your Ear when Lutes be old.

Loose the Flood—you shall find it patent—
Gush after Gush, reserved for you—
Scarlet Experiment! Sceptic Thomas!
Now, do you doubt that your Bird was true?

870

Finding is the first Act
The second, loss,
Third, Expedition for
The "Golden Fleece"

Fourth, no Discovery—
Fifth, no crew—
Finally, no Golden Fleece—
Jason—sham—too.

875

I stepped from Plank to Plank
A slow and cautious way
The Stars about my Head I felt
About my Feet the Sea.

I knew not but the next
Would be my final inch—
This gave me that precarious Gait
Some call Experience.

883

The Poets light but Lamps—
Themselves—go out—
The Wicks they stimulate—
If vital Light

Inhere as do the Suns—
Each Age a Lens
Disseminating their
Circumference—

884

An Everywhere of Silver
With Ropes of Sand
To keep it from effacing
The Track called land.

914

I cannot be ashamed
Because I cannot see
The love you offer—
Magnitude
Reverses Modesty

And I cannot be proud
Because a Height so high
Involves Alpine
Requirements
And Services of Snow.

963

A nearness to Tremendousness—
An Agony procures—
Affliction ranges Boundlessness—
Vicinity to Laws

Contentment's quiet Suburb—
Affliction cannot stay
In Acres—Its Location
Is Illocality—

994

Partake as doth the Bee,
Abstemiously.
The Rose is an Estate—
In Sicily.

997

Crumbling is not an instant's Act
A fundamental pause
Dilapidation's processes
Are organized Decays.

'Tis first a Cobweb on the Soul
A Cuticle of Dust
A Borer in the Axis
An Elemental Rust—

Ruin is formal—Devil's work
Consecutive and slow—
Fail in an instant, no man did
Slipping—is Crash's law.

1036

Satisfaction—is the Agent
Of Satiety—
Want—a quiet Commissary
For Infinity.

To possess, is past the instant
We achieve the Joy—
Immortality contented
Were Anomaly.

1072

Title divine—is mine!
The Wife—without the Sign!
Acute Degree—conferred on me—
Empress of Calvary!
Royal—all but the Crown!
Betrothed—without the swoon
God sends us Women—
When you—hold—Garnet to Garnet—
Gold—to Gold—
Born—Bridalled—Shrouded—
In a Day—
Tri Victory
"My Husband"—women say—
Stroking the Melody—
Is *this*—the way?

1129

Tell all the Truth but tell it slant—
Success in Circuit lies
Too bright for our infirm Delight
The Truth's superb surprise

As Lightning to the Children eased
With explanation kind
The Truth must dazzle gradually
Or every man be blind—

1196

To make routine a stimulus
Remember it can cease.
Capacity to terminate
Is a specific grace.

1212

A word is dead
When it is said,
Some say.

I say it just
Begins to live
That day.

1218

Let my first Knowing be of thee
With morning's warming Light—
And my first Fearing, lest Unknowns
Engulf thee in the night—

1226

The Popular Heart is a Cannon first—
Subsequent a Drum—
Bells for an Auxiliary
And an Afterward of Rum—

Not a Tomorrow to know its name
Nor a Past to stare—
Ditches for Realms and a Trip to Jail
For a Souvenir—

1333

A little Madness in the Spring
Is wholesome even for the King,
But God be with the Clown—
Who ponders this tremendous scene—
This whole Experiment of Green—
As if it were his own!

1463

A Route of Evanescence
With a revolving Wheel—
A Resonance of Emerald—
A Rush of Cochineal—
And every Blossom on the Bush
Adjusts its tumbled Head—
The mail from Tunis, probably,
An easy Morning's Ride—

1624

Apparently with no surprise
To any happy Flower
The Frost beheads it at its play—
In accidental power—
The blonde Assassin passes on—
The Sun proceeds unmoved
To measure off another Day
For an Approving God.

1651

A Word made Flesh is seldom
And tremblingly partook
Nor then perhaps reported
But have I not mistook
Each one of us has tasted
With ecstasies of stealth
The very food debated
To our specific strength—

A Word that breathes distinctly
Has not the power to die
Cohesive as the Spirit
It may expire if He—
"Made Flesh and dwelt among us"
Could condescension be
Like this consent of Language
This loved Philology

1732

My life closed twice before its close—
It yet remains to see
If Immortality unveil
A third event to me

So huge, so hopeless to conceive
As these that twice befell.
Parting is all we know of heaven,
And all we need of hell.

1755

To make a prairie it takes a clover and one bee,
One clover, and a bee,
And revery.
The revery alone will do,
If bees are few.

1760

Elysium is as far as to
The very nearest Room
If in that Room a Friend await
Felicity or Doom—

What fortitude the Soul contains,
That it can so endure
The accent of a coming Foot—
The opening of a Door—

That Love is all there is,
Is all we know of Love;
It is enough, the freight should be
Proportioned to the groove.

CELIA THAXTER
(1835–1894)

Imprisoned

Lightly she lifts the large, pure, luminous shell,
    Poises it in her strong and shapely hand.
"Listen," she says, "it has a tale to tell,
    Spoken in language you may understand."

Smiling, she holds it at my dreaming ear:
    The old, delicious murmur of the sea
Steals like enchantment through me, and I hear
    Voices like echoes of eternity.

She stirs it softly. Lo, another speech!
    In one of its dim chambers, shut from sight,
Is sealed the water that has kissed the beach
    Where the far Indian Ocean leaps in light.

Those laughing ripples, hidden evermore
    In utter darkness, plaintively repeat
Their lapsing on the glowing tropic shore,
    In melancholy whispers low and sweet.

O prisoned wave that may not see the sun!
    O voice that never may be comforted!
You cannot break the web that Fate has spun;
    Out of your world are light and gladness fled.

The red dawn nevermore shall tremble far
    Across the leagues of radiant brine to you;
You shall not sing to greet the evening star,
    Nor dance exulting under heaven's clear blue.

Inexorably woven is the weft
    That shrouds from you all joy but memory;
Only this tender, low lament is left
    Of all the sumptuous splendor of the sea.

Alone

The lilies clustered fair and tall;
I stood outside the garden wall;
I saw her light robe glimmering through
The fragrant evening's dusk and dew.

She stopped above the lilies pale;
Up the clear east the moon did sail;
I saw her bend her lovely head
O'er her rich roses blushing red.

Her slender hand the flowers caressed,
Her touch the unconscious blossoms blessed;
The rose against her perfumed palm
Leaned its soft cheek in blissful calm.

I would have given my soul to be
That rose she touched so tenderly!
I stood alone, outside the gate,
And knew that life was desolate.

MARK TWAIN [Samuel Clemens]
(1835–1910)

Ode to Stephen Dowling Bots

And did young Stephen sicken,
    And did young Stephen die?
And did the sad hearts thicken,
    And did the mourners cry?

No; such was not the fate of
    Young Stephen Dowling Bots;
Though sad hearts round him thickened,
    'Twas not from sickness' shots.

No whooping-cough did rack his frame,
    Nor measles drear, with spots;
Not these impaired the sacred name
    Of Stephen Dowling Bots.

Despised love struck not with woe
    That head of curly knots,
Nor stomach troubles laid him low,
    Young Stephen Dowling Bots.

O no. Then list with tearful eye,
    Whilst I his fate do tell.
His soul did from this cold world fly,
    By falling down a well.

They got him out and emptied him;
    Alas it was too late;
His spirit was gone for to sport aloft
    In the realms of the good and great.

THOMAS BAILEY ALDRICH
(1836–1906)

Fredericksburg

The increasing moonlight drifts across my bed,
And on the churchyard by the road, I know
It falls as white and noiselessly as snow. . . .
'T was such a night two weary summers fled;
The stars, as now, were waning overhead.
Listen! Again the shrill-lipped bugles blow
Where the swift currents of the river flow
Past Fredericksburg; far off the heavens are red
With sudden conflagration; on yon height,
Linstock in hand, the gunners hold their breath;
A signal rocket pierces the dense night,
Flings its spent stars upon the town beneath:
Hark!—the artillery massing on the right,
Hark!—the black squadrons wheeling down to Death!

Identity

Somewhere—in desolate wind-swept space—
 In Twilight-land—in No-man's-land—
Two hurrying Shapes met face to face,
 And bade each other stand.

"And who are you?" cried one a-gape,
 Shuddering in the gloaming light.
"I know not," said the second Shape,
 "I only died last night!"

Memory

My mind lets go a thousand things,
Like dates of wars and deaths of kings,
And yet recalls the very hour—
'T was noon by yonder village tower,
And on the last blue noon in May—
The wind came briskly up this way,
Crisping the brook beside the road;
Then, pausing here, set down its load
Of pine-scents, and shook listlessly
Two petals from that wild-rose tree.

CHARLOTTE L.F. GRIMKE
(1837–1914)

Wordsworth

Poet of the serene and thoughtful lay!
In youth's fair dawn, when the soul, still untried,
Longs for life's conflict, and seeks restlessly
Food for its cravings in the stirring songs,
The thrilling strains of more impassioned bards;
Or, eager for fresh joys, culls with delight
The flowers that bloom in fancy's fairy realm—
We may not prize the mild and steadfast ray
That streams from thy pure soul in tranquil song
But, in our riper years, when through the heat
And burden of the day we struggle on,
Breasting the stream upon whose shores we dreamed,

Weary of all the turmoil and the din
Which drowns the finer voices of the soul;
We turn to thee, true priest of Nature's fane,
And find the rest our fainting spirits need,—
The calm, more ardent singers cannot give;
As in the glare intense of tropic days,
Gladly we turn from the sun's radiant beams,
And grateful hail fair Luna's tender light.

ADAH ISAACS MENKEN
(c.1835–1868)

Infelix

Where is the promise of my years;
    Once written on my brow?
Ere errors, agonies and fears
Brought with them all that speaks in tears,
Ere I had sunk beneath my peers;
    Where sleeps that promise now?

Naught lingers to redeem those hours,
    Still, still to memory sweet!
The flowers that bloomed in sunny bowers
Are withered all; and Evil towers
Supreme above her sister powers
    Of Sorrow and Deceit.

I look along the columned years,
    And see Life's riven fane,
Just where it fell, amid the jeers
Of scornful lips, whose mocking sneers,
For ever hiss within mine ears
    To break the sleep of pain.

I can but own my life is vain
    A desert void of peace;
I missed the goal I sought to gain,
I missed the measure of the strain
That lulls Fame's fever in the brain,
    And bids Earth's tumult cease.

Myself! alas for theme so poor
    A theme but rich in Fear;
I stand a wreck on Error's shore,
A spectre not within the door,
A houseless shadow evermore,
    An exile lingering here.

SIDNEY LANIER
(1842–1881)

The Crystal

Ye companies of governor-spirits grave,
Bards, and old bringers-down of flaming news
From steep-walled heavens, holy malcontents,
Sweet seers, and stellar visionaries, all
That brood about the skies of poesy,
Full bright ye shine, insuperable stars.
Yet, if a man look hard upon you, none
With total lustre blazeth, no, not one
But hath some heinous freckle of the flesh
Upon his shining cheek, not one but winks
His ray, opaqued with intermittent mist
Of defect; yea, you masters all must ask
Some sweet forgiveness, which we leap to give,
We lovers of you, heavenly-glad to meet
Your largess so with love, and interplight
Your geniuses with our mortalities.

Thus unto thee, O sweetest Shakspere sole,
A hundred hurts a day I do forgive
('Tis little, but, enchantment! 'tis for thee):
Small curious quibble; Juliet's prurient pun
In the poor, pale face of Romeo's fancied death;
Cold rant of Richard; Henry's fustian roar
Which frights away that sleep he invocates;
Wronged Valentine's unnatural haste to yield;
Too-silly shifts of maids that mask as men
In faint disguises that could ne'er disguise—
Viola, Julia, Portia, Rosalind;
Fatigues most drear, and needless overtax
Of speech obscure that had as lief be plain;
Last I forgive (with more delight, because

'Tis more to do) the labored-lewd discourse
That e'en thy young invention's youngest heir
Besmirched the world with.

                    Father Homer, thee,
Thee also I forgive thy sandy wastes
Of prose and catalogue, thy drear harangues
That tease the patience of the centuries;
Thy sleazy scrap of story—but a rogue's
Rape of a light-o'-love—too soiled a patch
To broider with the gods.

                    Thee, Socrates,
Thou dear and very strong one, I forgive
Thy year-worn cloak, thine iron stringencies
That were but dandy upside-down, thy words
Of truth that mildlier spoke had mainlier wrought.

So, Buddha, beautiful! I pardon thee
That all the All thou hadst for needy man
Was Nothing, and thy Best of being was
But not to be.

                Worn Dante, I forgive
The implacable hates that in thy horrid hells
Or burn or freeze thy fellows, never loosed
By death, nor time, nor love.

                    And I forgive
Thee, Milton, those thy comic-dreadful wars
Where, armed with gross and inconclusive steel,
Immortals smite immortals mortalwise
And fill all heaven with folly.

                    Also thee,
Brave Æschylus, thee I forgive, for that
Thine eye, by bare bright justice basilisked,
Turned not, nor ever learned to look where Love
Stands shining.

                So, unto thee, Lucretius mine
(For oh, what heart hath loved thee like to this
That's now complaining?), freely I forgive
Thy logic poor, thine error rich, thine earth
Whose graves eat souls and all.

                                        Yea, all you hearts
Of beauty, and sweet righteous lovers large:
Aurelius fine, oft superfine; mild Saint
À Kempis, overmild; Epictetus,
Whiles low in thought, still with old slavery tinct;
Rapt Behmen, rapt too far; high Swedenborg,
O'ertoppling; Langley, that with but a touch
Of art hadst sung Piers Plowman to the top
Of English songs, whereof 'tis dearest now
And most adorable; Cædmon, in the morn
A-calling angels with the cow-herd's call
That late brought up the cattle; Emerson,
Most wise, that yet, in finding Wisdom, lost
Thy Self, sometimes; tense Keats, with angel's nerves,
Where men's were better; Tennyson, largest voice
Since Milton, yet some register of wit
Wanting—all, all, I pardon, ere 'tis asked,
Your more or less, your little mole that marks
You brother and your kinship seals to man.

But Thee, but Thee, O Sovereign Seer of time,
But Thee, O poets' Poet, Wisdom's Tongue,
But Thee, O man's best Man, O love's best Love,
O perfect life in perfect labor writ,
O all men's Comrade, Servant, King, or Priest—
What *if* or *yet* what mole, what flaw, what lapse,
What least defect or shadow of defect,
What rumor tattled by an enemy,
Of inference loose, what lack of grace,
Even in torture's grasp, or sleep's, or death's—
Oh, what amiss may I forgive in Thee,
Jesus, good Paragon, thou Crystal Christ?

Marsh Song—at Sunset

Over the monstrous shambling sea,
    Over the Caliban sea,
Bright Ariel-cloud, thou lingerest:
Oh wait, oh wait, in the warm red West,—
    Thy Prospero I'll be.

Over the humped and fishy sea,
    Over the Caliban sea,
O cloud in the West, like a thought in the heart
Of pardon, loose thy wing and start,
    And do a grace for me.

Over the huge and huddling sea,
   Over the Caliban sea,
Bring hither my brother Antonio,—Man,—
My injurer: night breaks the ban;
   Brother, I pardon thee.

from Sunrise

In my sleep I was fain of their fellowship, fain
   Of the live-oak, the marsh, and the main.
The little green leaves would not let me alone in my sleep;
Up-breathed from the marshes, a message of range and of sweep,
Interwoven with wafture of wild sea-liberties, drifting,
   Came through the lapped leaves sifting, sifting,
      Came to the gates of sleep.
   Then my thoughts, in the dark of the dungeon-keep
Of the Castle of Captives hid in the City of Sleep,
   Upstarted, by twos and by threes assembling:
      The gates of sleep fell a-trembling
Like as the lips of a lady that forth falter *yes,*
   Shaken with happiness:
   The gates of sleep stood wide.

I have waked, I have come, my beloved! I might not abide:
I have come ere the dawn, O beloved, my live-oaks, to hide
   In your gospelling glooms,—to be
As a lover in heaven, the marsh my marsh and the sea my sea.

   Tell me, sweet burly-bark'd, man-bodied Tree
   That mine arms in the dark are embracing, dost know
   From what fount are these tears at thy feet which flow?
They rise not from reason, but deeper inconsequent deeps.
   Reason's not one that weeps.
   What logic of greeting lies
Betwixt dear over-beautiful trees and the rain of the eyes?

O cunning green leaves, little masters! like as ye gloss
All the dull-tissued dark with your luminous darks that emboss
   The vague blackness of night into pattern and plan,
                  So,
   (But would I could know, but would I could know,)
With your question embroid'ring the dark of the question of man,—
So, with your silences purfling this silence of man
While his cry to the dead for some knowledge is under the ban,
      Under the ban,—
      So, ye have wrought me

Designs on the night of our knowledge,—yea, ye have taught me,
So,
That haply we know somewhat more than we know.

Ye lispers, whisperers, singers in storms,
Ye consciences murmuring faiths under forms,
Ye ministers meet for each passion that grieves,
Friendly, sisterly, sweetheart leaves,
Oh, rain me down from your darks that contain me,
Wisdoms ye winnow from winds that pain me,—
Sift down tremors of sweet-within-sweet
That advise me of more than they bring,—repeat
Me the woods-smell that swiftly but now brought breath
From the heaven-side bank of the river of death,—
Teach me the terms of silence,—preach me
The passion of patience, lift me,—impeach me,—
And there, oh there
As ye hang with your myriad palms upturned in the air,
Pray me a myriad prayer.

My gossip, the owl,—is it thou
That out of the leaves of the low-hanging bough,
As I pass to the beach, art stirred?
Dumb woods, have ye uttered a bird?

. . . .

The Raven Days

Our hearths are gone out, and our hearts are broken,
And but the ghosts of homes to us remain,
And ghostly eyes and hollow sighs give token
From friend to friend of an unspoken pain.

O, Raven Days, dark Raven Days of sorrow,
Bring to us, in your whetted ivory beaks,
Some sign out of the far land of To-morrow,
Some strip of sea-green dawn, some orange streaks.

Ye float in dusky files, forever croaking—
Ye chill our manhood with your dreary shade.
Pale, in the dark, not even God invoking,
We lie in chains, too weak to be afraid.

O Raven Days, dark Raven Days of sorrow,
    Will ever any warm light come again?
Will ever the lit mountains of To-morrow
    Begin to gleam across the mournful plain?

from Clover

. . . .

Now comes the Course-of-things, shaped like an Ox,
Slow browsing, o'er my hillside, ponderously—
The huge-brawned, tame, and workful Course-of-things,
That hath his grass, if earth be round or flat,
And hath his grass, if empires plunge in pain
Or faiths flash out. This cool, unasking Ox
Comes browsing o'er my hills and vales of Time,
And thrusts me out his tongue, and curls it, sharp
And sicklewise, about my poets' heads,
And twists them in, all—Dante, Keats, Chopin,
Raphael, Lucretius, Omar, Angelo,
Beethoven, Chaucer, Schubert, Shakspere, Bach,
And Buddha, in one sheaf—and champs and chews,
With slanty-churning jaws, and swallows down;
Then slowly plants a mighty forefoot out,
And makes advance to futureward, one inch.
So: they have played their part.

. . . .

The Mocking Bird

Superb and sole, upon a plumèd spray
    That o'er the general leafage boldly grew,
    He summ'd the woods in song; or typic drew
The watch of hungry hawks, the lone dismay
Of languid doves when long their lovers stray,
    And all birds' passion-plays that sprinkle dew
    At morn in brake or bosky avenue.
Whate'er birds did or dreamed, this bird could say.
Then down he shot, bounced airily along
The sward, twitched-in a grasshopper, made song
    Midflight, perched, primped, and to his art again.
    Sweet Science, this large riddle read me plain:
        How may the death of that dull insect be
        The life of yon trim Shakspere on the tree?

Song of the Chattahoochee

Out of the hills of Habersham,
  Down the valleys of Hall,
I hurry amain to reach the plain,
Run the rapid and leap the fall,
Split at the rock and together again,
Accept my bed, or narrow or wide,
And flee from folly on every side
With a lover's pain to attain the plain
  Far from the hills of Habersham,
  Far from the valleys of Hall.

All down the hills of Habersham,
  All through the valleys of Hall,
The rushes cried *Abide, abide,*
The willful waterweeds held me thrall,
The laving laurel turned my tide,
The ferns and the fondling grass said *Stay,*
The dewberry dipped for to work delay,
And the little reeds sighed *Abide, abide,*
  Here in the hills of Habersham,
  Here in the valleys of Hall.

High o'er the hills of Habersham,
  Veiling the valleys of Hall,
The hickory told me manifold
Fair tales of shade, the poplar tall
Wrought me her shadowy self to hold,
The chestnut, the oak, the walnut, the pine,
Overleaning, with flickering meaning and sign,
Said, *Pass not, so cold, these manifold*
  Deep shades of the hills of Habersham,
  These glades in the valleys of Hall.

And oft in the hills of Habersham,
  And oft in the valleys of Hall,
The white quartz shown, and the smooth brook-stone
Did bar me of passage with friendly brawl,
And many a luminous jewel lone
—Crystals clear or a-cloud with mist,
Ruby, garnet and amethyst—
Made lures with the lights of streaming stone
  In the clefts of the hills of Habersham,
  In the beds of the valleys of Hall.

But oh, not the hills of Habersham,
    And oh, not the valleys of Hall
Avail: I am fain for to water the plain.
Downward the voices of Duty call—
Downward, to toil and be mixed with the main,
The dry fields burn, and the mills are to turn,
And a myriad flowers mortally yearn,
And the lordly main from beyond the plain
    Calls o'er the hills of Habersham,
    Calls through the valleys of Hall.

The Marshes of Glynn

Glooms of the live-oaks, beautiful-braided and woven
With intricate shades of the vines that myriad-cloven
    Clamber the forks of the multiform boughs,—
        Emerald twilights,—
        Virginal shy lights,
Wrought of the leaves to allure to the whisper of vows,
When lovers pace timidly down through the green colonnades
    Of the dim sweet woods, of the dear dark woods,
        Of the heavenly woods and glades,
That run to the radiant marginal sand-beach within
        The wide sea-marshes of Glynn;—

    Beautiful glooms, soft dusks in the noon-day fire,—
    Wildwood privacies, closets of lone desire,
Chamber from chamber parted with wavering arras of leaves,—
Cells for the passionate pleasure of prayer to the soul that grieves,
    Pure with a sense of the passing of saints through the wood,
    Cool for the dutiful weighing of ill with good;—

O braided tusks of the oak and woven shades of the vine,
While the riotous noon-day sun of the June-day long did shine,
Ye held me fast in your heart and I held you fast in mine;
    But now when the noon is no more, and riot is rest,
    And the sun is a-wait at the ponderous gate of the West,
        And the slant yellow beam down the wood-aisle doth seem
        Like a lane into heaven that leads from a dream,—
Ay, now, when my soul all day hath drunken the soul of the oak,
And my heart is at ease from men, and the wearisome sound of
                        the stroke
    Of the scythe of time and the trowel of trade is low,
    And belief overmasters doubt, and I know that I know,
    And my spirit is grown to a lordly great compass within,

That the length and the breadth and the sweep of the marshes
                    of Glynn
Will work me no fear like the fear they have wrought me of yore
When length was fatigue, and when breadth was but bitterness
                    sore,
And when terror and shrinking and dreary unnamable pain
Drew over me out of the merciless miles of the plain,—
        Oh, now, unafraid, I am fain to face
        The vast sweet visage of space.
        To the edge of the wood I am drawn, I am drawn,
Where the gray beach glimmering runs, as a belt of the dawn,
        For a mete and a mark
        To the forest-dark:—
                So:
        Affable live-oak, leaning low,—
Thus—with your favor—soft, with a reverent hand,
(Not lightly touching your person, Lord of the land!)
Bending your beauty aside, with a step I stand
        On the firm-packet sand,
                Free
        By a world of marsh that borders a world of sea.
Sinuous southward and sinuous northward the shimmering band
    Of the sand-beach fastens the fringe of the marsh to the folds
                    of the land.
Inward and outward to northward and southward the beach-lines
                    linger and curl
As a silver-wrought garment that clings to and follows the firm sweet
                    limbs of a girl.
    Vanishing, swerving, evermore curving again into sight,
    Softly the sand-beach wavers away to a dim gray looping of light.
    And what if behind me to westward the wall of the woods
                    stands high?
    The world lies east: how ample, the marsh and the sea and
                    the sky!
    A league and a league of marsh-grass, waist-high, broad in the
                    blade,
        Green, and all of a height, and unflecked with a light or a shade,
        Stretch leisurely off, in a pleasant plain,
        To the terminal blue of the main.

    Oh, what is abroad in the marsh and the terminal sea?
        Somehow my soul seems suddenly free
        From the weighing of fate and the sad discussion of sin,
    By the length and the breadth and the sweep of the marshes of
                    Glynn.
Ye marshes, how candid and simple and nothing-withholding and free
Ye publish yourselves to the sky and offer yourselves to the sea!

Tolerant plains, that suffer the sea and the rains and the sun,
Ye spread and span like the catholic man who hath mightily won
    God out of knowledge and good out of infinite pain
    And sight out of blindness and purity out of a stain.

    As the marsh-hen secretly builds on the watery sod,
    Behold I will build me a nest on the greatness of God:
    I will fly in the greatness of God as the marsh-hen flies
    In the freedom that fills all the space 'twixt the marsh and the
                                        skies:
    By so many roots as the marsh-grass sends in the sod
    I will heartily lay me a-hold on the greatness of God:
    Oh, like to the greatness of God is the greatness within
    The range of the marshes, the liberal marshes of Glynn.

And the sea lends large, as the marsh: lo, out of his plenty the sea
    Pours fast: full soon the time of the flood-tide must be:
        Look how the grace of the sea doth go
    About and about through the intricate channels that flow
            Here and there,
            Everywhere,
Till his waters have flooded the uttermost creeks and the low-lying
                                        lanes,
        And the marsh is meshed with a million veins,
    That like as with rosy and silvery essences flow
        In the rose-and-silver evening glow.
        Farewell, my lord Sun!
    The creeks overflow: a thousand rivulets run
    'Twixt the roots of the sod; the blades of the marsh-grass stir;
Passeth a hurrying sound of wings that westward whirr;
Passeth, and all is still; and the currents cease to run;
    And the sea and the marsh are one.

        How still the plains of the waters be!
        The tide is in his ecstasy.
        The tide is at his highest height:
            And it is night.

    And now from the Vast of the Lord will the waters of sleep
        Roll in on the souls of men,
        But who will reveal to our waking ken
        The forms that swim and the shapes that creep
            Under the waters of sleep?
And I would I could know what swimmeth below when the tide
                                        comes in
    On the length and the breadth of the marvellous marshes of
                                        Glynn.

A Ballad of Trees and the Master

Into the woods my Master went,
    Clean forspent, forspent.
Into the woods my Master came,
    Forspent with love and shame.
But the olives they were not blind to Him,
The little gray leaves were kind to Him:
The thorn-tree had a mind to Him
    When into the woods He came.

Out of the woods my Master went,
    And He was well content.
Out of the woods my Master came,
    Content with death and shame.
When Death and Shame would woo Him last,
From under the trees they drew Him last:
'Twas on a tree they slew Him—last
    When out of the woods He came.

SONGS, HYMNS, SPIRITUALS, AND CAROLS:
1859–1870

Dixie's Land
(Daniel Decatur Emmett, 1859)

I wish I was in de land ob cotton,
Old times dar am not forgotten;
Look away, look away, look away, Dixie Land!
In Dixie Land, whar I was born in,
Early on one frosty mornin';
Look away, look away, look away, Dixie Land!

Chorus
Den I wish I was in Dixie, hooray, hooray!
In Dixie Land I'll take my stand,
To lib and die in Dixie;
Away, away, away down south in Dixie;
Away, away, away down south in Dixie.

Old Missus marry Will-de-weaber,
Willium was a gay deceaber;
Look away, look away, look away, Dixie Land!
But when he put his arm around 'er,
He smiled as fierce as a forty-pounder;
Look away, look away, look away, Dixie Land!

His face was sharp as a butcher's cleaber,
But dat did not seem to greab 'er;
Look away, look away, look away, Dixie Land!
Old Missus acted de foolish part,
And died for a man dat broke her heart;
Look away, look away, look away, Dixie Land!

Now, here's a health to the next Old Missus,
An' all de gals dat want to kiss us;
Look away, look away, look away, Dixie Land!
But if you want to drive 'way sorrow,
Come and hear dis song tomorrow;
Look away, look away, look away, Dixie Land!

Dar's buckwheat cakes an' Ingen' batter
Makes you fat or a little fatter;
Look away, look away, look away, Dixie Land!
Den hoe it down and scratch your grabble,
To Dixie's Land I'm bound to trabble;
Look away, look away, look away, Dixie Land!

Battle Hymn of the Republic
(Julia Ward Howe, 1862)

Mine eyes have seen the glory of the coming of the Lord:
He is trampling out the vintage where the grapes of wrath are stored;
He hath loosed the fateful lightning of his terrible swift sword:
       His truth is marching on.
       Glory, glory hallelujah,
       Glory, glory hallelujah,
       Glory, glory hallelujah,
       His truth is marching on.

I have seen Him in the watch-fires of a hundred circling camps;
They have builded Him an altar in the evening dews and damps;
I can read His righteous sentence by the dim and flaring lamps.
       His day is marching on.

I have read a fiery gospel, writ in burnished rows of steel:
"As ye deal with my contemners, so with you my grace shall deal;
Let the Hero, born of woman, crush the serpent with his heel,
        Since God is marching on."

He has sounded forth the trumpet that shall never call retreat;
He is sifting out the hearts of men before His judgment-seat:
Oh! be swift, my soul, to answer Him! be jubilant, my feet!
        Our God is marching on.

In the beauty of the lilies Christ was born across the sea,
With a glory in his bosom that transfigures you and me:
As he died to make men holy, let us die to make men free,
        While God is marching on.

When Johnny Comes Marching Home
("Louis Lambert" [Patrick S. Gilmore], 1863)

When Johnny comes marching home again, hurrah, hurrah,
We'll give him a hearty welcome then, hurrah, hurrah;
The men will cheer, the boys will shout,
The ladies, they will all turn out,
And we'll all feel gay when Johnny comes marching home.

When You and I Were Young, Maggie
(George W. Johnson, 1866)

I wandered today to the hill, Maggie,
To watch the scene below,
The creek and the old rusty mill, Maggie,
Where we sat in the long, long ago.
The green grove is gone from the hill, Maggie,
Where first the daisies sprung;
The old rusty mill is still, Maggie,
Since you and I were young.

Chorus
And now we are aged and gray, Maggie,
The trials of life nearly done,
Let us sing of the days that are gone, Maggie,
When you and I were young.

They say I am feeble with age, Maggie,
My steps are less sprightly than then;
My face is a well-written page, Maggie,
But time alone was the pen.
They say we are aged and gray, Maggie,
As spray by the white breakers flung,
But to me you're as fair as you were, Maggie,
When you and I were young.

Nobody Knows de Trouble I've Had
(Unknown, 1867)

One morning I was a-walking down,
Oh, yes, Lord!
I saw some berries a-hanging down,
Oh, yes, Lord!

Chorus
Nobody knows de trouble I've had,
Nobody knows but Jesus;
Nobody knows de trouble I've had,
Sing glory hallelu!

I pick de berry and I suck de juice,
Oh, yes, Lord!
Just as sweet as the honey in de comb,
Oh, yes, Lord!

Sometimes I'm up, sometimes I'm down,
Oh, yes, Lord!
Sometimes I'm almost on de groun',
Oh, yes, Lord!

What makes ole Satan hate me so?
Oh, yes, Lord!
Because he got me once and he let me go,
Oh, yes, Lord!

Rock O' My Soul
(Unknown, 1867)

Rock o' my soul in de bosom of Abraham,
Rock o' my soul in de bosom of Abraham.
Rock o' my soul in de bosom of Abraham,
Lord, Rock o' my soul. (King Jesus)

He toted the young lambs in his bosom,
He toted the young lambs in his bosom,
And leave the old sheep alone.

Many Thousand Gone
(Unknown, 1867)

No more auction block for me,
No more, no more;
No more auction block for me,
Many thousand gone.

No more peck o' corn for me,
No more, no more;
No more peck o' corn for me,
Many thousand gone.

No more driver's lash for me,
No more, no more;
No more driver's lash for me,
Many thousand gone.

No more pint o' salt for me,
No more, no more;
No more pint o' salt for me,
Many thousand gone.

No more hundred lash for me,
No more, no more;
No more hundred lash for me,
Many thousand gone.

No more mistress' call for me,
No more, no more;
No more mistress' call for me,
Many thousand gone.

Michael Row the Boat Ashore
(Unknown, 1867)

Then you'll hear the horn they blow,
Michael haul the boat ashore, Hallelujah!
Michael haul the boat ashore, Hallelujah!

Then you'll hear the trumpet sound,
Michael haul the boat ashore, Hallelujah!
Michael haul the boat ashore, Hallelujah!

Trumpet sound the world around,
Michael haul the boat ashore, Hallelujah!
Michael haul the boat ashore, Hallelujah!

Trumpet sound for rich and poor,
Michael haul the boat ashore, Hallelujah!
Michael haul the boat ashore, Hallelujah!

Trumpet sound the jubilee,
Michael haul the boat ashore, Hallelujah!
Michael haul the boat ashore, Hallelujah!

Trumpet sound for you and me,
Michael haul the boat ashore, Hallelujah!
Michael haul the boat ashore, Hallelujah!

O Little Town of Bethlehem
(Phillips Brooks, 1868)

O little town of Bethlehem,
How still we see thee lie!
Above thy deep and dreamless sleep
The silent stars go by:
Yet in thy dark streets shineth
The everlasting light;
The hopes and fears of all the years
Are met in thee tonight.

For Christ is born of Mary,
And gathered all above,
While mortals sleep, the angels keep
Their watch of wond'ring love.
O morning stars, together
Proclaim the holy birth!

And praises sing to God the King,
And peace to men on earth!

How silently, how silently,
The wondrous gift is given!
So God imparts to human hearts
The blessings of his heaven.
No ear may hear his coming,
But in this world of sin,
Where meek souls will receive him, still
The dear Christ enters in.

O holy Child of Bethlehem,
Descend to us, we pray,
Cast out our sin, and enter in,
Be born in us to-day!
We hear the Christmas angels
The great glad tidings tell;
O come to us, abide with us,
Our Lord Emmanuel!

There Is a Balm in Gilead
(Unknown)

Sometimes I feel discouraged, and think my work's in vain.
But then the Holy Spirit revives my soul again.

Refrain
There is a balm in Gilead to make the world whole;
There is a balm in Gilead to heal the sin-sick soul.

Don't ever feel discouraged, for Jesus is your friend,
and if you look for knowledge he'll never refuse to lend.

If you can't preach like Peter, if you can't pray like Paul,
just tell the love of Jesus, and say he died for all.

V

THE ERA OF RECONSTRUCTION AND EXPANSION: 1870–1900

Emma Lazarus
(1849–1887)

The New Ezekiel

What, can these dead bones live, whose sap is dried
    By twenty scorching centuries of wrong?
Is this the House of Israel, whose pride
Is as a tale that's told, an ancient song?
Are these ignoble relics all that live
    Of psalmist, priest, and prophet? Can the breath
Of very heaven bid these bones revive,
    Open the graves and clothe the ribs of death?

Yea, Prophesy, the Lord hath said. Again
    Say to the wind, Come forth and breathe afresh,
Even that they may live upon these slain,
    And bone to bone shall leap, and flesh to flesh.
The Spirit is not dead, proclaim the word,
    Where lay dead bones, a host of armed men stand!
I ope your graves, my people, saith the Lord,
    And I shall place you living in your land.

The New Colossus

Not like the brazen giant of Greek fame,
With conquering limbs astride from land to land;
Here at our sea-washed, sunset gates shall stand
A mighty woman with a torch, whose flame
Is the imprisoned lightning, and her name
Mother of Exiles. From her beacon-hand
Glows world-wide welcome; her mild eyes command
The air-bridged harbor that twin cities frame.
"Keep, ancient lands, your storied pomp!" cries she
With silent lips. "Give me your tired, your poor,
Your huddled masses yearning to breathe free,
The wretched refuse of your teeming shore.
Send these, the homeless, tempest-tost to me,
I lift my lamp beside the golden door!"

423

JAMES WHITCOMB RILEY
(1849–1916)

Little Orphant Annie

INSCRIBED WITH ALL FAITH AND AFFECTION
To all the little children:—The happy ones; and sad ones;
The sober and the silent ones; the boisterous and glad ones;
The good ones—Yes, the good ones, too; and all the lovely bad ones.

Little Orphant Annie's come to our house to stay,
An' wash the cups an' saucers up, an' brush the crumbs away,
An' shoo the chickens off the porch, an' dust the hearth, an' sweep,
An' make the fire, an' bake the bread, an' earn her board-an'-keep;
An' all us other children, when the supper-things is done,
We set around the kitchen fire an' has the mostest fun
A-list'nin' to the witch-tales 'at Annie tells about,
An' the Gobble-uns 'at gits you
                Ef you
                    Don't
                        Watch
                            Out!

Wunst they wuz a little boy wouldn't say his prayers,—
An' when he went to bed at night, away up-stairs,
His Mammy heerd him holler, an' his Daddy heerd him bawl,
An' when they turn't the kivvers down, he wuzn't there at all!
An' they seeked him in the rafter-room, an' cubby-hole, an' press,
An' seeked him up the chimbly-flue, an' ever'-wheres, I guess;
But all they ever found wuz thist his pants an' roundabout:—
An' the Gobble-uns 'll git you
                Ef you
                    Don't
                        Watch
                            Out!

An' one time a little girl 'ud allus laugh an' grin,
An' make fun of ever' one, an' all her blood-an'-kin;
An' wunst, when they was "company," an' ole folks wuz there,
She mocked 'em an' shocked 'em, an' said she didn't care!
An' thist as she kicked her heels, an' turn't to run an' hide,
They wuz two great big Black Things a-standin' by her side,
An' they snatched her through the ceilin' 'fore she knowd what she's
    about!
An' the Gobble-uns 'll git you

Ef you
    Don't
        Watch
           Out!

An' little Orphant Annie says, when the blaze is blue,
An' the lamp-wick sputters, an' the wind goes *woo-oo*!
An' you hear the crickets quit, an' the moon is gray,
An' the lightnin'-bugs in dew is all squenched away,—
You better mind yer parunts, an' yer teachurs fond an' dear,
An' churish them 'at loves you, an' dry the orphant's tear,
An' he'p the pore an' needy ones 'at clusters all about,
Er the Gobble-uns 'll git you
    Ef you
        Don't
           Watch
             Out!

ELLA WHEELER WILCOX
(1850–1919)

Solitude

Laugh, and the world laughs with you;
    Weep, and you weep alone;
For the sad old earth must borrow its mirth,
    But has trouble enough of its own.
Sing, and the hills will answer;
    Sigh, it is lost on the air;
The echoes bound to a joyful sound,
    But shrink from voicing care.

Rejoice, and men will seek you;
    Grieve, and they turn and go;
They want full measure of all your pleasure,
    But they do not need your woe.
Be glad, and your friends are many;
    Be sad, and you lose them all,—
There are none to decline your nectared wine,
    But alone you must drink life's gall.

Feast, and your halls are crowded;
    Fast, and the world goes by.
Succeed and give, and it helps you live,
    But no man can help you die.
For there is room in the halls of pleasure
    For a large and lordly train,
But one by one we must all file on
    Through the narrow aisles of pain.

HENRIETTA CORDELIA RAY
(1850–1916)

My Spirit's Complement

Thy life hath touched the edges of my life,
All glistening and moist with sunlit dew.
They touched, they paused,—then drifted wide apart,
Each gleaming with a rare prismatic hue.

'Twas but a touch! the edges of a life
Alone encolored with the rose, yet lo!
Each fibre started into strange unrest,
And then was stilled, lulled to a rhythmic flow.

Perchance our spirits clasp on some fair isle,
Bright with the sheen of reveries divine;
Or list'ning to such strains as chant the stars,
In purest harmony their tendrils twine.

God grant our souls may meet in Paradise,
After the mystery of life's sweet pain;
And find the strange prismatic hues of earth
Transmuted to the spotless light again.

EDWIN MARKHAM
(1852–1940)

The Man with the Hoe

Bowed by the weight of centuries he leans
Upon his hoe and gazes on the ground,
The emptiness of ages in his face,
And on his back the burden of the world.
Who made him dead to rapture and despair,
A thing that grieves not and that never hopes,
Stolid and stunned, a brother to the ox?
Who loosened and let down this brutal jaw?
Whose was the hand that slanted back this brow?
Whose breath blew out the light within this brain?
Is this the Thing the Lord God made and gave
To have dominion over sea and land;
To trace the stars and search the heavens for power;
To feel the passion of Eternity?
Is this the Dream He dreamed who shaped the suns
And marked their ways upon the ancient deep?
Down all the stretch of Hell to its last gulf
There is no shape more terrible than this—
More tongued with censure of the world's blind greed—
More filled with signs and portents for the soul—
More fraught with menace to the universe.

What gulfs between him and the seraphim!
Slave of the wheel of labor, what to him
Are Plato and the swing of Pleiades?
What the long reaches of the peaks of song,
The rift of dawn, the reddening of the rose?
Through this dread shape the suffering ages look;
Time's tragedy is in that aching stoop;
Through this dread shape humanity betrayed,
Plundered, profaned and disinherited,
Cries protest to the Judges of the World,
A protest that is also prophecy.

O masters, lords and rulers in all lands,
Is this the handiwork you give to God,
This monstrous thing distorted and soul-quenched?
How will you ever straighten up this shape;
Touch it again with immortality;
Give back the upward looking and the light;

Rebuild in it the music and the dream;
Make right the immemorial infamies,
Perfidious wrongs, immedicable woes?

O masters, lords and rulers in all lands,
How will the Future reckon with this Man?
How answer his brute question in that hour
When whirlwinds of rebellion shake the world?
How will it be with kingdoms and with kings—
With those who shaped him to the thing he is—
When this dumb Terror shall reply to God,
After the silence of the centuries?

EDITH M. THOMAS
(1854–1925)

Frost To-Night

Apple-green west and an orange bar,
And the crystal eye of a lone, one star . . .
And, "Child, take the shears and cut what you will.
Frost to-night—so clear and dead-still."

Then, I sally forth, half sad, half proud,
And I come to the velvet, imperial crowd,
The wine-red, the gold, the crimson, the pied,—
The dahlias that reign by the garden-side.

The dahlias I might not touch till to-night!
A gleam of the shears in the fading light,
And I gathered them all,—the splendid throng,
And in one great sheaf I bore them along.

In my garden of Life with its all-late flowers,
I heed a Voice in the shrinking hours:
"Frost to-night—so clear and dead-still . . ."
Half sad, half proud, my arms I fill.

LIZETTE WOODWORTH REESE
(1856–1935)

Rachel

No days that dawn can match for her
    The days before her house was bare;
Sweet was the whole year with the stir
    Of young feet on the stair.

Once was she wealthy with small cares,
    And small hands clinging to her knees;
Now is she poor, and, weeping, bears
    Her strange, new hours of ease.

Renunciation

Loose hands and part: I am not she you sought,
    The fair one whom in all our dreams you see,
    But something more of earth and less than she,
That crowded her an instant from your thought.
Blameless we face the fate this hour has brought.
    Unwitting I took hers; I set you free
    From all that you unwitting gave to me;
Seek her and find her; I do grudge her naught.
Love, after daylight, dark; so there is left
    This season stripped of you; but yet I know,
        Remembering the old, I cannot make
These new days bitter or myself bereft.
    I know, O love, that I do love you so,
        While peace is yours my true heart cannot break!

To Life

Unpetal the flower of me,
And cast it to the gust;
Betray me if you will;
Trample me to dust.

But that I should go bare,
But that I should go free
Of any hurt at all—
Do not this thing to me.

Crows

Earth is raw with this one note,
　　This tattered making of a song,
Narrowed down to a crow's throat,
　　Above the willow-trees that throng

The crooking field from end to end,
　　Fixed as the sun, the grave, this sound;
Of what the weather has to spend
　　As much a part as sky or ground.

The primal yellow of that flower,
　　The tansy making August plain;
And the stored wildness of this hour
　　It sucks up like a bitter rain.

Miss it we would, were it not here,
　　Simple as water, rough as spring,
It hurls us at the point of spear,
　　Back to some naked, early thing.

Listen now. As with a hoof
　　It stamps an image on the gust;
Chimney by chimney a lost roof
　　Starts for a moment from its dust.

SAMUEL ALFRED BEADLE
(1857–1932)

Words

Words are but leaves to the tree of mind;
　　Where breezy fancy plays;
Or echoes from the souls which find
　　Expression's subtle ways.

A beaming lamp to idea's feet
　　Where sentinel thought abides;
Or a guide to the soul's retreat,
　　Where master man presides.

A jewel trembling on the tongue,
    The index of the heart;
The black mask from the spirit wrung,
    Revealing every part.

A ship upon the sea of life,
    With all her sails aswell;
Her cargo being the bread of life,
    Or the cindered dross of hell.

GEORGE MARION McCLELLAN
(1860–1934)

A September Night

The full September moon sheds floods of light,
And all the bayou's face is gemmed with stars
Save where are dropped fantastic shadows down
From sycamores and moss-hung cypress trees.
With slumberous sound the waters half asleep
Creep on and on their way, twixt rankish reeds,
Through marsh and lowlands stretching to the gulf.
Begirt with cotton fields Anguilla sits
Half bird-like dreaming on her summer nest
Amid her spreading figs, and roses still
In bloom with all their spring and summer hues.
Pomegranates hang with dapple cheeks full ripe,
And over all the town a dreamy haze
Drops down. The great plantations stretching far
Away are plains of cotton downy white.
O, glorious is this night of joyous sounds
Too full for sleep. Aromas wild and sweet,
From muscadine, late blooming jessamine,
And roses, all the heavy air suffuse.
Faint bellows from the alligators come
From swamps afar, where sluggish lagoons give
To them a peaceful home. The katydids
Make ceaseless cries. Ten thousand insects' wings
Stir in the moonlight haze and joyous shouts
Of Negro song and mirth awake hard by
The cabin dance. O, glorious is this night.
The summer sweetness fills my heart with songs
I cannot sing, with loves I cannot speak.

BLISS CARMAN
(1861–1929)

A Vagabond Song

There is something in the autumn that is native to my blood—
Touch of manner, hint of mood;
And my heart is like a rhyme,
With the yellow and the purple and the crimson keeping time.

The scarlet of the maples can shake me like a cry
Of bugles going by.
And my lonely spirit thrills
To see the frosty asters like a smoke upon the hills.

There is something in October sets the gypsy blood astir;
We must rise and follow her,
When from every hill of flame
She calls and calls each vagabond by name.

LOUISE IMOGEN GUINEY
(1861–1920)

from The Knight Errant

(Donatello's Saint George)

. . . .

Oh, give my youth, my faith, my sword,
Choice of the heart's desire:
A short life in the saddle, Lord!
Not long life by the fire.

Forethought and recollection
Rivet mine armour gay!
The passion for perfection
Redeem my failing way!
The arrows of the upper slope
From sudden ambush cast,
Rain quick and true, with one to ope
My Paradise at last!

I fear no breathing bowman,
But only, east and west,
The awful other foeman
Impowered in my breast.
The outer fray in the sun shall be,
The inner beneath the moon;
And may Our Lady lend to me
Sight of the Dragon soon!

Borderlands

Through all the evening,
All the virginal long evening,
Down the blossomed aisle of April it is dread to walk alone;
For there the intangible is nigh, the lost is ever-during;
And who would suffer again beneath a too divine alluring,
Keen as the ancient drift of sleep on dying faces blown?

Yet in the valley,
At a turn of the orchard alley,
When a wild aroma touched me in the moist and moveless air,
Like breath indeed from out Thee, or as airy vesture round Thee,
Then was it I went faintly, for fear I had nearly found Thee,
O Hidden, O Perfect, O Desired! O first and final Fair!

The Wild Ride

I hear in my heart, I hear in its ominous pulses
All day, on the road, the hoofs of invisible horses,
All night, from their stalls, the importunate pawing and neighing.

Let cowards and laggards fall back! but alert to the saddle
Weather-worn and abreast, go men of our galloping legion,
With a stirrup-cup each to the lily of women that loves him.

The trail is through dolour and dread, over crags and morasses;
There are shapes by the way, there are things that appal or entice us:
What odds? We are Knights of the Grail, we are vowed to the riding.

Thought's self is a vanishing wing, and joy is a cobweb,
And friendship a flower in the dust, and glory a sunbeam:
Not here is our prize, nor, alas! after these our pursuing.

A dipping of plumes, a tear, a shake of the bridle,
A passing salute to this world and her pitiful beauty:
We hurry with never a word in the track of our fathers.

(I hear in my heart, I hear in its ominous pulses
All day, on the road, the hoofs of invisible horses,
All night, from their stalls, the importunate pawing and neighing.)

We spur to a land of no name, out-racing the storm-wind;
We leap to the infinite dark like sparks from the anvil.
Thou leadest, O God! All's well with Thy troopers that follow.

GEORGE SANTAYANA
(1863–1952)

O World, thou choosest not the better part

O World, thou choosest not the better part!
It is not wisdom to be only wise,
And on the inward vision close the eyes,
But it is wisdom to believe the heart.
Columbus found a world, and had no chart.
Save one that faith deciphered in the skies;
To trust the soul's invincible surmise
Was all his science and his only art.
Our knowledge is a torch of smoky pine
That lights the pathway but one step ahead
Across a void of mystery and dread.
Bid, then, the tender light of faith to shine
By which alone the mortal heart is led
Unto the thinking of the thought divine.

To W.P.

I
Calm was the sea to which your course you kept,
Oh, how much calmer than all southern seas!
Many your nameless mates, whom the keen breeze
Wafted from mothers that of old have wept.
All souls of children taken as they slept—

Are your companions, partners of your ease,
And the green souls of all these autumn trees
Are with you through the silent spaces swept.
Your virgin body gave its gentle breath
Untainted to the gods. Why should we grieve,
But that we merit not your holy death?
We shall not loiter long, your friends and I;
Living you made it goodlier to live,
Dead you will make it easier to die.

2
With you a part of me hath passed away;
For in the peopled forest of my mind
A tree made leafless by this wintry wind
Shall never don again its green array.
Chapel and fireside, country road and bay,
Have something of their friendliness resigned;
Another, if I would, I could not find,
And I am grown much older in a day.
But yet I treasure in my memory
Your gift of charity, and young heart's ease,
And the dear honour of your amity;
For these once mine, my life is rich with these.
And I scarce know which part may greater be,—
What I keep of you, or you rob from me.

from Normal Madness

. . . .

When I discover that the substance of the beautiful is a certain rhythm
and harmony in motion, as the atoms dance in circles through the void
(and what else should the substance of the beautiful be if it has a
substance at all?) far from destroying the beautiful in the realm of
appearance my discovery raises its presence there to a double dignity; for
its witchery, being a magic birth, is witchery indeed; and in its parent
nature, whose joy it is, proves her fertility. I deny nothing. Your
Olympian victory and your trembling steeds, spattered with foam, and
your strong lithe hand detaining them before the altar of Apollo, while
you receive the crown—how should science delete these verses from the
book of experience or prove that they were never sung? But where is
their music now? What was it when passing? A waking dream. Yes, and
grief also is a dream, which if it leaves a trace leaves not one of its own
quality, but a transmuted and serene image of sorrow in this realm of
memory and truth. As the grief of Priam in Homer and the grief of

Achilles, springing from the dreadful madness of love and pride in their two bosoms, united in the divine ecstasy of the poet, so all the joys and grief of illusion unite and become a strange ecstasy in a sane mind. What would you ask of philosophy? To feed you on sweets and lull you in your errors in the hope that death may overtake you before you understand anything? Ah, wisdom is sharper than death and only the brave can love her. When in the thick of passion the veil suddenly falls, it leaves us bereft of all we thought ours, smitten and consecrated to an unearthly revelation, walking dead among the living, not knowing what we seem to know, not loving what we seem to love, but already translated into an invisible paradise where none of the things are, but one only companion, smiling and silent, who by day and night stands beside us and shakes his head gently, bidding us say Nay, nay, to all our madness. Did you think, because I would not spare you, that I never felt the cold steel? Has not my own heart been pierced? Shed your tears, my son, shed your tears. The young man who has not wept is a savage, and the old man who will not laugh is a fool.

RICHARD HOVEY
(1864–1900)

The Sea Gypsy

I am fevered with the sunset,
I am fretful with the bay,
For the wander-thirst is on me
And my soul is in Cathay.

There's a schooner in the offing,
With her topsails shot with fire,
And my heart has gone aboard her
For the Islands of Desire.

I must forth again to-morrow!
With the sunset I must be
Hull down on the trail of rapture
In the wonder of the sea.

MADISON CAWEIN
(1865–1914)

Uncalled

As one, who, journeying westward with the sun,
Beholds at length from the up-towering hills,
Far-off, a land unspeakable beauty fills,
Circean peaks and vales of Avalon:
And, sinking weary, watches, one by one,
The big seas beat between; and knows it skills
No more to try; that now, as Heaven wills,
This is the helpless end, that all is done:
So 'tis with him, whom long a vision led
In quest of Beauty; and who finds at last
She lies beyond his effort; all the waves
Of all the world between them: while the dead,
The myriad dead, who people all the past
With failure, hail him from forgotten graves.

Deserted

The old house leans upon a tree
    Like some old man upon a staff:
The night wind in its ancient porch
    Sounds like a hollow laugh.

The heaven is wrapped in flying clouds
    As grandeur cloaks itself in gray:
The starlight flitting in and out,
    Glints like a lanthorn ray.

The dark is full of whispers. Now
    A fox-hound howls: and through the night,
Like some old ghost from out its grave,
    The moon comes misty white.

JAMES EDWIN CAMPBELL
(1867–1896)

Mors et Vita

Into the soil a seed is sown,
Out of the soul a song is wrung,
Out of the shell a pearl is gone,
Out of the cage a bird is flown,
    Out of the body, a soul!

Unto a tree the seed is grown,
Wide in the world the song is sung,
The pearl in a necklace gleams more fair,
The bird is flown to a sweeter air,
And Death is half and Life is half,
    And the two make up the whole!

W.E.B. DU BOIS
(1868–1963)

A Litany at Atlanta

*Done at Atlanta
in the Day of Death, 1906*

O Silent God, Thou whose voice afar in mist and mystery hath left our ears an-hungered in these fearful days—
Hear us, good Lord!

Listen to us, Thy children: our faces dark with doubt are made a mockery in Thy sanctuary. With uplifted hands we front Thy heaven, O God, crying:
We beseech Thee to hear us, good Lord!

We are not better than our fellows, Lord, we are but weak and human men. When our devils do deviltry, curse Thou the doer and the deed: curse them as we curse them, do to them all and more than ever they have done to innocence and weakness, to womanhood and home.
Have mercy upon us, miserable sinners!

And yet whose is the deeper guilt? Who made these devils? Who nursed them in crime and fed them on injustice? Who ravished and debauched their mothers and their grandmothers? Who bought and sold their crime, and waxed fat and rich on public iniquity?

Thou knowest, good God!

Is this Thy Justice, O Father, that guile be easier than innocence, and the innocent crucified for the guilt of the untouched guilty?

Justice, O judge of men!

Wherefore do we pray? Is not the God of the fathers dead? Have not seers seen in Heaven's halls Thine hearsed and lifeless form stark amidst the black and rolling smoke of sin, where all along bow bitter forms of endless dead?

Awake, Thou that sleepest!

Thou are not dead, but flown afar, up hills of endless light through blazing corridors of suns, where worlds do swing of good and gentle men, of women strong and free—far from the cozenage, black hypocrisy and chaste prostitution of this shameful speck of dust!

Turn again, O Lord, leave us not to perish in our sin!

From lust of body and lust of blood,
Great God, deliver us!

From lust of power and lust of gold,
Great God, deliver us!

From the leagued lying of despot and of brute,
Great God, deliver us!

A city lay in travail, God our Lord, and from her loins sprang twin Murder and Black Hate. Red was the midnight; clang, crack and cry of death and fury filled the air and trembled underneath the stars when church spires pointed silently to Thee. And all this was to sate the greed of greedy men who hide behind the veil of vengeance!

Bend us Thine ear, O Lord!

In the pale, still morning we looked upon the deed. We stopped our ears and held our leaping hands, but they—did they not wag their heads and leer and cry with bloody jaws: *Cease from Crime!* The word was mockery, for thus they train a hundred crimes while we do cure one.

Turn again our captivity, O Lord!

Behold this maimed and broken thing; dear God, it was an humble black man who toiled and sweat to save a bit from the pittance paid him. They told him: *Work and Rise.* He worked. Did this man sin? Nay, but some one told how some one said another did—one whom he had never seen nor known. Yet for that man's crime this man lieth maimed and murdered, his wife naked to shame, his children, to poverty and evil.

Hear us, O Heavenly Father!

Doth not this justice of hell stink in Thy nostrils, O God? How long shall the mounting flood of innocent blood roar in Thine ears and pound in our hearts for vengeance? Pile the pale frenzy of blood-crazed brutes who do such deeds high on Thine altar, Jehovah Jireh, and burn it in hell forever and forever!

Forgive us, good Lord; we know not what we say!

Bewildered we are, and passion-tost, mad with the madness of a mobbed and mocked and murdered people; straining at the armposts of Thy Throne, we raise our shackled hands and charge Thee, God, by the bones of our stolen fathers, by the tears of our dead mothers, by the very blood of Thy crucified Christ: *What meaneth this?* Tell us the Plan; give us the Sign!

Keep not Thou silence, O God!

Sit no longer blind, Lord God, deaf to our prayer and dumb to our dumb suffering. Surely Thou too art not white, O Lord, a pale, bloodless, heartless thing?

Ah! Christ of all the Pities!

Forgive the thought! Forgive these wild, blasphemous words. Thou are still the God of our black fathers, and in Thy soul's soul sit some soft darkenings of the evening, some shadowings of the velvet night.

But whisper—speak—call, great God, for Thy silence is white terror to our hearts! The way, O God, show us the way and point us the path.

Whither? North is greed and South is blood; within, the coward, and without, the liar. Whither? To death?

Amen! Welcome dark sleep!

Whither? To life? But not this life, dear God, not this. Let the cup pass from us, tempt us not beyond our strength, for there is that clamoring and clawing within, to whose voice we would not listen, yet shudder lest we must, and it is red, Ah! God! It is a red and awful shape.

Selah!

In yonder East trembles a star.

Vengeance is mine; I will repay, saith the Lord!

Thy will, O Lord, be done!
Kyrie Eleison!

Lord, we have done these pleading, wavering words.
We beseech Thee to hear us, good Lord!

We bow our heads and hearken soft to the sobbing of women and
little children.
We beseech Thee to hear us, good Lord!

Our voices sink in silence and in night.
Hear us, good Lord!

In night, O God of a godless land!
Amen!

In silence, O Silent God.
Selah!

WILLIAM VAUGHN MOODY
(1869–1910)

Gloucester Moors

A mile behind is Gloucester town
Where the fishing fleets put in,
A mile ahead the land dips down
And the woods and farms begin.
Here, where the moors stretch free
In the high blue afternoon,
Are the marching sun and talking sea,
And the racing winds that wheel and flee
On the flying heels of June.

Jill-o'er-the-ground is purple blue,
Blue is the quaker-maid,
The wild geranium holds its dew
Long in the boulder's shade.
Wax-red hangs the cup
From the huckleberry boughs,
In barberry bells the grey moths sup,
Or where the choke-cherry lifts high up
Sweet bowls for their carouse.

Over the shelf of the sandy cove
Beach-peas blossom late.
By copse and cliff the swallows rove
Each calling to his mate.
Seaward the sea-gulls go,
And the land-birds all are here;
That green-gold flash was a vireo,
And yonder flame where the marsh-flags grow
Was a scarlet tanager.

This earth is not the steadfast place
We landsmen build upon;
From deep to deep she varies pace,
And while she comes is gone.
Beneath my feet I feel
Her smooth bulk heave and dip;
With velvet plunge and soft upreel
She swings and steadies to her keel
Like a gallant, gallant ship.

These summer clouds she sets for sail,
The sun is her masthead light,
She tows the moon like a pinnace frail
Where her phosphor wake churns bright.
Now hid, now looming clear,
On the face of the dangerous blue
The star fleets tack and wheel and veer,
But on, but on does the old earth steer
As if her port she knew.

God, dear God! Does she know her port,
Though she goes so far about?
Or blind astray, does she make her sport
To brazen and chance it out?
I watched when her captains passed:
She were better captainless.
Men in the cabin, before the mast,
But some were reckless and some aghast,
And some sat gorged at mess.

By her battened hatch I leaned and caught
Sounds from the noisome hold,—
Cursing and sighing of souls distraught
And cries too sad to be told.
Then I strove to go down and see;
But they said, "Thou art not of us!"
I turned to those on the deck with me

And cried, "Give help!" But they said, "Let be:
Our ship sails faster thus."

Jill-o'er-the-ground is purple blue,
Blue is the quaker-maid,
The alder-clump where the brook comes through
Breeds cresses in its shade.
To be out of the moiling street
With its swelter and its sin!
Who has given to me this sweet,
And given my brother dust to eat?
And when will his wage come in?

Scattering wide or blown in ranks,
Yellow and white and brown,
Boats and boats from the fishing banks
Come home to Gloucester town.
There is cash to purse and spend,
There are wives to be embraced,
Hearts to borrow and hearts to lend,
And hearts to take and keep to the end,—
O little sails, make haste!

But thou, vast outbound ship of souls,
What harbor town for thee?
What shapes, when thy arriving tolls,
Shall crowd the banks to see?
Shall all the happy shipmates then
Stand singing brotherly?
Or shall a haggard ruthless few
Warp her over and bring her to,
While the many broken souls of men
Fester down in the slaver's pen,
And nothing to say or do?

The Bracelet of Grass

The opal heart of afternoon
Was clouding on to throbs of storm,
Ashen within the ardent west
The lips of thunder muttered harm,
And as a bubble like to break
Hung heaven's trembling amethyst,
When with the sedge-grass by the lake
I braceleted her wrist.

And when the ribbon grass was tied,
Sad with the happiness we planned,
Palm linked in palm we stood awhile
And watched the raindrops dot the sand;
Until the anger of the breeze
Chid all the lake's bright breathing down,
And ravished all the radiancies
From her deep eyes of brown.

We gazed from shelter on the storm,
And through our hearts swept ghostly pain
To see the shards of day sweep past,
Broken, and none might mend again.
Broken, that none shall ever mend;
Loosened, that none shall ever tie.
O the wind and the wind, will it never end?
O the sweeping past of the ruined sky!

Faded Pictures

Only two patient eyes to stare
Out of the canvas. All the rest—
The warm green gown, the small hands pressed
Light in the lap, the braided hair.

That must have made the sweet low brow
So earnest, centuries ago,
When some one saw it change and glow—
All faded! Just the eyes burn now.

I dare say people pass and pass
Before the blistered little frame,
And dingy work without a name
Stuck in behind its square of glass.

But I, well, I left Raphael
Just to come drink these eyes of hers,
To think away the stains and blurs
And make all new again and well.

Only, for tears my head will bow,
Because there on my heart's last wall,
Scarce on tint left to tell it all,
A picture keeps its eyes, somehow.

Edwin Arlington Robinson
(1869–1935)

Walt Whitman

The master-songs are ended, and the man
That sang them is a name. And so is God
A name; and so is love, and life, and death,
And everything. But we, who are too blind
To read what we have written, or what faith
Has written for us, do not understand:
We only blink, and wonder.

Last night it was the song that was the man,
But now it is the man that is the song.
We do not hear him very much to-day:
His piercing and eternal cadence rings
Too pure for us—too powerfully pure,
Too lovingly triumphant, and too large;
But there are some that hear him, and they know
That he shall sing to-morrow for all men,
And that all time shall listen.

The master-songs are ended? Rather say
No songs are ended that are ever sung,
And that no names are dead names. When we write
Men's letters on proud marble or on sand,
We write them there forever.

Luke Havergal

Go to the western gate, Luke Havergal,
There where the vines cling crimson on the wall,
And in the twilight wait for what will come.
The leaves will whisper there of her, and some,
Like flying words, will strike you as they fall;
But go, and if you listen she will call.
Go to the western gate, Luke Havergal—
Luke Havergal.

No, there is not a dawn in eastern skies
To rift the fiery night that's in your eyes;
But there, where western glooms are gathering,
The dark will end the dark, if anything:
God slays Himself with every leaf that flies,

And hell is more than half of paradise.
No, there is not a dawn in eastern skies—
In eastern skies.

Out of a grave I come to tell you this,
Out of a grave I come to quench the kiss
That flames upon your forehead with a glow
That blinds you to the way that you must go.
Yes, there is yet one way to where she is,
Bitter, but one that faith may never miss.
Out of a grave I come to tell you this—
To tell you this.

There is the western gate, Luke Havergal,
There are the crimson leaves upon the wall.
Go, for the winds are tearing them away,—
Nor think to riddle the dead words they say,
Nor any more to feel them as they fall;
But go, and if you trust her she will call.
There is the western gate, Luke Havergal—
Luke Havergal.

Richard Cory

Whenever Richard Cory went down town,
We people on the pavement looked at him:
He was a gentleman from sole to crown,
Clean favored, and imperially slim.

And he was always quietly arrayed,
And he was always human when he talked;
But still he fluttered pulses when said,
"Good-morning," and he glittered when he walked.

And he was rich—yes, richer than a king—
And admirably schooled in every grace:
In fine, we thought that he was everything
To make us wish that we were in his place.

So on we worked, and waited for the light,
And went without the meat, and cursed the bread;
And Richard Cory, one calm summer night,
Went home and put a bullet through his head.

Miniver Cheevy

Miniver Cheevy, child of scorn,
    Grew lean while he assailed the seasons;
He wept that he was ever born,
    And he had reasons.

Miniver loved the days of old
    When swords were bright and steeds were prancing;
The vision of a warrior bold
    Would set him dancing.

Miniver sighed for what was not,
    And dreamed, and rested from his labors;
He dreamed of Thebes and Camelot,
    And Priam's neighbors.

Miniver mourned the ripe renown
    That made so many a name so fragrant;
He mourned Romance, now on the town,
    And Art, a vagrant.

Miniver loved the Medici,
    Albeit he had never seen one;
He would have sinned incessantly
    Could he have been one.

Miniver cursed the commonplace
    And eyed a khaki suit with loathing;
He missed the mediæval grace
    Of iron clothing.

Miniver scorned the gold he sought,
    But sore annoyed was he without it;
Miniver thought, and thought, and thought,
    And thought about it.

Miniver Cheevy, born too late,
    Scratched his head and kept on thinking;
Miniver coughed, and called it fate,
    And kept on drinking.

For a Dead Lady

No more with overflowing light
Shall fill the eyes that now are faded,
Nor shall another's fringe with night
Their woman-hidden world as they did.
No more shall quiver down the days
The flowing wonder of her ways,
Whereof no language may requite
The shifting and the many-shaded.

The grace, divine, definitive,
Clings only as a faint forestalling;
The laugh that love could not forgive
Is hushed, and answers to no calling;
The forehead and the little ears
Have gone where Saturn keeps the years;
The breast where roses could not live
Has done with rising and with falling.

The beauty, shattered by the laws
That have creation in their keeping,
No longer trembles at applause,
Or over children that are sleeping;
And we who delve in beauty's lore
Know all that we have known before
Of what inexorable cause
Makes Time so vicious in his reaping.

Eros Turannos

She fears him, and will always ask
    What fated her to choose him;
She meets in his engaging mask
    All reasons to refuse him;
But what she meets and what she fears
Are less than are the downward years,
Drawn slowly to the foamless weirs
    Of age, were she to lose him.

Between a blurred sagacity
    That once had power to sound him,
And Love, that will not let him be
    The Judas that she found him,
Her pride assuages her almost,
As if it were alone the cost.—

He sees that he will not be lost,
    And waits and looks around him.

A sense of ocean and old trees
    Envelops and allures him;
Tradition, touching all he sees,
    Beguiles and reassures him;
And all her doubts of what he says
Are dimmed with what she knows of days—
Till even prejudice delays
    And fades, and she secures him.

The falling leaf inaugurates
    The reign of her confusion:
The pounding wave reverberates
    The dirge of her illusion;
And home, where passion lived and died,
Becomes a place where she can hide,
While all the town and harbor side
    Vibrate with her seclusion.

We tell you, tapping on our brows,
    The story as it should be,—
As if the story of a house
    Were told, or ever could be;
We'll have no kindly veil between
Her visions and those we have seen,—
As if we guessed what hers have been,
    Or what they are or would be.

Meanwhile we do no harm; for they
    That with a god have striven,
Not hearing much of what we say,
    Take what the god has given;
Though like waves breaking it may be
Or like a changed familiar tree,
Or like a stairway to the sea
    Where down the blind are driven.

Mr. Flood's Party

Old Eben Flood, climbing alone one night
Over the hill between the town below
And the forsaken upland hermitage
That held as much as he should ever know
On earth again of home, paused warily.

The road was his with not a native near;
And Eben, having leisure, said aloud,
For no man else in Tillbury Town to hear:

"Well, Mr. Flood, we have the harvest moon
Again, and we may not have many more;
The bird is on the wing, the poet says,
And you and I have said it here before.
Drink to the bird." He raised up to the light
The jug that he had gone so far to fill,
And answered huskily: "Well, Mr. Flood,
Since you propose it, I believe I will."

Alone, as if enduring to the end
A valiant armor of scarred hopes outworn,
He stood there in the middle of the road
Like Roland's ghost winding a silent horn.
Below him, in the town among the trees,
Where friends of other days had honored him,
A phantom salutation of the dead
Rang thinly till old Eben's eyes were dim.

Then, as a mother lays her sleeping child
Down tenderly, fearing it may awake,
He set the jug down slowly at his feet
With trembling care, knowing that most things break;
And only when assured that on firm earth
It stood, as the uncertain lives of men
Assuredly did not, he paced away,
And with his hand extended paused again:

"Well, Mr. Flood, we have not met like this
In a long time; and many a change has come
To both of us, I fear, since last it was
We had a drop together. Welcome home!"
Convivially returning with himself,
Again he raised the jug up to the light;
And with an acquiescent quaver said:
"Well, Mr. Flood, if you insist, I might.

"Only a very little, Mr. Flood—
For auld lang syne. No more, sir; that will do."
So, for the time, apparently it did,
And Eben evidently thought so too;
For soon amid the silver loneliness
Of night he lifted up his voice and sang,

Secure, with only two moons listening,
Until the whole harmonious landscape rang—

"For auld lang syne." The weary throat gave out,
The last word wavered, and the song was done.
He raised again the jug regretfully
And shook his head, and was again alone.
There was not much that was ahead of him,
And there was nothing in the town below—
Where strangers would have shut the many doors
That many friends had opened long ago.

The Man Against the Sky

Between me and the sunset, like a dome
Against the glory of a world on fire,
Now burned a sudden hill,
Bleak, round, and high, by flame-lit height made higher,
With nothing on it for the flame to kill
Save one who moved and was alone up there
To loom before the chaos and the glare
As if he were the last god going home
Unto his last desire.

Dark, marvelous, and inscrutable he moved on
Till down the fiery distance he was gone,
Like one of those eternal, remote things
That range across a man's imaginings
When a sure music fills him and he knows
What he may say thereafter to few men,—
The touch of ages having wrought
An echo and a glimpse of what he thought
A phantom or a legend until then;
For whether lighted over ways that save,
Or lured from all repose,
If he go on too far to find a grave,
Mostly alone he goes.

Even he, who stood where I had found him,
On high with fire all round him,
Who moved along the molten west,
And over the round hill's crest
That seemed half ready with him to go down,
Flame-bitten and flame-cleft,
As if there were to be no last thing left
Of a nameless unimaginable town,—

Even he who climbed and vanished may have taken
Down to the perils of a depth not known,
From death defended though by men forsaken,
The bread that every man must eat alone;
He may have walked while others hardly dared
Look on to see him stand where many fell;
And upward out of that, as out of hell,
He may have sung and striven
To mount where more of him shall yet be given,
Bereft of all retreat,
To sevenfold heat,—
As on a day when three in Dura shared
The furnace, and were spared
For glory by that king of Babylon
Who made himself so great that God, who heard,
Covered him with long feathers, like a bird.

Again, he may have gone down easily,
By comfortable altitudes, and found,
As always, underneath him solid ground
Whereon to be sufficient and to stand
Possessed already of the promised land,
Far stretched and fair to see:
A good sight, verily,
And one to make the eyes of her who bore him
Shine glad with hidden tears.
Why question of his ease of who before him,
In one place or another where they left
Their names as far behind them as their bones,
And yet by dint of slaughter toil and theft,
And shrewdly sharpened stones,
Carved hard the way of his ascendency
Through deserts of lost years?
Why trouble him now who sees and hears
Nor more than what his innocence requires,
And therefore to no other height aspires
Than one at which he neither quails nor tires?
He may do more by seeing what he sees
Than others eager for iniquities;
He may, by seeing all things for the best,
Incite futurity to do the rest.

Or with an even likelihood,
He may have met with atrabilious eyes
The fires of time on equal terms and passed
Indifferently down, until at last
His only kind of grandeur would have been,

Apparently, in being seen.
He may have had for evil or for good
No argument; he may have had no care
For what without himself went anywhere
To failure or to glory, and least of all
For such a stale, flamboyant miracle;
He may have been the prophet of an art
Immovable to old idolatries;
He may have been a player without a part,
Annoyed that even the sun should have the skies
For such a flaming way to advertise;
He may have been a painter sick at heart
With Nature's toiling for a new surprise;
He may have been a cynic, who now, for all
Of anything divine that his effete
Negation may have tasted,
Saw truth in his own image, rather small,
Forebore to fever the ephemeral,
Found any barren height a good retreat
From any swarming street,
And in the sun saw power superbly wasted:
And when the primitive old-fashioned stars
Came out again to shine on joys and wars
More primitive, and all arrayed for doom,
He may have proved a world a sorry thing
In his imagining,
And life a lighted highway to the tomb.

Or, mounting with infirm unsearching tread,
His hopes to chaos led,
He may have stumbled up there from the past,
And with an aching strangeness viewed the last
Abysmal conflagration of his dreams,—
A flame where nothing seems
To burn but flame itself, by nothing fed;
And while it all went out,
Not even the faint anodyne of doubt
May then have eased a painful going down
From pictured heights of power and lost renown,
Revealed at length to his outlived endeavor
Remote and unapproachable forever;
And at his heart there may have gnawed
Sick memories of a dead faith foiled and flawed
And long dishonored by the living death
Assigned alike by chance
To brutes and hierophants;
And anguish fallen on those he loved around him

May once have dealt the last blow to confound him,
And so have left him as death leaves a child,
Who sees it all too near;
And he who knows no young way to forget
May struggle to the tomb unreconciled.
Whatever suns may rise or set
There may be nothing kinder for him here
Than shafts and agonies;
And under these
He may cry out and stay on horribly;
Or, seeing in death too small a thing to fear,
He may go forward like a stoic Roman
Where pangs and terrors in his pathway lie,—
Or, seizing the swift logic of a woman,
Curse God and die.

Or maybe there, like many another one
Who might have stood aloft and looked ahead,
Black-drawn against wild red,
He may have built, unawed by fiery gules
That in him no commotion stirred,
A living reason out of molecules
Why molecules occurred,
And one for smiling when he might have sighed
Had he seen far enough,
And in the same inevitable stuff
Discovered an odd reason too for pride
In being what he must have been by laws
Infrangible and for no kind of cause.
Deterred by no confusion or surprise
He may have seen with his mechanic eyes
A world without a meaning, and had room,
Alone amid magnificence and doom,
To build himself an airy monument
That should, or fail him in his vague intent,
Outlast an accidental universe—
To call it nothing worse—
Or, by the burrowing guile
Of Time disintegrated and effaced,
Like once-remembered mighty trees go down
To ruin, of which by man may now be traced
No part sufficient even to be rotten,
And in the book of things that are forgotten
Is entered as a thing not quite worth while.
He may have been so great
That satraps would have shivered at his frown,

And all he prized alive may rule a state
No larger than a grave that holds a clown;
He may have been a master of his fate,
And of his atoms,—ready as another
In his emergence to exonerate
His father and his mother;
He may have been a captain of a host,
Self-eloquent and ripe for prodigies,
Doomed here to swell by dangerous degrees,
And then give up the ghost.
Nahum's great grasshoppers were such as these,
Sun-scattered and soon lost.

Whatever the dark road he may have taken,
This man who stood on high
And faced alone the sky,
Whatever drove or lured or guided him—
A vision answering a faith unshaken,
An easy trust assumed of easy trials,
A sick negation born of weak denials,
A crazed abhorrence of an old condition,
A blind attendance on a brief ambition,—
Whatever stayed him or derided him,
His way was even as ours;
And we, with all our wounds and all our powers,
Must each await alone at his own height
Another darkness or another light;
And there, of our poor self dominion reft,
If inference and reason shun
Hell, Heaven, and Oblivion,
May thwarted will (perforce precarious,
But for our conservation better thus)
Have no misgiving left
Of doing yet what here we leave undone?
Or if unto the last of these we cleave,
Believing or protesting we believe
In such an idle and ephemeral
Florescence of the diabolical,—
If, robbed of two fond old enormities,
Our being had no onward auguries,
What then were this great love of ours to say
For launching other lives to voyage again
A little farther into time and pain,
A little faster in a futile chase
For a kingdom and a power and a Race
That would have still in sight

A manifest end of ashes and eternal night?
Is this the music of the toys we shake
So loud,—as if there might be no mistake
Somewhere in our indomitable will?
Are we no greater than the noise we make
Along one blind atomic pilgrimage
Whereon by crass chance billeted we go
Because our brains and bones and cartilage
Will have it so?
If this we say, then let us all be still
About our share in it, and live and die
More quietly thereby.

Where was he going, this man against the sky?
You know not, nor do I.
But this we know, if we know anything:
That we may laugh and fight and sing
And of our transience here make offering
To an orient Word that will not be erased,
Or, save in incommunicable gleams
Too permanent for dreams,
Be found or known.
No tonic and ambitious irritant
Of increase or of want
Has made an otherwise insensate waste
Of ages overthrown
A ruthless, veiled, implacable foretaste
Of other ages that are still to be
Depleted and rewarded variously
Because a few, by fate's economy,
Shall seem to move the world the way it goes;
No soft evangel of equality,
Safe cradled in a communal repose
That huddles into death and may at last
Be covered well with equatorial snows—
And all for what, the devil only knows—
Will aggregate an inkling to confirm
The credit of a sage or of a worm,
Or tell us why one man in five
Should have a care to stay alive
While in his heart he feels no violence
Laid on his humor and intelligence
When infant Science makes a pleasant face
And waves again that hollow toy, the Race;
No planetary trap where souls are wrought
For nothing but the sake of being caught

And sent again to nothing will attune
Itself to any key of any reason
Why man should hunger through another season
To find out why 'twere better late than soon
To go away and let the sun and moon
And all the silly stars illuminate
A place for creeping things,
And those that root and trumpet and have wings,
And herd and ruminate,
Or dive and flash and poise in rivers and seas,
Or by their loyal tails in lofty trees
Hang screeching lewd victorious derision
Of man's immortal vision.

Shall we, because Eternity records
Too vast an answer for the time-born words
We spell, whereof so many are dead that once
In our capricious lexicons
Were so alive and final, hear no more
The Word itself, the living word
That none alive has ever heard
Or ever spelt,
And few have ever felt
Without the fears and old surrenderings
And terrors that began
When Death let fall a feather from his wings
And humbled the first man?
Because the weight of our humility,
Wherefrom we gain
A little wisdom and much pain,
Falls here too sore and there too tedious,
Are we in anguish or complacency,
Not looking far enough ahead
To see by what mad couriers we are led
Along the roads of the ridiculous,
To pity ourselves and laugh at faith
And while we curse life bear it?
And if we see the soul's dead end in death,
Are we to fear it?
What folly is here that has not yet a name
Unless we say outright that we are liars?
What have we seen beyond our sunset fires
That lights again the way by which we came?
Why pay we such a price, and one we give
So clamoringly, for each racked empty day
That leads one more last human hope away,

As quiet fiends would lead past our crazed eyes
Our children to an unseen sacrifice?
If after all that we have lived and thought,
All comes to Nought—
If there be nothing after Now,
And we be nothing anyhow,
And we know that,—why live?
'Twere sure but weaklings' vain distress
To suffer dungeons where so many doors
Will open on the cold eternal shores
That look sheer down
To the dark tideless floods of Nothingness
Where all who know may drown.

JESSE RITTENHOUSE
(1869–1948)

Debt

My debt to you, Belovéd,
    Is one I cannot pay
In any coin of any realm
    On any reckoning day;

For where is he shall figure
    The debt, when all is said,
To one who makes you dream again
    When all the dreams were dead?

Or where is the appraiser
    Who shall the claim compute,
Of one who makes you sing again
    When all the songs were mute?

GEORGE STERLING
(1869–1926)

Aldebaran at Dusk

Thou art the star for which all evening waits—
    O star of peace, come tenderly and soon
    Nor heed the drowsy and enchanted moon,
Who dreams in silver at the eastern gates
Ere yet she brim with light the blue estates
    Abandoned by the eagles of the noon.
    But shine thou swiftly on the darkling dune
And woodlands where the twilight hesitates.

Above that wide and ruby lake to-West,
    Wherein the sunset waits reluctantly,
        Stir silently the purple wings of Night.
She stands afar, upholding to her breast,
    As mighty murmurs reach her from the sea,
        Thy lone and everlasting rose of light.

The Black Vulture

Aloof within the day's enormous dome,
    He holds unshared the silence of the sky.
    Far down his bleak, relentless eyes descry
The eagle's empire and the falcon's home—
Far down, the galleons of sunset roam;
    His hazards on the sea of morning lie;
    Serene, he hears the broken tempest sigh
Where cold sierras gleam like scattered foam.

And least of all he holds the human swarm—
    Unwitting now that envious men prepare
        To make their dream and its fulfillment one,
When, poised above the caldrons of the storm,
    Their hearts, contemptuous of death, shall dare
        His roads between the thunder and the sun.

EDGAR LEE MASTERS
(1869–1950)

Petit, the Poet

Seeds in a dry pod, tick, tick, tick,
Tick, tick, tick, like mites in a quarrel—
Faint iambics that the full breeze wakens—
But the pine tree makes a symphony thereof.
Triolets, villanelles, rondels, rondeaus,
Ballades by the score with the same old thought:
The snows and the roses of yesterday are vanished;
And what is love but a rose that fades?
Life all around me here in the village:
Tragedy, comedy, valor and truth,
Courage, constancy, heroism, failure—
All in the loom, and oh what patterns!
Woodlands, meadows, streams and rivers—
Blind to all of it all my life long.
Triolets, villanelles, rondels, rondeaus,
Seeds in a dry pod, tick, tick, tick,
Tick, tick, tick, what little iambics,
While Homer and Whitman roared in the pines.

Many Soldiers

The idea danced before us as a flag;
The sound of martial music;
The thrill of carrying a gun;
Advancement in the world on coming home;
A glint of glory, wrath for foes;
A dream of duty to country or to God.
But these were things in ourselves, shining before us,
They were not the power behind us,
Which was the Almighty hand of Life,
Like fire at earth's centre making mountains,
Or pent up waters that cut them through.
Do you remember the iron band
The blacksmith, Shack Dye, welded
Around the oak on Bennet's lawn,
From which to swing a hammock,
That daughter Janet might repose in, reading
On summer afternoons?

And that the growing tree at last
Sundered the iron band?
But not a cell in all the tree
Knew aught save that it thrilled with life,
Nor cared because the hammock fell
In the dust with Milton's Poems.

from Chicago

This is the city of great doges hidden
In guarded offices and country places.
The city strives against the things forbidden
By the doges, on whose faces
The city at large never looks;
Doges who could accomplish if they would
In a month the city's beauty and good.
Yet this city in a hundred years has risen
Out of a haunt of foxes, wolves and rooks,
And breaks asunder now the bars of the prison
Of dead days and dying. It has spread
For many a rood its boundaries, like the sprawled
And fallen Hephæstos, and has tenanted
Its neighborhoods increasing and unwalled
With peoples from all lands.
From Milwaukee Avenue to the populous mills
Of South Chicago, from the Sheridan Drive
Through forests where the water smiles
To Harlem for miles and miles.
It reaches out its hands,
Powerful and alive
With dreams to touch to-morrow, which it wills
To dawn and which shall dawn . . .
And like lights that twinkle through the stench
And putrid mist of abattoirs,
Great souls are here, separate and withdrawn,
Companionless, whom darkness cannot quench.
Seeing they are the chrysalis which must feed
Upon its own thought and the life to be,
Its flight among the stars.
Beauty is here, like half protected flowers,
Blooms and will cast its multiplying seed,
Until one mass of color shall succeed
The shaley places of these arid hours.

. . . .

Cities of the Plain

Where are the cabalists, the insidious committees,
The panders who betray the idiot cities
For miles and miles toward the prairie sprawled,
Ignorant, soulless, rich,
Smothered in fumes of pitch?

Rooms of mahogany in tall skyscrapers
See the unfolding and the folding up
Of ring-clipped papers,
And letters which keep drugged the public cup.
The walls hear whispers and the semi-tones
Of voices in the corner, over telephones
Muffled by Persian padding, gemmed with brass spittoons.
Butts of cigars are on the glass-topped table,
And through the smoke, gracing the furtive Babel,
The bishop's picture blesses the picaroons,
Who start or stop the life of millions moving
Unconscious of obedience, the plastic
Yielders to satanic and dynastic
Hands of reproaching and approving.

Here come knights armed,
But with their arms concealed,
And rubber heeled.
Here priests and wavering want are charmed.
And shadows fall here like the shark's
In messages received or sent.
Signals are flying from the battlement.
And every president
Of rail, gas, coal and oil, the parks,
The receipt of custom knows, without a look,
Their meaning as the code is in no book.
The treasonous cracksmen of the city's wealth
Watch for the flags of stealth!

Acres of coal lie fenced along the tracks.
Tracks ribbon the streets, and beneath the streets
Wires for voices, fire, thwart the plebiscites,
And choke the counsel and symposiacs
Of dreamers who have pity for the backs
That bear and bleed.
All things are theirs: tracks, wires, streets and coal,
The church's creed,
The city's soul,
The city's sea-girt loveliness,

The merciless and meretricious press.
Far up in watch-tower, where the news is printed,
Gray faces and bright eyes, weary and cynical
Discuss fresh wonders of the old cabal.
But nothing of its work in type is hinted:
Taxes are high! The mentors of the town
Must keep their taxes down
On buildings, presses, stocks
In gas, oil, coal and docks.
The mahogany rooms conceal a spider man
Who holds the taxing bodies through the church,
And knights with arms concealed. The mentors search
The spider man, the master publican,
And for his friendship silence keep,
Letting him herd the populace like sheep
For self and for the insatiable desires
Of coal and tracks and wires;
Pick judges, legislators,
And tax-gatherers.
Or name his favorites, whom they name
The slick and sinistral,
Servitors of the cabal,
For praise, which seems the equivalent of fame:
Giving to the delicate-handed crackers
Of priceless safes, the spiritual slackers,
The flash and thunder of front pages!
And the gulled millions stare and fling their wages
Where they are bidden, helpless and emasculate.
And the unilluminate,
Whose brows are brass,
Who weep on every Sabbath day
For Jesus riding on an ass,
Scarce know the ass is they,
Now ridden by his effigy,
The publican with Jesus' painted mask,
Along a way where fumes of odorless gas
First spur, then fell them from the task.

Through the parade run swift the psychic cackle
Like thorns beneath a boiling pot that crackle.
And the angels say to Yahveh looking down
From the alabaster railing, on the town,
O, cackle, cackle, cackle, crack and crack
We wish we had our little Sodom back!

from Henry C. Calhoun

. . . .

On the way to the grove you'll pass the Fates,
Shadow-eyed, bent over their weaving.
Stop for a moment, and if you see
The thread of revenge leap out of the shuttle,
Then quickly snatch from Atropos
The shears and cut it, lest your sons,
And the children of them and their children
Wear the envenomed robe.

AMERICAN INDIAN POETRY:
1870–1900

Song of Sequence
(Navajo)

Young Woman Who Becomes a Bear set fire in the mountains
In many places: as she journeyed on
There was a line of burning mountains.
The Otter set fire in the waters
In many places: as he journeyed on
There was a line of burning waters.

Invocation to Dsilyi N'eyani
(Navajo)

Reared Within the Mountains!
Lord of the Mountains!
Young Man!
Chieftain!
I have made your sacrifice.
I have prepared a smoke for you.
My feet restore thou for me.
My legs restore thou for me.
My body restore thou for me.
My mind restore thou for me.
My voice thou restore for me.
Restore all for me in beauty.
Make beautiful all that is before me.
Make beautiful all that is behind me.

It is done in beauty.
It is done in beauty.
It is done in beauty.
It is done in beauty.

The Whole World is Coming
(Sioux)

The whole world is coming.
A nation is coming, a nation is coming,
The Eagle has brought the message to the tribe.
The father says so, the father says so.
Over the whole earth they are coming.
The buffalo are coming, the buffalo are coming,
The Crow has brought the message to the tribe,
The father says so, the father says so.

from The Walum Olum or Red Score
(Lenape)

A great land and a wide land was the east land,
A land without snakes, a rich land, a pleasant land.
Great Fighter was chief, toward the north.
At the Straight river, River-Loving was chief.
Becoming-Fat was chief at Sassafras land.
All the hunters made wampum again at the great sea.
Red-Arrow was chief at the stream again.
The Painted-Man was chief at the Mighty Water.
The Easterners and the Wolves go northeast.
Good-fighter was chief, and went to the north.
The Mengwe, the Lynxes, all trembled.
Again an Affable was chief, and made peace with all.
All were friends, all were united, under this great chief.
Great-Beaver was chief, remaining in Sassafras land.
White-Body was chief in the sea shore.
Peace-Maker was chief, friendly to all.
He-Makes-Mistakes was chief, hurriedly coming.
At this time whites came on the Eastern sea.

. . . .

Much-Honored was chief; he was prosperous.
Well-Praised was chief; he fought at the south.
He fought in the land of the Talega and Koweta.
White-Otter was chief; a friend of the Talamatans.
White-Horn was chief; he went to the Talega,
To the Hilini, to the Shawnees, to the Kanawhas.
Coming-as-a-Friend was chief; he went to the Great Lakes,
Visiting all his children, all his friends.
Cranberry-Eater was chief, friend of the Ottawas.
North-Walker was chief; he made festivals.
Slow-Gatherer was chief at the shore.
As three were desired, three those were who grew forth.
The Unami, the Minsi, the Chikini.
The Unami, the Minsi, the Chikini.
Man-Who-Fails was chief; he fought the Mengwe.
He-is-Friendly was chief; he scared the Mengwe.
Saluted was chief; thither,
Over there, on the Scioto, he had foes.
White-Crab was chief; a friend of the shore.
Watcher was chief; he looked toward the sea.
At this time, from north and south, the whites came.
They are peaceful; they have great things [ships]; who are they?

SONGS, SPIRITUALS, HYMNS, AND POPULAR POEMS:
1870–1900

Frankie and Johnny
(Unknown, 1870–75)

Frankie and Johnny were lovers, O lordy how they could love.
Swore to be true to each other, true as the stars above;
He was her man but he done her wrong, so wrong.

. . . .

Frankie went down to the corner, to buy a glass of beer;
She says to the fat bartender, "Has my lovinest man been here?
He was my man but he's done me wrong, so wrong."

Frankie went down to the pawn shop, she bought herself a little
                                        forty-four
She aimed it at the ceiling, shot a big hole in the floor;
"Where is my man, he's doin' me wrong, so wrong?"

466

. . . .

Frankie went down to the hotel, looked in the window so high,
There she saw her lovin' Johnny a-lovin' up Alice Bly;
He was her man but he done her wrong, so wrong.

Frankie went down to the hotel, she rang that hotel bell,
"Stand back all of you floozies or I'll blow you all to hell,
I want my man, he's doin' me wrong, so wrong."

Frankie threw back her kimono, she took out her forty-four.
Root-a-toot-toot, three times she shot, right through that hardwood
floor,
She shot her man, 'cause he done her wrong, so wrong.

. . . .

Bring out your long black coffin, bring out your funeral clo'es;
Bring back Johnny's mother; to the churchyard Johnny goes.
He was her man but he done her wrong, so wrong.

. . . .

Oh bring on your rubber-tired hearses, bring on your rubber-tired
hacks,
They're takin' Johnny to the buryin' groun' an' they won't bring a bit
of him back;
He was her man but he done her wrong, so wrong.

. . . .

John Henry
(Unknown, 1873)

John Henry tol' his cap'n
Dat a man wuz a natural man,
An' befo' he'd let dat steam drill run him down,
He'd fall dead wid a hammer in his han',
He'd fall dead wid a hammer in his han'.

Cap'n he sez to John Henry:
"Gonna bring me a steam drill 'round;
Take that steel drill out on the job,
Gonna whop that steel on down,
Gonna whop that steel on down."

John Henry sez to his cap'n:
"Send me a twelve-poun' hammer aroun',
A twelve-poun' hammer wid a fo'-foot handle,
An' I beat yo' steam drill down,
An' I beat yo' steam drill down."

. . . .

John Henry went down de railroad
Wid a twelve-poun' hammer by his side,
He walked down de track but he didn' come back,
'Cause he laid down his hammer an' he died,
'Cause he laid down his hammer an' he died.

. . . .

John Henry had a 'ooman,
De dress she wo' wuz blue.
De las' words I heard de pore gal say:
"John Henry, I ben true to yo',
John Henry, I ben true to yo'."

. . . .

Home on the Range
(Brewster Higley, c. 1876)

O give me a home where the buffalo roam,
Where the deer and the antelope play.
Where seldom is heard a discouraging word,
And the skies are not cloudy all day.

Chorus
Home, home on the range,
Where the deer and the antelope play.
Where seldom is heard a discouraging word,
And the skies are not cloudy all day.

Where the air is so pure, the zephyrs so free,
And the breezes so balmy and light.
Then I would not exchange my home on the range
For all of your cities so bright.

The redman was pressed from this part of the West,
And he's likely no more to return
To the banks of the Red River, where seldom, if ever,
Their flickering campfires burn.

How often at night when the heavens are bright
With the light from the glittering stars,
Have I stood there amazed, and asked as I gazed,
If their glory exceeds that of ours.

I love the wild flowers in this dear land of ours,
And the curlew I love to hear scream.
I love the white rocks and the antelope flocks
That graze on the mountaintops green.

O give me a land where the bright diamond sand
Flows leisurely down the stream.
Where the graceful white swan goes gliding along,
Like a maid in a heavenly dream.

That I would not exchange my home on the range,
Where the deer and the antelope play.
Where seldom is heard a discouraging word,
And the skies are not cloudy all day.

What a Friend We Have in Jesus
(Joseph Scriven, 1876)

What a Friend we have in Jesus,
All our sins and griefs to bear!
What a privilege to carry
Every thing to God in prayer!
O what peace we often forfeit,
O what needless pain we bear,
All because we do not carry,
Every thing to God in prayer!

Have we trials and temptations?
Is there trouble anywhere?
We should never be discouraged,
Take it to the Lord in prayer.
Can we find a friend so faithful,
Who will all our sorrows share?
Jesus knows our every weakness,
Take it to the Lord in prayer.

Are we weak and heavy laden,
Cumbered with a load of care?—
Precious Savior, still our refuge,—
Take it to the Lord in prayer.
Do thy friends despise, forsake thee?
Take it to the Lord in prayer,
In His arms He'll take and shield thee,
Thou wilt find a solace there.

Carry Me Back to Old Virginny
(James A. Bland, 1878)

Carry me back to old Virginny,
There's where the cotton and the corn and tatoes grow,
There's where the birds warble sweet in the springtime,
There's where this old darkey's heart am long'd to go.
There's where I labor'd so hard for old massa,
Day after day in the field of yellow corn,
No place on earth do I love more sincerely
Than old Virginny, the state where I was born.

Chorus
Carry me back to old Virginny,
There's where the cotton and the corn and tatoes grow,
There's where the birds warble sweet in the springtime,
There's where this old darkey's heart am long'd to go.

Carry me back to old Virginny,
There let me live 'till I wither and decay,
Long by the old Dismal Swamp have I wander'd,
There's where this old darkey's life will pass away.
Massa and missis have long gone before me,
Soon we will meet on that bright and golden shore,
There we'll be happy and free from all sorrow,
There's where we'll meet and we'll never part no more.

Polly Wolly Doodle
(Unknown, 1883)

Oh, I went down South for to see my Sal,
Sing Polly-wolly-doodle all the day;
My Sally am a spunky gal,
Sing Polly-wolly-doodle all the day.

Fare thee well, farewell, fare thee well, farewell,
Fare thee well my fairy fay,
For I'm going to Louisiana,
For to see my Susyanna,
Sing Polly-wolly-doodle all the day.

Oh, my Sal, she am a maiden fair,
Sing Polly-wolly-doodle all the day;
With curly eyes and laughing hair,
Sing Polly-wolly-doodle all the day.

Behind de barn, down on my knees,
Sing Polly-wolly-doodle all the day;
I thought I heard a chicken sneeze,
Sing Polly-wolly-doodle all the day.

He sneezed so hard wid de whoopin' cough,
Sing Polly-wolly-doodle all the day;
He sneezed his head an' tail right off.
Sing Polly-wolly-doodle all the day.

Oh My Darling Clementine
(Percy Montrose, 1884)

In a cabin, in a cañon,
An excavation for a mine;
Dwelt a miner, a Forty-niner,
And his daughter Clementine.

Chorus
Oh my darling, oh my darling,
Oh my darling Clementine,
You are lost and gone forever,
Drefful sorry, Clementine.

She drove her ducklets, to the river,
Ev'ry morning just at nine;
She stubb'd her toe against a sliver,
And fell into the foaming brine.

I saw her lips above the water,
Blowing bubbles soft and fine;
Alas for me, I was no swimmer,
And so I lost my Clementine.

Casey at the Bat
(Ernest Lawrence Thayer, 1888)

The outlook wasn't brilliant for the Mudville nine that day:
The score stood four to two with but one inning more to play.
And then when Cooney died at first, and Barrows did the same,
A sickly silence fell upon the patrons of the game.

A straggling few got up to go in deep despair. The rest
Clung to that hope which springs eternal in the human breast;
They thought if only Casey could but get a whack at that—
We'd put up even money now with Casey at the bat.

But Flynn preceded Casey, as did also Jimmy Blake,
And the former was a lulu and the latter was a cake;
So upon that stricken multitude grim melancholy sat,
For there seemed but little chance of Casey's getting to the bat.

But Flynn let drive a single, to the wonderment of all,
And Blake, the much despis-ed, tore the cover off the ball;
And when the dust had lifted, and the men saw what had occurred,
There was Jimmy safe at second and Flynn a-hugging third.

Then from 5,000 throats and more there rose a lusty yell;
It rumbled through the valley, it rattled in the dell;
It knocked upon the mountain and recoiled upon the flat,
For Casey, mighty Casey, was advancing to the bat.

There was ease in Casey's manner as he stepped into his place;
There was pride in Casey's bearing and a smile on Casey's face.
And when, responding to the cheers, he lightly doffed his hat,
No stranger in the crowd could doubt 'twas Casey at the bat.

Ten thousand eyes were on him as he rubbed his hands with dirt;
Five thousand tongues applauded when he wiped them on his shirt.
Then while the writhing pitcher ground the ball into his hip,
Defiance gleamed in Casey's eye, a sneer curled Casey's lip.

And now the leather-covered sphere came hurtling through the air,
And Casey stood a-watching it in haughty grandeur there.
Close by the sturdy batsman the ball unheeded sped—
"That ain't my style," said Casey. "Strike one," the umpire said.

From the benches black with people, there went up a muffled roar,
Like the beating of the storm-waves on a stern and distant shore.
"Kill him! Kill the umpire!" shouted some one on the stand;
And it's likely they'd have killed him had not Casey raised his hand.

With a smile of Christian charity great Casey's visage shone;
He stilled the rising tumult; he bade the game go on;
He signaled to the pitcher, and once more the spheroid flew;
But Casey still ignored it, and the umpire said, "Strike two."

"Fraud!" cried the maddened thousands, and echo answered fraud;
But one scornful look from Casey and the audience was awed.
They saw his face grow stern and cold, they saw his muscles strain,
And they knew that Casey wouldn't let that ball go by again.

The sneer is gone from Casey's lip, his teeth are clenched in hate;
He pounds with cruel violence his bat upon the plate.
And now the pitcher holds the ball, and now he lets it go,
And now the air is shattered by the force of Casey's blow.

Oh, somewhere in this favored land the sun is shining bright;
The band is playing somewhere, and somewhere hearts are light,
And somewhere men are laughing, and somewhere children shout;
But there is no joy in Mudville—mighty Casey has struck out.

I Been Working on the Railroad
(Unknown, 1894)

I been working on the railroad,
I been working night and day;
I been working on the railroad,
Just to pass the time away;
Don't you hear the captain shouting,
Won't you rise up so early in the morn;
Don't you hear the captain shouting,
Dinah, blow your horn.

The Sidewalks of New York
(James W. Blake, 1894)

Down in front of Casey's
Old brown wooden stoop,
On a summer's evening,
We formed a merry group;
Boys and girls together,
We would sing and waltz,
While Giuseppe played the organ
On the sidewalks of New York.

East Side, West Side,
All around the town,
The tots sang "Ring a rosie,"
"London Bridge is falling down";
Boys and girls together,
Me and Mamie O'Rorke
Tripped the light fantastic
On the sidewalks of New York.

That's where Johnny Casey
And little Jimmy Crowe,
With Jakey Krause, the baker,
Who always had the dough,
Pretty Nellie Shannon,
With a dude as light as cork,
First picked up the waltz step
On the sidewalks of New York.

Things have changed since those times,
Some are up in "G,"
Others, they are on the hog,
But they all feel just like me;
They would part with all they've got
Could they but once more walk
With their best girl and have a twirl
On the sidewalks of New York.

When the Saints Go Marching In
(Unknown, 1896)

Oh, When the Saints Go Marching In,
Oh, When the Saints Go Marching In,
Lord, I want to be in that number,
When the Saints Go Marching In.

Oh, When the Saints Go Marching In,
Oh, When the Saints Go Marching In,
I will meet them all up in heaven,
When the Saints Go Marching In.

Oh, When the Saints Go Marching In,
Oh, When the Saints Go Marching In,
We will be in line for that judgment,
When the Saints Go Marching In.

I Never Saw a Purple Cow
(Gelett Burgess, 1898)

I never saw a Purple Cow,
    I never hope to see one;
But I can tell you, anyhow,
    I'd rather see than be one.

VI

THE ADVENT OF
THE MODERN:
1901–1922

STEPHEN CRANE
(1871–1900)

from THE BLACK RIDERS

III
In the desert
I saw a creature, naked, bestial,
Who, squatting upon the ground,
Held his heart in his hands,
And ate of it.
I said, "Is it good, friend?"
"It is bitter—bitter," he answered;
"But I like it
Because it is bitter,
And because it is my heart."

XXIV
I saw a man pursuing the horizon;
Round and round they sped.
I was disturbed at this;
I accosted the man.
"It is futile," I said,
"You can never—"
"You lie," he cried,
And ran on.

from WAR IS KIND

I
Do not weep, maiden, for war is kind.
Because your lover threw wild hands toward the sky
And the affrighted steed ran on alone,
Do not weep.
War is kind.

> Hoarse, booming drums of the regiment,
> Little souls who thirst for fight,
> These men were born to drill and die.
> The unexplained glory flies above them,
> Great is the battle-god, great, and his kingdom—
> A field where a thousand corpses lie.

Do not weep, babe, for war is kind.
Because your father tumbled in the yellow trenches,
Raged at his breast, gulped and died,
Do not weep.
War is kind.

> Swift blazing flag of the regiment,
> Eagle with crest of red and gold,
> These men were born to drill and die.
> Point for them the virtue of slaughter,
> Make plain to them the excellence of killing
> And a field where a thousand corpses lie.

Mother whose heart hung humble as a button
On the bright splendid shroud of your son,
Do not weep.
War is kind.

VI
I explain the silvered passing of a ship at night,
The sweep of each sad lost wave,
The dwindling boom of the steel thing's striving,
The little cry of a man to a man,
A shadow falling across the greyer night,
And the sinking of the small star;
Then the waste, the far waste of waters,
And the soft lashing of black waves
For long and in loneliness.

Remember, thou, O ship of love,
Thou leavest a far waste of waters,
And the soft lashing of black waves
For long and in loneliness.

XXI
A man said to the universe:
"Sir, I exist!"
"However," replied the universe,
"The fact has not created in me
A sense of obligation."

JAMES WELDON JOHNSON
(1871–1938)

O Black and Unknown Bards

O black and unknown bards of long ago,
How came your lips to touch the sacred fire?
How, in your darkness, did you come to know
The power and beauty of the minstrels' lyre?
Who first from midst his bonds lifted his eyes?
Who first from out the still watch, lone and long,
Feeling the ancient faith of prophets rise
Within his dark-kept soul, burst into song?

Heart of what slave poured out such melody
As "Steal away to Jesus"? On its strains
His spirit must have nightly floated free,
Though still about his hands he felt his chains.
Who heard great "Jordan roll"? Whose starward eye
Saw chariot "swing low"? And who was he
That breathed that comforting, melodic sigh,
"Nobody knows de trouble I see"?

What merely living clod, what captive thing,
Could up toward God through all its darkness grope,
And find within its deadened heart to sing
These songs of sorrow, love and faith, and hope?
How did it catch that subtle undertone,
That note in music heard not with the ears?
How sound the elusive reed so seldom blown,
Which stirs the soul or melts the heart to tears.

Not that great German master in his dream
Of harmonies that thundered amongst the stars
At the creation, ever heard a theme
Nobler than "Go down, Moses." Mark its bars
How like a mighty trumpet-call they stir
The blood. Such are the notes that men have sung
Going to valorous deeds; such tones there were
That helped make history when Time was young.

There is a wide, wide wonder in it all,
That from degraded rest and servile toil
The fiery spirit of the seer should call
These simple children of the sun and soil.
O black slave singers, gone, forgot, unfamed,
You—you alone, of all the long, long line
Of those who've sung untaught, unknown, unnamed,
Have stretched out upward, seeking the divine.

You sang not deeds of heroes or of kings;
No chant of bloody war, no exulting paean
Of arms-won triumphs; but your humble strings
You touched in chord with music empyrean.
You sang far better than you knew; the songs
That for your listeners' hungry hearts sufficed
Still live—but more than this to you belongs:
You sang a race from wood and stone to Christ.

Lift Every Voice and Sing

Lift every voice and sing
Till earth and heaven ring,
Ring with the harmonies of Liberty;
Let our rejoicing rise
High as the listening skies,
Let it resound loud as the rolling sea.
Sing a song full of the faith that the dark past has taught us,
Sing a song full of the hope that the present has brought us,
Facing the rising sun of our new day begun
Let us march on till victory is won.

Stony the road we trod,
Bitter the chastening rod,
Felt in the days when hope unborn had died;
Yet with a steady beat,
Have not our weary feet
Come to the place for which our fathers sighed?
We have come over a way that with tears has been watered,
We have come, treading our path through the blood of the
                                                    slaughtered,
Out from the gloomy past,
Till now we stand at last
Where the white gleam of our bright star is cast.

God of our weary years,
God of our silent tears,
Thou who has brought us thus far on the way;
Thou who has by Thy might
Let us into the light,
Keep us forever in the path, we pray.
Lest our feet stray from the places, our God, where we met Thee,
Lest, our hearts drunk with the wine of the world, we forget Thee;
Shadowed beneath Thy hand,
May we forever stand.
True to our God,
True to our native land.

LOLA RIDGE
(1871–1941)

from The Alley

Because you are four years old
the candle is all dressed up in a new frill.
And stars nod to you through the hole in the curtain,
(except the big stiff planets
too fat to move about much,)
and you curtsey back to the stars
when no one is looking.
You feel sorry for the poor wooden chair
that knows it isn't nice to sit on,
and no one is sad but mama.
You don't like mama to be sad
when you are four years old,
so you pretend
you like the bitter gold-pale tea—
you pretend
if you don't drink it up pretty quick
a little gold-fish
will think it is a pond
and come and get born in it.

. . . .

Paul Laurence Dunbar
(1872–1906)

Sympathy

I know what the caged bird feels, alas!
    When the sun is bright on the upland slopes;
When the wind stirs soft through the springing grass,
And the river flows like a stream of glass;
    When the first bird sings and the first bud opes,
And the faint perfume from its chalice steals—
I know what the caged bird feels!

I know why the caged bird beats his wing
    Till its blood is red on the cruel bars;
For he must fly back to his perch and cling
When he fain would be on the bough a-swing;
    And a pain still throbs in the old, old scars
And they pulse again with a keener sting—
I know why he beats his wing!

I know why the caged bird sings, ah me,
    When his wing is bruised and his bosom sore,—
When he beats his bars and he would be free;
It is not a carol of joy or glee,
    But a prayer that he sends from his heart's deep core,
But a plea, that upward to Heaven he flings—
I know why the caged bird sings!

We Wear the Mask

We wear the mask that grins and lies,
It hides our cheeks and shades our eyes—
This debt we pay to human guile;
With torn and bleeding hearts we smile
And mouth with myriad subtleties.

Why should the world be over-wise,
In counting all our tears and sighs?
Nay, let them only see us, while
    We wear the mask.

We smile, but oh great Christ, our cries
To Thee from tortured souls arise.
We sing, but oh the clay is vile
Beneath our feet, and long the mile;
But let the world dream otherwise,
        We wear the mask!

When All Is Done

When all is done, and my last word is said,
And ye who loved me murmur, "He is dead,"
Let no one weep, for fear that I should know,
And sorrow too that ye should sorrow so.

When all is done and in the oozing clay,
Ye lay this cast-off hull of mine away,
Pray not for me, for, after long despair,
The quiet of the grave will be a prayer.

For I have suffered loss and grievous pain,
The hurts of hatred and the world's disdain,
And wounds so deep that love, well-tried and pure,
Had not the pow'r to ease them or to cure.

When all is done, say not my day is o'er,
And that thro' night I seek a dimmer shore:
Say rather that my morn has just begun,—
I greet the dawn and not a setting sun,
        When all is done.

The Paradox

I am the mother of sorrows,
    I am the ender of grief;
I am the bud and the blossom,
    I am the late-falling leaf.

I am thy priest and thy poet,
    I am thy serf and thy king;
I cure the tears of the heartsick,
    When I come near they shall sing.

White are my hands as the snowdrop;
 Swart are my fingers as clay;
Dark is my frown as the midnight,
 Fair is my brow as the day.

Battle and war are my minions,
 Doing my will as divine;
I am the calmer of passions,
 Peace is a nursling of mine.

Speak to me gently or curse me,
 Seek me or fly from my sight;
I am thy fool in the morning,
 Thou art my slave in the night.

Down to the grave will I take thee,
 Out from the noise of the strife;
Then shalt thou see me and know me—
 Death, then, no longer, but life.

Then shalt thou sing at my coming,
 Kiss me with passionate breath,
Clasp me and smile to have thought me
 Aught save the foeman of Death.

Come to me, brother, when weary,
 Come when thy lonely heart swells;
I'll guide thy footsteps and lead thee
 Down where the Dream Woman dwells.

The Poet

He sang of life, serenely sweet,
 With, now and then, a deeper note.
 From some high peak, nigh yet remote,
He voiced the world's absorbing beat.

He sang of love when earth was young,
 And Love, itself, was in his lays.
 But ah, the world, it turned to praise
A jingle in a broken tongue.

GUY WETMORE CARRYL
(1873–1904)

The Patrician Peacocks and the Overweening Jay

Once a flock of stately peacocks
    Promenaded on a green,
There were twenty-two or three cocks,
    Each as proud as seventeen,
And a glance, however hasty,
Showed their plumage to be tasty;
Wheresoever one was placed, he
    Was a credit to the scene.

Now their owner had a daughter
    Who, when people came to call,
Used to say, "You'd reelly oughter
    See them peacocks on the mall."
Now this wasn't to her credit,
And her callers came to dread it,
For the way the lady said it
    Wasn't *recherché* at all.

But a jay that overheard it
    From his perch upon a fir
Didn't take in how absurd it
    Was to every one but her;
When they answered, "You don't tell us!"
And to see the birds seemed zealous
He became extremely jealous,
    Wishing, too, to make a stir.

As the peacocks fed together
    He would join them at their lunch,
Culling here and there a feather
    Till he'd gathered quite a bunch;
Then this bird, of ways perfidious,
Stuck them on him most fastidious
Till he looked uncommon hideous,
    Like a Judy or a Punch.

But the peacocks, when they saw him,
    One and all began to haul,
And to harry and to claw him
    Till the creature couldn't crawl;
While their owner's vulgar daughter,

When her startled callers sought her,
And to see the struggle brought her,
    Only said, "They're on the maul."

It was really quite revolting
    When the tumult died away,
One would think he had been moulting
    So dishevelled was the jay;
He was more than merely slighted,
He was more than disunited,
He'd been simply dynamited
    In the fervor of the fray.

And THE MORAL of the verses
    Is: That short men can't be tall.
Nothing sillier or worse is
    Than a jay upon a mall,
And the jay opiniative
Who, because he's imitative,
Thinks he's highly decorative
    Is the biggest jay of all.

ROBERT FROST
(1874–1963)

Storm Fear

When the wind works against us in the dark,
And pelts with snow
The lower chamber window on the east,
And whispers with a sort of stifled bark,
The beast,
'Come out! Come out!'—
It costs no inward struggle not to go,
Ah, no!
I count our strength,
Two and a child,
Those of us not asleep subdued to mark
How the cold creeps as the fire dies at length,—
How drifts are piled,
Dooryard and road ungraded,
Till even the comforting barn grows far away,

And my heart owns a doubt
Whether 'tis in us to arise with day
And save ourselves unaided.

from MOUNTAIN INTERVAL

Hyla Brook

By June our brook's run out of song and speed.
Sought for much after that, it will be found
Either to have gone groping underground
(And taken with it all the Hyla breed
That shouted in the mist a month ago,
Like ghost of sleigh bells in a ghost of snow)—
Or flourished and come up in jewelweed,
Weak foliage that is blown upon and bent,
Even against the way its waters went.
Its bed is left a faded paper sheet
Of dead leaves stuck together by the heat—
A brook to none but who remember long.
This as it will be seen is other far
Than with brooks taken otherwhere in song.
We love the things we love for what they are.

from The Hill Wife

IV. THE OFT-REPEATED DREAM

She had no saying dark enough
    For the dark pine that kept
Forever trying the window latch
    Of the room where they slept.

The tireless but ineffectual hands
    That with every futile pass
Made the great tree seem as a little bird
    Before the mystery of glass!

It never had been inside the room,
    And only one of the two
Was afraid in an oft-repeated dream
    Of what the tree might do.

V. THE IMPULSE

It was too lonely for her there,
    And too wild,
And since there were but two of them,
    And no child,

And work was little in the house,
    She was free,
And followed where he furrowed field,
    Or felled tree.

She rested on a log and tossed
    The fresh chips,
With a song only to herself
    On her lips.

And once she went to break a bough
    Of black alder.
She strayed so far she scarcely heard
    When he called her—

And didn't answer—didn't speak—
    Or return.
She stood, and then she ran and hid
    In the fern.

He never found her, though he looked
    Everywhere,
And he asked at her mother's house
    Was she there.

Sudden and swift and light as that
    The ties gave,
And he learned of finalities
    Besides the grave.

The Lockless Door

It went many years,
But at last came a knock,
And I thought of the door
With no lock to lock.

I blew out the light,
I tiptoed the floor,
And raised both hands
In prayer to the door.

But the knock came again.
My window was wide;
I climbed on the sill
And descended outside.

Back over the sill
I bade a "Come in"
To whatever the knock
At the door may have been.

So at a knock
I emptied my cage
To hide in the world
And alter with age.

The Need of Being Versed in Country Things

The house had gone to bring again
To the midnight sky a sunset glow.
Now the chimney was all of the house that stood,
Like a pistil after the petals go.

The barn opposed across the way,
That would have joined the house in flame
Had it been the will of the wind, was left
To bear forsaken the place's name.

No more it opened with all one end
For teams that came by the stony road
To drum on the floor with scurrying hoofs
And brush the mow with the summer load.

The birds that came to it through the air
At broken windows flew out and in,
Their murmur more like the sigh we sigh
From too much dwelling on what has been.

Yet for them the lilac renewed its leaf,
And the aged elm, though touched with fire;
And the dry pump flung up an awkward arm;
And the fence post carried a strand of wire.

For them there was really nothing sad.
But though they rejoiced in the nest they kept,
One had to be versed in country things
Not to believe the phoebes wept.

Mending Wall

Something there is that doesn't love a wall,
That sends the frozen-ground-swell under it,
And spills the upper boulders in the sun;
And makes gaps even two can pass abreast.
The work of hunters is another thing:
I have come after them and made repair
Where they have left not one stone on a stone,
But they would have the rabbit out of hiding,
To please the yelping dogs. The gaps I mean,
No one has seen them made or heard them made,
But at spring mending-time we find them there.
I let my neighbor know beyond the hill;
And on a day we meet to walk the line
And set the wall between us once again.
We keep the wall between as we go.
To each the boulders that have fallen to each.
And some are loaves and some so nearly balls
We have to use a spell to make them balance:
'Stay where you are until our backs are turned!'
We wear our fingers rough with handling them.
Oh, just another kind of outdoor game,
One on a side. It comes to little more:
There where it is we do not need the wall:
He is all pine and I am apple orchard.
My apple trees will never get across
And eat the cones under his pines, I tell him.
He only says, 'Good fences make good neighbors.'
Spring is the mischief in me, and I wonder
If I could put a notion in his head:

'*Why* do they make good neighbors? Isn't it
Where there are cows? But here there are no cows.
Before I built a wall I'd ask to know
What I was walling in or walling out,
And to whom I was like to give offense.
Something there is that doesn't love a wall,
That wants it down.' I could say 'Elves' to him,
But it's not elves exactly, and I'd rather
He said it for himself. I see him there
Bringing a stone grasped firmly by the top
In each hand, like an old-stone savage armed.
He moves in darkness as it seems to me,
Not of woods only and the shade of trees.
He will not go behind his father's saying,
And he likes having thought of it so well
He says again, 'Good fences make good neighbors.'

The Death of the Hired Man

Mary sat musing on the lamp-flame at the table
Waiting for Warren. When she heard his step,
She ran on tip-toe down the darkened passage
To meet him in the doorway with the news
And put him on his guard. 'Silas is back.'
She pushed him outward with her through the door
And shut it after her. 'Be kind,' she said.
She took the market things from Warren's arms
And set them on the porch, then drew him down
To sit beside her on the wooden steps.

'When was I ever anything but kind to him?
But I'll not have the fellow back,' he said.
'I told him so last haying, didn't I?
If he left then, I said, that ended it.
What good is he? Who else will harbor him
At his age for the little he can do?
What help he is there's no depending on.
Off he goes always when I need him most.
He thinks he ought to earn a little pay,
Enough at least to buy tobacco with,
So he won't have to beg and be beholden.
"All right," I say, "I can't afford to pay
Any fixed wages, though I wish I could."
"Someone else can." "Then someone else will have to."
I shouldn't mind his bettering himself
If that was what it was. You can be certain,

When he begins like that, there's someone at him
Trying to coax him off with pocket-money,—
In haying time, when any help is scarce.
In winter he comes back to us. I'm done.'

'Sh! not so loud: he'll hear you,' Mary said.

'I want him to: he'll have to soon or late.'

'He's worn out. He's asleep beside the stove.
When I came up from Rowe's I found him here,
Huddled against the barn-door fast asleep,
A miserable sight, and frightening, too—
You needn't smile—I didn't recognize him—
I wasn't looking for him—and he's changed.
Wait till you see.'

                    'Where did you say he'd been?'

'He didn't say. I dragged him to the house,
And gave him tea and tried to make him smoke.
I tried to make him talk about his travels.
Nothing would do: he just kept nodding off.'

'What did he say? Did he say anything?'

'But little.'

                'Anything? Mary, confess
He said he'd come to ditch the meadow for me.'

'Warren!'

                'But did he? I just want to know.'

'Of course he did. What would you have him say?
Surely you wouldn't grudge the poor old man
Some humble way to save his self-respect.
He added, if you really care to know,
He meant to clear the upper pasture, too.
That sounds like something you have heard before?
Warren, I wish you could have heard the way
He jumbled everything. I stopped to look
Two or three times—he made me feel so queer—
To see if he was talking in his sleep.
He ran on Harold Wilson—you remember—
The boy you had in haying four years since.

He's finished school, and teaching in his college.
Silas declares you'll have to get him back.
He says they two will make a team for work:
Between them they will lay this farm as smooth!
The way he mixed that in with other things.
He thinks young Wilson a likely lad, though daft
On education—you know how they fought
All through July under the blazing sun,
Silas up on the cart to build the load,
Harold along beside to pitch it on.'

'Yes, I took care to keep well out of earshot.'

'Well, those days trouble Silas like a dream.
You wouldn't think they would. How some things linger!
Harold's young college boy's assurance piqued him.
After so many years he still keeps finding
Good arguments he sees he might have used.
I sympathize. I know just how it feels
To think of the right thing to say too late.
Harold's associated in his mind with Latin.
He asked me what I thought of Harold's saying
He studied Latin like the violin
Because he liked it—that an argument!
He said he couldn't make the boy believe
He could find water with a hazel prong—
Which showed how much good school had ever done him.
He wanted to go over that. But most of all
He thinks if he could have another chance
To teach him how to build a load of hay—'

'I know, that's Silas' one accomplishment.
He bundles every forkful in its place,
And tags and numbers it for future reference,
So he can find and easily dislodge it
In the unloading. Silas does that well.
He takes it out in bunches like big birds' nests.
You never see him standing on the hay
He's trying to lift, straining to lift himself.'

'He thinks if he could teach him that, he'd be
Some good perhaps to someone in the world.
He hates to see a boy the fool of books.
Poor Silas, so concerned for other folk,
And nothing to look backward to with pride,
And nothing to look forward to with hope,
So now and never any different.'

Part of a moon was falling down the west,
Dragging the whole sky with it to the hills.
Its light poured softly in her lap. She saw it
And spread her apron to it. She put out her hand
Among the harp-like morning-glory strings,
Taut with the dew from garden bed to eaves,
As if she played unheard some tenderness
That wrought on him beside her in the night.
'Warren,' she said, 'he has come home to die:
You needn't be afraid he'll leave you this time.'

'Home,' he mocked gently.

                    'Yes, what else but home?
It all depends on what you mean by home.
Of course he's nothing to us, any more
Than was the hound that came a stranger to us
Out of the woods, worn out upon the trail.'

'Home is the place where, when you have to go there,
They have to take you in.'

                  'I should have called it
Something you somehow haven't to deserve.'

Warren leaned out and took a step or two,
Picked up a little stick, and brought it back
And broke it in his hand and tossed it by.
'Silas has better claim on us you think
Than on his brother? Thirteen little miles
As the road winds would bring him to his door.
Silas has walked that far no doubt today.
Why doesn't he go there? His brother's rich,
A somebody—director in the bank.'

'He never told us that.'

                  'We know it though.'

'I think his brother ought to help, of course.
I'll see to that if there is need. He ought of right
To take him in, and might be willing to—
He may be better than appearances.
But have some pity on Silas. Do you think
If he had any pride in claiming kin
Or anything he looked for from his brother,
He'd keep so still about him all this time?'

'I wonder what's between them.'

                              'I can tell you.
Silas is what he is—we wouldn't mind him—
But just the kind that kinsfolk can't abide.
He never did a thing so very bad.
He don't know why he isn't quite as good
As anybody. Worthless though he is,
He won't be made ashamed to please his brother.'

'I can't think Si ever hurt anyone.'

'No, but he hurt my heart the way he lay
And rolled his old head on that sharp-edged chair-back.
He wouldn't let me put him on the lounge.
You must go in and see what you can do.
I made the bed up for him there tonight.
You'll be surprised at him—how much he's broken.
His working days are done; I'm sure of it.'

'I'd not be in a hurry to say that.'

'I haven't been. Go, look, see for yourself.
But, Warren, please remember how it is:
He's come to help you ditch the meadow.
He has a plan. You mustn't laugh at him.
He may not speak of it, and then he may.
I'll sit and see if that small sailing cloud
Will hit or miss the moon.'

                              It hit the moon.
Then there were three there, making a dim row,
The moon, the little silver cloud, and she.

Warren returned—too soon, it seemed to her,
Slipped to her side, caught up her hand and waited.

'Warren?' she questioned.

                              'Dead,' was all he answered.

After Apple-Picking

My long two-pointed ladder's sticking through a tree
Toward heaven still,
And there's a barrel that I didn't fill
Beside it, and there may be two or three
Apples I didn't pick upon some bough.
But I am done with apple-picking now.
Essence of winter sleep is on the night,
The scent of apples: I am drowsing off.
I cannot rub the strangeness from my sight
I got from looking through a pane of glass
I skimmed this morning from the drinking trough
And held against the world of hoary grass.
It melted, and I let it fall and break.
But I was well
Upon my way to sleep before it fell,
And I could tell
What form my dreaming was about to take.
Magnified apples appear and disappear,
Stem end and blossom end,
And every fleck of russet showing clear.
My instep arch not only keeps the ache,
It keeps the pressure of a ladder-round.
I feel the ladder sway as the boughs bend.
And I keep hearing from the cellar bin
The rumbling sound
Of load on load of apples coming in.
For I have had too much
Of apple-picking: I am overtired
Of the great harvest I myself desired.
There were ten thousand thousand fruit to touch,
Cherish in hand, lift down, and not let fall.
For all
That struck the earth,
No matter if not bruised or spiked with stubble,
Went surely to the cider-apple heap
As of no worth.
One can see what will trouble
This sleep of mine, whatever sleep it is.
Were he not gone,
The woodchuck could say whether it's like his
Long sleep, as I describe its coming on,
Or just some human sleep.

The Road Not Taken

Two roads diverged in a yellow wood,
And sorry I could not travel both
And be one traveler, long I stood
And looked down one as far as I could
To where it bent in the undergrowth;

Then took the other, as just as fair,
And having perhaps the better claim,
Because it was grassy and wanted wear;
Though as for that the passing there
Had worn them really about the same,

And both that morning equally lay
In leaves no step had trodden black.
Oh, I kept the first for another day!
Yet knowing how way leads on to way,
I doubted if I should ever come back.

I shall be telling this with a sigh
Somewhere ages and ages hence:
Two roads diverged in a wood, and I—
I took the one less traveled by,
And that has made all the difference.

The Oven Bird

There is a singer everyone has heard,
Loud, a mid-summer and a mid-wood bird,
Who makes the solid tree trunks sound again.
He says that leaves are old and that for flowers
Mid-summer is to spring as one to ten.
He says the early petal-fall is past
When pear and cherry bloom went down in showers
On sunny days a moment overcast;
And comes that other fall we name the fall.
He says the highway dust is over all.
The bird would cease and be as other birds
But that he knows in singing not to sing.
The question that he frames in all but words
Is what to make of a diminished thing.

Birches

When I see birches bend to left and right
Across the lines of straighter darker trees,
I like to think some boy's been swinging them.
But swinging doesn't bend them down to stay
As ice-storms do. Often you must have seen them
Loaded with ice a sunny winter morning
After a rain. They click upon themselves
As the breeze rises, and turn many-colored
As the stir cracks and crazes their enamel.
Soon the sun's warmth makes them shed crystal shells
Shattering and avalanching on the snow-crust—
Such heaps of broken glass to sweep away
You'd think the inner dome of heaven had fallen.
They are dragged to the withered bracken by the load,
And they seem not to break; though once they are bowed
So low for long, they never right themselves:
You may see their trunks arching in the woods
Years afterwards, trailing their leaves on the ground
Like girls on hands and knees that throw their hair
Before them over their heads to dry in the sun.
But I was going to say when Truth broke in
With all her matter-of-fact about the ice-storm
I should prefer to have some boy bend them
As he went out and in to fetch the cows—
Some boy too far from town to learn baseball,
Whose only play was what he found himself,
Summer or winter, and could play alone.
One by one he subdued his father's trees
By riding them down over and over again
Until he took the stiffness out of them,
And not one but hung limp, not one was left
For him to conquer. He learned all there was
To learn about not launching out too soon
And so not carrying the tree away
Clear to the ground. He always kept his poise
To the top branches, climbing carefully
With the same pains you use to fill a cup
Up to the brim, and even above the brim.
Then he flung outward, feet first, with a swish,
Kicking his way down through the air to the ground.
So was I once myself a swinger of birches.
And so I dream of going back to be.
It's when I'm weary of considerations,
And life is too much like a pathless wood
Where your face burns and tickles with the cobwebs

Broken across it, and one eye is weeping
From a twig's having lashed across it open.
I'd like to get away from earth awhile
And then come back to it and begin over.
May no fate willfully misunderstand me
And half grant what I wish and snatch me away
Not to return. Earth's the right place for love:
I don't know where it's likely to go better.
I'd like to go by climbing a birch tree,
And climb black branches up a snow-white trunk
Toward heaven, till the tree could bear no more,
But dipped its top and set me down again.
That would be good both going and coming back.
One could do worse than be a swinger of birches.

'Out, Out—'

The buzz saw snarled and rattled in the yard
And made dust and dropped stove-length sticks of wood,
Sweet-scented stuff when the breeze drew across it.
And from there those that lifted eyes could count
Five mountain ranges one behind the other
Under the sunset far into Vermont.
And the saw snarled and rattled, snarled and rattled,
As it ran light, or had to bear a load.
And nothing happened: day was all but done.
Call it a day, I wish they might have said
To please the boy by giving him the half hour
That a boy counts so much when saved from work.
His sister stood beside them in her apron
To tell them 'supper.' At the word, the saw,
As if to prove saws knew what supper meant,
Leaped out at the boy's hand, or seemed to leap—
He must have given the hand. However it was,
Neither refused the meeting. But the hand!
The boy's first outcry was a rueful laugh,
As he swung toward them holding up the hand
Half in appeal, but half as if to keep
The life from spilling. Then the boy saw all—
Since he was old enough to know, big boy
Doing a man's work, though a child at heart—
He saw all spoiled. 'Don't let him cut my hand off—
The doctor, when he comes. Don't let him, sister!'
So. But the hand was gone already.
The doctor put him in the dark of ether.
He lay and puffed his lips out with his breath.

And then—the watcher at his pulse took fright.
No one believed. They listened at his heart.
Little—less—nothing!—and that ended it.
No more to build on there. And they, since they
Were not the one dead, turned to their affairs.

ROBERT W. SERVICE
(1874–1958)

The Cremation of Sam McGee

There are strange things done in the midnight sun
    By the men who moil for gold;
The Arctic trails have their secret tales
    That would make your blood run cold;
The Northern Lights have seen queer sights,
    But the queerest they ever did see
Was that night on the marge of Lake Lebarge
    I cremated Sam McGee.

Now Sam McGee was from Tennessee, where the cotton blooms
                                        and blows.
Why he left home in the South to roam 'round the Pole, God
                                        only knows.
He was always cold, but the land of gold seemed to hold him
                                        like a spell;
Though he'd often say in his homely way that "he'd sooner
                                        live in hell."

On a Christmas Day we were mushing our way over the Dawson trail.
Talk of your cold! through the parka's fold it stabbed like a
                                        driven nail.
If our eyes we'd close, then the lashes froze till sometimes we
                                        couldn't see;
It wasn't much fun, but the only one to whimper was Sam McGee.

And that very night, as we lay packed tight in our robes beneath
                                        the snow,
And the dogs were fed, and the stars o'erhead were dancing
                                        heel and toe,
He turned to me, and "Cap," says he, "I'll cash in this trip, I guess;
And if I do, I'm asking that you won't refuse my last request."

Well, he seemed so low that I couldn't say no; then he says with a
                                        sort of moan:
"It's the cursèd cold, and it's got right hold till I'm chilled clean
                                        through to the bone.
Yet 'tain't being dead—it's my awful dread of the icy grave that pains;
So I want you to swear that, foul or fair, you'll cremate my last
                                        remains."

A pal's last need is a thing to heed, so I swore I would not fail;
And we started on at the streak of the dawn; but God! he looked
                                        ghastly pale.
He crouched on the sleigh, and he raved all day of his home in
                                        Tennessee;
And before nightfall a corpse was all that was left of Sam McGee.

There wasn't a breath in that land of death, and I hurried,
                                        horror-driven,
With a corpse half hid that I couldn't get rid, because of a
                                        promise given;
It was lashed to the sleigh, and it seemed to say: "You may tax your
                                        brawn and brains,
But you promised true, and it's up to you to cremate those
                                        last remains."

Now a promise made is a debt unpaid, and the trail has its
                                        own stern code.
In the days to come, though my lips were dumb, in my heart how I
                                        cursed that load.
In the long, long night, by the lone firelight, while the huskies, round
                                        in a ring,
Howled out their woes to the homeless snows—O God! how I
                                        loathed the thing.

And every day that quiet clay seemed to heavy and heavier grow;
And on I went, though the dogs were spent and the grub was
                                        getting low;
The trail was bad, and I felt half mad, but I swore I would not
                                        give in;
And I'd often sing to the hateful thing, and it hearkened with a grin.

Till I came to the marge of Lake Lebarge, and a derelict there lay;
It was jammed in the ice, but I saw in a trice it was called the
                                        "Alice May."
And I looked at it, and I thought a bit, and I looked at my frozen
                                        chum;
Then "Here," said I, with a sudden cry, "is my cre-ma-tor-eum."

Some planks I tore from the cabin floor, and I lit the boiler fire;
Some coal I found that was lying around, and I heaped
                                  the fuel higher;
The flames just soared, and the furnace roared—such a blaze
                                  you seldom see;
And I burrowed a hole in the glowing coal, and I stuffed in
                                  Sam McGee.

Then I made a hike, for I didn't like to hear him sizzle so;
And the heavens scowled, and the huskies howled, and the wind
                                  began to blow.
It was icy cold, but the hot sweat rolled down my cheeks, and I
                                  don't know why;
And the greasy smoke in an inky cloak went streaking down the sky.

I do not know how long in the snow I wrestled with grisly fear;
But the stars came out and they danced about ere again
                                  I ventured near;
I was sick with dread, but I bravely said: "I'll just take a peep inside.
I guess he's cooked, and it's time I looked"; . . . then the door I
                                  opened wide.

And there sat Sam, looking cool and calm, in the heart of
                                  the furnace roar;
And he wore a smile you could see a mile, and he said:
                                  "Please close that door.
It's fine in here, but I greatly fear you'll let in the cold and storm—
Since I left Plumtree, down in Tennessee, it's the first time
                                  I've been warm."

There are strange things done in the midnight sun
    By the men who moil for gold;
The Arctic trails have their secret tales
    That would make your blood run cold;
The Northern Lights have seen queer sights,
    But the queerest they ever did see
Was that night on the marge of Lake Lebarge
    I cremated Sam McGee.

"EDWARD E. PARAMORE, JR."

(*fl. 1923*)

The Ballad of Yukon Jake

BEGGING ROBERT W. SERVICE'S PARDON

Oh the North Countree is a hard countree
That mothers a bloody brood;
And its icy arms hold hidden charms
For the greedy, the sinful and lewd.
And strong men rust, from the gold and the lust
That sears the Northland soul,
But the wickedest born, from the Pole to the Horn,
Is the Hermit of Shark-Tooth Shoal.

Now Jacob Kaime was the Hermit's name
In the days of his pious youth,
Ere he cast a smirch on the Baptist Church
By betraying a girl named Ruth.
But now men quake at "Yukon Jake,"
The Hermit of Shark-Tooth Shoal,
For that is the name that Jacob Kaime
Is known by from Nome to the Pole.
He was just a boy and the parson's joy
(Ere he fell for the gold and the muck),
And had learned to pray, with the hogs and the hay
On a farm near Keokuk.
But a Service tale of illicit kale,
And whisky and women wild,
Drained the morals clean as a soup tureen
From this poor but honest child.
He longed for the bite of a Yukon night
And the Northern Light's weird flicker,
Or a game of stud in the frozen mud,
And the taste of raw red licker.
He wanted to mush along in the slush,
With a team of husky hounds,
And to fire his gat at a beaver hat
And knock it out of bounds.

So he left his home for the hell-town Nome,
On Alaska's ice-ribbed shores,
And he learned to curse and to drink, and worse,
Till the rum dripped from his pores,
When the boys on a spree were drinking it free

In a Malamute saloon
And Dan Megrew and his dangerous crew
Shot craps with the piebald coon;
When the Kid on his stool banged away like a fool
At a jag-time melody,
And the barkeep vowed, to the hard-boiled crowd,
That he'd cree-mate Sam McGee—

Then Jacob Kaime, who had taken the name
Of Yukon Jake, the Killer,
Would rake the dive with his forty-five
Till the atmosphere grew chiller.
With a sharp command he'd make 'em stand
And deliver their hard-earned dust,
Then drink the bar dry of rum and rye,
As a Klondike bully must.
Without coming to blows he would tweak the nose
Of Dangerous Dan Megrew,
And, becoming bolder, throw over his shoulder
The lady that's known as Lou.

Oh, tough as a steak was Yukon Jake—
Hard-boiled as a picnic egg.
He washed his shirt in the Klondike dirt,
And drank his rum by the keg.
In fear of their lives (or because of their wives)
He was shunned by the best of his pals,
An outcast he, from the comradery
Of all but wild animals.
So he bought him the whole of Shark-Tooth Shoal,
A reef in the Bering Sea,
And he lived by himself on a sea lion's shelf
In lonely iniquity.

But, miles away, in Keokuk, Ia.,
Did a ruined maiden fight
To remove the smirch from the Baptist Church
By bringing the heathen Light;
And the Elders declared that all would be spared
If she carried the holy words
From her Keokuk home to the hell-town Nome
To save those sinful birds.

So, two weeks later, she took a freighter,
For the gold-cursed land near the Pole,
But Heaven ain't made for a lass that's betrayed—
She was wrecked on Shark-Tooth Shoal!
All hands were tossed in the Sea, and lost—
All but the maiden Ruth,
Who swam to the edge of the sea lion's ledge
Where abode the love of her youth.
He was hunting a seal for his evening meal
(He handled a mean harpoon)
When he saw at his feet, not something to eat,
But a girl in a frozen swoon,
Whom he dragged to his lair by her dripping hair,
And he rubbed her knees with gin.
To his great surprise, she opened her eyes
And revealed—his Original Sin!

His eight-months beard grew stiff and weird,
And it felt like a chestnut burr,
And he swore by his gizzard, and the Arctic blizzard
That he'd do right by her.
But the cold sweat froze on the end of her nose
Till it gleamed like a Tecla pearl,
While her bright hair fell, like a flame from hell,
Down the back of the grateful girl.
But a hopeless rake was Yukon Jake,
The hermit of Shark-Tooth Shoal!
And the dizzy maid he rebetrayed
And wrecked her immortal soul! . . .
Then he rowed her ashore, with a broken oar,
And he sold her to Dan Megrew
For a husky dog and some hot eggnog,
As rascals are wont to do.
Now ruthless Ruth is a maid uncouth
With scarlet cheeks and lips,
And she sings rough songs to the drunken throngs
That come from the sealing ships.
For a rouge-stained kiss from this infamous miss
They will give a seal's sleek fur,
Or perhaps a sable, if they are able;
It's much the same to her.

Oh, the North Countree is a rough countree,
That mothers a bloody brood;
And its icy arms hold hidden charms
For the greedy, the sinful and lewd.
And strong men rust, from the gold and the lust

That sears the Northland soul,
But the wickedest born from the Pole to the Horn
Was the Hermit of Shark-Tooth Shoal!

TRUMBULL STICKNEY
(1874–1904)

Mnemosyne

It's autumn in the country I remember.

How warm a wind blew here about the ways!
And shadows on the hillside lay to slumber
During the long sun-sweetened summer-days.

It's cold abroad the country I remember.

The swallows veering skimmed the golden grain
At midday with a wing aslant and limber;
And yellow cattle browsed upon the plain.

It's empty down the country I remember.

I had a sister lovely in my sight:
Her hair was dark, her eyes were very sombre;
We sang together in the woods at night.

It's lonely in the country I remember.

The babble of our children fills my ears,
And on our hearth I stare the perished ember
To flames that show all starry thro' my tears.

It's dark about the country I remember.

There are the mountains where I lived. The path
Is slushed with cattle-tracks and fallen timber,
The stumps are twisted by the tempests' wrath.

But that I knew these places are my own,
I'd ask how came such wretchedness to cumber
The earth, and I to people it alone.

It rains across the country I remember.

Live Blindly

Live blindly and upon the hour. The Lord,
Who was the Future, died full long ago.
Knowledge which is the Past is folly. Go,
Poor child, and be not to thyself abhorred.
Around thine earth sun-wingèd winds do blow
And planets roll; a meteor draws his sword;
The rainbow breaks his seven-coloured chord
And the long strips of river-silver flow:
Awake! Give thyself to the lovely hours.
Drinking their lips, catch thou the dream in flight
About their fragile hairs' aërial gold.
Thou art divine, thou livest,—as of old
Apollo springing naked to the light,
And all his island shivered into flowers.

At Sainte-Marguerite

The gray tide flows and flounders in the rocks
Along the crannies up the swollen sand.
Far out the reefs lie naked—dunes and blocks
Low in the watery wind. A shaft of land
Going to sea thins out the western strand.

It rains, and all along and always gulls
Career sea-screaming in and weather-glossed.
It blows here, pushing round the cliff; in lulls
Within the humid stone a motion lost
Ekes out the flurried heart-beat of the coast.

It blows and rains a pale and whirling mist
This summer morning. I that hither came—
Was it to pluck this savage from the schist,
This crazy yellowish bloom without a name,
With leathern blade and tortured wiry frame?

Why here alone, away, the forehead pricked
With dripping salt and fingers damp with brine,
Before the offal and the derelict
And where the hungry sea-wolves howl and whine,
Live human hours? now that the columbine

Stands somewhere shaded near the fields that fall
Great starry sheaves of the delighted year,
And globing rosy on the garden wall
The peach and apricot and soon the pear
Drip in the teasing hand their sugared tear.

Inland a little way the summer lies.
Inland a little and but yesterday
I saw the weary teams, I heard the cries
Of sicklemen across the fallen hay,
And buried in the sunburned stacks I lay

Tasting the straws and tossing, laughing soft
Into the sky's great eyes of gold and blue
And nodding to the breezy leaves aloft
Over the harvest's mellow residue.
But sudden then—then strangely dark it grew.

How good it is, before the dreary flow
Of cloud and water, here to lie alone
And in this desolation to let go
Down the ravine one with another, down
Across the surf to linger or to drown

The loves that none can give and none receive,
The fearful asking and the small retort,
The life to dream of and the dream to live!
Very much more is nothing than a part,
Nothing at all and darkness in the heart.

I would my manhood now were like the sea.—
Thou at high-tide, when compassing the land
Thou find'st the issue short, questioningly
A moment poised, thy floods then down the strand
Sink without rancour, sink without command,

Sink of themselves in peace without despair,
And turn as still the calm horizon turns,
Till they repose little by little nowhere
And the long light unfathomable burns
Clear from the zenith stars to the sea-ferns.

Thou are thy Priest, thy Victim and thy God.
Thy life is bulwarked with a thread of foam,
And of the sky, the mountains and the sod
Thou askest nothing, evermore at home
In thy own self's perennial masterdom.

He Said: "If in His Image I was Made"

He said: "If in his image I was made,
I am his equal and across the land
We two should make our journey hand in hand
Like brothers dignified and unafraid."
And God that day was walking in the shade.
To whom he said: "The world is idly planned,
We cross each other, let us understand
Thou who thou art, I who I am," he said.
Darkness came down. And all that night was heard
Tremendous clamour and the broken roar
Of things in turmoil driven down before.
Then silence. Morning broke, and sang a bird.
He lay upon the earth, his bosom stirred;
But God was seen no longer any more.

JOSEPHINE PRESTON PEABODY
(1874–1922)

After Music

I saw not they were strange, the ways I roam,
    Until the music called, and called me thence,
And tears stirred in my heart as tears may come
To lonely children straying far from home,
    Who know not how they wandered so, nor whence.

If I might follow far and far away
    Unto the country where these songs abide,
I think my soul would wake and find it day,
Would tell me who I am, and why I stray,—
    Would tell me who I was before I died.

A Far-Off Rose

O far-off rose of long ago,
    An hour of sweet, an hour of red,
To live, to breathe, and then to go
    Into the dark ere June was dead!

Why say they: Roses shall return
    With every year as years go on?
New springtime and strange bloom, my rose,
    And alien June; but thou art gone.

AMY LOWELL
(1874–1925)

Solitaire

When night drifts along the streets of the city,
And sifts down between the uneven roofs,
My mind begins to peek and peer.
It plays at ball in odd, blue Chinese gardens,
And shakes wrought dice-cups in Pagan temples
Amid the broken flutings of white pillars.
It dances with purple and yellow crocuses in its hair,
And its feet shine as they flutter over drenched grasses.
How light and laughing my mind is,
When all good folk have put out their bedroom candles,
And the city is still.

Meeting-House Hill

I must be mad, or very tired,
When the curve of a blue bay beyond a railroad track
Is shrill and sweet to me like sudden springing of a tune,
And the sight of a white church above thin trees in a city square
Amazes my eyes as though it were the Parthenon.
Clear, reticent, superbly final,
With the pillars of its portico refined to a cautious elegance,
It dominates the weak trees,
And the shot of its spire
Is cool and candid,
Rising into an unresisting sky.
Strange meeting-house
Pausing a moment upon a squalid hill-top.
I watch the spire sweeping the sky,
I am dizzy with the movement of the sky;
I might be watching a mast
With its royals set full
Straining before a two-reef breeze.

I might be sighting a tea-clipper,
Tacking into the blue bay,
Just back from Canton
With her hold full of green and blue porcelain
And a Chinese coolie leaning over the rail
Gazing at the white spire
With dull, sea-spent eyes.

A Lady

You are beautiful and faded,
Like an old opera tune
Played upon a harpsichord;
Or like the sun-flooded silks
Of an eighteenth-century boudoir.

In your eyes
Smoulder the fallen roses of outlived minutes,
And the perfume of your soul
Is vague and suffusing,
With the pungence of sealed spice-jars.
Your half-tones delight me,
And I grow mad with gazing
At your blent colors.

My vigor is a new-minted penny,
Which I cast at your feet.
Gather it up from the dust
That its sparkle may amuse you.

Wind and Silver

Greatly shining,
The Autumn moon floats in the thin sky;
And the fish-ponds shake their backs and flash their dragon scales
As she passes over them.

GERTRUDE STEIN
(1874–1946)

from BEE TIME VINE

from Yet Dish

I
Put a sun in Sunday, Sunday.
Eleven please ten hoop. Hoop.
Cousin coarse in coarse in soap.
Cousin coarse in soap sew up. soap.
Cousin coarse in sew up soap.

II
A lea ender stow sole lightly.
Not a bet beggar.
Nearer a true set jump hum,
A lamp lander so seen poor lip.

III
Never so round.
A is a guess and a piece.
A is a sweet cent sender.
A is a kiss slow cheese.
A is for age jet.

IV
New deck stairs.
Little in den little in dear den.

V
Polar pole.
Dust winder.
Core see.
A bale a bale o a bale.

VI
Extravagant new or noise peal extravagant.

VII
S a glass.
Roll ups.

VIII

Powder in wails, powder in sails, powder is all next to it is does wait sack rate all goals like chain in clear.

IX

Negligible old star.
Pour even.
It was a sad per cent.
Does on sun day.
Watch or water.
So soon a moon or a old heavy press.

X

Pearl cat or cat or pill or pour check.
New sit or little.
New sat or little not a wad yet.
Heavy toe heavy sit on head.

XI

Ex, ex, ex.
Bull it bull it bull it bull it.
Ex Ex Ex.

XII

Cousin plates pour a y shawl hood hair.
No see eat.

XIII

They are getting, bad left log lope, should a court say stream, not a dare long beat a soon port.

XIV

Colored will he.
Calamity.
Colored will he
Is it a soon. Is it a soon. Is it a soon. soon. Is it a soon. soon.

XV

Nobody's ice.
Nobody's ice to be knuckles.
Nobody's nut soon.
Nobody's seven picks.
Picks soap stacks.
Six in set on seven in seven told, to top.

XVI
A spread chin shone.
A set spread chin shone.

XVII
No people so sat.
Not an eider.
Not either. Not either either.

. . . .

from TENDER BUTTONS

A Frightful Release

A bag which was left and not only taken but turned away was not found. The place was shown to be very like the last time. A piece was not exchanged, not a bit of it, a piece was left over. The rest was mismanaged.

A Purse

A purse was not green, it was not straw color, it was hardly seen and it had a use a long use and the chain, the chain was never missing, it was not misplaced, it showed that it was open, that is all that it showed.

A Mounted Umbrella

What was the use of not leaving it there where it would hang what was the use if there was no chance of ever seeing it come there and show that it was handsome and right in the way it showed it. The lesson is to learn that it does show it, that it shows it and that nothing, that there is nothing, that there is no more to do about it and just so much more is there plenty of reason for making an exchange.

A Cloth

Enough cloth is plenty and more, more is almost enough for that and besides if there is no more spreading is there plenty of room for it. Any occasion shows the best way.

More

An elegant use of foliage and grace and a little piece of white cloth and oil.

Wondering so winningly in several kinds of oceans is the reason that makes red so regular and enthusiastic. The reason that there is more snips are the same shining very colored rid of no round color.

from Rooms

. . . .

A light in the moon the only light is on Sunday. What was the sensible decision. The sensible decision was that notwithstanding many declarations and more music, not even notwithstanding the choice and a torch and a collection, notwithstanding the celebrating hat and a vacation and even more noise than cutting, notwithstanding Europe and Asia and being overbearing, not even notwithstanding an elephant and a strict occasion, not even withstanding more cultivation and some seasoning, not even with drowning and with the ocean being encircling, not even with more likeness and any cloud, not even with terrific sacrifice of pedestrianism and a special resolution, not even more likely to be pleasing. The care with which the rain is wrong and the green is wrong and the white is wrong, the care with which there is a chair and plenty of breathing. The care with which there is incredible justice and likeness, all this makes a magnificent asparagus, and also a fountain.

RIDGELY TORRENCE
(1875–1950)

The Son
(Southern Ohio Market Town)

I heard an old farm-wife,
    Selling some barley,
Mingle her life with life
    And the name "Charley."

Saying: "The crop's all in,
    We're about through now;
Long nights will soon begin,
    We're just us two now.

"Twelve bushels at sixty cents,
    It's all I carried—
He sickened making fence;
    He was to be married—

"It feels like frost was near—
    His hair was curly.
The spring was late that year,
    But the harvest early."

ANNA HEMPSTEAD BRANCH
(1875–1937)

Ere the Golden Bowl is Broken

He gathered for His own delight
    The sparkling waters of my soul.
A thousand creatures, bubbling bright—
    He set me in a golden bowl.

From the deep cisterns of the earth
    He bade me up—the shining daughter—
And I am exquisite with mirth,
    A brightening and a sunlit water.

The wild, the free, the radiant one,
    A happy bubble I did glide.
I poised my sweetness to the sun
    And there I sleeked my silver side.

Sometimes I lifted up my head
    And globed the moonlight with my hands,
Or thin as flying wings I spread
    Angelic wildness through the sands.

Then, woven into webs of light,
    I breathed, I sighed, I laughed aloud,
And lifting up my pinions bright
    I shone in Heaven, a bird-white cloud.

Then did I dance above the mead,
    And through the crystal fields would run,
And from my scarlet splendors breed
    The golden thunders of the sun.

Beneath the whitening stars I flew
    And floated moon-like on the breeze,
Or my frail heart was piercéd through
    With sharp sweet flowers of the trees.

Of giant crags I bear the scars,
    And I have swept along the gale,
Such multitudes as are the stars,
    My myriad faces rapt and pale.

As savage creatures strong and free
    Make wild the jungle of the wood,
The starry powers that sport in me
    Habit my silver solitude.

From out my smallness, soft as dew,
    That utter fastness, stern and deep,
Terrible meanings look at you
    Like visions from the eyes of sleep.

I cannot leap—I cannot run—
    I only glimmer, soft and mild,
A limpid water in the sun,
    A sparkling and a sunlit child.

What stranger ways shall yet be mine
    When I am spilled, you cannot see.
But now you laugh to watch me shine,
    And smooth the hidden stars in me.

Lightly you stroke my silver wing—
    The folded carrier of my soul.
A soft, a shy, a silent thing,
    A water in a golden bowl!

Connecticut Road Song

In the wide and rocky pasture where the cedar trees are gray,
The briar rose was growing with the blueberry and bay.
The girls went forth to pick them and the lads went out to play,
But I had to get to Stonington before the break of day.

And when I came to Stonington, she was a town of pride.
"Come in," they said, "and labor, and be at home and bide.
For gold shall be thy wage," but 't was past the hour of morn—
And I had to get to Jordan while the dew was on the thorn.

There is a girl at Jordan, she sweetly smiled at me,
As pale as are the berries on the gray cedar tree.
And "Oh," she cried, "thou traveler, come bide awhile with me,"
But I had to get to Lebanon while light was in the tree.

The pale church spires of Lebanon shone sweet upon the sky.
The Sabbath bells were ringing, the parson passed me by.
"Oh wait, traveler, wait, for you've need to say a prayer,"
But I had to be in Wallingford while noon was in the air.

The road that leads to Wallingford, it runs through mire and stone.
I was parched with the dust, I was bleeding and alone.
"My lad, you will die, if you do not tarry here."
But I had to get to Killingworth while day was on the mere.

And when I got to Killingworth I heard the people say
"He has come to bring the news from a hundred miles away."
But I had not any news and not any time to stay,
For I had to be at Jericho before the end of day.

And when I came to Jericho I heard the people call,
"Do you run to save a city that you will not wait at all?"
"I run to save no city, yet must I leave you soon,
For I have to be in Windsor with the rising of the moon."

And when I got to Windsor, then was I spent for bread.
"Come in," they cried, "poor traveler! and be thou comforted.
What strange great need is on thee that makes thee journey so?"
But I had to be in Coventry ere yet the moon was low.

For a strange great need was on me that I should hunt the rain,
And take into my body a breakage and a pain;
That I should tame the sunset and goad the hurrying plain,
And that the leagues behind me should lie a thousand slain.

Wherefore, ye men of Coventry, if ye desire to stay,
Lay not your curb upon me, that love the open way.
For I want to smell the dew, the blueberry and the bay,
And I have to get to Colchester before the break of day.

WILLIAM STANLEY BRAITHWAITE
(1878–1962)

Rhapsody

I am glad daylong for the gift of song,
For time and change and sorrow;
For the sunset wings and the world-end things
Which hang on the edge of tomorrow.
I am glad for my heart whose gates apart
Are the entrance-place of wonders,
Where dreams come in from the rush and din
Like sheep from the rains and thunders.

CARL SANDBURG
(1878–1967)

Chicago

    Hog Butcher for the World,
    Tool Maker, Stacker of Wheat,
    Player with Railroads and the Nation's Freight Handler;
    Stormy, husky, brawling,
    City of the Big Shoulders:

They tell me you are wicked and I believe them, for I have seen your
    painted women under the gas lamps luring the farm boys.
And they tell me you are crooked and I answer: Yes, it is true I have
    seen the gunman kill and go free to kill again.
And they tell me you are brutal and my reply is: On the faces of
    women and children I have seen the marks of wanton hunger.
And having answered so I turn once more to those who sneer at this
    my city, and I give them back the sneer and say to them:
Come and show me another city with lifted head singing so proud to
    be alive and coarse and strong and cunning.
Flinging magnetic curses amid the toil of piling job on job, here is a
    tall bold slugger set vivid against the little soft cities;
Fierce as a dog with tongue lapping for action, cunning as a savage
    pitted against the wilderness,
        Bareheaded,
        Shoveling,
        Wrecking,

Planning,
Building, breaking, rebuilding,
Under the smoke, dust all over his mouth, laughing with white teeth,
Under the terrible burden of destiny laughing as a young man laughs,
Laughing even as an ignorant fighter laughs who has never lost a
battle,
Bragging and laughing that under his wrist is the pulse, and under his
ribs the heart of the people,
Laughing!
Laughing the stormy, husky, brawling laughter of Youth, half-naked,
sweating, proud to be Hog Butcher, Tool Maker, Stacker of
Wheat,
Player with Railroads and Freight Handler to the Nation.

Fog

The fog comes
on little cat feet.

It sits looking
over harbor and city
on silent haunches
and then moves on.

Bones

Sling me under the sea.
Pack me down in the salt and wet.
No farmer's plow shall touch my bones.
No Hamlet hold my jaws and speak
How jokes are gone and empty is my mouth.
Long, green-eyed scavengers shall pick my eyes,
Purple fish play hide-and-seek,
And I shall be song of thunder, crash of sea,
Down on the floors of salt and wet.
Sling me . . . under the sea.

Cool Tombs

When Abraham Lincoln was shoveled into the tombs, he forgot the
copperheads and the assassin . . . in the dust, in the cool tombs.

And Ulysses Grant lost all thought of con men and Wall Street, cash
and collateral turned ashes . . . in the dust, in the cool tombs.

Pocahontas' body, lovely as a poplar, sweet as a red haw in November
   or a pawpaw in May, did she wonder? does she remember? . . .
   in the dust, in the cool tombs?

Take any streetful of people buying clothes and groceries, cheering a
   hero or throwing confetti and blowing tin horns . . . tell me if
   the lovers are losers . . . tell me if any get more than the
   lovers . . . in the dust . . . in the cool tombs.

Grass

Pile the bodies high at Austerlitz and Waterloo,
Shovel them under and let me work—
         I am the grass; I cover all.

And pile them high at Gettysburg
And pile them high at Ypres and Verdun.
Shovel them under and let me work.
Two years, ten years, and passengers ask the conductor:
         What place is this?
         Where are we now?

         I am the grass.
         Let me work.

Haze

Keep a red heart of memories
Under the great gray rain sheds of the sky,
Under the open sun and the yellow gloaming embers.
Remember all paydays of lilacs and songbirds;
All starlights of cool memories on storm paths.

Out of this prairie rise the faces of dead men.
They speak to me. I can not tell you what they say.

Other faces rise on the prairie.
                  They are the unborn. The future.

Yesterday and tomorrow cross and mix on the skyline.
The two are lost in a purple haze. One forgets. One waits.

In the yellow dust of sunsets, in the meadows of vermilion eight
o'clock
June nights . . . the dead men and the unborn children speak to
me . . . I can not tell you what they say . . . you listen and you
know.

I don't care who you are, man:
I know a woman is looking for you
and her soul is a corn-tassel kissing a south-west wind.

(The farm-boy whose face is the color of brick-dust, is calling the
cows; he will form the letter X with crossed streams of milk from
the teats; he will beat a tattoo on the bottom of a tin pail with X's
of milk.)

I don't care who you are, man:
I know sons and daughters looking for you
And they are gray dust working toward star paths
And you see them from a garret window when you laugh
At your luck and murmur, "I don't care."

I don't care who you are, woman:
I know a man is looking for you
And his soul is a south-west wind kissing a corn-tassel.

(The kitchen girl on the farm is throwing oats to the chickens and the
buff of their feathers says hello to the sunset's late maroon.)

I don't care who you are, woman:
I know sons and daughters looking for you
And they are next year's wheat or the year after hidden in the dark
and loam.

My love is a yellow hammer spinning circles in Ohio, Indiana. My
love is a redbird shooting flights in straight lines in Kentucky and
Tennessee. My love is an early robin flaming an ember of copper
on her shoulders in March and April. My love is a graybird living
in the eaves of a Michigan house all winter. Why is my love
always a crying thing of wings?

On the Indiana dunes, in the Mississippi marshes, I have asked: Is it
only a fishbone on the beach?
Is it only a dog's jaw or a horse's skull whitening in the sun? Is the
red heart of man only ashes? Is the flame of it all a white light
switched off and the power-house wires cut?

Why do the prairie roses answer every summer? Why do the changing
repeating rains come back out of the salt sea wind-blown? Why
do the stars keep their tracks? Why do the cradles of the sky rock
new babies?

ADELAIDE CRAPSEY
(1878–1914)

November Night

Listen . . .
With faint dry sound,
Like steps of passing ghosts,
The leaves, frost-crisp'd, break from the trees
And fall.

Triad

These be
three silent things:
The falling snow . . . the hour
Before the dawn . . . the mouth of one
Just dead.

Susanna and the Elders

"Why do
You thus devise
Evil against her?" "For that
She is beautiful, delicate;
Therefore."

Night Winds

The old
Old winds that blew
When chaos was, what do
They tell the clattered trees that I
Should weep?

The Warning

Just now,
Out of the strange
Still dusk . . . as strange, as still . . .
A white moth flew . . . Why am I grown
So cold?

DON MARQUIS
(1878–1937)

The Coming of Archy

the circumstances of Archy's first appearance are narrated in the
following extract from the Sun Dial column of the New York *Sun*.

Dobbs Ferry possesses a rat which slips out of his lair at night and
runs a typewriting machine in a garage. Unfortunately, he has always
been interrupted by the watchman before he could produce a complete
story.

It was at first thought that the power which made the typewriter run
was a ghost, instead of a rat. It seems likely to us that it was both a ghost
and a rat. Mme. Blavatsky's ego went into a white horse after she passed
over, and someone's personality has undoubtedly gone into this rat. It is
an era of belief in communications from the spirit land.

And since this matter had been reported in the public prints and
seriously received we are no longer afraid of being ridiculed, and we do
not mind making a statement of something that happened to our own
typewriter only a couple of weeks ago.

We came into our room earlier than usual in the morning, and
discovered a gigantic cockroach jumping about upon the keys.

He did not see us, and we watched him. He would climb painfully
upon the framework of the machine and cast himself with all his force
upon a key, head downward, and his weight and the impact of the blow
were just sufficient to operate the machine, one slow letter after another.
He could not work the capital letters, and he had a great deal of
difficulty operating the mechanism that shifts the paper so that a fresh
line may be started. We never saw a cockroach work so hard or perspire
so freely in all our lives before. After about an hour of this frightfully
difficult literary labor he fell to the floor exhausted, and we saw him
creep feebly into a nest of the poems which are always there in
profusion.

Congratulating ourself that we had left a sheet of paper in the machine the night before so that all this work had not been in vain, we made an examination, and this is what we found:

expression is the need of my soul
i was once a vers libre bard
but i died and my soul went into the body of a cockroach
it has given me a new outlook upon life
i see things from the under side now
thank you for the apple peelings in the wastepaper basket
but your paste is getting so stale i cant eat it
there is a cat here called mehitabel i wish you would have
removed she nearly ate me the other night why dont she
catch rats that is what she is supposed to be for
there is a rat here she should get without delay

most of these rats here are just rats
but this rat is like me he has a human soul in him
he used to be a poet himself
night after night i have written poetry for you
on your typewriter
and this big brute of a rat who used to be a poet
comes out of his hole when it is done
and reads it and sniffs at it
he is jealous of my poetry
he used to make fun of it when we were both human
he was a punk poet himself
and after he reads it he sneers
and then he eats it

i wish you would have mehitabel kill that rat
or get a cat that is onto her job
and i will write you a series of poems showing how things look
to a cockroach
that rats name is freddy
the next time freddy dies i hope he wont be a rat
but something smaller i hope i will be a rat
in the next transmigration and freddy a cockroach
i will teach him to sneer at my poetry then

dont you ever eat any sandwiches in your office
i havent had a crumb of bread for i dont know how long
or a piece of ham or anything but apple parings
and paste leave a piece of paper in your machine
every night you can call me archy

Vachel Lindsay
(1879–1931)

General William Booth Enters into Heaven

I
(Bass drum beaten loudly.)
Booth led boldly with his big bass drum—
(Are you washed in the blood of the Lamb?)
The Saints smiled gravely and they said: "He's come."
(Are you washed in the blood of the Lamb?)
Walking lepers followed, rank on rank,
Lurching bravos from the ditches dank,
Drabs from the alleyways and drug fiends pale—
Minds still passion-ridden, soul-powers frail:—
Vermin-eaten saints with moldy breath,
Unwashed legions with the ways of Death—
(Are you washed in the blood of the Lamb?)

(Banjos.)
Every slum had sent its half-a-score
The round world over. (Booth had groaned for more.)
Every banner that the wide world flies
Bloomed with glory and transcendent dyes.
Big-voiced lasses made their banjos bang,
Tranced, fanatical they shrieked and sang:—
"Are you washed in the blood of the Lamb?"
Hallelujah! It was queer to see
Bull-necked convicts with that land make free.
Loons with trumpets blowed a blare, blare, blare
On, on upward thro' the golden air!
(Are you washed in the blood of the Lamb?)

2
(Bass drum slower and softer.)
Booth died blind and still by faith he trod,
Eyes still dazzled by the ways of God.
Booth led boldly, and he looked the chief
Eagle countenance in sharp relief,
Beard a-flying, air of high command
Unabated in that holy land.

(Sweet flute music.)
Jesus came from out the court-house door,
Stretched his hands above the passing poor.
Both saw not, but led his queer ones there
Round and round the mighty court-house square.
Then, in an instant all that blear review
Marched on spotless, clad in raiment new.
The lame were straightened, withered limbs uncurled
And blind eyes opened on a new, sweet world.

(Bass drum louder.)
Drabs and vixen in a flash made whole!
Gone was the weasel-head, the snout, the jowl!
Sages and sybils now, and athletes clean,
Rulers of empires, and of forests green!

(Grand chorus of all instruments. Tambourines to the foreground.)
The hosts were sandalled, and their wings were fire!
(Are you washed in the blood of the Lamb?)
But their noise played havoc with the angel-choir.
(Are you washed in the blood of the Lamb?)
Oh, shout Salvation! It was good to see
Kings and Princes by the Lamb set free.
The banjos rattled and the tambourines
Jing-jing-jingled in the hands of Queens.

(Reverently sung, no instruments.)
And when Booth halted by the curb for prayer
He saw his Master thro' the flag-filled air.
Christ came gently with a robe and crown
For Booth the soldier, while the throng knelt down.
He saw King Jesus. They were face to face,
And he knelt a-weeping in that holy place.
Are you washed in the blood of the Lamb?

Abraham Lincoln Walks at Midnight

It is portentous, and a thing of state
That here at midnight, in our little town
A mourning figure walks, and will not rest,
Near the old court-house pacing up and down,

Or by his homestead, or in shadowed yards
He lingers where his children used to play,
Or through the market, on the well-worn stones
He stalks until the dawn-stars burn away.

A bronzed, lank man! His suit of ancient black,
A famous high top-hat and plain worn shawl
Make him the quaint great figure that men love,
The prairie-lawyer, master of us all.

He cannot sleep upon his hillside now.
He is among us:—as in times before!
And we who toss and lie awake for long
Breathe deep, and start, to see him pass the door.

His head is bowed. He thinks on men and kings.
Yea, when the sick world cries, how can he sleep?
Too many peasants fight, they know not why,
Too many homesteads in black terror weep.

The sins of all the war-lords burn his heart.
He sees the dreadnaughts scouring every main.
He carries on his shawl-wrapped shoulders now
The bitterness, the folly and the pain.

He cannot rest until a spirit-dawn
Shall come;—the shining hope of Europe free:
The league of sober folk, the Workers' Earth,
Bringing long peace to Cornland, Alp and Sea.

It breaks his heart that kings must murder still,
That all his hours of travail here for men
Seem yet in vain. And who will bring white peace
That he may sleep upon his hill again?

The Leaden-Eyed

Let not young souls be smothered out before
They do quaint deeds and fully flaunt their pride.
It is the world's one crime its babes grow dull,
Its poor are ox-like, limp and leaden-eyed.

Not that they starve, but starve so dreamlessly,
Not that they sow, but that they seldom reap,
Not that they serve, but have no gods to serve,
Not that they die but that they die like sheep.

WALLACE STEVENS
(*1879–1955*)

Peter Quince at the Clavier

1
Just as my fingers on these keys
Make music, so the selfsame sounds
On my spirit make a music, too.

Music is feeling, then, not sound;
And thus it is that what I feel,
Here in this room, desiring you,

Thinking of your blue-shadowed silk,
Is music. It is like the strain
Waked in the elders by Susanna.

Of a green evening, clear and warm,
She bathed in her still garden, while
The red-eyed elders watching, felt

The basses of their beings throb
In witching chords, and their thin blood
Pulse pizzicati of Hosanna.

2
In the green water, clear and warm,
Susanna lay.
She searched
The touch of springs,
And found
Concealed imaginings.
She sighed,
For so much melody.

Upon the bank, she stood
In the cool
Of spent emotions.
She felt, among the leaves,
The dew
Of old devotions.

She walked upon the grass,
Still quavering.
The winds were like her maids,
On timid feet,
Fetching her woven scarves,
Yet wavering.

A breath upon her hand
Muted the night.
She turned—
A cymbal crashed,
And roaring horns.

3
Soon, with a noise like tambourines,
Came her attendant Byzantines.

They wondered why Susanna cried
Against the elders by her side;
And as they whispered, the refrain
Was like a willow swept by rain.

Anon, their lamps' uplifted flame
Revealed Susanna and her shame.

And then, the simpering Byzantines
Fled, with a noise like tambourines.

4
Beauty is momentary in the mind—
The fitful tracing of a portal;
But in the flesh it is immortal.
The body dies; the body's beauty lives.
So evenings die, in their green going,
A wave, interminably flowing.
So gardens die, their meek breath scenting
The cowl of winter, done repenting.
So maidens die, to the auroral
Celebration of a maiden's choral.
Susanna's music touched the bawdy strings
Of those white elders; but, escaping,
Left only Death's ironic scraping.
Now, in its immortality, it plays
On the clear viol of her memory.
And makes a constant sacrament of praise.

Disillusionment of Ten O'clock

The houses are haunted
By white night-gowns.
None are green,
Or purple with green rings,
Or green with yellow rings,
Or yellow with blue rings.
None of them are strange,
With socks of lace
And beaded ceintures.
People are not going
To dream of baboons and periwinkles.
Only, here and there, an old sailor,
Drunk and asleep in his boots,
Catches tigers
In red weather.

Sunday Morning

1
Complacencies of the peignoir, and late
Coffee and oranges in a sunny chair,
And the green freedom of a cockatoo
Upon a rug mingle to dissipate
The holy hush of ancient sacrifice.
She dreams a little, and she feels the dark
Encroachment of that old catastrophe,
As a calm darkens among water-lights.
The pungent oranges and bright, green wings
Seem things in some procession of the dead,
Winding across wide water, without sound.
The day is like wide water, without sound,
Stilled for the passing of her dreaming feet
Over the seas, to silent Palestine,
Dominion of the blood and sepulchre.

2
Why should she give her bounty to the dead?
What is divinity if it can come
Only in silent shadows and in dreams?
Shall she not find in comforts of the sun,
In pungent fruit and bright, green wings, or else
In any balm or beauty of the earth,
Things to be cherished like the thought of heaven?
Divinity must live within herself:

Passions of rain, or moods in falling snow;
Grievings in loneliness, or unsubdued
Elations when the forest blooms; gusty
Emotions on wet roads on autumn nights;
All pleasures and all pains, remembering
The bough of summer and the winter branch.
These are the measures destined for her soul.

3
Jove in the clouds had his inhuman birth.
No mother suckled him, no sweet land gave
Large-mannered motions to his mythy mind
He moved among us, as a muttering king,
Magnificent, would move among his hinds,
Until our blood, commingling, virginal,
With heaven, brought such requital to desire
The very hinds discerned it, in a star.
Shall our blood fail? Or shall it come to be
The blood of paradise? And shall the earth
Seem all of paradise that we shall know?
The sky will be much friendlier then than now,
A part of labor and a part of pain,
And next in glory to enduring love,
Not this dividing and indifferent blue.

4
She says, "I am content when wakened birds,
Before they fly, test the reality
Of misty fields, by their sweet questionings;
But when the birds are gone, and their warm fields
Return no more, where, then, is paradise?"
There is not any haunt of prophecy,
Nor any old chimera of the grave,
Neither the golden underground, nor isle
Melodious, where spirits gat them home,
Nor visionary south, nor cloudy palm
Remote on heaven's hill, that has endured
As April's green endures; or will endure
Like her remembrance of awakened birds,
Or her desire for June and evening, tipped
By the consummation of the swallow's wings.

5

She says, "But in contentment I still feel
The need of some imperishable bliss."
Death is the mother of beauty; hence from her,
Alone, shall come fulfilment to our dreams
And our desires. Although she strews the leaves
Of sure obliteration on our paths,
The path sick sorrow took, the many paths
Where triumph rang its brassy phrase, or love
Whispered a little out of tenderness,
She makes the willow shiver in the sun
For maidens who were wont to sit and gaze
Upon the grass, relinquished to their feet.
She causes boys to pile new plums and pears
On disregarded plate. The maidens taste
And stray impassioned in the littering leaves.

6

Is there no change of death in paradise?
Does ripe fruit never fall? Or do the boughs
Hang always heavy in that perfect sky,
Unchanging, yet so like our perishing earth,
With rivers like our own that seek for seas
They never find, the same receding shores
That never touch with inarticulate pang?
Why set the pear upon those river-banks
Or spice the shores with odors of the plum?
Alas, that they should wear our colors there,
The silken weavings of our afternoons,
And pick the strings of our insipid lutes!
Death is the mother of beauty, mystical,
Within whose burning bosom we devise
Our earthly mothers waiting, sleeplessly.

7

Supple and turbulent, a ring of men
Shall chant in orgy on a summer morn
Their boisterous devotion to the sun,
Not as a god, but as a god might be,
Naked among them, like a savage source.
Their chant shall be a chant of paradise,
Out of their blood, returning to the sky;
And in their chant shall enter, voice by voice,
The windy lake wherein their lord delights,
The trees, like serafin, and echoing hills,
That choir among themselves long afterward.
They shall know well the heavenly fellowship

Of men that perish and of summer morn.
And whence they came and whither they shall go
The dew upon their feet shall manifest.

8

She hears, upon that water without sound,
A voice that cries, "The tomb in Palestine
Is not the porch of spirits lingering.
It is the grave of Jesus, where he lay."
We live in an old chaos of the sun,
Or old dependency of day and night,
Or island solitude, unsponsored, free,
Of that wide water, inescapable.
Deer walk upon our mountains, and the quail
Whistle about us their spontaneous cries;
Sweet berries ripen in the wilderness;
And, in the isolation of the sky,
At evening, casual flocks of pigeons make
Ambiguous undulations as they sink,
Downward to darkness, on extended wings.

Domination of Black

At night, by the fire,
The colors of the bushes
And of the fallen leaves,
Repeating themselves,
Turned in the room,
Like the leaves themselves
Turning in the wind.
Yes: but the color of the heavy hemlocks
Came striding.
And I remembered the cry of the peacocks.

The colors of their tails
Were like the leaves themselves
Turning in the wind,
In the twilight wind.
They swept over the room,
Just as they flew from the boughs of the hemlocks
Down to the ground.
I heard them cry—the peacocks.
Was it a cry against the twilight
Or against the leaves themselves
Turning in the wind,

Turning as the flames
Turned in the fire,
Turning as the tails of the peacocks
Turned in the loud fire,
Loud as the hemlocks
Full of the cry of the peacocks?
Or was it a cry against the hemlocks?

Out of the window,
I saw how the planets gathered
Like the leaves themselves
Turning in the wind.
I saw how the night came,
Came striding like the color of the heavy hemlocks
I felt afraid.
And I remembered the cry of the peacocks.

Thirteen Ways of Looking at a Blackbird

1
Among twenty snowy mountains,
The only moving thing
Was the eye of the blackbird.

2
I was of three minds,
Like a tree
In which there are three blackbirds.

3
The blackbird whirled in the autumn winds.
It was a small part of the pantomime.

4
A man and a woman
Are one.
A man and a woman and a blackbird
Are one.

5
I do not know which to prefer,
The beauty of inflections
Or the beauty of innuendoes,
The blackbird whistling
Or just after.

6
Icicles filled the long window
With barbaric glass.
The shadow of the blackbird
Crossed it, to and fro.
The mood
Traced in the shadow
An indecipherable cause.

7
O thin men of Haddam,
Why do you imagine golden birds?
Do you not see how the blackbird
Walks around the feet
Of the women about you?

8
I know noble accents
And lucid, inescapable rhythms;
But I know, too,
That the blackbird is involved
In what I know.

9
When the blackbird flew out of sight,
It marked the edge
Of one of many circles.

10
At the sight of blackbirds
Flying in a green light,
Even the bawds of euphony
Would cry out sharply.

11
He rode over Connecticut
In a glass coach.
Once, a fear pierced him,
In that he mistook
The shadow of his equipage
For blackbirds.

12
The river is moving.
The blackbird must be flying.

13
It was evening all afternoon.
It was snowing
And it was going to snow.
The blackbird sat
In the cedar-limbs.

Metaphors of a Magnifico

Twenty men crossing a bridge,
Into a village,
Are twenty men crossing twenty bridges,
Into twenty villages,
Or one man
Crossing a single bridge into a village.

This is old song
That will not declare itself . . .

Twenty men crossing a bridge,
Into a village,
Are
Twenty men crossing a bridge
Into a village.

That will not declare itself
Yet is certain as meaning . . .

The boots of the men clump
On the boards of the bridge.
The first white wall of the village
Rises through fruit-trees.
Of what was it I was thinking?

So the meaning escapes.

The first white wall of the village . . .
The fruit-trees . . .

Anecdote of the Jar

I placed a jar in Tennessee,
And round it was, upon a hill.
It made the slovenly wilderness
Surround that hill.

The wilderness rose up to it,
And sprawled around, no longer wild.
The jar was round upon the ground
And tall and of a port in air.

It took dominion everywhere.
The jar was gray and bare.
It did not give of bird or bush,
Like nothing else in Tennessee.

The Snow Man

One must have a mind of winter
To regard the frost and the boughs
Of the pine-trees crusted with snow;

And have been cold a long time
To behold the junipers shagged with ice,
The spruces rough in the distant glitter

Of the January sun; and not to think
Of any misery in the sound of the wind,
In the sound of a few leaves,

Which is the sound of the land
Full of the same wind
That is blowing in the same bare place

For the listener, who listens in the snow,
And, nothing himself, beholds
Nothing that is not there and the nothing that is.

Le Monocle de Mon Oncle

"Mother of heaven, regina of the clouds,
O sceptre of the sun, crown of the moon,
There is not nothing, no, no, never nothing,
Like the clashed edges of two words that kill."
And so I mocked her in magnificent measure.
Or was it that I mocked myself alone?
I wish that I might be a thinking stone.
The sea of spuming thought foists up again
The radiant bubble that she was. And then
A deep up-pouring from some saltier well
Within me, bursts its watery syllable.

II

A red bird flies across the golden floor.
It is a red bird that seeks out his choir
Among the choirs of wind and wet and wing.
A torrent will fall from him when he finds.
Shall I uncrumple this much-crumpled thing?
I am a man of fortune greeting heirs;
For it has come that thus I greet the spring.
These choirs of welcome choir for me farewell.
No spring can follow past meridian.
Yet you persist with anecdotal bliss
To make believe a starry *connaissance*.

III

Is it for nothing, then, that old Chinese
Sat tittivating by their mountain pools
Or in the Yangtse studied out their beards?
I shall not play the flat historic scale.
You know how Utamoro's beauties sought
The end of love in their all-speaking braids.
You know the mountainous coiffures of Bath.
Alas! Have all the barbers lived in vain
That not one curl in nature has survived?
Why, without pity on these studious ghosts,
Do you come dripping in your hair from sleep?

IV

This luscious and impeccable fruit of life
Falls, it appears, of its own weight to earth.
When you were Eve, its acrid juice was sweet,
Untasted, in its heavenly, orchard air.
An apple serves as well as any skull
To be the book in which to read a round,
And is as excellent, in that it is composed
Of what, like skulls, comes rotting back to ground.
But it excels in this, that as the fruit
Of love, it is a book too mad to read
Before one merely reads to pass the time.

V

In the high west there burns a furious star.
It is for fiery boys that star was set
And for sweet-smelling virgins close to them.
The measure of the intensity of love
Is measure, also, of the verve of earth.
For me, the firefly's quick, electric stroke
Ticks tediously the time of one more year.

And you? Remember how the crickets came
Out of their mother grass, like little kin,
In the pale nights, when your first imagery
Found inklings of your bond to all that dust.

VI

If men at forty will be painting lakes
The ephemeral blues must merge for them in one,
The basic slate, the universal hue.
There is a substance in us that prevails.
But in our amours amorists discern
Such fluctuations that their scrivening
Is breathless to attend each quirky turn.
When amorists grow bald, then amours shrink
Into the compass and curriculum
Of introspective exiles, lecturing.
It is a theme for Hyacinth alone.

VII

The mules that angels ride come slowly down
The blazing passes, from beyond the sun.
Descensions of their tinkling bells arrive.
These muleteers are dainty of their way.
Meantime, centurions guffaw and beat
Their shrilling tankards on the table-boards.
This parable, in sense, amounts to this:
The honey of heaven may or may not come,
But that of earth both comes and goes at once.
Suppose these couriers brought amid their train
A damsel heightened by eternal bloom.

VIII

Like a dull scholar, I behold, in love,
An ancient aspect touching a new mind.
It comes, it blooms, it bears its fruit and dies.
This trivial trope reveals a way of truth.
Our bloom is gone. We are the fruit thereof.
Two golden gourds distended on our vines,
Into the autumn weather, turned grotesque.
We hang like warty squashes, streaked and rayed,
The laughing sky will see the two of us
Washed into rinds by rotting winter rains.

IX

In verses wild with motion, full of din,
Loudened by cries, by clashes, quick and sure
As the deadly thought of men accomplishing
Their curious fates in war, come, celebrate
The faith of forty, ward of Cupido.
Most venerable heart, the lustiest conceit
Is not too lusty for your broadening.
I quiz all sounds, all thoughts, all everything
For the music and manner of the paladins
To make oblation fit. Where shall I find
Bravura adequate to this great hymn?

X

The fops of fancy in their poems leave
Memorabilia of the mystic spouts,
Spontaneously watering their gritty soils.
I am a yeoman, as such fellows go.
I know no magic trees, no balmy boughs,
No silver-ruddy, gold-vermilion fruits.
But, after all, I know a tree that bears
A semblance to the thing I have in mind.
It stands gigantic, with a certain tip
To which all birds come sometime in their time.
But when they go that tip still tips the tree.

XI

If sex were all, then every trembling hand
Could make us squeak, like dolls the wished-for words.
But note the unconscionable treachery of fate,
That makes us weep, laugh, grunt and groan, and shout
Doleful heroics, pinching gestures forth
From madness or delight, without regard
To that first, foremost law. Anguishing hour!
Last night, we sat beside a pool of pink,
Clippered with lilies scudding the bright chromes,
Keen to the point of starlight, while a frog
Boomed from his very belly odious chords.

XII

A blue pigeon it is, that circles the blue sky,
On sidelong wing, around and round and round.
A white pigeon it is, that flutters to the ground,
Grown tired of flight. Like a dark rabbi, I
Observed, when young, the nature of mankind,
In lordly study. Every day, I found
Man proved a gobbet in my mincing world.

Like a rose rabbi, later, I pursued,
And still pursue, the origin and course
Of love, but until now I never knew
That fluttering things have so distinct a shade.

The Emperor of Ice-Cream

Call the roller of big cigars,
The muscular one, and bid him whip
In kitchen cups concupiscent curds.
Let the wenches dawdle in such dress
As they are used to wear, and let the boys
Bring flowers in last month's newspapers.
Let be be finale of seem.
The only emperor is the emperor of ice-cream.

Take from the dresser of deal.
Lacking the three glass knobs, that sheet
On which she embroidered fantails once
And spread it so as to cover her face.
If her horny feet protrude, they come
To show how cold she is, and dumb.
Let the lamp affix its beam.
The only emperor is the emperor of ice-cream.

The Comedian as the Letter C

I. THE WORLD WITHOUT IMAGINATION

Nota: man is the intelligence of his soil,
The sovereign ghost. As such, the Socrates
Of snails, musician of pears, principium
And lex. Sed quaeritur: is the same wig
Of things, the nincompated pedagogue,
Preceptor to the sea? Crispin at sea
Created, in his day, a touch of doubt.
An eye most apt in gelatines and jupes,
Berries of villages, a barber's eye,
An eye of land, of simple salad-beds,
Of honest quilts, the eye of Crispin, hung
On porpoises, instead of apricots,
And on silentious porpoises, whose snouts

Dibbled in waves that were mustachios,
Inscrutable hair in an inscrutable world.

One eats one paté, even of salt, quotha.
It was not so much the lost terrestrial,
The snug hibernal from that sea and salt,
That century of wind in a single puff.
What counted was mythology of self,
Blotched out beyond unblotching. Crispin,
The lutanist of fleas, the knave, the thane,
The ribboned stick, the bellowing breeches, cloak
Of China, cap of Spain, imperative haw
Of hum, inquistorial botanist,
And general lexicographer of mute
And maidenly greenhorns, now beheld himself,
A skinny sailor peering in the sea-glass.
What word split up in clickering syllables
And storming under multitudinous tones
Was name for this short-shanks in all that brunt?
Crispin was washed away by magnitude.
The whole of life that still remained in him
Dwindled to one sound strumming in his ear,
Ubiquitous concussion, slab and sigh,
Polyphony beyond his baton's thrust.

Could Crispin stem verboseness in the sea,
The old age of a watery realist,
Triton, dissolved in shifting diaphanes
Of blue and green? A wordy, watery age
That whispered to the sun's compassion, made
A convocation, nightly, of the sea-stars,
And on the clopping foot-ways of the moon
Lay grovelling. Triton incomplicate with that
Which made him Triton, nothing left of him,
Except in faint, memorial gesturings,
That were like arms and shoulders in the waves,
Here, something in the rise and fall of wind
That seemed hallucinating horn, and here,
A sunken voice, both of remembering
And of forgetfulness, in alternate strain.

Just so an ancient Crispin was dissolved.
The valet in the tempest was annulled.
Bordeaux to Yucatan, Havana next,
And then to Carolina. Simple jaunt.
Crispin, merest minuscule in the gales,
Dejected his manner of the turbulence.

The salt hung on his spirit like a frost,
The dead brine melted in him like a dew
Of winter, until nothing of himself
Remained, except some starker, barer self
In a starker, barer world, in which the sun
Was not the sun because it never shone
With bland complaisance on pale parasols,
Beetled, in chapels, on the chaste bouquets.
Against his pipping sounds a trumpet cried
Celestial sneering boisterously. Crispin
Became an introspective voyager.

Here was the veritable ding an sich, at last,
Crispin confronting it, a vocable thing,
But with a speech belched out of hoary darks
Noway resembling his, a visible thing.
And excepting negligible Triton, free
From the unavoidable shadow of himself
That lay elsewhere around him. Severance
Was clear. The last distortion of romance
Forsook the insatiable egotist. The sea
Severs not only lands but also selves.
Here was no help before reality.
Crispin beheld and Crispin was made new.
The imagination, here, could not evade,
In poems of plums, the strict austerity
Of one vast, subjugating, final tone.
The drenching of stale lives no more fell down.
What was this gaudy, gusty panoply?
Out of what swift destruction did it spring?
It was caparison of wind and cloud
And something given to make whole among
The ruses that were shattered by the large.

II. CONCERNING THE THUNDERSTORMS OF YUCATAN

In Yucatan, the Maya sonneteers
Of the Caribbean amphitheatre,
In spite of hawk and falcon, green toucan
And jay, still to the night-bird made their plea,
As if raspberry tanagers in palms,
High up in orange air, were barbarous.
But Crispin was too destitute to find
In any commonplace the sought-for aid.

He was a man made vivid by the sea,
A man come out of luminous traversing,
Much trumpeted, made desperately clear,
Fresh from discoveries of tidal skies,
To whom oracular rockings gave no rest.
Into a savage color he went on.
How greatly had he grown in his demesne,
This auditor of insects! He that saw
The stride of vanishing autumn in a park
By way of decorous melancholy; he
That wrote his couplet yearly to the spring,
As dissertation of profound delight,
Stopping, on voyage, in a land of snakes,
Found his vicissitudes had much enlarged
His apprehension, made him intricate
In moody rucks, and difficult and strange
In all desires, his destitution's mark.
He was in this as other freemen are,
Sonorous nutshells rattling inwardly.
His violence was for aggrandizement
And not for stupor, such as music makes
For sleepers halfway waking. He perceived
That coolness for his heat came suddenly,
And only, in the fables that he scrawled
With his own quill, in its indigenous dew,
Of an æsthetic tough, diverse, untamed,
Incredible to prudes, the mint of dirt,
Green barbarism turning paradigm.
Crispin foresaw a curious promenade
Or, nobler, sensed an elemental fate,
And elemental potencies and pangs,
And beautiful barenesses as yet unseen,
Making the most of savagery of palms,
Of moonlight on the thick, cadaverous bloom
That yuccas breed, and of the panther's tread.
The fabulous and its intrinsic verse
Came like two spirits parleying, adorned
In radiance from the Atlantic coign,
For Crispin and his quill to catechize.
But they came parleying of such an earth,
So thick with sides and jagged lops of green,
So intertwined with serpent-kin encoiled
Among the purple tufts, the scarlet crowns,
Scenting the jungle in their refuges,
So streaked with yellow, blue and green and red
In beak and bud and fruity gobbet-skins,
That earth was like a jostling festival

Of seeds grown fat, too juicily opulent,
Expanding in the gold's maternal warmth.
So much for that. The affectionate emigrant found
A new reality in parrot-squawks.
Yet let that trifle pass. Now, as this odd
Discoverer walked through the harbor streets
Inspecting the cabildo, the façade
Of the cathedral, making notes, he heard
A rumbling, west of Mexico, it seemed,
Approaching like a gasconade of drums.
The white cabildo darkened, the façade,
As sullen as the sky, was swallowed up
In swift, successive shadows, dolefully.
The rumbling broadened as it fell. The wind,
Tempestuous clarion, with heavy cry,
Came bluntly thundering, more terrible
Than the revenge of music on bassoons.
Gesticulating lightning, mystical,
Made pallid flitter. Crispin, here, took flight.
An annotator has his scruples, too.
He knelt in the cathedral with the rest,
This connoisseur of elemental fate,
Aware of exquisite thought. The storm was one
Of many proclamations of the kind,
Proclaiming something harsher than he learned
From hearing signboards whimper in cold nights
Or seeing the midsummer artifice
Of heat upon his pane. This was the span
Of force, the quintessential fact, the note
Of Vulcan, that a valet seeks to own,
The thing that makes him envious in phrase.

And while the torrent on the roof still droned
He felt the Andean breath. His mind was free
And more than free, elate, intent, profound
And studious of a self possessing him,
That was not in him in the crusty town
From which he sailed. Beyond him, westward, lay
The mountainous ridges, purple balustrades,
In which the thunder, lapsing in its clap,
Let down gigantic quavers of its voice,
For Crispin to vociferate again.

The book of moonlight is not written yet
Nor half begun, but, when it is, leave room
For Crispin, fagot in the lunar fire,
Who, in the hubbub of his pilgrimage
Through sweating changes, never could forget
That wakefulness or meditating sleep,
In which the sulky strophes willingly
Bore up, in time, the somnolent, deep songs.
Leave room, therefore, in that unwritten book
For the legendary moonlight that once burned
In Crispin's mind above a continent.
America was always north to him,
A northern west or western north, but north,
And thereby polar, polar-purple, chilled
And lank, rising and slumping from a sea
Of hardy foam, receding flatly, spread
In endless ledges, glittering, submerged
And cold in a boreal mistiness of the moon.
The spring came there in clinking pannicles
Of half-dissolving frost, the summer came,
If ever, whisked and wet, not ripening,
Before the winter's vacancy returned.
The myrtle, if the myrtle ever bloomed,
Was like a glacial pink upon the air.
The green palmettoes in crepuscular ice
Clipped frigidly blue-black meridians,
Morose chiaroscuro, gauntly drawn.

How many poems he denied himself
In his observant progress, lesser things
Than the relentless contact he desired;
How many sea-masks he ignored; what sounds
He shut out from his tempering ear; what thoughts,
Like jades affecting the sequestered bride;
And what descants, he sent to banishment!
Perhaps the Arctic moonlight really gave
The liaison, the blissful liaison,
Between himself and his environment,
Which was, and if, chief motive, first delight,
For him, and not for him alone. It seemed
Illusive, faint, more mist than moon, perverse,
Wrong as a divagation to Peking,
To him that postulated as his theme
The vulgar, as his theme and hymn and flight,

A passionately niggling nightingale.
Moonlight was an evasion, or, if not,
A minor meeting, facile, delicate.

Thus he conceived his voyaging to be
An up and down between two elements,
A fluctuating between sun and moon,
A sally into gold and crimson forms,
As on this voyage, out of goblinry,
And then retirement like a turning back
And sinking down to the indulgences
That in the moonlight have their habitude.
But let these backward lapses, if they would,
Grind their seductions on him, Crispin knew
It was a flourishing tropic he required
For his refreshment, an abundant zone,
Prickly and obdurate, dense, harmonious,
Yet with a harmony not rarefied
Nor fined for the inhibited instruments
Of over-civil stops. And thus he tossed
Between a Carolina of old time,
A little juvenile, an ancient whim,
And the visible, circumspect presentment drawn
From what he saw across his vessel's prow.

He came. The poetic hero without palms
Or jugglery, without regalia.
And as he came he saw that it was spring,
A time abhorrent to the nihilist
Or searcher for the fecund minimum.
The moonlight fiction disappeared. The spring,
Although contending featly in its veils,
Irised in dew and early fragrancies,
Was gemmy marionette to him that sought
A sinewy nakedness. A river bore
The vessel inward. Tilting up his nose,
He inhaled the rancid rosin, burly smells
Of dampened lumber, emanations blown
From warehouse doors, the gustiness of ropes,
Decays of sacks, and all the arrant stinks
That helped him round his rude æsthetic out.
He savored rankness like a sensualist.
He marked the marshy ground around the dock,
The crawling railroad spur, the rotten fence,
Curriculum for the marvelous sophomore.
It purified. It made him see how much
Of what he saw he never saw at all.

He gripped more closely the essential prose
As being, in a world so falsified,
The one integrity for him, the one
Discovery still possible to make,
To which all poems were incident, unless
That prose should wear a poem's guise at last.

IV: THE IDEA OF A COLONY

Nota: his soil is man's intelligence.
That's better. That's worth crossing seas to find
Crispin in one laconic phrase laid bare
His cloudy drift and planned a colony.
Exit the mental moonlight, exit lex,
Rex and principium, exit the whole
Shebang. Exeunt omnes. Here was prose
More exquisite than any tumbling verse:
A still new continent in which to dwell.
What was the purpose of his pilgrimage,
Whatever shape it took in Crispin's mind,
If not, when all is said, to drive away
The shadow of his fellows from the skies,
And, from their stale intelligence released,
To make a new intelligence prevail?
Hence the reverberations in the words
Of his first central hymns, the celebrants
Of rankest trivia, tests of the strength
Of his æsthetic, his philosophy,
The more invidious, the more desired:
The florist asking aid from cabbages,
The rich man going bare, the paladin
Afraid, the blind man as astronomer,
The appointed power unwielded from disdain.
His western voyage ended and began.
The torment of fastidious thought grew slack,
Another, still more bellicose, came on.
He, therefore, wrote his prolegomena,
And, being full of the caprice, inscribed
Commingled souvenirs and prophecies.
He made a singular collation. Thus:
The natives of the rain are rainy men.
Although they paint effulgent, azure lakes,
Their azure has a cloudy edge, their white
And pink, the water bright that dogwood bears.
And in their music showering sounds intone.

On what strange froth does the gross Indian dote,
What Eden sapling gum, what honeyed gore,
What pulpy dram distilled of innocence,
That streaking gold should speak in him
Or bask within his images and words?
If these rude instances impeach themselves
By force of rudeness, let the principle
Be plain. For application Crispin strove,
Abhorring Turk as Esquimau, the lute
As the marimba, the magnolia as rose.

Upon these premises propounding, he
Projected a colony that should extend
To the dusk of a whistling south below the south,
A comprehensive island hemisphere.
The man in Georgia waking among pines
Should be pine-spokesman. The responsive man,
Planting his pristine cores in Florida,
Should prick thereof, not on the psaltery,
But on the banjo's categorical gut,
Tuck, tuck, while the flamingoes flapped his bays.
Sepulchral señors, bibbing pale mescal,
Oblivious to the Aztec almanacs,
Should make the intricate Sierra scan.
And dark Brazilians in their cafés,
Musing immaculate, pampean dits,
Should scrawl a vigilant anthology,
To be their latest, lucent paramour.
These are the broadest instances. Crispin,
Progenitor of such extensive scope,
Was not indifferent to smart detail.
The melon should have apposite ritual,
Performed in verd apparel, and the peach,
When its black branches came to bud, belle day,
Should have an incantation. And again,
When piled on salvers its aroma steeped
The summer, it should have a sacrament
And celebration. Shrewd novitiates
Should be the clerks of our experience.

These bland excursions into time to come,
Related in romance to backward flights,
However prodigal, however proud,
Contained in their afflatus the reproach
That first drove Crispin to his wandering.
He could not be content with counterfeit,
With masquerade of thought, with hapless words

That must belie the racking masquerade,
With fictive flourishes that preordained
His passion's permit, hang of coat, degree
Of buttons, measure of his salt. Such trash
Might help the blind, not him, serenely sly.
It irked beyond his patience. Hence it was,
Preferring text to gloss, he humbly served
Grotesque apprenticeship to chance event,
A clown, perhaps, but an aspiring clown.
There is a monotonous babbling in our dreams
That makes them our dependent heirs, the heirs
Of dreamers buried in our sleep, and not
The oncoming fantasies of better birth.
The apprentice knew these dreamers. If he dreamed
Their dreams, he did it in a gingerly way.
All dreams are vexing. Let them be expunged.
But let the rabbit run, the cock declaim.

Trinket pasticcio, flaunting skyey sheets,
With Crispin as the tiptoe cozener?
No, no: veracious page on page, exact.

V: A NICE SHADY HOME

Crispin as hermit, pure and capable,
Dwelt in the land. Perhaps if discontent
Had kept him still the prickling realist,
Choosing his element from droll confect
Of was and is and shall or ought to be,
Beyond Bordeaux, beyond Havana, far
Beyond carked Yucatan, he might have come
To colonize his polar planterdom
And jig his chits upon a cloudy knee.
But his emprize to that idea soon sped.
Crispin dwelt in the land and dwelling there
Slid from his continent by slow recess
To things within his actual eye, alert
To the difficulty of rebellious thought
When the sky is blue. The blue infected will.
It may be that the yarrow in his fields
Sealed pensive purple under its concern.
But day by day, now this thing and now that
Confined him, while it cosseted, condoned,
Little by little, as if the suzerain soil
Abashed him by carouse to humble yet

Attach. It seemed haphazard denouement.
He first, as realist, admitted that
Whoever hunts a matinal continent
May, after all, stop short before a plum
And be content and still be realist.
The words of things entangle and confuse.
The plum survives its poems. It may hang
In the sunshine placidly, colored by ground
Obliquities of those who pass beneath,
Harlequined and mazily dewed and mauved
In bloom. Yet it survives in its own form,
Beyond these changes, good, fat, guzzly fruit.
So Crispin hasped on the surviving form,
For him, of shall or ought to be in is.

Was he to bray this in profoundest brass
Arointing his dreams with fugal requiems?
Was he to company vastest things defunct
With a blubber of tom-toms harrowing the sky?
Scrawl a tragedian's testament? Prolong
His active force in an inactive dirge,
Which, let the tall musicians call and call,
Should merely call him dead? Pronounce amen
Through choirs infolded to the outmost clouds?
Because he built a cabin who once planned
Loquacious columns by the ructive sea?
Because he turned to salad-beds again?
Jovial Crispin, in calamitous crape?
Should he lay by the personal and make
Of his own fate an instance of all fate?
What is one man among so many men?
What are so many men in such a world?
Can one man think one thing and think it long?
Can one man be one thing and be it long?
The very man despising honest quilts
Lies quilted to his poll in his despite.
For realist, what is is what should be.

And so it came, his cabin shuffled up,
His trees were planted, his duenna brought
Her prismy blonde and clapped her in his hands,
The curtains flittered and the door was closed.
Crispin, magister of a single room,
Latched up the night. So deep a sound fell down
It was as if the solitude concealed
And covered him and his congenial sleep.

So deep a sound fell down it grew to be
A long soothsaying silence down and down.
The crickets beat their tambours in the wind,
Marching a motionless march, custodians.

In the presto of the morning, Crispin trod,
Each day, still curious, but in a round
Less prickly and much more condign than that
He once thought necessary. Like Candide,
Yeoman and grub, but with a fig in sight,
And cream for the fig and silver for the cream,
A blonde to tip the silver and to taste
The rapey gouts. Good star, how that to be
Annealed them in their cabin ribaldries!
Yet the quotidian saps philosophers
And men like Crispin like them in intent,
If not in will, to track the knaves of thought.
But the quotidian composed as his,
Of breakfast ribands, fruits laid in their leaves,
The tomtit and the cassia and the rose,
Although the rose was not the noble thorn
Of crinoline spread, but of a pining sweet,
Composed of evenings like cracked shutters flung
Upon the rumpling bottomness, and nights
In which those frail custodians watched,
Indifferent to the tepid summer cold,
While he poured out upon the lips of her
That lay beside him, the quotidian
Like this, saps like the sun, true fortuner.
For all it takes it gives a humped return
Exchequering from piebald fiscs unkeyed.

VI: AND DAUGHTERS WITH CURLS

Portentous enunciation, syllable
To blessed syllable affined, and sound
Bubbling felicity in cantilene,
Prolific and tormenting tenderness
Of music, as it comes to unison,
Forgather and bell boldly Crispin's last
Deduction. Thrum with a proud douceur
His grand pronunciamento and devise.

The chits came for his jigging, bluet-eyed,
Hands without touch yet touching poignantly,
Leaving no room upon his cloudy knee,
Prophetic joint, for its diviner young.
The return to social nature, once begun,
Anabasis or slump, ascent or chute,
Involved him in midwifery so dense
His cabin counted as phylactery,
Then place of vexing palankeens, then haunt
Of children nibbling at the sugared void,
Infants yet eminently old, then dome
And halidom for the unbraided femes,
Green crammers of the green fruits of the world,
Bidders and biders for its ecstasies,
True daughters both of Crispin and his clay.
All this with many mulctings of the man,
Effective colonizer sharply stopped
In the door-yard by his own capacious bloom.
But that this bloom grown riper, showing nibs
Of its eventual roundness, puerile tints
Of spiced and weathery rouges, should complex
The stopper to indulgent fatalist
Was unforeseen. First Crispin smiled upon
His goldenest demoiselle, inhabitant,
She seemed, of a country of the capuchins,
So delicately blushed, so humbly eyed,
Attentive to a coronal of things
Secret and singular. Second, upon
A second similar counterpart, a maid
Most sisterly to the first, not yet awake
Excepting to the motherly footstep, but
Marvelling sometimes at the shaken sleep.
Then third, a thing still flaxen in the light,
A creeper under jaunty leaves. And fourth,
Mere blusteriness that gewgaws jollified,
All din and gobble, blasphemously pink.
A few years more and the vermeil capuchin
Gave to the cabin, lordlier than it was,
The dulcet omen fit for such a house.
The second sister dallying was shy
To fetch the one full-pinioned one himself
Out of her botches, hot embosomer.
The third one gaping at the orioles
Lettered herself demurely as became
A pearly poetess, peaked for rhapsody.
The fourth, pent now, a digit curious.

Four daughters in a world too intricate
In the beginning, four blithe instruments
Of differing struts, four voices several
In couch, four more personæ, intimate
As buffo, yet divers, four mirrors blue
That should be silver, four accustomed seeds
Hinting incredible hues, four selfsame lights
That spread chromatics in hilarious dark,
Four questioners and four sure answerers.

Crispin concocted doctrine from the rout.
The world, a turnip once so readily plucked,
Sacked up and carried overseas, daubed out
Of its ancient purple, pruned to the fertile main,
And sown again by the stiffest realist,
Came reproduced in purple, family font,
The same insoluble lump. The fatalist
Stepped in and dropped the chuckling down his craw,
Without grace or grumble. Score this anecdote
Invented for its pith, not doctrinal
In form though in design, as Crispin willed,
Disguised pronunciamento, summary,
Autumn's compendium, strident in itself
But muted, mused, and perfectly revolved
In those portentous accents, syllables,
And sounds of music coming to accord
Upon his lap, like their inherent sphere,
Seraphic proclamations of the pure
Delivered with a deluging onwardness.
Or if the music sticks, if the anecdote
Is false, if Crispin is a profitless
Philosopher, beginning with green brag,
Concluding fadedly, if as a man
Prone to distemper he abates in taste,
Fickle and fumbling, variable, obscure,
Glozing his life with after-shining flicks,
Illuminating, from a fancy gorged
By apparition, plain and common things,
Sequestering the fluster from the year,
Making gulped potions from obstreperous drops,
And so distorting, proving what he proves
Is nothing, what can all this matter since
The relation comes, benignly, to its end?

So may the relation of each man be clipped.

O Florida, Venereal Soil

A few things for themselves,
Convolvulus and coral,
Buzzards and live-moss,
Tiestas from the keys,
A few things for themselves,
Florida, venereal soil,
Disclose to the lover.

The dreadful sundry of this world,
The Cuban, Polodowsky,
The Mexican women,
The negro undertaker
Killing the time between corpses
Fishing for crayfish . . .
Virgin of boorish births,

Swiftly in the nights,
In the porches of Key West,
Behind the bougainvilleas,
After the guitar is asleep,
Lasciviously as the wind,
You come tormenting,
Insatiable,

When you might sit,
A scholar of darkness,
Sequestered over the sea,
Wearing a clear tiara
Of red and blue and red,
Sparkling, solitary, still,
In the high sea-shadow.

Donna, donna, dark,
Stooping in indigo gown
And cloudy constellations,
Conceal yourself or disclose
Fewest things to the lover—
A hand that bears a thick-leaved fruit,
A pungent bloom against your shade.

To the One of Fictive Music

Sister and mother and diviner love,
And of the sisterhood of the living dead
Most near, most clear, and of the clearest bloom,
And of the fragrant mothers the most dear
And queen, and of diviner love the day
And flame and summer and sweet fire, no thread
Of cloudy silver sprinkles in your gown
Its venom of renown, and on your head
No crown is simpler than the simple hair.

Now, of the music summoned by the birth
That separates us from the wind and sea,
Yet leaves us in them, until earth becomes,
By being so much of the things we are,
Gross effigy and simulacrum, none
Gives motion to perfection more serene
Than yours, out of our imperfections wrought,
Most rare, or ever of more kindred air
In the laborious weaving that you wear.

For so retentive of themselves are men
That music is intensest which proclaims
The near, the clear, and vaunts the clearest bloom,
And of all vigils musing the obscure,
That apprehends the most which sees and names,
As in your name, an image that is sure,
Among the arrant spices of the sun,
O bough and bush and scented vine, in whom
We give ourselves our likest issuance.

Yet not too like, yet not so like to be
Too near, too clear, saving a little to endow
Our feigning with the strange unlike, whence springs
The difference that heavenly pity brings.
For this, musician, in your girdle fixed
Bear other perfumes. On your pale head wear
A band entwining, set with fatal stones.
Unreal, give back to us what once you gave:
The imagination that we spurned and crave.

To the Roaring Wind

What syllable are you seeking,
Vocalissimus,
In the distances of sleep?
Speak it.

WITTER BYNNER
(1881–1968)

Tiles

Chinese magicians had conjured their chance,
And they hunted, with their hooded birds of glee,
The heat that rises from the summer-grass
And shakes against the sea.
And when they had caught a wide expanse
In nets of careful wizardry,
They coloured it like molten glass
For roofs, imperially,
With blue from a cavern, green from a morass
And yellow from weeds in the heart of the sea,
And they laid long rows on the dwellings of romance
In perfect alchemy—
And before they ascended like a peal of brass,
They and their tiptoeing hawks of glee
Had topped all China with a roof that slants
And shakes against the sea.

The Highest Bidder

To the highest bidder,
Your birthplace, Walt Whitman,
Under the hammer . . .
The old farm on Paumanok north of Huntington,
Its trees,
Its leaves of grass!

Voices bid and counterbid over those ninety acres . . .
And your own voice among them, like an element,
Roaring and outbidding.

Opus 6

If I were only dafter
  I might be making hymns
To the liquor of your laughter
  And the lacquer of your limbs.

But you turn across the table
  A telescope of eyes,
And it lights a Russian sable
  Running circles in the skies . . .

Till I go running after,
  Obeying all your whims—
For the liquor of your laughter
  And the lacquer of your limbs.

ANNE SPENCER
(1882–1975)

Letter to My Sister

It is dangerous for a woman to defy the gods;
To taunt them with the tongue's thin tip,
Or strut in the weakness of mere humanity,
Or draw a line daring them to cross;
The gods own the searing lightning,
The drowning waters, tormenting fears
And anger of red sins.

Oh, but worse still if you mince timidly—
Dodge this way or that, or kneel or pray,
Be kind, or sweat agony drops
Or lay your quick body over your feeble young;
If you have beauty or none, if celibate
Or vowed—the gods are Juggernaut,
Passing over . . . over . . .

This you may do:
Lock your heart, then, quietly,
And lest they peer within,
Light no lamp when dark comes down
Raise no shade for sun;
Breathless must your breath come through
If you'd die and dare deny
The gods their god-like fun.

KAHLIL GIBRAN
(1883–1931)

The Madman *(Prologue)*

You ask me how I became a madman. It happened thus:
One day, long before many gods were born, I woke from a deep sleep
and found all my masks were stolen,—the seven masks I have fashioned
and worn in seven lives,—I ran maskless through the crowded streets
shouting, "Thieves, thieves, the cursed thieves."

Men and women laughed at me and some ran to their houses in
fear of me.

And when I reached the market place, a youth standing on a house-
top cried, "He is a madman." I looked up to behold him; the sun kissed
my own naked face for the first time. For the first time the sun kissed my
own naked face and my soul was inflamed with love for the sun, and I
wanted my masks no more. And as if in a trance I cried, "Blessed,
blessed are the thieves who stole my masks."

Thus I became a madman.

And I have found both freedom and safety in my madness; the
freedom of loneliness and the safety from being understood, for those
who understand us enslave something in us.

But let me not be too proud of my safety. Even a Thief in a jail is
safe from another thief.

ARTHUR DAVISON FICKE
(1883–1945)

The Three Sisters

Gone are the three, those sisters rare
    With wonder-lips and eyes ashine.
One was wise and one was fair,
    And one was mine.

Ye mourners, weave for the sleeping hair
    Of only two, your ivy vine.
For one was wise and one was fair,
    But one was mine.

Sonnet

There are strange shadows fostered of the moon,
More numerous than the clear-cut shade of day . . .
Go forth, when all the leaves whisper of June,
Into the dusk of swooping bats at play;
Or go into that late November dusk
When hills take on the noble lines of death,
And on the air the faint, astringent musk
Of rotting leaves pours vaguely troubling breath.
Then shall you see shadows whereof the sun,
Knows nothing—aye, a thousand shadows there
Shall leap and flicker and stir and stay and run,
Like petrels of the changing foul or fair;
Like ghosts of twilight, of the moon, of him
Whose homeland lies past each horizon's rim . . .

WILLIAM CARLOS WILLIAMS
(1883–1963)

from KORA IN HELL: IMPROVISATIONS

from II, 1

Why go further? One might conceivably rectify the rhythm, study all out and arrive at the perfection of a tiger lily or a china doorknob. One might lift all out of the ruck, be a worthy successor to—the man in the moon. Instead of breaking the back of a willing phrase why not try to follow the wheel through—approach death at a walk, take in all the scenery. There's as much reason one way as the other and then—one never knows—perhaps we'll bring back Euridice—this time!

from XIV, 2

Some fools once were listening to a poet reading his poem. It so happened that the words of the thing spoke of gross matters of the everyday world such as are never much hidden from a quick eye. Out of these semblances, and borrowing certain members from fitting masterpieces of antiquity, the poet began piping up his music, simple fellow, thinking to please his listeners. But they getting the whole matter sadly muddled in their minds made such a confused business of listening that not only were they not pleased at the poet's exertions but no sooner had he done than they burst out against him with violent imprecations.

from XXIV, 2

Pathology literally speaking is a flower garden. Syphilis covers the body with salmon-red petals. The study of medicine is an inverted sort of horticulture. Over and above all this floats the philosophy of disease which is a stern dance. One of its most delightful gestures is bringing flowers to the sick.

from XXV, 1

There's force to this cold sun, makes beard stubble stand shinily. We look, we pretend great things to our glass—rubbing our chin: This is a profound comedian who grimaces deeds into slothful breasts. This is a sleepy president, without followers save oak leaves—but their coats are of the wrong color. This is a farmer—plowed a field in his dreams and since that time—goes stroking the weeds that choke his furrows. This is a poet left his own country—

———

from The Wanderer: A Rococo Study
[*First Version*]

PATERSON—THE STRIKE

At the first peep of dawn she roused me
Trembling at those changes the night saw,
For brooding wretchedly in a corner
Of the room to which she had taken me—
Her old eyes glittering fiercely—
Go! she said and I hurried shivering
Out into the deserted streets of Paterson.

    That night she came again, hovering
In rags within the filmy ceiling—
Great Queen, bless me with your tatters!
You are blest! Go on!

        Hot for savagery,
I went sucking the air! Into the city,
Out again, baffled, on to the mountain!
Back into the city!
        Nowhere
The subtle! Everywhere the electric!

A short bread-line before a hitherto empty tea shop:
No questions—all stood patiently,
Dominated by one idea: something
That carried them as they are always wanting to be carried,
But what is it, I asked those nearest me,
This thing heretofore unobtainable
That they seem so clever to have put on now?

Why since I have failed them can it be anything
But their own brood? Can it be anything but brutality?
On that at least they're united! That at least
Is their bean soup, their calm bread and a few luxuries!

But in me more sensitive, marvelous old queen,
It sank deep into the blood, that I rose upon
The tense air enjoying the dusty fight!
Heavy wrought drink were the low foreheads,
The flat heads with the unkempt black or blond hair!

Below the skirt the ugly legs of the young girls
Pistons too powerful for delicacy!
The women's wrists, the men's arms, red,
Used to heat and cold, to toss quartered beeves
And barrels and milk cans and crates of fruit!
Faces all knotted up like burls on oaks,
Grasping, fox snouted, thick lipped,
Sagging breasts and protruding stomachs,
Rasping voices, filthy habits with the hands.

Nowhere you! Everywhere the electric!

Ugly, venomous, gigantic!
Tossing me as a great father his helpless
Infant till it shriek with ecstasy
And its eyes roll and its tongue hangs out—!

I am at peace again, old queen, I listen clearer now.

GRoTEsqUe

The city has tits in rows.
The country is in the main—male,
It butts me with blunt stub-horns,
Forces me to oppose it
Or be trampled.

The city is full of milk
And lies still for the most part.
These crack skulls
And spill brains
Against her stomach.

Spring Strains

In a tissue-thin monotone of blue-grey buds
crowded erect with desire against
the sky—
⠀⠀⠀⠀⠀tense blue-grey twigs
slenderly anchoring them down, drawing
them in—

⠀⠀⠀⠀⠀two blue-grey birds chasing
a third struggle in circles, angles,
swift convergings to a point that bursts
instantly!

⠀⠀⠀⠀⠀Vibrant bowing limbs
pull downward, sucking in the sky
that bulges from behind, plastering itself
against them in packed rifts, rock blue
and dirty orange!

⠀⠀⠀⠀⠀⠀⠀⠀⠀⠀⠀⠀⠀⠀⠀⠀But—
(Hold hard, rigid jointed trees!)
the blinding and red-edged sun-blur—
creeping energy, concentrated
counterforce—welds sky, buds, trees,
rivets them in one puckering hold!

Sticks through! Pulls the whole
counter-pulling mass upward, to the right,
locks even the opaque, not yet defined
ground in a terrific drag that is
loosening the very tap-roots!

On a tissue-thin monotone of blue-grey buds
two blue-grey birds, chasing a third,
at full cry! Now they are
flung outward and up—disappearing suddenly!

A Coronal

New books of poetry will be written
New books and unheard of manuscripts
will come wrapped in brown paper
and many and many a time
the postman will bow

and sidle down the leaf-plastered steps
thumbing over other men's business.

But we ran ahead of it all.
One coming after
could have seen her footprints
in the wet and followed us
among the stark chestnuts.

Anemones sprang where she pressed
and cresses
stood green in the slender source—
And new books of poetry
will be written, leather-colored oakleaves
many and many a time.

The Widow's Lament in Springtime

Sorrow is my own yard
where the new grass
flames as it has flamed
often before but not
with the cold fire
that closes round me this year.
Thirtyfive years
I lived with my husband.
The plumtree is white today
with masses of flowers.
Masses of flowers
load the cherry branches
and color some bushes
yellow and some red
but the grief in my heart
is stronger than they
for though they were my joy
formerly, today I notice them
and turned away forgetting.
Today my son told me
that in the meadows,
at the edge of the heavy woods
in the distance, he saw
trees of white flowers.
I feel that I would like
to go there
and fall into those flowers
and sink into the marsh near them.

To Mark Anthony in Heaven

This quiet morning light
reflected, how many times
from grass and trees and clouds
enters my north room
touching the walls with
grass and clouds and trees.
Anthony,
trees and grass and clouds.
Why did you follow
that beloved body
with your ships at Actium?
I hope it was because
you knew her inch by inch
from slanting feet upward
to the roots of her hair
and down again and that
you saw her
above the battle's fury—
clouds and trees and grass—

For then you are
listening in heaven.

from Spring and All

I
By the road to the contagious hospital
under the surge of the blue
mottled clouds driven from the
northeast—a cold wind. Beyond, the
waste of broad, muddy fields
brown with dried weeds, standing and fallen

patches of standing water
the scattering of tall trees

All along the road the reddish
purplish, forked, upstanding, twiggy
stuff of bushes and small trees
with dead, brown leaves under them
leafless vines—

Lifeless in appearance, sluggish
dazed spring approaches—

They enter the new world naked,
cold, uncertain of all
save that they enter. All about them
the cold, familiar wind—
Now the grass, tomorrow
the stiff curl of wildcarrot leaf

One by one objects are defined—
It quickens: clarity, outline of leaf

But now the stark dignity of
entrance—Still, the profound change
has come upon them: rooted, they
grip down and begin to awaken

VI
No that is not it
nothing that I have done
nothing
I have done

is made up of
nothing
and the diphthong

ae

together with
the first person
singular
indicative

of the auxiliary
verb
to have

everything
I have done
is the same

if to do
is capable
of an
infinity of
combinations

involving the
moral
physical
and religious

codes

for everything
and nothing
are synonymous
when

energy *in vacuo*
has the power
of confusion

which only to
have done nothing
can make
perfect

XVIII
The pure products of America
go crazy—
mountain folk from Kentucky

or the ribbed north end of
Jersey
with its isolate lakes and

valleys, its deaf-mutes, thieves
old names
and promiscuity between

devil-may-care men who have taken
to railroading
out of sheer lust of adventure—

and young slatterns, bathed
in filth
From Monday to Saturday

to be tricked out that night
with gauds
from imaginations which have no

peasant traditions to give them
character
but flutter and flaunt

sheer rags—succumbing without
emotion
save numbed terror

under some hedge of choke-cherry
or viburnum—
which they cannot express—

Unless it be that marriage
perhaps
with a dash of Indian blood

will throw up a girl so desolate
so hemmed round
with disease or murder

that she'll be rescued by an
agent—
reared by the state and

sent out at fifteen to work in
some hard-pressed
house in the suburbs—

some doctor's family, some Elsie—
voluptuous water
expressing with broken

brain the truth about us—
her great
ungainly hips and flopping breasts

addressed to cheap
jewelry
and rich young men with fine eyes

as if the earth under our feet
were
an excrement of some sky

and we degraded prisoners
destined
to hunger until we eat filth

while the imagination strains
after deer
going by fields of goldenrod in

the stifling heat of September
Somehow
it seems to destroy us

it is only in isolate flecks that
something
is given off

No one
to witness
and adjust, no one to drive the car

XXVI
The crowd at the ball game
is moved uniformly

by a spirit of uselessness
which delights them—

all the exciting detail
of the chase

and the escape, the error
the flash of genius—

all to no end save beauty
the eternal—

So in detail they, the crowd,
are beautiful

for this
to be warned against

saluted and defied—
It is alive, venomous

it smiles grimly
its words cut—

The flashy female with her
mother, gets it—

The Jew gets it straight—it
is deadly, terrifying—

It is the Inquisition, the
Revolution

It is beauty itself
that lives

day by day in them
idly—

This is
the power of their faces

It is summer, it is the solstice
the crowd is

cheering, the crowd is laughing
in detail

permanently, seriously
without thought

SARA TEASDALE
(1884–1933)

I Shall not Care

When I am dead and over me bright April
    Shakes out her rain-drenched hair,
Tho' you should lean above me broken-hearted,
    I shall not care.

I shall have peace, as leafy trees are peaceful
    When rain bends down the bough,
And I shall be more silent and cold-hearted
    Than you are now.

I love too much; I am a river
    Surging with spring that seeks the sea,
I am too generous a giver,
    Love will not stoop to drink of me.

His feet will turn to desert places
  Shadowless, reft of rain and dew,
Where stars stare down with sharpened faces
  From heavens pitilessly blue.

And there at midnight sick with faring,
  He will stoop down in his desire
To slake the thirst grown past all bearing
  In stagnant water keen as fire.

Let It Be Forgotten

Let it be forgotten, as a flower is forgotten,
  Forgotten as a fire that once was singing gold,
Let it be forgotten for ever and ever,
  Time is a kind friend, he will make us old.

If anyone asks, say it was forgotten
  Long and long ago,
As a flower, as a fire, as a hushed footfall
  In a long forgotten snow.

On the Dunes

If there is any life when death is over,
  These tawny beaches will know much of me,
I shall come back, as constant and as changeful
  As the unchanging, many-colored sea.

If life was small, if it has made me scornful,
  Forgive me; I shall straighten like a flame
In the great calm of death, and if you want me
  Stand on the sea-ward dunes and call my name.

The Long Hill

I must have passed the crest a while ago
  And now I am going down—
Strange to have crossed the crest and not to know,
  But the brambles were always catching the hem of my gown.

All the morning I thought how proud I should be
    To stand there straight as a queen,
Wrapped in the wind and the sun with the world under me—
    But the air was dull, there was little I could have seen.

It was nearly level along the beaten track
    And the brambles caught in my gown—
But it's no use now to think of turning back,
    The rest of the way will be only going down.

DONALD EVANS
(1884–1921)

Dinner at the Hotel
de la Tigresse Verte

1—Terrace
As they sat sipping their glasses in the courtyard
Of the Hotel de la Tigresse Verte,
With their silk-swathed ankles softly kissing,
They were certain that they had forever
Imprisoned fickleness in the vodka—
They knew they had found the ultimate pulse of love.

Story upon story, the dark windows whispered down
To them from above, and over the roof's edge
Danced a grey moon.

The woman pressed her chicken-skin fan against her breast
And through her ran trepidant mutinies of desire
With treacheries of emotion. Her voice vapoured:
"In which room shall it be to-night, darling?"
His eyes swept the broad facade, the windows,
Tier upon tier, and his lips were regnant:
"In every room, my beloved!"

2—Loyalty
I am kissing your wayward feet—
The rumours of flight are broken,
Your hands are a dear pale token.
I adore you to touch me, sweet,
And now are the frail vows spoken.

576

It is bravely the words are said,
Faith is a flash on our faces—
We mock as the mummer traces
The dawn when the month is dead,
Loyalty mussed like your laces.

EZRA POUND
(1885–1972)

Sestina: Altaforte

LOQUITUR: *En* Bertrans de Born.
    Dante Alighieri put this man in hell for that he was a stirrer up of
    strife.
    Eccovi!
    Judge ye!
    Have I dug him up again?
The scene is at his castle, Altaforte. "Papiols" is his jongleur.
"The Leopard," the *device* of Richard Coeur de Lion.

I
Damn it all! all this our South stinks peace.
You whoreson dog, Papiols, come! Let's to music!
I have no life save when the swords clash.
But ah! when I see the standards gold, vair, purple, opposing
And the broad fields beneath them turn crimson,
Then howl I my heart nigh mad with rejoicing.

II
In hot summer have I great rejoicing
When the tempests kill the earth's foul peace,
And the lightnings from black heav'n flash crimson,
And the fierce thunders roar me their music
And the winds shriek through the clouds mad, opposing,
And through all the riven skies God's swords clash.

III
Hell grant soon we hear again the swords clash!
And the shrill neighs of destriers in battle rejoicing,
Spiked breast to spiked breast opposing!
Better one hour's stour than a year's peace
With fat boards, bawds, wine and frail music!
Bah! there's no wine like the blood's crimson!

IV

And I love to see the sun rise blood-crimson.
And I watch his spears through the dark clash
And it fills all my heart with rejoicing
And pries wide my mouth with fast music
When I see him so scorn and defy peace,
His lone might 'gainst all darkness opposing.

V

The man who fears war and squats opposing
My words for stour, hath no blood of crimson
But is fit only to rot in womanish peace
Far from where worth's won and the swords clash
For the death of such sluts I go rejoicing;
Yea, I fill all the air with my music.

VI

Papiols, Papiols, to the music!
There's no sound like to swords swords opposing,
No cry like the battle's rejoicing
When our elbows and swords drip the crimson
And our charges 'gainst "The Leopard's" rush clash.
May God damn for ever all who cry "Peace!"

VII

And let the music of the swords make them crimson!
Hell grant soon we hear again the swords clash!
Hell blot black for alway the thought "Peace"!

The Seafarer

May I for my own self song's truth reckon,
Journey's jargon, how I in harsh days
Hardship endured oft.
Bitter breast-cares have I abided,
Known on my keel many a care's hold,
And dire sea-surge, and there I oft spent
Narrow nightwatch nigh the ship's head
While she tossed close to cliffs. Coldly afflicted,
My feet were by frost benumbed.
Chill its chains are; chafing sighs
Hew my heart round and hunger begot
Mere-weary mood. Lest man know not
That he on dry land loveliest liveth,
List how I, care-wretched, on ice-cold sea,
Weathered the winter, wretched outcast

Deprived of my kinsmen;
Hung with hard ice-flakes, where hail-scur flew,
There I heard naught save the harsh sea
And ice-cold wave, at whiles the swan cries,
Did for my games the gannet's clamour,
Sea-fowls' loudness was for me laughter,
The mews' singing all my mead-drink.
Storms, on the stone-cliffs beaten, fell on the stern
In icy feathers; full oft the eagle screamed
With spray on his pinion.
                    Not any protector
May make merry man faring needy.
This he little believes, who aye in winsome life
Abides 'mid burghers some heavy business,
Wealthy and wine-flushed, how I weary oft
Must bide above brine.
Neareth nightshade, snoweth from north,
Frost froze the land, hail fell on earth then,
Corn of the coldest. Nathless there knocketh now
The heart's thought that I on high streams
The salt-wavy tumult traverse alone.
Moaneth alway my mind's lust
That I fare forth, that I afar hence
Seek out a foreign fastness.
For this there's no mood-lofty man over earth's midst,
Not though he be given his good, but will have in his youth greed;
Nor his deed to the daring, nor his king to the faithful
But shall have his sorrow for sea-fare
Whatever his lord will.
He hath not heart for harping, nor in ring-having
Nor winsomeness to wife, nor world's delight
Nor any whit else save the wave's slash,
Yet longing comes upon him to fare forth on the water.
Bosque taketh blossom, cometh beauty of berries,
Fields to fairness, land fares brisker,
All this admonisheth man eager of mood,
The heart turns to travel so that he then thinks
On flood-ways to be far departing.
Cuckoo calleth with gloomy crying,
He singeth summerward, bodeth sorrow,
The bitter heart's blood. Burgher knows not—
He the prosperous man—what some perform
Where wandering them widest draweth.
So that but now my heart burst from my breastlock,
My mood 'mid the mere-flood,
Over the whale's acre, would wander wide.
On earth's shelter cometh oft to me,

Eager and ready, the crying lone-flyer,
Whets for the whale-path the heart irresistibly,
O'er tracks of ocean; seeing that anyhow
My lord deems to me this dead life
On loan and on land, I believe not
That any earth-weal eternal standeth
Save there be somewhat calamitous
That, ere a man's tide go, turn it to twain.
Disease or oldness or sword-hate
Beats out the breath from doom-gripped body.
And for this, every earl whatever, for those speaking after—
Laud of the living, boasteth some last word,
That he will work ere he pass onward,
Frame on the fair earth 'gainst foes his malice,
Daring ado, . . .
So that all men shall honour him after
And his laud beyond them remain 'mid the English,
Aye, for ever, a lasting life's-blast,
Delight 'mid the doughty.
                              Days little durable,
And all arrogance of earthen riches,
There come now no kings nor Ceasars
Nor gold-giving lords like those gone.
Howe'er in mirth most magnified,
Whoe'er lived in life most lordliest,
Drear all this excellence, delights undurable!
Waneth the watch, but the world holdeth.
Tomb hideth trouble, The blade is layed low.
Earthly glory ageth and seareth.
No man at all going the earth's gait,
But age fares against him, his face paleth,
Grey-haired he groaneth, knows gone companions,
Lordly men, are to earth o'ergiven,
Nor may he then the flesh-cover, whose life ceaseth,
Nor eat the sweet nor feel the sorry,
Nor stir hand nor think in mid heart,
And though he strew the grave with gold,
His born brothers, their buried bodies
Be an unlikely treasure hoard.

An Immorality

Sing we for love and idleness,
Naught else is worth the having.

Though I have been in many a land,
There is naught else in living.

And I would rather have my sweet,
Though rose-leaves die of grieving,

Than do high deeds in Hungary
To pass all men's believing.

A Virginal

No, no! Go from me. I have left her lately.
I will not spoil my sheath with lesser brightness,
For my surrounding air hath a new lightness;
Slight are her arms, yet they have bound me straitly
And left me cloaked as with a gauze of æther;
As with sweet leaves; as with subtle clearness.
Oh, I have picked up magic in her nearness
To sheathe me half in half the things that sheathe her.
No, no! Go from me. I have still the flavour,
Soft as spring wind that's come from birchen bowers.
Green come the shoots, aye April in the branches,
As winter's wound with her sleight hand she staunches,
Hath of the trees a likeness of the savour:
As white their bark, so white this lady's hours.

Portrait d'une Femme

Your mind and you are our Sargasso Sea,
London has swept about you this score years
And bright ships left you this or that in fee:
Ideas, old gossip, oddments of all things,
Strange spars of knowledge and dimmed wares of price.
Great minds have sought you—lacking someone else.
You have been second always. Tragical?
No. You preferred it to the usual thing:
One dull man, dulling and uxorious,
One average mind—with one thought less, each year.
Oh, you are patient, I have seen you sit
Hours, where something might have floated up.

And now you pay one. Yes, you richly pay.
You are a person of some interest, one comes to you
And takes strange gain away:
Trophies fished up; some curious suggestion;
Fact that leads nowhere; and a tale or two,
Pregnant with mandrakes, or with something else
That might prove useful and yet never proves,
That never fits a corner or shows use,
Or finds its hour upon the loom of days:
The tarnished, gaudy, wonderful old work;
Idols and ambergris and rare inlays,
These are your riches, your great store; and yet
For all this sea-hoard of deciduous things,
Strange woods half sodden, and new brighter stuff:
In the slow float of differing light and deep,
No! there is nothing! In the whole and all,
Nothing that's quite your own.
                    Yet this is you.

In a Station of the Metro

The apparition of these faces in the crowd;
Petals on a wet, black bough.

Alba

As cool as the pale wet leaves
                    of lily-of-the-valley
She lay beside me in the dawn.

L'Art, 1910

Green arsenic smeared on an egg-white cloth,
Crushed strawberries! Come, let us feast our eyes.

Ancient Music

Winter is icummen in,
Lhude sing Goddamm,
Raineth drop and staineth slop,
And how the wind doth ramm!
                    Sing: Goddamm.
Skiddeth bus and sloppeth us,

An ague hath my ham.
Freezeth river, turneth liver,
                     Damn you, sing: Goddamm.
Goddamm, Goddamm, 'tis why I am, Goddamm,
                     So 'gainst the winter's balm.
Sing goddamm, damm, sing Goddamm,
Sing goddamm, sing goddamm, DAMM.

from Hugh Selwyn Mauberley
(LIFE AND CONTACTS)

"VOCAT ÆSTUS IN UMBRAM"
           Nemesianus, Ec. IV.

E. P.
ODE POUR L'ELECTION DE SON SEPULCHRE

I
For three years, out of key with his time,
He strove to resuscitate the dead art
Of poetry; to maintain "the sublime"
In the old sense. Wrong from the start—

No, hardly but, seeing he had been born
In a half savage country, out of date;
Bent resolutely on wringing lilies from the acorn;
Capaneus; trout for factitious bait;

Ἴδμεν γάρ τοι πάνθ', ὅσ' ἐνὶ Τροίῃ
Caught in the unstopped ear;
Giving the rocks small lee-way
The chopped seas held him, therefore, that year.

His true Penelope was Flaubert,
He fished by obstinate isles;
Observed the elegance of Circe's hair
Rather than the mottoes on sun-dials.

Unaffected by "the march of events,"
He passed from men's memory in *l'an trentiesme
De son eage;* the case presents
No adjunct to the Muses' diadem.

II
The age demanded an image
Of its accelerated grimace,
Something for the modern stage,
Not, at any rate, an Attic grace;

Not, not certainly, the obscure reveries
Of the inward gaze;
Better mendacities
Than the classics in paraphrase!

The "age demanded" chiefly a mould in plaster,
Made with no loss of time,
A prose kinema, not, not assuredly, alabaster
Or the "sculpture" of rhyme.

III
The tea-rose tea-gown, etc.
Supplants the mousseline of Cos,
The pianola "replaces"
Sappho's barbitos.

Christ follows Dionysus,
Phallic and ambrosial
Made way for macerations;
Caliban casts out Ariel.

All things are a flowing,
Sage Heracleitus says;
But a tawdry cheapness
Shall outlast our days.

Even the Christian beauty
Defects—after Samothrace;
We see τό καλόν
Decreed in the market place.

Faun's flesh is not to us,
Nor the saint's vision.
We have the press for wafer;
Franchise for circumcision.

All men, in law, are equals.
Free of Peisistratus,
We choose a knave or an eunuch
To rule over us.

O bright Apollo,
τίν' ἄνδρα, τίν ἥρωα, τίνα θεόν,
What god, man, or hero
Shall I place a tin wreath upon!

IV
These fought in any case,
and some believing,
                    pro domo, in any case . .

Some quick to arm,
some for adventure,
some from fear of weakness,
some from fear of censure,
some for love of slaughter, in imagination,
learning later . . .

some in fear, learning love of slaughter;
Died some, pro patria,
                    non "dulce" non "et decor" . .
walked eye-deep in hell
believing in old men's lies, then unbelieving
came home, home to a lie,
home to many deceits,
home to old lies and new infamy;
usury age-old and age-thick
and liars in public places.

Daring as never before, wastage as never before.
Young blood and high blood,
fair cheeks, and fine bodies;

fortitude as never before

frankness as never before,
disillusions as never told in the old days,
hysterias, trench confessions,
laughter out of dead bellies.

V
There died a myriad,
And of the best, among them,
For an old bitch gone in the teeth,
For a botched civilization,

Charm, smiling at the good mouth,
Quick eyes gone under earth's lid,

For two gross of broken statues,
For a few thousand battered books.

. . . .

ENVOI (1919)

Go, dumb-born book,
Tell her that sang me once that song of Lawes;
Hadst thou but song
As thou hast subjects known,
Then were there cause in thee that should condone
Even my faults that heavy upon me lie,
And build her glories their longevity.

Tell her that sheds
Such treasure in the air,
Recking naught else but that her graces give
Life to the moment,
I would bid them live
As roses might, in magic amber laid,
Red overwrought with orange and all made
One substance and one colour
Braving time.

Tell her that goes
With song upon her lips
But sings not out the song, nor knows
The maker of it, some other mouth,
May be as fair as hers,
Might, in new ages, gain her worshippers,
When our two dusts with Waller's shall be laid,
Siftings on siftings in oblivion,
Till change hath broken down
All things save Beauty alone.

I
Turned from the "eau-forte
Par Jaquemart"
To the strait head
Of Messalina:

"His true Penelope
Was Flaubert,"
And his tool
The engraver's.

Firmness,
Not the full smile,
His art, but an art
In profile;

Colourless
Pier Francesca,
Pisanello lacking the skill
To forge Achaia.

II
*"Qu'est ce qu'ils savent de l'amour, et qu'est ce qu'ils peuvent
comprendre?*
*S'ils ne comprennent pas la poésie, s'ils ne sentent pas la musique,
qu'est ce qu'ils peuvent comprendre de cette passion en comparaison
avec laquelle la rose est grossière et le parfum des violettes un
tonnerre?"*

CAID ALI

For three years, diabolus in the scale,
He drank ambrosia,
All passes, ANANGKE prevails,
Came end, at last, to that Arcadia.

He had moved amid her phantasmagoria,
Amid her galaxies,
NUKTIS 'AGALMA

*   *   *   *   *   *   *

Drifted . . . drifted precipitate,
Asking time to be rid of . . .
Of his bewilderment; to designate
His new found orchid . . .

To be certain . . . certain . . .
(Amid ærial flowers) . . . time for arrangements—
Drifted on
To the final estrangement;

Unable in the supervening blankness
To sift TO AGATHON from the chaff
Until he found his sieve . . .
Ultimately, his seismograph:

—Given that is his "fundamental passion"
This urge to convey the relation
Of eye-lid and cheek-bone
By verbal manifestations;

To present the series
Of curious heads in medallion—

He had passed, inconscient, full gaze,
The wide-banded irises
And botticellian sprays implied
In their diastasis;

Which anæthesis, noted a year late,
And weighed, revealed his great affect,
(Orchid), mandate
Of Eros, a retrospect.
*   *   *
Mouths biting empty air,
The still stone dogs,
Caught in metamorphosis, were
Left him as epilogues.

"THE AGE DEMANDED"

(Vide Poem II, page 584)

For this agility chance found
Him of all men, unfit
As the red-beaked steeds of
The Cytheræan for a chain bit.

The glow of porcelain
Brought no reforming sense
To his perception
Of the social inconsequence.

Thus, if her colour
Came against his gaze,
Tempered as if
It were through a perfect glaze

He made no immediate application
Of this to relation of the state
To the individual, the month was more temperate
Because this beauty had been.

        The coral isle, the lion-coloured sand
        Burst in upon the porcelain revery:
        Impetuous troubling
        Of his imagery.

Mildness, amid the neo-Nietzschean clatter,
His sense of graduations,
Quite out of place amid
Resistance to current exacerbations,

Invitation, mere invitation to perceptivity
Gradually led him to the isolation
Which these presents place
Under a more tolerant, perhaps, examination.

By constant elimination
The manifest universe
Yielded an armour
Against utter consternation,

A Minoan undulation,
Seen, we admit, amid ambrosial circumstances
Strengthened him against
The discouraging doctrine of chances,

And his desire for survival,
Faint in the most strenuous moods,
Became an Olympian *apathein*
In the presence of selected perceptions.

A pale gold, in the aforesaid pattern,
The unexpected palms
Destroying, certainly, the artist's urge,
Left him delighted with the imaginary
Audition of the phantasmal sea-surge,

Incapable of the least utterance or composition,
Emendation, conservation of the "better tradition,"
Refinement of medium, elimination of superfluities
August attraction or concentration.

Nothing, in brief, but maudlin confession,
Irresponse to human aggression,
Amid the precipitation, down-float
Of insubstantial manna,
Lifting the faint susurrus
Of his subjective hosannah.

Ultimate affronts to human redundancies;

Non-esteem of self-styled "his betters"
Leading, as he well knew,
To his final
Exclusion from the world of letters.

IV
Scattered Moluccas
Not knowing, day to day,
The first day's end, in the next noon;
The placid water
Unbroken by the Simoon;

Thick foliage
Placid beneath warm suns,
Tawn fore-shores
Washed in the cobalt of oblivions;

Or through dawn-mist
The grey and rose
Of the juridical
Flamingoes;

A consciousness disjunct,
Being but this overblotted
Series
Of intermittences;

Coracle of Pacific voyages,
The unforecasted beach;
Then on an oar
Read this:

"I was
And I no more exist;
Here drifted
An hedonist."

MEDALLION

Luini in porcelain!
The grand piano
Utters a profane
Protest with her clear soprano.

The sleek head emerges
From the gold-yellow frock
As Anadyomene in the opening
Pages of Reinach.

Honey-red, closing the face-oval,
A basket-work of braids which seem as if they were
Spun in King Minos' hall
From metal, or intractable amber;

The face-oval beneath the glaze,
Bright in its suave bounding-line, as,
Beneath half-watt rays,
The eyes turn topaz.

The River-Merchant's Wife:
A Letter

While my hair was still cut straight across my forehead
I played about the front gate, pulling flowers.
You came by on bamboo stilts, playing horse,
You walked about my seat, playing with blue plums.
And we went on living in the village of Chokan:
Two small people, without dislike or suspicion.

At fourteen I married My Lord you.
I never laughed, being bashful.
Lowering my head, I looked at the wall.
Called to, a thousand times, I never looked back.

At fifteen I stopped scowling,
I desired my dust to be mingled with yours
Forever and forever and forever.
Why should I climb the look out?

At sixteen you departed,
You went into far Ku-to-yen, by the river of swirling eddies,
And you have been gone five months.
The monkeys make sorrowful noise overhead.

You dragged your feet when you went out.
By the gate now, the moss is grown, the different mosses,
Too deep to clear them away!
The leaves fall early this autumn, in wind.
The paired butterflies are already yellow with August
Over the grass in the West garden;
They hurt me. I grow older.
If you are coming down through the narrows of the river Kiang,
Please let me know beforehand,
And I will come out to meet you
                    As far as Cho-fu-Sa.

Night Litany

O Dieu, Purifiez nos coeurs!
  Purifiez nos coeurs!

Yea the lines hast thou laid unto me
        in pleasant places,
And the beauty of this thy Venice
        hast thou shown unto me
Until is its loveliness become unto me
        a thing of tears.

O God, what great kindness
        have we done in times past
        and forgotten it,
That thou givest this wonder unto us,
        O God of waters?

O God of the night,
        What great sorrow
Cometh unto us,
        That thou thus repayest us
Before the time of its coming?

O God of silence,
        Purifiez nos coeurs,
        Purifiez nos coeurs,
For we have seen
The glory of the shadow of the
        likeness of thine handmaid,

Yea, the glory of the shadow
        of thy Beauty hath walked
Upon the shadow of the waters
In this thy Venice.
        And before the holiness
Of the shadow of thy handmaid
        Have I hidden mine eyes,
        O God of waters.

O God of silence,
        Purifiez nos coeurs,
        Purifiez nos coeurs,
O God of waters,
        make clean our hearts within us,
        For I have seen the

Shadow of this thy Venice
Floating upon the waters,
                    And thy stars

Have seen this thing, out of their far courses
Have they seen this thing.
                    O God of waters,
Even as are thy stars
Silent unto us in their far-coursing,
Even so is mine heart
                    become silent within me.

                    Purifiez nos coeurs
O God of the silence,
                    Purifiez nos coeurs
O God of waters.

Sandalphon

And these about me die,
Because the pain of the infinite singing
Slayeth them.
Yet that have sung of the pain of the earth-horde's
        age-long crusading,
Ye know somewhat the strain,
        the sad-sweet wonder-pain of such singing.
And therefore ye know after what fashion
This singing hath power destroying.

Yea, these about me, bearing such song in homage
Unto the Mover of Circles,
Die for the might of their praising,
And the autumn of their marcescent wings
Maketh ever new loam for my forest;
And these grey ash trees hold within them
All the secrets of whatso things
They dreamed before their praises,
And in this grove my flowers,
Fruit of prayerful powers,
Have first their thought of life
            And then their being.

Ye marvel that I die not! *forsitan!*
Thinking me kin with such as may not weep,
Thinking me part of them that die for praising
—Yea, though it be praising,
Past the power of man's mortality to
Dream or name its phases,
—Yea, though it chaunt and paean
Past the might of earth-dwelt
Soul to think on,
—Yea, though it be praising
As these the winged ones die of.

Ye think me one insensate
                else die I also
Sith these about me die,
And if I, watching
Ever the multiplex jewel, or beryl and jasper
    and sapphire,
Make of these prayers of earth ever new flowers;
Marvel and wonder!
Marvel and wonder even as I,
Giving to prayer new language
And causing the words to speak
Of the earth-horde's age-lasting longing,
Even as I marvel and wonder, and know not,
Yet keep my watch in the ash wood.

from QUIA PAUPER AMAVI

from Three Cantos

. . . .

III

Another one, half-cracked: John Heydon,
Worker of miracles, dealer in levitation,
"Servant of God and secretary of nature,"
The half transparent forms, in a trance at Bulverton:
"Decked all in green," which sleeves of yellow silk
Slit to the elbow, slashed with various purples,
(Thus in his vision.) Her eyes were green as glass,
Dangling a chain of emeralds, promised him—
Her foot was leaf-like, and she promised him
The way of holiest wisdom.

"Omniformis
Omnis intellectus est": thus he begins
By spouting half of Psellus; no, not "Daemonibus,"
But Porphyry's "Chances," the 13th chapter,
That every intellect is omniform.
"A daemon is a substance in the locus of souls."
Munching Ficino's mumbling Platonists.

Valla, more earth and sounder rhetoric,
Prefacing praise to his Pope, Nicholas:
A man of parts skilled in the subtlest sciences;
A patron of the arts, of poetry; and of a fine discernment.
A catalogue, his jewels of conversation.
"Know then the Roman speech: a sacrament"
Spread for the nations, eucharist of wisdom,
Bread of the liberal arts.
                              Ha! Sir Blancatz,
Sordello would have your heart up, give it to all the princes;
Valla, the heart of Rome,
                              sustaining speech,
Set out before the people. "Nec bonus
Christianus" (in the Elegantiae) "ac bonus Tullianus."
Shook the church. Marius, Du Bellay, wept for the buildings;
Baldassar Castiglione saw Raphael
"Lead back the soul into its dead, waste dwelling,"
Laniato corpore. Lorenzo Valla
"Broken in middle life? Bent to submission?
Took a fat living from the Papacy"
(That's in Villari, but Burckhardt's statement's different).
"More than the Roman city the Roman speech"
Holds fast its part among the ever living.
"Not by the eagles only was Rome measured."
"Wherever the Roman speech was, there was Rome."
Wherever the speech crept, there was mastery,
Spoke with the law's voice, while your greek logicians. . . .
More greeks than one! Doughty's "Divine Homeros"
Came before sophistry. Justinopolitan, uncatalogued,
One Andreas Divus gave him in latin,
In Officina Wecheli, M.D. three "X's." eight,
Caught up his cadence, word and syllable:
"Down to the ships we went, set mast and sail,
Black keel and beasts for bloody sacrifice,
Weeping we went."
I've strained my ear for *-ensa, -ombra,* and *-ensa,*
And cracked my wit on delicate canzoni,
                              Here's but rough meaning:
"And then went down to the ship, set keel to breakers,

Forth on the godly sea,
We set up mast and sail on the swart ship,
Sheep bore we aboard her, and our bodies also,
Heavy with weeping; and winds from sternward
Bore us out onward with bellying canvas,
Circe's this craft, the trim-coifed goddess.
Then sat we amidships—wind jamming the tiller—
Thus with stretched sail
                    we went over sea till day's end.
Sun to his slumber, shadows o'er all the ocean,
Came we then to the bounds of deepest water,
To the Kimmerian lands and peopled cities
Covered with close-webbed mist, unpierced ever
With glitter of sun-rays,
Nor with stars stretched, nor looking back from heaven,
Swartest night stretched over wretched men there,
The ocean flowing backward, came we then to the place
Aforesaid by Circe.
Here did they rites, Perimedes and Eurylochus,
And drawing sword from my hip
I dug the ell-square pitkin,
Poured we libations unto each the dead,
First mead and then sweet wine, water mixed with white flour,
Then prayed I many a prayer to the sickly death's-heads,
As set in Ithaca, sterile bulls of the best
For sacrifice, heaping the pyre with goods.
Sheep, to Tiresias only; black and bell sheep.
Dark blood flowed in the fosse,
Souls out of Erebus, cadaverous dead,
Of brides, of youths, and of much-bearing old;
Virgins tender, souls stained with recent tears,
Many men mauled with bronze lance-heads,
Battle spoil, bearing yet dreary arms,
These many crowded about me,
With shouting, pallor upon me, cried to my men for more beasts.
Slaughtered the herds, sheep slain of bronze,
Poured ointment, cried to the gods,
To Pluto the strong, and praised Proserpine,
Unsheathed the narrow sword,
I sat to keep off the imperious, impotent dead
Till I should hear Tiresias.
But first Elpenor came, our friend Elpenor,
Unburied, cast on the wide earth,
Limbs that we left in the house of Circe,
Unwept, unwrapped in sepulchre, since toils urged other.
Pitiful spirit, and I cried in hurried speech:
"Elpenor, how art thou come to this dark coast?

Com'st thou a-foot, outstripping seamen?"
                                    And he in heavy speech:
"Ill fate and abundant wine! I slept in Circe's ingle,
Going down the long ladder unguarded, I fell against the buttress,
Shattered the nerve-nape, the soul sought Avernus.
But thou, O King, I bid remember me, unwept, unburied,
Heap up mine arms, be tomb by sea-board, and inscribed:
'*A man of no fortune and with a name to come.*'
And set my oar up, that I swung mid fellows."

Came then another ghost, whom I beat off, Anticlea,
And then Tiresias, Theban,
Holding his golden wand, knew me and spoke first:
"Man of ill hour, why come a second time,
Leaving the sunlight, facing the sunless dead, and this joyless region?
Stand from the fosse, move back, leave me my bloody bever,
And I will speak you true speeches."
                                    And I stepped back,
Sheathing the yellow sword. Dark blood he drank then,
And spoke: "Lustrous Odysseus
Shalt return through spiteful Neptune, over dark seas,
Lose all companions." Foretold me the ways and the signs.
Came then Anticlea, to whom I answered:
"Fate drives me on through these deeps. I sought Tiresias.
Told her the news of Troy. And thrice her shadow
                                    Faded in my embrace."
Lie quiet Divus. Then had he news of many faded women,
Tyro, Alcmena, Chloris,
Heard out their tales by that dark fosse, and sailed
By sirens and thence outward and away,
And unto Circe. Buried Elpenor's corpse.
Lie quiet Divus, plucked from a Paris stall
With a certain Cretan's "Hymni Deorum";
The thin clear Tuscan stuff
                    Gives way before the florid mellow phrase,
Take we the goddess, Venerandam
Auream coronam habentem, pulchram. . . .
Cypri munimenta sortita est, maritime,
Light on the foam, breathed on by Zephyrs
And air-tending Hours, mirthful, orichalci, with golden
Girdles and breast bands, thou with dark eyelids,
Bearing the golden bough of Argicida.

ELINOR WYLIE
(1885–1928)

Wild Peaches

1

When the world turns completely upside down
You say we'll emigrate to the Eastern Shore
Aboard a river-boat from Baltimore;
We'll live among wild peach trees, miles from town.
You'll wear a coonskin cap, and I a gown
Homespun, dyed butternut's dark gold color.
Lost, like your lotus-eating ancestor,
We'll swim in milk and honey till we drown.

The winter will be short, the summer long,
The autumn amber-hued, sunny and hot,
Tasting of cider and scuppernong;
All seasons sweet, but autumn best of all.
The squirrels in their silver fur will fall
Like falling leaves, like fruit, before your shot.

2

The autumn frosts will lie upon the grass
Like bloom on grapes of purple-brown and gold.
The misted early mornings will be cold;
The little puddles will be roofed with glass.
The sun, which burns from copper into brass,
Melts these at noon, and makes the boys unfold
Their knitted mufflers; full as they can hold,
Fat pockets dribble chestnuts as they pass.

Peaches grow wild, and pigs can live in clover;
A barrel of salted herrings lasts a year;
The spring begins before the winter's over.
By February you may find the skins
Of garter snakes and water moccasins
Dwindled and harsh, dead-white and cloudy-clear.

3

When April pours the colors of a shell
Upon the hills, when every little creek
Is shot with silver from Chesapeake
In shoals new-minted by the ocean swell,
When strawberries go begging, and the sleek

Blue plums lie open to the blackbird's beak,
We shall live well—we shall live very well.

The months between the cherries and the peaches
Are brimming cornucopias which spill
Fruits red and purple, somber-bloomed and black;
Then, down rich fields and frosty river beaches
We'll trample bright persimmons, while we kill
Bronze partridge, speckled quail, and canvas-back.

4
Down to the Puritan marrow of my bones
There's something in this richness that I hate.
I love the look, austere, immaculate,
Of landscapes drawn in pearly monotones.
There's something in my very blood that owns
Bare hills, cold silver on a sky of slate,
A thread of water, churned to milky spate
Streaming through slanted pastures fenced with stones.

I love those skies, thin blue or snow gray,
Those fields sparse-planted, rendering meager sheaves;
That spring, briefer than apple-blossom's breath,
Summer, so much too beautiful to stay,
Swift autumn, like a bonfire of leaves,
And sleepy winter, like the sleep of death.

Spring Pastoral

Liza, go steep your long white hands
In the cool waters of that spring
Which bubbles up through shiny sands
The color of a wild-dove's wing.

Dabble your hands, and steep them well
Until those nails are pearly white
Now rosier than a laurel bell;
Then come to me at candle-light.

Lay your cold hands across my brows,
And I shall sleep, and I shall dream
Of silver-pointed willow boughs
Dipping their fingers in a stream.

GEORGIA JOHNSON
(1886–1966)

I Want to Die While You Love Me

I want to die while you love me,
    While yet you hold me fair,
While laughter lies upon my lips
    And lights are in my hair.

I want to die while you love me,
    And bear to that still bed,
Your kisses turbulent, unspent,
    To warm me when I'm dead.

I want to die while you love me,
    Oh, who would care to live
Till love has nothing more to ask
    And nothing more to give!

I want to die while you love me
    And never, never see
The glory of this perfect day
    Grow dim or cease to be.

JOYCE KILMER
(1886–1918)

Trees

I think that I shall never see
A poem lovely as a tree.

A tree whose hungry mouth is prest
Against the earth's sweet flowing breast;

A tree that looks at God all day,
And lifts her leafy arms to pray;

A tree that may in Summer wear
A nest of robins in her hair;

Upon whose bosom snow has lain;
Who intimately lives with rain.

Poems are made by fools like me,
But only God can make a tree.

H. D. [HILDA DOOLITTLE]
(1886–1961)

Heat

O wind, rend open the heat,
cut apart the heat,
rend it to tatters.

Fruit cannot drop
through this thick air—
fruit cannot fall into heat
that presses up and blunts
the points of pears
and rounds the grapes.

Cut the heat—
plough through it,
turning it on either side
of your path.

Orchard

I saw the first pear
as it fell—
the honey-seeking, golden-banded,
the yellow swarm
was not more fleet than I,
(spare us from loveliness)
and I fell prostrate
crying:
you have flayed us
with your blossoms,
spare us the beauty
of fruit-trees.

The honey-seeking
paused not,
the air thundered their song,
and I alone was prostrate.

O rough-hewn
god of the orchard,
I bring you an offering—
do you, alone unbeautiful,
son of the god,
spare us from loveliness:

these fallen hazel-nuts,
stripped late of their green sheaths,
grapes, red-purple,
their berries
dripping with wine,
pomegranates already broken,
and shrunken figs
and quinces untouched,
I bring you as offering.

Oread

Whirl up, sea—
whirl your pointed pines.
splash your great pines
on our rocks,
hurl your green over us,
cover us with your pools of fir.

The Islands

I
What are the islands to me,
what is Greece,
what is Rhodes, Samos, Chios,
what is Paros facing west,
what is Crete?

What is Samothrace,
rising like a ship,
what is Imbros rending the storm-waves
with its breast?

What is Naxos, Paros, Milos,
what the circle about Lycia,
what, the Cyclades'
white necklace?

What is Greece—
Sparta, rising like a rock,
Thebes, Athens,
what is Corinth?

What is Euboia
with its island violets,
what is Euboia, spread with grass,
set with swift shoals,
what is Crete?

What are the islands to me,
what is Greece?

2
What can love of land give to me
that you have not—
what do the tall Spartans know,
and gentler Attic folk?

What has Sparta and her women
more than this?
What are the islands to me
if you are lost—
what is Naxos, Tinos, Andros,
and Delos, the clasp
of the white necklace?

3
What can love of land give to me
that you have not,
what can love of strife break in me
that you have not?

Though Sparta enter Athens,
Thebes wrack Sparta,
each changes as water,
salt, rising to wreak terror
and fall back.

4
'What has love of land given to you
that I have not?'

I have questioned Tyrians
where they sat
on the black ships,
weighted with rich stuffs,
I have asked the Greeks
from the white ships,
and Greeks from ships whose hulks
lay on the wet sand, scarlet
with great beaks.
I have asked bright Tyrians
and tall Greeks—
'what has love of land given you?'
And they answered—'peace.'

5
But beauty is set apart,
beauty is cast by the sea,
a barren rock,
beauty is set about
with wrecks of ships,
upon our coast, death keeps
the shallows—death waits
clutching toward us
from the deeps.

Beauty is set apart,
the winds that slash its beach,
swirl the coarse sand
upward toward the rocks.

Beauty is set apart
from the islands
and from Greece.

6
In my garden
the winds have beaten
the ripe lilies;
in my garden, the salt
has wilted the first flakes
of young narcissus,
and the lesser hyacinth,

and the salt has crept
under the leaves of the white hyacinth.

In my garden
even the wind-flowers lie flat,
broken by the wind at last.

7
What are the islands to me
if you are lost,
what is Paros to me
if your eyes draw back,
what is Milos
if you take fright of beauty,
terrible, torturous, isolated,
a barren rock?

What is Rhodes, Crete,
what is Paros facing west,
what, white Imbros?

What are the islands to me
if you hesitate,
what is Greece if you draw back
from the terror
and cold splendour of song
and its bleak sacrifice?

Song

You are as gold
as the half-ripe grain
that merges to gold again,
as white as the white rain
that beats through
the half-opened flowers
of the great flower tufts
thick on the black limbs
of an Illyrian apple bough.

Can honey distill such fragrance
as your bright hair—
for your face is as fair as rain,
yet as rain that lies clear
on white honey-comb,

lends radiance to the white wax,
so your hair on your brow
casts light for a shadow.

Pear Tree

Silver dust
lifted from the earth,
higher than my arms reach,
you have mounted,
O silver,
higher than my arms reach
you front us with great mass;

no flower ever opened
so staunch a white leaf,
no flower ever parted silver
from such rare silver;

O white pear,
your flower-tufts,
thick on the branch,
bring summer and ripe fruits
in their purple hearts.

Lethe

Nor skin nor hide nor fleece
    Shall cover you,
Nor curtain of crimson nor fine
Shelter of cedar-wood be over you,
    Nor the fir-tree
    Nor the pine.

Nor sight of whin nor gorse
    Nor river-yew,
Nor fragrance of flowering bush,
Nor wailing of reed-bird to waken you,
    Nor of linnet,
    Nor of thrush.

Nor word nor touch nor sight
    Of lover, you
Shall long through the night but for this:
The roll of the full tide to cover you
    Without question,
    Without kiss.

JOHN GOULD FLETCHER
(1886–1950)

Clipper Ships

Beautiful as a tiered cloud, skysails set and shrouds twanging, she
    emerges from the surges that keep running away before day on the
    low Pacific shore. With the roar of the wind blowing half a gale after,
    she heels and lunges, and buries her bows in the smother, lifting
    them swiftly, and scattering the glistening spray-drops from her jib-
    sails with laughter. Her spars are cracking, her royals are half split-
    ting, her lower stun-sail booms are bent aside, like bowstrings ready
    to loose, and the water is roaring into her scuppers, but she still
    staggers out under a full press of sail, her upper trucks enkindled by
    the sun into shafts of rosy flame.
Oh, the anchor is up and the sails they are set, and it's 'way Rio; 'round
    Cape Stiff and up to Boston, ninety days hauling at the ropes: the
    decks slope and the stays creak as she lurches into it, sending her jib
    awash at every thrust, and a handful of dust and a thirst to make you
    weep, are all we get for being two years away to sea.
Topgallant stunsail has carried away! Ease the spanker! The anchor is
    rusted on the deck. Men in short duck trousers, wide-brimmed straw
    hats, with brown mahogany faces, pace up and down, spinning the
    wornout yarns they told a year ago. Some are coiling rope; some
    smoke; "Chips" is picking oakum near the boats. Ten thousand
    miles away lies their last port. In the rigging climbs a hairy monkey,
    and a green parakeet screams at the masthead. In the dead calm of a
    boiling noonday near the line, she lifts her spread of shining canvas
    from heel to truck, from jib o' jib to ringtail, from moonsails to
    watersails. Men have hung their washing in the stays so she can get
    more way on her. She ghosts along before an imperceptible breeze,
    the sails hanging limp in the cross-trees, and clashing against the
    masts. She is a proud white albatross skimming across the ocean,
    beautiful as a tiered cloud. Oh, a Yankee ship comes down the river;
    blow, boys, blow; her yards and masts they shine like silver; blow,

my bully boys, blow; she's a crack ship, a dandy clipper, nine hundred miles from land; she's a down-Easter from Massachusetts, and she's bound to the Rio Grande!

Where are the men who put to sea in her on her first voyage? Some have piled their bones in California among the hides; some died frozen off the Horn in snowstorms; some slipped down between two greybacks, when the yards were joggled suddenly. Still she glistens beautifully, her decks snow-white with constant scrubbing as she sweeps into some empty sailless bay which sleeps all day, where the wild deer skip away when she fires her eighteen-pounder, the sound reverberating about the empty hills. San Francisco? No: San Francisco will not be built for a dozen years to come. Meanwhile she hums with the tumult of loading. The mutineers, even, are let out of their irons and flogged and fed. Every day from when the dawn flares up red amid the hills to the hour it drops dead to westward, men walk gawkily, balancing on their heads the burden of heavy, stiff hides. Now the anchor is up and the sails they are set, and it's 'way Rio. Boston girls are pulling at the ropes: only three months of trouble yet: time for us to go!

Beautiful as a tiered cloud she flies out seaward, and on her decks loaf and stumble a luckless crowd; the filthy sweepings of the stews. In a week, in a day, they have spent a year's wages, swilling it away and letting the waste of it run down among the gutters. How were these deadbeats bribed to go? Only the Ann Street runners know. Dagos, Dutchmen, Souwegians, niggers, crimp-captured greenhorns, they loaf up on the afterdeck, some of them already wrecks, so sick they wish they had never been born. Before them all the "old man" calls for a bucket of salt water to wash off his shore face. While he is at it, telling them how he will haze them till they are dead if they try soldiering, but it will be good grub and easy work if they hand, reef, and steer, and heave the lead, his officers are below, rummaging through the men's dunnage, pulling out heavers, prickers, rum bottles, sheath knives, and pistols. On each grizzled half-cowed face appears something between a sheepish grin, a smirk of fear, a threat of treachery, and the dogged resignation of a brute. But the mate—Bucko Douglas is his name—is the very same that booted three men off the masthead when they were shortening sail in the teeth of a Cape Horn snorter. Two of them fell into the sea, and the third was tossed still groaning into the water. Only last night the captain stuck his cigar butt into one poor swabber's face for not minding the compass, and gave Jim Baines a taste of ratline hash for coming up on deck with dirty hands. Meanwhile under a grand spread of canvas, one hundred feet from side to side, the ship rides up the parallels. From aloft through the blue stillness of a tropic night, crammed with stars, with thunder brewing in the horizon, a mournful echo rises and swells:

Oh, my name is hanging Johnny,
Hooray, hooray!
Oh, my name is hanging Johnny,
So hang, boys, hang.

The "Great Republic," launched before thirty thousand people, her main truck overlooking the highest steeple of the town, the eagle at her bows, and colours flying, now in her first and last port, is slowly dying. She is a charred hulk, with toppling masts, seared gliding, and blistered sides. The "Alert" no more slides pertly through the bergs of the Horn. The desolate barrens of Staten Land, where no man was ever born, hold her bones. The Black Baller "Lightning," that took eighty thousand dollars' worth of cargo around the world in one quick trip, was hurled and ripped to pieces on some uncharted reef or other. The "Dreadnought" disappeared in a hurricane's smother of foam. The "Sovereign of the Seas," that never furled her topsails for ten years, was sheared clean amidships by the bows of an iron steamer as she left her last port. The slaver, "Bald Eagle," cut an unlucky career short when she parted with her anchor and piled up on the Paracels where the pirate junks are waiting for every ship that swells out over the horizon. The "Antelope" was caught off the Grand Ladrone in the northeast monsoon; she's gone. The "Flying Cloud," proud as she was of beating every ship that carried the Stars and Stripes or the St. George's flag, could not race faster than a thunderbolt that fell one day on her deck and turned her to a cloud of flame—everything burned away but her fame! No more will California hear the little "Pilgrim's" parting cheer. The crew took to an open boat when their ship was scuttled by a privateer. So they die out, year after year. Sometimes the lookout on a great steamer wallowing and threshing through the heavy seas by night, sees far off on his lee quarter something like a lofty swinging light. Beautiful as a tiered cloud, a ghostly clipper-ship emerges from the surges that keep running away before day on the low Pacific shore. Her upper works are enkindled by the sun into shafts of rosy flame. Swimming like a duck, steering like a fish, easy yet dry, lively yet stiff, she lifts cloud on cloud of crowded stainless sail. She creeps abeam, within hail, she dips, she chases, she outpaces like a mettlesome racer the lumbering tea-kettle that keeps her company. Before she fades into the weather quarter, the lookout cries: "Holy Jiggers, are you the Flying Dutchman, that you go two knots to our one?" Hoarsely comes back this answer from the sail: "Challenge is our name: America our nation: Bully Waterman our master: we can beat Creation."

And it's 'way Rio;
Way—hay—hay, Rio;
O, fare you well, my pretty young girl,
For we're bound to the Rio Grande.

MARIANNE MOORE

(1887–1972)

Poetry

I, too, dislike it: there are things that are important beyond
        all this fiddle.
  Reading it, however, with a perfect contempt for it, one
        discovers in
  it after all, a place for the genuine.
      Hands that can grasp, eyes
      that can dilate, hair that can rise
        if it must, these things are important not because a

high-sounding interpretation can be put upon them but be-
        cause they are
  useful. When they become so derivative as to become
        unintelligible,
  the same thing may be said for all of us, that we
      do not admire what
      we cannot understand: the bat
        holding on upside down or in quest of something to

eat, elephants pushing, a wild horse taking a roll, a tireless
        wolf under
  a tree, the immovable critic twitching his skin like a horse
        that feels a flea, the base-
  ball fan, the statistician—
      nor is it valid
      to discriminate against "business documents and

school-books"; all these phenomena are important. One
        must make a distinction
  however: when dragged into prominence by half poets,
        the result is not poetry,
  nor till the poets among us can be
      "literalists of
      the imagination"—above
        insolence and triviality and can present

for inspection, "imaginary gardens with real toads in them,"
        shall we have
  it. In the meantime, if you demand on the one hand,
  the raw material of poetry in
      all its rawness and
      that which is on the other hand
        genuine, you are interested in poetry.

T.S. ELIOT
(1888–1965)

Preludes

I
The winter evening settles down
With smell of steaks in passageways.
Six o'clock.
The burnt-out ends of smoky days.
And now a gusty shower wraps
The grimy scraps
Of withered leaves about your feet
And newspapers from vacant lots;
The showers beat
On broken blinds and chimney-pots,
And at the corner of the street
A lonely cab-horse steams and stamps.
And then the lighting of the lamps.

II
The morning comes to consciousness
Of faint stale smells of beer
From the sawdust-trampled street
With all its muddy feet that press
To early coffee-stands.
With the other masquerades
That time resumes,
One thinks of all the hands
That are raising dingy shades
In a thousand furnished rooms.

III
You tossed a blanket from the bed,
You lay upon your back, and waited;
You dozed, and watched the night revealing
The thousand sordid images
Of which your soul was constituted;
They flickered against the ceiling.
And when all the world came back
And the light crept up between the shutters
And you heard the sparrows in the gutters,
You had such a vision of the street
As the street hardly understands;
Sitting along the bed's edge, where

You curled the papers from your hair,
Or clasped the yellow soles of feet
In the palms of both soiled hands.

IV
His soul stretched tight across the skies
That fade behind a city block,
Or trampled by insistent feet
At four and five and six o'clock;
And short square fingers stuffing pipes,
And evening newspapers, and eyes
Assured of certain certainties,
The conscience of a blackened street
Impatient to assume the world.

    I am moved by fancies that are curled
Around these images, and cling:
The notion of some infinitely gentle
Infinitely suffering thing.

    Wipe your hand across your mouth, and laugh;
The worlds revolve like ancient women
Gathering fuel in vacant lots.

The Love Song of J. Alfred Prufrock

S'io credesse che mia risposta fosse
A persona che mai tornasse al mondo,
Questa fiamma staria senza piu scosse.
Ma perciocche giammai di questo fondo
Non tornò vivo alcun, s'i'odo il vero,
Senza tema d'infamia ti rispondo.

 Let us go then, you and I,
When the evening is spread out against the sky
Like a patient etherised upon a table;
Let us go, through certain half-deserted streets,
The muttering retreats
Of restless nights in one-night cheap hotels
And sawdust restaurants with oyster-shells:
Streets that follow like a tedious argument
Of insidious intent
To lead you to an overwhelming question . . .
Oh, do not ask, "What is it?"
Let us go and make our visit.

In the room the women come and go
Talking of Michelangelo.

The yellow fog that rubs its back upon the window-panes,
The yellow smoke that rubs its muzzle on the window-panes
Licked its tongue into the corners of the evening.
Lingered upon the pools that stand in drains,
Let fall upon its back the soot that falls from chimneys,
Slipped by the terrace, made a sudden leap,
And seeing that it was a soft October night,
Curled once about the house, and fell asleep.

And indeed there will be time
For the yellow smoke that slides along the street,
Rubbing its back upon the window-panes;
There will be time, there will be time
To prepare a face to meet the faces that you meet;
There will be time to murder and create,
And time for all the works and days of hands
That lift and drop a question on your plate;
Time for you and time for me,
And time yet for a hundred indecisions,
And for a hundred visions and revisions,
Before the taking of a toast and tea.

In the room the women come and go
Talking of Michelangelo.

And indeed there will be time
To wonder, "Do I dare?" and, "Do I dare?"
Time to turn back and descend the stair,
With a bald spot in the middle of my hair—
(They will say: "How his hair is growing thin!")
My morning coat, my collar mounting firmly to the chin,
My necktie rich and modest, but asserted by a simple pin—
(They will say: "But how his arms and legs are thin!")
Do I dare
Disturb the universe?
In a minute there is time
For decisions and revisions which a minute will reverse.

For I have known them all already, known them all:—
Have known the evenings, mornings, afternoons,
I have measured out my life with coffee spoons;
I know the voices dying with a dying fall
Beneath the music from a farther room.
    So how should I presume?

And I have known the eyes already, known them all—
The eyes that fix you in a formulated phrase,
And when I am formulated, sprawling on a pin,
When I am pinned and wriggling on the wall,
Then how should I begin
To spit out all the butt-ends of my days and ways?
    And how should I presume?

And I have known the arms already, known them all—
Arms that are braceleted and white and bare
[But in the lamplight, downed with light brown hair!]
Is it perfume from a dress
That makes me so digress?
Arms that lie along a table, or wrap about a shawl.
    And should I then presume?
    And how should I begin?

                  *   *   *

Shall I say, I have gone at dusk through narrow streets
And watched the smoke that rises from the pipes
Of lonely men in shirt-sleeves, leaning out of windows? . . .

I should have been a pair of ragged claws
Scuttling across the floors of silent seas.

                  *   *   *

And the afternoon, the evening, sleeps so peacefully!
Smoothed by long fingers,
Asleep . . . tired . . . or it malingers,
Stretched on the floor, here beside you and me.
Should I, after tea and cakes and ices,
Have the strength to force the moment to its crisis?
But though I have wept and fasted, wept and prayed,
Though I have seen my head [grown slightly bald] brought in upon a
                                            platter,
I am no prophet—and here's no great matter;
I have seen the moment of my greatness flicker,
And I have seen the eternal Footman hold my coat, and snicker,
And in short, I was afraid.

And would it have been worth it, after all,
After the cups, the marmalade, the tea,
Among the porcelain, among some talk of you and me,
Would it have been worth while,
To have bitten off the matter with a smile,
To have squeezed the universe into a ball
To roll it toward some overwhelming question,

To say: "I am Lazarus, come from the dead,
Come back to tell you all, I shall tell you all"—
If one, settling a pillow by her head,
   Should say: "That is not what I meant at all.
   That is not it, at all."

And would it have been worth it, after all,
Would it have been worth while,
After the sunsets and the dooryards and the sprinkled streets,
After the novels, after the teacups, after the skirts that trail
                              along the floor—
And this, and so much more?—
It is impossible to say just what I mean!
But as if a magic lantern threw the nerves in patterns on a screen:
Would it have been worth while
If one, settling a pillow or throwing off a shawl,
And turning toward the window, should say:
   "That is not it at all,
   That is not what I meant, at all."

*   *   *

No! I am not Prince Hamlet, nor was meant to be;
Am an attendant lord, one that will do
To swell a progress, start a scene or two,
Advise the prince; no doubt, an easy tool,
Deferential, glad to be of use,
Politic, cautious, and meticulous;
Full of high sentence, but a bit obtuse;
At times, indeed, almost ridiculous—
Almost, at times, the Fool.

I grow old . . . I grow old . . .
I shall wear the bottoms of my trousers rolled.

Shall I part my hair behind? Do I dare to eat a peach?
I shall wear white flannel trousers, and walk upon the beach.
I have heard the mermaids singing, each to each.

I do not think that they will sing to me.

I have seen them riding seaward on the waves
Combing the white hair of the waves blown back
When the wind blows the water white and black.

We have lingered in the chambers of the sea
By sea-girls wreathed with seaweed red and brown
Till human voices wake us, and we drown.

Morning at the Window

They are rattling breakfast plates in basement kitchens,
And along the trampled edges of the street
I am aware of the damp souls of housemaids
Sprouting despondently at area gates.

The brown waves of fog toss up to me
Twisted faces from the bottom of the street,
And tear from a passer-by with muddy skirts
An aimless smile that hovers in the air
And vanishes along the level of the roofs.

Gerontion

Thou hast nor youth nor age
But as it were an after dinner sleep
Dreaming of both.

Here I am, an old man in a dry month,
Being read to by a boy, waiting for rain.
I was neither at the hot gates
Nor fought in the warm rain
Nor knee deep in the salt marsh, heaving a cutlass,
Bitten by flies, fought.
My house is a decayed house,
And the Jew squats on the window sill, the owner,
Spawned in some estaminet of Antwerp,
Blistered in Brussels, patched and peeled in London.
The goat coughs at night in the field overhead;
Rocks, moss, stonecrop, iron, merds.
The woman keeps the kitchen, makes tea,
Sneezes at evening, poking the peevish gutter.
                    I an old man,
A dull head among windy spaces.

Signs are taken for wonders. "We would see a sign!"
The word within a word, unable to speak a word,
Swaddled with darkness. In the juvenescence of the year
Came Christ the tiger

In depraved May, dogwood and chestnut, flowering judas,
To be eaten, to be divided, to be drunk
Among whispers; by Mr. Silvero
With caressing hands, at Limoges
Who walked all night in the next room;

By Hakagawa, bowing among the Titians;
By Madame de Tornquist, in the dark room
Shifting the candles; Fräulein von Kulp
Who turned in the hall, one hand on the door. Vacant shuttles
Weave the wind. I have no ghosts,
An old man in a draughty house
Under a windy knob.

After such knowledge, what forgiveness? Think now
History has many cunning passages, contrived corridors
And issues, deceives with whispering ambitions,
Guides us by vanities. Think now
She gives when our attention is distracted
And what she gives, gives with such supple confusions
That the giving famishes the craving. Gives too late
What's not believed in, or if still believed,
In memory only, reconsidered passion. Gives too soon
Into weak hands, what's thought can be dispensed with
Till the refusal propagates a fear. Think
Neither fear nor courage saves us. Unnatural vices
Are fathered by our heroism. Virtues
Are forced upon us by our impudent crimes.
These tears are shaken from the wrath-bearing tree.

The tiger springs in the new year. Us he devours. Think at last
We have not reached conclusion, when I
Stiffen in a rented house. Think at last
I have not made this show purposelessly
And it is not by any concitation
Of the backward devils.
I would meet you upon this honestly.
I that was near your heart was removed therefrom
To lose beauty in terror, terror in inquisition.
I have lost my passion: why should I need to keep it
Since what is kept must be adulterated?
I have lost my sight, smell, hearing, taste and touch:
How should I use them for your closer contact?

These with a thousand small deliberations
Protract the profit of their chilled delirium,
Excite the membrane, when the sense has cooled,
With pungent sauces, multiply variety
In a wilderness of mirrors. What will the spider do,
Suspend its operations, will the weevil
Delay? De Bailhache, Fresca, Mrs. Cammel, whirled
Beyond the circuit of the shuddering Bear
In fractured atoms. Gull against the wind, in the windy straits

Of Belle Isle, or running on the Horn,
White feathers in the snow, the Gulf claims,
And an old man driven by the Trades
To a sleepy corner.

                              Tenants of the house,
Thoughts of a dry brain in a dry season.

The Hippopotamus

The broad-backed hippopotamus
Rests on his belly in the mud;
Although he seems so firm to us
He is merely flesh and blood.

Flesh and blood is weak and frail,
Susceptible to nervous shock;
While the True Church can never fail
For it is based upon a rock.

The hippo's feeble steps may err
In compassing material ends,
While the True Church need never stir
To gather in its dividends.

The 'potamus can never reach
The mango on the mango-tree;
But fruits of pomegranate and peach
Refresh the Church from over sea.

At mating time the hippo's voice
Betrays inflexions hoarse and odd,
But every week we hear rejoice
The Church, at being one with God.

The hippopotamus' day
Is passed in sleep; at night he hunts;
God works in a mysterious way—
The Church can sleep and feed at once.

I saw the 'potamus take wing
Ascending from the damp savannas,
And quiring angels round him sing
The praise of God, in loud hosannas.

Blood of the Lamb shall wash him clean
And him shall heavenly arms enfold,
Among the saints he shall be seen
Performing on a harp of gold.

He shall be washed as white as snow,
By all the martyr'd virgins kist,
While the True Church remains below
Wrapt in the old miasmal mist.

The Waste Land

"Nam Sibyllam quidem Cumis ego ipse oculis meis vidi in ampulla pendere, et cum illi pueri dicerent: Σίβυλλα τί θέλεις respondebat illa: ἀποθανεῖν θέλω."

FOR EZRA POUND
il miglior fabbro

I. THE BURIAL OF THE DEAD

April is the cruellest month, breeding
Lilacs out of the dead land, mixing
Memory and desire, stirring
Dull roots with spring rain.
Winter kept us warm, covering
Earth in forgetful snow, feeding
A little life with dried tubers.
Summer surprised us, coming over the Starnbergersee
With a shower of rain; we stopped in the colonnade,
And went on in sunlight, into the Hofgarten,
And drank coffee, and talked for an hour.
Bin gar keine Russin, stamm' aus Litauen, echt deutsch.
And when we were children, staying at the archduke's,
My cousin's, he took me out on a sled,
And I was frightened. He said, Marie,
Marie, hold on tight. And down we went.
In the mountains, there you feel free.
I read, much of the night, and go south in the winter.

What are the roots that clutch, what branches grow
Out of this stony rubbish? Son of man,
You cannot say, or guess, for you know only
A heap of broken images, where the sun beats,
And the dead tree gives no shelter, the cricket no relief,

And the dry stone no sound of water. Only
There is a shadow under this red rock,
(Come in under the shadow of this red rock),
And I will show you something different from either
Your shadow at morning striding behind you
Or your shadow at evening rising to meet you;
I will show you fear in a handful of dust.
            Frisch weht der Wind
            Der Heimat zu
            Mein Irisch Kind,
            Wo weilest du?
"You gave me hyacinths first a year ago;
"They called me the hyacinth girl."
—Yet when we came back, late, from the hyacinth garden,
Your arms full, and your hair wet, I could not
Speak, and my eyes failed, I was neither
Living nor dead, and I knew nothing,
Looking into the heart of light, the silence.
Oed' und leer das Meer.

Madame Sosostris, famous clairvoyante,
Had a bad cold, nevertheless
Is known to the wisest woman in Europe,
With a wicked pack of cards. Here, said she,
Is your card, the drowned Phoenician Sailor,
(Those are pearls that were his eyes. Look!)
Here is Belladona, the Lady of the Rocks,
The lady of situations.
Here is the man with three staves, and here the Wheel,
And here is the one-eyed merchant, and this card,
Which is blank, is something he carries on his back,
Which I am forbidden to see. I do not find
The Hanged Man. Fear death by water.
I see crowds of people, walking round in a ring.
Thank you. If you see dear Mrs. Equitone,
Tell her I bring the horoscope myself:
One must be so careful these days.

Unreal City,
Under the brown fog of a winter dawn,
A crowd flowed over London Bridge, so many,
I had not thought death had undone so many.
Sighs, short and infrequent, were exhaled,
And each man fixed his eyes before his feet.
Flowed up the hill and down King William Street,
To where Saint Mary Woolnoth kept the hours
With a dead sound on the final stroke of nine.

There I saw one I knew, and stopped him crying: "Stetson!
"You who were with me in the ships at Mylae!
"That corpse you planted last year in your garden,
"Has it begun to sprout? Will it bloom this year?
"Or has the sudden frost disturbed its bed?
"Oh keep the Dog far hence, that's friend to men,
"Or with his nails he'll dig it up again!
"You! hypocrite lecteur!—mon semblable,—mon frère!"

II. A GAME OF CHESS

The Chair she sat in, like a burnished throne,
Glowed on the marble, where the glass
Held up by standards wrought with fruited vines
From which a golden Cupidon peeped out
(Another hid his eyes behind his wing)
Doubled the flames of sevenbranched candelabra
Reflecting light upon the table as
The glitter of her jewels rose to meet it,
From satin cases poured in rich profusion;
In vials of ivory and coloured glass
Unstoppered, lurked her strange synthetic perfumes,
Unguent, powdered, or liquid—troubled, confused
And drowned the sense in odours; stirred by the air
That freshened from the window, these ascended
In fattening the prolonged candle-flames,
Flung their smoke into the laquearia,
Stirring the pattern on the coffered ceiling.
Huge sea-wood fed with copper
Burned green and orange, framed by the coloured stone,
In which sad light a carvèd dolphin swam.
Above the antique mantel was displayed
As though a window gave upon the sylvan scene
The change of Philomel, by the barbarous king
So rudely forced; yet there the nightingale
Filled all the desert with inviolable voice
And still she cried, and still the world pursues,
"Jug Jug" to dirty ears.
And other withered stumps of time
Were told upon the walls; staring forms
Leaned out, leaning, hushing the room enclosed.
Footsteps shuffled on the stair.
Under the firelight, under the brush, her hair
Spread out in fiery points
Glowed into words, then would be savagely still.

"My nerves are bad to-night. Yes, bad. Stay with me.
"Speak to me. Why do you never speak. Speak.
        "What are you thinking of? What thinking? What?
"I never know what you are thinking. Think."

I think we are in rats' alley
Where the dead men lost their bones.

"What is that noise?"
                        The wind under the door.
"What is that noise now? What is the wind doing?"
                        Nothing again nothing.
                                        "Do
"You know nothing? Do you see nothing? Do you remember
"Nothing?"

    I remember
Those are pearls that were his eyes.
"Are you alive, or not? Is there nothing in your head?"
                                            But
O O O O that Shakespeherian Rag—
It's so elegant
So intelligent
"What shall I do now? What shall I do?"
"I shall rush out as I am, and walk the street
"With my hair down, so. What shall we do to-morrow?
"What shall we ever do?"
                        The hot water at ten.
And if it rains, a closed car at four.
And we shall play a game of chess,
Pressing lidless eyes and waiting for a knock upon the door.

When Lil's husband got demobbed, I said—
I didn't mince my words, I said to her myself,
Hurry up please its time
Now Albert's coming back, make yourself a bit smart.
He'll want to know what you done with that money he gave you
To get yourself some teeth. He did, I was there.
You have them all out, Lil, and get a nice set,
He said, I swear, I can't bear to look at you.
And no more can't I, I said, and think of poor Albert,
He's been in the army four years, he wants a good time,
And if you don't give it him, there's others will, I said.
Oh is there, she said. Something o' that, I said.
Then I'll know who to thank, she said, and give me a straight look.
Hurry up please its time
If you don't like it you can get on with it, I said.

Others can pick and choose if you can't.
But if Albert makes off, it won't be for lack of telling.
You ought to be ashamed, I said, to look so antique.
(And her only thirty-one.)
I can't help it, she said, pulling a long face,
It's them pills I took, to bring it off, she said.
(She's had five already, and nearly died of young George.)
The chemist said it would be all right, but I've never been the same.
You are a proper fool, I said.
Well, if Albert won't leave you alone, there it is, I said,
What you get married for if you don't want children?
HURRY UP PLEASE ITS TIME
Well, that Sunday Albert was home, they had a hot gammon,
And they asked me in to dinner, to get the beauty of it hot—
HURRY UP PLEASE ITS TIME
HURRY UP PLEASE ITS TIME
Goonight Bill. Goonight Lou. Goonight May. Goonight.
Ta ta. Goonight. Goonight.
Good night, ladies, good night, sweet ladies, good night, good night.

III. THE FIRE SERMON

The river's tent is broken: the last fingers of leaf
Clutch and sink into the wet bank. The wind
Crosses the brown land, unheard. The nymphs are departed.
Sweet Thames, run softly, till I end my song.
The river bears no empty bottles, sandwich papers,
Silk handkerchiefs, cardboard boxes, cigarette ends
Or other testimony of summer nights. The nymphs are departed.
And their friends, the loitering heirs of City directors;
Departed, have left no addresses.
By the waters of Leman I sat down and wept . . .
Sweet Thames, run softly till I end my song,
Sweet Thames, run softly, for I speak not loud or long.
But at my back in a cold blast I hear
The rattle of the bones, and chuckle spread from ear to ear.

A rat crept softly through the vegetation
Dragging its slimy belly on the bank
While I was fishing in the dull canal
On a winter evening round behind the gashouse
Musing upon the king my brother's wreck
And on the king my father's death before him.
White bodies naked on the low damp ground
And bones cast in a little low dry garret,

Rattled by the rat's foot only, year to year.
But at my back from time to time I hear
The sound of horns and motors, which shall bring
Sweeney to Mrs. Porter in the spring.
O the moon shone bright on Mrs. Porter
And on her daughter
They wash their feet in soda water
Et O ces voix d'enfants, chantant dans la coupole!

Twit twit twit
Jug jug jug jug jug jug
So rudely forc'd.
Tereu

Unreal City
Under the brown fog of a winter noon
Mr. Eugenides, the Smyrna merchant
Unshaven, with a pocket full of currants
C.i.f. London: documents at sight,
Asked me in demotic French
To luncheon at the Cannon Street Hotel
Followed by a weekend at the Metropole.

At the violet hour, when the eyes and back
Turn upward from the desk, when the human engine waits
Like a taxi throbbing waiting,
I Tiresias, though blind, throbbing between two lives,
Old man with wrinkled female breasts, can see
At the violet hour, the evening hour that strives
Homeward, and brings the sailor home from sea,
The typist home at teatime, clears her breakfast, lights
Her stove, and lays out food in tins.
Out of the window perilously spread
Her drying combinations touched by the suns' last rays,
On the divan are piled (at night her bed)
Stockings, slippers, camisoles, and stays.
I Tiresias, old man with wrinkled dugs
Perceived the scene, and foretold the rest—
I too awaited the expected guest.
He, the young man carbuncular, arrives,
A small house agent's clerk, with one bold stare,
One of the low on whom assurance sits
As a silk hat on a Bradford millionaire.
The time is now propitious, as he guesses,
The meal is ended, she is bored and tired,
Endeavours to engage her in caresses
Which still are unreproved, if undesired.

Flushed and decided, he assaults at once;
Exploring hands encounter no defence;
His vanity requires no response,
And makes a welcome of indifference.
(And I Tiresias have foresuffered all
Enacted on this same divan or bed;
I who have sat by Thebes below the wall
And walked among the lowest of the dead.)
Bestows one final patronising kiss,
And gropes his way, finding the stairs unlit. . . .

She turns and looks a moment in the glass,
Hardly aware of her departed lover;
Her brain allows one half-formed thought to pass:
"Well now that's done: and I'm glad it's over."
When lovely woman stoops to folly and
Paces about her room again, alone,
She smoothes her hair with automatic hand,
And puts a record on the gramophone.

"This music crept by me upon the waters"
And along the Strand, up Queen Victoria Street.
O City city, I can sometimes hear
Beside a public bar in Lower Thames Street,
The pleasant whining of a mandoline
And a clatter and a chatter from within
Where fishmen lounge at noon: where the walls
Of Magnus Martyr hold
Inexplicable splendour of Ionian white and gold.

        The river sweats
        Oil and tar
        The barges drift
        With the turning tide
        Red sails
        Wide
        To leeward, swing on the heavy spar.
        The barges wash
        Drifting logs
        Down Greenwich reach
        Past the Isle of Dogs.
                Weialala leia
                Wallala leialala

Elizabeth and Leicester
Beating oars
The stern was formed
A gilded shell
Red and gold
The brisk swell
Rippled both shores
Southwest wind
Carried down stream
The peal of bells
White towers
                    Weialala leia
                    Wallala leialala

"Trams and dusty trees.
Highbury bore me. Richmond and Kew
Undid me. By Richmond I raised my knees
Supine on the floor of a narrow canoe."

"My feet are at Moorgate, and my heart
Under my feet. After the event
He wept. He promised 'a new start.'
I made no comment. What should I resent?"

"On Margate Sands.
I can connect
Nothing with nothing.
The broken fingernails of dirty hands.
My people humble people who expect
Nothing."
                    la la

To Carthage then I came

Burning burning burning burning
O Lord Thou pluckest me out
O Lord Thou pluckest

burning

IV. DEATH BY WATER

Phlebas the Phoenician, a fortnight dead,
Forgot the cry of gulls, and the deep sea swell
And the profit and loss.
                              A current under sea
Picked his bones in whispers. As he rose and fell
He passed the stages of his age and youth
Entering the whirlpool.
                              Gentile or Jew
O you who turn the wheel and look to windward,
Consider Phlebas, who was once handsome and tall as you.

V. WHAT THE THUNDER SAID

After the torchlight red on sweaty faces
After the frosty silence in the gardens
After the agony in stony places
The shouting and the crying
Prison and palace and reverberation
Of thunder of spring over distant mountains
He who was living is now dead
We who were living are now dying
With a little patience

Here is no water but only rock
Rock and no water and the sandy road
The road winding above among the mountains
Which are mountains of rock without water
If there were water we should stop and drink
Amongst the rock one cannot stop or think
Sweat is dry and feet are in the sand
If there were only water amongst the rock
Dead mountain mouth of carious teeth that cannot spit
Here one can neither stand nor lie nor sit
There is not even silence in the mountains
But dry sterile thunder without rain
There is not even solitude in the mountains
But red sullen faces sneer and snarl
From doors of mudcracked houses
                              If there were water
  And no rock
  If there were rock
  And also water
  And water

A spring
A pool among the rock
If there were the sound of water only
Not the cicada
And dry grass singing
But sound of water over a rock
Where the hermit-thrush sings in the pine trees
Drip drop drip drop drop drop drop
But there is no water

Who is the third who walks always beside you?
When I count, there are only you and I together
But when I look ahead up the white road
There is always another one walking beside you
Gliding wrapt in a brown mantle, hooded
I do not know whether a man or a woman
—But who is that on the other side of you?

What is that sound high in the air
Murmur of maternal lamentation
Who are those hooded hordes swarming
Over endless plains, stumbling in cracked earth
Ringed by the flat horizon only
What is the city over the mountains
Cracks and reforms and bursts in the violet air
Falling towers
Jerusalem Athens Alexandria
Vienna London
Unreal

A woman drew her long black hair out tight
And fiddled whisper music on those strings
And bats with baby faces in the violet light
Whistled, and beat their wings
And crawled head downward down a blackened wall
And upside down in air were towers
Tolling reminiscent bells, that kept the hours
And voices singing out of empty cisterns and exhausted wells.

In this decayed hole among the mountains
In the faint moonlight, the grass is singing
Over the tumbled graves, about the chapel
There is the empty chapel, only the wind's home.
It has no windows, and the door swings,
Dry bones can harm no one.
Only a cock stood on the rooftree
Co co rico co co rico

In a flash of lightning. Then a damp gust
Bringing rain

Ganga was sunken, and the limp leaves
Waited for rain, while the black clouds
Gathered far distant, over Himavant.
The jungle crouched, humped in silence.
Then spoke the thunder
DA
Datta: what have we given?
My friend, blood shaking my heart
The awful daring of a moment's surrender
Which an age of prudence can never retract
By this, and this only, we have existed
Which is not to be found in our obituaries
Or in memories draped by the beneficent spider
Or under seals broken by the lean solicitor
In our empty rooms
DA
Dayadhvam: I have heard the key
Turn in the door once and turn once only
We think of the key, each in his prison
Thinking of the key, each confirms a prison
Only at nightfall, aetheral rumours
Revive for a moment a broken Coriolanus
DA
Damyata: The boat responded
Gaily, to the hand expert with sail and oar
The sea was calm, your heart would have responded
Gaily, when invited, beating obedient
To controlling hands
                           I sat upon the shore
Fishing, with the arid plain behind me
Shall I at least set my lands in order?
London Bridge is falling down falling down falling down
Poi s'ascose nel foco che gli affina
Quando fiam uti chelidon—O swallow swallow
Le Prince d'Aquitaine à la tour abolie
These fragments I have shored against my ruins
Why then Ile fit you. Hieronymo's mad againe.
Datta. Dayadhvam. Damyata.
        Shantih   shantih   shantih

_____

Notes on "THE WASTE LAND"

Not only the title, but the plan and a good deal of the incidental symbolism of the poem were suggested by Miss Jessie L. Weston's book on the Grail legend: *From Ritual to Romance* (Cambridge). Indeed, so deeply am I indebted, Miss Weston's book will elucidate the difficulties of the poem much better than my notes can do; and I recommend it (apart from the great interest of the book itself) to any who think such elucidation of the poem worth the trouble. To another work of anthropology I am indebted in general, one which has influenced our generation profoundly; I mean *The Golden Bough;* I have used especially the two volumes *Adonis, Attis, Osiris.* Anyone who is acquainted with these works will immediately recognise in the poem certain references to vegetation ceremonies.

I. THE BURIAL OF THE DEAD

Line 20. Cf. Ezekiel II, i.

23. Cf. Ecclesiastes XII, v.

31. V. Tristan und Isolde, I, verses 5–8.

42. Id. III, verse 24.

46. I am not familiar with the exact constitution of the Tarot pack of cards, from which I have obviously departed to suit my own convenience. The Hanged Man, a member of the traditional pack, fits my purpose in two ways: because he is associated in my mind with the Hanged God of Frazer, and because I associate him with the hooded figure in the passage of the disciples to Emmaus in Part V. The Phoenician Sailor and the Merchant appear later; also the "crowds of people," and Death by Water is executed in Part IV. The Man with Three Staves (an authentic member of the Tarot pack) I associate, quite arbitrarily, with the Fisher King himself.

60. Cf. Baudelaire:
"Fourmillante cité, cité pleine de rêves,
"Où le spectre en plein jour raccroche le passant."

63. Cf. Inferno III, 55–57:
". . . . . si lunga tratta
di gente, ch'io non avrei mai creduto
che morte tanta n'avesse disfatta."

64. Cf. Inferno IV, 25–27:
"Quivi, secondo che per ascoltare,
"non avea pianto, ma' che di sospiri,
"che l'aura eterna facevan tremare."

68. A phenomenon which I have often noticed.

74. Cf. the Dirge in Webster's *White Devil.*

76. V. Baudelaire, Preface to *Fleurs du Mal.*

II. A GAME OF CHESS

77. Cf. *Antony and Cleopatra,* II, ii, l. 190.
92. Laquearia. V. *Aeneid,* I, 726:
    dependent lychni laquearibus aureis incensi, et noctem flammis
    funalia vincunt.
98. Sylvan scene. V. Milton, *Paradise Lost,* IV, 140.
99. V. Ovid, *Metamorphoses,* VI, Philomela.
100. Cf. Part III, l. 204.
115. Cf. Part III, l. 195.
118. Cf. Webster: "Is the wind in that door still?"
126. Cf. Part I, l. 37, 48.
138. Cf. the game of chess in Middleton's *Women beware Women.*

III. THE FIRE SERMON

176. V. Spenser, *Prothalamion.*
192. Cf. *The Tempest,* I, ii.
196. Cf. Marvell, *To His Coy Mistress.*
197. Cf. Day, *Parliament of Bees:*
    "When of the sudden, listening, you shall hear,
    "A noise of horns and hunting, which shall bring
    "Actaeon to Diana in the spring,
    "Where all shall see her naked skin . . ."
199. I do not know the origin of the ballad from which these lines are taken: it was reported to me from Sydney, Australia.
202. V. Verlaine, *Parsifal.*
210. The currants were quoted at a price "carriage and insurance free to London"; and the Bill of Lading etc. were to be handed to the buyer upon payment of the sight draft.
218. Tiresias, although a mere spectator and not indeed a "character," is yet the most important personage in the poem, uniting all the rest. Just as the one-eyed merchant, seller of currants, melts into the Phoenician Sailor, and the latter is not wholly distinct from Ferdinand Prince of Naples, so all the women are one woman, and the two sexes meet in Tiresias. What Tiresias *sees,* in fact, is the substance of the poem. The whole passage from Ovid is of great anthropological interest:
'. . . Cum Iunone iocos et maior vestra profecto est
Quam, quae contingit maribus,' dixisse, 'voluptas.'
Illa negat; placuit quae sit sententia docti
Quaerere Tiresiae: venus huic erat utraque nota.
Nam duo magnorum viridi coeuntia silva
Corpora serpentum baculi violaverat ictu
Deque viro factus, mirabile, femina septem
Egerat autumnos; octavo rursus eosdem

Vidit et 'est vestrae si tanta potentia plagae,'
Dixit 'ut auctoris sortem in contraria mutet,
Nunc quoque vos feriam!' percussis anguibus isdem
Forma prior rediit genetivaque venit imago.
Arbiter hic igitur sumptus de lite iocosa
Dicta Iovis firmat; gravius Saturnia iusto
Nec pro materia fertur doluisse suique
Iudicis aeterna damnavit lumina nocte,
At pater omnipotens (neque enim licet inrita cuiquam
Facta dei fecisse deo) pro lumine adempto
Scire futura dedit poenamque levavit honore.

221. This may not appear as exact as Sappho's lines, but I had in mind the "longshore" or "dory" fisherman, who returns at nightfall.

253. V. Goldsmith, the song in *The Vicar of Wakefield.*

257. V. *The Tempest,* as above.

264. The interior of St. Magnus Martyr is to my mind one of the finest among Wren's interiors. See *The Proposed Demolition of Nineteen City Churches:* (P. S. King & Son, Ltd.).

266. The Song of the (three) Thames-daughters begins here. From line 292 to 306 inclusive they speak in turn. V. *Götterdämmerung,* III, i: the Rhine-daughters.

279. V. Froude, *Elizabeth,* Vol. I, ch. iv, letter of De Quadra to Philip of Spain:

"In the afternoon we were in a barge, watching the games on the river. (The queen) was alone with Lord Robert and myself on the poop, when they began to talk nonsense, and went so far that Lord Robert at last said, as I was on the spot there was no reason why they should not be married if the queen pleased."

293. Cf. *Purgatorio,* V, 133:

"Ricorditi di me, che son la Pia;
"Siena mi fe', disfecemi Maremma."

307. V. St. Augustine's *Confessions:* "to Carthage then I came, where a cauldron of unholy loves sang all about mine ears."

308. The complete text of the Buddha's Fire Sermon (which corresponds in importance to the Sermon on the Mount) from which these words are taken, will be found translated in the late Henry Clarke Warren's *Buddhism in Translation* (Harvard Oriental Series). Mr. Warren was one of the great pioneers of Buddhist studies in the Occident.

IV. DEATH BY WATER

309. From St. Augustine's *Confessions* again. The collocation of these two representatives of eastern and western asceticism, as the culmination of this part of the poem, is not an accident.

In the first part of Part V three themes are employed: the journey to Emmaus, the approach to the Chapel Perilous (see Miss Weston's book) and the present decay of eastern Europe.

357. This is *Turdus aonalaschkae pallasii,* the hermit-thrush which I have heard in Quebec Province. Chapman says *(Handbook of Birds of Eastern North America)* "it is most at home in secluded woodland and thickety retreats. . . . Its notes are not remarkable for variety or volume, but in purity and sweetness of tone and exquisite modulation they are unequalled." Its "water-dripping song" is justly celebrated.

360. The following lines were stimulated by the account of one of the Antarctic expeditions (I forget which, but I think one of Shackleton's): it was related that the party of explorers, at the extremity of their strength, had the constant delusion that there was *one more member* than could actually be counted.

366–76. Cf. Hermann Hesse, *Blick ins Chaos:* "Schon ist halb Europa, schon ist zumindest der halbe Osten Europas auf dem Wege zum Chaos, fährt betrunken im heiligem Wahn am Abgrund entlang und singt dazu, singt betrunken und hymnisch wie Dmitri Karamasoff sang. Ueber diese Lieder lacht der Bürger beleidigt, der Heilige und Seher hört sie mit Tränen."

401. "Datta, dayadhvam, damyata" (Give, sympathise, control). The fable of the meaning of the Thunder is found in the *Brihadaranyaka— Upanishad,* 5, 1. A translation is found in Deussen's *Sechzig Upanishads des Veda,* p. 489.

407. Cf. Webster, *The White Devil,* V, vi:
". . . . . they'll remarry
Ere the worm pierce your winding-sheet, ere the spider
Make a thin curtain for your epitaphs."

411. Cf. *Inferno,* XXXIII, 46:
"ed io sentii chiavar l'uscio di sotto
all'orribile torre."
Also F. H. Bradley, *Appearance and Reality,* p. 346.
"My external sensations are no less private to myself than are my thoughts or my feelings. In either case my experience falls within my own circle, a circle closed on the outside; and, with all its elements alike, every sphere is opaque to the others which surround it. . . . In brief, regarded as an existence which appears in a soul, the whole world for each is peculiar and private to that soul."

424. V. Weston: *From Ritual to Romance;* chapter on the Fisher King.

427. V. *Purgatorio,* XXVI, 148.
" 'Ara vos prec per aquella valor
'que vos guida al som de l'escalina,
'sovegna vos a temps de ma dolor.'
Poi s'ascose nel foco che gli affina."

428. V. *Pervigilium Veneris.* Cf. Philomela in Parts II and III.
429. V. Gerard de Nerval, Sonnet *El Desdichado.*
431. V. Kyd's *Spanish Tragedy.*
433. Shantih. Repeated as here, a formal ending to an Upanishad. "The Peace which passeth understanding" is our equivalent to this word.

The Boston Evening Transcript

The readers of the *Boston Evening Transcript*
Sway in the wind like a field of ripe corn.

When evening quickens faintly in the street,
Wakening the appetites of life in some
And to others bringing the *Boston Evening Transcript,*
I mount the steps and ring the bell, turning
Wearily, as one would turn to nod good-bye to La Rochefoucauld,
If the street were time and he at the end of the street,
And I say, 'Cousin Harriet, here is the *Boston Evening Transcript.'*

Conversation Galante

I observe: 'Our sentimental friend the moon!
Or possibly (fantastic, I confess)
It may be Prester John's balloon
Or an old battered lantern hung aloft
To light poor travellers to their distress.'
    She then: 'How you digress!'

And I then: 'Someone frames upon the keys
That exquisite nocturne, with which we explain
The night and moonshine; music which we seize
To body forth our own vacuity.'
    She then: 'Does this refer to me?'
    'Oh no, it is I who am inane.'

'You, madam, are the eternal humorist,
The eternal enemy of the absolute,
Giving our vagrant moods the slightest twist!
With your air different and imperious
At a stroke our mad poetics to confute—'
    And—'Are we then so serious?'

La Figlia che Piange

O quam te memorem virgo . . .

Stand on the highest pavement of the stair—
Lean on a garden urn—
Weave, weave the sunlight in your hair—
Clasp your flowers to you with a pained surprise—
Fling them to the ground and turn
With a fugitive resentment in your eyes:
But weave, weave the sunlight in your hair.

So I would have had him leave,
So I would have had her stand and grieve,
So he would have left
As the soul leaves the body torn and bruised,
As the mind deserts the body it has used.
I should find
Some way incomparably light and deft,
Some way we both should understand,
Simple and faithless as a smile and shake of the hand.

She turned away, but with the autumn weather
Compelled my imagination many days,
Many days and many hours:
Her hair over her arms and her arms full of flowers.
And I wonder how they should have been together!
I should have lost a gesture and a pose.
Sometimes these cogitations still amaze
The troubled midnight and the noon's repose.

FENTON JOHNSON
(1888–1958)

Children of the Sun

We are children of the sun,
      Rising sun!
Weaving Southern destiny,
Waiting for the mighty hour
When our Shiloh shall appear
With the flaming sword of right,
With the steel of brotherhood,

And emboss in crimson die
Liberty!   Fraternity!

We are the star-dust folk,
    Striving folk!
Sorrow songs have lulled to rest;
Seething passions wrought through wrongs,
Led us where the moon rays dip
In the night of dull despair,
Showed us where the star gleams shine,
And the mystic symbols glow—
Liberty!   Fraternity!

We have come through cloud and mist,
    Mighty men!
Dusk has kissed our sleep-born eyes,
Reared for us a mystic throne
In the splendor of the skies,
That shall always be for us,
Children of the Nazarene,
Children who shall ever sing
Liberty!   Fraternity!

Tired

I am tired of work; I am tired of building up somebody
    else's civilization.
Let us take a rest, M'lissy Jane.
I will go down to the Last Chance Saloon, drink a gallon
    or two of gin, shoot a game or two of dice and
    sleep the rest of the night on one of Mike's barrels.
You will let the old shanty go to rot, the white people's
    clothes turn to dust, and the Calvary Baptist Church
    sink to the bottomless pit.
You will spend your days forgetting you married me and
    your nights hunting the warm gin Mike serves the
    ladies in the rear of the Last Chance Saloon.
Throw the children into the river; civilization has given
    us too many. It is better to die than it is to grow
    up and find out that you are colored.
Pluck the stars out of the heavens. The stars mark our
    destiny. The stars marked my destiny.
I am tired of civilization.

ALAN SEEGER
(1888–1916)

I Have a Rendez-Vous with Death

I have a rendezvous with Death
At some disputed barricade,
When Spring comes back with rustling shade
And apple blossoms fill the air—
I have a rendezvous with Death
When Spring brings back blue days and fair.

It may be he shall take my hand,
And lead me into his dark land,
And close my eyes and quench my breath—
It may be I shall pass him still.
I have a rendezvous with Death
On some scarred slope of battered hill,
When Spring comes round again this year
And the first meadow flowers appear.

God knows 'twere better to be deep
Pillowed in silk and scented down,
Where Love throbs out in blissful sleep,
Pulse nigh to pulse, and breath to breath,
Where hushed awakenings are dear . . .
But I've a rendezvous with Death
At midnight in some flaming town,
When Spring trips north again this year;
And I to my pledged word am true,
I shall not fail that rendezvous.

CONRAD AIKEN
(1889–1973)

Chance Meetings

In the mazes of loitering people, the watchful and furtive,
The shadows of tree-trunks and shadows of leaves,
In the drowse of the sunlight, among the low voices,
I suddenly face you,

Your dark eyes return for a space from her who is with you,
They shine into mine with a sunlit desire,
They say an 'I love you, what star do you live on?'
They smile and then darken,

And silent, I answer 'You too—I have known you,—I love you!—'
And the shadows of tree-trunks and shadows of leaves
Interlace with low voices and footsteps and sunlight
To divide us forever.

Miracles

Twilight is spacious, near things in it seem far,
And distant things seem near.
Now in the green west hangs a yellow star.
And now across old waters you may hear
The profound gloom of bells among still trees,
Like a rolling of huge boulders beneath seas.

Silent as thought in evening contemplation
Weaves the bat under the gathering stars.
Silent as dew, we seek new incarnation,
Meditate new avatars.
In a clear dusk like this
Mary climbed up the hill to seek her son,
To lower him down from the cross, and kiss
The mauve wounds, every one.

Men with wings
In the dusk walked softly after her.
She did not see them, but may have felt
The winnowed air around her stir;
She did not see them, but may have known
Why her son's body was light as a little stone.
She may have guessed that other hands were there
Moving the watchful air.

Now, unless persuaded by searching music
Which suddenly opens the portals of the mind,
We guess no angels,
And are contented to be blind.
Let us blow silver horns in the twilight,
And lift our hearts to the yellow star in the green,
To find perhaps, if, while the dew is rising,
Clear things may not be seen.

E.E. CUMMINGS
(1894–1962)

the Cambridge ladies who live in furnished souls

the Cambridge ladies who live in furnished souls
are unbeautiful and have comfortable minds
(also,with the church's protestant blessings
daughters,unscented shapeless spirited)
they believe in Christ and Longfellow,both dead,
are invariably interested in so many things—
at the present writing one still finds
delighted fingers knitting for the is it Poles?
perhaps. While permanent faces coyly bandy
scandal of Mrs. N and Professor D
. . . . the Cambridge ladies do not care,above
Cambridge if sometimes in its box of
sky lavender and cornerless,the
moon rattles like a fragment of angry candy

O sweet spontaneous

O sweet spontaneous
earth how often have
the
doting

       fingers of
prurient philosophers pinched
and
poked

thee
, has the naughty thumb
of science prodded
thy

   beauty .how
often have religions taken
thee upon their scraggy knees
squeezing and

buffeting thee that thou mightest conceive
gods
      (but
true

to the incomparable
couch of death thy
rhythmic
lover

      thou answerest

them only with

        spring)

Buffalo Bill 's

Buffalo Bill 's
defunct
      who used to
      ride a watersmooth-silver
                stallion
and break onetwothreefourfive pigeonsjustlikethat
                          Jesus

he was a handsome man
              and what i want to know is
how do you like your blueeyed boy
Mister Death

Picasso

Picasso
you give us Things
which
bulge: grunting lungs pumped full of sharp thick mind

you make us shrill
presents always
shut in the sumptuous screech of
simplicity

(out of the
black unbunged
Something gushes vaguely a squeak of planes
or

between squeals of
Nothing grabbed with circular shrieking tightness
solid screams whisper.)
Lumberman of The Distinct

your brain's
axe only chops hugest inherent
Trees of Ego,from
whose living and biggest

bodies lopped
of every
prettiness

you hew form truly

CLAUDE MCKAY
(1890–1948)

The Harlem Dancer

Applauding youths laughed with young prostitutes
And watched her perfect, half-clothed body sway;
Her voice was like the sound of blended flutes
Blown by black players upon a picnic day.
She sang and danced on gracefully and calm,
The light gauze hanging loose about her form;
To me she seemed a proudly-swaying palm
Grown lovelier for passing through a storm.
Upon her swarthy neck black, shiny curls
Profusely fell; and, tossing coins in praise,
The wine-flushed, bold-eyed boys, and even the girls,
Devoured her with their eager, passionate gaze;
But, looking at her falsely-smiling face
I knew her self was not in that strange place.

Harlem Shadows

I hear the halting footsteps of a lass
  In Negro Harlem when the night lets fall
Its veil. I see the shapes of girls who pass
  Eager to heed desire's insistent call:
Ah, little dark girls, who in slippered feet
  Go prowling through the night from street to street.

Through the long night until the silver break
  Of day the little gray feet know no rest,
Through the lone night until the last snow-flake
  Has dropped from heaven upon the earth's white breast,
The dusky, half-clad girls of tired feet
  Are trudging, thinly shod, from street to street.

Ah, stern harsh world, that in the wretched way
  Of poverty, dishonor and disgrace,
Has pushed the timid little feet of clay.
  The sacred brown feet of my fallen race!
Ah, heart of me, the weary, weary feet
  In Harlem wandering from street to street.

The Lynching

His spirit is smoke ascended to high heaven.
His father, by the cruelest way of pain,
Had bidden him to his bosom once again;
The awful sin remained still unforgiven.
All night a bright and solitary star
(Perchance the one that ever guided him,
Yet gave him up at last to Fate's wild whim)
Hung pitifully o'er the swinging char.
Day dawned, and soon the mixed crowds came to view
The ghastly body swaying in the sun:
The women thronged to look, but never a one
Showed sorrow in her eyes of steely blue;
And little lads, lynchers that were to be,
Danced round the dreadful thing in fiendish glee.

EDNA ST. VINCENT MILLAY
(1892–1950)

from Renascence

All I could see from where I stood
Was three long mountains and a wood;
I turned and looked another way,
And saw three islands in a bay.
So with my eyes I traced the line
Of the horizon, thin and fine,
Straight around till I was come
Back to where I'd started from;
And all I saw from where I stood
Was three long mountains and a wood.
Over these things I could not see;
These were the things that bounded me;
And I could touch them with my hand,
Almost, I thought, from where I stand.
And all at once things seemed so small
My breath came short, and scarce at all.
But, sure, the sky is big, I said;
Miles and miles above my head;
So here upon my back I'll lie
And look my fill into the sky.
And so I looked, and, after all,
The sky was not so very tall.
The sky, I said, must somewhere stop,
And—sure enough!—I see the top!
The sky, I thought, is not so grand;
I 'most could touch it with my hand!
And reaching up my hand to try,
I screamed to feel it touch the sky.
I screamed, and—lo!—Infinity
Came down and settled over me;
Forced back my scream into my chest,
Bent back my arm upon my breast,
And, pressing of the Undefined
The definition on my mind,
Held up before my eyes a glass
Through which my shrinking sight did pass
Until it seemed I must behold
Immensity made manifold;
Whispered to me a word whose sound

Deafened the air for worlds around,
And brought unmuffled to my ears
The gossiping of friendly spheres,
The creaking of the tented sky,
The ticking of Eternity.
I saw and heard, and knew at last
The How and Why of all things, past,
And present, and forevermore.
The Universe, cleft to the core,
Lay open to my probing sense
That, sick'ning, I would fain pluck thence
But could not,—nay! But needs must suck
At the great wound, and could not pluck
My lips away till I had drawn
All venom out.—Ah, fearful pawn!
For my omniscience paid I toll
In infinite remorse of soul.
All sin was of my sinning, all
Atoning mine, and mine the gall
Of all regret. Mine was the weight
Of every brooded wrong, the hate
That stood behind each envious thrust,
Mine every greed, mine every lust.
And all the while for every grief,
Each suffering, I craved relief
With individual desire,—
Craved all in vain! And felt fierce fire
About a thousand people crawl;
Perished with each,—then mourned for all!
A man was starving in Capri;
He moved his eyes and looked at me;
I felt his gaze, I heard his moan,
And knew his hunger as my own.
I saw at sea a great fog bank
Between two ships that struck and sank;
A thousand screams the heavens smote;
And every scream tore through my throat.
No hurt I did not feel, no death
That was not mine; mine each last breath
That, crying, met an answering cry
From the compassion that was I.
All suffering mine, and mine its rod;
Mine, pity like the pity of God.
Ah, awful weight! Infinity
Pressed down upon the finite Me!
My anguished spirit, like a bird,

Beating against my lips I heard;
Yet lay the weight so close about
There was no room for it without.
And so beneath the weight lay I
And suffered death, but could not die.

. . . .

LANGSTON HUGHES
(1902–1967)

The Negro Speaks of Rivers

I've known rivers:
I've known rivers ancient as the world and older than the flow
    of human blood in human veins.

My soul has grown deep like the rivers.

I bathed in the Euphrates when dawns were young.
I built my hut near the Congo and it lulled me to sleep.
I looked upon the Nile and raised the pyramids above it.
I heard the singing of the Mississippi when Abe Lincoln went
    down to New Orleans, and I've seen its muddy bosom turn
    all golden in the sunset.

I've known rivers:
Ancient, dusky rivers.

My soul has grown deep like the rivers.

I Sing for the Animals
(Teton Sioux)

Out of the earth
I sing for them,
A Horse nation
I sing for them.
Out of the earth
I sing for them,
The animals
I sing for them.

Carrying My Mind Around
(Tlingit)

My own mind is very hard to me.
It is just as if I were carrying my mind around.
What is the matter with you?

Haida Cradle-Song

Whence have you fallen, have you fallen? Whence have you
    fallen, have you fallen?
Did you fall, fall, fall, fall, from the top of the salmon-berry
    bushes?

First Song of the Thunder
(Navaho "Mountain Chant")

Thonah! Thonah!
There is a voice above,
The voice of the thunder.
Within the dark cloud,
Again and again it sounds,
Thonah! Thonah!

Thonah! Thonah!
There is a voice below,
The voice of the grasshopper.
Among the plants,
Again and again it sounds,
Thonah! Thonah!

The Creation of the Earth
(Navaho)

Earth Magician shapes this world.
    Behold what he can do!
Round and smooth he molds it.
    Behold what he can do!
Earth Magician makes the mountains.
    Heed what he has to say!
He it is that makes the mesas.
    Heed what he has to say.
Earth Magician shapes this world;
    Earth Magician makes its mountains;
Makes all larger, larger, larger.
    Into the earth the Magician glances;
Into its mountains he may see.

Corn Ceremony
(Apache)

At the east where the black water lies stands the large corn, with
    staying roots, its large stalk, its red silk, its long leaves, its tassel
    dark and spreading, on which there is the dew.
At the sunset where the yellow water lies stands the large pumpkin
    with its tendrils, its long stem, its wide leaves, its yellow top on
    which there is pollen.

Song of the Pleiades
(Pawnee)

Look as they rise, rise
Over the line where sky meets the earth;
Pleiades!
Lo! They ascending, come to guide us,
Leading us safely, keeping us one;
Pleiades,
Teach us to be, like you, united.

Arrow Song

Scarlet
    Is its head.

SONGS OF THE MODERN ERA:
1900–1922

A Bird in a Gilded Cage
(Arthur J. Lamb, 1900)

The ball-room was filled with fashions throng,
It shone with a thousand lights,
And there was a woman who passed along,
The fairest of all the sights,
A girl to her lover then softly sighed,
There's riches at her command;
But she married for wealth, not for love he cried,
Though she lives in a mansion grand.

Chorus
She's only a bird in a gilded cage,
A beautiful sight to see,
You may think she's happy and free from care,
She's not, though she seems to be,
'Tis sad when you think of her wasted life,
For youth cannot mate with age,
And her beauty was sold,
For an old man's gold,
She's a bird in a gilded cage.

I stood in a church-yard just at eve',
When sunset adorned the west,
And looked at the people who'd come to grieve,
For loved ones now laid at rest,
A tall marble monument marked the grave,
Of one who'd been fashion's queen,
And I thought she is happier here at rest,
Than to have people say when seen.

Give My Regards to Broadway
(George M. Cohan, 1904)

Did you ever see two Yankees part upon a foreign shore,
When the good ship's just about to start for Old New York once
more?
With tear-dimmed eye they say good-bye, they're friends with out a
doubt;
When the man on the pier shouts,
"Let them clear,"
As the ship strikes out.

Chorus
Give my regards to Broadway,
Remember me to Herald Square,
Tell all the gang at Forty-Second Street,
That I will soon be there;
Whisper of how I'm yearning,
To mingle with the old time throng,
Give my regards to old Broadway and say
That I'll be there e'er long.

Say hello to dear old Coney Isle, if there you chance to be,
When you're at the Waldorf have a smile and charge it up to me;
Mention my name ev'ry place you go, as 'round the town you roam;
Wish you'd call on my gal,
Now remember, old pal,
When you get back home.

His Eye Is on the Sparrow
(Mrs. C. D. Martin, 1905)

Why should I feel discouraged,
Why should the shadows come,
Why should my heart be lonely
And long for Heav'n and home,
When Jesus is my portion?
My constant Friend is He:
His eye is on the sparrow,
And I know He watches me;
His eye is on the sparrow,
And I know He watches me.

"Let not your heart be troubled,"
His tender word I hear,
And resting on His goodness,
I lose my doubts and fears:
Tho' by the path He leadeth
But one step I may see:
His eye is on the sparrow,
And I know He watches me;
His eye is on the sparrow,
And I know He watches me.

Whenever I am tempted,
Whenever clouds arise,
When songs give place to sighing,
When hope within me dies,
I draw the closer to Him,
From care He sets me free;
His eye is on the sparrow,
And I know He cares for me;
His eye is on the sparrow,
And I know He cares for me.

Take Me Out to the Ball Game
(Jack Norworth, 1908)

Katie Casey was base-ball mad,
Had the fever and had it bad;
Just to root for the home town crew,
Ev'ry sou Katie blew.
On a Saturday, her young beau called to see if she'd like to go,
To see a show but Miss Kate said "no,
I'll tell you what you can do:"

Chorus
Take me out to the ball game,
Take me out with the crowd
Buy me some peanuts and cracker jack,
I don't care if I never get back,
Let me root, root, root for the home team,
If they don't win it's a shame
For it's one, two, three strikes, you're out, at the old ball game.

Katie Casey saw all the games,
Knew the players by their first names;
Told the umpire he was wrong, all along good and strong
When the score was just two to two,
Katie Casey knew what to do,
Just to cheer up the boys she knew,
She made the gang sing this song:
(*Chorus*)

Casey Jones
(*Wallace Saunders, 1909*)

Come all you rounders, for I want you to hear,
The story of a brave engineer.
Casey Jones was the rounder's name.
On a big eight wheeler of a mighty fame.

Caller called Casey 'bout half-past four,
He kissed his wife at the station door,
Climbed to the cab with the orders in his hand,
He says, "This is my trip to the holy land."

Out of South Memphis yard on the fly,
Heard the fireman say, "You got a white eye."
Well, the switchmen knew by the engine moan
That the man at the throttle was Casey Jones.

The rain was comin' down five or six weeks.
The railroad track was like the bed of a creek.
They slowed her down to a thirty mile gait
And the south-bound mail was eight hours late.

Fireman says, "Casey, you're runnin' too fast,
You run that block board the last station you passed."
Casey says, "I believe we'll make it though,
For she steams a lot better than I ever know."

Casey says, "Fireman, don't you fret,
Keep knockin' at the fire door, don't give up yet,
I'm going to run her till she leaves the rail,
Or make it on time with the south-bound mail."

Around the curve and down the dump,
Two locomotives was a bound to jump,
Fireman hollered, "Casey, it's just ahead,
We might jump and make it but we'll all be dead."

Around the curve comes a passenger train,
Casey blows the whistle, tells the fireman, "Ring the bell,"
Fireman jumps and says "Good-by,
Casey Jones, You're bound to die."

Well Casey Jones was all right.
He stuck to his duty day and night.
They loved his whistle and his ring number three,
And he came into Memphis on the old I. C.

Fireman goes down the depot track,
Begging his honey to take him back,
She says, "Oranges on the table, peaches on the shelf,
You're a goin' to get tired sleepin' by yourself."

Mrs. Casey Jones was a sittin' on the bed.
Telegram comes that Casey is dead.
She says, "Children, go to bed, and hush your cryin',
'Cause you got another papa on the Frisco line."

Headaches and heartaches and all kinds of pain.
They ain't apart from a railroad train.
Stories of brave men, noble and grand,
Belong to the life of a railroad man.

Let Me Call You Sweetheart
(Beth Slater Whitson, 1910)

I am dreaming
Dear of you
Day by day
Dreaming when the skies are blue
When they're gray;
When the silv'ry moonlight gleams
Still I wander on in dreams
In a land of love, it seems
Just with you.

Chorus
Let me call you "Sweetheart"
I'm in love with you
Let me hear you whisper that you love me too
Keep the love-light glowing
In your eyes so true
Let me call you "Sweetheart"
I'm in love with you.

Longing for you all the while
More and more
Longing for the sunny smile,
I adore;
Birds are singing far and near
Roses blooming ev'rywhere
You, alone, my heart can cheer
You just you.

Alexander's Ragtime Band
(Irving Berlin, 1911)

Oh, ma honey,
Oh, ma honey,
Better hurry and let's meander,
Ain't you goin',
Ain't you goin',
To the leader man, ragged meter man?
Oh, ma honey,
Oh, ma honey,
Let me take you to Alexander's grand stand, brass band,
Ain't you comin' along?

Come on and hear,
Come on and hear
Alexander's ragtime band,
Come on and hear,
Come on and hear,
It's the best band in the land,
They can play a bugle call like you never heard before,
So natural that you want to go to war;
That's just the bestest band what am, honey lamb,
Come on along,
Come on along,
Let me take you by the hand,
Up to the man,
Up to the man who's the leader of the band,
And if you care to hear the Swanee River played in ragtime,
Come on and hear,
Come on and hear
Alexander's ragtime band.

Oh, ma honey,
Oh, ma honey,
There's a fiddle with notes that screeches,
Like a chicken,
Like a chicken,
And the clarinet is a colored pet,
Come and listen,
Come and listen,
To a classical band what's peaches, come now, somehow,
Better hurry along.

Whiffenpoof Song
(Meade Minnigerode, George S. Pomeroy, and Ted B. Galloway, 1911)

To the table down at Mory's, to the place where Louis dwells,
To the dear old Temple Bar we love so well,
Sing the Whiffenpoofs assembled with their glasses raised on high,
And the magic of their singing casts its spell.

Yes, the magic of their singing of the songs we love so well,
"Shall I wasting," and "Mavoureen," and the rest;
We will serenade our Louis while life and voice shall last,
Then we'll pass and be forgotten with the rest.

We're poor little lambs who have lost our way:
Baa! Baa! Baa!
We're little black sheep who have gone astray:
Baa! Baa! Baa!
Gentlemen songsters off on a spree,

Damned from here to eternity;
God have mercy on such as we:
Baa! Baa! Baa!

The Old Rugged Cross
(George Bennard, 1913)

On a hill far away stood an old rugged cross,
The emblem of suff'ring and shame;
And I love that old cross, where the dearest and best
For a world of lost sinners was slain.

Chorus
So I'll cherish the old rugged cross,
Till my trophies at last I lay down;
I will cling to the old rugged cross,
And exchange it some day for a crown.

Oh, that old rugged cross, so despised by the world,
Has a wondrous attraction for me;
For the dear Lamb of God left His glory above,
To bear it to dark Calvary.

In the old rugged cross, stained with blood so divine,
A wondrous beauty I see;
For 'twas on that old cross Jesus suffered and died,
To pardon and sanctify me.

To the old rugged cross, I will ever be true,
Its shame and reproach gladly bear;
Then He'll call me some day to my home far away,
Where His glory forever I'll share.

St. Louis Blues
(W. C. Handy, 1914)

I hate to see de ev'nin' sun go down,
Hate to see de ev'nin' sun go down.
'Cause my baby, he done lef' dis town.
Feelin' tomorrow lak I feel today,
Feel tomorrow lak I feel today.
I'll pack my trunk, make ma get away.
St. Louis woman wid her diamon' rings
Pulls dat man roun' by her apron strings.
'Twant for powder an' for store bought hair
De man I love would not gone nowhere.

Chorus
Got de St. Louis Blues jes' as blue as ah can be,
Dat man got a heart lak a rock cast in the sea.
Or else he wouldn't have gone so far from me.
Dog-gone it!

Been to de gypsy to get ma fortune tole,
To de gypsy done got ma fortune tole.
'Cause I'm most wile 'bout ma Jelly roll.
Gypsy done tole me, "Don't you wear no black,"
Yes, she done tole me, "Don't you wear no black."

Go to St. Louis, you can win him back.
Help me to Cairo, make St. Louis by ma-self,
Git to Cairo, find ma ole friend Jeff.
Gwine to pin maself close to his side,
If ah flag his train, I sho' can ride.

Chorus
I loves dat man lak a school-boy loves his pie,
Lak a Kentucky Col'nel loves his mint an' rye.
I'll love ma baby till the day ah die.

You ought to see dat stovepipe brown of mine,
Lak he owns de Dimon' Joseph line.
He'd make a cross-eyed o' man go stone blind,
Blacker than midnight, teeth lak flags of truce,
Blackest man in de whole St. Louis.
Blacker de berry, sweeter is the juice.
About a crap game he knows a pow'ful lot,
But when work-time comes he's on de dot.
Gwine to ask him for a cold ten-spot.
What it takes to git it, he's certainly got.

Chorus
A black-headed gal make a freight train jump the track.
Said a black-headed gal make a freight train jump the track,
But a long tall gal makes a preacher ball the jack.

Extra choruses
Lawd, a blonde-headed woman makes a good man leave the town,
I said blonde-headed woman makes a good man leave the town,
But a red-head woman makes a boy slap his papa down.

O ashes to ashes and dust to dust,
I said ashes to ashes and dust to dust,
If my blues don't get you my jazzing must.

Oh! How I Hate to Get up in the Morning
(Irving Berlin, 1918)

The other day I chanced to meet a soldier friend of mine,
He'd been in camp for sev'ral weeks and he was looking fine;
His muscles had developed and his cheeks were rosy red,
I asked him how he liked the life and that is what he said:

Chorus
"Oh! how I hate to get up in the morning,
Oh! how I'd love to remain in bed;
For the hardest blow of all, is to hear the bugler call;
You've got to get up, you've got to get up, you've got to get up this morning!
Some day I'm going to murder the bugler,
Some day they're gong to find him dead;
I'll amputate his reveille, and step upon it heavily,
And spend the rest of my life in bed."

A bugler in the army is the luckiest of men,
He wakes the boys at five and then goes back to bed again;
He doesn't have to blow again until the afternoon,
If ev'ry thing goes well with me I'll be a bugler soon.

Chorus
"Oh! how I hate to get up in the morning,
Oh! how I'd love to remain in bed;
For the hardest blow of all, is to hear the bugler call;
You've got to get up, you've got to get up, you've got to get up this morning!
Oh! boy the minute the battle is over,
Oh! boy the minute the foe is dead;
I'll put my uniform away, and move to Philadelphia,
And spend the rest of my life in bed."

Look for the Silver Lining
(Jerome Kern, 1920)

Please don't be offended if I preach to you a while,
Tears are out of place in eyes that were meant to smile.
There's a way to make your very biggest troubles small,
Here's the happy secret of it all:

Chorus
Look for the silver lining
Whene'er a cloud appears in the blue.
Remember somewhere the sun is shining
And so the right thing to do is make it shine for you.
A heart full of joy and gladness
Will always banish sadness and strife
So always look for the silver lining
And try to find the sunny side of life.

As I wash my dishes, I'll be following your plan,
Till I see the brightness in ev'ry pot and pan.
I am sure your point of view will ease the daily grind,
So I'll keep repeating in my mind:
(*Chorus*)

Stairway to Paradise
(*B. G. De Sylva and Arthur Francis, 1900–1922*)

All you preachers
Who delight in panning the dancing teachers,
Let me tell you there are a lot of features
Of the dance that carry you through
The Gates of Heaven.

It's madness
To be always sitting around in sadness,
When you could be learning the Steps of Gladness.
(You'll be happy when you can do
Just six or seven.)

Begin today. You'll find it nice:
The quickest way to Paradise.
When you practice,
Here's the thing to do—
Simply say as you go:

Refrain
I'll build a Stairway to Paradise,
With a new Step ev'ry day.
I'm going to get there at any price;
Stand aside, I'm on my way!
I got the blues,
And up above it's so fair;
Shoes,
Go on and carry me there!
I'll build a Stairway to Paradise
With a new Step ev'ry day.

NOTES

I THE COLONIAL ERA: TO 1775

John Smith (c.1580–1631) is better known as a colonist, explorer, and adventurer than as a poet. He offered his services to the *Mayflower* colonists, but they took along his book instead. It was called *A Description of New England* (1616). His poem "The Sea Marke" appeared in *Advertisements for the Unexperienced Planters of New England, or Anywhere* . . . (London, 1631). The rest of Smith's small poetic output can be found in *The Complete Works of Captain John Smith*, 3 vols., ed. Philip L. Barbour (1986), vol. 3.

"The Sea Marke": Smith's image here is of a wreck, a ship aground in shallow water, abandoned, with some parts of her still sticking up out of the water to serve as a beacon and a warning to others. Like John Winthrop's image of the city on a hill, Smith's image of the wreck insists on the visibility, the vulnerability, and the exemplary nature of the colonial experiment.

day of Dome: Judgment Day

Roger Williams (1603–1683) was a clergyman and the founder of Rhode Island. Born in England, he came to Massachusetts in 1630. He was banished from the colony in 1635, founding Providence, Rhode Island, the following year on the principle of religious toleration. See *The Complete Writings of Roger Williams*, ed. J. Trumbull et al., 7 vols. (1866–1874, 1963).

"Of Eating and Entertainment": This poem appeared in *A Key Into the Language of America* (1643), which is primarily a dictionary of the Narragansett language. In Williams's text the lines are preceded by the following: "It is a strange truth that a man shall generally find more free entertainment and refreshing amongst these barbarians than amongst thousands that call themselves Christians."

ravens: see I Kings 17:6.

Anne Bradstreet (c.1612–1672), America's first major poet, was born Anne Dudley in England. She came to Massachusetts in 1630 with her husband, Simon Bradstreet, who was later governor of the colony. Bradstreet's poems were published, probably without her knowledge, in England as *The Tenth Muse Lately Sprung up in America* (1650), the first volume of poems by a woman published in English. Bradstreet's stylistic roots are in the English Renaissance and in the work of the Huguenot (French Protestant) poet Guillaume du Bartas, author of a major Creation epic in two parts: *La Sepmaine* and *La Seconde Sepmaine.* Bradstreet's great theme is the difficult balance of the Puritan Way—that is, how to live in the world without being of it; her greatest achievements are those poems in which emotionally charged personal or domestic loyalties struggle with public, rational, theological loyalties. It is clear that Anne Bradstreet sometimes felt rebellious: but Puritanism itself was rebellious, and so it was possible for her to be both a woman and a Puritan. Her best poems remind us, as Roy Harvey Pearce once put it, that "the power of American poetry from the beginning has derived from the poet's inability or refusal, at some depth of consciousness, wholly to accept his culture's system of values." The standard edition is *The Complete Works of Anne Bradstreet,* ed. J. McElrath and A. Robb (1981).

"Contemplations": On "the white stone," see Revelations 2:17, Geneva Version.

"Anagrams": These poems are not by Bradstreet herself but were composed by an unknown hand for her first book. The anagram was a favored Puritan genre: the meaning of a person's life could be coaxed out of the name itself. Thus a minor poet named John Fiske got "all mine will sing" out of the name William Snelling.

Michael Wigglesworth (1631–1705) was born in England, came to America in 1638, and became a clergyman in Malden, Massachusetts, in 1656. *The Day of Doom,* a long poem in ballad meter published in 1662, has been called the first American best-seller. It is a vivid, pictorially literal account of the Day of Judgment as seen in the light of Calvinist theology, set to the hearty gallop of adroitly handled ballad meter. It was an enormous success: the first edition numbered eighteen hundred copies, or one for every twenty New England colonists. Copies of early editions are now virtually impossible to locate; they may all have been simply read to pieces. The standard edition is *The Poems of Michael Wigglesworth,* ed. Ronald A. Bosco (1989).

"The Day of Doom": In sophisticated English and American verse from Chaucer to Arnold, the standard poetic line is iambic pentameter, rhymed or unrhymed. But in popular poetry, from "O Western Wind" and "Barbara Allen" to the Protestant hymns, Mother Goose, and Emily Dickinson, the standard line has been ballad meter: 4-3-4-3 if cast in four-line stanzas, or "fourteeners," 7-7 if cast as couplets.

John Cotton of 'Queen's Creek' (1640–1669), not to be confused with the Puritan clergyman John Cotton of England and New England (1585–1652), was a planter in York County, Virginia. Very little is known about him; he is thought to be the author of *The History of Bacons and Ingram's Rebellion*, written in 1677, published in 1814. The most recent edition is in Charles M. Andrews, *Narratives of the Insurrections, 1675–1690* (1915).

"Bacons Epitaph": The subject is Nathaniel Bacon, leader of a rebellion against the governor and Assembly of Virginia in 1676.

Edward Taylor (1642–1729) was born in England, came to America in 1668, and was the minister at Westfield, Massachusetts (at that time a frontier community) from 1671 to 1729. Except for a fragment of one poem, Taylor's Puritan poetry was not published until the 1930s, when his manuscripts were discovered in the Yale University library. Taylor's powerful, compressed baroque style has strong affinities with the English Metaphysical poets, but his intended audience was limited to himself and to God. He and Bradstreet are without much question the best seventeenth-century American poets. The standard edition is *The Poems of Edward Taylor,* ed. Donald Stanford (1960).

"Prologue": hand, *handle;* glore, *glory*

Gods Determinations: Fillitted, *adorned with ribbons;* Smaragdine, *emerald green;* Selvedge, *border;* fet, *fetched*

Preparatory Meditations: Each of these poems was written as a personal preparation for the sacrament of communion, the Eucharist. This, Taylor's central subject, also lies at the heart of Christianity. His language is strong and concrete, his syntax is knotted, and his lines seethe with a confined restless energy that seeks to yoke the physical and the spiritual through language. Like Bradstreet, Taylor is at his best when giving us the personal experience of an individual in a Puritan world.

"The Reflexion": Trencher, *wooden plate;* bin, *been;* Sprindge, *spread*

Meditation 6: enfoile, *to coat with thin sheet of metal*

Meditation 22: Mullipuff, *puffball fungus*

Meditation 35: Spruice, *spruce;* Peart, *pert;* Pronown, *pronoun*

"The Likenings of Edward Taylor": This gathering of metaphors and similes from Taylor's work has been made—and titled—for this anthology in order to foreground Taylor's inventiveness—and compulsiveness.

Meditation 3: Catch, *receptacle*

Meditation 39: Bubs, *pustules;* Snaffle, *simple bridle bit*

Meditation 18: Shittim, *acacia* (Hebrew)

Meditation 25: pericarde, *sac enclosing the heart*

Richard Steere (1643–1721), an English-born merchant, settled in New London, Connecticut, in 1685. His *Monumental Memorial of Marine Mercy,* the best sea-deliverance poem of the period, appeared in 1684. It tells the story of a passage by ship from New England back to England. The ship was of a type called a pink; its name was *Adventure.* After many difficulties the ship reaches England, but the wind is so great, the sailors are almost unable to anchor. In the selection reprinted here the crew throws out three anchors, one after the other. None of them holds. Finally the crew is down to a very small anchor, called a kedging anchor, usually used only to move a ship about on a calm day. Steere's poem may be contrasted with Smith's "The Sea Marke."

Thomas Maule (c.1645–1724), a Quaker merchant, was born in England and settled in Salem, Massachusetts, in 1688. Prosperous, well regarded, and a troublemaker, he was a burr under the Puritan saddle. This sally appeared in *An Abstract of a Letter to Cotton Mather* (1701) and shows that the Puritans did not always have it their own way. The name Maule figures prominently in Nathaniel Hawthorne's 1851 historical novel about colonial Salem, *The House of the Seven Gables.*

Ebenezer Cooke (1667–c.1732) was born in England and came to Maryland in the late seventeenth century, where he became the colony's self-appointed poet laureate. His main work, *The Sot–weed Factor,* appeared in 1708. A distinguishing feature of the poem is its Hudibrastic rhyme, a smart, deft, exaggerated rhyme used by Samuel Butler in his *Hudibras,* and much favored by Byron, Ogden Nash, and other wits. Byron once rhymed "intellectual" with "henpecked you all."

"The Sot-weed Factor": A sot-weed factor is a tobacco merchant.

Benjamin Franklin (1706–1790) was born in Boston, the youngest son of the youngest son for five generations back. Despite having no formal education past age ten, he became one of the leading men of his time, with major accomplishments in politics, science, and letters. His verse is collected in *The Writings of Benjamin Franklin,* ed. Albert H. Smyth (1905–7).

Jane Colman Turell (1708–1735) was born in Massachusetts and married Ebenezer Turell, the minister in Medford, in 1726. Her poetry appears in *Memoirs of the Life and Death of the Pious and Ingenious Mrs Jane Turell* (1735), edited by her husband. Her graceful neoclassical verse is capable of enthusiastic love poetry as well as the more predictable Horatian moderation.

"The Cameleon Lover" appeared anonymously in the *South-Carolina Gazette,* no. 10 (March 11, 1732). The reply, by "Sable," appeared in the same paper, no. 11 (March 18, 1732). In this early, elegant exchange on the subject of race relations, "Sable" has the last word, invoking, in a striking phrase, "Love . . . the Monarch Passion of the Mind."

Francis Hopkinson (1737–1791), born in Philadelphia, was a poet, a politician, a signer of the Declaration of Independence, and designer of the American flag. His Revolutionary War poems, such as *The Battle of the Kegs* (1779), were widely read at the time. *The Miscellaneous Essays and Occasional Writings of Francis Hopkinson* (Philadelphia, 1792), 3 vols., is incomplete. While most of his verse is impossible to read now, except as a historical example of what once passed for poetry, the short selection here suggests that Hopkinson had a real feeling for country life and that he could, upon occasion, rise to a good subject.

Daniel Bliss (1740–1806), a Tory lawyer in Concord, Massachusetts, is supposed to have written this epitaph for a client, a former slave belonging to Benjamin Barron, a local shoemaker. John Jack bought his freedom in 1761. The headstone with this text is in the Old Burying Ground in Concord center. As an ironic and pointed set of observations on freedom, it stands comparison with many other longer and less witty pieces.

"The Country School," in the version printed here, comes from *American Poems* (1793), edited by Elihu H. Smith, the first anthology of American poetry. Smith noted that the poem "is extracted from *The New Hampshire Spy.*" Its colloquial realism is a welcome relief from the overwhelmingly formal qualities of most colonial poetry.

> Gizzard: When Sampson spells this word "G,I,Z," the point depends on the reader knowing that the letter *z* used to be pronounced "izzard."

Songs and Hymns: To 1775

"The Lord to Mee a Shepherd Is": This song comes from *The Bay Psalm Book* (1640), the first book printed in the American colonies. It marks the high point of Puritan literary theory and, at the same time, the low point of Puritan poetic practice. The preface presents an excellent argument for the plain style, a style that was to have a lasting legacy in American writing:

> If therefore the verses are not always so smooth and elegant as some may desire or expect, let them consider that God's altar needs not our polishings, for we have respected rather a plain translation than to smooth our verses with the sweetness of any paraphrases, and so have attended conscience rather than elegance, fidelity rather than poetry.

The altar was rough-hewn indeed. The psalms were taken almost word for word from the Bible and chopped into ballad meter; it was lack of skill, not ballad meter itself, that was responsible for the primitive result.

"A Whaling Song": John Osborn (1713–1753) was born on Cape Cod, in Sandwich, Massachusetts. He later moved to Middletown, Connecticut, where he practiced as a physician. "A Whaling Song" will be recognized as an early version of a song usually called "The Greenland Whaler." Our text is from *Specimens of American Poetry,* ed. Samuel Kettell (Boston, 1829), vol. 1.

"Christ the Apple-Tree": Said to be an American production, this hymn or song, with its innocent, almost medieval spirit, was first published in England in 1761, then reprinted in *Divine Hymns,* ed. Joshua Smith (1804). Our text is from *Hymns as Poetry.*

"Springfield Mountain": The original manuscript is dated 1761. Springfield Mountain, now known as Wilbraham Mountain, is in Massachusetts. We often assume that ballads and folk songs are communal productions, arising spontaneously from "the folk." Yet many can be traced back to a single author. This ballad, for example, has been attributed to one Irma Townsend Ireland.

"Let Tyrants Shake": William Billings (1746–1800) was born in Boston and was the first American to apply for a copyright. A compiler, composer, and author, he died in poverty and was buried in an unmarked grave. Written in 1770, this poem was a colonial war hymn.

"Wak'd by the Gospel's . . .": Samson Occom (1723–1792) was a Mohegan Indian, born in Mohegan, a village near New London, Connecticut. Occom converted to Christianity and learned Latin, Greek, and Hebrew as well as English. He taught at New London, at Montauk, and in Oneida County, New York. He also preached in the British Isles, raising the money that became the basis of Dartmouth College's endowment. This hymn, which was widely sung during the nineteenth century, is dated to 1774. Our text is from E. S. Ninde, *Story of the American Hymn* (1921). It is not the earliest example of an American Indian using a European poetic form. In 1678 an Indian known to us now only by the name Eliazar was a senior at Harvard College, where he wrote a Latin elegy as an obituary for Thomas Thatcher; it was printed in Cotton Mather's *Magnalia Christi Americana.* See Harold Jantz, *The First Century of New England Verse* (1943, reprinted 1962).

II REVOLUTION AND THE EARLY REPUBLIC: 1775-1825

John Trumbull (1750–1831) was born in Westbury, Connecticut, went to Yale, studied law in Boston with John Adams, and settled in Hartford in 1781, where he became a judge both of the Superior Court and of the Supreme Court of Errors. He was one of a group of poets known as the Connecticut Wits, which also included Joel Barlow and Timothy Dwight. The Wits favored long poetic forms and wrote prosy, abstract, overregular verse. Trumbull is remembered for *The Anarchiad* and *The Progress of Dulness* as well as *M'Fingal,* which appeared in 1775. *M'Fingal* is a mock epic; its attitude toward the American Revolution is complex. Trumbull, in common with the other Connecticut Wits (with the notable exception of Barlow) was essentially conservative. He was an American patriot but was profoundly uneasy about populism and rebellion. He seems half contemptuous of his hero, M'Fingal, whom he presents as a satire of the mythical heroes of the would-be epic poems of James McPherson. McPherson (who knew no Gaelic) claimed that his concoctions were translations from a shadowy "Ossian," an early Celtic epic poet. The poems created a sensation (because they seemed to provide Europe with its own indigenous epics), impressing, among others, Goethe and Jefferson. They have been shown to be more like Mark Twain's description of the dinosaur in the museum, "half a dozen bones and a dozen barrels of plaster."

Philip Freneau (1752–1832) was born in New York City, of French Huguenot descent. After graduating from Princeton, he became a sea captain, then a journalist, editing the highly partisan ultra-Jeffersonian *National Gazette.* George Washington despised him, calling him "that rascal, Freneau." Jefferson said that Freneau's paper "saved our Constitution, which was fast galloping into monarchy." Famous in his time as a poet of the Revolution, he was also an important pre-Romantic, an outspoken Deist, and a poet of nature. He outlived his era, retiring to Monmouth County, New Jersey, after a second career at sea. He was found frozen to death in a snowbank after a raging snowstorm on December 18, 1832. He was at the time nearly forgotten. The standard edition of his work is *Poems of Philip Freneau,* ed. F. L. Pattee (1903).

"The House of Night": The lurid light and eerie setting of this poem strongly foreshadow the work of Edgar Allan Poe.

"The British Prison Ship": Freneau was captured by the British during the Revolution in 1780; his experience aboard a prison hulk provided the basis for this poem.

"Epitaph for Jonathan Robbins": This is a minor masterpiece of mock outrage. Robbins was in fact a British citizen, and Freneau knew it.

Phillis Wheatley (c.1753–1784) was born in Africa, probably in the Gambia–Senegal region. Kidnapped in 1761, she was brought to Boston and purchased by John Wheatley. Her writings began to appear in newspapers and magazines in 1767. *Poems on Various Subjects* appeared in 1773, the same year she traveled to England. She was freed in 1773 or 1774. Thereafter, and ironically, her fortunes declined. She married a freedman, John Peters, and spent her last months working in a boarding house. Her chosen poetic forms are drawn almost entirely from the standard eighteenth-century neoclassical English repertoire. The standard edition is *The Poems of Phillis Wheatley*, ed. J. D. Mason, Jr. (1989).

Joel Barlow (1754–1812) was born in Redding, Connecticut, and graduated from Yale. He was at first associated with the more or less conservative, Federalist "Connecticut Wits." His years in Europe and his friendship with Thomas Paine converted him to support for radical democracy. Barlow aspired, in *The Vision of Columbus* (1787) and in *The Columbiad* (1807), to write a New World epic with New World material. His heroic mythic founders are the Inca Manco Capac and his consort Oella, who are seen as bringers of civilization (in the good sense) and are praised for their introduction of a modern, rational sun worship. The boldness of Barlow's poetic design was not matched by his verse itself, with two exceptions. His mock epic "The Hasty Pudding" still has a witty warmth, and his periodic attacks on tyrannical governments and authoritarian religions can rise to a sort of splendid rhythmic wrath. Appointed minister to France in 1812, Barlow died while chasing Napoleon across Europe trying to get a treaty signed. The standard edition is *The Works of Joel Barlow*, 2 vols., ed. William K. Bottorf and A. L. Ford (1970).

Songs and Hymns: 1775–1825

"Yankee Doodle": Little is known about this most famous song of the American Revolution. The earliest manuscript is dated 1775; the earliest known printing is in a Scottish collection, around 1778.

"The Yankee Man-of-War": The origin of this spirited composition is unknown, but the poem itself has not gone unnoticed. It was printed in E. C. Stedman's *An American Anthology* (1900) and has appeared in collections of American naval verse. It tells part of the story of John Paul Jones's cruise in the *Ranger* through St. George's Channel and the Irish Sea in 1778.

"See! How the Nations . . .": Richard Allen (1760–1831) was born a slave in Philadelphia. He became a Methodist, purchased his freedom, and was instrumental in founding the African Methodist Episcopal Church, of which he was the first bishop. See J. M. Spencer, *Black Hymnody* (1992), from which our text is taken.

"I Love Thy Kingdom . . .": Timothy Dwight (1752–1817) was the grandson of Jonathan Edwards and a president of Yale. He was an influential clergyman and one of the Connecticut Wits. His other poetry includes *The Conquest of Canaan* (1785) and *Greenfield Hill* (1794). *The Conquest of Canaan* is no longer readable.

"Poor Wayfaring Stranger": This poem is identified as a "Post Revolutionary camp-meeting hymn" in *Hymns as Poetry,* ed. T. Ingram and D. Newton (1956).

"Walk Softly": This poem and "I Will Bow . . ." are identified as early Shaker hymns in *Hymns as Poetry.*

"Home, Sweet Home": John Howard Payne (1791–1852) was a New York dramatist. This sentimental song is, rather improbably, from his *Clari: or The Maid of Milan* (1823), which was set as an opera by Sir Henry Bishop.

"O Thou, to Whom . . .": John Pierpont (1785–1866) was born in Connecticut and became a Unitarian minister in Boston in 1819. A radical among the liberals, he advocated antislavery, pacifism, and temperance. His poetry includes *Airs of Palestine* (1812) and *The Anti-Slavery Poems of John Pierpont* (1843). He is best known now as the author of "Jingle Bells." J. P. Morgan was his grandson.

III YOUNG AMERICA: THE ROMANTIC ERA: 1826–1859

William Cullen Bryant (1794–1878), was born in Cummington, Massachusetts, and attended the village school. He studied Latin and Greek with nearby clergymen and entered the sophomore class at Williams College when he was sixteen. He withdrew before graduating, hoping to study at Yale, but instead he studied law privately. He was admitted to the bar and practiced law in Great Barrington, Massachusetts, for nine years. He never liked the practice of law, however, and moved to New York in 1825, where he became one of the editors of the New York *Evening Post* in 1826. He soon acquired complete editorial control and principal ownership of the paper. For the next fifty years he was a formidable voice in public affairs. He had first become famous with "Thanatopsis," written at Cummington when he was eighteen and published in 1817 in the *North American Review*. Besides his *Poems* (1821), he published many volumes of verse, the last being *Poetical Works* (1876). He translated the *Iliad* (1870) and the *Odyssey* (1871–72). His chief theme was nature, and he was often compared with Wordsworth, who was a major influence on him.

"Thanatopsis": The title of this poem means "view of death." It originally began on line 17, with "Yet a few days . . . ," and ended on line 66 with "and make their bed with thee." The opening and closing lines were added later to make a frame, which the poem may not actually need.

"To Cole, the Painter . . .": Thomas Cole, founder of the Hudson River School, was a friend of Bryant's. Landscape painting and landscape in poetry were both popular in early nineteenth-century America, and the painters and poets strongly influenced one another.

Lydia [Howard Huntley] Sigourney (1791–1865) was born in Norwich, Connecticut. She settled in Hartford, where she opened a school for girls and married a Hartford merchant. Sigourney wrote more than two thousand articles for some three hundred periodicals and published sixty-seven books, beginning with *Moral Pieces in Prose and Verse* (1815). She became an enormously popular and influential poet, often compared to the British poet Felicia Hemans. Her instinct for women's issues was especially keen. A great many nineteenth-century poems emulated the tone and feelings expressed in her "Death of an Infant."

George Moses Horton (c.1797–c.1883) was born the slave of William Horton in Northampton County, North Carolina. He moved to Chapel Hill, where his literary abilities were quickly recognized, though in a unique way: He wrote love poems for use by the students there (twenty-five cents for a moderate one, fifty for a passionate one). His first book, *The Hope of Liberty,* appeared in 1829; his last, *Naked Genius,* in 1865.

Edward Coote Pinkney (1802–1828) was born in London. During his short life he served in the U.S. Navy, edited the *Marylander,* and brought out a volume, *Poems* (1825), that was praised by Poe.

Ralph Waldo Emerson (1803–1882) was born in Boston, attended Harvard, and then entered the ministry. After the tragic death of his young wife, Ellen Tucker, in 1831, he left the ministry and, after a trip to Europe, started life again as a freelance lecturer and writer. He remarried and with his new wife, Lidian (née Lydia) Jackson, settled in Concord, Massachusetts, in 1835. He became a regular lecturer on the new lyceum circuit, giving some fifteen hundred lectures over the next thirty years. He wrote essays and books, edited the journal *The Dial,* and became a defining figure of Transcendentalism, which is, at its core, the belief that there is more in the human mind than can be accounted for simply by experience; that there is intuition as well as tuition. But Emerson's deepest ambition was to be a poet; poetry was the activity on which he always placed the highest value. His *Poems* appeared in 1846, and *May-Day and Other Pieces* in 1867. His poetry had an immediate and major impact on Walt Whitman and Emily Dickinson, and on many other American poets since. His conception of poetry, as he put it forward in his poems and in his essay "The Poet," has had an enormous influence. Emerson believed that poetry is a process rather than a product. "Genius," he once said, "is the activity that repairs the decay of things." His interest in the processes of poetry corresponded to a lack of interest in most of the formal features of verse. "It is not meter, but a meter making argument that makes a poem," he wrote. He thought that poetry is everywhere in the world, that it is the poet's job to capture it in words. The true poet, he thought, is a sayer, a namer, rather than a maker. For him, the need for expression is universal and as basic a human drive as sex. The poet is not an isolated, unique kind of being but a representative of us all: "He stands among partial men for the complete man, and apprises us not of his wealth, but of the common wealth." Emerson's basic belief that art is a process found its best expression in his comment that "art is the path of the creator to his work." His essay "The Poet" appeared in *Essays, Second Series* (1844). The best edition of his poetry is *Collected Poems and Translations,* ed. Harold Bloom and Paul Kane (1994).

"The Sphinx": Emerson once explained his intention in this poem: "The perception of identity unites all things and explains one by another, and the most rare and strange is equally facile as the most common. But if the mind live only in particulars, and see only difference, (wanting the power to see the whole—all in each) then the world addresses to this mind a question it cannot answer, and each new fact tears it in pieces."

"Dirge": Of Emerson's four brothers, two (Charles and Edward) had died in their twenties.

"Threnody": Loss was the ground-note of Emerson's life. This poem is his effort to come to terms with one of his greatest losses, the death of his five-year-old son Waldo in 1842.

"Boston Hymn": Emerson read this poem at the opening of a huge meeting in Boston's Music Hall on January 1, 1863, to celebrate the first day of Emancipation.

"Poet": The second quatrain of this name shows how short the distance is between Emerson and Dickinson.

Sarah Helen Whitman (1803–1878) was born Sarah Helen Power in Rhode Island. She married John Winslow Whitman, who died in 1833. She met Edgar Allan Poe in 1848. They were engaged, but Poe died in 1849. Her *Hours of Life and Other Poems* was published in 1848.

Elizabeth Oakes-Smith (1806–1893) had her first major success with a long poem, *The Sinless Child,* published in 1842. She was active in advocating women's rights; her *Woman and Her Needs* appeared in 1851. Her husband was the humor writer Seba Smith.

John Greenleaf Whittier (1807–1892) was born near Haverhill, Massachusetts, descended from French Huguenots through both the Whittiers and the Greenleafs. (Anne Bradstreet and Philip Freneau also had Huguenot connections; this is an underexamined strain in American poetry.) A Quaker, educated in local district schools, Whittier early on came under the influence of Robert Burns and Lord Byron and decided to become a poet. His first poem, "The Exile's Departure," was published in William Lloyd Garrison's *Newburyport Free Press* in 1826. In 1830 he went to Hartford, Connecticut, to edit the *New England Review.* His first book, of short stories and poems, called *Legends of New England,* appeared in 1831. Whittier was an active abolitionist. In 1835 he was mobbed in Concord, New Hampshire, for his views; in 1838 another mob burned the building in Philadelphia where he ran his newspaper, the *Pennsylvania Freeman.* Whittier was always a journalist and editor as well as a poet. In 1843 he was elected to the Massachusetts state senate. Like Henry David Thoreau, he opposed the Mexican War. His early fame was as a confrontational prophet, defying both church and state in the cause of freedom. Later this image of him was replaced by that of a benign old singer of harmless country themes. His antislavery verse was collected in *Voices of Freedom* (1846); his best-known volume was *Snow-Bound* (1866). The standard edition is *The Poetical Works of Whittier* (1894).

"Ichabod": The title refers to Daniel Webster; the poem records Whittier's reaction to Webster's March 7, 1850, speech endorsing the Fugitive Slave Act.

"Abraham Davenport": The famous Dark Day of New England occurred on May 19, 1780.

"The Slave-Ships": This poem is based on the voyage of the French ship *Le Rodeur,* which sailed from Africa in April 1819.

Henry Wadsworth Longfellow (1807–1882) was born in Portland, Maine, and graduated from Bowdoin College in the spectacular class of 1825, along with Nathaniel Hawthorne and Franklin Pierce. He went to Europe, learned French, Spanish, and Italian, then returned to teach at Bowdoin. He was appointed professor of Romance languages at Harvard, but in 1835, before taking up this position, he made another trip to Europe; his young wife died in the same year. He came under the influence of German Romanticism, especially the poems of Novalis. His first volume of poems, *Voices of the Night* (Novalis had written a "Hymn to the Night") appeared in 1839. In 1841 he brought out *Ballads and Other Poems,* containing among others "The Wreck of the Hesperus," which quickly made him famous. He taught at Harvard for eighteen years, but his "poetic dreams were shaded by French irregular verbs," and as Wilbert Snow notes, "he longed for freedom." He quit teaching in 1854 to devote himself to poetry; many of his later books were best-sellers. *Evangeline* is said to have "reached almost every literate home in America." *Hiawatha,* published in 1855, based on Henry Rowe Schoolcraft's work on the *Algic Researches* and set in a meter suggested by the newly published Finnish epic *Kalevala,* was an enormous success. Longfellow lived in a grand home in Cambridge; he knew everyone and entertained lavishly. One day in 1861 his wife, Frances Appleton, was at home standing too close to the hearth; her dress caught fire, and she was burned to death. In the years that followed, Longfellow translated Dante's *Divine Comedy* and wrote *Tales of a Wayside Inn* (the first poem of which is "Paul Revere's Ride") and, in 1872, *Christus: A Mystery*. Longfellow has been condescended to as a "fireside poet" and a mere metrist. Others have said that reading his poems provides one with a good general education. But Longfellow's sheer poetic abilities, lyrical and narrative, are unmistakable, and his work refuses to die. He is America's great poet of loss. The standard edition is *Poetical Works* (1904).

"A Psalm of Life": The first of Longfellow's poems to become widely known, it was translated into many languages. It was, for example, heard on the lips of a dying soldier at Sebastopol during the Crimean War.

"The Wreck of the Hesperus": The schooner *Hesperus* was actually wrecked on the ledges off Cape Ann, the headland on which Gloucester, Massachusetts, sits. But a nearby reef called Norman's Woe proved irresistible to the poet.

"Excelsior": This poem was set to music, and the refrain was provided with a silly translation ("upidee, upida"). It was still being belted out in the 1950s by students at Exeter Academy at the last chapel before every long vacation.

"The Cross of Snow": This poem is about the death of Longfellow's wife in 1861.

"The Children's Hour": J. P. Morgan acquired a major collection of American literary manuscripts because it contained the manuscript of this poem, which, like many of Longfellow's individual poems, is still in print.

Hiawatha: This poem has been much abused as an early example of "Judeo-Christian-Disney" culture, but the judgment is unfair. The material of the poem was drawn from Schoolcraft's *Algic Researches* and other respectable sources, and though the meter was taken from the *Kalevala,* it has a strong resemblance to a verse form used in the New World in Aztec or Nahuatl poetry.

"Michael Angelo": This poem was never finished; the fragments show Longfellow with impressive power even at the end of his life.

Lucretia Davidson (1808–1825) was born in Plattsburgh, New York, and attended Emma Willard's Female Academy in Troy and Miss Gilbert's in Albany. She died at age sixteen; her poetry was published in *Amir Khan and Other Poems,* ed. Margaret Davidson (1829).

Edgar Allan Poe (1809–1849) was born in Boston to an English mother and an American father of Scotch-Irish descent, both of whom were actors. Poe's life was haunted by disaster. His father disappeared, and his mother died in Richmond, Virginia, when the boy was two. He was raised by John and Frances Allan of Richmond and spent the years 1815–20 in England with them. Poe attended the University of Virginia for one term in 1826. His foster father seems to have been stingy, and Poe owed the school money when he arrived. To raise money, he took to gambling but lost heavily. John Allan refused to cover his debts, which amounted to around $2,500. Poe left school and traveled to Boston as Henri Le Rennet, then joined the U.S. Army under the name Edgar A. Perry and was assigned to Battery H of the First U.S. Artillery at Fort Independence in Boston Harbor. From 1827 to 1831 he was a soldier as well as a poet. His *Tamerlane* was published in Boston in 1827, his *Al Aaraaf* in Baltimore in 1829, and his *Poems* in New York in 1831. After leaving the army, Poe became a magazine editor, living in Baltimore, New York, Richmond, and Philadelphia, editing and writing for the *Southern Literary Messenger, Burton's Gentleman's Magazine, Graham's Lady's and Gentleman's Magazine,* and the *Broadway Journal.* In 1836 he married his fourteen-year-old cousin, Virginia Clemm. She fell dangerously ill in 1841 and died six years later. Nothing went right for Poe except his writing. His magazine jobs ended badly, he alienated friends and supporters, and physically and mentally his health was often borderline. After his death his reputation was systematically blackened by, of all people, his own literary executor, Rufus Griswold. Yet Poe has been enormously influential. He was praised and translated by Charles Baudelaire, and later by Stéphane Mallarmé and Paul Verlaine; his influence on American poetry is incalculable. With his emphasis on intensity of effect, the concentrated duration of *excited* attention, and the "totality of . . . impression," Poe reflected and significantly spurred the growing emphasis on the short poem as a norm for poetry. He even suggested that the *Iliad* was probably "intended as a series of lyrics; but, granting the epic intention . . . the work is based in an imperfect sense of Art." Behind the decline of the long poem lies the growing significance of the novel, which was usurping its role—and its audience. Against Poe, there stand—surely more formidably than *The Columbiad*—Whitman, Melville's *Clarel,* Hart Crane, Williams's *Paterson,* and Pound's *Cantos.* But aside from the long and short of it, there is the quality that his criticism does not deal with overtly: his literally hypnotic, cadenced exploration of the realm of dream and the dreaming "I." His poems, like his stories, have been read and loved and memorized by generations of readers who care nothing for critical fashion or even the history of literature. Their response forms part of what Erich Heller has called the course of poetry since the Renaissance: "the Discovery and Colonisation of Inwardness." Poe is one of its heroic explorers. The standard edition of his poetry is *Collected Works of Edgar Allan Poe,* ed. T. O. Mabbott (1969), vol. 1.

"To Helen": This poem was inspired by Poe's affection for Jane Stith Stanard.

"Israfel": Some printings of the poem include the following epigraph from Sale's translation of the Koran: "And the angel Israfel, whose heartstrings are a lute, and who has the sweetest voice of all God's creatures."

"The Haunted Palace": This allegorical poem appears in Poe's story "The Fall of the House of Usher."

"The Raven": This most famous of Poe's poems appeared in 1845 and caused a literary sensation.

Oliver Wendell Holmes (1809–1894) was born in Cambridge, Massachusetts, went to Harvard, studied in Paris hospitals, and received his M.D. from Harvard in 1836. He practiced and taught medicine at Dartmouth, then at Harvard, where he was also dean. Active in the founding of the *Atlantic Monthly,* which he named, he was famous as a man of letters, an occasional poet, and a wit, best known for *The Autocrat of the Breakfast-Table* (1858). The standard edition of his poetry is *The Poetical Works of Oliver Wendell Holmes,* Cambridge ed., rev. and with a new introduction by Eleanor Tilton (1975).

"Aestivation": Holmes labeled this "an unpublished poem by my late Latin tutor."

"Ballad of the Oysterman": This poem is a comic retelling of the Hero and Leander story.

"The Deacon's Masterpiece": This poem is generally supposed to be a parable of the breakdown of Calvinism.

"The Last Leaf": This poem portrays Major Thomas Melvill, a Revolutionary War veteran and grandfather of Herman Melville, who added the final *e* to the family name.

"Old Ironsides": The USS *Constitution,* nicknamed Old Ironsides, was scheduled for demolition but saved, in part by this poem, which was printed in the Boston *Daily Advertiser.*

"Peau de Chagrin . . .": The name comes from the title of a novel by Balzac about a magic skin that shrinks as one makes wishes. The analogy is to a bond from which one clips coupons at regular intervals. The coupons, which are redeemed for cash, represent the interest the bond produces.

Thomas Holley Chivers (1809–1858) was born in Georgia and earned his M.D. at Transylvania University in Lexington, Kentucky, but he soon abandoned medicine for authorship. He became a good friend of Poe. His earlier "Isadore" and other poems may have influenced Poe; Poe's work certainly influenced Chivers. Each charged the other with plagiarism, a controversy that continued after Poe's death. Chivers published twelve books, including *The Lost Pleiad and Other Poems* (1845). Poe's original estimate of Chivers, that he was "one of the best and one of the worst poets in America," is at least half right.

Margaret Fuller (1810–1850), born in Cambridgeport, Massachusetts, was associated with Emerson and the Transcendentalists, editing the *Dial.* After moving to New York, she became a full-time critic for the *New York Tribune.* An advocate of women's rights, she later moved to Italy, where she took up the cause of the Roman Revolution. She died in a shipwreck off Fire Island on her way back to the United States. Her poems are in *The Essential Margaret Fuller,* ed. Jeffrey Steele (1992).

Frances S. Osgood (1811–1859), born in Boston, grew up in Hingham, Massachusetts. After marrying painter Samuel Osgood, she lived in England for five years, where she published *A Wreath of Wild Flowers from New England* (1838). Returning to the United States, she became a popular poet, well known in New York circles. She was romantically involved with Poe and was a friend of Poe's literary executor, Rufus Griswold. Her poetry was collected in *Osgood's Poetical Works* (1880).

Ellen Sturgis Hooper (1812–1848) was born in Boston, the second child of the merchant William Sturgis, who by 1825 controlled half the American shipping to China. A Transcendentalist, she was a friend of Margaret Fuller's and contributed eleven poems to the *Dial.* See Perry Miller, *The American Transcendentalists* (1957).

Jones Very (1813–1880) was born in Salem, Massachusetts. His mother, Lydia Very, was a forceful materialist, atheist, and disciple of Fanny Wright. His father was a sea captain who took his eleven-year-old son on a trip to the North Sea, where the boy walked the walls of Kronborg Castle, the "Elsinore" of *Hamlet.* Very graduated from Harvard, and during a prolonged period of religious exaltation from 1833 to 1840 (1837–39 were the peak years), he wrote what many now consider the finest sonnets produced in the United States. His poetry was edited by Emerson as *Essays and Poems* (1839). But his vision soon clouded, and his rapture drained away. He held pastoral positions briefly in Eastport, Maine, and North Beverly, Massachusetts, but was too shy to be a good preacher. He returned to his native town and lived on, in the shadow of his lost rapture, as a mild retired Unitarian minister until 1880. A friend observed that "he moved in Salem like Dante among the Florentines: a man who had seen God." The standard edition is *Jones Very: The Complete Poems,* ed. Helen R. Deese (1993).

Christopher Cranch (1813–1892) was born in Alexandria, Virginia, and became a magazine editor and a painter as well as a poet. He was also a Unitarian minister at Bangor and Portland, Maine, and at Richmond, St. Louis, Cincinnati, and Louisville. In 1841 he turned to painting full time. Sympathetic to Transcendentalism and to the Brook Farm experiment in communal living, he wrote poems for the *Dial,* drew witty caricatures, and translated the *Aeneid* (1872). In 1873 he moved to Cambridge, Massachusetts. His first volume was *Poems* (1844); the standard edition is *Collected Poems of Christopher Cranch,* ed. J. M. DeFalco (1971).

"Enosis": The title is the Greek word for "unity, union, combination into one." The poem has often appeared under the misleading and erroneous title "Gnosis," meaning "knowing." It was one of William James's favorite poems.

Henry David Thoreau (1817–1862) lived in his native Concord, Massachusetts, for his entire life, except for a few short trips. He went to Harvard, where, as a senior, he heard Longfellow lecture on poetry, giving special emphasis to what was early, primitive, and heroic. After college Thoreau became first a disciple, then a friend of Emerson's. Emerson praised the young man's poetry, calling it "the purest strain, and the loftiest, I think, that has yet pealed from this unpoetic American forest." Thoreau became best known for his prose, especially *Walden,* but his best poems have a bleached-bone simplicity, a wavelike rhythm, and a clean narrative drive. Thoreau himself liked the kind of poem that has an unmistakable tone of experienced emotion, the kind of poem that "is drawn out from under the feet of the poet—his whole weight has rested on this ground." His poems appeared in the *Dial* and in his books. The standard edition is *Collected Poems of Henry Thoreau,* ed. C. Bode, enlarged ed. (1965).

"Light-Winged Smoke": This poem appears in *Walden.*

"I Am a Parcel of Vain Strivings": Tradition has it that when he was a senior at Harvard, Thoreau tossed this poem, wrapped around some flowers, through the window of Lucy Brown, a Concord woman somewhat older than he was and the sister of Emerson's wife, née Lydia Jackson.

William Ellery Channing (1818–1901) was a nephew of the celebrated Boston minister of the same name. Ellery the poet lived in Concord and was a friend and—with his dog, Professor—a walking companion of Emerson and Thoreau. His occupation was once listed, in an official census, as "a do-nothing." His *Poems* (1843) was followed by *Poems Second Series* (1847).

AMERICAN INDIAN POEMS: 1826–1859

A large number of works can be classed as American Indian or Native American poetry. Aztec or Nahuatl poetry was being written down by the mid-1520s, and many texts of both Nahuatl and Mayan poetry date from the middle of the sixteenth century. The Iroquois "Ritual of Condolence" was written down in the mid–eighteenth century, the Navajo "Night Chant" at the end of the nineteenth. Yet like much Native American ceremonial poetry, both poems are older than the earliest attempts to write them down. Our selections are limited to pieces that appeared in English during the period covered. For others, see, for example, John Bierhorst, *Four Masterworks of American Indian Literature* (1974).

"Chant to the Fire-fly": This transcription and translation of a Chippewa (Ojibwa) original was done by Henry Rowe Schoolcraft.

"From the South": Both versions are recorded by Schoolcraft in *Historical and Statistical Information Respecting . . . the Indian Tribes of the United States,* 6 vols. (1851–57).

Songs, Hymns, Spirituals, Carols, and Parlor Poems: 1826–1859

"The Lament of the Captive": Richard Henry Wilde (1798–1846), born in Ireland, was a lawyer, a congressman from Georgia, and a professor of law as well as a poet. The "Lament . . . ," published without his knowledge in 1819, was part of a projected epic on the Seminole War.

"A Visit from St. Nicholas": This poem by Clement Moore (1779–1863) was first published in the *Troy Sentinel* on December 23, 1823.

"The Old Oaken Bucket": This poem by Samuel Woodworth (1785–1842), originally titled "The Bucket," appeared in *Melodies, Duets, Songs, and Ballads* (1826).

"Mary Had a Little Lamb": Sarah Josepha Hale (1788–1879), the distinguished editor of *Ladies' Magazine* and *Godey's Lady's Book,* wrote and published this poem in 1830 in *Poems for Our Children.*

"America": Samuel Francis Smith (1808–1895) wrote this poem in 1831 while he was a student at Andover Theological Seminary. It was first published in Mason's *The Choir.* Smith's work was collected in *Poems of Home and Country* (1895).

"Woodman . . .": George Pope Morris (1802–1864) went riding with a friend one day to see the old oak in front of his friend's family home. The current owner was sharpening his ax to cut the tree down, as it was too near the road, and he needed firewood. The friend, "in great agitation," paid the man ten dollars to let the tree stand. The poem originally appeared as "The Oak" in the New York *Mirror* for January 17, 1837.

"The Blue Tail Fly": Another version has the familiar refrain,

> Jimmy cracked corn and I don't care,
> Jimmy cracked corn and I don't care,
> Jimmy cracked corn and I don't care,
> The Master's gone away.

"Oh, Susanna!": This song by Pittsburgh songwriter Stephen Foster (1826–1864) was first published anonymously in *Songs of the Sable Harmonists* in 1848. Foster wrote more than 175 songs, many of which appeared under the name "E. P. Christy" in various editions of *Ethiopian Melodies.*

"It Came Upon the Midnight Clear": Edmund Hamilton Sears (1810–1876) was a Unitarian clergyman who served pulpits in Lancaster, Wayland, and Weston, Massachusetts. He wrote this lovely Christmas carol in 1850. He fell out of a tree in 1874 and died two years later.

"Listen to the Mocking Bird": Septimus Winner wrote this under the pseudonym "Alice Hawthorne" in 1855.

IV THE CIVIL WAR ERA: 1860–1870

Walt Whitman (1819–1892), born in Huntington, New York, on Long Island, was a teacher, typesetter, journalist, and editor as well as a poet. He was of mainly English and Dutch extraction; he had no formal schooling beyond his thirteenth year. He was associated, during the late 1830s and the 1840s, with a great many newspapers in Brooklyn and Manhattan, including the *Aurora,* the *Sun,* the *Tattler, Brother Jonathan,* the *Statesman,* the *Democrat,* the *American Review,* the *Columbian,* the *Democratic Review,* and the *Brooklyn Eagle.* His early verse is conventional in the extreme; the free verse that was to make *Leaves of Grass* (1855) so unusual seems to have been formulated during a short space of time, possibly the month of March 1850. Two weeks after Daniel Webster's "Seventh of March Speech" endorsing the Fugitive Slave Act, Whitman attacked Webster in a poem called "Blood Money" in irregular lines resembling biblical "verses." "Resurgemus," later retitled "Europe, the 72nd and 73rd Years of These States" and included in *Leaves of Grass,* was published in the *New York Tribune* on June 21, 1850. These details matter because Whitman is the inventor of modern free verse, and his influence has been—and continues to be—enormous. When he self-published *Leaves of Grass* in 1850, he sent a copy to Emerson, who responded with an astonishing letter of praise. "I am not blind to the wonderful worth of *Leaves of Grass,*" it went in part. "I find it the most extraordinary piece of wit and wisdom that America has yet contributed. . . . I greet you at the beginning of a great career." Whitman's poetry changed the course of modern poetry. Not only is he the inventor of modern free verse and the originator of the subjective epic (the *modern* subjective epic; Dante has a prior claim here), Whitman is the first modern poet to celebrate sex openly and explicitly in his work. He did more than anyone else to make modern city life a subject for poetry. He had a strong homoerotic streak, and while he was praised in the nineteenth century as "The Good Grey Poet," he is fast becoming known now as "The Good Gay Poet." Neither of these tags does him full justice. He lived for a time in Washington, D.C., and served tirelessly in Civil War hospitals. It has been argued that the war was the central event of his life. He is by general consent one of the two most original American poets yet, the other being Emily Dickinson. The standard edition is *The Collected Writings of Walt Whitman,* ed. G. W. Allen and S. Bradley (1961).

"Song of Myself": This was the first poem in the first (1855) edition of *Leaves of Grass.* Like all the other poems in that edition, it was untitled. Together with Wordsworth's *The Prelude,* it marks the beginning of the modern subjective epic. But while the subject is "I," it is a representative "I," standing for everyone and committed to Emerson's idea that poetry inheres in all people and all things. "The United States themselves are essentially the greatest poem," Whitman wrote. His free verse has been regarded as the inevitable poetic result of the democratic idea: free verse for a free people. No class lines and no formal structures translate into no fixed line length and no fixed stanza pattern. The poet delivers reality: "Stop this day and night with me and you shall possess the original of all poems." Like Emerson, Whitman doubted that literary forms themselves meant much. "No one," he wrote, "will get at my verses who insists upon viewing them as a literary performance, or as aiming mainly towards art or aestheticism." Some critics have insidiously suggested that Whitman's monologism is only *masked* by polyphony; at bottom, the only voice is his own, feigning other voices like a ventriloquist, ever awake, watching over everything and everyone in Orwellian fashion.

"Europe, the 72nd and 73rd Years of These States": This was the first-written of the poems in Whitman's first edition, and the first he wrote in free verse. The subject matter here is, significantly, the revolutions of 1848.

"Cavalry Crossing a Ford": This poem employs an essentially cinematic technique, the juxtaposition of images without perceptible editorial comment.

"When Lilacs Last . . .": This and the next poem are both elegies for Abraham Lincoln, though Lincoln is never mentioned by name. This elegy, which along with Milton's "Lycidas" and Shelley's "Adonais" is among the finest in English, is essentially organized along musical lines. The symbols of the bird, the star, and the lilac recur repeatedly in a poem that is more elaborately constructed than it looks.

James Russell Lowell (1819–1891) was born and died in the same house, Elmwood, in Cambridge, Massachusetts. His father, Charles, was a Unitarian minister. His mother, Harriet Brackett Spence, may have been related to the hero of the old Scottish "ballad of Sir Patrick Spens." At Harvard he was elected class poet, but when he went to chapel afterward, rose, and bowed, smiling to all sides as though in acknowledgment of the honor, the Harvard authorities "rusticated" him for this uppity behavior to Concord and the custody of Reverend Barzillai Frost until commencement. He graduated from Harvard in 1838, tried law, then turned to literature. His *A Year's Life* appeared in 1841, his *Poems* in 1844. In the same year he married Maria White, whose strong views on abolition were largely responsible for Lowell's swing from conservative to radical politics and sentiments. He followed Longfellow as professor of Romance languages at Harvard, being appointed in 1855 and staying on there until 1886. An active critic as well as poet, Lowell was the first editor of the *Atlantic Monthly,* from 1857 to 1861.

"A Fable for Critics": This poem first appeared in 1848.

The Biglow Papers: Lowell wrote two series of Biglow Papers, satirical verses in Yankee dialect. The first series, published in 1848, opposed the Mexican War; the second series, published in the *Atlantic Monthly,* supported the North in the Civil War. The narrator is a young farmer named Hosea Biglow.

"The 'Cruetin Sarjunt'": This portrait of a recruiting sergeant is part of the introduction to *The Biglow Papers.*

Herman Melville (1819–1891) was born in New York City; his father's family was English, his mother's Dutch. Herman had Revolutionary War heroes on both family's sides. (See the note to Oliver Wendell Holmes's "The Last Leaf" on page 675.) Melville's father declared bankruptcy, then died when the boy was twelve. He went to school until he was fifteen, then did a little clerking, a little farming, and a little teaching. When he was twenty, he shipped as a cabin boy to Liverpool and made one round trip. In January 1841 he shipped for the South Seas on the whaler *Acushnet;* the trip became the basis of *Moby-Dick.* He turned to poetry after writing most of the novels for which he is best known. "Herman has taken to writing poetry," his wife told her mother in 1859. "You need not tell anyone, for you know how such things get around." *Battle Pieces and Aspects of the War* appeared in 1866; *Clarel,* a long narrative poem about a trip to the Holy Land, in 1876; *John Marr and Other Sailors* in 1888; and *Timoleon* in 1891. *Clarel* was published at the expense of his uncle, Peter Gansevoort. The latter two volumes were financed by the author and published in editions of twenty-five copies each. Melville's poetry was neglected, as was Melville himself during his later years. The standard edition of *Clarel* is that edited by H. Hayford et al. (1991). The other poems here are from *Collected Poems of Herman Melville,* ed. H. Vincent (1947).

"The Portent": Melville's image of the hanged John Brown should be compared with John Smith's "The Sea Marke," which opens this anthology.

"The House-Top . . .": This poem is about the New York draft riots of July 11–13, 1863, which seemed to Melville to bear out Calvin's dark assessment of human nature.

"The Martyr": This is Melville's Lincoln poem.

"The Maldive Shark" and "The Berg": Both poems amply illustrate Melville's contention, in *Moby-Dick,* that the world has two sides, and that the dark half was "formed in fright."

"Monody": This poem is thought to be about Nathaniel Hawthorne. Melville and Hawthorne became close friends when both were living in the Berkshires, in western Massachusetts.

Clarel: Melville's immense poem is about a modern trip to the Holy Land, or what is now Israel. The poem has four parts, 150 cantos, and is eighteen thousand lines long. It is about a young American named Clarel who is on a pilgrimage through the ancient ruins of Palestine with a group of companions. While the main interest of the poem lies in the exchanges between the sharply delineated characters, our selections are entirely set pieces, in which a single speech or a short exchange is self-explanatory. Perhaps most interesting about *Clarel* is Melville's lack of interest in conventional verse and five-foot lines and his use of a new, compressed, four-foot, stripped-down poetic line. Melville's vision is not lyrical; neither is his best verse.

"Epilogue": The references to Darwin and Luther underscore the strongly intellectual nature of the poem. Melville's lifelong struggle with the problem of belief was best summed up by his friend Hawthorne, who observed that Melville "could neither believe, nor be entirely comfortable in his unbelief."

Alice Cary (1820–1871) was born near Cincinnati. She and her sister Phoebe (also a poet) published *Poems of Alice and Phoebe Cary* in 1849. Later the sisters moved to New York. The work of Alice Cary was admired by Rufus Griswold, Poe, and Whittier.

Ann Plato (c.1820–?) lived in Hartford, Connecticut, and in 1841 published *Essays: Including Biographies and Miscellaneous Pieces, In Prose and Poetry,* with an introduction by Reverend James W.C. Pennington, her pastor at the Colored Congregational Church of Hartford. Almost nothing else is known about this African-American poet.

Joshua McCarter Simpson (c.1820–1876), a freeborn African-American from Morgan County, Ohio, was at first largely self-taught. He attended Oberlin College from 1844 to 1848, married, and settled in Zanesville, Ohio. His poetry was published in *The Emancipation Car* in 1874.

Frederick Goddard Tuckerman (1821–1873) was born in Massachusetts, attended Harvard (where Jones Very was his tutor), and practiced law briefly before withdrawing to live as a recluse. He published one volume, *Poems,* in 1860. In the 1930s he was effectively discovered by Witter Bynner, who edited his *Sonnets* (1931). The standard edition is *The Complete Poems of Frederick Goddard Tuckerman,* ed. M. Scott Momaday (1965).

F[rances] E[llen] W[atkins] Harper (1824–1911) was born to free parents in Baltimore. She became a teacher, then moved to Philadelphia, where she soon became a major lecturer and activist for education, civil rights, and temperance. She spoke and published widely; her verse alone comprises eleven volumes. See especially *Poems on Miscellaneous Subjects,* 2nd ed. (1854) and *Poems* (1871).

Lucy Larcom (1824–1893) grew up in Beverly, Massachusetts, the daughter of a retired shipmaster. She read poetry, learned German, and contributed to the *Lowell Offering,* a magazine by and for the millworkers of Lowell. Larcom taught at Wheaton Seminary (later Wheaton College) from 1854 to 1862 and in 1868 published her first book of poems. She was an editor and a critic, collaborating with Whittier on several projects in the 1870s. Her autobiography is called *A New England Girlhood* (1889).

Charles Godfrey Leland (1824–1903) was a Philadelphia editor and author. One of his early teachers was Bronson Alcott; he later studied at the College of New Jersey, in Heidelberg, and in Munich. His "Hans Breitmann's Barty" appeared in *Graham's Magazine* in May 1857. His comic poems were collected and printed after his death as *Hans Breitmann's Ballads* (1914).

Bayard Taylor (1825–1878) was a traveler, a very successful journalist and popular writer, and a poet. Born in Pennsylvania of Quaker stock, his first book was a volume of romantic verse, *Ximena* (1844). In addition to a wide range of original poetry, he produced a translation of Goethe's *Faust* in 1870–71, for which he is now best known.

Rose Terry Cooke (1827–1892) grew up in Hartford, Connecticut, where her mother made her memorize a page from the dictionary every day. She graduated from the Hartford Female Seminary at age sixteen, becoming first a teacher, then a significant and popular writer of short stories as well as of poetry. Her *Poems* appeared in book form in 1861 and again in 1881.

Henry Timrod (1828–1867) was born in Charleston, South Carolina, of German and Scotch-Irish descent on his father's side (his paternal grandfather was named Heinrich Dimroth) and Anglo-Swiss descent on his mother's. He was educated at Franklin College (now the University of Georgia). He published one volume of poems during his lifetime, *Poems* (1860). On March 1, 1862, he enlisted in Company B of the 30th South Carolina Regiment. He served as a clerk (his regiment fought at Shiloh) and as a correspondent but was discharged in December 1862, suffering from incipient tuberculosis. He married Kate

Goodwin in February 1864, but a year later Columbia was burned and his livelihood destroyed. His son Willie, his "single rose-bud in a crown of thorns," died. As an editor, he lived a life of want and poverty, summing up his condition in an 1866 letter as "beggary, starvation, death, bitter grief, utter want of hope." Timrod was called the laureate of the Confederacy; his poems were collected and published in 1873 and again, as *Complete Poems,* in 1899.

"Ethnogenesis": The title means "birth of a nation" and refers to the Confederate States of America. The poem was written in February 1861.

"Ode Sung at Magnolia Cemetery": This poem was written in 1867, shortly before Timrod's own death.

Helen Hunt Jackson (1830–1885) was born Helen Fiske in Amherst, Massachusetts. Her first husband, Edward Hunt, blew himself up in the Brooklyn Navy Yard while testing a torpedo he had invented. Once she turned to poetry, her work attracted the attention of Emerson. In 1873 she married a Quaker banker from Colorado who supported her writing. She was a lifelong friend of Emily Dickinson and wrote two important books about Native Americans, *A Century of Dishonor* (1881) and *Ramona* (1884).

Emily Dickinson (1830–1886) was also born in Amherst. Her mother, Emily Norcross, was a quiet woman, rarely mentioned by her daughter. Her father, Edward Dickinson, was treasurer of Amherst College and a formidable presence who read "lonely and rigorous books" on Sundays and stepped "like Cromwell when he [got] the kindlings." The poet was educated at Amherst Academy and—for a year—at Mount Holyoke Female Seminary, where she was the lone holdout in a protracted and blistering religious revival conducted at the school. Except for a few trips (one to Philadelphia in 1854), she spent her entire life in Amherst, the last twenty-five years as a virtual recluse. She wrote more than 1,750 poems, of which only some seven were published during her lifetime, "none of them with clear consent" (P. Rosenbaum). She is now usually considered one of the most important American poets. Her poetry is metrically based in hymn meter; most of her poems use four-line stanzas with eight syllables in the first line, six in the second, eight in the third, and six again in the fourth. (There is, to be sure, some variation; some stanzas are 4-4-4-4.) While this formal base may seem almost impossibly limited, it should be remembered that hymn meter—also called fourteeners, when four lines are printed as two, each having seven poetic feet—is the great meter of most popular poetry in English, the meter of Mother Goose and of most ballads and songs and folk poetry. What is so astonishing is the immense technical subtlety with which Dickinson combines this simple form with her unparalleled lyrical—and intellectual—intensity. There is no pressure of chant in Dickinson; there is pressure of thought—and unrelenting resistance to the facile. Despite the overwhelming frequency of "I," "me," and "my," no poet in English can surprise us with her choice of words as consistently as Dickinson can. During a meeting with Thomas Wentworth Higginson, Dickinson gave this definition of poetry: "If I read a book and it makes my whole body so cold no fire can ever warm me, I know that is poetry. If I feel physically as if the top of my head were taken off, I know that is poetry. These are the only ways I know it. Is there any other way?" Two volumes of her poems, edited by Mabel Todd and T. W. Higginson, appeared in 1890 and 1891; more followed. The standard edition is Thomas Johnson's *The Poems of Emily Dickinson,* 3 vols. (1958).

216: The second version of this poem is an excellent example of Dickinson's common practice of punctuating mainly with dashes.

288: Napoleon's final question, after hearing all the recommendations for a person, was "Yes, but is he somebody?"

Celia Thaxter (1835–1894), was born in Portsmouth, New Hampshire, moving to the Isles of Shoals when she was four because her father, disappointed in his run for governor, had himself appointed lighthouse keeper there. Thaxter was educated at home. When her father opened a hotel for summer visitors on Appledore in 1848, writers and painters (Thoreau, Whittier, Lowell, Hunt, Hassam) began to spend time there. Thaxter became a writer of poetry, stories, and children's literature. Her first poem was published in the *Atlantic* in March 1861, and her first volume, *Poems,* appeared in 1872.

Mark Twain (Samuel Clemens, 1835–1910) was born in Florida, Missouri, and grew up in Hannibal, which provided him with the background for *The Adventures of Tom Sawyer* (1876) and *The Adventures of Huckleberry Finn* (1884).

"Ode to Stephen Dowling Bots": Twain's satire on the sentimental poetry of the time appears in *Huckleberry Finn.* The crowning touch in this parody of incompetence is the change of rhythm in the next-to-last line.

Thomas Bailey Aldrich (1836–1906) was born in Portsmouth, New Hampshire, the scene of his novel *The Story of a Bad Boy.* He became a poet and a newspaper correspondent, then an editor, moving to Boston in 1865. He was a prolific writer in many genres; he edited the *Atlantic* from 1881 to 1890. His first volume of poems was *The Bells* (1855). The standard edition is *The Writings of Thomas Bailey Aldrich* (1907).

"Fredericksburg": The title refers to one of the bloodiest battles in the bloody Civil War.

Charlotte L. F[orten] Grimke (1837–1914) was born in Philadelphia and moved to Salem, Massachusetts, in 1853. She was educated at the Higginson School and the Salem Normal School. Afterward she taught on St. Helena Island, South Carolina, then settled in Washington, D.C. She was active in the abolition movement and later in the struggle for racial equality. For her poetry, see Anna J. Cooper, *Life and Writings of the Grimke Family* (1951), vol. 2.

Adah Isaacs Menken (c.1835–1868), born near New Orleans, was a celebrated actress as well as a poet. Reliable information about her early life is scarce. Her father may have been Auguste Theodore, a mulatto; he or her mother may have been Jewish. She married A. I. Menken in 1856 and thereafter a number of other men. Moving to New York, she became a popular actress. At Pfaff's, the bohemian center of New York, she met Walt Whitman, Ada Clare, and many others. She was a huge success in England in the stage version of Byron's *Mazeppa,* and she came to know Dickens, Swinburne, and Rossetti. In Paris she was a sensation in *Les Pirates de la Savane.* Menken is buried in Montmartre under a marble monument with an inscription from Swinburne. Her poems appeared in *Infelicia* (1868).

Sidney Lanier (1842–1881) descended from a long line of musicians, probably including a Huguenot musician who fled France for England and found a place in the household of Queen Elizabeth. Born in Macon, Georgia, Lanier was raised a Calvinist and a Presbyterian and was educated at Oglethorpe University. He served in the Confederate Army; his company, the Macon Volunteers, saw action at Malvern Hill. Lanier was a mounted scout, then a signal officer on blockade runners. He was captured and held prisoner at Point Lookout, Maryland. He became a flutist in the Peabody Orchestra in Baltimore and brought out a volume, *Poems,* in 1877. He was also a novelist, essayist, and lecturer on English literature at Johns Hopkins University. Lanier's *The Science of English Verse* remains a valiant attempt to link poetry to music, with its emphasis on poetry and time rather than stress—that is to say, on quantitative rather than accentual meter. The standard edition of his work is the *Centennial Edition* (1945); vol. 1, *Poems and Poem Outlines,* is edited by C. R. Anderson.

"Sunrise": This poem was written in the last months of Lanier's life, when he had a body temperature of 104 degrees.

"The Raven Days": "Raven Days" are the time just after the war, when, as Lanier wrote Bayard Taylor, "Pretty much the whole of life has been merely not dying."

"The Marshes of Glynn": Not only is this a splendid example of Lanier's ideas about the music of poetry and a major religious poem, it is a great poetic achievement in its own right.

SONGS, HYMNS, SPIRITUALS, AND CAROLS: 1859–1870

"Dixie's Land": The war song of the Confederacy was originally written in 1859 for Bryant's Minstrels, of which Daniel Emmett was a member. *Dixie* may be a corruption of the name Jeremiah Dixon, one of the surveyors of the Mason-Dixon Line.

"Battle Hymn of the Republic": Julia Ward Howe wrote the lyrics at the suggestion of J. F. Clarke, when Clarke and Howe were visiting McClellan's troops in December 1861. It is sung to the tune of "John Brown's Body," which is ascribed to William Steffe some five years earlier.

"Rock O' My Soul": This song and **"Michael Row the Boat Ashore"** were first printed in *Slave Songs of the United States* (New York: A. Simpson, 1867) but were most likely composed earlier.

"O Little Town of Bethlehem": This carol was composed by Phillips Brooks, an Episcopalian churchman and social reformer in Boston.

V THE ERA OF RECONSTRUCTION AND EXPANSION: 1870–1900

Emma Lazarus (1849–1887) was born in New York City of Sephardic Jewish stock; her parents were Moses and Esther (Nathan) Lazarus. The precocious young poet was privately educated at home. Her first volume, *Poems and Translations* (1866), was published when she was seventeen. Emerson became interested in her work, and they became friends. Around 1880 she became interested in immigration issues and in Jewish affairs. In 1881 she brought out her *Poems and Ballads of Heinrich Heine*. An 1882 volume is called *Songs of a Semite*. The *Poems of Emma Lazarus* was published in 2 volumes in 1889.

> "The New Colossus": Composed in 1883 to help raise funds for the Statue of Liberty, the sonnet was inscribed on the base of the completed statue in 1886.

James Whitcomb Riley (1849–1916), born in Greenfield, Indiana, started life as a "house, sign, and ornamental painter." He traveled with a group of painters called the Graphics and soon "covered all the barns and fences in the state with advertisements." He then became a journalist and a poet. He wrote popular poems for the *Indianapolis Journal* under the pseudonym "Benj. F. Johnson of Boone." In 1883 he published *The Old Swimmin' Hole and 'Leven More Poems,* the first of many volumes. His Hoosier dialect poems became enormously popular, and he himself became a well-known platform reader and entertainer. His poems are collected in *The Complete Works of James Whitcomb Riley,* ed. E. H. Eitel, 6 vols. (1913).

Ella Wheeler Wilcox (1850–1919) was born in Johnstown Center, near Madison, Wisconsin. Her parents, Marius and Sarah (Pratt) Wheeler, had emigrated from Vermont. Wilcox began to write early; before she was ten, she had written a novel for her sister. Her first real success was *Poems of Passion* (1883), which was turned down by a Chicago publisher. The rejection brought her notoriety; her poems were said to have "out-Swinburned Swinburne and out-Whitmaned Whitman." She became famous, wrote a poem a day for a newspaper syndicate, and published in all some forty-six books. In 1918 she toured the army camps in France, reciting poetry and "delivering talks on sexual problems." She became ill and returned home to die at her summer home in Short Beach, Connecticut. Her *Collected Poems* appeared in 1924.

Henrietta Cordelia Ray (1850–1916), daughter of Charlotte Augusta (Burrough) and Charles Bennett Ray was born and educated in New York City. Her father was a well-known abolitionist, editor, minister, and civic leader. Ray earned a master's degree in pedagogy from the University of the City of New York in 1891, then taught for thirty years in the public schools. Her volume *Sonnets* was published in 1893 and her *Poems* in 1910.

Edwin Markham (1852–1940) was born in Oregon City, Oregon. After a lonely childhood, he attended Christian College in Santa Rosa, California, and became a Christian socialist, a Swedenborgian, and a teacher. In 1886 he saw Jean-François Millet's painting *The Man with the Hoe*. The poem he wrote about it was published in the *San Francisco Examiner* and quickly brought him international fame. His book *The Man with the Hoe and Other Poems* (1899) was translated into forty languages. In later life he wrote articles for *Cosmopolitan* against child labor and verses for a Boston greeting-card firm; he compiled an immense ten-volume anthology of poetry. He was, his biographer notes, "guest of honor at great numbers of celebrations of every type."

Edith Matilda Thomas (1854–1925) was born in Ohio; her father, a farmer and teacher, was Welsh. She attended Geneva Normal School and, for a semester, Oberlin College. She moved to New York, where she met Helen Hunt Jackson, who praised her poems; later Thomas became an editor for the *Century Dictionary* and for *Harper's*. Her poetry includes *Lyrics and Sonnets* (1887) and *The Inverted Torch* 1890; in 1926 the poet Jesse Rittenhouse edited her *Selected Poems*.

Lizette Woodworth Reese (1856–1935) was born in Baltimore; her mother was German, her father Welsh. She taught in the Baltimore public schools, in what were then called English-German schools, in the high school for African-American children, and in the Western high school for girls. Her first volume, *A Branch of May* (1887), brought her recognition and the friendship of the influential critic and anthologist Edmund Clarence Stedman. Many volumes followed, including *Selected Poems* (1926) and a long poem, *Little Henrietta*, in 1927. For her epitaph she wrote, "The long day sped, / A roof, a bed; / No years, / No tears." Her best poems, currently undervalued, have, like her epitaph, lyric intensity, drive, and compression.

Samuel Alfred Beadle (1857–1932) was born in Atlanta and studied and practiced law in Mississippi. He wrote *Sketches from Life in Dixie* (1899) and *Lyrics of the Underworld* (1912).

George Marion McClellan (1860–1934), born in Belfast, Tennessee, was a minister and teacher as well as a poet. He took his B.A. and M.A. from Fisk University and a bachelor of divinity degree from Hartford Theological Seminary. He taught for twenty years in the Louisville schools. He published *Poems* (1895), retitled *Songs of a Southerner* (Boston, 1896), and *The Path of Dreams* (1916).

Bliss Carman (1861–1929) was born in Canada and was declared Canada's poet laureate in 1928. But after 1888 he made his home in New York and in New Canaan, Connecticut. He collaborated with Richard Hovey in *Songs from Vagabondia* (1894) and two sequels. He wrote more than twenty subsequent volumes.

Louise Imogen Guiney (1861–1920) was born in Roxbury, now part of Boston. One March day in 1877, her father, Irish born and a hero of the American Civil War, removed his hat, knelt in the street, crossed himself, and died. The image stayed with his daughter. Guiney graduated from Elmhurst, the convent school of the Order of the Sacred Heart in Providence, Rhode Island. Her first volume of poetry, *Songs at the Start,* appeared in 1884. After two trips to England, she settled in Oxford in 1901. She was much interested in Catholic poetry; her anthology *Recusant Poets* was published after her death. See E. M. Tenison, *Louise Imogen Guiney: Her Life and Works* (1923).

George Santayana (1863–1952) was born in Spain and came to Boston in 1872. He graduated from Harvard in 1886 and took a Ph.D. there in 1889. Thereafter he was a philosophy professor at Harvard, though he lived in Europe much of the time after 1914. His main fame is as a philosopher, but he also had an extensive literary career, starting with *Sonnets and Other Verses* (1894) and including a fine novel, *The Last Puritan* (1935). He issued a *Collected Poems* in 1923.

> "Normal Madness": This moving bit of prose poetry is taken from the conclusion of the dialogue of the same name in Santayana's *Dialogues in Limbo* (1925).

Richard Hovey (1864–1900) was born in Normal, Illinois, and grew up in Washington, D.C. He went to Dartmouth, where he wrote songs and poems that are still remembered. In 1887 he met Bliss Carman, with whom he would later collaborate on the *Vagabondia* poems. In later life he undertook an ambitious cycle of poem-dramas on Arthurian themes, known as the *Lancelot and Guenevere* cycle. For the last two years of his life he was a lecturer at Barnard College.

Madison Cawein (1865–1914) was born in Louisville, Kentucky, of Huguenot stock. As a young man, he worked as a cashier in a pool room, writing Romantic verse. His first volume, *Blooms of the Berry* (1887), was praised by William Dean Howells. He published thirty-five more volumes while making a living at real estate and in stocks. In 1907 he brought out a five-volume *Poems of Madison Cawein*. He died at forty-nine, falling in the bathroom and striking his head on the side of the tub.

James Edwin Campbell (1867–1896) was born in Pomeroy, Ohio, and became a schoolteacher, then a principal. He moved to Chicago and worked for the *Times Herald*. He was writing dialect poems before they were popularized by his friend Paul Laurence Dunbar. He published *Driftings and Gleanings* in 1887 and *Echoes from the Cabin and Elsewhere* in 1895.

W[illiam] E[dward] B[urghardt] Du Bois (1868–1963), famous as an educator, editor, and writer, was born in Great Barrington, Massachusetts. A student of William James, he became a professor of economics and history at Atlanta University. He led the Niagara Movement and was one of the founders of the NAACP in 1909, which he renounced in 1948 as too conservative. In 1961 he joined the Communist Party. In 1962 he moved to Ghana and became a citizen. He edited the magazine *Crisis* from 1910 to 1934. His best-known book is *The Souls of Black Folk* (1903).

"A Litany at Atlanta": Occasioned by the Atlanta race riot of 1906, this powerful prophetic poem is reminiscent of Isaiah and of Whitman and Frederick Douglass. It is a sort of *Job,* but with Job not surrounded by his friends, but spoken—sung—prayed for—by a supreme psalmist.

William Vaughn Moody (1869–1910) was born in Spencer, Indiana; his father was a steamboat captain. Moody graduated from Harvard and taught in the English department there and at the University of Chicago until 1907, when he turned to writing full time. Moody was short in stature, wore a small pointed beard, and exhibited a certain academic aloofness. He was a playwright as well as a poet. His first verse drama, *The Masque of Judgment,* appeared in 1900, his *Poems* in 1901. R. M. Lovett edited a *Selected Poems of William Vaughn Moody* in 1931.

Edwin Arlington Robinson (1869–1935) was born in Head Tide, Maine, and grew up in Gardiner, Maine. His father was Scotch Irish; his mother was descended from Anne Bradstreet's sister. His life was one of compound misfortune. He went to Harvard but was called home in 1892 to attend his dying father. His patrimony disappeared in the panic of 1893. Three years later his mother died of black diphtheria in a quarantined house. Next, his two older brothers died of mysterious ailments compounded by narcotics and alcohol. If his personal life was a hell, his writing went badly, too. One magazine, *Lippincott's,* kept a poem of his for twelve years. An editor named Small Maynard left and forgot the manuscript of his volume of poems, *Captain Craig,* in a Boston whorehouse. Robinson's biographer notes acidly that perhaps Maynard found the whorehouse so like a publishing house that he got confused. The madam kept the manuscript and returned it to Maynard on his next visit; only then did Robinson get it back. When the book was eventually published, it was met with silence: no praise, no criticism—nothing. Robinson said the hardest thing to bear was that he did not exist as a poet. He was eventually rescued by President Theodore Roosevelt, who had somehow found time to read and even to review his work. Roosevelt also got him a job with the New York Customs Office. In later years Robinson's life improved. He lived in New York City, writing long Arthurian poems, plays, and psychoanalytic studies. He never followed the Modernist line struck out by Pound, Eliot, and others. Instead, like Robert Frost (and in Frost's phrase), Robinson was content with the old way to be new. Few poems in English can match, say, "Eros Turannos" in psychological power and in dark finery of language. In 1921 appeared his *Collected Poems*, which won the first of three Pulitzer prizes awarded to him. The volume was reissued with additions in 1937. Robinson died of cancer at age sixty-six.

"Richard Cory": Robinson was leery of poems preserved in what he called "anthological pickle." This would be a good example, if it were not such a good poem.

"The Man Against the Sky": This is a minor masterwork of a modern Stoic sensibility.

Jesse Rittenhouse (1869–1948) was born in Mount Morris, New York. An influential anthologist and for ten years (1905–1915) poetry editor of the *New York Times Book Review,* she was instrumental in founding the Poetry Society of America in 1910. She was a close friend of Edgar Lee Masters, Vachel Lindsay, and Amy Lowell. Her own poems appeared in *The Door of Dreams* (1918), *The Lifted Cup* (1921), and *The Secret Bird* (1930).

George Sterling (1869–1926) was born in Sag Harbor, New York. After finishing school, he moved to Oakland, California, where he met Ambrose Bierce, who became his mentor. Sterling was a colorful bohemian figure; he looked like Dante and cut a wide social swath. He published many volumes of poetry, the best of which is collected in *Selected Poems* (1923). He died a suicide.

Edgar Lee Masters (1869–1950) was born in Garnett, Kansas, though his family soon moved to Illinois. His father was a lawyer of English descent, his mother the daughter of a Methodist minister in Vermont. Lee, as the young man was called, became a lawyer, moved to Chicago, and embraced Populism, Governor John P. Altgeld, and William Jennings Bryan. He joined the law firm of Clarence Darrow and, like him, defended the defenseless. As a poet he was largely unknown until 1914, when a series of 244 epitaphs under the pseudonym "Webster Ford" were revealed to be by Masters. The poems were reprinted as *Spoon River Anthology,* a volume that, by 1940, had gone through seventy editions and been translated into eight other languages. *The New Spoon River,* an extension, appeared in 1924. Masters also wrote novels, more poetry, biographies (of Lincoln, Vachel Lindsay, Whitman, and Mark Twain), and a poetic survey of American history called *Domesday Book*. His *Selected Poems* appeared in 1925. He died in his sleep at the Pine Manor Convalescent Home in Melrose, Pennsylvania, on March 5, 1950.

"Petit, the Poet": The *Spoon River Anthology* is roughly modeled on the *Greek Anthology* (a collection of over 6,000 short poems—many of them epitaphs from the 7th century BCE to the tenth century CE). It consists entirely of autobiographical epitaphs in which the inhabitants of an imagined town give summaries of their lives, one by one.

AMERICAN INDIAN POETRY: 1870–1900

For extensive selections, bibliographies, and context, see A. Grove Day, *The Sky Clears* (1951) and Jerome Rothenberg, *Shaking the Pumpkin: Traditional Poetry of the Indian North Americas* (1972).

"The Walum Olum": This is a traditional rendering of Lenape history.

SONGS, SPIRITUALS, HYMNS, AND POPULAR POEMS: 1870–1900

"John Henry": The legend of John Henry seems to have originated around 1870. He may have been a real person who competed with a real steam drill. For the full story as well as many variants, see G. B. Johnson's *John Henry: Tracking Down a Negro Legend* (1931).

"Home on the Range": Alan Lomax said that the music for this song was obtained in 1910 "from the negro proprietor of a low drinking and gambling dive in the slum district of San Antonio." It was published in Lomax's *Cowboy Songs* that year.

"Casey at the Bat": Ernest Lawrence Thayer (1863–1940) was born in Lawrence, Massachusetts, and studied philosophy at Harvard with William James. He wrote "Casey" in 1888 for William Randolph Hearst and the *San Francisco Examiner*. Thayer was not a writer; he managed his family's woolen mills in Worcester. An entertainer named William De Wolf Hopper took up the poem, delivering it some ten thousand times, making it America's best-known comic poem and the national poem about the national sport.

"I Been Working on the Railroad": This lyric was first published in the eighth edition of *Carmina Princetonia* (Newark, N.J., 1894). Of a possible earlier existence in the oral tradition of Black laborers, nothing certain is known.

"I Never Saw a Purple Cow": Gelett Burgess (1866–1951) was born in Boston and attended MIT. In San Francisco he started a magazine called *The Lark,* the first number of which contained "The Purple Cow." Burgess later moved to New York, wrote more than thirty-five books, and became a well-known figure in Greenwich Village. Among the words he contributed to the English language are *goop, bromide,* and *blurb.*

VI THE ADVENT OF THE MODERN: 1901–1922

Stephen Crane (1871–1900) was born in Newark, spent a year each at Lafayette College and Syracuse University, then moved to New York. There he worked as a journalist and wrote *Maggie, A Girl of the Streets* (1893) and *The Red Badge of Courage* (1895). His 1895 volume of poems, *The Black Riders,* was influenced by his reading of Dickinson. Crane's starkness, his bitterness, and his powerful irregularity mark him as an important harbinger of Modernism. In 1898 he went to England, where he befriended Joseph Conrad, H. G. Wells, and others. Another volume of poems, *War is Kind,* appeared in 1899. Crane developed tuberculosis, dying at twenty-nine of a hemorrhage at Badenweiler in the Black Forest.

James Weldon Johnson (1871–1938) was born in Jacksonville, Florida, and was educated at Jacksonville's Stanton Institute, the largest Florida high school for African-Americans, and at Atlanta University. He was the first African-American admitted to the Florida bar. He was also a skilled musician, and with his brother Rosamond he wrote a musical, *Toloso,* a satire on American imperialism; it was not produced. He and his brother also wrote a great many songs. In 1906 he turned from music and the stage to the foreign service; he was U.S. consul in Venezuela and Nicaragua. He moved to New York, where he became active in politics and in the founding of the NAACP. A leader of the Harlem Renaissance, he wrote *The Autobiography of an Ex-Colored Man* (1912) and many other books. His own poems appeared in *Fifty Years and Other Poems* (1917) and in *God's Trombones* (1927). He also edited the influential *Book of American Negro Poetry* (1922, enlarged ed. 1931) and, with his brother, two collections of spirituals. He was killed in an auto accident on June 26, 1938.

"Lift Every Voice and Sing": This poem has become known as the Black American anthem.

Lola Ridge (1871–1941) was born in Ireland and lived in Australia before coming to the United States in 1907. Her *The Ghetto and Other Poems* (1918) shows the influence of Imagism (see the note on Ezra Pound, page 700). Among her other books is *Firehead* (1929), inspired by the Sacco-Vanzetti case.

Paul Laurence Dunbar (1872–1906) was born in Dayton, Ohio, to parents who had been slaves in Kentucky; his father had escaped to Canada, then returned to fight in the 55th Massachusetts Regiment. After graduating high school Dunbar ran an elevator in Dayton for four dollars a week. His first book of poems, *Oak and Ivy,* was published in 1893; he sold copies on his elevator for a dollar each. His second book, *Majors and Minors* (1895), was prominently praised by Howells, after which Dunbar's career took off. He lectured, visited England, worked in the Library of Congress, and wrote more poetry, especially *Lyrics of Lowly Life* (1896). His *Complete Poems* appeared in 1913.

"The Poet": Dunbar wrote both dialect and nondialect poetry and came to regret the public's preference for the former.

Guy Wetmore Carryl (1873–1904) was born in New York City and became a journalist and editor. From 1896 to 1902 he lived in Paris, writing for various magazines. In 1898 he published *Fables for the Frivolous,* following it with *Mother Goose for Grown-Ups* (1900) and *Grimm Tales Made Gay* (1902). After he returned to the United States, his bungalow in Swampscott, Massachusetts, burned down; Carryl died of complications arising from injuries he sustained fighting the fire.

Robert Frost (1874–1963) was born in San Francisco but moved to New England at age ten. He attended Dartmouth and Harvard, each only briefly, worked in mills, did journalism, taught, and then turned to farming. He lived in England for three years, starting in 1912; his first book, *A Boy's Will* (1913), was published there. The publication of *North of Boston* (1914) brought him recognition, after which he returned to live on a New Hampshire farm. *Mountain Interval* appeared in 1916, and his *Collected Poems* in 1930. He continued to write poems and plays and to teach (at Amherst, Harvard, and the University of Michigan). He read "The Gift Outright" at John F. Kennedy's inauguration and is one of the few modern poets to figure importantly in the popular imagination. (Others include T. S. Eliot, Sylvia Plath, and Maya Angelou.) Frost's subject matter is often country life, and his poetic techniques are mostly traditional. Yet the leavening of irony is everywhere in Frost, like the neoclassical flash in "Oh lord, forgive my little jokes on thee / And I'll forgive thy great big one on me." He seems often to prefer nature to humankind, but he could also write that "nothing not made with hands is . . . sacred." The preface to his *Collected Poems,* "The Figure a Poem Makes," makes a strong pitch for content: "All that can be done with words is soon told. . . . Theme alone can steady us down." He likened the wild indirections of Modernism to "kicking ourselves from one chance suggestion to another in all directions as of a hot afternoon in the life of a grasshopper." A poem, he says, "begins in delight, and ends in wisdom. . . .

Like a piece of ice on a hot stove, the poem must ride on its own melting." Reflecting on the "wonder of unexpected supply," he said that "like Giants we are always hurling experience ahead of us to pave the future with against the day when we may want to strike a line of purpose across it for somewhere."

Robert W. Service (1874–1958) is not an American poet: he has been hijacked for this anthology. He was born in Preston, England, and moved to Canada in 1894. He worked in a bank, spent eight years in the Yukon, and must be considered a Canadian poet. He is included here because his poems have been wildly popular in the United States and because, as he tells us, Sam McGee was from Tennessee.

"Edward E. Paramore, Jr." (fl. 1923) is unknown except for this poem, which can be traced back as far as Tom Masson's *Annual for 1923* (Doubleday, Doran and Co.). "The Ballad of Yukon Jake," sometimes known as "The Hermit of Shark-Tooth Shoal," is the poetic equivalent of barroom piano, and is still treasured by many readers for its wacky, irreverent rhymes.

Trumbull Stickney (1874–1904) was born in Switzerland and grew up in Wiesbaden, Florence, Nice, and New York. He attended Harvard, then the Sorbonne, where he was the first American to attain the *doctorat-ès-lettres.* He taught Greek at Harvard until his death at age thirty. His *Poems* (1905) were published posthumously by other members of the so-called "Harvard School," which included George Santayana, George Cabot Lodge, and William Vaughn Moody. Stickney's verse was not in the line that led to Modernism, but the best of it retains a haunting power.

Josephine Preston Peabody (1874–1922), was born in New York and went to Radcliffe, where she came under the influence of William Vaughn Moody. She wrote lyric poetry; her first volume was *The Wayfarers* (1898). She also wrote poetic dramas, the first of which was *Fortune and Men's Eyes* (1900). *The Piper* (1910) was a great success, winning the Stratford-on-Avon competition. Her *Collected Poems and Plays* appeared in 1927.

Amy Lowell (1874–1925), born in Brookline, Massachusetts, was a collateral descendant of James Russell Lowell. After her first book of poetry, *A Dome of Many-Coloured Glass* (1912), appeared, she became associated with Ezra Pound and the Imagist movement. (See the note on Pound, page 700.) Together with John Gould Fletcher, Lowell was also an exponent of polyphonic prose. Her books include *Sword Blades and Poppy Seed* (1914), *Men, Women, and Ghosts* (1916), *Can Grande's Castle* (1918), and *Pictures of the Floating World* (1919), as well as critical studies and a biography of John Keats.

Gertrude Stein (1874–1946) was born in Allegheny, Pennsylvania, and spent her early years in Vienna, Paris, and Oakland, California. She went to Radcliffe, where she studied with William James, whose ideas about consciousness form the basis of her thought. James described consciousness as an unending stream of ideas, impressions, and images—a much richer and more various display than could be adequately expressed in standard English. The modern literary technique known as stream of consciousness started with James and found its most complete proponent in Stein. (Contemporary with but independent of James's probing was Édouard Dujardin's *Les Lauriers sont coupés* [1888], translated as *We'll to the Woods No More* by Stuart Gilbert, the exegete of Joyce, in 1938.) Intending a career in psychology, Stein went to Johns Hopkins Medical School in 1897. Bored by routine courses, however, she failed her final exams and, rather than retake them, moved abroad, settling in Paris in 1903 with her brother Leo. After 1909 Alice B. Toklas was her companion. Stein's home became a center for Modernism in literature and painting. She created her own legend in *The Autobiography of Alice B. Toklas* (1933). She is buried in Père Lachaise cemetery in Paris, where her birthplace is spelled "Allfghany."

"Yet Dish": Published in Paris in 1913 in the volume *Bee Time Vine,* this poem is Stein's "portrait of the Jews"; the title is a transyllabification of "Yiddish." In another place Stein rendered the handwriting on the wall, "Mene, mene, tekel, upharsin" as "Many many tickle you for them."

Ridgely Torrence (1875–1950) was born in Xenia, Ohio, and attended Miami University in Ohio and Princeton. He then went to New York, where he met E. C. Stedman and started a literary career. In 1899 he published *The House of a Hundred Lights.* He worked at the New York Public Library and later, from 1920 to 1933, as poetry editor for the *New Republic.* He had a great gift for friendship, becoming a lifelong friend of E. A. Robinson and many others.

"The Son": Perhaps loss is *the* great American theme. Compare Frost's 'Out, Out—', Robinson's "Eros Turannos," Longfellow's "My Lost Youth," and Emerson's "Threnody."

Anna Hempstead Branch (1875–1937), a New York poet, wrote lyric poems gathered in *The Heart of the Road* (1901), *The Shoes That Danced* (1906), and other volumes. Her long poem *Nimrod* (1910) was much praised by Alfred Kreymborg, author of the influential history of American poetry *Our Singing Strength* (1929), and her poem "The Monk in the Kitchen" was once much anthologized. Her graceful combination of lyricism and narrative endures; witness her modern ballad of Connecticut.

William Stanley Braithwaite (1878–1962) was born in Boston, of West Indian parents. He was for many years an editor for the Boston *Transcript.* He edited an annual *Anthology of Magazine Verse* from 1913 to 1929. In his editing and in his own verse, he was more concerned with poetry as such than with what we have since come to think of as Black or African-American poetry. His own work appeared in *Lyrics of Life and Love* (1904) and *The House of Falling Leaves* (1908). His *Selected Poems* appeared in 1948.

Carl Sandburg (1878–1967) was born in Galesburg, Illinois. He worked at various jobs and was in and out of college. He was briefly in the army; he farmed; he worked as a gandy dancer for a railroad. He moved to Chicago in 1905, where he became a socialist and an organizer. Some of his poems were printed in Harriet Monroe's *Poetry: A Magazine of Verse,* and he soon brought out, in 1916, *Chicago Poems.* Sandburg had a long and varied career. He wrote a major biography of Lincoln, he collected American folk songs (in *The American Songbag,* 1927) and he wrote children's stories (*Rootabaga Stories,* 1922). In 1945 he moved to Flat Rock, North Carolina, where he spent his last years. No one forgets the first time reading "Chicago" or "Fog." Like Frost's, Sandburg's gate into poetry is open to anyone. His poetry could be called Populist Modernism, reminding us that the Modernist achievement, like a pyramid, rests on a very broad base.

Adelaide Crapsey (1878–1914) was born in New York City and raised in Rochester. She graduated from Vassar in 1901 and became a teacher; in 1911 she took an appointment at Smith. Her volume *Verse* (1915) came out after her death. She is best known for her use of the cinquain—a five-line stanza of two, four, six, eight, and two syllables that resembles Japanese haiku.

Don Marquis (1878–1937) was born Donald Robert Perry Marquis in Walnut, Illinois. He spent one year at Knox College, then worked as a teacher, a reporter, a clerk, and an actor before Joel Chandler Harris made him assistant editor of *Uncle Remus's Magazine.* He moved to New York in 1909. The poems that eventually made up *archy and mehitabel* (1927) began to appear in "The Sun Dial" column in the New York *Sun* in 1912. The poems are all written in lower case because they were composed on an old typewriter by a cockroach, archy, who had to hurl his whole body at each key in order to make the machine work, and he had no way to press the shift key while throwing himself at a letter key. Modernism revived the spirit of satire, and some of the best Modernist writing is often right at the edge of self-satire.

Vachel Lindsay (1879–1931) was born in Springfield, Illinois. He became interested in religion, poetry, and art, attended Hiram College in Ohio and the New York School of Art, where he studied with Robert Henri. In the spring of 1906, he began a walking tour of the South, exchanging a poem—"The Tree of Laughing Bells"—in return for bed and board. He wrote this journey up later in *A Handy Guide for Beggars* (1916). His first book was *General William Booth Enters into Heaven and Other Poems* (1913), but it was his second book, *The Congo and other Poems* (1914), that brought him fame. He was a great platform reader; he was the first American invited to read his poems at Oxford. His chanting of his own verses made a powerful impression, and he became a sort of legendary figure. Returning at last to Springfield, he committed suicide on December 5, 1931.

"General William Booth . . .": Booth was the founder of the Salvation Army.

Wallace Stevens (1879–1955) was born in Reading, Pennsylvania, and attended Harvard. Afterward he tried journalism and law before settling into insurance. In 1909 he married Elsie Kachel, whose profile was used for the head of Liberty by the sculptor who designed the Liberty dime. He moved from New York to Hartford in 1916. Stevens befriended the young Modernist poets, including William Carlos Williams and Donald Evans. He wrote poetry and published in magazines, but no book appeared until *Harmonium* in 1923. The revised *Harmonium* of 1931 established his reputation. Stevens's life balanced public and private concerns. He lived in Hartford and loved Key West. He was the dean of bond surety underwriting in America—and one of its leading poets to boot. There was always more to Stevens than met the eye, although what met the eye was plenty. At six foot two and somewhere near three hundred pounds, dressed always in a gray suit and with a serious look, he was a man you got out of the way for. A tough executive whose letters were sometimes just one word long (No!), he had expensive tastes and appetites. He liked cold roast beef, half an inch thick, covered with English mustard. He loved tea, French wine, California dried fruit, big grapes, and cigars made in Tampa. He walked back and forth from home to work and was known to go miles out of his way for a good cinnamon bun. He wrote a lot about Key West, and much of his supposed exoticism is just a sober account of Key West life. He gave Connecticut much of what mythology that cool state possesses. He has a fair claim to being the greatest of the Moderns. He is without question the great Modern poet of the imagination, the richest heir of Romanticism. When he won the National Book Award in 1955, he said in his response, "Humble as my actual contribution to poetry may be, and however modest my experience of poetry has been, I have learned through that contribution and by the aid of that experience of the greatness that lay beyond, the power over the mind that lies in the mind itself, the incalculable expanse of the imagination as it reflects itself in us and about us." His *Collected Poems* appeared in 1954, and *Opus Posthumous* in 1957. The Library of America volume *Wallace Stevens: Collected Poetry and Prose*, ed. Frank Kermode and Joan Richardson, is indispensable.

Witter Bynner (1881–1968) graduated from Harvard in 1902. He wrote in many styles and opened himself to many influences, from Whitman to Chinese verse. In 1916 Bynner (writing under the name Emanuel Morgan) collaborated with Arthur Davison Ficke (writing under the name Anne Knish) on a hoax, a book of Modernist experimental poems called *Spectra,* complete with theoretical manifesto. Their aim, they wrote in the preface, was to speak to the mind of a "process of diffraction by which are disarticulated the several colored and other rays of which light is composed." A poem, then, "is to be regarded as a prism, upon which the colorless white light of infinite existence falls and is broken up into glowing, beautiful, and intelligible hues." Because others were taken in, and because *Spectra* was taken seriously before it was unmasked, Bynner's serious work has not been properly appreciated, despite an edition of his *Selected Poems* edited by Richard Wilbur in 1978.

Anne Spencer (1882–1975) lived in Lynchburg, Virginia, and was the librarian of Dunbar High School. For many years she published her poems only in magazines. In 1970 the Friendship Press published her *African Panorama.* Underappreciated even now, her best work has a strange calm power.

Kahlil Gibran (1883–1931), whose Arabic name was Jubrān Kahlīl Jubrān, was born in Syria but lived in New York after 1912. His early writings were in Arabic, his later ones in English. His style contains elements of Blake, Nietzsche, and the Bible. *The Prophet* (1923) attained wide popularity—phrases from it have entered the popular culture ("Let there be spaces in your togetherness").

Arthur Davison Ficke (1883–1945) was born in Iowa. His early volumes of neo-Romantic poetry include *From the Isles* (1907), *The Happy Princess* (1907), *The Earth Passion* (1908), and *The Man on the Hilltop* (1915). In 1916 he collaborated with Witter Bynner in the *Spectra* hoax, writing pseudo-Modernist poems under the name Anne Knish. (See the note on Bynner, page 698.) In later life he wrote a novel, *Mrs. Morton of Mexico,* as well as more volumes of poetry, including *Mountain against Mountain* (1929) and *Tumultuous Shore* (1942).

William Carlos Williams (1883–1963) was born in Rutherford, New Jersey. His father, English born, was raised in the West Indies. His mother, Puerto Rico born, studied art in Paris. Williams went to school in Rutherford, Geneva, Paris, and New York. He studied medicine at the University of Pennsylvania, where he met Ezra Pound, Hilda Doolittle, and the painter Charles Demuth. He interned in New York City from 1906 to 1909; his first book, *Poems,* appeared in 1909. Now and henceforward he would combine his writing and medical careers. He turned to Modernism, impelled by Pound, by Imagism, by Alfred North Whitehead's *Science and the Modern World,* by the Armory Show of 1913, and by painters and photographers in Walter Arensberg's circle. (Arensberg, now remembered as an early collector of Cubist paintings, was a poet himself and a patron of new poets.) Williams's concern for the direct and the concrete is expressed in his saying "no ideas but in things." His emphasis on American culture and lifeways as distinct from European, his interest in American speech, and his commitment to the plain style set him in opposition to the work of Stevens and Eliot. Indeed, Williams thought of his poetic world as the polar opposite of Eliot's, and he said in his *Autobiography* (1951) that "The Waste Land" "wiped out our world as if an atom bomb had been dropped upon it." Something of Williams's attitude toward Eliot can be learned from the following invented exchange in a Williams letter of 1945.

"Christ: In my house there are many mansions.
Eliot: I'll take the corner room on the second floor overlooking the lawns and the river. And WHO is this rabble that follows you about?
Christ: Oh, some of the men I've met in my travels.
Eliot: Well, if I'm to follow you I'd like to know something more of your sleeping arrangements.
Christ: Yes, sir."

Williams's work, says David Perkins, "can be read as a demonstration that here, now, and everywhere the world is always fresh, full, and vivid." Looking back, we can see now that the poetry of Williams has had, if anything, more influence than Eliot's—to which one might add, however, that he was hardly given to hygienic homilies or uplift.

Kora in Hell: One effect of the rise of free verse was fresh attention given to poetic prose. John Gould Fletcher, George Santayana, and Gertrude Stein are other examples of this phenomenon.

Sara Teasdale (1884–1933), born and educated in St. Louis, was a precocious child. After a trip to Europe she settled in Chicago. Vachel Lindsay courted her for many years. She brought out *Sonnets to Duse and Other Poems* (1907) and *Helen of Troy and Other Poems* (1911). In 1914 she married a businessman, Ernest Filsinger, who is said to have known most of her poems by heart before he met her. They were divorced in 1929. Teasdale's later years were spent in New York, and she was always unhappy. A little more than a year after Lindsay's death, she was found drowned in her bath. Her volumes include *Rivers to the Sea* (1915), *Love Songs* (1917), and *Flame and Shadow* (1920).

Donald Evans (1884–1921) was born in Philadelphia and lived in New York City, where he became a Greenwich Village journalist, music critic, and poet. His ironic and urbane poetry, prefiguring Stevens and Eliot, appeared in a number of volumes, including *Discords* (1912), *Two Deaths in the Bronx* (1916), and *Ironica* (1919). Anyone who wonders just how original Eliot's "Prufrock" and the opening of "The Waste Land" are might want to read Evans's sophisticated and dramatic "Dinner at the Hotel de la Tigresse Verte." Evans committed suicide in 1921.

Ezra Pound (1885–1972) was born in Hailey, Idaho. His grandfather, Thaddeus Pound, had been a railroad builder, acting governor of Wisconsin, and an anti-bank Populist. On his mother's side he was distantly related to Longfellow. When Ezra was six, the Pound family moved to a suburb of Philadelphia. He attended the University of Pennsylvania, where he met William Carlos Williams and Hilda Doolittle (to whom he became "informally" engaged). Transferring to Hamilton College, he graduated in 1905. He took an M.A. from Pennsylvania in 1906 and found a job at Wabash College—then lost it as the result of a minor scandal. He sailed for Europe in March 1908, the year he published his first book, *A Lume Spento.* He became a fast friend of Yeats (Pound married Dorothy Shakespear, the daughter of Yeats's friend Olivia Shakespear), T. E. Hulme, and T. S. Eliot. Pound was soon at the center of literary Modernism, inventing first Imagism and then Vorticism. He defined the *image,* for the purposes of modern poetry, as "that which presents an intellectual and emotional complex in an instant of time. . . . It is better to present one Image in a lifetime than to produce voluminous works." He laid out a three-point program for Imagism in the magazine *Poetry* in March 1913: "1. Direct treatment of the 'thing,' whether subjective or objective. 2. To use absolutely no word that did not contribute to the presentation. 3. As regarding rhythm: to compose in sequence of the musical phrase, not in sequence of a metronome." Vorticism grew out of Pound's friendship with the painter and novelist Wyndham Lewis and the sculptor Henri Gaudier-Brzeska; in some ways it was an extension of Imagism. The Image, Pound now held, "is a radiant node or cluster; it is what I can and must perforce call a VORTEX, from which, and through which, and into which ideas are constantly rushing." Pound was London editor of *Poetry* from 1912, literary editor of *The Egoist* from 1914 to 1919, foreign editor of *The Little Review* from 1917 to 1919, and music and art critic for *The New Age*. His influence was enormous. In later years he came to admire Mussolini and made anti-American radio broadcasts during World War II. After the war, charged with treason in the United States, he was confined for twelve years in St. Elizabeth's Hospital, a mental institution in Washington, D.C. On his release he moved back to Italy, where he spent the rest of his life. Pound remains a figure of incalculable importance. He literally redefined poetry for modernity. Poetry, he said, "is simply language charged to the utmost degree with meaning." He observed that there are three ways to charge language. First is what he called "melopoeia, wherein the words are charged over and above their plain meaning, with some musical property, which directs the bearing or trend of that meaning." Second is "phanopoeia" (the trombone terminology is a nuisance, but the distinctions matter), which is "a casting of images upon the visual imagination." Third is "logopoeia," defined as "the dance of the intellect among words, that is to say, it employs words not only for their direct meaning, but it takes account in a special way of habits of usage, of the context we expect to find with the word, its usual concomitants, of its known acceptances, and of ironical play." As late as 1942 he seems to have said, in an Italian interview, that where Eliot excelled him in logopoeia, he excelled Eliot in melopoeia. The best editions of his work are *Selected Poems of Ezra Pound* (1949) and *The Cantos,* 6th printing (1977).

"The Seafarer": This translation, published in 1912, of the Old English poem is, by common consent, the most brilliant modern rendering ever done from that language.

"In a Station of the Metro": This perfect Imagist poem, reminiscent of haiku, simply juxtaposes the thing and its image. No comment is made or needed.

"Hugh Selwyn Mauberley (Life and Contacts)": This 1920 sequence Pound called "a farewell to London." As a poem made of assembled pieces, it is a sort of precursor of Eliot's "The Waste Land"; to highlight that, we have given the 1921 text of "Mauberley" (Boni and Liveright), but with the 1920 titling of the first part. That titling is the central issue of later discussions of the relation between Pound the author, Pound's persona in the first part, and the Mauberley who is the protagonist of the second part.

"VOCAT ÆSTUS IN UMBRAM": "The heat invites us to the shade." This epigraph is taken from the fourth eclogue of the third-century Latin poet Nemesianus. Nemesianus was a Carthaginian, which adds impact to Pound's words on his own antecedents in the second stanza: "he had been born / in a half savage country."

"E. P. / ODE POUR L'ELECTION DE SON SEPULCHRE": In line 8, Capaneus: See *The Thebaid* of Statius (X: 826–939; III: 598–699), as well as Ovid's *Metamorphoses* (I: 151–62) and, not least, the defiant Capaneus, supine on fiery sands in Dante's Hell, who yet outcries, "That which I was in life, I am in death" *(Inferno, XIV: 51).*

Ἴδμεν γάρ τοι πάνθ᾽, ὅσ᾽ ἐνὶ Τροίῃ [Idmen gar toi panth hos eni Troie(i)]: "For we know all that at Troy . . ." referring to the Sirens' song, Pound omits the last word in Homer's line *(Odyssey,* XII:189), εὐρείη [eureie], which means "wide," to give the line a more decasyllabic feel. The iota subscript in "Τροίῃ" gives us a neat bilingual chime with "lee-way."

L'an trentiesme / De son eage: "The thirtieth year of his age." The phrase is adapted from the beginning of François Villon's *Grant testament,* where it is not *"his* age" but *"mon* trentiesme eage."

τό καλόν: "The beautiful."

τίν᾽ ἀοδρα, τίν ἦρωα, τίνα θεόν, [tin᾽ andra, tin heroa, tina theon]: "What man, what hero, what god." This line takes off from Pindar's *Olympian* II: "what god, what hero, what man shall we sing?" The Greek *tin* plays off against the "tin wreath" of the last line. Pound was an ardent debunker of Pindar, but he praised Sappho and her "barbitos" (a kind of lyre) as in the first stanza of this poem.

"1920 (Mauberley)": Pound later inverted this to "Mauberley 1920" and added *"Vacuos exercet aera morsus"* as epigraph to explain the penultimate line of this part, "mouths biting empty air," based on the hound in Ovid, *Metamorphoses* VII, 782–91: "as he bites, his teeth / snap shut on empty air . . ."

II. CAID ALI is a pseudonym for Pound.
ANANGKE (or more correctly ANAGKE—but not so in most editions): necessity, destiny.
NUKTIS 'AGALMA: Night's ornament—indebted to Bion's *Bucolics,* frag. 8.
TO AGATHON. The good—i.e., what was best in him.

"Canto III": The *Cantos* are Pound's major work. The *Finnegan's Wake* of modern poetry, they are always mentioned, often praised, and too infrequently read. Pound thought of the *Cantos* as a sort of modern epic, defining epic as "a poem that includes history." He worked on the *Cantos* from about 1917 until the end of his life; the first ones appeared in *Quia pauper amavi* (1919). The canto printed here was the third one; later it was revised and became, in 1925, what is now Canto I, beginning with the line "And then went down to the ship."

Elinor Wylie (1885–1928) was born in Somerville, New Jersey, but was raised in Rosemont, a suburb of Philadelphia. She had superior schooling, European travels, and summers at Mount Desert, Maine; she married the son of an admiral in 1905. In 1910 she bolted from her fashionable life, eloping to England with Horace Wylie, whom she married in 1916. In 1921 she moved to New York; her poems appeared in many magazines and in *Nets to Catch the Wind* (1921) and *Black Armour* (1923). After her divorce from Wylie in 1923, she married William Rose Benét, who published her *Collected Poems* (1932) and *Collected Prose* (1933).

Georgia Johnson (1886–1966) was born in Atlanta and studied music at Oberlin College. She became a schoolteacher, moving with her husband to Washington, D.C. Her books include *The Heart of a Woman* (1918), *Bronze* (1922), *An Autumn Love Cycle* (1928), and *Share My World* (1962).

[Alfred] Joyce Kilmer (1886–1918) was born in New Brunswick, New Jersey. He was a poet, journalist, and critic and was on the staff of the *Standard Dictionary* from 1909 to 1912. His books include *Summer Love* (1911), *Trees and Other Poems* (1914), and *Main Street* (1917). He was killed in the second battle of the Marne.

"Trees": This poem was first published in the magazine *Poetry* in 1913.

H.D.[Hilda Doolittle] (1886–1961) was born in Bethlehem, Pennsylvania, and educated in Philadelphia; she attended Bryn Mawr in 1904 and 1905. During this time she met Marianne Moore, William Carlos Williams, and Ezra Pound, who was her early love as she was his. (See her *to torment: A memoir of Ezra Pound*, which includes his early love poems to her, which he grouped as "Hilda's Book." H.D.'s indelible memoir, written in 1958, was published in 1979.) She moved to England in 1911, became a member of the Imagist group, and married Richard Aldington. Her poems appeared in *Poetry* in 1913, poems she signed, at Pound's suggestion, as "H.D. Imagiste"—and it was as H.D. that, from then on, she preferred to be known. Her work appeared in Pound's *Des Imagistes* (1914). Her first book was *Sea Garden* (1916); her *Collected Poems* appeared in 1925 and in another edition in 1940. In the wake of a mental breakdown after World War II, she moved to Switzerland, where she lived and wrote until her death in a Zurich hospital in 1961. H.D.'s early work was and often still is considered the purest example of Imagism. In her later work, with which we are still catching up, she gives us a Greek world that is part classical, part romantic, and all modern. (For the Freudian ingredient of her "modern-ity," see her 1956 prose work *Tribute to Freud*—whose patient she was.)

John Gould Fletcher (1886–1950) was born in Little Rock, Arkansas, and went to Harvard. There he read Arthur Symons and became interested in the French Symbolists. In 1908 he went to Europe; five years later he met Pound and the Imagists. Fletcher and Amy Lowell together developed a kind of prose poetry they called polyphonic prose. Lowell found a publisher for his *Irradiations: Sand and Spray* (1915). In later years he returned to the United States and to Arkansas, met John Crowe Ransom and the Fugitive Group, and became much interested in southern regionalism and agrarianism.

Marianne Moore (1887–1972) was born in Kirkwood, Missouri, moved to Pennsylvania, and attended Bryn Mawr. She made her home in Greenwich Village in 1918, where she became friends with William Carlos Williams, Lola Ridge, e.e. cummings, and others. Her first book, *Poems,* appeared (in England) in 1921. In 1925 she became the editor of the *Dial.* She moved to Brooklyn in 1929, became an avid Dodgers fan, and brought out *Selected Poems* in 1935. Most of the work of this accomplished and influential poet was written after that volume was published. Her *Complete Poems* appeared in 1981, and her *Complete Prose* in 1986.

T[homas] S[tearns] Eliot (1888–1965) was born in St Louis. His father, Henry Ware Eliot, was a manufacturer of bricks; his mother, Charlotte Champe Stearns, was a volunteer social worker and amateur writer. Eliot went to Smith Academy in St. Louis, spent a year at Milton Academy in Massachusetts, then entered Harvard in 1906; in 1908 he discovered the French Symbolist poet Jules Laforgue. Impressed by the anti-Romantic teaching of Irving Babbitt and, most of all, by the poetry of Dante ("the most persistent and deepest influence on my verse"), Eliot wrote poetry and became an editor of the *Harvard Advocate.* In 1911 he enrolled as a graduate student in philosophy at Harvard. He left for Europe in 1914 and completed his Ph.D. dissertation (published in 1964 as *Knowledge and Experience in the Philosophy of F.H. Bradley*), but he never took the degree itself. In the fall of 1914 he had met Pound, who sent Eliot's "Prufrock" to Harriet Monroe for the magazine *Poetry,* where it was published in 1915. That same year Eliot met and married Vivien Haigh-Wood. *Prufrock and Other Observations* appeared in 1917. "The Waste Land," heavily edited by Pound, appeared in 1922; it has been perhaps the most discussed of all modern poems. Eliot worked at Lloyds Bank and later at the publishing house of Faber and Faber. He was also the leading critic of his day; his emphasis on the self-sufficiency of the work became the leading tenet of the so-called New Critics. Two comments by Eliot on the work of others cast indispensable light on his own poetic practice. Writing about James Joyce's *Ulysses,* Eliot said that Joyce used myth to manipulate "a continuous parallel between contemporaneity and antiquity. . . . It is simply a way of controlling, of ordering, of giving a shape and a significance to the immense panorama of futility and anarchy which is contemporary history." And in his preface to his translation of Saint-John

Perse's *Anabasis*, Eliot said, "The obscurity of the poem, on first readings, is due to the suppression of 'links of the chain' or explanatory and connecting matter, and not to incoherence or the love of cryptogram. The justification of the abbreviation of method is that the sequence of images coincides and concentrates into one intense impression [in this case] of barbaric civilization. The reader has to allow the images to fall into his memory without questioning the reasonableness of each at the moment, so that, at the end, a total effect is produced." In 1927 Eliot became a British subject and converted to Anglo-Catholicism. He wrote verse plays, such as *Murder in the Cathedral*, that were successful. In the late 1930s and early 1940s he wrote *Four Quartets*, which many consider his finest work. Ten years after the death of his first wife, Eliot married Esme Valerie Fletcher, who had long been his secretary. His ashes are buried in East Coker in Somerset. His epitaph reads "Of your charity / pray for the repose / of the soul of / Thomas Stearns Eliot / Poet."

"The Love Song of J. Alfred Prufrock": The epigraph is from Dante. It says:

"If I thought my reply were meant for one
who ever could return into the world,
this flame would stir no more; and yet, since none—
if what I hear is true—ever returned
alive from this abyss, then without fear
of facing infamy, I answer you."

These words are spoken by Guido de Montefeltro, who is in the eighth circle of Hell for perverting human reason by fraud (*Inferno*, Canto XXVII).

We have printed the later version of "Gerontion," where "jew" is capitalized "Jew," a correction by Eliot himself, "mitigating" his anti-Semitism (often less blatant than Pound's), though he did allow the lower-case "jew" of "Dirge" (a section dropped from the final "Waste Land") to keep a lower-case "jew" when the "Waste Land" early drafts were later printed. A penetrating discussion is now to be found in Anthony Julius, *T. S. Eliot, Anti-semitism, and Literary Form*, 1995.

"The Waste Land": Eliot's original draft of this poem was heavily edited by Ezra Pound who, according to Eliot, turned "a jumble of good and bad passages into a poem." Eliot dedicated the poem to Pound, "the better maker." Originally the epigraph was to be from Joseph Conrad, "The horror, the horror," but Pound objected. The existing epigraph is from Petronius; it says, "With my own eyes I saw the Sibyl suspended in a glass bottle at Cumae, and when the boys said to her, 'Sibyl, what's the matter?' she would always respond, 'I yearn to die.'" Eliot's own notes on the poem follow the poem itself, as he first printed them. The longest quote in Eliot's notes (to line 218) is a passage from Ovid (*Metamorphoses*, III, 320–338 but best begun at I. 318):

" . . . . The story goes
that meanwhile, in his home on high, great Jove,
his spirits warmed by nectar, set aside
his heavy cares and jested pleasantly
with Juno—she was also idle then.
'The pleasure love allots to you,' he said,
'is greater than the pleasure given men.'
But she contested that. And they agreed
to let Tiresias decide, for he
knew love both as a woman and a man.

Tiresias had once struck with his staff
two huge snakes as they mated in the forest;
for that, he had been changed—a thing of wonder—
from man to woman. Seven autumns passed,
and still that change held fast. But at the eighth,
he came upon those serpents once again.
He said: 'If he who strikes you can be changed
into his counter-state, then this time, too,
I'll strike at you.' His stout staff dealt a blow;
and he regained the shape he had before,
the shape the Theban had when he was born.

And when he had been summoned to decide
ths jesting controversy, he took sides
with Jove. The story goes that Juno grieved
far more than she had any right to do,
more than was seemly in a light dispute.
And she condemned to never-ending night
the judge whose verdict found her in the wrong.
But then almighty Jove (though no god can
undo what any other god has done),
to mitigate Tiresias' penalty,
his loss of sight, gave him the power to see
the future, pairing pain with prophecy."

Quotes from Dante are cited in the note to Line 293 (*Purg.* V, 133–134), "May you remember me, who am La Pia / Siena made—Maremma unmade—me"; Line 412 (*Inf.* XXXIII, 46–47). ". . . I heard them nailing up the door / of that appalling tower"; and Line 428 (*Purg.* XXVI, 145–148), " 'Now, by the Power that conducts you to / the summit of the stairway, I pray you: / remember, at time opportune, my pain!' / Then in the fire that refines, he hid."

Fenton Johnson (1888–1958) was born in Chicago and attended the University of Chicago. He was a poet, playwright, editor, and publisher, active in the Chicago Renaissance that paralleled that of Harlem. His first book of poems, *A Little Dreaming,* came out in 1914. *Visions of the Dusk* appeared in 1915, and *Songs of the Soil* in 1916.

Alan Seeger (1888–1916) was born in New York and went to Harvard. In Paris at the start of World War I, he enlisted in the French Foreign Legion. He was killed at Belloy-en-Santerre, during the battle of the Somme. His *Poems* appeared in 1916.

"I Have a Rendez-Vous with Death": This poem was first published in the *North American Review* in October 1916.

Conrad Aiken (1888–1973) was born in Savannah, Georgia. When he was eleven, his father shot himself and his mother. Aiken was sent to live in New England, where he went first to Concord Academy, then to Harvard, where he read Arthur Symons and Walt Whitman. He was impressed by Santayana and became friendly with T. S. Eliot. His first book of poems, *Earth Triumphant and Other Tales in Verse,* appeared in 1914. In 1921 he moved to England. He wrote for the *New Yorker,* the *New Republic,* and many other magazines; he published fiction, criticism, autobiography, and poetry. He edited anthologies of American verse and of Emily Dickinson (1924). His *Collected Poems* appeared in 1954.

E[dward] E[stlin] Cummings (1894–1962) was born in Cambridge, Massachusetts, and went to Harvard. In France he volunteered for the Norton Harjes Ambulance Corps. He was confined in a French concentration camp (on an unfounded charge), which became the basis for his first book, *The Enormous Room* (1922). His first book of poems, *Tulips and Chimneys,* came out in 1923. His wit, his defense of the individual, his satirical view of society, his lowercase compulsion, and his wild typography are all in the service of real poetic ability, and his work endures.

Claude McKay (1890–1948) was born in Jamaica, where he published, in 1912, *Songs of Jamaica.* He moved to the United States in 1912 to study at Tuskegee and at Kansas State University. He moved to New York and became part of the literary life there. After a year in London—and an English volume called *Spring in New Hampshire* (1920)—he returned to the United States, became associate editor of the *Liberator,* and published *Harlem Shadows* (1922). He wrote novels and an autobiography; his *Selected Poems* appeared in 1953.

Edna St. Vincent Millay (1892–1950) was born in Rockland, Maine. Her poem "Renascence" was published in November 1912 in the *Lyric Year.* She graduated from Vassar in 1917, the year of her book *Renascence and Other Poems.* She lived in Greenwich Village, bringing out *A Few Figs from Thistles* in 1920. She became prominent and wrote many books; she moved to Austerlitz, New York, and spent summers on Ragged Island in Maine's Casco Bay. Her *Collected Sonnets* appeared in 1941, her *Collected Lyrics* in 1943.

Langston Hughes (1902–1967) was born in Joplin, Missouri, and lived in Lawrence, Kansas, in the home of his grandmother Mary Langston, whose first husband had been an associate of John Brown and had died at Harper's Ferry. After living in Cleveland and, for a year, in Mexico, he entered Columbia University. He had read Dunbar, Whitman, and Sandburg. In 1921 he published "The Negro Speaks of Rivers" in W.E.B. Du Bois's *Crisis*. After seeing the west coast of Africa and Paris, he returned to the United States and published his first book, *The Weary Blues,* in 1926. He became a major figure in the Harlem Renaissance. His complex life took him to Cuba, Russia, Spain, and Carmel, California. His career had ups and downs and took various political turnings, but he was as deeply beloved and admired as any African-American writer of his time.

SONGS OF THE MODERN ERA: 1900–1922.

"Casey Jones": The original version of this song was probably by Wallace Saunders, an African-American. See Norm Cohen, *Long Steel Rail* (1981).

"Whiffenpoof Song": The refrain of this famous Yale song was lifted from Kipling's poem "Gentlemen-Rankers." A ranker is a soldier in the ranks or an officer who rose from the ranks.

"St. Louis Blues": Elizabeth Bishop used to cite the first line of this W. C. Handy classic as her favorite line of iambic pentameter.

ABOUT THE EDITORS

ALLEN MANDELBAUM is an acclaimed poet and translator. His verse has been seen as "precise, inspired" *(Parnassus)*, "marvelously original" (James Wright), "a verbal paradise" *(Denver Quarterly)*. His verse translation of the *Aeneid* was deemed "brilliant" (Bernard M. W. Knox) and won the National Book Award; his *Metamorphoses* of Ovid was a finalist for the Pulitzer Prize in poetry; his *Divine Comedy* translation was named "the Dante of choice" (Hugh Kenner, *Harper's*) and seen as "a miracle . . . a model (an encyclopedia) for poets" (Charles Simic); and his *Odyssey* was called "splendid . . . outstripping all competitors" (Anthony A. Long). A recipient of the Order of Merit of the Republic of Italy, of honorary degrees from Purdue, the University of Cassino, and the University of Turin, and of numerous international awards, he is now the W. R. Kenan Professor of Humanities at Wake Forest University.

ROBERT D. RICHARDSON, JR., is the biographer and cultural historian who—most recently—has given us *Emerson: The Mind on Fire* ("a splendid book," *The New Yorker;* "exciting," *The Washington Post;* "immensely valuable," *Times Literary Supplement;* "the definitive biography of Emerson," David M. Robinson) and *Thoreau: A Life of the Mind* ("absorbing . . . splendidly written," *The Boston Globe*). His earlier volumes were *Myth and Literature in the American Renaissance* and *The Rise of Modern Mythology: 1680–1860* (with Burton Feldman). He has been a Guggenheim and a Huntington Library Fellow, a recipient of the Melcher Prize, the Francis Parkman Prize, and—in 1998—an Academy Award in Literature from the American Academy of Arts and Letters. He taught for years at the University of Denver and has been a visiting professor at Harvard, Yale, the Graduate Center of CUNY, and Wesleyan University.

INDEX OF POETS

INDEX OF TITLES

INDEX OF FIRST LINES

A great land and a wide land was the east land, 465
Ah, broken is the golden bowl, 184
A Heart a Fly buzz—when I died, 379
Ah! These under-formings in the mind, 331
Alas! our pleasant moments fly, 95
A light in the moon the only light is on Sunday, 517
A line in long array where they wind betwixt green islands, 297
A little madness in the Spring, 396
All Dull, my Lord, my Spirits flat, and dead, 25
All houses wherein men have lived and died, 161
All I could see from where I stood, 644
All Men have Follies, which they blindly trace, 42
"All ready?" cried the captain, 137
All things are current found, 219
All things must have an end, 169
All you preachers who delight in panning the dancing teachers, 659
Aloof within the day's enormous dome, 459
Aloofe, aloofe, and come no neare the dangers doe appeare, 3
A lovely morning, without the glare of the sun, 151
Alter! When the Hills do, 389
A mile behind is Gloucester town, 441
Am I thy Gold? Or Purse, Lord, for thy Wealth, 22
Among the twenty snowy mountains, 537
An Anagram, 16
And change with hurried hand has swept these scenes, 340
And did young Stephen sicken, 399
And these about me die, 594
A nearness to Tremendousness, 393
An Everywhere of Silver, 392
Announced by all the trumpets of the sky, 102
A noiseless patient spider, 308
An old man bending I come among new faces, 298

An old man in a lodge within a park, 153
Another one, half-cracked, 595
Any fool can make a rule, 220
A Pit indeed of Sin: No water's here, 27
Apparently with no suprise, 396
Applauding youths laughed with young prostitutes, 642
Apple-green west and an orange bar, 428
April is the cruellest month, 620
A purse was not green, it was not straw color, it was hardly seen and it had a use a long use and the chain, 516
A Route of Evanescence, 396
As cool as the pale wet leaves of lily-of-the-valley, 582
As cruel as a Turk: whence came, 334
As I ebb'd with the ocean of life, 294
As I was a-gwine down the road, 234
As one, who, journeying westward with the sun, 437
As they sat sipping their glasses in the courtyard, 576
A Thought went up my mind today, 388
A throe upon the features, 359
At least—to pray—is left—is left, 381
At night, by the fire, 536
At the first peep of dawn she roused me, 565
A Visitor in Marl, 375
A Wife—at Daybreak I shall be, 379
A word is dead, 395
A Word made Flesh is seldom, 396
Ay, Democracy, 334
Ay, tear her tattered ensign down, 207

Beautiful as a tiered cloud, 608
Because you are four years old, 483
Between me and the sunset, like a dome, 451
Between the dark and the daylight, 155
Beware! The Israelite of old, who tore, 150
Booth led boldly with his big bass drum, 528

Me from Myself—to banish, 386
Mid pleasures and palaces though we may roam, 82
Mine and yours, 101
Mine eyes have seen the glory of the coming of the Lord, 414
Miniver Cheevy, child of scorn, 447
Mother of heaven, regina of the clouds, 540
Much Madness is divinest Sense, 377
My Blessed Lord, that Golden Linck that joyns, 25
My country tis of thee, 226
My debt to you, Beloved, 458
My jacket old, with narrow seam, 328
My life closed twice before its close, 397
My Life had stood—a Loaded Gun, 390
My life has been the poem I would have writ, 220
My life is like the summer rose, 223
My long two-pointed ladder's sticking through a tree, 498
My memory is short and braine is dry, 14
My Metaphors are but dull Tacklings tag'd, 26
My mind lets go a thousand things, 401
My own mind is very hard to me, 647
My Sin my Sin, My God, these Cursed Dregs, 29

Nature centres into balls, 125
Nearer, my God, to thee, 228
New books of poetry will be written, 567
New England first a wilderness was found, 68
Night-dreams trace on Memory's wall, 124
Noble gods at the board, 333
No! Cover not the fault, 340
No days that dawn can match for her, 429
No more auction block for me, 417
No more the scarlet maples flash and burn, 215
No more with overflowing light, 448

No, no! Go from me. I have left her lately, 581
No Rack can torture me, 374
Nor strange it is, to United States who walk in bonds, 341
No sleep. The sultriness pervades the air, 323
Nota: man is the intelligence of his soil, 544
Nothing that is shall perish utterly, 177
Not like the brazen giant of Greek fame, 423
Not probable—the barest Chance, 370
Not sometimes, but to him that heeds the whole, 339
Now comes the Course-of-things, shaped like an Ox, 408

O Black and unknown bards of long ago, 481
O Captain! my Captain!, 307
O Dieu, Purifiez nos coeurs!, 593
O'er the hills far away, at the birth of the morn, 42
O far-off rose of long ago, 511
Of Course—I prayed, 373
Often I think of the beautiful town, 159
Oft have I seen at some cathedral door, 153
O give me a home where the buffalo roam, 468
Oh, don't you remember sweet Betsey from Pike, 237
Oh, Give my youth, my faith, my sword, 432
Oh, I went down South for to see my Sal, 470
Oh, ma honey, 654
Oh never on that mountain, 346
Oh the North Countree is a hard countree, 505
Old Eben Flood, climbing alone one night, 449
Old Joe is gone, who saw hot Percy goad, 318
O little town of Bethlehem, 418
On a hill far away stood an old rugged cross, 655
Once a flock of stately peacocks, 487

Once upon a midnight dreary, while I
  pondered, weak and weary, 185
One morning I was a-walking down,
  416
One must have a mind of winter, 540
One's-Self I sing, a simple separate
  person, 243
Only two patient eyes to stare, 444
On one fix'd point all nature moves,
  64
On Springfield Mountains there did
  dwell, 48
On such a night, or such a night, 360
On the beach at night, 292
On the fourth day of his fasting, 163
On the way to the grove you'll pass
  the Fates, 464
O Silent God, Thou whose voice afar
  in mist and mystery hath left our
  ears an-hungered in these fearful
  days, 438
O sweet spontaneous earth how often
  have the doting, 640
O Thou, to whom, in ancient time, 82
Our hearths are gone out, and our
  hearts are broken, 407
Out of the bosom of the Air, 155
Out of the earth, 647
Out of the hills of Habersham, 409
Over and over, like a Tune, 373
Over the monstrous shambling sea,
  405
O when you come in summer time,
  230
O wind, rend open the heat, 602
O World, thou choosest not the better
  part, 434

Pain—has an Element of Blank, 386
Partake as doth the Bee, 393
Perhaps I asked too large, 371
Phlebas the Phoenician, a fortnight
  dead, forgot the cry of gulls, 628
Phoebus, sitting one day in a laurel
  tree's shade, 309
Picasso you give us things, 641
Pile the bodies high at Austerlitz and
  Waterloo, 523
Please don't be offended if I preach
  to you a while, 658

Poet of the serene and thoughtful lay,
  401
Publication—is the Auction, 388
Put a sun in Sunday, Sunday, 514
Put to the door—the school's begun,
  43

Rabbi Ben Levi, on the Sabbath, read,
  174
Reader, If thou be a Christian and a
  Freeman, 65
Reared within the Mountains, 464
Rock o' my soul in de bosom of
  Abraham, 416
Roof and spire and darkened vane,
  216

Safe in their Alabaster Chambers, 364
Salmon Brook, Penichook, 218
Satisfaction—is the Agent, 394
Science! true daughter of Old Time
  thou art, 178
Seeds in a dry pod, tick, tick, tick,
  460
See! how the nations rage together, 78
She fears him, and will always ask, 448
She had no saying dark enough, 489
Shot gold, maroon and violet, dazzling
  silver, emerald, fawn, 308
Silver dust lifted from the earth, 607
Since Every Quill is silent to Relate,
  36
Sing we for love and idleness, 581
Sister and mother and diviner love,
  559
Skimming lightly, wheeling still, 323
Skins of flayed authors, husks of dead
  reviews, 199
Skirting the river road, 296
Sleep sweetly in your humble graves,
  357
Sling me under the sea, 522
So fallen! so lost! the light withdrawn,
  134
Soft through the silent air descend the
  feathery snow-flakes, 151
Some keep the Sabbath going to
  Church, 369
Something there is that doesn't love a
  wall, 492

To him who in the love of Nature
holds, 87
To lose one's faith—surpass, 373
To make a prairie, it takes a clover
and one bee, 397
To make One's Toilette—after Death,
379
To sing of Wars, of Captaines, and of
Kings, 14
To the highest bidder, 560
To the States or any one of them,
Resist much, obey little, 143
To the table down at Mory's, to the
place where Louis dwells, 655
Trembling I write my dream, and
recollect, 58
Triumph—may be of several kinds,
378
Turned from the "eau—forte Par
Jaquemart," 587
Twas the night before Christmas,
when all through the house, 223
Twenty men crossing a bridge, 539
Twilight is spacious, near things in it
seem far, 639
Two hulks on Hudson's stormy bosom
lie, 60
Two roads diverged in a yellow wood,
499
Two swimmers wrestled on the spar,
362

Unpetal the flower of me, 429

Vainly my heart had with thy sorceries
striven, 126
Vigil strange I kept on the field one
night, 297

Wak'd by the gospel's joyful sound, 50
We are children of the sun, 636
We're married, they say, and you
think you have won me, 336
We wear the mask the grins and lies,
484
We were forty miles from Albany, 234
What, can these dead bones live,
whose sap is dried, 423
What a friend we have in Jesus, 469
What are the islands to me, 603

What is it makes thy sound unto my
ear, 209
What Soft-Cherubic Creatures, 375
What syllable are you seeking, 560
When, Lord, I seeke to shew thy
praises, then, 26
When Abraham Lincoln was shoveled
into the tombs, 522
When all is done, and my last word is
said, 485
When breezes are soft and skies are
fair, 90
Whence have you fallen, have you
fallen, 647
Whenever Richard Cory went down
town, 446
When I am dead and over me bright
April, 574
When I see birches bend to left and
right, 500
When I was a beggarly boy, 321
When Johnny comes marching home
again, hurrah, hurrah, 415
When lilacs last in the dooryard
bloom'd, 300
When night drifts along the streets of
the city, 512
When ocean-clouds over inland hills,
322
When spring returns with western
gales, 46
When the charms of spring awaken,
235
When the wind works against us in
the dark, 488
When the world turns completely
upside down, 599
When thy Bright Beams, my Lord, do
strike mine Eye, 24
When we assemble here to worship
God, 81
When Yankies, skill'd in martial rule,
55
Where are the cabalists, the insidious
committees, 462
Where is the promise of my years, 402
Where is the world we roved, Ned
Bunn, 326
While an intrinsic ardor prompts to
write, 67

PERMISSIONS